METHODS AND MATERIALS FOR TEACHING THE GIFTED

METHODS AND MATERIALS FOR TEACHING THE GIFTED

EDITED BY

Frances A. Karnes

AND

Suzanne M. Bean

PRUFROCK PRESS, INC.

Prufrock Press, Inc.
P.O. Box 8813
Waco, Texas 76714-8813
(800) 998-2208
Fax (800) 240-0333
http://www.prufrock.com

Dedication

We dedicate this book to our families: Ray, John, Leighanne, and Mary Ryan, Mark, Meriweather, and Hudson for their love and support and to Christopher Karnes, for his special love and guidance.

This book is also dedicated to all gifted learners who need differentiated instruction to reach their potential.

TABLE OF CONTENTS

SECTION IV
SUPPORTING AND ENHANCING
GIFTED PROGRAMS

PREFACE

The purpose of this book is to give strategies and resources for differentiating the instruction of gifted learners. Although there is general agreement in the field of gifted education as to the need to modify regular instruction to more appropriately address the unique characteristics and behaviors of gifted learners, this book is one of the first to focus on specific ways differentiation can be accomplished. Methods are given for developing appropriate learning environments, blending advanced content with instructional processes, and selecting products that match the needs of this population of students. The text also gives an array of current books, teaching materials, web sites, and other resources for teaching gifted students.

After determining the chapters to be included in the book, the editors selected contributors from across the nation who have specific expertise in the areas defined and are recognized leaders in the field of gifted education. The goal is to provide readers with current information about best practices for gifted learners from experts who have developed and tested these best practices.

We begin this book by revisiting the characteristics and needs of gifted learners, for these understandings have a critical role in determining appropriate learning environments, content, processes, products, and resources for this population. While the introductory chapter gives an excellent summary of the nature and needs of gifted learners, the editors believe that more information may be necessary as a prerequisite to this text in order to give educators the essential understandings about gifted learners so that they may work more effectively with them. Therefore, this text would best be used following a text/course about the general characteristics and needs of gifted learners.

The first section of the book offers chapters that address the unique needs of gifted learners and plan appropriate learning environments for them. The second section features chapters focusing on instructional planning, to include content, process, and product differentiation for gifted learners. Also included is a chapter on writing units that are appropriate for gifted learners. The culmination of this section is a chapter on evaluating learner and program outcomes. The third section of the text provides chapters on specific strategies for best practices with gifted learners. From critical and creative thinking to strategies for research, independent study, and mentorships, rich and substantive ideas are highlighted. Also included in this section are chapters on affective education, leadership development, and cooperative learning for gifted learners. The fourth section presents often-neglected areas of importance in supporting and enhancing programs for gifted learners: public relations and advocacy, locating funding sources, and finding appropriate resources and materials. Though these areas may not be considered critical to the daily work of teachers, they are critical to the overall success and defensibility of strong gifted programs and services.

Educators in all areas can benefit from this book. Certainly, pre-service and in-service teachers in elementary and secondary schools who are training to work with gifted learners in specialized programs could use this book for instructional planning. Many sections of the text might also be used by coordinators of gifted programs as they conduct staff development programs to address the needs of various groups. General classroom teachers may also find it helpful as they prepare to individualize their instruction to meet the needs of gifted learners. Other school personnel, such as administrators, counselors, and school psychologists, could use the book to increase their understanding about gifted students and to develop strong programs for them. Parents of gifted students may use the book to assist them in their own home instruction or to compare these best practices with what is offered for their children in specialized programs for the gifted.

ACKNOWLEDGEMENTS

There are many people who have made valuable contributions to this book. We deeply appreciate the enthusiastic encouragement and guidance of Joel McIntosh at Prufrock Press. Also, to Jim and Christy Kendrick, we express sincere gratitude for the patience and support in helping us prepare this manuscript. We are especially indebted to the chapter contributors who have offered their expertise across the many dimensions of teaching gifted learners. A special word of thanks is given to Carolyn Foil at the University of Southern Mississippi and Lane Sample and Ivey McKellar at Mississippi University for Women for their editing and technical writing assistance. And to our administrators and colleagues at The University of Southern Mississippi and Mississippi University for Women, we thank you for the continued support of this and of our other professional endeavors.

SECTION I

CHARACTERISTICS AND NEEDS OF GIFTED LEARNERS

CHAPTER 1

Gifted and Talented Learners

Many, Varied, Unique, and Diverse

SALLY M. REIS
University of Connecticut

MELISSA A. SMALL
Neag Center for Gifted Education
and Talent Development, Storrs, CT

*J*ulia is a smart sixth grader who continuously brings home A's in all subjects on her report card. Teachers frequently comment on her aptitude as well as her achievement. She has many friends, and her teachers have mentioned her promising leadership ability. Though quite task-committed when it comes to her homework, she has a tendency to procrastinate on longer projects. Her finished products, especially those that are computer-related, are usually nothing less than exceptional for her grade level, and her test scores are extremely high.

Justin, a 10th grader, is less than interested in school. Though achievement test scores have indicated he is well above grade level, especially in verbal areas, his grades in high school have been B's and C's. He recently designed the logo and painted the entranceway sign for a local business, a project few teachers at his school knew about but which had drawn many positive comments and praise from community members. Justin has quite a few friends, although he also enjoys time by him-

1

self, which he usually spends producing graphic design work for his high school's yearbook, pen and ink sketches for his parents' holiday cards, and paintings for his art portfolio.

Based on these brief case studies, which of these two students would be considered "gifted and talented?" Julia? Justin? Both? Neither? Do the "gifted and talented" learners in our classrooms exhibit characteristics which, if understood, would help us to better meet their educational needs? An awareness of the traits and characteristics of gifted and talented learners is essential in a discussion of methods, materials, and resources appropriate for developing their potential. However, as the title of this chapter implies, gifted and talented learners are not a homogeneous group. To the contrary, they are many, varied, and unique. Several researchers who have studied gifted and talented learners agree that "there is no one portrait of a gifted student. Talents and strengths among the gifted vary as widely as they do with any sample of students drawn from a so-called average population" (Schmitz & Galbraith, 1985, p. 13). Lovecky (1992), concurred, finding that "gifted children differ from each other as much as they differ from average children" (p. 18). Clark (1988) also discussed the unique differences in characteristics of gifted and talented learners, indicating

> as a human being develops higher levels of functioning, many unique patterns and traits emerge. For that reason, the education of groups of gifted individuals is not an easy task. They are not a homogeneous group. (pp. 122–123)

Despite this variability, some common characteristics can be found of many in this population. As Passow (1981) wrote, "Despite the tremendous variation which exists among a group of gifted and talented children, they do have many characteristics which differentiate them from other learners" (p. 3). The purpose of this chapter is to discuss general characteristics of gifted and talented learners as identified in the research literature. The attempt here is not to provide a checklist by which students may be classified as "gifted and talented," but rather to provide educators with an overview of the characteristics they may observe in some high ability students. These characteristics may vary by gender, or socio-cultural group or they may be manifested differently among gifted children with disabilities, with different linguistic backgrounds, or among previously high-achieving students who have begun to underachieve. A better understanding of the generally recognized attributes of gifted and talented learners may enable educators to provide appropriate opportunities for special gifts and talents in the students they serve.

Giftedness and Talent: An Introduction

For many years, psychometricians and psychologists, following in the footsteps of Terman (1916), equated giftedness with high IQ. This "legacy" survives to the present day, in that giftedness and high IQ continue to be equated in some conceptions of giftedness. Since that early time, however, other researchers (e.g., Cattell, Guilford, and Thurstone) have argued that intellect cannot be expressed in such a unitary manner and have suggested more multifaceted approaches to intelligence (Wallace & Pierce, 1992). Research conducted in the 1980s and 1990s has provided data supporting notions of multiple components to intelligence. This is particularly evident in the reexamination of "giftedness" by Sternberg and Davidson (1986) in their edited *Conceptions of Giftedness*. The 16 different conceptions of giftedness presented (those of Albert & Runco [1986]; Bamberger [1986]; Borkowski & Peck [1986]; Csikszentmihalyi & Robinson [1986]; Davidson [1986]; Feldhusen [1986]; Feldman & Benjamin [1986]; Gallagher & Courtright [1986]; Gruber [1986]; Haensly, Reynolds, & Nash [1986]; Jackson & Butterfield [1986]; Renzulli [1986]; Stanley & Benbow [1986]; Sternberg [1986]; Tannenbaum [1986]; and Walters & Gardner [1986]), although distinct, are interrelated in several ways. Most of the investigators define giftedness in terms of multiple qualities, not all of which are intellectual. IQ scores are often viewed as inadequate measures of giftedness. Motivation, high self-concept, and creativity are key qualities in many of these broadened conceptions of giftedness (Siegler & Kotovsky, 1986).

Howard Gardner's (1983) theory of multiple intelligences (MI) and Joseph Renzulli's (1978) "three ring" definition of gifted behavior serve as precise examples of multifaceted and well-researched conceptualizations of intelligence and giftedness. Gardner's definition of an intelligence is "the ability to solve problems, or create products, that are valued within one or more cultural settings" (Gardner, 1993, p. x). Within his MI theory, he articulates at least seven specific intelligences: linguistic, musical, logical-mathematical, spatial, bodily-kinesthetic, interpersonal, and intrapersonal. Gardner believes that people are much more comfortable using the term "talents" and "intelligence" is generally reserved to describe linguistic or logical "smartness" however, he does not believe that certain human abilities should arbitrarily qualify as "intelligence" over others (e.g., language as an intelligence vs. dance as a talent) (Gardner, 1993).

Renzulli's (1978) definition, which defines gifted behaviors rather than gifted individuals, is composed of three components as follows:

> Gifted behavior consists of behaviors that reflect an interaction among three basic clusters of human traits—above average ability, high levels of task commitment, and high levels of creativity. Individuals capable of developing gifted behavior are those possessing or capable of developing this composite set of traits and applying them to any potentially valuable area of human performance. Persons who manifest or are capable of developing an interaction among the three clusters require a wide variety of educational opportunities and services that are not ordinarily provided through regular instructional programs. (Renzulli & Reis, 1997, p. 8)

Characteristics which may be manifested in Renzulli's three clusters are presented in Figure 1.

The United States federal government also subscribed to a multifaceted approach to giftedness as early as 1972 when the Marland Report definition was passed (Public Law 91–230, section 806). The Marland, or "U.S. Department of Education," definition has dominated most states' definitions of giftedness and talent (Passow & Rudnitski, 1993). The most recent federal definition was cited in the Jacob K. Javits Gifted and Talented Students Education Act of 1988 and is discussed in the most recent national report on the state of gifted and talented education:

> Children and youth with outstanding talent perform or show the potential for performing at remarkably high levels of accomplishment when compared with others of their age, experience, or environment. These children and youth exhib-

it high performance capability in intellectual, creative, and/or artistic areas, possess an unusual leadership capacity, or excel in specific academic fields. They require services or activities not ordinarily provided by the schools. Outstanding talents are present in children and youth from all cultural groups, across all economic strata, and in all areas of human endeavor. (U.S. Department of Education, 1993, p. 26)

Above Average Ability (general)
- high levels of abstract thought
- adaptation to novel situations
- rapid and accurate retrieval of information

Above Average Ability (specific)
- applications of general abilities to specific area of knowledge
- capacity to sort out relevant from irrelevant information
- capacity to acquire and use advanced knowledge and strategies while pursuing a problem

Task Commitment
- capacity for high levels of interest, enthusiasm
- hard work and determination in a particular area
- self-confidence and drive to achieve
- ability to identify significant problems within an area of study
- setting high standards for one's work

Creativity
- fluency, flexibility, and originality of thought
- open to new experiences and ideas
- curious
- willing to take risks
- sensitive to aesthetic characteristics

Figure 1. Taxonomy of Behavioral Manifestations of Giftedness According to Renzulli's "Three-Ring" Definition of Gifted Behaviors

Note. Adapted from *The Schoolwide Enrichment Model: A How-to Guide for Educational Excellence* (2nd ed.), (p. 9), by J. S. Renzulli and S. M. Reis, 1997, by Mansfield Center, CT: Creative Learning Press. Copyright 1997 by Creative Learning Press. Adapted with permission.

Though many school districts adopt this or other broad definitions as their philosophy, others still only pay attention to "intellectual" ability when both identifying and serving students. And, even though we have more diverse definitions of giftedness and intelligence today, many students with gifts and talents go unrecognized and underserved (Hishinuma & Tadaki, 1996; Kloosterman, 1997) perhaps due to the differing characteristics found in intellectually gifted, creatively gifted, and diverse gifted learners.

Characteristics of Individuals
With High Intellectual Ability or Potential

A discussion of "high intellectual ability or potential" and "high creative ability or potential" is presented in two separate sections because existing research and discussion often identify two broad categories, which Renzulli (1986) appropriately referred to as either "schoolhouse giftedness" or "creative/productive giftedness." Schoolhouse giftedness refers to test-taking, lesson-learning, or academic giftedness. Individuals who fall into this category generally score well on more traditional intellectual or cognitive assessments and perform well in school. Creative/productive giftedness, on the other hand, is reflected in individuals who tend to be producers (rather than consumers) of original knowledge, materials, or products, and who employ thought processes that tend to be inductive, integrated, and problem oriented. Results of a recent longitudinal study provide research which supports Renzulli's distinction between schoolhouse giftedness and creative/productive giftedness. Perleth, Sierwald, and Heller (1993), in their Munich Longitudinal Study of Giftedness (1985–1989) focusing on a large number of secondary students, found clear differences between students who demonstrated creative/productive as opposed to schoolhouse giftedness. Renzulli believes that both types of giftedness should be developed and that an interaction exists between them (Renzulli & Reis, 1985). This interaction is discussed in later sections of the chapter.

Cognitive and Affective Characteristics

Clark's (1988) extensive list of the characteristics of gifted students is widely cited. Figure 2 summarizes these characteristics, which are often manifested by intellectually or academically gifted students in majority cultures. Again, this list should not serve as an exclusive checklist for identification, as any individual will probably not exhibit all of these characteristics. Lists such as this one may provide information about students who may be in need of special services or modifications in their academic, counseling, or extracurricular programs.

Other researchers have also compiled similar, though less extensive, lists of characteristics which seek to define the intellectually gifted learner. Feldhusen (1989) indicated characteristics, similar to those described by Renzulli and Clark, that gifted learners

- have the ability to learn more rapidly than average ability students;
- are able to deal with complex and abstract concepts;
- are ahead of age-mates in basic skills;
- have advanced verbal ability; and
- have a developed use of thinking skills.

Based upon anecdotal evidence from her work with intellectually talented children, Hannell (1991) discussed the following cognitive and affective characteristics of intellectually-able children:

- sophisticated ability to evaluate own performance;
- search for ordered complexity, undiagnosed specific learning difficulties;
- incompatibility of intellectual and emotional developmental levels; and
- overall lack of experience with failure.

Though these are not necessarily negative characteristics, their presence may result in frustrations and difficulties for gifted children, both in the personal and academic arenas.

In research about gifted students from multicultural and diverse backgrounds, Frasier and Passow (1994) refer to "general/common attributes of giftedness"—traits, aptitudes, and behaviors consistently identified by researchers as common to all gifted students. They note that these basic elements of giftedness

Cognitive (Thinking) Characteristics
- retention of large quantities of information
- advanced comprehension
- varied interests and high curiosity
- high level of language development and verbal ability
- unusual capacity for processing information
- flexible thought processes
- accelerated pace of thought processes
- comprehensive synthesis of ideas
- early ability to delay closure
- ability to see unusual relationships
- ability to generate original ideas and solutions
- capacity to integrate ideas and disciplines
- early differential patterns for thought processing
- early ability to use and form conceptual frameworks
- evaluative approach toward self and others
- unusual intensity
- persistent and goal-directed behavior

Affective (Feeling) Characteristics
- large accumulation of information about emotions
- unusual sensitivity to the feelings of others
- keen sense of humor
- heightened self awareness, feelings of being different
- idealism and sense of justice
- inner locus of control
- unusual emotional depth and intensity
- high expectations of self/others
- perfectionism
- strong need for consistency between values/actions
- advanced levels of moral judgment

Physical (Sensation) Characteristics
- heightened sensory awareness
- unusual discrepancy between physical and intellectual development
- low tolerance for lag between their standards and their athletic skills

Intuitive Characteristics
- early involvement and concern for intuitive knowing
- open to intuitive experiences
- creativity apparent in all areas of endeavor
- ability to predict
- interest in future

Societal Characteristics
- strongly motivated by self-actualization needs
- advanced capacity for conceptualizing and solving societal problems
- leadership
- involvement with the metaneeds of society (i.e., justice, truth, beauty)

Figure 2. Clark's Differentiating Characteristics of Gifted Students

---

Note. From *Growing Up Gifted* (3rd ed.), (p. 126–132), by B. Clark, 1988, Columbus, OH: Merrill Publishing. Copyright 1988 by Prentice-Hall. Adapted with permission of Prentice-Hall of Prentice-Hall, Inc., Upper Saddle River, NJ.

are similar across cultures (though each is not displayed by every student). A listing of these attributes may be found in Figure 3. Each of these common characteristics may be manifested in different ways in different students; educators should be especially careful in attempting to identify these characteristics in students from diverse backgrounds (i.e., disadvantaged, different ethnic or racial backgrounds, etc.), as specific behavioral manifestations of the characteristics may vary with context (Frasier & Passow, 1994). Further issues related to diverse gifted learners will be discussed later in this chapter.

Social and Emotional Issues

Do intellectually gifted learners have unique affective, social, and emotional characteristics as well? As indicated in Figure 2, Clark

(1988) delineated differential affective and societal characteristics of gifted individuals, as well as cognitive characteristics. Roeper (1996) believed the gifted individual is emotionally different from others in a holistic sense, rather than in trait-level differences. She wrote "the gifted child is emotionally different from others," "the self of the gifted child is structured differently," they have a more complex view of the world, their depth of awareness is different, that there is a "gifted personality structure," and gifted children have an emotional need to develop themselves and master the world (p. 18).

Although some researchers, such as Feldhusen (1989), assured us that gifted children do not have more social-emotional problems than average children, others disagree and claim that unique characteristics of intellectually able individuals may pose challenges to social and emotional balance and adjustment and leave these individuals somewhat vulnerable. Common characteristics which, though neutral in and of themselves, may prove to be somewhat problematic, include those summarized in Figure 4.

These personality/affective characteristics interact with intellectual traits and talents of the individual as well (Silverman, 1993). Depending on the interaction of characteristics and the strength of the displayed traits, these characteristics may be crucial when dealing with the psychological development of certain intellectually able

---

- motivation
- communication skills
- well-developed memory
- insight
- imagination/creativity
- advanced ability to deal with symbol systems

- advanced interests
- problem-solving ability
- inquiry
- reasoning
- sense of humor

Figure 3. Common Attributes of Giftedness

Note[1]. From *Towards a New Paradigm for Identifying Talent Potential,* (p. 49–51), by M. M. Frasier and A. H. Passow, 1994, Storrs, CT: University of Connecticut, The National Research Center on the Gifted and Talented. Copyright 1994 by National Research Center on the Gifted and Talented. Adapted with permission.

individuals. Although possible vulnerabilities or negative consequences resulting from these traits are cited in research and textbooks dealing with this subject, many of them can actually have a positive impact on an individual's social and emotional well-being, if developed in a healthy manner. For example, in a recent study by Schuler (1997) dealing with perfectionism in gifted adolescents, she found examples of healthy perfectionism in the participants, as

- perceptiveness (Lovecky, 1992, 1993; Schmitz & Galbraith, 1985)
- high involvement and preoccupation; need to understand (Schmitz & Galbraith, 1985; Silverman, 1993)
- heightened sensitivity (Coleman, 1996; Lovecky, 1992, 1993; Schmitz & Galbraith, 1985; Silverman, 1993; Swart, 1993)
- perfectionism (Coleman, 1996; Lovecky, 1992; Reis, 1987; Schmitz & Galbraith, 1985; Schuler, 1997; Silverman, 1993)
- uneven integration of intellectual abilities (Schmitz & Galbraith, 1985)
- emotional intensity (Lovecky, 1992; Silverman, 1993; Swart, 1993)
- feelings and early awareness of being different (Coleman, 1996; Lovecky, 1992; Swart, 1993)
- asynchronous development of physical, intellectual, social, emotional aspects (Lovecky, 1992; Swart, 1993)
- anxiety caused by advanced knowledge (Coleman, 1996)
- early adolescence (some children, especially highly gifted, may skip the latency stage of development) (Swart, 1993)
- need for mental stimulation (Silverman, 1993)
- entelechy—a particular type of motivation where there is a desire to become all one is capable of becoming (Lovecky, 1992, 1993)
- need for precision (Silverman, 1993)
- nonconformity and questioning of authority (Silverman, 1993; Swart, 1993)
- excitability and overexcitability (Dabrowski, 1938; Lovecky, 1992, 1993)
- tendency toward introversion (Silverman, 1993)

Figure 4. Social and Emotional Characteristics of Gifted Children That May Pose Challenges

defined by students doing their personal best and wanting to consistently do well.

Social and emotional stress can also result when high ability students are teased by their peers and are subjected to peer pressure regarding their intellectual abilities. Many of our brightest students learn to not answer in class, to stop raising their hands, and to minimize their abilities in order to avoid pressures of being labeled as a "nerd," "dweeb," or "dork." Consider the experiences of an exceptional student who pleaded with her school board to save the gifted program:

> In my 12 years in school, I have been placed in many "average" classes—especially up until the junior high school level—in which I have been spit on, ostracized, and verbally abused for doing my homework on a regular basis, for raising my hand in class, and particularly for receiving outstanding grades. (Peters, 1990, p. 10)

Opportunities for students to spend time with others of similar ability who recognize and appreciate their talents and academically positive behaviors can be essential in enabling students to understand and deal with these peer pressures (Rogers, 1991). Individual, group, or family counseling, whether formal or informal, may be needed for some individuals to cope with issues brought about by their differences.

Characteristics of Individuals
With High Creative Ability or Potential

The ways in which academically gifted and creatively gifted students vary have been discussed by many researchers and educators, and most who have studied the area would probably agree with Sternberg and Lubart's (1993) assertion that the "academically successful children of today are not necessarily the creatively gifted adults of tomorrow" (p. 12). Individuals with high intelligence may or may not have high creative ability or potential as well (Davis & Rimm, 1998; Renzulli & Reis, 1985). There is evidence, however, to suggest a relationship between the constructs. The "threshold concept" discussed by MacKinnon (1978), describes a base level (an IQ of about 120) of intelligence as essential for creative productivity. Beyond that threshold, there is no relationship between creativity and intelligence as measured by IQ tests (Davis & Rimm, 1998; Sternberg & Lubart, 1993).

What are the traits that help define an individual with high creative ability or potential? Gardner's (1993) conception of a creative individual is one who "regularly solves problems or fashions products in a domain, and whose work is considered both novel and acceptable by knowledgeable members of a field" (p. xvii). Creativity should not be regarded as a construct in the mind or personality of an individual, rather it is something that emerges from the interactions of intelligence (personal profile of compentences), domain (disciplines or crafts within a culture), and field (people and institutions that judge quality within a domain) (Gardner, 1993).

Sternberg and Lubart (1993) view creativity as a type of giftedness in itself, rather than as one dimension of intelligence. They propose that a person's "resources" for creativity allow a process of creative production to occur. Because they believe that six separate resources combine to interactively yield creativity, they find creative giftedness to be a rare occurrence because so many components must interact at once. Sternberg and Lubart's six "resources" succinctly describe many of the traits of creative individuals.

Intellectual Processes. Creatively gifted people excel in problem definition, using insight (selective encoding, selective comparison, and selective combination) to solve problems and divergent thought as a problem solving strategy. These intellectual processes of creatively gifted learners are all immeasurable by traditional IQ tests.

Knowledge. Knowledge of the domain allows for one to identify areas where new and novel work is needed. To some extent, knowledge may serve as a hindrance to creativity, as too much of it can limit ability to have fresh ideas.

Intellectual (Cognitive) Styles. Creatively gifted people tend to prefer a legislative style (creating, formulating, and planning) and a global mode of processing information (thinking abstractly, generalizing, and extrapolating). Both of these styles are encouraged through approaches such as the Schoolwide Enrichment Model (Renzulli & Reis, 1985, 1997).

Personality. Five key personality attributes are important to creative giftedness: tolerance of ambiguity, moderate risk-taking, willingness to surmount obstacles and persevere, willingness to grow, and belief in self and ideas.

Motivation. A task-focused orientation (drive or goal that leads a person to work on a task, as opposed to a goal-focused orientation [extrinsic motivators, rewards, or recognition] which leads people to see a task as a means to an end) exists often in creatively gifted individuals. (See also Renzulli, 1978.)

Environmental Context. Environmental resources play into creativity as well. Implications for educators include providing surroundings which promote creativity, a reward system for creative ideas, and an evaluation of creative products by appropriate audiences. (See also Renzulli & Reis, 1985, 1997.)

Davis (1992) also provides a list of characteristics of individuals with high creative ability or potential, after reviewing many lists of personality characteristics compiled by researchers (see Figure 5). Additionally, he compiled a list of traits not uncommon in creative students, which may be considered more "negative" (see Figure 5). These traits may tend to upset the parents and educators, as well as some of the peers of creative children, since they lead to behaviors not considered appropriate in traditional classrooms. A challenge exists for educators and parents to identify these characteristics of creativity in children and to channel creative energy into constructive outlets (Davis & Rimm, 1998) by encouraging playfulness, flexibility, and the production of wild and unusual ideas (Torrance, 1962).

In summary, creatively gifted and talented children may exhibit different characteristics than academically gifted children. Those with high academic abilities have the potential to develop creative gifts and talents, yet many creatively gifted students do not necessarily display high academic performance in school.

Developmental Considerations

Developmental issues are important to consider in attempting to recognize and advance talents and abilities in individuals. Traits and behaviors unique to learners of varying age levels may provide clues regarding the manifestations of talent at different ages.

The Young Gifted Child

Early signs of precocity exist in some children. Parents are quite capable of describing early behaviors, though they may not necessarily identify the behaviors as precocious. Because of this, parents should be viewed by educators as important sources of information about children's talents (Robinson, 1987). Early language development, advanced gross motor competence, and early reading are precocious behaviors easily identified and assessed in young children. In general, though, assessing advanced abilities and talents in young children proves quite difficult and unreliable, especially when using

---

Positive Characteristics

- original
- independent
- energetic
- keen sense of humor

- artistic
- perceptive

- aware of their own creativeness
- willing to take risks
- curious
- attracted to complexity and novelty
- open-minded
- need for privacy, alone time

Negative Characteristics

- rebelliousness

- stubbornness
- low interest in details
- forgetfulness
- carelessness and disorganization with unimportant matters

- indifference to common conventions
- questioning rules and authority
- tendency to be emotional
- absentmindedness

Figure 5. Positive and Negative Characteristics of Creativity

---

Note. From *Creativity is Forever* (3rd ed.), (p. 68–80), by G. A. Davis, 1992, Dubuque, IA: Kendall/Hunt. Copyright 1992 by Kendall/Hunt. Adapted with permission.

traditional intelligence tests. According to Robinson (1987), several researchers have found that strength in very early novelty preferences, visual attention, and visual recognition memory during infancy can be somewhat effective predictors of intelligence in childhood. Because little research exists in this area (as compared to research on older gifted students), parents and teachers should "keep our views broad and flexible if we are to identify reliable and significant indices of precocious development" (Robinson, 1987, p. 162).

Some gifted young children have been described as having emotional intensity and emotional sensitivity. Dabrowski (1938) suggested that gifted children release emotional tension through five overexcitabilities (intellectual, imaginational, emotional, psy-

Table 1. Overexcitability Behaviors

Behavior	Definition
Intellectual overexcitability behaviors	Curiosity, asking probing questions, concentration, problem solving, theoretical thinking
Imaginational overexcitability behaviors	Fantasy play, imaginative thinking, daydreaming, dramatic perception
Emotional overexcitability behaviors	Concern for others, timidity and shyness, fear and anxiety, intensity of feeling
Psychomotor overexcitability behaviors	Marked enthusiasm, rapid speech, impulsive actions
Sensual overexcitability behaviors	Sensory pleasures, appreciation of sensory aspects of experiences

Note. From "Psychological intensities in young gifted children," by B. Tucker and N. L. Hafenstein, 1997, *Gifted Child Quarterly, 41*, p. 70. Copyright 1997 by National Association for the Gifted and Talented. Adapted with permission.

chomotor, and sensual). A recent study by Tucker and Hafenstein (1997) using qualitative case study methodology with five young gifted children provides evidence to the existence of the five overexcitabilities in these children via manifestations of behaviors associated with the overexcitabilities. These young children displayed the behaviors listed in Table 1. The results of the study certainly support the work of Dabrowski (1938) and can serve as a guideline for possible behaviors which may be seen in young gifted children.

Feldman (1993) conducted research on child prodigies, which he defines as children (usually younger than 10 years old) who are performing at the levels of highly skilled adults in demanding fields. He considers prodigious talent to be a distinct form of giftedness and has found prodigies to have highly focused talent, extreme motivation to develop the talent, and unusual self-confidence in their ability to do so. Psychometric intelligence plays a role in the development of a prodigy, but not a central one (Feldman, 1993).

The Gifted Adolescent

Along with the multitude of issues faced by any adolescent, particular social and career choice issues may present unique challenges to gifted and talented teenagers. In addition, talented adolescents may have certain qualities that other teenagers do not. Csikszentmihalyi, Rathunde, and Whalen (1993) conducted an in-depth longitudinal study of 200 talented teenagers. They identified a strong core of personal attributes which distinguished the talented teenagers in their study from their average counterparts: intellectual curiosity, active reception of information from the world, strong desire to achieve, perseverance to attain their goals, preference for leading and controlling, desire to display accomplishments and gain other's attention, and little questioning of their own worth. Some personality attributes were displayed by only one gender. For example, talented male teens, in comparison to average male teens, valued stability and predictability more, preferred to avoid physical risks, enjoyed arguments more, and had an unusual need for social recognition. The talented female teens, when compared to their average counterparts, were less inclined to identify with values seen often as "feminine" (orderliness, neatness, and predictability). Overall, the researchers found that the cluster of attributes which described the talented teens suggested an "autotelic" (self-directed or self-rewarding) personality. The teens in this study

> entered adolescence with personality attributes well suited to the difficult struggle of establishing their mastery over a domain: a desire to achieve, persistence, and a curiosity and openness to experience. (Csikszentmihalyi, et al., 1993, p. 82)

Karnes and McGinnis (1996) also found support for differences between academically talented adolescents and average adolescents. Their study showed that their sample of academically talented adolescents indicated a more internal locus of control than average students. Locus of control is the extent to which an individual sees that their own behavior causes subsequent reinforcement; an individual perceiving reinforcement as contingent upon his or her own behavior or characteristics is said to have an internal locus of control.

Baker (1996) discussed several issues and pressures that affect gifted adolescents, noting that much of the evidence comes from anecdotal literature. There are conflicting data regarding the stress of academic achievement for gifted adolescents versus their average counterparts. Other stressors may include pressure for success from self (perfectionism) or from others, including parents; feeling different from others; boredom (which may lead to underachievement, acting out, and so forth); extreme sensitivity (may internalize or elaborate minor things); multipotentiality (with regard to extracurricular activities, issues of spreading themselves too thin versus missing out on projects and activities they may like and be good at); vocational choice issues (stress due to multiple interests and potential in multiple areas); and competition (some may fear competition, others feel used in order for a team to win, and so forth). Baker (1996) conducted a recent study in which academically gifted, exceptionally academically gifted, and academically average adolescents were evaluated regarding levels and types of these everyday stressors. Interestingly, Baker found few differences between gifted and nongifted adolescents, concluding that both gifted and nongifted teens experience similar levels and types of stressors.

However, exceptionally gifted girls were found to be more perfectionistic than average girls; this was the only significant difference found.

Diverse Gifted and Talented Learners

Culturally and Linguistically Diverse Gifted and Talented Learners

Case Study: Nakesha

Nakesha, who lives in a large urban city in the northeast, reads at a fourth-grade level and often finishes a 50-page paperback book in the hour. She reads to herself before she falls asleep each night. The next day in school she is bored and sleepy; on several occasions she has begged her parents to let her stay home and read. It's only September, and she is becoming distracted in school, rarely finishes her assignments, and on two occasions, Nakesha's parents, who came to this island from Puerto Rico where they were born, have been called by Nakesha's teacher. The problem with Nakesha is that she is six years old and in first grade. Only one other student in her classroom reads. While her peers learn beginning sounds, Nakesha is left on her own and spends most of her time in school finishing her assigned work in a fraction of the time it takes other students to finish their work and learning to daydream and pass the time. There is a gifted program in Nakesha's school, but it provides services for identified students who are in fourth grade. The teacher in the program spends only a day and a half at Nakesha's school, which is one of the three schools that she travels to each week. No mandate exists to provide services to gifted students in the state in which Nakesha lives, and there is no certification for teachers who work in gifted programs. The teacher who provides services to students in Nakesha's school has had no formal training or coursework, but she has attended a few staff development sessions and one conference on gifted students. Nakesha's parents watch as their child, who was excited about learning and motivated to begin first grade, gradually begins to dislike school and starts crying each morning as she gets ready to leave their apartment. By the time Nakesha finished first grade, she had become bored by school and disinterested in learning.

The decade of the 1980s was marked by an increasing interest in atypical gifted learners, who are described generally as consisting of ethnic, racial, and linguistic minorities, the economically disadvantaged, gifted females, gifted underachievers, and the gifted/disabled. In these populations, the identification of giftedness may be masked by other characteristics and prejudices (Bireley, Languis, & Williamson, 1992). During the last two decades, researchers in the field of gifted education have increasingly turned their attention to the underrepresentation of some populations in gifted programs, such as those mentioned above. Ethnic, racial, and linguistic minorities have also been targeted by federal and state policies. For example, the Jacob K. Javits Gifted and Talented Students Education Act of 1988 established that "outstanding talents are present in children and youth from all cultural groups, across all economic strata, and in all areas of human endeavor" (U.S. Department of Education, 1993, p. 26).

The pervasive disparity in the proportion of culturally and linguistically diverse (limited English proficient [LEP], bilingual, and English as a Second Language [ESL]) students identified and served in programs for the gifted is the major concern of several researchers and educators in gifted education (Maker, 1983; Mitchell, 1988). The primary reason cited for their underrepresentation is the absence of adequate assessment procedures and programming efforts (Frasier, García, & Passow, 1995; Frasier & Passow, 1994; Kitano & Espinosa, 1995). The U.S. Department of Education (1993) report, *National Excellence: A Case for Developing America's Talent*, states that "special efforts are required to overcome the barriers to achievement that many economically disadvantaged and minority students face" (p. 28). Various sections in this report also address the need to identify talents in youngsters of different socioeconomic and cultural backgrounds. In this regard, although several efforts have been made in the last decade to overcome these limitations, school districts and individuals still find themselves lacking systematic research support to design and implement a more equitable system of identifying these students. However, careful attention needs to be devoted to the relevance of the current checklists of traits and characteristics leading to the identification of advanced students. For instance, teacher judgment poses difficulties in referring and identifying culturally and linguistically diverse students due to negative teacher attitudes, resistance, or unsatisfactory knowledge of the manifestations of giftedness in these students. It is crucial that educators hold positive and high expectations toward their bilingual/LEP and culturally diverse students and become aware of the family culture, which may differ greatly from majority families. It is also critical that unique characteristics of each population be included as a part of the identification process.

Recognizing this need to acknowledge characteristics of different cultures in the identification of talent among diverse groups, Maker and Schiever (1989) created several tables listing the common attributes of giftedness, cultural values specific to certain racial or ethnic groups, and the behavioral manifestations of giftedness one might observe in a student from a particular group. Their tables, summarizing characteristics of gifted students of Hispanic, Native American Indian, Asian American, and low socioeconomic status background, have been condensed and displayed in Table 2.

Recently, researchers at The National Research Center on the Gifted and Talented completed a three-year study of 35 economically disadvantaged, ethnically diverse, talented high school students who either achieved or underachieved in their urban high school (Reis, Hébert, Díaz, Maxfield, & Ratley, 1995). Researchers used qualitative methods and found the participants exhibited a number of common personal characteristics including motivation and inner will, positive use of problem solving, independence, realistic aspirations, heightened sensitivity to each other and the world around them, and appreciation of cultural diversity. Despite what could be considered prejudice leveled against them, the participants in this study consistently echoed a determination to succeed.

Rosa, one of the participants in the study, said she had experienced various types of prejudice in her community, and occasionally in academic experiences. Rosa believed she experienced prejudice because of her intelligence and Puerto Rican decent. This prejudice, from teachers as well as students, occurred in school and during her participation in the summer programs for high achieving students at some of the most prestigious private schools in the state. She explained, "I know that people will occasionally look at me and say, when they find out that I'm smart, 'How can that be? She's Puerto Rican'" (Reis, et al., 1995, p. 102).

Table 2. Characteristics of Giftedness and Cultural Values of Minorities, and Possible Behavioral Manifestations of Giftedness Resulting From Their Interaction

Absolute Aspects of Giftedness	Characteristic Cultural Values	Behavioral Differences
HISPANICS		
Leadership	Collaborative rather than competitive dynamic	Accomplishes more, works better in small groups than individually
Emotional depth and intensity	"Abrazo," a physical or spiritual index of personal support	Requires touching, eye contact, feeling of support to achieve maximum productivity
NATIVE AMERICAN INDIANS		
Unusual sensitivity to expectations and feelings of others	Collective self— the Tribe	Is a good mediator
Creativity in endeavors	Traditions, heritage, beliefs	Makes up stories or poems
ASIAN AMERICANS		
High expectations of self	Confucianist ethic—people can be improved by proper effort and instruction	Academic orientation and achievement
Perfectionism	Conformity, correctness, respect for and obedience to authority	Patience and willingness for drill and rote exercises; decreased risk taking and creative expression

LOW SOCIOECONOMIC STATUS GROUPS

Persistent, goal-directed behavior	Survival in circumstances	"Streetwiseness," community-based entrepreneurship
Accelerated pace of thought processes	Physical punishment, blunt orders rather than discussion	Manipulative behavior, scapegoating

Note. From *Critical Issues in Gifted Education: Defensible Programs for Cultural and Ethnic Minorities* (Vol. II), (p. 4, 78, 152, 211), by C. J. Maker and S. W. Schiever, 1989, Austin, TX: PRO-ED. Copyright 1989 by PRO-ED. Adapted with permission.

Each of the high achieving participants in this study referred to an internal motivation that kept them driven to succeed in their urban environment. One participant referred to this drive as an "inner will," which contributed to the strong belief in self. Resilience was also exhibited by many of the participants in this study, as the majority came from homes which had been affected by periodic or regular unemployment of one or more parents, poverty, family turmoil caused by issues such as alcohol, drugs, and mental illness, and other problems. All participants also lived in a city plagued by violence, drugs, poverty, and crime. Their school district has often been called one of the worst in the country and had the dubious distinctions of having the state eliminate the local board of education and take over the schools. Despite these challenges, the majority of the high achieving participants in this study developed the resilience necessary to overcome problems associated with their families, their school, and their environment. The courage and resilience they displayed seems remarkable, and yet they simply accepted their circumstances and took advantage of the opportunities given to them.

These culturally diverse gifted students and those who are acquiring English represent a heterogeneous group. According to Kitano and Espinosa (1995), "Their diversity suggests a need for a broad range of programs that provide options for different levels of primary and English language proficiency, different subject-matter interests, and talent areas" (p. 237). These authors call for new strategies for identifying diverse gifted students, including developmental curriculum and enriched programs that evoke a gifted student's potential, broader conceptions of intelligence, alternative definitions of giftedness, and assessment models developed for specific populations.

Gifted Females

What factors cause some smart young girls with hopes and dreams to become self-fulfilled, talented women in their later lives? For the last two decades, educators have speculated on the answers to this question, and while some research has addressed the issue, much more is needed. In this section, several issues related to the characteristics of gifted and talented girls in school are discussed.

Some research (Arnold, 1995; Bell, 1989; Cramer, 1989; Hany, 1994; Kline & Short, 1991; Kramer, 1991; Leroux, 1988; Perleth & Heller, 1994; Reis, 1987, 1998; Reis & Callahan, 1989; Subotnik, 1988) has indicated that gifted females begin to lose self-confidence in elementary school, which continues through college and graduate school. They increasingly doubt their intellectual competence, perceive themselves as less capable than they actually are, and believe that boys can rely on innate ability while they themselves must work hard. Talented girls, it is also said, choose more often to work in groups and are more concerned about teacher reactions, more likely to adapt to adult expectations, and less likely than boys to describe themselves or to be described as autonomous and independent. But some bright girls also use affiliations and their relationships to assess their level of ability to achieve at higher levels and often believe that their grades will be higher if their teachers like them.

Reis (1998) recently completed a comprehensive analysis of gifted females and offered numerous suggestions on how their needs can be better met across the lifespan. She studied research on talented girls' social and emotional development through elementary and secondary school and concluded that achievement of girls is good in school but that self-confidence and self-perceived abilities decrease and that achievement in life is lower than males of comparable ability. Some gifted females value their own personal achievements less as they get older, which may indicate that the aging process has a negative impact on both the achievement and the self-confidence of gifted females. Reis (1998) also found, however, that as gifted females approach middle to later age, many of the conflicts they faced as young women decrease and they are able to excel.

Previous research indicated that being identified as having talents or being bright may even be problematic for females because of adverse social consequences (Buescher, Olszewski, & Higham, 1987; Eccles, Midgley, & Adler, 1984; Kerr, Colangelo, & Gaeth 1988; Kramer, 1991). Some adolescent females believe that it is a social disadvantage to be smart because of the potential negative reactions this may generate from others. Many bright young women deliberately understate their abilities in order to avoid being seen as physically unattractive or lacking in social competence (Reis, 1998). Some researchers have concluded that our society's general increase in negativity toward academic achievement affects even the higher achieving students in junior and senior high school. This may cause some male and female students to try to be like everyone else and, under no circumstances, to appear different by working for good, but not outstanding, grades (Reis, 1998).

Recent research indicated in some situations high ability females do view their achievement and talents more positively. African-American talented males and females in an urban school district expressed great support for the achievement ideology; and in one study by Ford (1992), gifted females believed they had the highest teacher feedback on their efforts. Similar findings emerged in research conducted by Reis et al. (1995) on talented female adolescents in an urban environment. In another study, girls were encouraged by their parents to go to college and to continue achieving but were not actively encouraged to pursue specific careers (Reis, Callahan, & Goldsmith, 1996). And Spielhagen (1996) found that 45 young talented females, who had participated in programs for talented youth, were clearly aware of their abilities and did not deny or hide their potential. They also demonstrated a more balanced view of female achievement, understanding that achievement in school and life does not always take the same form. It is clear that characteristics of gifted and talented girls vary by age, cultural group, and circumstance; and we cannot always generalize from one population to another or use one characteristic from one gifted girl to describe another. Too many intervening variables affect the complex reasons that one girl grows up to be self-confident and able to achieve, while another of similar ability does not.

Gifted Students With Disabilities

Historically, the exceptionality of gifted students with disabilities was mentioned at a national conference on handicapped gifted held in 1976; in 1977 the category "gifted handicapped" was added to ERIC indices (Yewchuk & Bibby, 1989). During the last 20 years, some research has contributed to our understanding of the special needs of these exceptional young children; however, it is still clear that students with disabilities are more often recognized for handicaps, not gifts (Schmitz & Galbraith, 1985; Schwartz, 1994; Yewchuk & Bibby, 1989). Research about this population is ongoing and will be briefly discussed by specific exceptionality.

Gifted and Talented Students With Hearing Disabilities. Teachers judged children with hearing impairments to exhibit similar characteristics of giftedness to hearing peers, except for academic achievement, which may be delayed for four or five years. Yewchuk and Bibby (1989) concluded that "giftedness in both hearing and hearing impaired populations is manifested in similar ways" (p. 48), including an eagerness to learn, visual skills, superior recall, quick understanding, superior reasoning ability, expressive language, and so forth.

Gifted and Talented Students With Cerebral Palsy. Willard-Holt (1994) explored the experiences of two talented students who have cerebral palsy and were not able to communicate with speech. Using qualitative cross-case methodology, she found that these students demonstrated the following characteristics of giftedness: advanced academic abilities (especially math and verbal skills), broad knowledge base, quickness of learning and recall, sense of humor, curiosity, insight, desire for independence, use of intellectual skills to cope with disability, and maturity (shown in high motivation, goal orientation, determination, patience, and recognition of their own limitations). Several educational factors contributed to the development of these characteristics in these students, such as willingness of the teachers to accommodate for the disabilities, mainstreaming with nondisabled students, individualization and opportunities for student choice, and hands-on experiences.

Gifted and Talented Students With Learning Disabilities. During the last two decades, increasing attention has been given to the perplexing problem of high ability talented students who also have learning disabilities. The specific research concerning high ability students with learning disabilities began following the passage of PL 94–142, when the expanded emphasis on the education of students with disabilities created an interest in students who were gifted but also demonstrated learning disabilities. Although the literature has addressed this topic, problems still exist regarding the identification and provision of support services and programs for this population. Research on high ability students with learning disabilities continues to be difficult because of problems in defining each population. The fields of gifted education and education of students with learning disabilities have long been separated by their own definitions of the population to be served, as well as by their separate professional organizations, journals, and recommended educational practices. Practitioners in both fields have indicated that their respective federal definitions are inadequate (Boodoo, Bradley, Frontera, Pitts, & Wright, 1989; Renzulli, 1978; Taylor, 1989; Vaughn, 1989; Ysseldyke & Algozzine, 1983).

Baum and Owen (1988), in a study of 112 high ability or LD students in grades 4–6 using discriminant analyses, found the major characteristic distinguishing high ability/LD students from both LD/average and high ability (non-LD) groups was a heightened sense of inefficacy in school. The high ability/LD students in their study also displayed high levels of creative potential, along with a tendency to behave disruptively and to achieve low levels of academic success. Also, 36% of the students in their study, who had been identified as having a learning disability, simultaneously demonstrated behaviors associated with giftedness. Baum (1990) later identified four recommendations for gifted students with learning

disabilities: encourage compensation strategies, encourage awareness of strengths and weaknesses, focus on developing the child's
gift, and provide an environment that values individual differences.

After a thorough review of the literature on gifted/LD students,
Reis, Neu, and McGuire (1995) compiled a list of characteristics of
gifted/LD students which may hamper their identification as being
gifted. These characteristics are the result between the interaction of
their high abilities and their learning disabilities and include those
listed in Figure 6. These researchers also identified several characteristic strengths of gifted students with learning disabilities, which
are also listed in Figure 6.

Some high ability students with reading disabilities may display
different characteristics including
- high verbal or visual-motor aptitude;
- possible creativity; boredom with grade level or below grade
  level reading;
- variable scores on achievement tests in reading sections;
- improved performance with compensation strategies (heard
  information, word processor, spell-checkers, additional time for
  assignments);
- low tolerance for frustration with rote/drill reading tasks; possible inattention; and
- unrealistically high or low self-concept (Hishinuma & Tadaki,
  1996).

High ability students with math disabilities may display a set of different characteristics including
- high verbal aptitude;
- possible creativity;
- boredom with grade level or below grade level math;
- variable scores on achievement tests in math sections;
- improved performance with compensation (emphasis on word
  problems, calculator use, additional time for assignments);
- low tolerance for frustration with rote/drill math tasks;
- possible inattention; and
- unrealistically high or low self-concept (Hishinuma & Tadaki,
  1996).

Students who exhibit characteristics of both the gifted and
learning disabled populations pose quandaries for educators. The

Characteristics Which Hamper Identification as Gifted

- frustration with inability to master certain academic skills
- learned helplessness
- general lack of motivation
- disruptive classroom behavior
- perfectionism
- supersensitivity
- failure to complete assignments
- lack of organizational skills
- demonstration of poor listening and concentration skills
- deficiency in tasks emphasizing memory and perceptual abilities
- low self-esteem
- unrealistic self-expectations
- absence of social skills with some peers

Characteristic Strengths

- advanced vocabulary use
- exceptional analytic abilities
- high levels of creativity
- advanced problem-solving skills
- ability to think of divergent ideas and solutions
- specific aptitude (artistic, musical, or mechanical)
- wide variety of interests
- good memory
- task commitment
- spatial abilities

Figure 6. Characteristics of Gifted Students With Learning Disabilities

Note. From *Talent in Two Places: Case Studies of High Ability Students with Learning Disabilities Who Have Achieved,* (p. 16–17), by S. M. Reis, T. W. Neu and J. M. McGuire, 1995, Storrs, CT: University of Connecticut, The National Research Center on the Gifted and Talented. Copyright 1995 by NRC/GT. Adapted with permission.

misconceptions, definitions, and expected outcomes for these types of students further complicate the issues facing appropriate programming for this population (Baum, Owen, & Dixon, 1991; Olenchak & Renzulli, 1989; Whitmore, 1986). Awareness of these students' needs is becoming more common with both the teachers of the gifted and the teachers of LD students, yet most school districts have no provision for intervention programs for this group (Boodoo et al., 1989).

Gifted and Talented Students With ADHD. Children with ADHD (attention deficit hyperactivity disorder) and gifted children may exhibit similar behaviors (inattention, high energy level, impulsivity). There seems to be mounting evidence that many children being identified as having ADHD are also very bright and creative (Cramond, 1995; Webb & Latimer, 1993).

To distinguish whether a gifted student may also have ADHD, the school and home situation and settings must be closely monitored because gifted children typically will not display similar behaviors in all settings (home, school, music lessons, etc.). Gifted students may experience inattention due to not being appropriately challenged, and a high energy level may be demonstrated only in areas of intense interest. One characteristic difference which is often noted in ADHD children is that they usually show variability in the quality of their performance on specific tasks, whereas gifted students are more consistent with their level of effort and performance, especially when they are interested and challenged. Of course, gifted children may also have ADHD; but a careful professional evaluation is needed to make this diagnosis, followed by appropriate medical, psychological, and curricular and instructional modifications (Webb & Latimer, 1993).

Underachieving Gifted Learners

Case Study: Mark

Mark's work in school had frustrated both of his parents for years. Always a child of remarkably high potential, Mark's grades had fluctuated in elementary, junior, and senior high school. Mark took advanced math classes in school and achieved a near perfect score on the math section of the SAT, taken during his junior year of high school. However, he was labeled an "underachiever" because of his variable attitudes toward school. He always did well on his exams, even when he had done none of the assigned work in class. He simply lost credit for every bit of homework and classwork that he did not do.

The problem wasn't that Mark was idle. In fact, his parents pleaded with him to go to bed in the evening because he was reading books about artificial intelligence or pursuing his own interests, which happened to be designing software and building computers. In his senior year, Mark received recruitment letters from the best colleges in the country because of his SAT scores; but, unfortunately, he did not graduate from high school, failing both English and history. He did not like his teachers, and the work was too easy in the lower-track classes to which he had been assigned because of his lack of effort in earlier years and his variable performance in his classes. Not graduating from high school was, for Mark, the lesser of two fates. The worse fate, in his opinion, was pretending to be interested in boring, uninspiring classes taught by teachers he believed did not care about him.

Almost 15 years have passed since Mark flunked his senior year of high school, and a happier ending has unfolded. After a few years of switching jobs and searching for the right school and the right program, Mark started college part-time, despite the fact that he did not have a high school diploma. Eight years later, he had completed both his Bachelor's and Master's degrees in Systems Engineering, and he is currently working on sophisticated software design as an engineer. The reversal of his underachievement occurred when he made up his own mind that it was time to succeed academically and that he wanted to succeed and also when he found the right academic program for himself. He didn't get high grades in every class, but he learned to put out the minimum effort necessary to pass required classes which were not in his major area, which in turn enabled him to continue taking the classes he loved.

Student performance that falls noticeably short of potential, especially for young people with high ability, is bewildering and perhaps the most frustrating of all challenges both teachers and parents face. According to a 1990 national needs assessment survey conducted by The National Research Center on the Gifted and Talented, most educators of gifted identified the problem of underachievement as their number one concern (Renzulli, Reid, & Gubbins, 1991).

Some students underachieve or fail in school for obvious reasons: excessive absences from school, poor performance, disruptive behavior, low self-esteem, family problems, and poverty. In addition to the risk factors which clearly predict the reasons why most students fail, another long-standing problem which causes underachievement in gifted or high potential students is the totally inappropriate curriculum and content, which some of them encounter on a daily basis. The hundreds of hours spent each month in classrooms where students rarely encounter new or challenging curricula, the boredom of being assigned routine tasks mastered long ago, the low levels of discussion, and the mismatch of content to students' ability lead to frustration on the parts of many of our brightest students. In fact, dropping out of school is the only way that some students believe they can address these issues effectively.

Gallagher (1991) discussed characteristics of personal-psychological underachievers, indicating that the characteristics identified by Terman and Oden in their 1947 study of 300 men have been confirmed by several subsequent researchers (Butler-Por, 1987; Rimm, 1986; and Whitmore, 1980). Those characteristics include lack of self-confidence, inability to persevere, absence of integration toward goals, and feelings of inferiority. Hishinuma and Tadaki (1996) also identified specific characteristics of gifted underachievers, which may provide helpful insights for educators regarding the performance of some of their students. These characteristics include

- high or variable abilities, especially verbal, visual/motor, or both;
- good knowledge, memory, and motivation in areas of strength and interest;
- possible creative talents;
- low course grades relative to ability;
- variable scores on standardized achievement tests;
- preference for nontraditional rewards;
- poor organization and time management;
- lack of homework production; and
- unrealistically low or high self-concept.

Summary

In the past, the general approach to the study of gifted persons could easily lead the casual reader to believe that giftedness is an absolute condition that is magically bestowed upon a person in much the same way that nature endows us with blue eyes, red hair, or a dark complexion (Renzulli, 1980). This position is not supported by the current research cited in this chapter. There are multiple lists of traits and characteristics—some for girls and some for boys; some for students from the majority culture, others for students from diverse cultural backgrounds. For too many years, we have pretended that we can identify the traits of gifted children in an absolute and unequivocal fashion. Many people have been led to believe that certain individuals have been endowed with a golden chromosome that makes him or her "a gifted person." This belief has further led to the mistaken idea that all we need to do is find the right combination of traits that prove the existence of this "gift." The further use of terms such as "the truly gifted," "the highly gifted," the "moderately gifted," and the "borderline gifted" only serve to confound the issue. The misuse of the concept of giftedness has given rise to a great deal of criticism and confusion about both identification and programming, and the result of so many mixed messages being sent to educators and the public at large is that both groups now have a justifiable skepticism about the credibility of the gifted education movement and our ability to both define and offer services that are qualitatively different from general education.

Most of the confusion and controversy surrounding characteristics of giftedness can be placed into proper perspective if we examine a few key questions.

- Do we use specific characteristics of one group of people to identify another group? Are the characteristics of giftedness reflected in high ability Puerto Rican students in Hartford, CT, the same characteristics of giftedness as those demonstrated by above average Mexican students in Texas?
- Are there characteristics common to each group? If so, how are they exhibited?
- What happens to a child who consistently manifests these characteristics when he or she is in the primary grades but

who learns to underachieve in school because of an unchallenging curriculum?

- What about a gifted child with a learning disability whose disability masks his or her talents?
- Are characteristics of giftedness static (you have or you don't have them) or are they dynamic (they vary within persons and among learning/performance situations)?

These questions have led us to advocate a fundamental change in the ways the characteristics and traits of giftedness should be viewed in the future. We believe that the characteristics of any advanced learners must be identified within various population groups. That is, we should attempt to identify the characteristics of talented students within each educational context and population. This information should be used to help us differentiate between all students and those who need different levels of service or a continuum of services (Renzulli & Reis, 1997) in school to realize their potential. This shift might appear insignificant, but we believe that it has implications for the way that we think about the characteristics of giftedness and the ways in which we should structure our identification and programming endeavors. This change may also provide the flexibility in both identification and programming endeavors that will encourage the inclusion of diverse students in our programs.

Defining our populations, then deciding which services are offered to all students and what is qualitatively necessary for gifted students based on the traits of the population, will help us to develop programs that are internally consistent. At a very minimum, we must understand that giftedness is manifested by different traits in different populations, and we must develop programs which reflect the diversity of talent in our culture.

References

Albert, R. S., & Runco, M. A. (1986). The achievement of eminence: A model based on a longitudinal study of exceptionally gifted boys and their families. In R. J. Sternberg & J. E. Davidson (Ed.), *Conceptions of giftedness* (pp. 332–357). Cambridge, England: Cambridge University Press.

Arnold, K. D. (1995). The lives of female high school valedictorians in the 1980s. In K. D. Hulbert & D. T. Schuster (Eds.), *Women's lives through time: Educated American women of the 20th century* (pp. 393–414). San Francisco: Jossey-Bass.

Baker, J. A. (1996). Everyday stressors of academically gifted adolescents. *The Journal of Secondary Gifted Education, 7*, 356–368.

Bamberger, J. (1986). Cognitive issues in the development of musically gifted children. In R. J. Sternberg & J. E. Davidson (Ed.), *Conceptions of giftedness* (pp. 388–413). Cambridge, England: Cambridge University Press.

Baum, S. (1990). *Gifted but learning disabled: A puzzling paradox.* (Report No. EDD00036). Washington, DC: Office of Educational Research. (ERIC Document Reproduction Service No. EC231805)

Baum, S., & Owen, S. V. (1988). High ability/learning disabled students: How are they different? *Gifted Child Quarterly, 32*, 321–325.

Baum, S., Owen, S. V., & Dixon, J. (1991). *To be gifted and learning disabled: From definitions to practical intervention strategies.* Mansfield Center, CT: Creative Learning Press.

Bell, L. A. (1989). Something's wrong here and it's not me: Challenging the dilemmas that block girls' success. *Journal for the Education of the Gifted, 12*, 118–130.

Bireley, M., Languis, M., & Williamson, T. (1992). Physiological uniqueness: A new perspective on the learning disabled/gifted child. *Roeper Review, 15*, 101–107.

Boodoo, G. M., Bradley, C. L., Frontera, R. L., Pitts, J. R., & Wright, L. P. (1989). A survey of procedures used for identifying gifted learning disabled children. *Gifted Child Quarterly, 33*, 110–114.

Borkowski, J. G., & Peck, V. A. (1986). Causes and consequences of metamemory in gifted children. In R. J. Sternberg & J. E. Davidson (Ed.), *Conceptions of giftedness* (pp. 182–200). Cambridge, England: Cambridge University Press.

Buescher, T. M., Olszewski, P., & Higham, S. J. (1987, April). *Influences on strategies adolescents use to cope with their own recognized talents* (Report No. EC 200 755). Baltimore, MD: Society for Research in

Child Development. (ERIC Document Reproduction Service No. ED288285)

Butler-Por, N. (1987). *Underachievers in school.* New York: Wiley & Sons.

Clark, B. (1988). *Growing up gifted* (3rd ed.). Columbus, OH: Merrill.

Coleman, M. R. (1996). Recognizing social and emotional needs of gifted students. *Gifted Child Today, 19*(3), 36–37.

Cramer, R. H. (1989). Attitudes of gifted boys and girls toward math: A qualitative study. *Roeper Review, 11,* 128–130.

Cramond, B. (1995). *The coincidence of attention deficit hyperactivity disorder and creativity.* Storrs, CT: University of Connecticut, The National Research Center on the Gifted and Talented.

Csikszentmihalyi, M., Rathunde, K., & Whalen, S. (1993). *Talented teenagers: The roots of success and failure.* Cambridge, England: Cambridge University Press.

Csikszentmihalyi, M., & Robinson, R. E. (1986). Culture, time, and the development of talent. In R. J. Sternberg & J. E. Davidson (Ed.), *Conceptions of giftedness* (pp. 264–284). Cambridge, England: Cambridge University Press.

Dabrowski, K. (1938). Typy wzmozonej pobudliwosci psychicznej (Types of increased psychic excitability). *Biul. Inst. Hig. Psychicznej, 1*(3–4), 3–26.

Davidson, J. E. (1986). The role of insight in giftedness. In R. J. Sternberg & J. E. Davidson (Ed.), *Conceptions of giftedness* (pp. 201–222). Cambridge, England: Cambridge University Press.

Davis, G. A. (1992). *Creativity is forever* (3rd ed.). Dubuque, IA: Kendall/Hunt.

Davis, G. A., & Rimm, S. B. (1998). *Education of the gifted and talented* (4th ed.). Boston, MA: Allyn & Bacon.

Eccles, J., Midgley, C. & Adler, T. F. (1984). Grade-related changes in the school environment: Effects on achievement motivation. In J. Nicholls (Ed.), *Advances in motivation and achievement* (Vol. 3, pp. 283–331). Greenwich, CT: JAI Press.

Feldhusen, J. F. (1986). A concept of giftedness. In R. J. Sternberg & J. E. Davidson (Ed.), *Conceptions of giftedness* (pp. 112–127). Cambridge, England: Cambridge University Press.

Feldhusen, J. F. (1989). Why the public schools will continue to neglect the gifted. *Gifted Child Today, 12*(2), 56–59.

Feldman, D. H. (1993). Child prodigies: A distinctive form of giftedness. *Gifted Child Quarterly, 37,* 188–193.

Feldman, D. H., & Benjamin, A. C. (1986). Giftedness as a developmentalist sees it. In R. J. Sternberg & J. E. Davidson (Ed.), *Conceptions of giftedness* (pp. 285–305). Cambridge, England: Cambridge University Press.

Ford, D. Y. (1992). Determinants of underachievement as perceived by gifted, above–average, and average Black students. *Roeper Review, 13,* 27–32.

Frasier, M. M., García, J. H., & Passow, A. H. (1995). *A review of assessment issues in gifted education and their implications for identifying gifted minority students.* Storrs, CT: University of Connecticut, The National Research Center on the Gifted and Talented.

Frasier, M. M., & Passow, A. H. (1994). *Towards a new paradigm for identifying talent potential.* Storrs, CT: University of Connecticut, The National Research Center on the Gifted and Talented.

Gallagher, J. J. (1991). Personal patterns of underachievement. *Journal for the Education of the Gifted, 14,* 221–233.

Gallagher, J. J., & Courtright, R. D. (1986). The educational definition of giftedness and its policy implications. In R. J. Sternberg & J. E. Davidson (Ed.), *Conceptions of giftedness* (pp. 93–111). Cambridge, England: Cambridge University Press.

Gardner, H. (1983). *Frames of mind: The theory of multiple intelligences.* New York: Basic Books.

Gardner, H. (1993). *Frames of mind: The theory of multiple intelligences* (10th-anniversary ed.). New York: Basic Books.

Gruber, H. E. (1986). The self-construction of the extraordinary. In R. J. Sternberg & J. E. Davidson (Ed.), *Conceptions of giftedness* (pp. 247–263). Cambridge, England: Cambridge University Press.

Haensly, P., Reynolds, C. R., & Nash, W. R. (1986). Giftedness: Coalescence, context, conflict, and commitment. In R. J. Sternberg & J. E. Davidson (Ed.), *Conceptions of giftedness* (pp. 128-148). Cambridge, England: Cambridge University Press.

Hannell, G. (1991). The complications of being gifted. *Gifted Education International, 7,* 126–128.

Hany, E. A. (1994). The development of basic cognitive components of technical creativity: A longitudinal comparison of children and youth with high and average intelligence. In R. F. Subotnik & K. D. Arnold (Eds.), *Beyond Terman: Contemporary longitudinal studies of giftedness and talent* (pp. 115–154). Norwood, NJ: Ablex.

Hishinuma, E., & Tadaki, S. (1996). Addressing diversity of the gifted/at risk: Characteristics for identification. *Gifted Child Today, 19*(5), 20–25, 28–29, 45, 50.

Jackson, N. E., & Butterfield, E. C. (1986). A conception of giftedness designed to promote research. In R. J. Sternberg & J. E. Davidson (Ed.), *Conceptions of giftedness* (pp. 151–181). Cambridge, England: Cambridge University Press.

Karnes, F. A., & McGinnis, J. C. (1996). Self-actualization and locus of control with academically talented adolescents. *The Journal of Secondary Gifted Education, 7*, 369–372.

Kerr, B., Colangelo, N., & Gaeth, J. (1988). Gifted adolescents' attitudes toward their giftedness. *Gifted Child Quarterly, 32*, 245–247.

Kitano, M. K., & Espinosa, R. (1995). Language diversity and giftedness: Working with gifted English language learners. *Journal for the Education of the Gifted, 18*, 234–254.

Kline, B. E., & Short, E. B. (1991). Changes in emotional resilience: Gifted adolescent females. *Roeper Review, 13*, 118–121.

Kloosterman, V. (1997). *Talent identification and development in high ability, Hispanic, bilingual students in an urban elementary school.* Unpublished doctoral dissertation, University of Connecticut, Storrs.

Kramer, L. R. (1991). The social construction of ability perceptions: An ethnographic study of gifted adolescent girls. *Journal of Early Adolescence, 11*, 340–362.

Leroux, J. A. (1988). Voices from the classroom: Academic and social self-concepts of gifted adolescents. *Journal for the Education of the Gifted, 11*, 3–18.

Lovecky, D. V. (1992). Exploring social and emotional aspects of giftedness in children. *Roeper Review, 15*, 18–25.

Lovecky, D. V. (1993). The quest for meaning: Counseling issues with gifted children and adolescents. In L. K. Silverman (Ed.), *Counseling the gifted and talented* (pp. 29–50). Denver, CO: Love.

MacKinnon, D. W. (1978). Educating for creativity: A modern myth? In G. A. Davis & J. A. Scott (Eds.), *Training creative thinking.* Melbourne, FL: Kreiger.

Maker, C. J. (1983). Quality education for gifted minority students. *Journal for the Education of the Gifted, 6*, 140–153.

Maker, C. J., & Schiever, S. W. (1989). *Critical issues in gifted education: Defensible programs for cultural and ethnic minorities* (Volume II). Austin, TX: PRO-ED.

Marland, S. P. Jr., (1972). *Education of the gifted and talented: Report to Congress of the United States by the U.S. Commissioner of Education and background papers submitted to the U.S. Office of Education*, 2 vols. Washington, DC: U.S. Government Printing Office (Government Documents, Y4.L 11/2: G36).

Mitchell, B. M. (1988). The last national assessment of gifted education. *Roeper Review, 10*, 239–240.

Olenchak, F. R., & Renzulli, J. S. (1989). The effectiveness of the school-wide enrichment model on selected aspects of elementary school change. *Gifted Child Quarterly, 33*, 36–46

Passow, A. H. (1981). The four curricula of the gifted and talented: Toward a total learning environment. *Gifted Child Today, 4*(5), 2–7.

Passow, A. H., & Rudnitski, R. A. (1993). *State policies regarding education of the gifted as reflected in legislation and regulation.* Storrs, CT: University of Connecticut, The National Research Center on the Gifted and Talented.

Perleth, C., & Heller, K. A. (1994). The Munich longitudinal study of giftedness. In R. F. Subotnik & K. D. Arnold (Eds.), *Beyond Terman: Contemporary longitudinal studies of giftedness and talent* (pp. 77–114). Norwood, NJ: Ablex.

Perleth, C., Sierwald, W., & Heller, K. A. (1993). Selected results of the Munich longitudinal study of giftedness: The multidimensional/typological giftedness model. *Roeper Review, 15,* 149–155.

Peters, P. (1990, July). TAG student defends programs against critic. [Letter to the editor]. *The Register Citizen* (Torrington, CT), 10.

Public Law 94–142. (1975). Education for all handicapped children act 613 (a) (4), s.6, 94 Cong. 1st session, June. Report No. 94-168.

Reis, S. M. (1987). We can't change what we don't recognize: Understanding the special needs of gifted females. *Gifted Child Quarterly, 31,* 83–89.

Reis, S. M. (1998). *Work left undone: Choices and compromises of talented females.* Mansfield Center, CT: Creative Learning Press.

Reis, S. M., & Callahan, C. M. (1989). Gifted females: They've come a long way—or have they? *Journal for the Education of the Gifted, 12,* 99–117.

Reis, S. M., Callahan, C. M., & Goldsmith, D. (1996). Attitudes of adolescent gifted girls and boys toward education, achievement, and the future. In K. D. Arnold, K. D. Noble, & R. F. Subotnik (Eds.), *Remarkable women: Perspectives on female talent development* (pp. 209–224). Cresskill, NJ: Hampton Press.

Reis, S. M., Hébert, T. P., Díaz, E. I., Maxfield, L. R., & Ratley, M. E. (1995). *Case studies of talented students who achieve and underachieve in an urban high school.* Storrs, CT: University of Connecticut, The National Research Center on the Gifted and Talented.

Reis, S. M., Neu, T. W., & McGuire, J. M. (1995). *Talent in two places: Case studies of high ability students with learning disabilities who have achieved.* Storrs, CT: University of Connecticut, The National Research Center on the Gifted and Talented.

Renzulli, J. S. (1978). What makes giftedness?: Reexamining a definition. *Phi Delta Kappan, 60,* 180–184.

Renzulli, J. S. (1980). Will the gifted child movement be alive and well in 1990? *Gifted Child Quarterly, 24,* 3–9.

Renzulli, J. S. (1986). The three-ring conception of giftedness: A developmental model for creative productivity. In R. J. Sternberg & J. E. Davidson (Eds.), *Conceptions of giftedness* (pp. 53–92). Cambridge, England: Cambridge University Press.

Renzulli, J. S., Reid, B. D., & Gubbins, E. J. (1991). *Setting an agenda: Research priorities for the gifted and talented through the year 2000.* Storrs, CT: University of Connecticut, The National Research Center on the Gifted and Talented.

Renzulli, J. S., & Reis, S. M. (1985). *The schoolwide enrichment model: A comprehensive plan for educational excellence.* Mansfield Center, CT: Creative Learning Press.

Renzulli, J. S., & Reis, S. M. (1997). *The schoolwide enrichment model: A how-to guide for educational excellence* (2nd ed.). Mansfield Center, CT: Creative Learning Press.

Rimm, S. (1986). *Underachievement syndrome: Causes and cures.* Watertown, WI: Apple.

Robinson, N. M. (1987). The early development of precocity. *Gifted Child Quarterly, 31,* 161–164.

Roeper, A. (1996). A personal statement of philosophy of George and Annemarie Roeper. *Roeper Review, 19,* 18–19.

Rogers, K. B. (1991). *The relationship of grouping practices to the education of the gifted and talented learner.* Storrs, CT: University of Connecticut, The National Research Center on the Gifted and Talented.

Schmitz, C. C., & Galbraith, J. (1985). *Managing the social and emotional needs of the gifted: A teacher's survival guide.* Minneapolis, MN: Free Spirit.

Schuler, P. A. (1997). *Characteristics and perceptions of perfectionism in gifted adolescents in a rural school environment.* Unpublished doctoral dissertation, University of Connecticut, Storrs.

Schwartz, L. L. (1994). *Why give "gifts" to the gifted?: Investing in a national resource.* Thousand Oaks, CA: Corwin Press.

Siegler, R. S., & Kotovsky, K. (1986). Two levels of giftedness: Shall ever the twain meet? In R. J. Sternberg & J. E. Davidson (Eds.), *Conceptions of giftedness* (pp. 417–435). Cambridge, England: Cambridge University Press.

Silverman, L. K. (1993). A developmental model for counseling the gifted. In L. K. Silverman (Ed.), *Counseling the gifted and talented* (pp. 51–78). Denver, CO: Love.

Spielhagen, F. R. (1996). Perceptions of achievement among high-potential females between 9 and 26 years of age. In K. D. Arnold, K. D. Noble, & R. F. Subotnik (Eds.), *Remarkable women: Perspectives on female talent development* (pp. 193–208). Cresskill, NJ: Hampton Press.

Stanley, J. C., & Benbow, C. P. (1986). Youths who reason exceptionally well mathematically. In R. J. Sternberg & J. E. Davidson (Ed.), *Conceptions of giftedness* (pp. 53–92). Cambridge, England: Cambridge University Press.

Sternberg, R. J. (1986). A triarchic theory of intellectual giftedness. In R. J. Sternberg & J. E. Davidson (Ed.), *Conceptions of giftedness* (pp. 223–243). Cambridge, England: Cambridge University Press.

Sternberg, R. J., & Davidson, J. E. (1986). *Conceptions of giftedness.* Cambridge, England: Cambridge University Press.

Sternberg, R. J., & Lubart, T. I. (1993). Creative giftedness: A multivariate investment approach. *Gifted Child Quarterly, 37,* 7–15.

Subotnik, R. F. (1988). The motivation to experiment: A study of gifted adolescents' attitudes toward scientific research. *Journal for the Education of the Gifted, 11,* 19–35.

Swart, R. S. (1993, March). Smart, talented, and ... failing: What educators, counselors, and therapists need to understand about gifted students. *Adolescence, 44–47.*

Tannenbaum, A. J. (1986). Giftedness: A psychosocial approach. In R. J. Sternberg & J. E. Davidson (Ed.), *Conceptions of giftedness* (pp. 21–52). Cambridge, England: Cambridge University Press.

Taylor, H. G. (1989). Learning disabilities. In E. J. Mash & R. Barkley (Eds.), *Treatment of childhood disorders* (pp. 347–380). New York: Guilford Press.

Terman, L. (1916). *The measurement of intelligence.* Boston: Houghton Miflin.

Terman, L., & Oden, M. (1947). *Genetic studies of genius* (Vol. 4). Stanford, CA: Stanford University Press.

Torrance, E. P. (1962). *Guiding creative talent.* Huntington, NY: Robert E. Krieger.

Tucker, B., & Hafenstein, N. L. (1997). Psychological intensities in young gifted children. *Gifted Child Quarterly, 41,* 66–75.

U.S. Department of Education, Office of Educational Research & Improvement. (1993). *National excellence: A case for developing America's talent.* Washington, DC: U.S. Government Printing Office.

Vaughn, S. (1989). Gifted learning disabilities: Is it such a bright idea? *Learning Disabilities Focus, 4*(2), 123–126.

Wallace, B., & Pierce, J. (1992). The changing nature of giftedness: An examination of various strategies for provision. *Gifted Education International, 8,* 4–9.

Walters, J., & Gardner, H. (1986). The crystallizing experience: Discovering an intellectual gift. In R. J. Sternberg & J. E. Davidson (Ed.), *Conceptions of giftedness* (pp. 306–331). Cambridge, England: Cambridge University Press.

Webb, J. T., & Latimer, D. (1993). ADHD and children who are gifted. *Exceptional Children, 60,* 183–184.

Whitmore, J. (1980). *Giftedness, conflict, and underachievement.* Boston: Allyn & Bacon.

Whitmore, J. (1986). Conceptualizing the issue of underserved populations of gifted students. *Journal for the Education of the Gifted, 10,* 141–153.

Willard-Holt, C. (1994). *Recognizing talent: Cross-case study of two high potential students with cerebral palsy.* Storrs, CT: University of Connecticut, The National Research Center on the Gifted and Talented.

Yewchuk, C. R., & Bibby, M. A. (1989). Identification of giftedness in severely and profoundly hearing impaired students. *Roeper Review, 12,* 42–48.

Ysseldyke, J. E., & Algozzine, B. (1983). LD or not LD: That's not the question. *Journal of Learning Disabilities, 16,* 29–31.

Author Note

1. The work reported herein was supported under the Education Research and Development Centers Program, PT/Award Number R206R50001, as administered by the Office of Educational Research and Improvement, U.S. Department of Education. The findings and opinions expressed do not reflect the positions or policies of the National Institute on the Education of At-Risk Students, the Office of Educational Research and Improvement, or the U.S. Department of Education. Permission to reproduce this material has been granted by The National Research Center on the Gifted and Talented, Joseph S. Renzulli, Director.

CHAPTER 2

Planning the Learning Environment

BARBARA G. HUNT
Mississippi University for Women

ROBERT W. SENEY
Mississippi University for Women

If teachers are to play the lead role in effectively helping students become self-directed learners, they must first embrace learning as their primary function: they must learn how they themselves learn and how they in turn can create learning environments.
—Susan J. Poulsen (1997, p. 7)—

In this chapter, the elements of creating an effective learning environment will be investigated. While process, product, and content are often intentionally modified, the importance of modifying the environment for students is often overlooked. At the same time, it is readily acknowledged that the environment affects students' learning. The way classrooms are structured reflects the teacher's thoughts and philosophies on how students learn and how the students, in turn, will perform. For example, if learning by investigation is the goal in the classroom, then the learning environment should be structured for exploration by providing many resources, opportunities for movement, and provisions for more interaction between students. If the purpose is to invite students to raise questions, to experiment, and to work cooperatively with others, then an environment that will enhance and facilitate these interactions should be designed. Carefully planned and differentiated activities may fall short of the teacher's goals and expectations if the students' learning environment is not also modified.

This chapter addresses the question, Now that the students have been identified, how should the learning environment be modified to reflect the unique needs of gifted and high potential learners?

The Modifications

Without needed modifications to the environment, opportunities are restricted and gifted students cannot develop their abilities effectively.
—C. June Maker and Aleene B. Nielson (1996, p. 23)—

In their text, *Curriculum Development and Teaching Strategies for Gifted Learners, Second Edition* (1996), C. June Maker and Aleene B. Nielson have provided guidelines to help the teacher make learning experiences appropriate for gifted learners. Basing their precepts on the "acid test" of relating curriculum and teaching strategies to the characteristics that make students different, they have provided an important guide. These guidelines are built upon the touchstones of modification: process, product, content, and environment.

While modifications in all four of these areas are important, an emphasis is placed upon modifying the environment:

> Learning environment modifications ... are prerequisites for making modifications in content, process, and product. The learning context shapes input, processing, and output. The environment affords certain kinds of learning experiences; when the environment is properly modified, great opportunities are afforded to its inhabitants. Without needed modifications to the environment, opportunities are restricted and gifted students cannot develop their abilities effectively. (Maker & Nielson, 1996, p. 23)

With this in mind, Maker and Nielson offer a set of "principles" to guide in modifying learning environments for gifted learners.

The environment should

1. be learner-centered rather than teacher- or content-centered;
2. focus on independence rather than emphasizing dependence;
3. be open rather than closed to new ideas, innovations, and exploration;
4. promote acceptance rather than judgment;
5. focus on complexity rather than simplicity;
6. provide for a variety of group options rather than one grouping as a general organization;
7. be flexible rather than having a rigid structure or chaotic lack of structure; and
8. provide for high mobility rather than low mobility (Maker & Nielson, 1996, p. 31).

These principles of the classroom are discussed in terms of a continuum with the most appropriate environment for gifted learners occurring near the extreme. By using these as guidelines environments are created which provide the comfort, autonomy, and opportunities gifted learners need for optimum growth and development.

Modifying the Environment

Modifying the environment will facilitate necessary changes in the three other areas: content, process, and products. For appropriate modifications to be made, the focus must be on gifted learners and the many differences that exist among these students. Learning styles, interests, learning needs, and characteristics must be taken into account when planning for gifted learners. Determining the learning styles and learning preferences are of primary importance. This issue is discussed later in this chapter.

Different Environmental Needs

In working with gifted learners, awareness of the diversity, even within a single classroom of gifted learners, becomes obvious. While these learners share many characteristics, there is a great deal of variety and diversity. Uniqueness becomes the key term. When dealing with special populations of gifted learners, there is almost a quantum leap in diversity. It is important to be aware of cultural differences, cultural values, the concept of giftedness within the context of specific cultures, and the behavioral differences exhibited and expected in other cultures.

It is also important for educators to identify their own attitudes and belief systems about minorities, socioeconomic status, and other cultures. Diversity must be valued, and potential contributions to the gifted classroom must be identified. In addition, cultural bridges have to be built within the classroom setting. These elements must be considered and must become key ingredients in the design of learning environments for gifted learners.

The Responsive Learning Environment

In an environment where each student is considered a unique individual, a positive self-concept can be developed naturally. Students can learn responsibility and an inner sense of control when expectations and opportunities for choice, sharing responsibility, and self-evaluation are a planned part of their day.
—Barbara Clark (1997, p. 331)—

Clark's work in the responsive learning environment (RLE) identifies key ingredients for designing appropriate settings. The RLE is approached from the point of view of optimizing learning. The seven areas of the teaching process that must be developed to optimize learning are
1. create a responsive learning environment;
2. integrate the intellectual processes during instruction;
3. differentiate the content;
4. assess the learner's knowledge, understanding, and interests;
5. individualize the instruction;
6. evaluate learning and teaching; and
7. reflect on the entire process and reform the learning plan to incorporate all new insights gained (Clark, 1997, p. 326).

RLE

The first step in providing optimal learning for all students and especially for meeting the unique needs of gifted learners is to create the responsive learning environment. It can be defined as a flexible environment that allows learners to pursue educational requirements and interests in depth and with a minimum of time limitations. Learners either have the opportunity to move at their own pace and work individually, or they are grouped with other students as learning needs require (Clark, 1997).

In order to evaluate a learning environment, Clark has developed a Responsive Learning Environment Checklist (see Figure 1). She also provides some guidelines for developing both the physical learning environment and the social-emotional learning environment. Her basic premise is to create "people space." This involves space that is inviting, flexible, and large enough to allow students to be engaged in a variety of instructional groupings at the same time. In short, the goal should be to "create a laboratory for learning" (Clark, 1997, p. 329).

Suggestions for creating usable physical space in the classroom are
1. take out furniture;
2. carpet areas of the room;
3. use floors, walls, window, closets, and drawers;
4. bring in comfortable, movable furniture;
5. use color to support learning; and
6. order materials at many levels in smaller numbers (Clark, 1997, p. 329).

Clark (1997) also provided suggestions for developing a safe and caring social-emotional setting. It is one in which students are free to be themselves, where it is safe to be smart. Gifted learners often have much more in common with their intellectual peers than they do with their chronological peers. They are often subject to teasing and negative attention from their peers. Therefore, a supportive environment must be created where gifted learners can express their thoughts and pursue their interests without distracting interference. In addition, this climate must be conducive to risk taking, exploration, and growth. In this supportive environment, students will be able to build trust in others and themselves, build self-confidence, address issues of giftedness, and know that the teacher is aware of the counseling needs of gifted students.

You will know that the physical environment is responsive when

1. There is space for students to simultaneously participate in a variety of activities.
2. Students have access to materials with a range of levels and topics.
3. There is space for the students to engage in a variety of instructional groupings, and flexible grouping is used.
4. There are areas supportive of student self-management.
5. Desks are not individually owned.
6. The classroom has a comfortable, inviting ambiance supportive of exploration, application, and personal construction of knowledge.

You will know that the social/emotional environment is responsive when

1. The emotional climate is warm and accepting.
2. The class operates with clear guidelines decided upon cooperatively.
3. Instruction is based on each individual student's needs and interests as assessed by the teacher from the student's interaction with the materials and the concepts.
4. Student activities, products, and ideas are reflected around the classroom.
5. Student choice is evident in planning, instruction, and products of evaluation.
6. Building and practicing affective skills are a consistent and valued part of the curriculum and of each teaching day.
7. Students and teachers show evidence of shared responsibility for learning.
8. Empowering language is evident between teacher and students and among students.
9. Students show evidence of becoming independent learners with skills of inquiry and self-evaluation.

Figure 1. A Responsive Learning Environment Checklist

Note. From *Growing Up Gifted* (5th ed.) (p. 328), by B. Clark, 1997, Upper Saddle River, NJ: Merrill. Used with permission.

The Psychological
and Social/Emotional Environment

*The goodness of fit, the appropriate coincidence of individual
characteristics and needs with an understanding and supportive environment, is crucial for proper development.*
—Franz J. Mönks (Mönks & Peters, 1992, p. 191)—

Gifted and Talented Students

What do gifted and talented students need for optimal adjustment to occur?

In order to create an environment for optimal adjustment, Leta
Hollingworth recommended grouping gifted students together, to
compact curriculum and to spend half a day for enrichment. This
allows for lively discussions and happier, more well-adjusted human
beings through meeting not only their cognitive needs but also their
equally important social and emotional needs (Silverman, 1990). In
order for the teacher of the gifted to create an optimal learning environment, he or she must collect as much information, through
cumulative records and different assessment instruments in order to
clearly answer, "Who are these gifted individuals?"

Learning Styles

Gifted students need to understand their learning styles and
their strengths and weaknesses. Griggs and Dunn (1984) found a
positive relationship between improvement in academic achievement, attitudes, and behaviors and accommodation of the student's learning style preferences in the classroom. Gifted students
appear to show evidence of preferring certain cognitive learning
styles. Gifted elementary students and junior high school students
show similar patterns for high tactile and kinesthetic and low
auditory preferences. Most gifted students prefer little structure,
less supervision, more independence, flexibility in learning, and
real life experiences to lectures, discussions, and more small group
or individual self-designed instructional opportunities (Clark,
1997).

Creative or divergent thinkers have a unique learning style. They are immersion learners, who want to find out everything about one subject at once. These thinkers are holistic and sometimes find the artificial boundaries around school subjects annoying. The ability to make something happen or the novelty of an idea is more often rewarding than the extrinsic reward system in our schools (Silverman, 1993).

Teachers need to use learning style instruments to get a clearer picture of the gifted students they teach. Silverman (1989) found that children who exhibit visual-spatial learning styles appear to have difficulties with risk taking and accepting failure; spatial learners can become panic-stricken if they do not know the answer; and introverts and visual-spatial learners find the computer an invaluable asset to learning.

Instruments to aid the teacher in assessing students' learning style preferences are found in the Teacher Resource Section at the end of this chapter.

Personality/Psychological Types (MBTI)

Personality (like biology) is not destiny. Talented students—in fact all students—need to recognize the shortcomings of their natural dispositions and to value as acquired skills specific techniques to help them become balanced adults. (Gallagher, 1990, p. 12)

The Myers-Briggs Type Indicator (MBTI) was the instrument used by Myers and McCaulley in 1985 (cited in Gallagher, 1990) to study the personality types of high school gifted students across the country. A total of 1,725 gifted learners' preferences was compared to a sample of adolescents' preferences in the general population. Several strong patterns occurred:

1. Almost 50% of the talented students were extroverts, and 50% introverts, while 63% of the general population were extroverts.
2. Over 75% of the talented sample preferred intuition to sensing, while only 32% of the general population preferred intuition.
3. Talented high school males equally preferred thinking (64%) with their nontalented male counterparts (61%), while 55% of the talented females preferred feeling; 66% of the nontalented high school females preferred feeling.

4. Talented students were more likely to prefer perceiving (61%) over judging, while 46% of the high school students preferred perceiving (Gallagher, 1990, p. 12).

Again the importance of uncovering these basic dispositions creates a new level of understanding of giftedness. Also, it gives the teacher of the gifted learner another tool to knowing their uniqueness in order to create a responsive environment.

Peer and Peer Relations

I made most of my friends in the advanced classes at school. Their goals were compatible with mine and that's what made me feel so comfortable around them.
    —Boy, 16 (Galbraith & Delisle, 1996, p. 212)—

I have a lot of trouble relating to kids my age. It's as though we're on a totally different wavelength. I prefer adult company over kid company because I can contribute in their conversations without being thought of as strange for knowing what's going on.
    —Billy, 14 (Galbraith & Delisle, 1996, p. 213)—

In an environmental support system, the internal world of the individual must be considered, and peer relationships are a vital element. Because of the gifted child's asynchronous development, an eight year old can find peers among early adolescents. The teacher of the gifted can help gifted learners with peer and social relationships through

1. providing more flexibility in schools to foster peer relationships (multi-age groups, adoption programs in which an older gifted child works with a younger gifted child, or small groups formed where personality and learning styles are considered);
2. promoting acceleration for some gifted learners (offer "survival courses" for grade level changes);
3. providing an effective counseling/advisement program (develop peer counseling);
4. incorporating self esteem development into the curriculum;
5. incorporating leadership and social skills into the curriculum;
6. developing programs that are sensitive to diversity (forming peer groups that are from diverse populations); and

7. understanding the special problems with peer relationships for adolescent gifted girls (utilize female role models and mentors) (Silverman, 1993).

In promoting positive social development, Roedell (1985) found that gifted children develop social skills more easily when they interact with their true peers. When gifted learners are grouped together in special classes, in summer programs (e.g., Governor Schools, Programs for Gifted), or in special schools (e.g., High Schools for Mathematics and Science, Vanguard High Schools), some teenagers report that, for the first time in years, they are able to meet, enjoy, and interact deeply with a peer.

Understanding Giftedness

Galbraith (1985) found that of the "eight great gripes of gifted children," number one was that no one explains what being gifted is all about. Kunkel, Chapa, Patterson, and Walling (1992) found the same number one complaint. If gifted children do not understand what giftedness is, how can we as teachers create an optimal learning environment?

A student's confusion about giftedness and its implications for his or her life was an abiding and overriding theme. Their ambivalence about giftedness manifested itself largely as an apparent eagerness to diminish their own uniqueness, enforce equality (e.g., "Everybody's gifted in their own way"), and broaden the definition of giftedness to include all variation in human ability. For adolescents in whom the most powerful social imperative is conformity, denial of giftedness may serve an important psychosocial function. The conflict, whether mild or intense, must be resolved by gaining ownership and responsibility for the recognized talent (p. 13).

Teachers of the gifted can encourage the emergence of self through self-acceptance. It may be helpful to incorporate a unit on being gifted, to study eminent gifted people, to teach leadership skills, to use self assessment tools, to incorporate counseling strategies, to study brain research, to incorporate role playing and problem solving directly related to giftedness, and to introduce mentors to these students.

Risk Taking

Life is either a daring adventure, or nothing.
        —Helen Keller (Source unknown)—

Many young gifted learners are willing to be risk takers, but gifted adolescents seem more cautious, while other adolescents become less cautious. This may be because gifted adolescents are more aware of consequences or more skilled at judging the advantages and disadvantages of the situation (Galbraith & Delisle, 1996).

In a responsive social/emotional environment, the gifted learner is more likely to take risks. Teaching these students how to accept mistakes and treat them as learning experiences can help them see the benefits of risk taking. Teaching gifted learners to be risk takers means letting them be open to criticism, give input, work under unstructured situations, and defend their ideas. Frank Williams' (1982) *Model for Implementing Cognitive-Affective Behaviorism in the Classroom* includes the element of risk taking. Some other strategies to implement risk taking into the curriculum are creative problem solving, synectics, SCAMPER, role playing, and debate (Mississippi State Department, 1994).

The Teacher of the Gifted and Talented Learner

To successfully meet gifted students' psychological and social/emotional needs, the teacher must develop a nurturing and positive environment. He or she is the key to establishing a supportive atmosphere where self-esteem can grow. A supportive environment is characterized by a general air of acceptance, confidence, mutual support, respect for effort, and reduction of tension and anxiety in the learning interaction. The effective teacher is involved with the dissemination of knowledge and becomes the facilitator in enhancing the students' self-esteem. Building a nonthreatening environment includes a harmonious relationship among the students, where all feel accepted and are encouraged to work together, help one another, and learn from each other. "Gifted students strengthen the inner locus of control by continuous encounters with the intrinsic values in learning from their own interests or from real need" (Clark, 1997, p. 291).

The gifted classroom needs to be a safe haven, a place where students can express their fears and dreams. The teacher must create an environment where gifted students learn to be considerate of others and accept their own social responsibilities in order to release their potential for self-fulfillment.

Characteristics and Competencies
of the Teacher of the Gifted and Talented Learner

As educators of gifted and talented students, it is the teacher's obligation to meet not only the cognitive needs of these children but the affective as well. Programs for the gifted cannot achieve excellence without teachers who possess personal characteristics and competencies to meet those needs. The characteristics, behaviors, and attitudes of effective teachers of the gifted student affect the learning environment. Roeper (1997) calls upon the educators of the gifted to "create an environment which allows the blossoming of the *Self*" (p. 1).

Research by Hansen and Feldhusen (1994) suggested that teachers who are trained in gifted education will develop skills deemed necessary by experts to teach gifted and talented students effectively. When compared to teachers not educated in gifted education, trained teachers showed an appreciation for giftedness, were flexible and highly intelligent, and showed the capacity to meet personal and social needs of gifted students.

Johnsen (1991) listed a set of 11 competencies that support the various roles that a teacher of gifted students might assume, four of which directly pertain to developing the psychological and social/emotional environment:

1. Understands the characteristics of gifted and talented students and the influence of these characteristics on their educational, psychological, and sociological development;

2. Understands strategies for modifying or designing learning experiences for gifted/talented students appropriate for nurturing creative and critical thinking;

3. Understands the effect of the interaction of various environmental and personality characteristics on the social/emotional development of gifted and talented students and strategies for addressing these effects; and

4. Understands program models and how these models adapt for gifted and talented students.

Gifted students know what characteristics they want in a teacher of the gifted. According to Galbraith (1983), gifted students want teachers who are flexible; have a good sense of humor; do not expect perfection; are willing to help; make learning fun and do not stick to the textbook; understand the pluses and minuses of giftedness; are inspiring; and do not pretend to know everything.

The Role of the Teacher of the Gifted and Talented Learner

Once in the classroom, the role of the teacher is one of providing differentiation to meet the cognitive and affective needs of gifted students. Silverman (1993) referred to the unique role of the teacher of the gifted as one that meets the psychological counseling needs of these students. Trained counselors with in-depth knowledge of gifted children's needs are in short supply; therefore, it is imperative that teachers of the gifted have special training to meet the affective development of these students (p. 181). Teachers of the gifted, in their role as teacher/counselor, need the following strengths:

1. awareness of the unique social and emotional needs of the gifted;
2. training in effective intervention techniques with gifted students;
3. sensitivity to affective issues;
4. availability to handle psychological issues daily in the classroom;
5. training to translate assessment information into program options; and
6. familiarity with gifted individuals who could serve as role models.

The teacher of the gifted has a wide spectrum of responsibilities to enhance the psychological and social/emotional environment of the classroom. He or she is a facilitator of learning, a model, a mentor, a collaborator, and a lifelong learner. To create a secure and positive environment for the gifted learner, the educator must collaborate with and gain the support of regular classroom teachers, counselors, administrators, parents, and the community. Only after these individuals are educated about gifted learners can a substantive and well-coordinated environment be established.

Counseling Needs of the Gifted Learner

The emotional aspects of giftedness lead to concerns about meeting the gifted learners' psychological and social/emotional needs. Silverman (1993) stated that "giftedness has an emotional as well as cognitive substructure: cognitive complexity gives rise to emotional depth" (p. 3). Not only do gifted learners think differently, but they also feel differently. In Silverman's book, *Counseling the Gifted and Talented*, she addressed a definition that highlights the internal experience of the gifted:

> Giftedness is *asynchronous development* in which advanced cognitive abilities and heightened intensity combine to create inner experiences and awareness that are qualitatively different from the norm. This asynchrony increases with higher intellectual capacity. The uniqueness of the gifted renders them particularly vulnerable and requires modifications in parenting, teaching, and counseling in order for them to develop optimally. (p. 3)

While the gifted child's intellectual or academic achievements may be more like those of older children or adults, his or her physical, psychomotor, and emotional development may be age appropriate. This lack of synchronicity creates greater inner tension and may affect children by a feeling of being "out of sync" (feeling that they are different or that they do not, should not, or cannot fit in) or "out of phase" (alienated and distant from a peer group with which to interact) (Silverman, 1993). The unique role of the teacher of the gifted is to meet some of the psychosocial counseling needs of these students. When the teacher acts as a teacher/counselor, there are multiple advantages to the student:

1. The gifted student can receive counseling assistance in the context of the regular classroom or specialized gifted setting, rather than being "taken out" for one or more type of activity.
2. The gifted student can begin to perceive his or her program as holistic, not segmented by concerns for affective issues separate from cognitive ones.

3. The gifted student can discuss common interests and problems in a small group of gifted peers with an adult who knows the student in another context.
4. The gifted student can receive reinforcement and encouragement on an ongoing basis rather than postponing it until a special appointment has been made (Silverman, 1993 p. 182).

Some counseling needs can be met by the teacher of the gifted who is aware of the special affective needs of the gifted learner:

1. understanding one's differences, yet recognizing one's similarities to others;
2. understanding how to accept and give criticism;
3. being tolerant of oneself and others;
4. developing an understanding of one's strengths and weaknesses; and
5. developing skills in areas that will nurture both cognitive and affective development (Silverman, 1993, p. 182).

Strategies that teachers may use to address the social and emotional needs of the gifted learner include role playing, tutorials, mentorships, internships, bibliotherapy, discussion groups, special projects, simulation, gaming, special interest clubs, skill development seminars, and career exploration (Silverman, 1993). These strategies can be used for preventive counseling.

A cautionary note needs to be addressed: teachers of the gifted who do not have training in counseling should be instructed in counselor/client ethics, particularly in regard to confidentiality. Teachers should be aware of all district policies related to counseling students. Noncounselor educators without training in counseling should seek advice from counselors, take course work in counseling, and attend conferences in order to gain knowledge about appropriate strategies and techniques. Teachers must realize their limitations in this important domain and be ready to recommend professional counseling for students with serious emotional problems. Until trained professionals are available, the teachers of the gifted are responsible for meeting the gifted students' emotional needs; therefore, it is important to know the essential elements of good counseling. Effective counselors ask pertinent questions, listen well, give honest feedback, sincerely respect the client and his or her problems, and enable the client to share deep feelings by providing a safe, confidential, nonjudgmental atmosphere

(Silverman, 1993). Because teachers of the gifted understand the special needs of the gifted and have established a trust relationship, gifted students may be willing to participate openly. One student put it this way:

> It is nothing more than having a person here to talk with who has dealt exclusively with people who are similar to you—not with the whole student body. That seems to be the key to having enough trust to let down the guard and be real. (Silverman, 1993, p. 126)

Strategies to Implement

Certain strategies promote a supportive social/emotional environment. Success of the strategies in the affective area relies on the attitude of the teacher. Integrating strategies to promote an optimal affective learning environment can include stress management, conflict resolution, bibliotherapy, behavior and classroom management, and grouping strategies.

Stress Management

Relaxation and reduction of tension are essential in optimizing the learning environment. Some characteristics common to gifted students, such as multipotentiality, intensity, and perceptivity, cause stressors not common to the general student population.

In a study evaluating everyday stressors experienced by academically gifted, exceptionally academically gifted, and academically average adolescents, Baker (1996) found the following stressors related to school significantly higher for gifted students when compared to average students: (1) thinking that it is important to do well in school; (2) others expecting me to know it all; (3) needing to be the best at everything; (4) pressuring myself to do well; (5) parents bothering me about grades; (6) teachers not liking me; (7) not doing as well in school as could have (pp. 364–365). Baker also found that gifted and exceptionally gifted adolescent girls reported higher levels of perfectionism compared to average adolescent girls. These data suggest the need for affective education and psychological interventions in gifted education.

Teachers of the gifted can help students learn to deal with stress through

1. recognizing stressors in their lives;
2. learning and accepting what it means to be gifted;
3. utilizing relaxation techniques (e.g., progressive relaxation, breathing exercises, deep muscle relaxation, imagery training);
4. developing time management skills;
5. setting goals;
6. utilizing problem-solving and decision-making strategies; and
7. understanding the importance of diet and exercise (Baker, 1996, pp. 364–366).

In a safe environment, the gifted student can express his or her emotions, brainstorm ways of releasing pent-up emotions, and quickly learn stress-reduction techniques that will help in different situations. Teachers of gifted students can assist them in coping through deep-breathing exercises, creative visualizations (e.g., the mountains or a favorite place), and soft music (e.g., baroque), all of which have calming effects. Biofeedback equipment is becoming more accessible and popular in schools, and gifted students quickly master the principles and learn to control their autonomic nervous system (Silverman, 1993, p. 102). Conflict resolution, a creative problem-solving technique, is a valuable tool in stress management. The teacher must be prepared to assist gifted learners in meeting and handling stress. The teacher's role is important in this sensitive area.

Conflict Resolution

Conflict is a natural part of life and can be positive if handled productively. The structural features of a conflict are usually described as issues, strategies, and outcomes (Ross & Conant, 1992). Issues include control of the physical or social environment. Strategies include physical and verbal tactics that can be both aggressive and nonaggressive. Killen and Turiel (1991) found that children were capable of resolving conflicts on their own and that adult intervention usually led to adult-generated resolutions. Also, children's conflicts tend to be more aggressive when an adult is present because adult-provided solutions are sometimes mistakes, inconsistent or biased in the resolutions they impose. Outcomes of a conflict may be (1) a resolved situation, as when children simply drop an issue; (2) an adult-imposed solution; (3) the submission of one child over the other; or (4) a mutually agreed upon solution achieved through bargaining, compromising, or finding alternate activities (Wilson, 1988).

Researchers have explored the relationships among the issues, strategies, and outcomes of children's conflicts. Issues often determine strategies (e.g., object conflicts tend to involve physical resistance, although as children grow older, they begin to use verbal protest more frequently). Strategies are then related to outcomes. Accommodating behaviors are associated with peaceful outcomes and with continued interaction following the conflict.

Once the teacher has created a nonthreatening environment where caring, cooperation, communication, self-expression, and appreciation of diversity is supported, conflict resolution skills can be taught. These skills build upon problem-solving and decision-making processes. The teacher establishes the groundwork through role playing that deals with a conflict, emphasizes listening skills, clarifies consequences, and teaches positive alternatives. An important skill in conflict resolution is negotiation: teaching students how to ask for what they want, how to hear what others need, and how to satisfy everyone through a win-win strategy. The last step is implementation of a plan, and again the teacher can help with negotiations. In a safe environment the gifted student can learn how to approach situations cooperatively and create allies out of opponents. Conflict resolution training tends to result in more frequent creative insights and greater task involvement (Silverman, 1993; Wheeler, 1994).

Bibliotherapy

Bibliotherapy is one of the most successful counseling tools available to teachers of the gifted. Bibliotherapy is the use of children's and young adult literature to help understand and solve personal problems (Frazier & McCannon, 1981). The use of literature helps students develop coping skills when dealing with life changes. It is especially useful when working with gifted learners who are perfectionists. Bibliotherapy shows gifted learners that they are not alone and that they can learn about themselves. Because gifted students are usually avid readers and are able to see metaphoric implications in the material, for both characters in the plot and for themselves, bibliotherapy is invaluable. Therapeutic reading enables the student to try various approaches vicariously without real life consequences (Frazier & McCannon, 1981). Bibliotherapy establishes trust between the student and adult, which can result in another bond for the teacher and gifted learner.

Book selection is important and the teacher should use the following criteria: (1) consult your librarian for good literature and resources; (2) select books that are concerned with the gifted but not necessarily about giftedness; and (3) select books in which readers can identify with the characters, themes, and conflicts (Kerr, 1992).

The teacher should follow these steps in bibliotherapy: (1) identify books sensitive to the student's needs; (2) use skill and insight to select books that give correct information but do not give a false sense of hope; (3) suggest rather than prescribe books; and (4) follow up with discussion, role playing, or creative activities.

Bibliotherapy requires the teacher of the gifted to use thoughtful planning, to carefully select books, and to know the individual needs of his or her students. "A book is not a pill that will cure if administered at the proper time; it is a starting point" (Adderholt-Elliott & Eller, 1989, p. 27). If bibliotherapy is to be an effective tool, the teacher must also read the book so that meaningful discussion can take place. The teacher must be a good listener, show tolerance of others' feelings, and must be empathetic and sincere to meet the psychological and social/emotional needs of the gifted student.

Behavior and Classroom Management

Even though we're gifted we still are human. We can make mistakes. No matter how smart we are supposed to be, inside we are just like everyone else.
—Matt, 12 (Schmitz & Galbraith, 1985, p. 21)—

Behavior

The teacher of the gifted needs to know characteristics of the gifted student, understand behavior, become proactive rather than reactive, set goals for positive behavior, build feelings of self-worth in students, use effective listening skills, and create an environment where the teacher and students express ideas and feelings openly. Again, a responsive social/emotional environment eliminates many behavioral problems through determining rules and guidelines together, basing instruction on individual's needs and interests, giving students choices, sharing responsibility, being flexible, encouraging independence, and showing acceptance for differences. Probably the most helpful advice when dealing with behavior management is to know the characteristics of the gifted student.

Lovecky (1992) explored the social/emotional aspects of giftedness. She described five social/emotional traits common to gifted students: divergent thinking ability, excitability, sensitivity, perceptiveness, and entelechy. Each one of these traits brings with it some behavior problems that need to be addressed by the teacher of the gifted.

Divergent thinkers prefer the unusual, original, and creative aspects of any topic. These students ask a lot of questions and march to a different drummer. Negative behaviors can be expressed through rebellion, inattentiveness, disorganization, refusal to participate in group work, and social ineptness. The teacher can use positive techniques to let them see the value in their uniqueness: give them creative outlets in their work, help them find someone who shares their ideas, and teach them organization and social skills.

The trait of excitability is expressed through high levels of energy, long concentration spans on topics of interest, powerful emotions, and the desire to take risks. Behavioral problems include inattentiveness to routine tasks, silliness, disruptive behavior (class clown), and competitiveness to the extreme. In this case, the teacher can use stress reduction, self-control, and self-pacing techniques. Creative problem solving through group dynamics is also valuable.

Sensitivity is a trait that is expressed through great passion (depth of feelings that color life experiences) and compassion (sense of caring for others, intense commitment to others). Problems arise for the teacher when the student withdraws from situations and people. The teacher can help the student understand the difference between empathy and sympathy and the difference between selfishness and asserting one's self.

The awareness of fairness, truth, and justice are traits of perceptiveness. Gifted students have clear values; they see truth as more important than feelings, and they are puzzled by those who do not understand. Negative behaviors result in intolerance of others, expectations of adults to practice what they preach, and fear of making wrong choices. The teacher can help gifted students see the limits of people and problems through teaching coping, compromise, and negotiation strategies. Empathy can be taught through studying the viewpoints of others.

Entelechy is expressed through traits of self-motivation, self-determination, high goal structure, and personal courage. The problems that arise with this trait are unwillingness to compromise, single mindedness, and rebelliousness. Again, the teacher of these students can help by finding an adult mentor or a true friend, showing students how to use their strengths in positive ways, and letting them see both sides of an issue (Lovecky, 1992). Being aware of the traits and other characteristics of the gifted student will make behavior management more viable for the teacher of the gifted.

Classroom Management

Classroom management is discussed in terms of two elements: the management of the "business" of the classroom and classroom discipline. Both of these elements are extremely important in a responsive learning environment. The management of learning must be designed with clear objectives in mind. Generally accepted objectives for gifted learners are

1. Students will be able to learn at their own level.
2. Students will be able to learn at their own pace.
3. Students will be able to assume responsibility for their own learning.

For these objectives to be achieved, a management plan for instruction and a plan for the physical lay-out of the classroom must be designed. These objectives provide the guidelines teachers need to plan their classroom. By using strategies such as independent study projects, contracts, group investigations, and research projects, students work with self-selected material at their own ability levels and are able to move at their own pace. As they plan their projects, they take on the responsibility for their own learning. The teacher as facilitator must provide the tools for recordkeeping, progress reports, and deadlines. Commercial plans exist, such as *The Management Plan for Individual and Small Group Investigations* designed by Renzulli and Reis, (1985) and are available from the Creative Learning Press; or the teacher can easily design his or her own management sheet. Items should include steps in the investigation, resources needed, ideas for a final product, and potential audiences. Other items that are appropriate for the project or are needed to meet the teacher's goals can be added.

In the classroom, the resources should be readily available and clearly labeled. Office letter boxes and trays provide both accessibility and organization. Art supplies and activities should be located in an area where they can be stored and used. Study carrels and small group study areas should be provided. Reference materials should be easily accessible and located. In and out boxes for assignments, questions, or requests should be provided. The overall layout of the room should be planned carefully for traffic flow to avoid distraction. In short, the room should be designed as a learning laboratory. It should be designed for the accomplishment of learning tasks and for student comfort.

The second element of classroom management is classroom discipline. Problems in classroom discipline will be minimized if appropriate, challenging learning activities are provided for gifted learners. However, it is important that clear expectations for students, which become the basis of classroom management, be delineated. Charles (1996) has suggested that a helpful way to view discipline is to see discipline as having three faces: (1) preventive, (2) supportive, and (3) corrective. If a careful program of preventive discipline has been designed, then the needs for both supportive and corrective discipline are diminished.

Charles (1996) offered the following suggestions for preventive discipline:

1. Make the curriculum as worthwhile and enjoyable as possible.
2. Remain the ultimate authority in the classroom.
3. With the students, create good rules for class conduct.
4. Continually emphasize good manners and abidance by the Golden Rule (p. 226).

Suggestions for supportive discipline include
1. Use signals directed to a student needing support.
2. Use physical proximity when signals are ineffective.
3. Restructure difficult work or provide help.
4. Inject humor into lessons that have become tiring.
5. Remove seductive objects.
7. Acknowledge good behavior in appropriate ways at appropriate times.
8. Request good behavior (p. 227).

Suggestions for corrective discipline are
1. Stop the misbehavior.
2. Invoke a consequence appropriate to the misbehavior.
3. Follow through consistently.
4. Redirect misbehavior in positive directions.
5. Be ready to invoke an insubordination rule (p. 228).

Each teacher must ultimately design his or her own personalized system of discipline. There is little need for corrective discipline when gifted learners are challenged, engaged in appropriate learning activities, allowed to assume responsibility for their own learning, and have the freedom to follow their own academic interests.

Grouping Strategies

I like working with bunches of brains.
—Sixth-Grade Girl (Hunt, 1994, p. 150)—

Ability grouping or homogeneous grouping has positive academic and social effects for the gifted, according to extensive research by Rogers (1991). In homogeneous classes, the gifted student faces mutual reinforcement of enthusiasm for academics or areas of interest. J. A. Kulik and C. L. Kulik (1982, 1987) found homogeneously grouped high-ability students, when compared to heterogeneously grouped high-ability students, did better academically and had a better attitude toward the subject. Hunt (1994), in a study of gifted sixth-grade mathematics students, found that the gifted in homogeneous groups had higher post achievement than gifted students in heterogeneous groups, gifted students completed more differentiated activities in homogeneous groups, and gifted students preferred working alone or not working in heterogeneous groups in mathematics. VanTassel-Baska (1992) stated, "The greater the commitment to serving gifted students, the greater the acceptance of advancing and grouping them appropriately" (p. 68).

Flexible grouping where gifted students are separated for part of the day or for particular classes is probably more acceptable and more effective overall. Flexible, homogeneous grouping provides peer stimulation, supports skill development, and meets specific cognitive and affective needs. Heterogeneous grouping develops social skills, introduces new experiences of information needed by the whole class, and builds a community of learners (Clark, 1997). "Among our goals must be providing experiences for individuals to continue their own educational progress *and* to learn from others, to meet their personal needs *and* to understand the needs of others, to learn to be independent and self-reliant *and* to have the skills of working with others" (Clark, 1997, pp. 212–213).

There are key characteristics when forming groups: composition, size, cohesion, and level of structure (Silverman, 1993). When working with groups of students (especially adolescents), the composition is important for success. By using interest inventories, learning style inventories, and test results, the teacher can blend personalities from knowledge of individual strengths and weaknesses (see Teachers Resource Section). It is important not to form groups of only highly aggressive, uncommunicative, or creatively gifted students. The size of the group is also important, usually three to five students per group; decision making is more effective when there are odd numbers. The togetherness or cohesion of the group is the "psychological glue" (Blocher, 1987, cited in Silverman, 1993). The use of group activities that enhance self-disclosure among members leads to successful groups. Letting students select a group name gives another level of mutual bonding. The feeling of solidarity creates an ambiance to the social/emotional and physical environment. Finally, the flexible structure approach to grouping allows different groups to be formed. Highly structured groups might be created for academics, while natural forming groups are created for discussions and problems dealing with the social/emotional needs of the students. Remember, groups are not successful unless social skills are modeled and taught by the teacher.

Assessment of Gifted and Talented Students

In designing an appropriate learning environment, the teacher needs assessment data to plan and to differentiate a student's program of study. In order to select academic options for gifted students, careful assessment of individual student ability, aptitude, interests, and personal values is essential. Collecting profile data on each gifted student and then translating it into a workable format for planning can prove helpful. Data from a student's cumulative records, screening and identification information, intelligence tests, portfolios, and affective instruments (e.g., learning styles, personality types) all combine to give the teacher a profile of the student. The counselor and teacher can work together to develop a plan, based on assessment information, that meets the academic as well as the social/emotional needs of the gifted student. This plan needs to address the following critical issues:

1. *Academic planning provides a blueprint for gifted students in negotiating a program of study that truly reflects their abilities and their interests.* In that sense it offers a built-in opportunity for students assessing their academic profiles at key stages. They are then able to build on their strengths and weaknesses in such a way that they can see progress and make changes or corrections in the planning process as needed based on good information.

2. *Academic planning is the vehicle through which comprehensive curricula and services can be made available to students and parents.* Many times schools offer a wide variety of opportunities, but these options are never fully explained and presented so that gifted students can see the importance of these options to their course of study. Assessing a student's test results (e.g., Torrance Tests of Creative Thinking) may open the door for participation in the arts as a co-curricular area of study. For instance, a student who demonstrated spatial abilities on an IQ test might find stimulation in a chess club, or a student who showed strong verbal and problem-solving skills might join the debate team.

3. *Academic planning influences the extent of articulation in programming for gifted students.* Without it, it would not be unusual to find a patchwork quilt model of program delivery. With

effective planning, students may put together an appropriate scope and sequence of offerings, thus eliminating the kind of fragmentation that is somewhat typical of the larger secondary school environment.

4. *Academic planning provides a way to enhance personalized education for gifted students.* This is particularly the case for students from special populations (e.g., minorities, low income, highly gifted, and twice-exceptional students) whose discrepant profiles and extraordinary needs may dictate annual review of an individualized program of study in all major areas.

5. *Early academic planning prevents the narrowing of options for gifted learners at important transition points in their program.* In the secondary curriculum there are several classes that serve to separate students in courses of study at essential stages in their academic development. The most notable courses are algebra and calculus in mathematics, physics in science, and foreign languages. If gifted students do not take these academic options at some point in their secondary experience, they could be penalized at the college level when attempting to enter into areas of mathematics, science, and foreign language at advanced levels. Absence of these courses can also narrow career options (Silverman, 1993, pp. 203–204).

Teachers must become more flexible in assessment of students. More trust should be put in the student's abilities to set goals and evaluate their own learning in order to meet their cognitive and affective needs.

Individual Education Plans (IEPs)

A planning document that makes the most of the student's aptitudes and abilities is the Individual Educational Plan (IEP). IEPs have traditionally been used in developing an academic plan for students with disabilities, but now they are being utilized in several states for gifted students' academic plans (Clark, 1997). An IEP is easy to plan based on the assessment profile of a gifted student. In addition to the profile data, objectives must be identified that will reflect the needs shown by the profile; activities must be planned to meet them; a time-

INDIVIDUAL EDUCATIONAL PROGRAMMING GUIDE

Strength - A - Lyzer

Prepared by: Joseph S. Renzulli
Linda H. Smith

NAME _____ AGE _____ TEACHER(S) _____

SCHOOL _____ GRADE ____ PARENT(S) _____

Individual Conference Dates And Persons Participating In Planning Of IEP

ABILITIES

INTELLIGENCE – APTITUDE – CREATIVITY

In the spaces below, enter the results of standardized test scores and circle all scores above the _____ percentile.

Test	Area	Date	Raw Score	Grade Equiv.	%ile

TEACHER RATINGS

In the spaces below, enter the scores from the Scale for Rating Behavioral Characteristics of Superior Students. Circle unusually high scores.

Scale	Score	Scale Group Mean	Group Score Mean
Learning			
Motivation			
Creativity			
Leadership			
Artistic			
Musical			
Dramatic			
Comm.: Precision			
Comm.: Expressive			
Planning			

END OF YEAR GRADES

Enter final grades for the past two years.

Reading		Art	
Mathematics		Foreign Language	
Language Arts		Other	
Social Studies		Other	
Science			
Music			

☐ Check here if additional assessment information is recorded on the reverse side.

INTERESTS

As a result of student responses to the Interest-A-Lyzer or other interest assessment procedures, indicate the general area(s) in which levels of interest seem to be High, Average and Low.

	H	A	L		H	A	L
Fine Arts/Crafts				Managerial			
Scientific/Technical				Business			
Literary/Writing				Historical			
Political/Judicial				Performing Arts			
Mathematical				Other			
Athletic				Other			

SPECIFIC AREAS OF INTEREST

As a result of indiv. val. discussions with the student, indicate particular topics, issues, or areas of study in which the student would like to do advanced level work.

LEARNING STYLES

Enter the scores from the Learning Styles Inventory in the spaces below. Circle the highest area(s).

Learning Style	Score	Learning Style	Score
Projects		Teaching Games	
Simulation		Independent Study	
Drill and Recitation		Programmed Instruction	
Peer Teaching		Lecture	
Discussion			

Comments regarding informal observations about Learning Styles and relationships between areas of interest and learning styles

SUMMARY AND RECOMMENDED ACTION BASED ON ASSESSMENT INFORMATION

In the space below summarize (1) strengths, interests, and learning styles, (2) areas in which remedial work or additional skill building appears to be warranted, and (3) specific higher mental processes and advanced skills that should be developed.

Copyright © 1978 by Creative Learning Press, Inc. PO Box 320 Mansfield Center, CT. 06250. All rights reserved.

Figure 2. Example of IEP

Note. From "Strength-a-Lyzer" (p. 77–78), by J. S. Renzulli and L. H. Smith, 1978b, Mansfield Center, CT: Creative Learning Press. Copyright 1978 by Creative Learning Press. Reprinted with permission.

INDIVIDUAL EDUCATIONAL PROGRAMMING GUIDE
The Compactor

Prepared by: Joseph S. Renzulli
Linda H. Smith

NAME _____ AGE _____ Individual Conference Dates And Persons Participating In Planning Of IEP

SCHOOL _____ GRADE _____ TEACHER(S) _____ PARENT(S) _____

CURRICULUM AREAS TO BE CONSIDERED FOR COMPACTING Provide a brief description of basic material to be covered during this marking period and the assessment information or evidence that suggests the need for compacting.	PROCEDURES FOR COMPACTING BASIC MATERIAL Describe activities that will be used to guarantee proficiency in basic curricular areas.	ACCELERATION AND/OR ENRICHMENT ACTIVITIES Describe activities that will be used to provide advanced level learning experiences in each area of the regular curriculum.

☐ Check here if additional information is recorded on the reverse side

Figure 3. Example of IEP

Note. From "*The Compactor*" (p. 77–78), by J. S. Renzulli and L. H. Smith, 1978a, Mansfield Center, CT: Creative Learning Press. Copyright 1978 by Creative Learning Press. Reprinted with permission.

line must be developed for implementation; and an evaluation must be conducted of the student's progress toward these objectives. Since an IEP is written in collaboration with the parents, regular education teachers, the gifted specialist, and other appropriate school personnel, a cooperative spirit is created that brings positive outcomes to all concerned (Clark, 1997). References for commercial IEP instruments can be found in the Teacher Resource Section at the end of this chapter. Several commercial IEP instruments can be used, or you can create your own district one. An example of an IEP is included in Figures 2 & 3 (Renzulli & Smith, 1978b, p. 77–78).

Portfolios

Like the particular qualities associated with a testing culture, authentic assessment doesn't automatically happen in the classroom ... an assessment culture means that teachers and students are continually asking themselves, How can I make use of this knowledge and feedback?
—Howard Gardner (Hart, 1994, p. 12)—

The portfolio is a powerful tool for authentic assessment. Assessment is authentic when it involves students in tasks that are worthwhile, significant, and meaningful and when students are actively involved in evaluating their own work. Authentic assessments are standard-setting, rather than standardized, assessment tools (Hart, 1994). Paulson, Paulson, and Meyer (1991) formulated this definition:

A portfolio is a purposeful collection of student work that exhibits the student's efforts, progress, and achievements in one or more areas. The collection must include student participation in selecting content, the criteria for selection, the criteria for judging merits, and evidence of student self-reflection. (p. 60)

The portfolio process will
1. project the purposes and types of portfolios;
2. collect and organize artifacts over time;
3. select key artifacts based on criteria;

4. interject personality through signature pieces;
5. reflect metacognitively on each item;
6. inspect to self-assess and align goals;
7. perfect and evaluate … and grade if you must;
8. connect and conference with others;
9. inject and eject artifacts continually to update; and
10. respect accomplishments and show with pride (Burke, Fogarty, & Belgrad, 1994).

Important elements of portfolio assessment are self-evaluation and reflection, which are particularly necessary for the gifted learner.

Student Self-Evaluation

Being gifted is like
 …being a leader and a follower all at the same time.
 having the world to yourself.
 sticking out like a sore thumb.
 being a Ruffles™ in a bag of Fritos.™
 opening the doors that others cannot.
 —Sixth-Grade Gifted Students (Hunt, 1984)—

Gifted students need to reflect on who they are academically and personally. Self-assessing academically can be done through portfolios, individual learning contracts, rubrics, checklists, learning logs, journals, and conferences between both peers and teachers. Individually and personally, gifted students need to assess their own learning style, personality type, and learning preferences (e.g., Multiple Intelligences).

The gifted student must understand his or her own giftedness. A student questionnaire (see Figure 4) lets the gifted student assess himself or herself personally (Schmitz & Galbraith, 1985). The Piers-Harris Children's Self-Concept Scale (Piers & Harris, 1969) can be another way that the gifted student can reflect on self. Teachers of the gifted are responsible in guiding these students in self-assessment and helping them find resources.

Galbraith and Delisle (1996) found gifted students can take charge of their education, are responsible for their own perfor-

Dear Students,

This questionnaire is about you—and I'd like you to fill it out so I can be a better teacher for this class. There are no "right" or "wrong" answers. The most important thing is to think honestly about the questions. You may remain anonymous if you wish and choose to skip some of the questions. But, try answering them all—you'll get more out of the exercise if you do. All answers will be kept strictly confidential, although we'll be talking about some of these questions later on as a group.

A. DEMOGRAPHICS

- your age _____   • your gender _____
- number of years in a gifted program or class
  (please circle one) 0 1 2 3 4 5 6 more

B. QUESTIONS YOU MAY ALREADY BE ASKING YOURSELF

1. What does gifted mean to you? _____
2. How do you feel about the label? _____
3. How were you selected for this class or program? _____
4. How do you feel about the selection process? _____
5. What do you think the purpose of this class/program is?

_____	I don't know	_____	Place where I'm not considered weird
_____	Harder work than other classes	_____	Learn something new
_____	More work than other classes	_____	Be stimulated to try new things
_____	More challenging or interesting work	_____	Nothing different from other classes
_____	Friendships with people like me	_____	Other (write it down)
_____	Place to have fun		_____

C. FEELINGS ABOUT YOURSELF

6. In what ways are you the same as most other kids your age? What things do you have in common? _____

7. In what ways are you different from most other kids your age? What makes you unique? _____

Figure 4. Example of Student Questionnaire

8. In terms of popularity ... (check one)
   _____ I have no close friends
   _____ I have one or two close friends
   _____ I have several (four or five) close friends
   _____ I have lots of close friends
   _____ I have tons of close friends and am liked by most everybody

9. In terms of how you feel about yourself ... (check one)
   _____ I hate myself
   _____ I don't like myself much
   _____ I like parts of myself, but dislike other parts
   _____ I feel okay about myself
   _____ Most of the time, I like myself a lot
   _____ I've always liked myself a whole lot

10. If there's one thing you'd like to change about yourself, it would be: _____

11. The best thing about you, as far as you're concerned, is: _____

D. CONFLICTS

12. Indicate how often you experience the following feelings or problems by circling 1, 2, 3, 4, or 5, based on this scale: 1 = not at all; 2 = hardly ever; 3 = sometimes; 4 = a lot; 5 = all the time

Feeling or Problem	How Frequently Felt?
a. I wonder what gifted means.	1 2 3 4 5
b. I wonder why they say I'm gifted, and what is expected of me.	1 2 3 4 5
c. School is too easy, boring.	1 2 3 4 5
d. Parents, teachers, and friends expect me to be perfect all the time.	1 2 3 4 5
e. Friends who really understand me are hard to find.	1 2 3 4 5
f. Kids often tease me about being smart (or for being interested in certain things, getting high grades, etc.).	1 2 3 4 5
g. I feel overwhelmed by the number of things I can understand or do.	1 2 3 4 5
h. I feel different, alienated, alone.	1 2 3 4 5
i. I worry about world problems, or problems in my family, and feel helpless to do anything about these problems.	1 2 3 4 5

Figure 4. Continued

13. What's your biggest problem or difficulty in life right now? _____

14. Generally, how do you feel about your life? (Make a slash somewhere along the continuum.) _____

|————————————————————————————————|

Feel extremely bad, upset,   Feel really great,
worried; think about dying.   confident, happy.

E. SUPPORT SYSTEMS

15. Who do you share your feelings or problems with when you're wondering what life is all about or who you are? Who do you go to—or like to be around—when things aren't so great? (Check all that apply.)

_____	friend	_____	school counselor
_____	mother	_____	camp counselor
_____	father	_____	official Big Brother or Big Sister
_____	sister		
_____	brother	_____	other grown-up (neighbor)
_____	other relative	_____	teacher
_____	pet (dog, cat)	_____	I prefer being alone
_____	coach	_____	I don't think about that kind of stuff
_____	clergy		

16. What do you do to feel good about yourself?

_____ think or study hard
_____ get some exercise (get on my bike, go for a run, head for the gym, dance)
_____ call up a friend on the phone
_____ write in a journal
_____ paint or do other artwork or crafts
_____ play an instrument
_____ work on a project (club, play, newspaper)
_____ play harder in sports

_____ earn some extra money
_____ get outdoors and go somewhere (shopping, park)
_____ watch TV
_____ talk to my parents
_____ talk to my teacher
_____ listen to music
_____ eat
_____ use relaxation techniques (yoga, meditation)
_____ other (please write it down)
_____

17. And, finally, if you could get this class/program to do or provide ONE THING for you, it would be: _____

• name (optional): _____

Note. From *Managing the Social and Emotional Needs of the Gifted,* (p. 47), by C. Schmitz and J. Galbraith, 1985, Minneapolis, MN: Free Spirit. Copyright 1985 by Free Spirit. Reprinted with permission.

Enrichment in the Classroom	A differentiated program of study is provided by the classroom teacher within the regular classroom without assistance from an outside resource or consultant.
Consultant-Teacher Program	Differentiated instruction is provided within the classroom by the classroom teacher with the assistance of a specially trained consultant teacher who provides extra materials and teaches small groups of children in the regular classroom.
Resource room/Pull-out	Gifted students leave the classroom on a regular basis for differentiated instruction provided by a specially trained teacher.
Interest Classes	Students volunteer for challenging classes on topics beyond or outside the regular curriculum.
Community Mentor Program	Gifted students interact on an individual basis with selected members of the community for an extended time period on a topic of special interest to the student.
Independent-study Program	Differentiated instruction consists of independent study projects supervised by a qualified teacher or mentor.
Special Class	Gifted students are grouped together for most of the day and receive instruction from a specially trained teacher.
Special School	Gifted students receive differentiated instruction in a specialized school established for that purpose.
Magnet School	A school is established that focuses on specific areas. Students with interest in a particular area are encouraged to volunteer for these programs even if they are outside the students' own neighborhood school.

Summer Program	Enrichment or fast paced summer programs that attract gifted students in art, mathematics, or general programs.
Acceleration	Allows you to move to a higher level of class work, skip a class, or entire grades.
Advanced Placement	AP classes are college-level courses taught in high schools by trained high school teachers. Provides a greater challenge and college credit.
Early College Entrance	Entrance into college, usually at end of the junior year, because of high grades and ACT/SAT scores.
Dual Enrollment	Students take college courses while they are enrolled in high school. This is sometimes available in special summer programs.

Figure 5. Program Options

From *Teaching the Gifted Child* (p. 89), by J. Gallagher and S. Gallagher, 1994, Boston: Allyn and Bacon. Copyright 1994 by Allyn and Bacon. Adapted with permission. *Gifted Kid's Survival Guide: A Teen Handbook.* (pp. 158–166), by J. Galbraith and J. R. Delisle, 1996, Minneapolis, MN: Free Spirit. Copyright 1996 by Free Spirit. Adapted with permission.

mance, and are competent and capable of assessing their educational options. Gifted students should ask themselves these questions when assessing their educational options:

1. Is the work in most of your classes too easy for you?
2. Is one specific subject too easy?
3. Do you have a special interest that isn't taught by any teachers: astronomy? paleontology? Chinese? computer networks?
4. Have you taken most of the courses required for graduation, and you're only a sophomore?
5. Are you planning on going to college? Do you want a head start?
6. Do you find you need more uninterrupted work time for projects that interest you?

7. Do you wish there were more gifted students in your classes?
8. Do you want to work independently more often?
9. Is there someone in your community you'd like to spend time with and learn from (Galbraith and Delisle, 1996, p. 158)?

The teacher of the gifted and the student need to work together to find course work, program options, and resources to answer these questions. Many schools offer a variety of possibilities to make school more meaningful and enjoyable for the gifted student. Some options to consider are shown in Figure 5.

> *It has finally dawned on me that if the system won't change, it's up to me to make my classes more interesting. Now, as a result of learning to do things differently, I can honestly say school is really looking up! All the action feels good—I'm having fun. I've realized I have more opportunities and choices available to me than most kids, all I have to do is go get them.*
> —Janice, 15 (Galbraith & Delisle, 1996, p. 148)—

Scheduling

Scheduling of students is at once a headache, a bone of contention, a wearisome task, and a matter of much debate. How can learning time for gifted students be appropriately scheduled? The question is easy—the answer is not. Many gifted learners are frustrated by segmented days and the lack of an appropriate block of time for uninterrupted study (Galbraith, 1983). Whatever the scheduling model that is used, the teacher of the gifted must work closely with general education teachers to reduce friction and ill will. In this section, two models are discussed that can provide adequate time for gifted learners: the resource room and block scheduling. However, both models are not without problems and criticism.

Block Scheduling

Another equally controversial scheduling method that is fast gaining acceptance and popularity is block scheduling. Several models of block scheduling exist, but their common goal is to allow more flexibility in the use of time. The outcomes of block scheduling have been very positive. In fact, block scheduling has answered some of the complaints of gifted students. Queen and Gaskey (1997) found that "the positive changes in the climate of schools on a block schedule stem in part from an increased ability to meet the needs of individual students" (p. 158). They also noted that schools that are using block scheduling have seen their students become more motivated toward exploration and discovery in class.

Canady and Rettig (1995) of the Curry School of Education at the University of Virginia have focused their research on the benefits of block scheduling. The goals they list for block scheduling are highly compatible with the goals for a responsive learning environment for gifted students. It may well be that many frustrations of gifted learners and their teachers would be solved in a block scheduling setting. The following are selected responses that may relate to concerns for gifted learners:

1. About 80% of the teachers in the school lecture less and gradually engage students in more active learning structures; therefore, students become less passive in their learning.
2. The number of students on the A/B Honor Roll increases.
3. To date, there is evidence that AP scores will hold or improve with block schedules.
4. In spite of some challenges that block scheduling presents, the majority of teachers reported that, after experiencing it for two or more years, they were favorable to it, and students were overwhelmingly positive (Canady & Rettig, 1995, p. 4).

Whatever model is selected and designed for a specific school or program, it is of vital importance that all teachers and administrators work together to provide appropriate extended time for gifted learners.

The Resource Room

Resource rooms are often coupled with pull-out programs. This is a model in which, for a portion of the day or a full day, students are pulled from the regular classroom and work with a trained teacher of the gifted in a classroom that is rich with resources and materials. Hickey (1990) identified concerns and recommendations by practicing classroom teachers for improvement of gifted programs. The disruption of class routines caused by pull-out programs was identified as a major concern. Another major concern was that "pull-out programs present scheduling problems" (Hickey, 1990). These teachers suggested a program model other than pull-out be used and that scheduling problems could be reduced by providing an "elective period" during the school day when gifted students could attend special classes. They also recommended that schedules be planned to benefit all teachers. Hickey also pointed out that these specific problems contribute to the conflict between gifted resource teachers and regular classroom teachers. These teachers "agreed that these problems can be alleviated, but that cooperation is needed in the areas of scheduling, communication, planning, and mutual concern for students" (Hickey, 1990).

Teachers of the gifted and administrators need to be aware of these conflicts and plan accordingly. The resource room can be the basis of a very effective program because it does allow for a larger block of time, and it provides a safe psychological environment in which gifted learners can interact without age peer scrutiny and teasing. The resource room is also a great setting for independent study. References, resources, materials, computers, and space for individual study are all provided in one setting. In addition, the teacher of the gifted is readily available for mentoring or guidance.

Another positive use of the resource room, especially for individual study, is created with the use of curriculum compacting (Renzulli & Reis, 1985). With this model, mastery of the regular curriculum is documented before the content is taught, and this allows the student to "buy free time" from the regular instruction. The student then uses this time to go to the resource room and work on individual or small group projects.

Summary

Leta Hollingworth believed that life was very precious, talent was a blessing to be nurtured and shared for the good of others, and that people were to be cherished and helped.
—M. C. T. Overton (Silverman, 1990, p. 172)—

In this chapter, the most appropriate learning environment for gifted students has been defined as a flexible environment that allows learners to pursue educational requirements and interests in-depth and with a minimum of time limitation. The importance of recognizing the diversity among gifted learners and modifying for their diverse needs has been discussed in terms of both the social/emotional and the physical environments. It has been noted that modification of the environment facilitates the curricular modifications that make learning appropriately differentiated for gifted students. An emphasis has been placed on the social/emotional learning environment. Each aspect of the environment has been discussed in terms of the contributions of both gifted learners and teachers of the gifted. This chapter has also emphasized the key role of the teacher in designing and maintaining a safe and nurturing environment for gifted learners. Various guidelines, models, strategies, and resources have been suggested to guide the teacher in designing the appropriate learning and social/emotional environment for gifted students. Hollingworth (Silverman, 1990) has articulated an important attitude in establishing the learning environment for gifted learners by emphasizing that we cherish these individuals and support them in their journeys to realize their full potential and to discover their true and unique selves.

Teacher Resources

Publications

Adderholdt-Elliott, M., & Eller, S. (1989, Fall). Counseling students who are gifted through bibliotherapy. *Teaching Exceptional Children,* 26–31.

American Association for Gifted Children. (1978). *On Being Gifted.* Reston, VA: Author.

Bennis, W., & Nanus, B. (1985). *Leaders: The strategies for taking charge.* New York: Harper & Row.

Brophy, J. E. (1979). Teacher behavior and student learning. *Educational Leadership, 37,* 33–38.

Brown, B. (1990). Peer group and peer cultures. In S. Shirley Feldman & G. R. Elliott (Eds.), *At the threshold: The developing adolescent.* (pp. 171–197). Cambridge, MA: Harvard University Press.

Burke, K., Fogarty, R., & Belgard, S. (1994). *The portfolio connection.* Palatine, IL: Skylight.

Butler, K. A. (1987). *Learning and teaching style in theory and practice.* Columbia, CT: The Learner's Dimension.

Butler, K. A. (1988). *It's all in your mind.* Columbia, CT: The Learner's Dimension.

Butterfield, S. M., Kaplan, S. N., Meeker, M., Renzulli, J. S., Smith, L. S., & Treffinger, D. (1979). *Developing IEP's for the gifted/talented.* Ventura, CA: Office of Ventura County Superintendent of Schools.

Charles, C. (1996). *Building classroom discipline.* White Plains, NY: Longman.

Charlesworth, E. A., & Nathan, R. G. (1982). *Stress management: A comprehensive guide to wellness.* New York: Ballantine Books.

Coleman, J. (1980). Friendship and peer group in adolescence. In J. Adelson (Ed.), *Handbook of adolescent psychology.* (pp. 408–431). New York: Wiley.

Corey, G. (1990). *Theory and practice of group counseling* (3rd ed.). Pacific Grove, CA: Brooks/Cole.

Covey, S. R. (1989). *The seven habits of highly effective people.* New York: Simon & Schuster.

Crosby, N., & Marten, E. (1981). *Discovering psychology.* Buffalo, NY: D.O.K.

Curwin, R. L., & Mendler, A. N. (1988). *Discipline with dignity.* Rochester, NY: Association for Supervision and Curriculum Development.

Delisle, J. R. (1987). *Gifted kids speak out: Hundreds of kids ages 6–13 talk about school, friends, their families, and future.* Minneapolis, MN: Free Spirit.

Delisle, J., & Galbraith, J. (1987). *The gifted survival guide II: A special to the original gifted kids survival guide (for ages 11–18).* Minneapolis, MN: Free Spirit.

Dunn, R., & Dunn, K. (1975). *Learning style inventory.* Lawrence, KS: Price Systems.

Farris, D. (1991). *Type tales.* Palo Alto, CA: Consulting Psychologists Press.

Galbraith, J., & Delisle, J. (1996). *The gifted kids' survival guide: A teen handbook. Revised, expanded, and updated edition.* Minneapolis, MN: Free Spirit.

Galbraith, J. (1983). *The gifted kids survival guide (for ages 11–18).* Minneapolis, MN: Free Spirit.

Gazda, G. M. (1989). *Group counseling: A developmental approach* (3rd ed.). Needham Heights, MA: Allyn & Bacon.

Gregorc, A. (1979). Learning/teaching styles: Their nature and effects. *Educational Leadership 36,* 234–237.

Halsted, J. (1988). *Guiding gifted readers from pre-school to high school: A handbook for parents, teachers, counselors, and librarians.* Columbus, OH: Ohio Psychology.

Hart, D. (1994). *Authentic assessment.* Menlo Park, CA: Addison-Wesley.

Hauser, P., & Nelson, G. A. (1988). *Books for the gifted child.* New York: R. R. Bowker.

Hooker, D., & Gallagher, R. (1984). *I am gifted, creative, & talented.* New York: Educational Design.

Johnson, D. W., & Johnson, F. P. (1987). *Joining together: Group theory and group skills* (3rd ed.). Englewood Cliffs, NJ: Prentice Hall.

Karnes, F. A., & Bean, S. M. (1990). *Process skills rating scales.* Buffalo, NY: United Educational Services.

Karnes, F. A., & Bean, S. M. (1993). *Girls and young women leading the way: 20 true stories about leadership.* Minneapolis, MN: Free Spirit.

Karnes, F. A., & Bean, S. M. (1995). *Leadership for students: A practical guide for ages 8–18.* Waco, TX: Prufrock Press.

Keirsey D., & Bates, M. (1978). *Please understand me: Character and temperament types.* Del Mar, CA: Prometheus Nemesis.

Kerr, B. A. (1994). *Smart girls* (Rev. ed.). Scottsdale, AZ: Gifted Psychology Press.

Kincher, J. (1995). *Psychology for kids, II: 40 fun experiments that help you learn about others.* Minneapolis, MN: Free Spirit.

Kulik, J. A. (1991). Findings on grouping are often distorted. *Educational Leadership, 46*(6), 67.

Lawrence, G. (1982). *People types and tiger stripes: A practical guide to learning styles* (2nd ed.). Gainesville, FL: Center for Applications of Psychological Type.

McCarthy, B. (1981). *The 4 MAT System: Teaching to learning styles with right/left mode techniques.* Barrington, IL: Excel.

Madigan, M. M. (1977). *Philosophers: A source guide for self-directed units.* Tucson, AZ: Zephyr Press.

Maker, J., & Neilson, A. (1996). *Curriculum development and teaching strategies for gifted learners* (2nd ed.). Austin, TX: PRO-ED.

Meisgeier, C., & Murphy, E. (1987). *Murphy-Meisgeier Type Indicator for Children.* Palo Alto, CA: Consulting Psychologists Press.

Myers, I. B., & Myers, P. B. (1980). *Gifts differing: Understanding personality type.* Palo Alto, CA: Davies-Black Publishing.

Pedersen, P. (1988). *A handbook for developing multicultural awareness.* Alexandria, VA: America Counseling Association.

Philpot, J. G. (1997). *Bibliotherapy for classroom use.* Nashville, TN: Incentive.

Polette, N. (1984). *Books and real life: A guide for gifted students and teachers.* Jefferson, NC: McFarland.

Polette, N., & Hamlin, M. (1980). *Exploring books with gifted children.* Littleton, CO: Libraries Unlimited.

Porter, A., & Brophy, J. (1988). Synthesis of research on good teaching. *Educational Leadership, 45*(8), 74–85.

Purkey, W. W., & Novak, J. (1984). *Inviting school success: A self-concept approach to teaching and learning.* (2nd ed.). Belmont, CA: Wadsworth.

Purkey, W. W., & Schmidt, J. J. (1987). *The inviting relationship: An expanded perspective for professional counseling.* Englewood Cliffs, NJ: Prentice-Hall.

Purkey, W. W., & Stanley, P. H. (1991). *Invitational teaching, learning, and living.* Washington, DC: National Education Association.

Reis, S. M., Burns, D. E., & Renzulli, J. S. (1992). *Curriculum compacting.* Mansfield Center, CT: Creative Learning Press.

Renzulli, J., & Smith, L. H. (1978). *Learning styles inventory.* Mansfield Center, CT: Creative Learning Press.

Roberts, G. C., & Guttormson, L. (1990). *You and stress: A survival guide for adolescence.* Minneapolis, MN: Free Spirit.

Rogers, K. (1991). *The relationship of grouping practices to the education of the gifted and talented learner.* Report to National Research Center on the Gifted and Talented, CT: University of Connecticut.

Sattler, J. M. (1988). *Assessment of children's intelligence and special abilities.* (3rd ed.). San Diego, CA: Jerome Sattler.

Schmitz, C. C., & Galbraith, J. (1985). *Managing the social and emotional needs of the gifted: A teacher's survival guide.* Minneapolis, MN: Free Spirit.

Scott, G. G. (1990). *Resolving conflicts with others and with yourself.* Oakland, CA: New Harbringer.

Seeley, A. E. (1994). *Portfolio assessment.* Westminister, CA: Teacher Created Materials.

Spredemann-Dreyer, S. S. (1989). *The bookfinder 4: When kids need books.* Circle Pines, MN: American Guidance Service.

Torrance, P., McCarthy, B., & Kolesinski, M. (1988). *Style of Learning and Thinking (SOLAT).* Bensenville, IL: Scholastic Testing Services.

Webb, J. T., & Meckstroth, J. T. (1982). *Guiding the gifted child.* Scottsdale, AZ: Gifted Psychology Press.

Weeks, D. (1992). *The eight essential steps to conflict resolution.* Los Angeles: Jeremy P. Tarcher.

Wilt, J. (1980). *A kid's guide to making friends.* Waco, TX: Educational Product Division, Word.

Yalom, I. D. (1985). *The theory and practice of group psychotherapy* (3rd ed.). New York: Basic Books.

Addresses

Myers-Briggs Type Indicator
Consulting Psychologists Press, Inc.
3803 East Bayshore Rd.
Palo Alto, CA 94303

Web Sites

America's Promise—http://www.americaspromise.org
The Alliance for Youth ensures access to the five fundamental resources necessary to enable young people to maximize their potential, live the American dream, and give back to society.

Amnesty International—http://www.amnesty.org
This site contains news, information, campaigns, library, and links.

Center for World Dialogue—http://www.worlddialogue.org
This site initiates dialogue on political, social, economic, and religious issues of global and regional concern.

Fund for Peace—http://www.fundforpeace.org
This site promotes education and research on global problems that threaten human survival and proposes practical solutions.

Institute for Global Communications—http://www.igc.org/igc
IGC's five online communities of activists and organizations are gateways to articles, headlines, features, and web links on progressive issues.

International Peace Bureau—http://www.ipb.org
This is the world's oldest international peace federation.

Search for Common Ground—http://www.sfcg.org
This site seeks workable solutions to divisive national and international conflicts.

References

Adderholt, E. M., & Eler, S. (1989, Fall). Counseling students who are gifted through bibliotherapy. *Teaching Exceptional Children, 26–31,* 50.

Baker, J. (1996, Winter). Everyday stressors of academically gifted adolescents. *Journal of Secondary Gifted Education, 7,* 356–368.

Blocher, D. H. (1987). *The professional counselor.* New York: MacMillan.

Burke, K., Fogarty, R., & Belgrad, S. (1994). *The mindful school: The portfolio connection.* Palatine, IL: IRI/Skylight.

Canady, R., & Rettig, M. (1995). The power of innovative scheduling. *Education Leadership, 53*(3), 4.

Charles, C. (1996). *Building classroom discipline.* White Plains, NY: Longman Publishers.

Clark, B. (1997). *Growing up gifted.* (5th ed.). Upper Saddle River, NJ: Merrill.

Frazier, M., & McCannon, C. (1981). Using bibliotherapy with gifted children. *Gifted Child Quarterly, 25,* 81–85.

Galbraith, J. (1983). *Gifted kids survival guide.* Minneapolis, MN: Free Spirit.

Galbraith, J. (1985). The eight great gripes of gifted kids: Responding to special needs. *Roeper Review, 8,* 15–18

Galbraith, J., & Delisle, J. R. (1996). *Gifted kid's survival guide: A teen handbook.* Minneapolis, MN: Free Spirit.

Gallagher, J., & Gallagher, S. (1994). *Teaching the gifted child.* Boston: Allyn and Bacon.

Gallagher, S. (1990, September/October). Personality patterns of the gifted. *Understanding Our Gifted, 3*(1), 1–13.

Griggs, S., & Dunn, R. (1984). Selected case studies of the learning style preferences of gifted students. *Gifted Child Quarterly, 28,* 115–119.

Hansen, J., & Feldhusen, J. (1994). Comparison of trained and untrained teachers of gifted students. *Gifted Child Quarterly, 38,* 115–121.

Hart, D. (1994). *Authentic assessment: A handbook for educators.* Menlo Park, CA: Addison-Wesley.

Hickey, G. (1990). Classroom teachers' concerns and recommendations for improvement of gifted programs. *Roeper Review, 12,* 265–268.

Hunt, B. (1984). Analogies of being gifted. *Chart Your Course, 3*(1), 19.

Hunt, B. (1994). The effect of homogeneous and heterogeneous grouping of gifted sixth-grade students on mathematics achievement and attitude (Doctoral dissertation, University of Houston, 1994). *Dissertation Abstracts International,* 9516742.

Johnsen, S. (1991, Fall). Excellence in the education of teachers of the gifted and talented. *TAGT Tempo, 9*(4), 6–12.

Kerr, B. (1990). Leta Hollingworth's legacy to counseling and guidance. *Roeper Review, 12*, 178–181.

Kerr, B. (1992). *A handbook for counseling the gifted and talented.* Alexandria, VA: American Counseling Association.

Killen, M., & Turiel, E. (1991, July). Conflict resolution in preschool social interactions. *Early Education and Development, 2*, 240–255.

Kulik, C., & Kulik, J. (1982). Research synthesis on ability grouping. *Educational Research, 39*, 619–621.

Kulik, J., & Kulik, C. (1987). Mastery testing and student learning: A meta-analysis. *Journal of Educational Technology Systems, 15*, 325–345.

Kunkel, M., Chapa, B., Patterson, G., & Walling, D. (1992). Experiences of giftedness "eight great gripes" six years later. *Roeper Review, 15*, 10–13.

Lovecky, D. (1992). Exploring social and emotional aspects of giftedness in children. *Roeper Review, 15*, 18–25.

Maker, C., & Nielson, A. (1996). *Curriculum development and teaching strategies for gifted learners,* (2nd Ed.). Austin, TX: PRO-ED.

Mississippi State Department. (1994). *Suggested teaching strategies for teachers of the intellectually gifted.* Jackson, MS: Office of Gifted Education Programs.

Mönks, F., & Peters, W. (1992). *Talent for the future.* Netherlands: Van Gorcum, Assen/Maastricht.

Myers, I. B., & McCaulley, M. H. (1985). *Manual: A guide to the development and use of the Myers-Briggs Type Indicator.* Palo Alto, CA: Consulting Psychologists Press.

Paulson, F., Paulson, P., & Meyer, C. (1991, February). What makes a portfolio a portfolio? *Educational Leadership,* 60–63.

Piers, E., & Harris, D. (1969). *The Piers-Harris Children's Self-Concept Scale.* Los Angeles, CA: Western Psychological Services.

Poulsen, S. (1997). What if … Teachers are also learners?. *Wingspread Journal, 19*(3) 7–8.

Queen, A., & Gaskey, K. (1997). Steps for improving school climate in block scheduling. *Phi Delta Kappan, 79*, 158–162.

Renzulli, J. S., & Reis, S. M. (1985). *The schoolwide enrichment model.* Mansfield Center, CT: Creative Learning Press.

Renzulli, J. S., & Smith, L. H. (1978a). *The compactor.* Mansfield Center, CT: Creative Learning Press.

Renzulli, J. S., & Smith, L. H. (1978b). *Strength-a-Lyzer.* Mansfield Center, CT: Creative Learning Press.

Roedell, W. (1985). Developing social competence in gifted preschool children. *Remedial and Special Education, 6*(4), 6–11.

Roeper, A. (1997). My hopes and my mission. *NAGC Counseling and Guidance Division Newsletter,* 1–3.

Rogers, K. (1991). *The relationship of grouping practices to the education of gifted and talented learner.* Report to National Research Center on the Gifted and Talented. CT: University of Connecticut.

Ross, H., & Conant, C. (1992). The social structure of early conflict: Interaction, relationships, and alliances. In C. Shantz & W. Hartup (Eds.), *Conflict in child and adolescent development,* 153–185. Cambridge, UK: Cambridge University Press.

Schmitz, C., & Galbraith, J. (1985). *Managing the social and emotional needs of the gifted.* Minneapolis, MN: Free Spirit.

Silverman, L. (1989). The visual-spatial learner. *Preventing School Failure, 34*(1), 15–20.

Silverman, L. (1990). Social and emotional education of the gifted: The discoveries of Leta Hollingworth. *Roeper Review, 12,* 171–177.

Silverman, L. (1993). *Counseling the gifted and talented.* Denver, CO: Love Publishing.

Van Tassel-Baska, J. (1992). Educational decision making on acceleration and grouping. *Gifted Child Quarterly, 36,* 68–72.

Wheeler, E. (1994). Peer conflicts in the classroom. *Childhood Education, 70,* 296–299.

Williams, F. (1982). *Classroom ideas book, Vol 2.* Buffalo, NY: D.O.K. Publishers.

Wilson, K. (1988). *The development of conflicts and conflict resolution.* Unpublished master's thesis, Pacific Oaks College, Pasadena, CA.

SECTION II

INSTRUCTIONAL PLANNING AND EVALUATION

An Analysis of Gifted Education Curriculum Models

JOYCE VANTASSEL-BASKA
The College of William and Mary

ELISSA F. BROWN
Chesapeake Bay Governor's School
Williamsburg, VA

Much of gifted education as a field rests on the approaches that are used to serve gifted students in schools and other contexts. Consequently, the importance of programmatic and curriculum models cannot be overestimated. The purpose of this chapter is to systematically review existing program/curriculum models in the field and to determine the evidence for their use and their effectiveness with gifted populations.

History of Curriculum Models

The history of curriculum development for the gifted has been fraught with problems, similar to the general history of curriculum development in this country. Some of the most successful curriculum models for gifted learners have been developed based on acceleration principles for advanced secondary students (VanTassel-Baska, 1998, pp. 232–236). Many educators worldwide perceive the International Baccalaureate program and the College Board Advanced Placement Program as representing the highest levels of academic attainment available. These programs are thought to provide important stepping stones to successful college work since they constitute the beginning entry levels of such work. Thus, one approach to curriculum development for the gifted may be seen as a "design down" model where all curricula at K–12 is organized to promote readiness for college and the process is both sped up and shortened along the way for the most apt.

Alternatives to this viewpoint abound, however, and tend to focus on learning beyond, or in lieu of, traditional academics. Most of the curriculum models cited in this chapter ascribe to an enriched view of curriculum development for the gifted, a view that addresses a broader conception of giftedness, taking into account principles of creativity, motivation, and independence as crucial constructs to the development of high ability. These enrichment views also tend to see process skills, such as critical thinking and creative problem solving, as central to the learning enterprise, with content choices being more incidental. Evidence of student work through high-quality products and performances is also typically highly valued in these models.

Most of the enrichment-oriented approaches to curriculum development for the gifted emanated from the early work of Leta Hollingworth and her curriculum template for New York City self-contained classes. Strongly influenced by Deweyian progressivism, she organized curriculum units that allowed students to discover connections about how the world worked and what the role of creative people is in societal progress by having students study biography and to promote the role of group learning through discussion and conversation about ideas (Hollingworth, 1926). In some respects, contemporary curricular development efforts fall short of Hollingworth's early work in scope, purpose, and delivery.

Accelerative approaches to learning owe much to the work of Terman and Oden (1947), Pressey (1949), and early developers of rapid learning classes that enabled bright students to progress at their own rates. Early educational examples of autodidacticism and tutorials also encouraged a view of learning that promoted independent interest and a self-modulated pace (VanTassel-Baska,

1995). Thus, current curriculum models are grounded in a history of research, development, and implementation of both accelerative and enrichment approaches, typically implemented in self-contained classes since the level of content instruction could be modified based on the group. Chief differentiation approaches, early in the history of this field, incorporated attention to differences between gifted and nongifted populations. One might argue that today's views of differentiation tend to center far more on individual differences among the gifted than on the group difference paradigm for curricula employed both in and out of school.

Definition of a Curriculum Model: Subjects for Analysis

One of the issues in the field of gifted education rests with the differences between a program model and a curriculum model. Several of the models that were researched in this study could be said to cut both ways: they met the criteria for a curriculum model, but they also worked as a broad program framework. Others were clearly developed with curriculum as the organizing principle. The operational definition of a curriculum model used for the study was one that had the following components:

A Framework for Curriculum Design and Development. The model had to provide a system for developing and designing an appropriate curriculum for the target population. As such, it had to identify elements of such a design and show how these elements interacted in a curriculum product.

Transferable and Usable in All Content Areas. The model had to be utilitarian in that it was easily applied to all major areas of school-based learning.

K–12 Applicability. The model had to be flexible in respect to the age groups to which it would be applied. The central elements would have to work for kindergarten-age gifted children, as well as high school students.

Applicable Across Schools and Grouping Settings. The model had to have relevance in multiple locations and learning settings. It would need to work in tutorials, as well as large classes.

Incorporates Differentiated Features for the Gifted/Talented Learner. The model had to spell out ways in which it responded to the particular needs of the gifted for curriculum and instruction.

If models met this definition, they were included in the study. Obviously, some well-known curricula such as *Man: A Course of Study* (MACOS) (Bruner, 1970) would be excluded because it was not developed with the target population in mind. Other curriculum models would be excluded because they focused in one subject area only, such as *Philosophy in the Classroom* (Lipman, Sharp, & Oscanyan, 1980) or *Junior Great Books.* Still others might be excluded because they were limited to particular grade levels, such as Advanced Placement (AP) or International Baccalaureate (IB). Originally, 20 models were identified and then sifted according to the definitional structure, yielding 11 models for continued analysis.

Criteria Used to Assess Model Effectiveness

At a second stage of the process, the researchers were interested in comparing the selected curriculum models according to criteria found in the curriculum literature to be important indicators of effectiveness. These criteria, taken together, constituted the basis for yielding the overall effectiveness of the model. The criteria employed were

Research Evidence to Support Use (Student Learning Impact). Studies have been conducted to document the effectiveness of the curriculum with target populations.

Application to Actual Curriculum (Products in Use). The model has been translated into teaching segments.

Quality of Curriculum Products Based on the Model. The curriculum products based on the model have been evaluated by appropriate audiences and show evidence of curriculum design features (goals, objectives, activities, assessment, resources).

Teacher Receptivity. Teachers have commented positively on the curriculum in implementation.

Teacher Training Component for Use of the Model. The model has a defined training package so that practitioners can learn how to implement it.

Ease of Implementation. The model shows evidence of feasible implementation.

Evidence of Application of Model in Practice. The model can be seen employed in various schools.

Sustainability. The model has been in operation in schools for at least three years.

Systemic (Operational in Respect to Elements, Input, Output, Interactions, and Boundaries). The model is definable as a system.

Alignment or Relationship to National Standards. The model has a defined relationship to the National Content Standards (e.g., American Association for the Advancement of Science, 1993; 1989; National Council of Teachers of English and the International Reading Association, 1996; National Research Council, 1996).

Relationship to School-Based Core Curricula. The model has a defined relationship to other curricular emphasis in schools.

Comprehensiveness. The model applies broadly to all areas and domains of curricula and to all types of gifted learners at all stages of development.

Evidence of Scope and Sequence Considerations. The model has been applied, using a progressive development of skills and concepts approach.

Longitudinal Evidence of Effectiveness With Gifted Students. The model has evidence of effectiveness over at least three years with a given student cohort.

Evidence of Use in Teacher-Developed Curricula (Planning and Organizing on Paper). The model shows evidence of being used to organize a new curriculum that is teacher-developed.

Methodology

The approach employed to carry out the study was organized around four phases. Phase I constituted the search for models that fit the definition described. Several comprehensive texts were reviewed for potential models. Moreover, additional searches were made in the broader literature. Once models were selected, Phase II constituted a review of both ERIC and Psychology Abstracts for research and program data about the models published from 1990 onward. The researchers determined that the models had to be contemporary and currently in use in order to be judged currently effective. Therefore, models written in roughly the last 10 years would be found in this limited year search. After such material was located for each model, it was decided to contact each model's developer to ensure that no research or technical data that were available had been overlooked. This phase of the study took five months, utilizing a written query followed up by a telephone call to nonrespondents. All developers were asked to corroborate our findings, using the same checklist of criteria described earlier. Three of the developers did not respond directly about their work. Several of the developers sent additional data and suggested changes in the rating of their work, based on this new information. The original developers' interpretations of the criteria for judgment of the work has been acknowledged in the text by the incorporation of key ideas and studies.

Limitations of the Study

While the curriculum study used established research procedures for investigation, there are clear limitations to the findings generated. No attempt was made to judge the technical adequacy of the various studies reported except where sample size or lack of comparison group was a clear problem. Consequently, meta-analytic techniques to arrive at effect sizes were not done, rendering the findings cautionary. A follow-up study should be conducted on the seven models that have yielded research evidence to ascertain the integrity of the research designs and the power of the findings.

Discussion

Each of the models is discussed in the following section according to the criteria used to assess effectiveness. The two mega-models are described first, those of Julian Stanley and Joe Renzulli, because both have defined the major curriculum efforts of the gifted education field since the middle 1970s, and both also represent well the persistent programmatic division in the field between accelerative and enrichment approaches. Moreover, each of these models has over a decade of research, development, and implementation behind it. None of the other models described in the study enjoy such longevity, widespread use, or research attention.

The Stanley Model of Talent Identification and Development

The overall purpose of the Stanley model is to educate for individual development over the lifespan. Major principles of the model include (1) the use of a secure and difficult testing instrument that taps into high-level verbal and mathematical reasoning to identify students; (2) a diagnostic testing-prescriptive instructional approach (DT-PI) in teaching gifted students through special classes, allowing for appropriate level challenge in instruction; (3) the use of subject matter acceleration and fast-paced classes in core academic areas, as well as advocacy for various other forms of acceleration; and (4) curriculum flexibility in all schooling. The model has been developed at key university sites across the country with some adoptions by local school districts that have established fast-paced classes.

The Study of Mathematically Precocious Youth (SMPY) officially started in September of 1971 at Johns Hopkins University (JHU) and now has been continued, since 1986, at Iowa State University. From 1972 through 1979, SMPY pioneered the concept of searching for youth who reason exceptionally well mathematically (i.e., a talent search). In 1980, the talent search was extended to verbally gifted youth by others at JHU. For the students identified by the talent searchers, SMPY provided educational facilitation by utilizing acceleration or curricular flexibility and by developing fast-paced academic programs. Gifted students in seventh and eighth grade can participate in these talent searches by taking the College Board's Scholastic Aptitude Test (SAT) or the ACT. Almost 150,000 gifted students do so every year. These centers and other universities and organizations also offer residential and commuter academic programs in several disciplines to qualified students.

The research work of SMPY has been strong over the past 27 years, with more than 300 published articles, chapters, and books about the model. Findings of these studies have consistently focused on the benefits of acceleration for continued advanced work in an area by precocious students (Stanley, Keating, & Fox, 1974), a clear rationale for the use of acceleration in intellectual development (Keating, 1976), and the long term positive repeated impacts of accelerative opportunities (Benbow & Arjmand, 1990). Case study research also has been undertaken to demonstrate how these processes affect individual students (Brody & Stanley, 1991). Other studies have focused more specifically on student gains from fast-paced classes (Lynch, 1992). The use of the model has been extensive across all of the United States and in selected foreign countries. Curriculum materials have been developed by talent search staff at various sites and by individual teachers in the summer and academic year programs. Especially noteworthy are the curriculum guides for teaching Advanced Placement courses developed at the Talent Identification Program (TIP) at Duke University. Strong use of articulated course materials are employed on the way to Advanced Placement coursework and testing in mathematics, science, and the verbal areas, including foreign language. These materials have been reviewed by practicing professionals and content specialists.

Over the entire 27 years of operation, the model has been well received by parents and students who constitute the major client groups; schools have been less receptive based on their conservative attitudes toward accelerative practices and the emphasis on highly gifted students in subject areas.

The model does not have a formal training component, although selection of teachers is a rigorous process carried out carefully in each university and school setting. Content expertise and work with highly gifted secondary students are primary considerations for selection. The model is easy to understand but difficult to implement in schools based on prevailing philosophies. The application of the model that has been most successful is in after-school and summer settings where students complete the equivalent of high school honors classes in three weeks.

The SMPY model has proven to be highly sustainable, exhibiting strong replication capacity. Even where countries do not conduct talent searches, students from those countries routinely attend summer programs at talent search universities.

Because the model is content-based, it aligns well with the National Content Standards, although some of the enrichment emphasis of the standards would be overlooked in implementation. SMPY represents core curricula on an accelerated and streamlined level. The model is not totally comprehensive in that it addresses students in grades 3–12 who reason exceptionally well mathematically and verbally. Some studies on spatially gifted students at those levels have also been conducted. Curriculum areas are comprehensive, including all of the 26 Advanced Placement course strands. Scope and sequence work has been articulated for grades 7–12 in some areas of learning. Northwestern University has developed a guide for educational options for grades 5–12.

Longitudinal data, collected over the past 20 years on 300 highly gifted students, have demonstrated the viability of the Stanley model in respect to the benefits of accelerative study, early identification of a strong talent area, and the need for assistance in educational decision making (Lubinski & Benbow, 1994). A 50-year follow-up study (1972–2022) is in progress at Iowa State University with 6,000 students in the sample. This study already rivals Terman's longitudinal study in respect to its longevity and exceeds it in regard to understanding the talent development process at work.

The Renzulli Schoolwide Enrichment Triad Model (SEM)

The Schoolwide Enrichment Model (SEM) evolved after 15 years of research and field testing by both educators and researchers (Renzulli, 1988). It combined the previously developed Enrichment Triad Model (Renzulli, 1977) with a more flexible approach to identifying high-potential students, the Revolving Door Identification Model (Renzulli, Reis, & Smith, 1981). This combination of services was initially field tested in 11 school districts of various types (rural, suburban, and urban) and sizes. The field tests resulted in the development of the SEM (Renzulli & Reis, 1985), which has been widely adopted throughout the country.

In the SEM, a talent pool of 15–20% of above-average ability/high-potential students is identified through a variety of measures, including achievement tests, teacher nominations, assessment of potential for creativity and task commitment, as well as alternative pathways of entrance (self-nomination, parent nomination, etc.). High achievement test scores and IQ scores automatically include a student in the talent pool, enabling those students who are underachieving in their academic school work to be considered.

Once students are identified for the talent pool, they are eligible for several kinds of services. First, interest and learning style assessments are used with talent pool students. Second, curriculum compacting is provided to all eligible students; that is, the regular curriculum is modified by eliminating portions of previously mastered content, and alternative work is substituted. Third, the Enrichment Triad Model offers three types of enrichment experiences: Type I, II, and III. Type III enrichment is usually more appropriate for students with higher levels of ability, interest, and task commitment.

Type I Enrichment consists of general exploratory experiences such as guest speakers, field trips, demonstrations, interest centers, and the use of audiovisual materials designed to expose students to new and exciting topics, ideas, and fields of knowledge not ordinarily covered in the regular curriculum. Type II Enrichment includes instructional methods and materials purposefully designed to promote the development of thinking, feeling, research, communication, and methodological processes. Type III Enrichment, the most advanced level of the model, is defined as investigative activities and artistic productions in which the learner assumes the role of a first-hand inquirer: thinking, feeling, and acting like a practicing professional, with involvement pursued at a level as advanced or professional as possible, given the student's level of development and age.

One comparative study (Heal, 1989) compared the effects of SEM to other enrichment models or strategies. Other studies report results using within-model comparisons (Delisle, 1981; Reis, 1981) or the SEM program as compared to no intervention (Karafelis, 1986; Starko, 1986). Because control or comparison groups of students participating in alternate or comparison models were not used, it is difficult to attribute various results to participation in the SEM.

Evaluation studies have been conducted in 29 school districts on the perceptions of the model with parents, teachers, and administrators. Researchers documented positive change in teacher attitudes toward student work.

Delcourt (1988) investigated characteristics related to creative/productive behavior in 18 high school students who consistently engaged in first-hand research on self-selected topics within or outside school. Starko (1986) also examined the effects of the Schoolwide Enrichment Model on student creative productivity. Results indicated that students who became involved in independent study projects in the SEM more often initiated their own creative products both *in and outside school* than did students in the comparison group. In addition, multiple creative products were linked to self-efficacy.

Several studies have examined the use of the model with underserved populations. Emerick (1988) investigated underachievement patterns of high-potential students. Baum (1985, 1988) examined highly able students with learning disabilities, identifying both characteristics and programmatic needs. Findings suggest positive effects of the model with these populations.

Compacting studies have sought to document the fact that gifted students are capable of rapidly progressing through regular school curriculum in order to spend time on Type III project work. Results demonstrate knowledge scores that were high or higher on in-grade standardized tests than noncompacted peers (Reis & Purcell, 1993).

Two SEM longitudinal studies have been conducted with 18 and 9 students, respectively. These studies showed that students in the sample maintained similar or identical career goals from their plans in high school, remained in major fields of study in college, and were satisfied in current project work. Moreover, the Type III process appeared to serve as important training for later productivity.

The SEM model is widely used in some form in schools nationally and internationally. Summer training on the model is available at the University of Connecticut, reportedly training more than 600 educators annually. Renzulli perceives that the model is closely linked to core curricula, offers a scope and sequence within Type II activities, and has the potential to be aligned with National Content Standards. Both teachers and selected students are especially enthusiastic about the model.

The Betts Autonomous Learner Model *Independent, in one area*

The autonomous learner model for the gifted and talented was developed to meet the diverse cognitive, emotional, and social needs of gifted and talented students in grades K–12 (Betts & Knapp, 1980). As the needs of gifted and talented students are met, gifted students will develop into autonomous learners who are responsible for the development, implementation, and evaluation of their own learning. The model is divided into five major dimensions: (1) orientation, (2) individual development, (3) enrichment activities, (4) seminars, and (5) in-depth study.

One of the criteria used for assessing the appropriateness of a curriculum model is the evidence of research to support its use with gifted and talented learners. To date, no research evidence of effectiveness has been shown with regard to this model's student learning impact or longitudinal effectiveness with gifted learners. However, several curriculum units and curriculum guides have been produced as a result of the dissemination of its ideas. One article reviewed and described the model by presenting guidelines for developing a process-based scope and sequence, as well as independent study programs for gifted learners (Betts & Neihart, 1986).

Regardless of the paucity of data on this model, it is one of the most widely recognized and used in the United States (Betts, 1986). Teachers have commented positively on its implementation. The model has been employed at selected sites in the United States and in other countries. Formal teacher training occurs in three-and five-day segments annually. Its design suggests a three-year timeline for model implementation. It does contain a degree of comprehensiveness in that the model applies broadly to all curriculum domains and ages of learners; however, it does not incorporate any features of accelerated learning, thereby limiting one aspect of its comprehensiveness.

Gardner's Multiple Intelligences

Multiple intelligences (MI) as a curriculum approach was built on a multidimensional concept of intelligence (Gardner, 1983). Seven areas of intelligence were defined in the original published work in 1983, with an eighth intelligence added by Gardner in

1995. They are (1) verbal/linguistic, (2) logical/mathematical, (3) visual/spatial, (4) musical/rhythmic, (5) bodily/kinesthetic, (6) interpersonal, (7) intrapersonal, and (8) naturalistic.

Evidence of research based on multiple intelligences translated into practice has recently been documented (Strahan, Summey, & Banks, 1996; Latham, 1997). Most of the research, however, lacks control groups; therefore, generalizations about the model are difficult to infer (Latham, 1997). Longitudinal evidence of effectiveness with gifted students over at least three years has not been documented, although some research has been conducted on incorporating multiple intelligences with other forms of curriculum models (Maker, Nielson, & Rogers, 1994).

The multiple intelligences approach has been used in the formation of new schools, in identifying individual differences, for curriculum planning and development, and as a way to assess instructional strategies. A plethora of curriculum materials has been produced and marketed based upon Multiple Intelligences (MI). This approach holds widespread appeal for many educators because it can be adapted for any learner, subject domain, or grade level. The model is not easy to implement and does require teacher training, financial resources, and time. Best-known project sites for the model are the Key School in Indianapolis, IN, and the Atlas Project in New York City. While the model has been readily adapted to curricula, it remains primarily a conception of intelligence applied broadly to school settings as a way to promote talent development for all learners.

Developer concerns about application fidelity of the ideas and variability in implementation quality are strong, leading to a new project specifically designed to monitor implementation of MI in classrooms nationally where positive impacts have been reported.

The Purdue Three-Stage Enrichment Model for Elementary Gifted Learners (PACE) and The Purdue Secondary Model for Gifted and Talented Youth

Feldhusen

The concept of a three-stage model, initiated by Feldhusen and his graduate students, was first introduced as a course design for university students in 1973. It evolved into the Three-Stage Model by

1979. It is primarily an ordered enrichment model that moves students from simple thinking experiences to complex independent activities (Feldhusen & Kolloff, 1986).

- Stage I focuses on the development of divergent and convergent thinking skills;
- Stage II provides development in creative problem solving; and
- Stage III allows students to apply research skills in the development of independent study skills.

The Purdue Secondary Model is a comprehensive structure for programming services at the secondary level. It has 11 components supporting enrichment and acceleration options, with each component designed to act as a guide for organizing opportunities for secondary gifted students. They are (1) counseling services, (2) seminars, (3) advanced placement courses, (4) honors classes, (5) math/science acceleration, (6) foreign languages, (7) arts, (8) cultural experiences, (9) career education, (10) vocational programs, and (11) extra-school instruction (Feldhusen & Robinson-Wyman, 1986).

Research has documented gains with regard to enhancement of creative thinking and self-concept using the Three-Stage Enrichment Model for Elementary Gifted Students (Kolloff & Feldhusen, 1984), and one study was conducted documenting limited long-term gains of the elementary program PACE (Moon, Feldhusen, & Dillon, 1994; Moon & Feldhusen, 1994).

The application and implementation of either the elementary or secondary models are not conclusive, yet they appear to be sustainable (Moon & Feldhusen, 1994). Teacher training has accompanied the site implementation of both the elementary and secondary models; however, it is difficult to ascertain the degree of widespread application beyond Indiana. Neither model utilizes a scope and sequence, and neither may be viewed as a comprehensive model in terms of applying broadly to all areas of the curriculum, all types of gifted learners, or to all stages of development.

The Kaplan Grid

The Grid was a model designed to facilitate the curriculum developer's task of deciding what constitutes a differentiated curriculum and how one can construct such a curriculum. The model uses the components of process, content, and product organized around a theme. Content is defined as "the relationship between economic, social, personal, and environmental displays of power, and the needs and the interests of individuals, groups, and societies (interdisciplinary)" (Kaplan, 1986). The process component utilizes productive thinking, research skills, and basic skills. The product component culminates the learning into a mode of communication.

Research evidence could not be found to support the effectiveness of this model with a target population. The quality of the curriculum products that have been produced based upon this model has not been reported in the literature. However, there has been extensive implementation of the approach at both state and local levels.

Teacher training has been conducted throughout the United States, initially through the National/State Leadership Training Institute and now independently by the developer so that practitioners can learn how to implement it. Thousands of teachers have developed their own curricula based upon the model. The Grid is intended as a developmental framework for curriculum planning for gifted learners, but it does not contain a scope and sequence. Additionally, within the model itself, no provisions are explicitly made for accelerated learning.

The Maker Matrix

The Maker matrix, developed to categorize content, process, environmental, and product dimensions of an appropriate curriculum for the gifted, represents a set of descriptive criteria that may be used to develop classroom-based curricula (Maker, 1982). Recent work on the model represents primarily an enhancement of its problem-solving component. The Discover project is a process for assessing problem solving in multiple intelligences. The problem-solving matrix incorporates a continuum of five problem types for use within each of the intelligences.

- Type I and II problems require convergent thinking.
- Type III problems are structured but allow for a range of methods to solve them and have a range of acceptable answers.
- Type IV problems are defined, but the learner selects a method for solving and establishing evaluation criteria for the solution.

- Type V problems are ill-structured, and the learner must define the problem, discover the method for solving, and establish criteria for creating a solution (Maker, Nielson, & Rogers, 1994).

The project is typically used by teachers for curriculum planning and assessing learner problem-solving abilities.

Research on problem types is currently underway involving 12 classrooms in a variety of settings. However, to date, the results have not been published. A pilot study has shown that use of the matrix enhances the process of problem solving (Maker, Rogers, Nielson, & Bauerle, 1996). Studies to evaluate the long-term validity of the process are in progress.

School systems in several states have applied the matrix as a framework for organizing and developing classroom level curricula. There is evidence of an individual teacher-developed curriculum, and teachers have been receptive to its use. Some training exists for its application. The sustainability of the matrix model for at least three years is not known. It is not comprehensive in nature, yet it does have a strong emphasis in its relationship to core subject domains.

The Meeker Structure of Intellect Model (SOI)

The Structure of Intellect Model (SOI) for gifted education was based upon a theory of human intelligence called the Structure of Intellect (SI) developed by J. P. Guilford (1967). The SI model of human intelligence describes 90 kinds of cognitive functions organized into content, operation, and product abilities. The SOI system applies Guilford's theory into the areas of assessment and training. The model is definable as a system and applies broadly to all types of gifted learners at varying developmental stages; but due to its comprehensiveness and emphasis on cognition, only a few sites have actually implemented the model. Those sites have used it for identifying students or for training teachers to view intelligence as a nonfixed entity.

Studies of the model do not include effectiveness data (Meeker, 1976); rather, they primarily focus on findings for its use as identification criteria, as a means for organizing information about a gifted child or as a means for overall program design. SOI has been successfully used in selected sites for identification with culturally diverse (Hengen, 1983) and preschool screening for multi-ethnic disadvantaged gifted studies (Bonne, 1985).

Although now somewhat dated, SOI offered a means of understanding students by delineating profiles of their intellectual abilities. It contained a teacher-training component that used teacher modules, designed to train one SOI ability at a time. Training materials included mini lesson plans for group teaching and self-help modules for individualized instruction with selected students (Meeker, 1969).

The Schlichter Models for Talents Unlimited Inc. and Talents Unlimited to the Secondary Power (TU²)

Talents Unlimited was based upon Guilford's (1967) research on the nature of intelligence. Taylor, Ghiselin, Wolfer, Loy, & Bourne (1964), also influenced by Guilford, authored the Multiple Talent Theory, which precipitated the development of a model to be employed in helping teachers identify and nurture students' multiple talents. Talents Unlimited features four major components:

- a description of specific skill abilities, or talents, in addition to academic ability that include productive thinking, communication, forecasting, decision making, and planning;
- model instructional materials;
- an in-service training program for teachers; and
- an evaluation system for assessing students' thinking skills development (Schlichter, 1986).

Talents Unlimited Inc. is the K–6 model, and Talents Unlimited to the Secondary Power is a model for grades 7–12.

Research has documented gains using the model in developing students' creative and critical thinking (Schlichter & Palmer, 1993). Additionally, there is evidence that the use of the model enhances academic skill development on standardized achievement tests (McLean & Chisson, 1980). However, no longitudinal studies have been conducted.

Staff development and teacher training constitute a strong component of the model. Teachers may become "certified" as Talents Unlimited trainers. Due to the strong emphasis on teacher training, Talents Unlimited has widespread applicable student use across the United States and worldwide. Part of its implementation success came as a result of funding and membership in the United States Office of Education, National Diffusion Network.

The model has been used most effectively as a classroom-based approach with all learners, thus rendering it less differentiated for the gifted in practice than some of the other models.

Sternberg's Triarchic Componential Model

Sternberg's Componential Model is based upon an information processing theory of intelligence (Sternberg, 1981). In the model, three components represent the mental processes used in thinking. The executive process component is used in planning, decision making, and monitoring performance. The performance component processes are used in executing the executive problem-solving strategies within domains. The knowledge-acquisition component is used in acquiring, retaining, and transferring new information. The interaction and feedback between the individual and his or her environment within any given context allows cognitive development to occur.

An initial study has shown the effectiveness of the triarchic model with students learning psychology in a summer program (Sternberg & Clinkenbeard, 1995). More recent work has been conducted in studies using psychology as the curriculum base with larger samples of students. Students continue to show growth patterns when assessment protocols are linked to measuring ability profiles (Sternberg, Ferrari, Clinkenbeard, & Grigorenko, 1996). Primary to these studies is the validation of the STAT (Sternberg Triarchic Abilities Test) and its utility for finding students strong on specific triarchic components. Other recent studies (Sternberg, Torff, & Grigorenko, 1998a, 1998b) focus on the use of triarchic instructional processes in classrooms at the elementary and middle school levels. Results suggest slightly stronger effects for triarchic instruction over traditional and critical-thinking approaches. Descriptions of teacher-created curricula and instructional instrumentation processes were limited but clearly are organized along discipline-specific lines of inquiry. Sustainability of the curriculum model beyond summer program implementation and pilot settings is not known.

There is not a packaged teacher-training or staff-development component, partially because the model is based upon a theory of intelligence rather than a deliberate curriculum framework. It is a systemic but not a comprehensive model with some applications in selected classrooms.

Van Tassel-Baska Integrated Curriculum Model (ICM)

The Van Tassel-Baska (1986) Integrated Curriculum Model (ICM) was specifically developed for high ability learners. It has three dimensions: (1) advanced content, (2) high-level process and product work, and (3) intra- and interdisciplinary concept development and understanding. Van Tassel-Baska, with funding from the Jacob Javits Program, used the ICM to develop specific curriculum frameworks and underlying units in language arts and science.

Research has been conducted to support the effectiveness of these curriculum units with gifted populations within a variety of educational settings. Specifically, significant growth gains in literary analysis and interpretation, persuasive writing, and linguistic competency in language arts have been demonstrated for experimental gifted classes using the developed curriculum units in comparison to gifted groups not using them (Van Tassel-Baska, Johnson, Hughes, & Boyce, 1996). Other studies have shown that using the problem-based science units embedded in an exemplary science curriculum significantly enhances the capacity for integrating higher-order process skills in science (Van Tassel-Baska, Bass, Reis, Poland, & Avery, 1998) regardless of the grouping approach employed. Further, research has documented positive change in teacher attitude, student motivational response, and school and district change (Van Tassel-Baska, Avery, Little & Hughes, 2000) as a result of using the ICM curriculum over three years.

Teacher training is an integral component of the ICM model. Training workshops have been conducted in 30 states, and the College of William and Mary offers training annually. There is a strong relationship to core subject domains, as well as national standards alignment. The curriculum, based on the model, was developed using the national standards work as a template. Alignment charts have been completed for national and state standards work in both language arts and science.

The ICM units are moderately comprehensive in that they span grades 2–8 in language arts and 2–8 in science. New language arts units developed in 1997–98 now offer K–11 coverage in language arts. The ICM model has been used for specific district curriculum development and planning.

There is evidence of broad-based application, but some questions remain regarding the ease of implementation of actual teaching units and the fidelity of implementation by teachers (Burruss, 1997). Some districts use the units as models for developing their own curricula. The developer reported that 100 school districts are part of a National Curriculum Network using both the science and language arts units. Data on student impact have been collected from over 100 classrooms nationally.

Studies of effectiveness are on-going in classrooms nationally. The curriculum is reported to be used in 45 states. Internationally, the model is being used in 15 countries with systematic unit development occurring in Australia in 1998.

Key Findings

An important part of the curriculum model analysis was also to compare the models to one another, using the same criteria as the basis for comparison. Some models were more organizational than curricular in nature, which helps teachers get started on differentiation in their classroom; others were more programmatic in nature and were intended as a defining framework in schools. Examples of the former were the Kaplan Grid and the Maker matrix, both heavily used by practitioners as designs for teacher-made materials. No studies of effectiveness have been conducted to date, however, to show the benefits of such models in practice with gifted learners. The Tannenbaum model, dropped at the second level of analysis, exemplified the programmatic framework model as a supraorganizer at the school level, not at the level of curriculum units or courses of study. Regrettably, no studies or evidence of application were found.

Only seven models showed evidence of research studies being conducted on them. Of those, only five of the models employed comparison groups where treatment might be attributed to the curriculum approach employed. The Stanley, Renzulli, Feldhusen, VanTassel-Baska, and Schlichter models all have some evidence of effectiveness with gifted populations in comparison to other treatments or no treatments. While the Talents Unlimited Model has some evidence of effectiveness, much of the research base is on nongifted populations.

Evidence for the translation of these curriculum models into effective practice varies considerably. Seven models have training packages that provide staff development for implementation, while only four models explicitly consider scope and sequence issues. Betts and Renzulli consider scope and sequence within their models. For Betts, it is in the movement from one stage to another; for Renzulli, it occurs within Type II activities. Stanley and VanTassel-Baska both have developed scope and sequence models linked to Advanced Placement work.

Data on curriculum and instructional practices with the gifted clearly favor advanced work in the subject areas of language arts, science, and mathematics, although the approach to content acceleration may vary. While both the Stanley and VanTassel-Baska models have elements of acceleration within them, only the Stanley model has empirically demonstrated its clear impact on learning over time.

Curricula organized around higher-order processes and independent study have yielded few studies of student impacts, nor are the findings across studies consistent. Even longitudinal studies, such as those of Feldhusen and Renzulli, have produced limited evidence of outcomes relevant to clear student gains. Limited sample size and other confounding variables, such as lack of comparison groups, also render these studies less credible.

Conclusions

A strong body of research evidence exists supporting the use of advanced curricula in core areas of learning at an accelerated rate for high-ability learners. Some evidence also exists that more enrichment-oriented models are effective. This conclusion has not changed much in the past 20 years (Daurio, 1979). Moreover, recent meta-analytic studies continue to confirm the superior learning effects of acceleration over enrichment in tandem with grouping the gifted (Kulik, 1993). In comparison to other strategies, such as independent study, various modes of grouping, and problem solving, acceleration not only shows performance gains but also has a powerful treatment effect, meaning that the gains are educationally, as well as statistically significant (Walberg, 1991). Despite the lack of convincing research to support their use, several of the enrichment models enjoy widespread popularity and are used extensively in schools.

General Implications

Several implications might be drawn from these findings, related to both research and practice in gifted education. Too frequently, it is assumed that if a model is written about and used enthusiastically, such popularity is sufficient for proclaiming its effectiveness. Nothing could be further from the truth. Research-based practice is critical to defensible gifted programs. Therefore, practitioners must proceed carefully in deciding on curricula for use in gifted programs. The evidence strongly suggests that content-based accelerative approaches should be employed in any curriculum used in school-based programs for the gifted and that schools need to apply curriculum models faithfully and thoroughly in order to realize their potential impacts over time.

In the area of research, it is clear that there is a limited base of coherent studies that can make claims about the efficacy of enriched approaches to curriculum for the gifted. Thus, an important direction for future research would be to conduct curriculum intervention studies testing these models, as well as to replicate existing studies to build a base of deeper understanding about what works well with gifted students in school programs. More research on differential student learning outcomes in gifted programs using different curricular approaches clearly needs to be undertaken.

Implications for Schools

Decisions about curriculum approaches and their implications for classrooms need to be made with a sense of "what works" for our best learners in schools. This chapter has delineated a set of criteria for considering the state of the art in curriculum interventions for gifted learners. These criteria are important considerations for schools in making curricular decisions. The fundamental questions upon which schools need to focus are

- Do gifted students show evidence of learning as a result of the curriculum approach? What is the nature and extent of the evidence and how credible is it?
- Is the curriculum approach currently being used in schools where we can talk to teachers and observe it in practice?
- Are classroom materials available to use in implementation?
- Is training available for school staff?

These questions are crucial to ask before schools decide what curriculum to employ for gifted populations. From a process perspective, school administrators of gifted programs might wish to do the following

1. Review each curriculum model with their staff, noting the advantages and disadvantages of each in a particular school context.
2. Visit schools using the most appropriate models (limit to three).
3. Review existing curriculum materials for the selected models with an eye to implementation issues.
4. Consider staffing match-ups. Who could teach each of the models based on background and experience?
5. Select one of the models for piloting in the school district for one year.
6. Secure appropriate training for teachers.
7. Provide additional planning time for implementation issues.
8. Provide follow-up classroom monitoring through visitation, videotaping, or peer/mentor coaching strategies.
9. Assess the effectiveness of the pilot based on student learning data and student and teacher feedback.

By following these processes in using research-based curriculum approaches, the level of curriculum services to gifted learners may become elevated over current practice.

Teacher Resources

Publications

Baum, S., Renzulli, J., & Hébert. T. P. (1995). Reversing under-achievement: Creative productivity as a systematic intervention. *Gifted Child Quarterly 39*, 224–235.

Benbow, C. P. (1986). SMPY's model for teaching mathematically precocious students. In J. S. Renzulli (Ed.), *Systems and models and programs for the gifted and talented* (pp. 1–25). Mansfield Center, CT: Creative Learning Press.

Benbow, C. P., Arjmand, O., & Walberg, H. J. (1991). Educational productivity predictors among mathematically talented students. *Journal of Educational Research, 84*, 215–223.

Benbow, C. P., & Lubinski, D. (1994). Individual differences amongst the mathematically gifted: Their educational and vocational implications. In N. Colangelo, S. G. Assouline, & D. L. Ambroson (Eds.), *Talent development* (Vol. 2, pp. 83–100). Dayton, OH: Ohio Psychology Press.

Benbow, C. P., & Lubinski, D. (1996). *Intellectual talent: Psychometric and social issues.* Baltimore: Johns Hopkins University Press.

Benbow, C. P., & Stanley, J. C. (1983). *Academic precocity.* Baltimore: Johns Hopkins University Press.

Benbow, C. P., & Stanley, J. C. (1996). Inequity in equity: How "equity" can lead to inequity for high-potential students. *Psychology Public Policy and Law, 2*, 249–292.

Betts, G. T., & Neihart, M. (1986). Implementing self-directed learning models for the gifted and talented. *Gifted Child Quarterly, 30*, 174–77.

Boyce, L. N., VanTassel-Baska, J., Burruss, J. D., Sher, B. T., & Johnson, D. T. (1997). A problem-based curriculum: Parallel learning opportunities for students and teachers. *Journal for the Education of the Gifted, 20*, 363–379.

Burns, D. (1988). The effects of group training activities on students' creative productivity. In J. S. Renzulli, *Technical report of research studies related to the revolving door identification model* (2nd ed., pp. 147–174). Storrs, CT: Research Report Series, School of Education, University of Connecticut.

Charlton, J. C., et al. (1994). Follow-up insights on rapid educational acceleration. *Roeper Review, 17*, 123–130.

Chissom, B. S., & McLean, J. E. (1979). *Talents unlimited program: Technical report summarizing research findings.* Mobile, AL: Mobile County Public Schools.

Cooper, C. (1983). *Administrators' attitudes toward gifted programs based on the enrichment triad/revolving door identification model: Case studies in decision making.* Unpublished doctoral dissertation, The University of Connecticut at Storrs.

Crump, W. D., Schlichter, C. L., & Palk, B. E. (1988). Teaching HOTS in the middle and high school: A district-level initiative in developing higher-order thinking skills. *Roeper Review, 10*, 205–211.

Daurio, S. (1978). Educational enrichment and acceleration. In J. C. Stanley, W. C. George, & C. H. Solano (Eds.), *Educational programs and intellectual prodigies* (pp. 90–120). Baltimore: Study of Mathematically Precocious Youth, Department of Psychology, Johns Hopkins University.

Delcourt, M. A. B. (1993). Creative productivity among secondary school students: Combining energy, interest, and imagination. *Gifted Child Quarterly, 37*, 23–31.

Delcourt, M. A. B. (1994). Characteristics of high-level creative productivity: A longitudinal study of students identified by Renzulli's three misconceptions of greatness. In R. Subotnik & K. D. Arnold (Eds.), *Beyond Terman contemporary longitudinal studies of giftedness and talent* (pp. 375–400). Norwood, NJ: Ablex.

Fasko, D., Jr. (1992). *Individual differences and multiple intelligences.* Paper presented at the annual meeting of the Mid-South Education Research Association, Knoxville, TN.

Feldhusen, J. F., & Kolloff, M. B. (1979). A rationale for career education activities in the Purdue Three-Stage model. *Roeper Review, 2*, 13–17.

Feldhusen, J. F., Kolloff, M. B., Cole, S., & Moon, S. (1988). A three-stage model for gifted education. *Gifted Child Today, 11*, 14–20.

Gallagher, S. A., Stepien, W. J., Sher, B. T., & Workman, D. (1995). Implementing problem-based learning in science classrooms. *School Science and Mathematics, 95*(3), 136–146.

Gardner, H. (1995). Reflections on multiple intelligences: Myths and messages. *Phi Delta Kappan, 77,* 200–203, 206–209.

Gardner, H., & Hatch, T. (1990). *Multiple intelligences go to school: Educational implications of the theory of multiple intelligences.* Technical Report No. 4. New York: Center for Technology in Education.

George, W. C. (1976). Accelerating mathematics instruction for the mathematically talented. *Gifted Child Quarterly, 20,* 246–261.

Hébert, T. P. (1993). Reflections at graduation: The long-term impact of elementary school experiences in created productivity. *Roeper Review, 16,* 22–28.

Hendricks, M. (1997, June). Yesterday's whiz kids: Where are they today? *Johns Hopkins Magazine, 49,* 31–36.

Johnson, D. T., Boyce, L. N., & VanTassel-Baska, J. (1995). Science curriculum review: Evaluation materials for high-ability learners. *Gifted Child Quarterly, 39,* 43–63.

Kolloff, M. B., & Feldhusen, J. F. (1981). PACE (Program for Academic and Creative Enrichment): An application of the Three-Stage Model. *G/C/T, 18,* 47–50.

Kolitch, E. R., & Brody, L. E. (1992). Mathematics acceleration of highly talented students: An evaluation. *Gifted Child Quarterly, 36,* 78–86.

Lupkowski, A. E., & Assouline, S. G. (1993). Identifying mathematically talented elementary students: Using the lower level of the SAT. *Gifted Child Quarterly, 37,* 118–123.

Lynch, S. J. (1990). Credit and placement issues for the academically talented: Following summer studies in science and mathematics. *Gifted Child Quarterly, 34,* 27–30.

Maker, C. J., & Nielson, A. B. (1995). *Teaching models in education of the gifted* (2nd ed.). Austin, TX: PRO-ED.

Maker, C. J., & King, M. A. (1996). *Nurturing giftedness in young children.* Reston, VA: Council for Exceptional Children.

Maker, C. J., & Nielson, A. G. (1996). *Curriculum development and teaching strategies for gifted learners.* (2nd ed.) Austin, TX: PRO-ED.

Mezynski, K., & Stanley, J. C. (1980). Advanced placement oriented calculus for high school students. *Journal for Research in Mathematics Education, 11,* 347–355.

Moon, S. M., Feldhusen, J. F., Powley, S., & Nidiffer, L. (1993). Secondary applications of the Purdue Three-Stage Model. *Gifted Child Today, 16*, 2–9.

Olenchak, F. R. (1990). School change through gifted education: Effects on elementary students' attitudes toward learning. *Journal for the Education of the Gifted, 14*, 66–78.

Olenchak, F. R. (1991). Assessing program effects for gifted/learning disabled students. In R. Swassing & A. Robinson (Eds.), *NAGC 1991 Research Briefs*. Washington, DC: National Association for Gifted Children.

Olenchak, F. R., & Renzulli, J. S. (1989). The effectiveness of the schoolwide enrichment model on selected aspects of elementary school change. *Gifted Child Quarterly, 33*, 36–46.

Reis, S. M., & Renzulli, J. S. (1982). A research report on the Revolving Door Identification Model: A case for the broadened conception of giftedness. *Phi Delta Kappan, 63*, 619–620.

Reis, S. M., & Schack, G. D. (1993). Differentiating products for the gifted and talented: The encouragement of independent learning. In C. J. Maker & D. Orzechowski-Harland (Eds.), *Critical issues in gifted education: Volume III. Programs for the gifted in regular classrooms* (pp. 161–186). Austin, TX: PRO-ED.

Renzulli, J. S. (1986). *Systems and models for developing programs for the gifted and talented.* Mansfield Center, CT: Creative Learning Press.

Renzulli, J. S., & Gable, R. K. (1976). A factorial study of the attitudes of gifted students toward independent study. *Gifted Child Quarterly, 20*, 91–99.

Renzulli, J. S., & Reis, S. (1994). Research related to the school wide enrichment triad model. *Gifted Child Quarterly, 38*, 7–20.

Roberts, C., Ingram, C., & Harris, C. (1992). The effects of special versus regular classroom programming on higher cognitive processes of intermediate elementary aged gifted and average ability students. *Journal for the Education of the Gifted, 15*, 332–343.

Rosnow, R. L. (1994). Intelligence and the epistemics of interpersonal acumen: Testing some implications of Gardner's theory. *Intelligence, 19*(1), 93–116.

Schack, G. D., Starko, A. J., & Burns, D. E. (1991). Self-efficacy and creative productivity: Three studies of above average ability children. *Journal of Research in Education, 1,* 44–52.

Schlichter, C. L. (1981). The multiple talent approach in mainstream and programs. *Exceptional Children, 48*(2), 144–150.

Schlichter, C. L. (1988). Thinking skills for all classrooms. *Gifted Child Today, 11*(2), 24–29.

Schlichter, C. L. (1989). More than a passing thought. *Teaching K–8, 19*(7), 55–57.

Schlichter, C. L. (1996). Creative and critical thinking: Not just enrichment. *THINK, 6*(3), 17–21.

Schlichter, C. L., Hobbs, D., & Crump, W. (1988). Extending talents unlimited to secondary schools. *Educational Leadership, 45*(7), 36–40.

Schlichter, C. L., Larkin, M. J., Casareno, A. B., Ellis, E. S., Gregg, M., Mayfield, P., & Rountree, B. (1997). Partners in enrichment: Preparing teachers for multiple ability classrooms. *Teaching Exceptional Children, 29*(4), 4–9.

Stanley, J. C. (1976a). Identifying and nurturing the intellectually gifted. *Phi Delta Kappan, 58,* 234–238.

Stanley, J. C. (1976b). Youths who reason extremely well mathematically: SMPY's accelerative approach. *Gifted Child Quarterly, 20,* 237–238.

Stanley, J. C. (1977). Rationale of the Study of Mathematically Precocious Youth (SMPY) during its first five years of promoting educational acceleration. In J. C. Stanley, W. C. George, & C. H. Solano (Eds.), *The gifted and the creative: A fifty year perspective* (pp. 73–112). Baltimore: Johns Hopkins University Press.

Stanley, J. C. (1978). SMPY's DT-PI mentor model: Diagnostic testing followed by prescriptive instruction. *Intellectually Talented Youth Bulletin, 4*(10), 7–8.

Stanley, J. C. (1981). Sex differences in mathematical reasoning ability. *Journal for the Education of the Gifted, 4,* 169–176.

Stanley, J. C. (1990). Finding and helping young people with exceptional mathematical reasoning ability. In M. J. A. Howe (Ed.), *Encouraging the development of exceptional skills and talents* (pp. 221–221). Leicester, England, UK: British Psychology Society.

Stanley, J. C. (1991a). An academic model for educating the mathematically talented. *Gifted Child Quarterly, 35,* 36–42.

Stanley, J. C. (1991b). A better model for residential high schools for talented youths. *Phi Delta Kappan, 72,* 471–473.

Stanley, J. C. (1993). Boys and girls who reason well mathematically. In G. Bock & K. Ackrill (Eds.), *The origins and development of high ability* (pp. 119–138). New York: Wiley.

Stanley, J. C. (1997). Varieties of intellectual talent. *Journal of Creative Behavior, 31,* 93–119.

Stanley, J. C., & Benbow, C. P. (1982). Educating mathematically precocious youths: Twelve policy recommendations. *Educational Researcher, 11,* 4–9.

Stanley, J. C., & Benbow, C. P. (1983). Intellectually talented students: The key is curricular flexibility. In S. P. Harris, G. Olson, & H. Stevenson (Eds.), *Learning and motivation in the classroom* (pp. 259–258). Hillsdale, NJ: Lawrence Erlbaum.

Stanley, J. C., & Benbow, C. P. (1986). Youths who reason exceptionally well mathematically. In R. J. Sternberg & J. E. Davidson (Eds.), *Conceptions of giftedness* (pp. 361–387). Cambridge, England: Cambridge University Press.

Stanley, J. C., Feng, C. D., & Zhu, X. (1989). Chinese youths who reason extremely well mathematically: Threat or bonanza? *Network News Views, 8,* 33–39.

Stanley, J. C., George W. C., & Solano, C. H. (Eds.). (1978). *Educational programs and intellectual prodigies.* Baltimore: Study of Mathematically Precocious Youth, Department of Psychology, Johns Hopkins University.

Swiatek, M. A. (1993). A decade of longitudinal research on academic acceleration through the study of mathematically precocious youth. *Roeper Review, 15,* 120–124.

Swiatek, M. A., & Benbow, C. P. (1991a). Ten-year longitudinal follow-up of ability-matched accelerated and unaccelerated gifted students. *Journal of Educational Psychology, 83,* 528–538.

Swiatek, M. A., & Benbow, C. P. (1991b). A 10–year longitudinal follow-up of participants in a fast-paced mathematics course. *Journal for Research in Mathematics Education, 22,* 138–150.

VanTassel-Baska, J., & Olszewski, P. O. (Eds.). (1989). *Patterns of influence on gifted learners: The home, the self, and the school.* New York: Teachers College Press.

VanTassel-Baska, J. (1982, April-May). Results of a Latin-based experimental study of the verbally precocious. *Roeper Review, 4,* 35–37.

Addresses

American Association for the Advancement of Science
1200 New York Ave., N.W.
Washington, DC 20005
(202) 326–6400

Advanced Placement Program Manuals
Duke University TIP
1121 W. Main St., Suite 100
Durham, NC 27701
(919) 683–1400

Each manual in the series contains suggestions for discussions, homework assignments, projects, reference materials, and test items that are appropriate for bright, capable students across all academic tracks. The manuals range from 275–475 pages in length and provide comprehensive course material for each subject area. TIP's AP manuals were designed and written by teachers with extensive experience in advanced placement and honors courses.

Bett's Formal Teacher Training
Division of Special Education
University of Northern Colorado
McKee Hall
Room 29, Box 141
Greeley, CO 80639
(970) 351-2691

Education Development Center
55 Chapel St.
Newton, MA 02458–1060
(800) 225-4276

Gardner's Multiple Intelligence Teacher Training
The Project Zero Classroom
Harvard Graduate School Education
321 Longfellow Hall
13 Appian Way
Cambridge, MA 02138
(617) 495-4342
http://www.pzweb.harvard.edu

The Great Books Foundation
35 E. Wacher Dr., Suite 2300
Chicago, IL 60601–2298
(800) 222-5870

Integrated Curriculum Model Training Workshops
and Summer Institute in Curriculum Development
Center for Gifted Education
The College of William and Mary
P.O. Box 8795
Williamsburg, VA 23187–8795

Kaplan Grid Teacher Training
Dr. Sandra N. Kaplan
10231–6 White Oak Ave.
Northridge, CA 91324
(213) 740-3291

Maker's Matrix Training
Special Education and Rehabilitation
College of Education
P.O. Box 210069
Tucson, AZ 85721–0069
(520) 621-8832

Meeker's Structure of Intellect Model Teacher Training
SOI Systems
45755 Goodpasture Rd.
Box D
Vida, OR 97488
(541) 896-3936

National Council for Teachers of English
1111 W. Kenyon Rd.
Urbana, IL 61801–1096
(877) 369-6283

National Academy Press
2101 Constitution Ave. N.W.
Lockbox 285
Washington, DC 20055
(888) 624-8373
(202) 334-3313

Northwestern University
Center for Talent Development
School of Education and Social Policy
617 Dartmouth Place
Evanston, IL 60208–4175
(847) 491-3782
fax (847) 467-4283

Purdue Three-Stage Enrichment Model
for Elementary Gifted Learners and the Purdue Secondary Model
for Gifted and Talented Youth Teacher Training
Gifted Education Resource Institute
Purdue University
1446 Liberal Arts and Education Building
West Lafayette, IN 47907–1446
(765) 494-7243

Renzulli's Summer Training
Neag Center for Education and Talent Development
3 Summers Program
362 Fairfield Rd., U-7
Storrs, CT 06269–2007
(860) 486-6013
fax (860) 486-2900

Talents Unlimited and Talents Unlimited
to the Secondary Power Teacher Training
Talents Unlimited Inc.
Mobile County Public Schools
109 South Cedar St.
Mobile, AL 36602
(334) 690-8060

Temple University Press
1601 N. Broad St.
USB Route 305
Philadelphia, PA 19122–6099
(800) 447-1656

References

American Association for the Advancement of Science. (1989). *Science for all Americans.* New York: Oxford University Press.

American Association for the Advancement of Science. (1993). *Benchmarks for science literacy.* New York: Oxford University Press.

Baum, S. (1985). *Learning disabled students with superior cognitive abilities: A validation study of descriptive behaviors.* Unpublished doctoral dissertation, The University of Connecticut at Storrs.

Baum, S. (1988). Enrichment program for the gifted learning disabled students. *Gifted Child Quarterly, 32,* 226–230.

Benbow, C. P., & Arjmand, O. (1990). Predictors of high academic achievement in mathematics and science by mathematically talented students: A longitudinal study. *Journal of Educational Psychology, 82,* 430–431.

Betts, G. T. (1986). The autonomous learner model for the gifted and talented. In J. S. Renzulli (Ed.), *Systems and models for developing programs for the gifted and talented* (pp. 27–56). Mansfield Center, CT: Creative Learning Press.

Betts, G., & Knapp, J. (1980). Autonomous learning and the gifted: A secondary model. In A. Arnold (Ed.), *Secondary programs for the gifted* (pp. 29–36). Ventura, CA: Ventura Superintendent of Schools Office.

Betts, G. T., & Neihart, M. (1986). Implementing self-directed learning models for the gifted and talented. *Gifted Child Quarterly, 30,* 174–177.

Bonne, R. (1985). *Identifying multi-ethnic disadvantaged gifted.* Brooklyn, NY: Community School District #19.

Brody, L. E., & Stanley, J. C. (1991). Young college students: Assessing factors that contribute to success. In W. T. Southern & E. D. Jones (Eds.), *Academic acceleration of gifted children.* New York: Teachers College Press.

Bruner, J. (Ed.). (1970). *Man: A course of study.* Newton, MA: Education Development Center.

Burruss, J. D. (1997, April). *Walking the talk: Implementation decisions made by teachers.* Chicago: American Educational Research Association (AERA).

Daurio, S. P. (1979). Education enrichment versus acceleration: A review of the literature. In W. C. Gregory, S. J. Cohn, and J. C. Stanley (Eds.), *Educating the gifted: Acceleration and enrichment* (pp. 13–63). Baltimore: Johns Hopkins University Press.

Delcourt, M. A. B. (1988). *Characteristics related to high levels of creative/productive behavior in secondary school students: A multi-case study.* Unpublished doctoral dissertation, The University of Connecticut at Storrs.

Delisle, J. R. (1981). *The revolving door identification model. Correlates of creative production.* Unpublished doctoral dissertation, The University of Connecticut at Storrs.

Emerick, L. (1988). *Academic underachievement among the gifted: Students' perceptions of factors relating to the reversal of the academic underachievement pattern.* Unpublished doctoral dissertation, The University of Connecticut at Storrs.

Feldhusen, J. F., & Kolloff, M. B. (1986). The Purdue Three-Stage Model for Gifted Education. In J. S. Renzulli (Ed.), *Systems and models for developing programs for the gifted and talented* (pp. 126–152). Mansfield Center, CT: Creative Learning Press.

Feldhusen, J. F., & Robinson-Wyman, A. (1986). The Purdue Secondary Model for gifted education. In J. S. Renzulli (Ed.), *Models for developing programs for the gifted and talented* (pp. 153–179). Mansfield Center, CT: Creative Learning Press.

Gardner, H. (1983). *Frames of mind: The theory of multiple intelligences.* New York: Basic Books.

Guilford, J. P. (1967). *The nature of human intelligence.* New York: McGraw-Hill.

Heal, M. M. (1989). *Student perceptions of labeling the gifted: A comparative case study analysis.* Unpublished doctoral dissertation, The University of Connecticut at Storrs.

Hengen, T. (1983). *Identification and enhancement of giftedness in Canadian Indians.* Paper presented at the annual meeting of the National Association for Gifted Children (NAGC), New Orleans, LA.

Hollingworth, L. (1926). *Gifted Children.* New York: World Book.

Kaplan, S. (1986). The Kaplan grid. In J. S. Renzulli (Ed.), *Systems and models for developing programs for the gifted and talented* (pp. 56–68). Mansfield Center, CT: Creative Learning Press.

Karafelis, P. (1986). *The effects of the tri-art drama curriculum on the reading comprehension of students with varying levels of cognitive ability.* Unpublished doctoral dissertation, The University of Connecticut at Storrs.

Keating, D. P. (Ed.). (1976). *Intellectual talent: Research and development.* Baltimore: Johns Hopkins University Press.

Kolloff, M. B., & Feldhusen, J. F. (1984). The effects of enrichment on self-concept and creative thinking. *Gifted Child Quarterly, 28,* 53–57.

Kulik, J. (1993). Meta analytic findings on grouping programs. *Gifted Child Quarterly, 36,* 73–77.

Latham, A. S. (1997). Quantifying MI's gains. *Educational Leadership, 55*(1), 84–85.

Lipman, M., Sharp, A. M., & Oscanyan, F. F. (1980). *Philosophy in the classroom.* Philadelphia, PA: Temple University Press.

Lubinski, D., & Benbow, C. P. (1994). The study of mathematically precocious youth: The first three decades of a planned 50-year study of intellectual talent. In R. Subotnik & K. D. Arnold (Eds.), *Beyond Terman contemporary longitudinal studies of giftedness and talent* (pp. 375–400). Norwood, NJ: Ablex.

Lynch, S. J. (1992). Fast-paced high school science for the academically talented: A six-year perspective. *Gifted Child Quarterly, 36,* 147–154.

Maker, C. J. (1982). *Curriculum development for the gifted.* Rockville, MD: Aspen.

Maker, C. J., Nielson, A. B., & Rogers, J. A. (1994). Multiple intelligences: Giftedness, diversity, and problem solving. *Teaching Exceptional Children, 27*(1), 4–19.

Maker, C. J., Rogers, J. A., Nielson, A. B., & Bauerle, P. R. (1996). Multiple intelligences, problem solving, and diversity in the general classroom. *Journal for the Education of the Gifted, 19,* 437–460.

McLean, J. E., & Chisson, B. S. (1980). *Talented unlimited program: Summary of research findings for 1979–80.* Mobile, AL: Mobile County Public Schools.

Meeker, M. (1969). *The structure of intellect: Its interpretation and uses.* Columbus, OH: Merrill.

Meeker, M. (1976). *A paradigm for special education diagnostics: The cognitive area.* (Report No. EC082519). Presented at AERA annual meeting. (ERIC Document Reproduction Service No. ED 121 010)

Moon, S., & Feldhusen, J. F. (1994). The program for academic and creative enrichment (PACE): A follow-up study 10 years later. In R. Subotnik & K. D. Arnold (Eds.) *Beyond Terman contemporary longitudinal studies of giftedness and talent* (pp. 375–400). Norwood, NJ: Ablex.

Moon, S. M., Feldhusen, J. F., & Dillon, D. R. (1994). Long-term effects of an enrichment program based on the Purdue Three-Stage Model. *Gifted Child Quarterly, 38,* 38–48.

National Council of Teachers of English and the International Reading Association. (1996). *Standards for the English language arts.* Urbana, IL: Author.

National Research Council. (1996). *National science education standards.* Washington, DC: National Academy Press.

Pressey, S. L. (1949). *Educational acceleration: Appraisal and basic problems.* Bureau of Educational Research Monographs (31). Columbus, OH: The Ohio State University Press.

Reis, S. M. (1981). *An analysis of the productivity of gifted students participating in programs using the Revolving Door Identification Model.* Unpublished doctoral dissertation, The University of Connecticut, Storrs.

Reis, S. M., & Purcell, J. H. (1993). An analysis of content elimination and strategies used by elementary classroom teachers in the curriculum compacting process. *Journal for the Education of the Gifted, 16,* 147–170.

Renzulli, J. S. (1977). *The enrichment triad model: A guide for developing defensible programs for the gifted and talented.* Mansfield Center, CT: Creative Learning Press.

Renzulli, J. S. (Ed.). (1988). *Technical report of research studies related to the revolving door identification model.* Storrs, CT: Bureau of Educational Research, The University of Connecticut.

Renzulli, J. S., & Reis, S. M. (1985). *The schoolwide enrichment model: A comprehensive plan for educational excellence.* Mansfield Center, CT: Creative Learning Press.

Renzulli, J. S., Reis, S. M., & Smith, L. (1981). The revolving-door model: A new way of identifying the gifted. *Phi Delta Kappan, 62,* 648–649.

Schlichter, C. (1986). Talents unlimited: Applying the multiple talent approach in mainstream and gifted programs. In J. S. Renzulli (Ed.), *Systems and models for developing programs for the gifted and talented.* Mansfield Center, CT: Creative Learning Press.

Schlichter, C. L., & Palmer, W. R. (Eds.). (1993). *Thinking smart: A premiere of the talents unlimited model.* Mansfield Center, CT: Creative Learning Press.

Stanley, J. C., Keating, D., & Fox, L. (1974). *Mathematical Talent.* Baltimore: Johns Hopkins University Press.

Starko, A. J. (1986). *The effects of the revolving door identification model on creative productivity and self-efficacy.* Unpublished doctoral dissertation, The University of Connecticut, Storrs.

Sternberg, R. (1981). A componential theory of intellectual giftedness. *Gifted Child Quarterly, 25*, 86–93.

Sternberg, R., & Clinkenbeard, P. R. (1995). The triadic model applied to identify, teach, and assess gifted children. *Roeper Review, 17*, 255–260.

Sternberg, R. J., Ferrari, M., Clinkenbeard, P., & Grigorenko, E. L. (1996). Identification, instruction, and assessment of gifted children: A construct validation of a triarchic model. *Gifted Child Quarterly, 40*, 129–137.

Sternberg, R. J., Torff, B., & Grigorenko, E. L. (1998a). Teaching for successful intelligence raises school achievement. *Phi Delta Kappan, 79*, 667–699.

Sternberg, R. J., Torff, B., & Grigorenko, E. L. (1998b). Teaching triarchically improves school achievement. *Journal of Educational Psychology, 90*, 374–384.

Strahan, D., Summey, H., & Banks, N. (1996). Teaching to diversity through multiple intelligences: Student and teacher responses to instructional improvement. *Research in Middle Level Education Quarterly, 19*(2), 43–65.

Tannenbaum, A. (1983). *Gifted children*. New York: MacMillan.

Taylor, C. W., Ghiselin, B., Wolfer, J., Loy, L., & Bourne, L. E., Jr. (1964). *Development of a theory of education from psychology and other basic research findings*. Final Report, USOE Cooperative Research Project, No. 621. Salt Lake City, UT: University of Utah.

Terman, L. M., & Oden, M. H. (1947). *The gifted child grows up*. Stanford University Press.

VanTassel-Baska, J. (1986). Effective curriculum and instruction models for talented students. *Gifted Child Quarterly, 30*, 164–169.

VanTassel-Baska, J. (1995). A study of life themes in Charlotte Brönte and Virginia Woolf. *Roeper Review, 18*, 14–19.

VanTassel-Baska, J. (1998). *Excellence in educating the gifted*. Denver, CO: Love.

VanTassel-Baska, J., Avery, L. D., Little, C. A., & Hughes, C. E. (2000). An evaluation of the implementation: The impact of the William and Mary units on schools. *Journal for the Education of the Gifted 23*, 244–272.

VanTassel-Baska, J., Bass, G. M., Ries, R. R., Poland, D. L., & Avery, L. D. (1998). A national study of science curriculum effectiveness with high ability students. *Gifted Child Quarterly, 42*, 200–211.

VanTassel-Baska, J., Johnson, D. T., Hughes, C. E., & Boyce, L. N. (1996). A study of the language arts curriculum effectiveness with gifted learners. *Journal for the Education of the Gifted, 19*, 461–480.

Walberg, H. (1991). Productive teaching and instruction: Assessing the knowledge base. In H. C. Waxman and H. J. Walberg (Eds.), *Effective teaching: Current research* (pp. 33–62). Berkeley, CA: McCutchan.

CHAPTER 4

Layering Differentiated Curriculum for the Gifted and Talented

SANDRA N. KAPLAN
University of Southern California

Introduction   A.E.M -

A gifted student reading a text that is two years beyond his or her current grade level is an example of differentiating the curriculum using ACCELERATION. A gifted student studying revolutions leading to the rise and fall of ancient civilizations in conjunction with the study of the core curriculum social studies unit on the American Revolution is an example of differentiating the curriculum through ENRICHMENT. A gifted student working with an engineer from the community to design a new means to restructure the freeway system to withstand expanding traffic problems and potential earthquake damage is an example of differentiating the curriculum using MENTORSHIPS. An elementary gifted student attending advanced mathematics classes at the high school each day is an example of differentiating the curriculum through ACCELERATION or ADVANCED STUDIES. A gifted student provided with classroom time to pursue his or her interest in geology by conducting an independent study is an example of differentiating the curriculum through both ENRICHMENT and ACCELERATION. A gifted student receiving computer-assisted instruction in science is an example of differentiating the curriculum through both ACCELERATION and ENRICHMENT.

These examples indicate that the meaning and implementation of differentiation of the curriculum is both broad and diverse. It has been said by many educators of the gifted that it is easier to define what differentiation of curriculum is not than it is to define what differentiation is. Differentiation is defined by the elements of the curriculum, such as the nature of the content to be studied or the skills to be mastered. Differentiation is not defined by program elements, such as when or where the curriculum is provided.

Over the years, the concept of differentiating the curriculum for gifted students has changed commensurate to the changes in the definition of giftedness, the contemporary emphasis in general education, and the political and parental responses to general and gifted education. The original need to differentiate the curriculum for gifted students was based on the recognized strengths of these learners and the acknowledged inadequacy of the regular or core curriculum to meet these needs. The discrepancy theory assesses the core curriculum against the traits of gifted students in order to determine what missing curricular elements would be responsive to the needs of gifted students. This comparative analysis between the needs, interests, and abilities of the gifted students and the content, processes, and product components of the core curriculum often has justified the need for a differentiated curriculum. If gifted students are recognized for their creative behaviors, the core curriculum is expected to support the development of creative expression. To the degree that the core curriculum correlates with the defined attributes of gifted students, the curriculum is perceived as either appropriately or inappropriately differentiated.

Curriculum; Content
           process
           product

1. Core Content
2.

A History of Differentiated Curriculum: 3.
A Perspective

The development of differentiated curriculum follows the definition and redefinition of the basic elements that comprise all curricula: content, process, and product. The development of all curricula is dependent on the same elements and answers to these questions: (1) What content do you want the students to know? (2) What skills or processes should the students master? (3) How should the students demonstrate understanding of the content and mastery of the skills through the products they create? Decisions to modify one, some, or all of these elements ultimately determine the differentiated nature of the core curriculum. The history of differentiated curriculum can be reconstructed from the decisions made to adjust the content, process, and product elements of the core curriculum.

An examination of the content, process, and product elements that form a learning experience provides the basis for telling the history of differentiation, for it is the interaction of these elements that form the curriculum (see Table 1).

The first real modification of basic learning experiences seemed to have paralleled the definition of taxonomies and strategies to

Table 1. Basic Elements Defining the Core Curriculum

Process: Thinking Skills	Content	Process: Research Skills	Product
Thinking Skill	Subject Matter	Research Skills and/or Resources	Culmination or Exhibition
List	The causes and effects of The Industrial Revolution	After reading the text, pages 42–49.	Write a paragraph to share the information.

develop higher-level thinking skills. The rationale for pursuing critical, creative, and problem-solving skills was responsive to the theoretical emphasis on developing gifted students as complex thinkers and the ready correlation between the traits of gifted students to be productive thinkers and the nature and scope of higher-level thinking skills. Thus, the primary change in the content, process, product curricular equation was to replace the process element, namely the thinking skills. Originally, the thinking skills in most of the core curricula were identified as basic or lower level thinking skills. This change enabled teachers responsible for the education of the gifted to pinpoint where in the teaching and learning of the core curriculum the needs of gifted students could be met. More importantly, the identification of the thinking skills in the definition of the curricular learning experience or objective provided substantive distinction of the curriculum as one that differed from the nature of the learning experiences constructed and presented to all students (see Table 2).

The next significant change in the equation to design curriculum was a process modification. It was the modification of the resources or research skills necessary for the input of content. This modification was a natural consequence of replacing lower order with higher-order thinking skills. For example, higher-order thinking skills demanded more and varied resources to build a richer background of information or content. It became apparent that students could not apply creative, critical, and problem-solving skills to simplistic content if these skills were

Table 2. Differentiating the Core: Modifying the Process Element—Thinking Skills

Process: Thinking Skills	Content	Process: Research Skills	Product
~~List~~ Judge with criteria	The causes and effects of the Industrial Revolution	After reading the text, pages 42–49.	Write a paragraph to share the information.

Table 3. Differentiating the Core:
Modifying the Process Element—Research Skills

Process: Thinking Skills	Content	Process: Research Skills	Product
Judge with criteria	The causes and effects of the Industrial Revolution	~~After reading the text, pages 42–49.~~ Interview an American history professor at the university; use the Internet; and read the text; chapter IV.	Write a paragraph to share the information.

to be practiced with efficacy. The use of more advanced and sophisticated resources was praised by both parents and students. Adjustments in the resources and research skills were tangible evidence that the gifted learner was being accelerated and enriched (see Table 3).

Modifying the product element in the curriculum equation was easy to accomplish. Modifications in the product element became the visible indicators of the effort and concern directed toward the gifted. In many instances, the flamboyancy of the product was believed to be equal to the quality of the gifted program and the recognition of the traits of giftedness. Long and exotic lists of unusual products were provided to teachers of the gifted as references for selecting products for gifted students to do beyond those traditionally completed by students to demonstrate their content understanding and skill mastery. For many gifted students, the modifications of products signified the grandiosity of their abilities. For many parents, the modifications of the product became synonymous with gifted education. And for many teachers, the modi-

Table 4. Differentiating the Core: Modifying the Product Element

Process: Thinking Skills	Content	Process: Research Skills	Product
Judge with criteria	The causes and effects of the Industrial Revolution	Interview an American history professor at the university; use the Internet; and read the text; chapter IV.	~~Write a paragraph to share the information.~~ Debate the positive and negative consequences due to the causes and effects of the Industrial Revolution.

fication of the product was the clearest means by which to justify their responsiveness to the needs of the gifted (see Figure 4).

The nature of the times, the maturity of gifted education, and the infusion of new theories and ideas about curriculum development all lended support to the idea that the modifications in what we wanted students to know—content areas—were imperative. The controversy centered on what significant modifications were to be made in the content element. Some educators of the gifted advocated the need to rethink the value of the core curriculum and entirely replace it. Others advocated on behalf of enriching the core curriculum by identifying more challenging and related content that could be distinctive, yet aligned, to the core. Many educators of the gifted advocated the need to maintain the core curriculum and modify the approach to learning it by emphasizing aspects of the discipline perceived to correlate more directly with the needs, interests, and abilities of gifted students. Currently, the modification of the core content still represents the area of greatest attention and concern in curriculum development for gifted learners.

One attempt to distinguish the appropriate means by which to modify the core curriculum was defined as a consequence of the collaborative work done by the California Department of Education and the California Association for the Gifted (1994). The basis of this work was supported by a Javits grant funded to the California Department of Education. An outcome of this work was the articulation of *depth* and *complexity* as two means by which the content element in the learning experience equation could be modified. The terms depth and complexity are replete in the literature describing differentiated curriculum. This contemporary view of these two terms attempts to specify their dimensions (see Table 5).

Table 5. Differentiating the Core: Modifying the Content Element

Process: Thinking Skills	Content	Process: Research Skills	Product
Judge with criteria	The causes and effects of the Industrial Revolution. The patterns in the behaviors and values of consumers and producers that contributed to the causes and subsequent effects of the Industrial Revolution.	Interview an American History professor at the university; use the Internet; and read the text; chapter IV.	Debate the positive and negative consequences due to the causes and effects of the Industrial Revolution.

Altering the content, process, or product dimensions of a curricula provides the opportunities to differentiate the core curriculum for gifted students. By using alternative content, process, or product dimensions identified appropriate for gifted learners, teachers can substitute one dimension for another: A basic skill for a higher-level critical thinking skill, a simple and concrete concept for a complex or universal concept, and a fundamental product such as a report for a more authentic medium of presentation such as the development of a questionnaire to conduct a survey. The altering of one or more dimensions in the curriculum equation not only demands an understanding of why these modifications are needed but, presents a delineation of the scope of options most appropriate to satisfying the needs of gifted students. Changing the content, process, and product dimensions is a means of attaining the clearly defined ends of learning for gifted students.

Modifications of each of the content, process, and product elements in the curriculum equation have significantly affected the definition of differentiating the core curriculum over time. The content, process, and product elements of the curriculum equation have allowed educators to address inquiries about the nature of a differentiated curriculum. It has enabled gifted students to participate without being penalized in both the differentiated and core curricula. However, the definition of differentiation is a constantly changing process. New demands in general education, analysis of the achievements of gifted students, and concerns for validation that a curriculum is responsive to the emerging definitions of intelligences and giftedness all pressure educators to reconsider consistently the meaning of differentiated curriculum.

The Layered Approach to Differentiate the Core Curriculum: Why Layered Approach?

The conception of a layered approach to differentiate the core curriculum for the gifted was derived from many factors. First, the idea for a layered approach came from the awareness of the ever-changing and increasing demands placed on teachers of the gifted. Second, the concept of a layered approach is a conse-

Table 6. Design for the Layered Curriculum

5	Theme	
6	Generalization	
1	Core	
2	Differentiated	
3	Classical	
4	Individualized	

quence of recognizing that gifted education needs to be more inclusive of existing curriculum theories. Last, the concept of a layered approach is related to the significant works of educators in the field of the gifted (see Table 6).

The concept of a layered approach to differentiate the curriculum for gifted students emerged from these concerns:

1. Gifted students should not be exonerated from the basic, regular, or core curriculum. While there was a time when the core curriculum was dismissed and devalued as an appropriate curriculum for gifted students, the articulation of national, state, and even local content and performance standards has shown the merit of the core curriculum. Data regarding the academic achievements of gifted students measured against their learning of core content indicates the need to reinforce rather than abolish the importance of this curriculum.

2. A single curriculum design cannot attend to all the needs of gifted students. Therefore, there was a need to conceptualize a

curriculum design to develop, as well as to implement, a differentiated curriculum that included many dimensions.

3. Linear expressions of curriculum have been found to inhibit the quality of the curriculum. A curriculum that emphasizes a linear progression of learning experiences or linear progress can deter the gifted student from becoming expert in particular areas of need or interest. Thus, a curriculum that provides alternative pathways for learning seems to have greater flexibility for the teacher and learner.

4. Educators need a curriculum structure that defines a field of curricular options and enables them to be responsive to groups, as well as to individual gifted students.

The layered curriculum approach emphasizes the acquisition of content. It is content dependent. The initial decisions made by curriculum developers revolve around the need to articulate the content. Decisions about the inclusion of creative, critical, or problem-solving skills are made only after the content has been defined. Similarly, decisions about the nature of products are deferred until the content has been defined. Processes and products do not lead content selection. Content selection determines the processes and products identified for the curriculum. Simply, there is enough evidence to warrant a more judicious concern for the content in a curriculum appropriate for gifted students and to relinquish the flamboyancy of product definition and the emphasis on higher-level thinking skills definition until the content has been determined. Thus, the plan to format a layered curriculum is a first step, and the consequence of following this format is the development of a content map that leads to other curriculum development sessions. The construction of learning experiences or objectives is dependent on the content map. Lessons are created from these learning experiences, resources are allocated, and assessment procedures and tools are decided. Both learning experiences (objectives) and lessons follow the development of the layered content map.

The Core Curriculum Layer

The first layer is the core curriculum, or that curriculum defined as the basic, rudimentary, or regular curriculum. This curriculum forms the basis of the layered curriculum design. The format for developing the layered curriculum content map is numbered to aid the curriculum developer to follow a step-by-step process. This numbered system defines the how-to of curriculum development. When the layered curriculum content map is complete, it is read from top to bottom without regard for the numbering system. In other words, the process used to develop the curriculum is not commensurate to the method used to read and consequently implement or instruct the curriculum. Derived from an accepted set of standards, the core curriculum outlines the fundamental expectations for gifted learners and does not exonerate them from basic learning because they are gifted or evidence readiness beyond grade-level expectations. The stress to differentiate the core curriculum sometimes has resulted in the absence rather than presence of the basic curriculum in order to ensure time and learning space, so to speak, for the more enriched or accelerated learning opportunities for the gifted students. Assessing the focus of the core curriculum for gifted learners becomes the most important role of the curriculum decision maker. Making sure that the questions regarding which concepts, principles, or theories of the core curriculum are most aligned to the needs, interests, and abilities of gifted students is crucial not only to determine the appropriateness of this layer of the curriculum for these learners but also to act as the determinant for decisions regarding all other layers of the curriculum.

This fifth-grade social studies standard is the foundation on which decisions about the suitability of the core content is made for gifted students. While the characteristics defining the nature of giftedness are primary factors dictating the needs of gifted learners, the appropriateness of the core content for gifted students also must parallel the philosophy of the gifted program. Many gifted programs exist without a specific definition of differentiation and without a specific definition of expectations or exit criteria distinguishing academic accomplishments from participation in the gifted program. The interaction of the needs of the gifted, the definition of differentiation, and the philosophy of the gifted program are the factors that ultimately shape the response to the standard and, subsequently, the core curriculum placed into this, the first layer of the layered curriculum (see Table 7).

Table 7. Layer One: The Core Curriculum Content

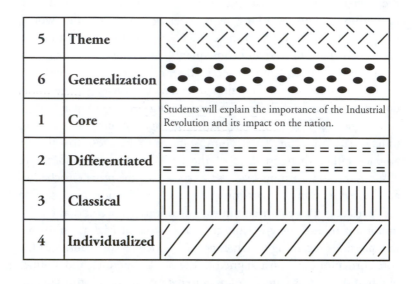

5	Theme	
6	Generalization	
1	Core	Students will explain the importance of the Industrial Revolution and its impact on the nation.
2	Differentiated	
3	Classical	
4	Individualized	

The Differentiated Curriculum Layer

Based on the dimensions of depth and complexity, this curriculum layer emphasizes the differentiation of the core curriculum. The dimensions of depth have been named to focus the teacher's and student's attention on increasingly more difficult, divergent, and abstract qualities of knowing a discipline or area of study. These can be introduced in descending order from simple to difficult, concrete to abstract, specific to general. They do not have to be included in every lesson or unit of study, nor do they necessarily need to be taught in the order in which they were introduced to the students. They are guides to developing questions and tasks that outline the essential understandings of subject matter. The dimensions of depth are not to be confused with the various levels of Bloom's taxonomy of educational objectives in the cognitive domain (1956). The dimensions define what students are to know: the levels of knowledge, comprehension, application, analysis, synthesis, and evaluation define the cognitive operations students are to employ with content.

Following are the dimensions of depth and complexity, the corresponding icons that symbolize them, and the definitions that explain them (see Figures 1 and 2). Complexity can be defined as the means by which knowledge is extended or broadened. The dimensions of complexity afford the teacher and the student with opportunities to identify the associations. Connections, relationships, and links exist within, between, and among areas or disciplines of study. It is these interactions that enable learners to extend or broaden their understanding of the knowledge. The icons that symbolize and the definitions for the dimensions of complexity are shown in Figure 2. The core and the differentiated layers are symbiotically related and are taught in tandem. While the core curriculum usually precedes the dimensions of depth and complexity, it is possible that the dimensions of depth and complexity can preface the core curriculum. How the layers are written in the curriculum format does not imply that they must be taught in the same way. In fact, many teachers do not understand that writing a curriculum in accord with a given format is intended to guide the development process and tell them what to think about as they construct the curriculum; it is not intended to tell them how to teach the very curriculum they are generating. The instructional plan for teaching the curriculum is described in activities and lessons derived from the curriculum format and should be included in a section that follows the design outlining the layers of the curriculum.

The Classical Curriculum Layer

This is perhaps the most controversial of the curriculum layers (see Table 8). In the context of this curriculum, the classical layer is based on a humanities approach to teaching the gifted. It is intended to present the teacher and the students with an orientation to subject areas that are often deferred due to the age of the student, the time involved in teaching these subjects, and, most importantly, the prevailing beliefs about who gifted students are and what they can learn or are supposed to learn at school. Another controversial aspect of this layer is that it is fraught with issues about what is classical education and what is considered to be a classic. Arguments

 **Language** of the disciplines refers to learning the specific specialized and technological terms associated with a specific area of study or discipline.

 Details refer to the learning of the specific attributes, traits, and characteristics that describe a concept, theory, principle, and even a fact.

 Patterns refer to recurring events represented by details.

 Trends refer to the factors that influence events.

 Unanswered questions refer to the ambiguities and gaps of information recognized within an area or discipline under study.

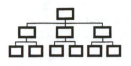 **Rules** refer to the natural or person-made structure or order of things that explain the phenomena within an area of study.

 Ethics refer to the dilemmas or controversial issues that plague an area of study or discipline.

 Big ideas refer to the generalizations, principles, and theories that distinguish themselves from the facts and concepts of the area or discipline under study.

Figure 1. Dimensions of Depth

Note. Definitions from *Differentiating the Core Curriculum and Instruction to Provide Advanced Learning Opportunities,* by S. Kaplan (California Department of Education and California Association for the Gifted), 1994, University of Southern California. Copyright 1994 by Sandra Kaplan. Icons from S. Kaplan, 1994, University of Southern California. Copyright 1994 by Sandra Kaplan. Reprinted with permission.

relate over time

Over time refers to the understanding of time as an agent of change and recognition that the passage of time changes our knowledge of things.

view from different perspectives

Points of view refer to the concept that there are different perspectives and that these perspectives alter the way ideas and objects are viewed and valued.

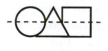

across disciplines

Disciplinary connections refer to both integrated and interdisciplinary links in the curriculum. Disciplinary connections can be made within, between, and among various areas of study or disciplines.

Figure 2. Dimensions of Complexity

Note. Definitions from *Differentiating the Core Curriculum and Instruction to Provide Advanced Learning Opportunities,* by S. Kaplan (California Department of Education and California Association for the Gifted), 1994, University of Southern California. Copyright 1994 by Sandra Kaplan. Icons from S. Kaplan, 1994, University of Southern California. Copyright 1994 by Sandra Kaplan. Reprinted with permission.

Table 8. Layer Two: Differentiating the Core Curriculum Content

5	Theme	
6	Generalization	
1	Core	Students will explain the importance of the Industrial Revolution and its impact on the nation.
2	Differentiated	Define how the *rules* between employer and employees, men and women in the family, and the status quo and reform were affected by events in this period of history.
3	Classical	
4	Individualized	

emerge regarding the inclusion of eastern versus western classics, old world versus contemporary classics, cultural representation in the selection and presentation of the classics, and the developmental appropriateness of the classics. Of course, there is always the argument about the justification of the classics in an already jam-packed curriculum that is hurrying to prepare students in prerequisite courses for the necessary tests to enter specialized programs and colleges.

The major objective of this layer is not to expect mastery of but rather to anticipate exposure to the classical ideas of philosophy, psychology, art, music, dance, sculpture, and political science. Much has been written about the need to expose gifted students to a variety of experiences; no one has clarified this point more than Renzulli in *The Enrichment Triad Model: A Guide for Developing Defensible Programs for the Gifted and Talented* (1977). The obligation of a curriculum to provide a sampling of nontraditional areas and disciplines of study is crucial if the concept of developing gifted students as lifelong learners is more than simply rhetoric. It is important to note that issues of both the quality and quantity of general versus specific studies for gifted students have never really reached consensus in the field. Many educators of the gifted will support the need for gifted students to specialize early in their academic careers, and others will fight for the gifted students' right to be introduced to the many and varied alternatives that are available for more intense study at a later time in their educational careers. Too often, gifted students select courses and areas of investigation later in their educational careers because they already have experienced success with them. They are hampered in their academic choices because they were not given the chance to see the broad range of academic areas and disciplines from which they can choose. One hopes that students will say, "I first found out about this when I was studying in the gifted program," as a direct result of their participation in the classical area of a layered curriculum designed for the gifted.

The selection of the classical area is dependent on both the core and differentiated curriculum layers. There must be a natural rather than contrived alignment of these layers. The relationship of the classics to the dimensions of depth or complexity and the core curriculum must be considered. The curriculum developer must perceive this layer as an interdependent yet individualistic member of the total curriculum. The entries on this layer of the curriculum should not have meaning as separate areas of study; rather, they have meaning only as they augment the understanding and stimulate investigations to enhance the core and differentiated layers. This layer of the curriculum also reinforces the use of technology as an integral feature of the curriculum planned for the gifted. However, it not intended to focus primarily on the use of computers. It is intended to include all aspects of media, from the use of the television to interviewing recognized experts. In this layer, technology is the tool that bridges the areas or disciplines under study with the real world by including contemporary resources as important reference materials. The inclusion of this layer in the curriculum is to ensure that gifted students understand the relationship between past learning and current happenings. Many of the gifted students have been rewarded for finding information from contemporary resources while not being held responsible for utilizing and inte-

Table 9. Layer Three: Classical Learning

5	Theme	////////////////////////
6	Generalization	••••••••••••••••••••••
1	Core	Students will explain the importance of the Industrial Revolution and its impact on the nation.
2	Differentiated	Define how the *rules* between employer and employees, men and women in the family, and the status quo and reform were affected by events in this period of history.
3	Classical	Investigate Kurt Lenin's psychological study describing the distribution of power in groups. Relate Plato's concept of differential roles in society (philosopher, kings, artisans, warriors, etc.) to the needs and interests of people in the industrialization of a society.
4	Individualized	////////////////////////

grating this newly found information into their school-based studies. This layer forces the connection between today's world and any subject or topic the gifted students are studying in the curriculum designed for them (see Table 9).

The Individualized Curriculum Layer

This layer is the formalized opportunity for gifted students to study further a teacher-selected defined topic within the core and differentiated curriculum layers or a topic that is student-selected and is an extension of the core curriculum. An important factor of this particular layer is that it affords gifted students the time to conduct an independent study that introduces learning-to-learning skills while simultaneously affording the student the time to delve

Table 10. Layer Four: Individualized Learning

5	Theme	
6	Generalization	
1	Core	Students will explain the importance of the Industrial Revolution and its impact on the nation.
2	Differentiated	Define how the *rules* between employer and employees, men and women in the family, and the status quo and reform were affected by events in this period of history.
3	Classical	Investigate Kurt Lenin's psychological study describing the distribution of power in groups. Relate Plato's concept of differential roles in society (philosopher, kings, artisans, warriors, etc.) to the needs and interests of people in the industrialization of a society.
4	Individualized	Select a specific topic of interest to investigate from among these areas: Inventions Standardizations Immigrants Unionism Supply and Demand Workers' Rights Form factual, analytic, and evaluative questions to organize and conduct a historical case study or descriptive type of study.

more independently and individualistically into a topic of choice. Unfortunately, this layer is a part and not the entire focus of the curriculum, so it is necessary to schedule time for the implementation of this layer without diminishing the other layers or demanding too little or too much from the students.

Self-discovery should be one of the outcomes derived from learning at this layer of the curriculum. The discovery of one's preferred learning style, the discovery of one's interests and abilities, as well as one's academic strengths and weaknesses represent the types of accomplishments students should acquire as they

Table 11. Layers Five and Six: Theme and Generalization

5	Theme	Systems
6	Generalization	Systems are made of parts that work together to accomplish a purpose. Systems follow rules and procedures.
1	Core	Students will explain the importance of the Industrial Revolution and its impact on the nation.
2	Differentiated	Define how the *rules* between employer and employees, men and women in the family, and the status quo and reform were affected by events in this period of history.
3	Classical	Investigate Kurt Lenin's psychological study describing the distribution of power in groups. Relate Plato's concept of differential roles in society (philosopher, kings, artisans, warriors, etc.) to the needs and interests of people in the industrialization of a society.
4	Individualized	Sam will study inventions. Melinda will study the effects of child labor.

work at this layer. In addition to these discoveries, gifted students should be aided in learning about how they allocate their study time, what types of intrinsic and extrinsic rewards are most conducive to sustained motivation and effort, and what types of activities seem to require independent versus dependent behaviors (see Table 10).

The Organizing Element or Theme and Generalization Curriculum Layer

This last layer (see Table 11) represents the organizing element for the curriculum or the initial theme statement in a debate or discussion. Its purpose is to excite the need to know, to prove, to judge with criteria, to differentiate between fact and opinion, and to note ambiguity. In other words, the generalization serves as the purpose for investigating, comprehending, and summarizing.

Following is a list of themes with some accompanying generalizations that have been used by teachers of the gifted in various programs throughout the country. The conventional wisdom derived from the usage of those themes and generalizations dictates the need to select a theme in accordance with age appropriateness, to develop a sequence of these themes so they are not repeated yearly and become redundant to students, and to understand as educators that there is no mastery of these themes because understanding them is a life-long pursuit.

Patterns
Generalizations:
- Patterns can be predictors.
- Some patterns are determined by nature; some patterns are person-made.

Change
Generalizations:
- Change can be planned or spontaneous.
- Change has a ripple effect.

Systems
Generalizations:
- Systems are made of parts that work together to perform a function.
- Systems interact.

Conflict
Generalizations:
- Conflict is inevitable.
- Conflict can lead to growth or can be generative.

Structure
Generalizations:
- Structure can follow function or function can follow structure.
- Structures are formed over time.

Power
Generalizations:
- Power can be destructive or constructive.
- Power can influence.

Relationships

Generalizations:
- Relationships are formed for many and varied purposes.
- Some relationships endure longer than others.

Adaptation

Generalizations:
- Adaptation is necessary for survival.
- Adaptation is a consequence of many factors that are bionic or abiotic.

Implementing the Layered Curriculum

Many factors ultimately determine the effectiveness of the curriculum developed for gifted students. Some of these factors have less to do with the structure and the scope of the curriculum and more to do with the milieu in which the curriculum is taught.

1. The curriculum for gifted students must be consonant with the purpose, philosophy, and structure of the gifted program. The implementation of a layered curriculum in a pull-out program has a very different effect and requires a different timeline than that same curriculum in a regular classroom with a cluster grouping of gifted students.

2. The curriculum should not have to compete with other types of curricula or programs developed or purchased to respond to the needs of the gifted. The implementation of a layered curriculum that has to compete with other programs is doomed to failure. Teachers who have to divide their loyalty between curricula that have incompatible philosophies opt to ignore the curricula given to them.

3. The curriculum for gifted students must be used as a whole with integrated and mutually reinforcing features or elements. The implementation of a layered curriculum in a situation where teachers are led to believe they can mix and match the elements to create their own eclectic curriculum is not appropriate. Such a disjointed selection of the incremental implementation of a layered curriculum abuses the integrity of the curriculum. It also makes the curriculum less appropriate to the needs of gifted students and to a comprehensive plan to

educate these learners. The lack of a comprehensive curriculum approach has been more injurious than helpful to the gifted.

4. The curriculum for gifted students must be accompanied by the resources that augment it. The implementation of a layered curriculum demands attention to surveying and gathering resources that are comprehensible, yet challenging, and clearly extend beyond those resources traditionally available to students. Teachers and students must understand that the layered curriculum requires materials that extend beyond the textbook yet are parallel to the textbooks used by all learners.

5. The curriculum for gifted students must be introduced with clarity within professional staff development activities. However, just providing staff development is insufficient to successful implementation of a curriculum for the gifted. The implementation of a layered curriculum requires a targeted set of staff development sessions within the context of a plan of action. This means that staff development sessions must be clearly defined by objectives that are expected to be translated into classroom practices. There needs to be some type of accountability that travels with the educator from the in-service venue to the classroom to ensure that what is discussed in staff development is practiced in the classroom. It has been noted that the failure of the curriculum is not always a consequence of a lack of in-service; rather, it is a consequence of the lack of following up after the in-service. On-site, in-classroom observations of the curriculum are crucial if they are to be practiced with efficacy.

6. The curriculum for the gifted needs to be understood for what it provides, as well as for what it does not provide. Many times, the curriculum for the gifted is blamed for the weaknesses of the gifted student and the inadequacies of the gifted program. The implementation of the layered curriculum cannot guarantee high SAT scores, motivated gifted students, or students who will be accepted to universities of their choice. The implementation of the layered curriculum can provide only what it has been designed to do:
    - develop the core curriculum;
    - provide for greater depth and complexity of the core curricular content;
    - introduce classical ideas of the past and correlate the past with the present;

- allow opportunities to study independently; and
- make connections within, between, and among areas and disciplines of study using a global theme and related generalizations.

Summary

The layered approach to differentiate the curriculum for gifted students is only one of many ways suggested to provide appropriate curricula for the gifted. There are many other models that can be used to develop or design differentiated curricula. Sometimes educators are confused when confronted by all the different models, theories, and philosophies available to differentiate the core curriculum for the gifted, and they ask for assistance in identifying the "best" from among these models. There are criteria that can be used to help teachers of the gifted, curriculum developers, and administrators select the model, theory, or philosophy to be used to define differentiated curriculum for the gifted. A design to differentiate the curriculum for the gifted should

- match the needs assessment data that answers the questions about the nature and needs of these students;
- match the program prototype selected to administer or implement the gifted program;
- match the competencies and the knowledge of the teachers of the gifted responsible for implementing the curriculum;
- match the expectations for both the general and gifted educational programs and reinforce rather than isolate gifted students from the basic educational program;
- match the understandings and interests of the parents of the gifted; and
- match the gifted students' expectations for their current and future educational aspirations.

References

Bloom, B. (Ed.). (1956). *Taxonomy of educational objectives: The classification of educational goals. Handbook I: Cognitive domain.* New York: Longman Green.

California Department of Education, & California Association for the Gifted. (1994). *Differentiating the core curriculum and instruction to provide advanced learning opportunities.* Sacramento, CA: California Department of Education.

Renzulli, J. (1977). *The enrichment triad model: A guide for developing defensible programs for the gifted and talent.* Mansfield Center, CT: Creative Learning Press.

CHAPTER 5

The Process Skills and the Gifted Learner

ROBERT W. SENEY

Mississippi University for Women

A key position in curriculum design for gifted learners is that adaptations must be made in content, process, product, and environment to appropriately differentiate for these students. The area of process skills has become most commonly associated with gifted learning and curriculum. Indeed, they have sometimes been popularly designated as "the curriculum for the gifted." In the big picture, this is unfortunate, but it is easy to see how this concept has developed. A major emphasis in learning programs for gifted learners is that these students should be trained to manipulate or use knowledge instead of concentrating on the acquisition of knowledge. The phrase "producer of knowledge and not just a user" typifies this appropriate attitude.

In order to become a producer, educators believed it was necessary to teach skills of processing. For students to manipulate knowledge, solve problems, and think critically and creatively, the focus highlighted process strategies, eventually becoming the educational center of the curriculum in many gifted programs. While they are important and the subject of this chapter, it is necessary to acknowledge at the onset that teaching the process skills in isolation, instead of in the context of high level or abstract content (either teacher-designated or student-selected), is inappropriate for gifted learners. Athletic skills or performance skills are not taught separately; and, as soon as possible, the skills are put into the game or the performance. This is just as true for the gifted learner and process skills. Simply put, process skills are taught in order for students to more appropriately handle advanced content that is the focus of their studies.

However, the process skills need to be investigated, and their importance for gifted learners should be emphasized. It must be noted that, in using the various skills, the procedures and models of these strategies must be taught. The phases, processes, and vocabulary of each of these approaches must be understood by the learner in order for these tools to be used effectively with advanced content. This progression of learning the skills and then applying them is readily seen in Betts' (Betts & Kercher, 1999) Autonomous Learner Model. Dimension Two of this model is Individual Development, which is divided into six basic areas: (1) inter/intra personal, (2) learning skills, (3) technology, (4) college and career involvement, (5) organizational skills, and (6) productivity. In learning skills, Betts (1985) listed 12 skill areas that should be taught for later use in becoming a self-directed learner.

Obviously, other program models depend heavily upon process skills. These models will be discussed in other chapters of this text but are briefly mentioned here. In Renzulli and Reis' (1985) Schoolwide Enrichment Model (formerly called the Enrichment Triad/Revolving Door Model), Type II activities are primarily process skills. Feldhusen's (1980) Purdue Three-Stage Model, in particular, relies heavily on process skills in both Stage 1 and Stage 2, and the application of process skills is found in Stage 3. Treffinger's Effective Independent Learner Model (1985) lists process development as one of the four major components of this model. The Multiple Talent Approach and Talents Unlimited (Schlichter, 1985) is itself not only a program model based on process skills but also a model for developing thinking skills. Other program models rely heavily upon process skills as well. The reader is referred to Renzulli's (1986) *Systems and Models for Developing Programs for the Gifted and Talented* for descriptions of other program models which rely heavily on process skills.

An emphasis on higher-level thinking skills has long been an accepted hallmark in designing appropriate curriculum for the gifted learner. It was in the gifted classroom that Bloom's *Taxonomy of Educational Objectives* (1956) became popular. This taxonomy, which has now "trickled" down into objectives and activities in the regular classroom, classifies thinking processes into six levels, each of which depends on the levels below it. The levels are (1) knowledge or recall, (2) comprehension, (3) application, (4) analysis, (5) synthesis, and (6) evaluation. In learning activities for the gifted, the focus of learning and curriculum has been on analysis, synthesis, and evaluation, the higher-level thinking skills. While all learners need exposure to all levels of thinking, gifted learners flourish and thrive on the higher-level thinking skills and are often frustrated when instruction focuses primarily at the knowledge and comprehension levels. A good description of strategies for using Bloom in the classroom can be found in Winebrenner (1992). Bloom's Taxonomy should still be considered a "primer" for gifted education, but in order to insure that curriculum is truly differentiated for gifted learners, it is important to look for more sophisticated and advanced strategies.

The purpose of this focus on the higher-level thinking skills is to guide students into thinking independently and help them "transfer these skills from one curriculum area to another and from one dimension (such as academic) to another dimension (such as their personal lives)" (VanTassel-Baska, 1994, p. 56). VanTassel-Baska (1994) suggested the following organization to ensure maximum internalization and transfer effect. The process skills must be (1) well-defined, (2) consistently addressed over time, (3) taught within basic content domains, as well as with intensity as a separate instructional set, (4) organized by scope and sequence from K–12, (5) modeled by the teacher in the classroom, and (6) employed as questioning techniques by the teacher (VanTassel-Baska, 1994, pp. 56–57).

Maker and Nielson's (1996) treatment of these eight modifications is recommended to the reader. They suggested a process modification that emphasizes higher levels of thinking, open-endedness, discovery learning, evidence of reasoning, freedom of choice, group interaction, pacing, and variety of processes. A synopsis of each process modification follows.

Process Modifications

Higher Levels of Thinking

There must be a change of instructional emphasis from the lower levels of thinking. As we move the instructional emphasis from the lower levels of thinking, memory, or recall to the higher levels of thinking, application, analysis, synthesis, and evaluation, we take an important step in building greater student involvement in learning. The emphasis becomes one of *using* information rather than focusing on the acquisition of facts and skills (Maker & Neilson, 1996).

Open-Endedness

This concept is different from the convergent-divergent emphasis found in much of the literature. Open-endedness requires a teacher attitude that is reflected in questioning techniques and the content of the questions. It also impacts the design of learning activities, materials, and the approach to evaluating student responses to questions. Maker and Nielson list these advantages to open questions. "They (a) encourage many students to give responses; (b) encourage student–to-student rather than teacher-to-student interaction patterns; (c) elicit more complete and more complex responses; (d) allow students to give knowledgeable answers; (e) encourage students to question themselves, their classmates, and their teachers; and (f) stimulate further thought and exploration of a topic" (Maker & Nielson, 1996 p.107).

Discovery Learning

The importance of discovery learning is that it helps students learn and "acquire knowledge that is uniquely their own because they discover it themselves" (Carin & Sund, 1980, p.100). This process requires the use of information as tools for inductive thinking. Students must find the meaning, structure, and organization of ideas. The primary mental processes of observing, classifying, labeling, describing, and inferring must be used as they draw conclusions and form generalizations. "Through doing, rather than listening, students learn to think inductively; to see a pattern among items, events, or phenomena that are presented (or observed); and to discern reasons why a particular pattern occurs" (Maker & Nielson, 1996, p. 110).

Evidence of Reasoning

It is important for gifted students to be able to explain the reasoning process or analysis that produced an answer. Three reasons are listed for this importance: (1) learners benefit from hearing or seeing how others analyze a problem; (2) it provides an opportunity to evaluate the processes, as well as the products of their thinking; and (3) it is important for students to be aware of their own mental processes in order to control and refine them (Maker & Nielson, 1996).

Freedom of Choice

"Gifted students need freedom to choose topics to study, methods to use in the process of manipulating and transforming information, the type of products to create, and the context of the learning environment in which to purse their studies" (Maker & Nielson, 1996 p.120). As freedom is provided for students, keep in mind the degree and kind of freedom allowed and the ability of the student to manage or profit from the freedom. The teacher must also be able to give up some control of part of the student's learning. While maximum freedom is seen in independent study, teachers can also use the element of choice in teacher directed activities as well (Maker & Nielson, 1996).

Group Interaction

"Group process and group interaction activities should be an integral part of curricula for gifted students" (Maker & Nielson,

1996 p. 126). These activities provide the opportunity to build group effectiveness and to assist individuals in developing skills in relating to others. Betts (1985) has suggested that group-building activities are an essential element in gifted programming. These activities provide the setting for learning important social and leadership skills (Maker & Nielson, 1996).

Pacing

Maker and Nielson (1996) consider pacing as one of the most important process modifications for gifted students. Pace of instruction refers to how quickly or slowly the information is presented in learning situations. Accelerated pacing refers to introducing of new material and/or skills in instruction and moving through the curriculum at a faster pace. In addition, it is generally recognized that gifted students do not need as much time to assimilate and process information. Modification of pacing should not be seen as cutting short student's thinking time. In fact, rapid movement through standard or required curriculum can provide more time for thinking and analysis (Maker & Nielson, 1996).

Variety of Processes

Variety of process refers to the number and types of learning procedures used. Teachers should use many different presentation strategies. Film, lectures, television, demonstrations, field trips, computer-based instruction, and learning centers are only a few ways in which information can be presented. Students should be encouraged to participate in discussions, learning games, independent research, and small group activities. The key to this modification is to discard the erroneous belief that all students must do the same thing at the same time (Maker & Nielson, 1996).

Maker and Nielson's (1996) treatment of these process skills, as summarized above, provides important lessons in differentiating learning for gifted students. Maker and Nielson see these processes as "crucial methodologies for manipulating content information and transforming it into personal knowledge" (p. 134). Some may not see "variety of processes" as a process skill as such, but it has been included in this synopsis of Maker and Nielson's work to emphasize that a variety of process skills and activities may be at work in the classroom at any given moment.

Critical Thinking

Critical thinking is addressed in detail in Parks' chapter, but it is important to note the interactions between critical thinking and process skills. Many of these skills are, in fact, models of critical thinking. The Creative Problem Solving Model (CPS) (Parnes, 1967) is a prime example. This model, with its unique combination of divergent and convergent thinking, demonstrates the interaction of critical thinking and processing. Models discussed later in other chapters project this same interaction. Other thinking models with this interaction are de Bono's (1986) Six Thinking Hats found in the *CoRT THINKING PROGRAM*, Harnadek's Critical Thinking and Mind Bender programs (1981a, 1981b), and Eberle and Stanish's (1995) *CPS for Kids,* to mention only a few. As various models are investigated, the importance of integrating critical thinking, learning processes, and significant content becomes obvious.

With this interaction of critical thinking and decision making, the work of Ennis (1964) provides some important guidelines. He suggested that students develop the following skills by judging whether a statement follows from the premises; something is an assumption; an observation statement is reliable; a simple generalization is warranted; a hypothesis is warranted; a theory is warranted; an argument depends on ambiguity; a statement is over vague or over specific; and an alleged authority is reliable (Ennis, 1964, pp. 600–610).

As students master these "judging" skills, they become adept in critical thinking, and these skills provide a taxonomy that moves them beyond Bloom.

The Constructivist Perspective

Constructivism is a theory about knowledge and learning that requires "a dramatic change in the focus of teaching by putting the students' own efforts to understand at the center of the educational enterprise" (Prawat, 1992, p. 357). This requires a learning setting in which "the traditional telling-listening relationship between teacher and student is replaced by one that is more complex and interactive" (p. 357). In the summary of Maker and Nielson's comments on discovery learning earlier in this chapter, the reader may well have been reminded of the theory of constructivism. This approach lends itself extremely well to education of gifted learners because it embodies many of the concepts that have been listed as important in learning activities for gifted learners. Brooks and Brooks (1993) suggested five principles of a constructivist pedagogy:

- posing problems of emerging relevance to students;
- structuring learning around primary concepts: the quest for essence;
- seeking and valuing students' points of view;
- adapting curriculum to address students' suppositions; and
- assessing student learning in the context of teaching (p. 33).

In this approach to learning, the teacher begins with a large question (the "umbrella" question) which prompts students to share their points of view. The teacher then encourages students to construct new understandings through probing questions and encouraging elaboration. Key phrases in this approach are *classifying, analyzing,* and *predicting.* With the focus on the learner, it is readily seen how appropriate this approach could be with gifted learners.

Process Skills

This section will focus on those skills that develop a student's ability to think, reason, search for knowledge, communicate, and interact effectively with others—specifically verbal communication skills. For the purpose of this discussion, the Process Skills Rating Scales (PSRS) developed by Karnes and Bean (1990) will be used as a guide. The PSRS, as seen in Table 1, obtain a rating of students' use of process skills. The scales can be used with elementary and secondary students and focus on those areas that will enhance students' ability to function well both in school and in the adult world.

Verbal Communication Skills

It is important for gifted learners to realize that the greatest ideas and solutions in the world are not worth anything unless they can be effectively communicated. The primary means of communicating those ideas is often through oral communication skills—the "ubiquitous" skills. These skills pervade every aspect of our lives. Oral communication is the primary form of communication. Even students who do not like to read or write find pleasure in talking both in informal and formal learning situations (Tchudi & Mitchell, 1999).

The importance of oral communication in the classroom and in the learning process cannot be ignored. Teacher talk is often seen as the most important talk in the classroom, but oral interaction between and among students may be more important, especially for gifted learners. Through oral communication, students assimilate new knowledge, make sense of it, and integrate it. By talking, students show us they can think and solve problems.

Talking is not only a medium for thinking but also an important means by which we learn how to think. From a Vygotskian perspective, thinking is an internal dialogue, an internalization of dialogues we've had with others. Our ability to think depends upon the many previous dialogues we have taken part in—we learn to think by participating in dialogue (Dudley-Marling & Sarle, 1991) Tchudi and Mitchell (1999) suggested a five-phase process to use oral communication as a learning tool:

Involving and Engaging. Teachers engage students in considering new material. Students use brainstorming or discuss what they know about a topic. The purpose is to give all students a chance to be heard and to get them to "buy into" the topic.

Exploring. Students in small groups begin to make sense of the information by sharing questions about the topic and discussing areas of interest.

Transforming. Students begin to focus their thinking and make decisions as they seek new understandings about the topic.

Table 1. Process Skills Rating Scales

Communication Skills	Descriptor
Verbal communication skills (speech)	A continuum of skills including the ability to express ideas in conversation and group discussion; to develop logically the points of a speech; to develop and deliver various types of speeches; and to obtain appropriate feedback.
Verbal communication skills (group discussion)	A continuum of skills including the ability to apply proper techniques for leading a group discussion; to keep the group focused on a topic; and to facilitate the contributions of the group members.
Verbal communication skills (interviewing)	A continuum of skills including the ability to construct appropriate interview questions; to develop a positive relationship with the respondent; and to analyze the information received.
Verbal communication skills (debate)	A continuum of skills including the ability to know various styles of debate; to identify appropriate materials for a debate; and to formulate and analyze rebuttals.
Written communication skills	A continuum of skills including the ability to write sentences and paragraphs; to evaluate writing; and to proofread and edit.

Receptive/nonverbal communication skills	A continuum of skills including the ability to listen with a purpose; to recognize nonverbal techniques to influence thinking; and to translate ideas from one verbal form to another.
Critical thinking and reasoning skills	A continuum of skills including the ability to solve problems independently; to identify cause-and-effect relationships; and to verify assumptions by using deductive reasoning.
Creative thinking skills	A continuum of skills including the ability to develop a flow of ideas; to combine unlike materials or ideas in unusual ways; and to plan for implementation of alternative solutions.
Personal growth and human relations skills	A continuum of skills including the ability to recognize a different point of view; to admit a mistake or failure; to evaluate the effects of personal decision on others.
Library research skills	A continuum of skills including the ability to compile a bibliography of books on a given subject; to locate and use periodicals; and to understand copyright laws.
Scientific research skills	A continuum of skills including the ability to develop inferences from observation and to synthesize collected data.

Table 1. Continued

Independent study skills	A continuum of skills including the ability to identify a topic; to establish a sequential work schedule; and to determine the appropriate format for the presentation of the independent study.

Note. From *Process Skills Rating Scales* (pp. 8–9), by F. A. Karnes and S. Bean, 1990, Buffalo, NY: United Educational Services. Copyright 1990 by Frances Karnes and Suzanne Bean. Reprinted with permission.

Presenting. Students make formal presentations before the larger group. The purpose is not only to inform but to allow the larger group to react to their thinking. (It is at this phase that the formal presentation skills are important.)

Reflecting. Students move back to their small groups and talk about what they have learned, how their learning was affected by interaction with other people, and the impact of the presentation on their thinking. (Tchudi & Mitchell, 1999, pp. 316–317)

Tchudi and Mitchell (1999) summarized their position on the importance of oral communication in learning by citing the work of the National Oracy Project (National Curriculum Council, 1991):

- We talk to make sense of the world and to try to exert some control over it.
- We talk in order to find out what others know and to share what we know.
- We talk in order to develop our thinking.
- We use talk to entertain, to tell stories or recite poetry, to create new roles and imaginative worlds.

- We use talk to evaluate our work, achievements, and learning.
- We use talk to demonstrate and to describe what we know or have found out. (Tchudi & Mitchell, 1999, p. 323)

The PSRS lists four areas of verbal communication: speech, group discussion, interviewing, and debate. These skills represent the basic presentation skills, and some appropriate resources for each of these areas are listed at the end of this chapter. It is important to note that, as we address these skills, oral communication involves both the speaker and the listener. It is the interaction of these two parties that is, in fact, communication. Galvin's (Galvin & Book, 1990) model (see Table 2) includes three elements: the speaker, the message, and the listener. The speaker and listener are affected by images, attitudes, and verbal or nonverbal delivery. Each of these elements can affect the communication.

Interviewing

The skills of interviewing are important for the gifted learner. Human resources are a significant element in primary research. Simply put, other people are valuable sources of information. Therefore, it is important that students know how to talk and listen to individuals in order to obtain and record this first-hand data. Sebranek, Meyer, and Kemper (1990) provided some helpful tips for better interviewing. They provide guidelines (see Figure 1) for the student before the interview, during the interview, and after the interview.

These tips should make the interview more comfortable and successful. Students not only will have discovered a great primary resource for their research but will have had the opportunity to expand their interpersonal skills.

Debate

The importance of debate for the gifted learner is that this skill provides the opportunity to research, define, and defend both sides of any given argument or issue. If the learner thinks of debate

Table 2. The Galvin Model

Speaker
The sender controls the message's content and organization. Physical and social image, attitudes toward the message and the receiver, and verbal and nonverbal delivery affect the way the speaker presents himself or herself. The sender is also affected by his or her level of creativity.

(See Cramond's chapter on creativity for more information on the importance of creativity for the speaker and the listener.)

Listener
Each listener has his or her own attitudes when receiving information. They can be indifferent, interested, or uninterested toward the message and can be neutral, friendly, or hostile to sender. The listener can receive information in a positive or negative way.

(Parks' chapter on thinking provides some important elements in how listeners process the sender's message.)

Message
The message is the link between the speaker and the listener, and the components of the message are occasion, content, and organization. Occasion includes reason, time, and place. Content encompasses the topic and materials, and organization includes ideas and words. Effective communicators use messages to draw the listener into an interactive process. Messages are constructed in order to inform, per-

suade, entertain, inspire, or exercise the vocal cords.

(Moore's chapter further explains the research skills that are important in developing the message.)

Interference	External and internal interference can cause breakdowns between the speaker and the listener.
Feedback	Communication is a two-way street between the speaker and listener linked through the message. A continuous exchange of feedback takes place between the two.

Note. From *Person to Person*, by K. Galvin and C. Book, 1990, Lincolnwood, IL: National Textbook Company, as cited in *Suggested Teaching Strategies for Teachers of the Intellectually Gifted*, (Speaking Skills, Section XXXII, p. 1) by Mississippi State Department of Education, 1994, Jackson, MS: Office of Gifted Education. Copyright 1994 by Office of Gifted Education. Reprinted with permission.

as arguing, he or she misses the point of this important strategy. Therefore, it is necessary to teach the accepted terminology and procedures for formal debate. In this process, many skills are brought together. The student must be able to research, distinguish between vital and unimportant information, support statements with valid evidence and sound reasoning, work cooperatively with other students, and present ideas in a clear and effective manner (Summers, Whan, & Rousee, 1963). In many ways, debate may be one of the richest opportunities for training in leadership.

In formal debate, the preparation phase is considered to be as important, maybe more so, than the formal debate itself. The O'Connor (1988) format is very helpful to the novice debater (see Figure 2). This clear and concise approach to debate brings this important skill into the reach of any gifted learner.

Before the Interview
- Carefully select the person who has the special knowledge in the area that is being researched.
- Write out all the questions that are to be asked.
- Make an appointment for a time and place that is convenient for the person to be interviewed.
- Inform the individual beforehand of the nature of your project.
- Study your topic beforehand so you will not be overwhelmed by new information and you will be an informed listener.
- Practice with your tape recorder so you know how to operate it and how to quickly and unobtrusively change tapes and batteries.
- Practice asking questions and writing down responses.

During the Interview
- Begin by introducing yourself, thanking your subject for the interview, and asking if it is all right to take notes or use a tape recorder.
- Ask a good first question and listen carefully.
- Keep eye contact with the subject and note the subject's facial expressions and gestures.
- Show that you are actively involved and interested in the topic by active listening.
- Do not interrupt your subject unless necessary.
- Before the interview is finished, review your notes for any clarification or follow-up questions.

After the Interview
- Thank the subject for the interview and offer to share a copy of the finished product.
- As soon as possible, write down everything you remember. Later, write a transcript of the interview from the tape.
- Double check any questionable facts or information with the subject or another authority before including it in the final product.
- Be sure that the subject gets a copy of the final work if requested.

Figure 1. Tips for Interviewing

Note. From *Write Source 2000* (pp. 405–407) by P. Sebranek, V. Meyer, & D. Kemper, 1990, Burlington, WS: Write Source Education. Copyright 1990 by D. C. Heath Company, a division of Houghton Mifflin Company. Used with permission of Great Source Education Group, Inc. All rights reserved.

Debate stimulates student interest in current issues, develops critical thinking ability, sharpens communication skills, and improves research abilities while demonstrating to students a method by which thoughtful, positive, and orderly change may be made in a democratic society (O'Connor, 1988).

The importance of debate for gifted learners cannot be overemphasized. In this process skill, there is a "celebration" of the other process skills and an opportunity to provide a truly appropriate challenge for gifted learners.

Summary

In this chapter, the importance of process skills in the education of the gifted has been discussed and noted with emphasis that they are tools to assist gifted learners in handling advanced content. These skills need to be taught in "isolation," but they should be applied to advanced content as quickly as possible. Betts' Autonomous Learner Model (Betts & Kercher, 1999) is a good example of this progression. Bloom's Taxonomy (1956) is a basic tool in education for the gifted, but in order to insure appropriate differentiation, other models should be identified.

The process modifications (Maker & Nielson, 1996) suggest the close connections between critical thinking and various process skills. The Ennis model (1964) is an appropriate model for critical thinking and decision making. The constructivist perspective is highly appropriate for gifted learners. Additional definitions of the process skills (Karnes & Bean, 1990) and notes on oral communication skills are supported in the work of Tchudi and Mitchell (1999), the Galvin Model (1990), and the Mississippi State Department of Education's *Suggested Teaching Strategies for Teachers of the Gifted* (1994). Tips for interviewing (Sebranek, Meyer, & Kemper, 1990) and the O'Connor model (1988) for debate contribute to the importance and pervasiveness of oral communication skills.

The use of process skills in differentiating for gifted learners should continue to play a major role in the education of gifted learners. While they are central to curricula for gifted learners, we

I. Preparation for the debate
    A. Analyze the proposition.
    B. Determine position.
        1. Affirmative
        2. Negative
    C. Assign responsibilities within the team.
    D. Build a case.
    E. Support the case.
        1. Research for evidence/proof
        2. Use logical reasoning
    F. Develop Strategies.
        1. Affirmative
        2. Negative
II. Participation in the debate contest.
    A. Select format.
        1. Standard format
        2. Cross-examination format
        3. Lincoln-Douglas format
    B. Present speeches.
        1. Constructive speeches
        2. Cross-examinations
        3. Rebuttals
    C. Judge effectiveness.

Figure 2. Tips for Debate

Note. From *Suggested Teaching Strategies for Teachers of Intellectually Gifted,* (section VII, p. 1), Mississippi State Department of Education, 1994, Jackson, MS: Office of Gifted Education. Copyright 1994 by the Office of Gifted Education. Reprinted with permission.

are shortchanging our gifted students if these skills become "the curricula for the gifted." If these students are to become "producers of knowledge and not just users," then the process skills must be taught to empower them to handle advanced content.

Teacher Resources

Publications

Benjamin, S. (1996). *The public speaking handbook.* Reading, MA: Addison-Wesley-Longman.

Berry, M. (1990). *Stepping into research.* Old Tappan, NJ: Prentice Hall.

Cray-Andrews, M., & Baum, S. (1992). *Creativity 1, 2, 3.* Unionville, NY: Royal Fireworks Press

Delisle, D., & Delisle, J. (1996). *Growing good kids.* Minneapolis, MN: Free Spirit.

Goodnight, L. (1987). *Getting started in debate.* Lincoln, IL: National Textbook.

Kincher, J. (1995). *Psychology for kids.* Minneapolis, MN: Free Spirit.

McCutcheon, R. (1991). *Can you find it?* Minneapolis, MN: Free Spirit.

McIntosh, J., & Meacham, A. (1992). *Creative problem solving in the classroom.* Waco, TX: Prufrock Press.

Otfinoski, S. (1997). *Speaking up, speaking out.* Brookfield, CT: Millbrook Press.

Romain, T. (1997). *How to do homework without throwing up.* Minneapolis, MN: Free Spirit.

Seymour, D., & Beardslee, E. (1990). *Critical thinking activities in patterns, imagery, logic.* White Plains, NY: Dale Seymour.

Standley, K. (1987). *How to study.* White Plains, NY: Dale Seymour.

Stanish, B. (1999). *The giving book.* Waco, TX: Prufrock Press.

Stay, B. (1996). *A guide to argumentative writing.* San Diego, CA: Greenhaven Press.

Stone, F. (1998). *Write makes might.* Waco, TX: Prufrock Press.

References

Betts, G. (1985). *Autonomous learner model for the gifted and talented learner.* Greeley, CO: ALPS.

Betts, G. T., & Kercher, J. K. (1999). *Autonomous learner model: Optimizing ability.* Greeley, CO: ALPS.

Bloom, B. (Ed.). (1956). *Taxonomy of educational objectives: The classification of educational goals. Handbook I: Cognitive domain.* New York: Longman Publishers.

Brooks, J., & Brooks, M. (1993). *The case for constructivist classrooms.* Alexandria, VA: Association for Supervision & Curriculum Development.

Carin, A., & Sund, R. (1980). *Teaching science through discovery* (4th ed.). Columbus, OH: Merrill.

de Bono, E. (1986). *CoRT THINKING PROGRAM.* New York: Pergamon Press.

Dudley-Marling, C., & Sarle, D. (1991). *When students have time to talk.* Portsmouth, NH: Heinemann.

Eberle, B., & Stanish, B. (1995). *CPS for kids.* Waco, TX: Prufrock Press.

Ennis, R. (1964). A definition of critical thinking. *The Reading Teacher, 18,* 599–612.

Feldhusen, J. (1980). *The three-stage model of course design.* Englewood Cliffs, NJ: Educational Technology.

Galvin, K., & Book, C. (1990). *Person to person.* Lincolnwood, IL: National Textbook.

Harnadek, A. (1981a). *Critical thinking: Books one and two.* Pacific Grove, CA: Critical Thinking Books & Software.

Harnadek, A. (1981b). *Mind bender: Books A, B, and C.* Pacific Grove, CA: Critical Thinking Books & Software.

Karnes, F. A., & Bean, S. M. (1990). *Process Skills Rating Scales.* Buffalo, NY: United Educational Services.

Maker, C. J., & Nielson, A. (1996). *Curriculum development and teaching strategies for gifted learners* (2nd ed). Austin, TX: PRO-ED.

Mississippi State Department of Education. (1994). *Suggested teaching strategies for teachers of the intellectually gifted.* Jackson, MS: Office of Gifted Education Programs.

National Curriculum Council. (1991). *National oracy project: Teaching talking and learning.* York, United Kingdom: Author.

O'Connor, J. (1988). *Speech: Exploring communication.* Englewood Cliffs, NJ: Prentice-Hall.

Parnes, S. (1967). *Creative behavior guidebook.* New York: Charles Scribner's Sons.

Prawat, R. (1992). Teachers' beliefs about teaching and learning: A constructivist perspective. *American Journal of Education, 110*(3), 354.

Renzulli, J. S. (Ed.). (1986). *Systems and models for developing programs for the gifted and talented.* Mansfield Center, CT: Creative Learning Press.

Renzulli, J. S., & Reis, S. J. (1985). *The schoolwide enrichment model.* Mansfield Center, CT: Creative Learning Press.

Schlichter, C. (1985). Talents unlimited: Applying the multiple talent approach in mainstream and gifted programs. In J. S. Renzulli (Ed.), *Systems and models for developing programs for the gifted and talented* (pp. 352–389). Mansfield Center, CT: Creative Learning Press.

Sebranek, P., Meyer, V., & Kemper, D. (1990). *Write source 2000.* Burlington, WS: Write Source Education.

Summers, H., Whan, F., & Rousee, T. (1963). *How to debate.* New York: H.W. Wilson.

Tchudi, S., & Mitchell, D. (1999). *Exploring and teaching the English language arts* (4th ed.). New York: Addison Wesley Longman.

Treffinger, D. (1985). Fostering effective, independent learning through individualized programming. In J. S. Renzulli (Ed.), *Systems and models for developing programs for the gifted and talented* (pp. 429–460). Mansfield Center, CT: Creative Learning Press.

VanTassel-Baska, J. (1994). *Comprehensive curriculum for gifted learners.* Boston, MA: Allyn & Bacon.

Winebrenner, S. (1992). *Teaching gifted kids in the regular classroom.* Minneapolis, MN: Free Spirit.

CHAPTER 6

Product Development for Gifted Students

KRISTEN R. STEPHENS
University of North Carolina—Charlotte

FRANCES A. KARNES
The University of Southern Mississippi

Introduction

*J*ulie, a second-grade girl, proudly wears the T-shirt that she designed to reflect the knowledge gained through the various units she explored during the school year. John, a seventh-grade boy, writes a script, designs a costume, and creates a set for a performance to depict the life, accomplishments, and impact of Abraham Lincoln on America. These are both examples of positive student products.

Meanwhile, David, an eighth-grade boy, writes his 10th book report this year. He has not been exposed to the variety of other products that could possibly be used to display his knowledge. Sarah, a fourth-grade girl, creates yet another unsuccessful poster. She has never been taught the elements of design that are necessary for the creation of a successful product.

Creative products are essential to curriculum for the gifted. This chapter provides teachers with the information necessary to assist students through the various stages of product development.

What is a Product?

Maker and Nielson (1996) define a product as "The tangible evidence of student learning" (p. 186). The transformation of knowledge into creative products is a critical goal for gifted students (Renzulli, 1977; Feldhusen & Kolloff, 1978). The types of products expected from students should be highly creative and perhaps abstract. In other words, products created by gifted students should be comparable to those made by professionals in the designated field. Furthermore, the products of gifted students should represent an application, analysis, and synthesis of knowledge acquired from their research.

Why is Product Development Important in Gifted Education?

The act of product development is multifaceted in scope and sequence; and through the production process, gifted students can develop, enhance, and evaluate a wide spectrum of content and process skills, thus adding to the advancement of self-esteem, self-analysis, and self-actualization. The content or knowledge displayed through products can encompass all areas of human endeavor and provide an integration of the arts, humanities, mathematics, science, literature, religion, and other subject matter. In addition, the process skills of creativity and creative problem solving, higher-level and critical thinking, oral and written communication, scientific and library research, and social and personal development will be refined with each new product created. Furthermore, the organizational skills of planning, time management, record keeping, and delegating will be enhanced, as they play a crucial role in the process of achieving the intended goal.

Through product design, gifted youth become responsible for their own learning, thus fostering independence and accountability. Moreover, product development allows learners to explore, investigate, design, and formulate their own ideas, feelings, and thoughts, which encourage risk-taking and stimulate creativity. Students are allowed to proceed at their own established pace through selected activities that accommodate their individually diverse learning styles. Finally, through research of a selected problem, presentation of solutions, and self-evaluation to assess demonstrated outcomes, students are exposed to authentic learning experiences.

Types of Products

Products have long been used to assess student progress. Unfortunately, many classrooms are still limited to products such as written reports and posters. However, the variety of products that students can create is abundant. Figure 1 lists an assortment of products that students can produce to display knowledge from their research (Karnes & Stephens, 2000).

The list of products in Figure 1 can be divided into several categories: written, visual, performance, oral, and multi-categorical products (Karnes & Stephens, 2000). Several examples of each type of product are displayed below.

Written: Letter of Inquiry, Persuasive Essay, Poem, Research Paper, Friendly Letter, Newspaper Story, Report, Business Letter, Description, Explanation, Story, Advertisement, Book Report, Classified Advertisement, Creative Writing, Critique, Diary, Dictionary, Editorial, Essay, Checklist, Script, Glossary, Journal, Magazine Article, Musical Composition, Play, Puppet Show, Questionnaire, Test, Worksheet, Book, Biography, and Song.

Visual: Book Jacket, Drawing, Poster, Story Map, Bar Graph, Concept Cube, Time Lines, Pie Chart, Tree Chart, Web, Collage, Flowchart, Venn Diagram, Advertisement, Blueprint, Brochure, Bulletin Board, Bullet Chart, Multimedia Project, Cross-Section, Film, Graph, Illustration, Map, Mobile, Mural, Cartoon, Story Board, Carving, Costume, Diorama, Photograph, Quilt, and Sculpture.

Performance: Dance, Monologue, Puppet Show, Demonstration, Skit, Dramatization, Simulation, Comedy Sketch, Experiment, Musical Performance, and Play.

Abstract
Acronym
Activity Sheet
Advertisement
Alphabet Book
Animation
Annotated Bibliography
Aquarium
Archive
Art Gallery
Autobiography
Banner
Bibliography
Biography
Big Book
Blueprint
Board Game
Book
Book Jacket
Bookmark
Book Review
Broadcast
Brochure
Budget
Bulletin Board
Bumper Sticker

Business Plan
Button
Campaign
Cartoon
Carving
Catalog
Celebration
Chart
Club
Coat of Arms
Collage
Collection
Coloring Book
Comedy Skit
Comic Strip
Commemorative Document
Commentary
Commercial
Competition
Computer Document
Computer Program
Conference
Construction
Cookbook
Cooked

Concoction
Costume
Crest
Critique
Cross Section
Crossword Puzzle
Dance
Database
Debate
Demonstration
Design
Diagram
Dialogue
Diary
Dictionary
Diorama
Display
Document
Documentary
Doll
Dramatization
Drawing
Editorial
Equation
Essay
Etching
Evaluation

Checklist
Event
Exhibit
Experiment
Fact File
Fairy Tale
Family Tree
Field Experience
Film
Flag
Flannel Board
Flip Book
Flow Chart
Flyer
Folder Game
Fractal
Game
Game Show
Geodesics
Geometric
Glossary
Graph
Graphic
Graphic Organizer
Greeting Card
Guest Speaker

Guide
Handbook
Hidden Picture
Histogram
Hologram
How to Book
Hypermedia
Hypothesis
Illuminated Manuscript
Illusion
Illustrated Story
Illustration
Index Cards
Instructions
Internet Search
Interview
Invention
Investigation
Itinerary
Jewelry
Jigsaw Puzzle
Jingle
Journal
Kit
Laser Show
Law

Learning Center
Lecture
Lesson
Letter
Limerick
List
Literary Analysis
Log
Logo
Logic Puzzle
Machine
Magazine
Magazine Article
Magic Show
Manual
Manuscript
Map with Key
Mask
Matrix
Menu
Metaphor
Mini-Center
Mobile
Mock Trial
Model
Monologue
Monument

Montage
Mosaic
Motto
Multimedia Presentation
Mural
Museum
Musical Composition
Musical Instrument
Musical Performance
Mystery
Narrative
Needlecraft
Newsletter
Newspaper
Novel
Origami
Oral Report
Organization
Ornament
Outline
Overhead Transparency
Packet

Painting
Pamphlet
Panel Discussion
Pantomime
Paper Mache
Pattern
Performance
Personal Experience
Petition
Photo Album
Photo Essay
Photograph
Photo Journalism
Pictograph
Pictorial Essay
Picture Dictionary
Picture Story
Pie Chart
Plan
Plaque

Play
Poem
Pointillism
Political Cartoon
Pop-Up Book
Portfolio
Portrait
Position Paper
Poster
Prediction
Presentation
Program
Project Cube
Prototype
Puppet
Puppet Show
Questionnaire
Quilt
Quotations
Radio Show

Rap
Rebus Story
Recipe
Recitation
Reenactment
Relief Map
Report
Riddle
Role Play
Routine
Rubber Stamp
Rubbing
Rubric
Samples
Sand Casting
Scavenger Hunt
Scenario
Science Fiction
Story
Scrapbook

Script
Sculpture
Self-Portrait
Seminar
Service Project
Shadow Box
Shadow Play
Short Story
Sign
Silk Screening
Simulation
Sketch
Skit
Slide Show
Sociogram
Song
Speech
Spreadsheet
Stage Setting
Stained Glass

Stamp
Stencil
Stitchery
Story
Story Board
Summary
Survey
Table
Tape Recording
Television Show
Terrarium
Tessellation
Test
Text Book
Theory
Three-D Model
Time Capsule
Timeline
Toy
Trademark

Travelogue
Triptych
Venn Diagram
Video
Video Game
Virtual Field Trip
Vocabulary List
Wall Hanging
Watercolor
Weaving
Webbing
Web Page
Woodworking
Word Puzzle
Written Paper

Figure 1. Product Ideas

Note. From *The Ultimate Guide for Student Product Development and Evaluation,* (p. 2), by F. A. Karnes and K. R. Stephens, 2000, Waco, TX: Prufrock Press. Copyright 2000 by Prufrock Press. Reprinted with permission.

Oral: Debate, Oral Report, Persuasive Speech, Round Table Discussion, Class Discussion, Mock Interview, Newscast, Oral Book Report, Informative Speech, Panel Discussion, Description/ Show and Tell, "How to" Talk, Reading to the Class, Audiotape, Conference Presentation, Documentary, Group Discussion, Lecture, Commentary, Seminar, Speech, and Trial.

Multi-Categorical: Exhibit, Game, Invention, Multimedia Slide Show, Oral History, Television Show, Video, Web Site, Broadcast, Computer Program, Museum, and Time Capsule.

Students' learning styles may influence which types of product they prefer creating. For example, a student who excels in writing may select a product from the written category of products, and one who enjoys hands-on activities would probably favor those products in the performance or multi-categorical areas.

To determine the type of product a student prefers, Kettle, Renzulli, and Rizza (1998) devised *My Way . . . An Expression Style Inventory*, an instrument used to gather information on the types of products students are interested in creating. Students are asked to rate their interests in various activities on a Likert-type scale. The *Expression Style Inventory* divides products into 10 different categories: written, oral, artistic, computer, audio-visual, commercial, service, dramatization, manipulative, and musical. Students determine which type of product they would most likely be interested in developing by adding up the total of their responses to the 50 items on the inventory.

Although information relating to the type of product a student would like to create is important, other circumstances must also be considered before selecting a product. For example, with what audiences will this product be shared, and what subject matter is the product attempting to display? While a puppet show may be appropriate to teach young children about the importance of recycling, it may not be suitable to convince community leaders about the necessity of a detailed plan to improve inner city environments.

Furthermore, it is important for teachers to encourage students to try creating a variety of products. Even though a student who is an outstanding artist prefers to engage in products involving drawing and painting, it is also important that he or she be assisted in developing his or her skills in other areas through the creation of an assortment of products. For example, he or she might include illustrations with a written story or design a set for a performance. Assisting gifted students in applying their strengths to a variety of areas encourages them to further see connections and expand their developing concepts.

Design and Product Development

Burnette, Norman, and Browning (1997) described design as "a way of thinking and doing that is both creative and practical ... and [is] the key to innovative thinking and invention" (p. 11). Before students begin their product endeavors, it is necessary that they have a preliminary knowledge of the processes, principles, and elements of design. Often times, it is assumed that students already possess most skills necessary for product design. However, they need prior instruction and guidance in such skills, from the basic uses of stencils, rulers, compasses, and protractor, to the selection of appropriate colors, sizes, and shapes, to the recognition of other aesthetic elements such as the more complex skills of super-imposed imaging, voice synthesizing, and computer-generated graphics.

An introduction to the design process will assist students in planning for future product development. Davis, Hawley, McMullan, and Spilka (1997) describe the following steps in the design process:
- identifying and defining the problem;
- gathering and analyzing information;
- determining performance criteria for successful solutions;
- generating alternative solutions and building prototypes;
- evaluating and selecting appropriate solutions;
- implementing choices; and
- evaluating outcomes.

Another model depicting the design process is the I/DEPPE/I model (Burnette, Norman, & Browning, 1997). This model is an acronym for the following dimensions:
- Intending: committing to a goal;
- Defining: identifying the problem;
- Exploring: generating possible solutions;
- Planning: making and communicating decisions;

- Producing: doing and making what is required;
- Evaluating: assessing the product and determining if you attained the goal; and
- Integrating: accommodating what was learned from the entire experience with previous knowledge.

Both of the above models almost mirror the stages involved in product development and creative problem solving.

In addition to an introduction to the design process, students should become familiar with the elements and principles of design. Elements such a color, line, value, shape, form, balance, and texture must be explored, as well as the principles of repetition, unity, emphasis, economy, proportion, and variety.

Instructional materials and other resources that assist in teaching the process, principles, and elements of design are listed at the end of this chapter. Consult with the arts or technology instructor or department for additional resources and information at your school.

Stages of Product Development

There are several stages a student goes through when creating a product. Each step assists students in developing and practicing numerous skills. These stages are as follows:
- formulation of a topic;
- organization of production aspects;
- transformation of content;
- communication through products;
- evaluation;
- celebration; and
- reflection (Karnes & Stephens, 2000).

Formulation of a Topic

The first stage in developing a product is selecting a topic to investigate. It may be selected through brainstorming or creating a web and can be content-specific, such as pirates, Egypt, wolves, or architecture. Or, it may be concept related, such as freedom, leadership, change, or cultures.

Narrow It Down. It is important for students to narrow the topic from broad to specific. For example, the topic of astronomy might be focused to the Big Dipper or black holes. This will assist students in focusing research questions to the selected topic.

Build New Knowledge. Students must be encouraged to select a topic from which they can learn new knowledge. One who has read every book about tornadoes and has already developed several products pertaining to tornadoes should select a different topic from which new knowledge can be gained.

Select an Area of Interest. Students should choose topics in which they have a genuine interest. This will serve as a motivator for the student to carry out product development to completion. Those who have been interested in tornadoes, for example, might find the topic of hurricanes fascinating as well.

Make Sure Resources Are Available. A topic should be selected that requires utilizing more than a single source of information during the research process. In other words, students must select a topic using a variety of sources including books, encyclopedias, Internet, films, interviews, newspapers, authentic documents, atlases, experiments, and so forth.

Organization of Production Aspects

The second phase, the organization stage, runs the length of the product-producing experience. Several organizational techniques can be utilized to help keep students focused and provide structure to daily activities relating to product development. For example, Figure 2 illustrates how students might document their production plan. Keep in mind, a well-developed organizational plan teaches students the necessity of setting and achieving both short and long term goals. The following are examples of some organizational techniques that can be applied by students.

Time Lines. Before getting too deep into a project, it is important to generate a time line with a reasonable date for project completion. For example, daily activities may be placed on a calendar to build time management skills. This will assist students in staying on task and will further allow them to visualize an end to their means. Furthermore, they should reflect on their accomplishments at the end of each day

Let's Get Organized!

Name: _____   Date: _____

Topic: _____   Product: _____

Description and components of proposed product	
Resources and contact people	
Criteria to meet: What are my goals?	
Materials I will need and where I might obtain them	

Possible audiences	<u>Within school</u>	<u>Outside school</u>

Figure 2. Product Planner

and evaluate their progress toward meeting established goals. By staying organized and working toward a projected date, students demonstrate the ability to be responsible for their own learning.

Logs. Students can record daily progress toward completion of goals and can plan activities for the next day in a project log. This will encourage students to think in advance about what materials they need to bring to the subsequent class session in order to complete the next planned stage of product development. Logs can be kept in a spiral notebook or on a product log form, which can be designed by the teacher or student. Such forms may require students to answer questions pertaining to current progress and future agendas. Sample questions on a product log form might include What did I accomplish today? What do I plan to do next class session? and What materials will I need to bring? By answering these questions, students will further enhance their organizational and planning skills.

Research Readiness. Research readiness is a term referring to the organizational activities that precede the research process. Research readiness can include generating a list of questions pertaining to the topic which will help guide research. The development of a KWL Chart (What I Know? What I Want to Know? What I Learned?) may be beneficial at this stage. Furthermore, students may want to produce a list of resources in which they might possibly locate the answers to formulated questions.

Determining Audiences. Before students decide what type of product will best convey their new knowledge, it is essential that they create a list of possible audiences with whom to share their creations. The characteristics of the audience, along with the information to be conveyed, will greatly influence the type and complexity of the product selected. Possible audiences might include peers, community leaders, younger students, retirement communities, the school board, clubs, and so forth.

Product Selection. Once the audience and presentation content have been selected, students can determine which type of product will be most suitable. Media are the mode through which ideas are communicated. Selecting appropriate forms of media may be a complicated step for some students. They often tend to select forms of media that reflect their particular learning style. For example, authors will write and artists will illustrate. Atwood (1974) described the three levels of media forms as demonstrative, representational, and symbolic. Demonstrative media, the most literal form of communication, might include displays, step-by-step procedures, and experiments. Representational media, which are used to represent reality when it is not easily displayed, might include sculptures, photographs, models, plays, and drawings. Symbolic media, which are considered translations of reality, might include speeches, advertisements, dances, graphs, maps, and computer programs. Depending on the content of the project and the audience, gifted students must decide what form of media is most suited to accurately communicate learned ideas. Sometimes the media that will best demonstrate, represent, or symbolize an idea may not be the type of media the student would have normally selected. Keeping a list of possible products, as found in Figure 1, may help students make varied ones that will communicate their thoughts most effectively.

Material Gathering. Once the product type has been selected, students should generate a list of needed materials in order to complete the proposed products. Students may need to make accommodations for certain materials due to expense and availability. These accommodations allow them to utilize their creative problem-solving abilities in authentic situations. Furthermore, materials that students first thought were appropriate may not work as planned. Through substitution and experimentation with alternate materials, they will enhance their problem-solving abilities.

Evaluation Criteria. Before creating their product, they should develop criteria with which to evaluate finished work. By establishing product criteria for evaluation early on, students are made aware of the standards set for themselves. Since product types vary from one to the other, different criteria will need to be established for each type. Students may consult with an expert in the topic field in order to develop a list of components and exemplary characteristics for the proposed product. For example, a cartographer or geography professor may be an excellent resource for a student who desires to create a map; a genealogist would provide information relating to the components and characteristics of an ideal family tree; and a local reporter may offer advice on how to conduct a professional-quality interview. Baker and Schacter (1996) suggested using adult expert performance as a benchmark for assessment. The Center for Research on Evaluation, Standards, and Student Testing (CRESST) employed expert models to assess student performance in a variety of content areas. In addition, Wiggins (1996) suggested that teachers look for "exemplars" or "anchors," which are examples of a particular product that demonstrate an exceptional standard. These "exemplars" can serve as a basis for setting performance standards. The following is a suggested list of specific products with the experts that may be consulted when developing evaluation criteria:

- blueprint/architect
- brochure/marketing consultant
- debate/speech-debate teacher
- exhibit/museum curator
- experiment/scientist
- family tree/genealogist
- magazine/editor
- map/cartographer or geography department
- musical composition/music professor
- photograph/photographer
- play/actor or professor of theater
- sculpture/local artist
- web page/computer expert

Experts are everywhere. Many can be found in your local community through the following sources:

- colleges and universities
- businesses
- clubs and organizations
- friends
- craft guilds
- local media
- Internet
- telephone directory
- library

The Internet provides a valuable source of experts if they cannot be found within your community. For instance, students can send questions related to a specific discipline to experts in that field. Here are a few examples:

Ask a Geologist
http://walrus.wr.usgs.gov/docs/ask-a-ge.html

Ask a Physicist
     http://www.wichita.edu/public/osbwww/public_html/o51.html
Ask an Astronomer
     http://www.twsu.edu/~obswww/o20.html
Ask Dr. Math
     http://forum.swarthmore.edu/dr.math/drmath.high.html
Ask a Scientist
     http://sln.fi.edu./tfi/publications/askexprt.html
Ask the Author
     http://mse.byu.edu/mse/Insci/286/communication/EmailAsk. html
Ask a Historian or an Archeologist
     http://www.cr.nps.gov/history/askhist.htm
Ask an Architect
     http://infopoint.theriver.com/aiasac/ask_welc.htm
Ask Dr. Universe
     http://www.vrd.org/locator/sites/DrUniverse.html
Ask Earth and Sky
     http://www.vrd.org/locator/sites/earthnsky.html
Ask a Hurricane Hunter
     http://www.vrd.org/locator/sites/hurricane.html
Ask a NASA Scientist
     http://www.vrd.org/locator/sites/highenergy.html
Ask a Reporter
     http://www.vrd.org/locator/sites/reporter.html
Ask a Volcanologist
     http://www.vrd.org/locator/sites/volcanologist.html
Ask the Optometrist
     http://www.vrd.org/locator/sites/optometrist.html
The Grammar Lady
     http://www.vrd.org/locator/sites/grammar.html
Ask a Linguist
     http://www.vrd.org/locator/sites/linguist.html
Ask an Astronaut
     http://www.vrd.org/locator/sites/astronaut.html
Ask a Zoo Keeper
     http://www.vrd.org/locator/sites/Animal.html
Ask an Ecologist
     http://www.vrd.org/locator/sites/ecologist.html

Ask an Entomologist
    http://www.vrd.org/locator/sites/bugnet.html
Ask about Careers
    http://www.vrd.org/locator/sites/industry.htm

Transformation of Content

Since the attainment of higher-level thinking skills is an essential focus in gifted programs, the type of products expected from students should be highly creative and perhaps abstract. Products should represent more than the mere acquisition of new knowledge. They should convey a genuine application of synthesis and analysis. This process of transformation allows the student to turn new knowledge into something more meaningful. Maker and Nielson (1996) outlined several elements of transformation: viewing from a different perspective, reinterpreting, elaborating, extending, and combining simultaneously. When evaluating a product, it is important to look for some of these elements in students' work. Students should turn learned content into their own creation instead of repeating or summarizing general information. Forster (1990) described the process of project development as "the act of surprising oneself with new ideas" (p. 40). The ultimate goal of product development is to transform student research into new thoughts, ideas, and perspectives. Transformation involves many steps and processes. These include

1. Research: The student locates, comprehends, and classifies information in order to gain knowledge.
2. Information Filtration: The student processes, interprets, refines, and extrapolates the knowledge and ideas gained from research.
3. Idea Generation: From the selected information, the student emphasizes and analyzes various elements, concepts, and ideas of interest.
4. Centralization: The student selects, decides, and focuses on a specific element or idea.
5. Reflection: The student considers, ponders, and judges the selected idea.
6. Manipulation: The student tests and experiments with the idea and changes, improves, and adapts it as necessary.

7. Execution: The student decides, organizes, prepares, and produces a product to display the idea.
8. Communication: The student shares, performs, displays, or disseminates the product to an authentic audience.

A model of the above transformation process appears in Figure 3.

Communication Through Products

During the communication stage, students share their ideas and products with a selected audience. Sharing the final product with an audience gives added purpose to the product. Instead of being stored in the back of a closet to collect dust, student products can provide valuable learning opportunities for many types of audiences.

Speaking Skills

Speaking skills will be enhanced through the continued exposure to a wide variety of audiences. Eye contact, clear speech, and confidence are a few components of an effective presentation. Students should become more comfortable with practice and experience in presenting their products and ideas. Never assume that a student who is unable to give an effective presentation has not synthesized and analyzed information from his or her study. Presenting the product in class should be the first step, followed by audiences within the school and community. Younger students will need time to feel comfortable expressing themselves in front of others. It may be advisable to keep audiences small and familiar for younger students until they build confidence presenting to larger, more unfamiliar groups.

Authentic Audiences

It is important for students to share their products and ideas with authentic audiences. These may vary from product to product and student to student. Potential audiences may be peers, teachers, family members, topic experts, clubs, the school board, retirement community, or councilmen, to name a few. Students should be involved in selecting the audience.

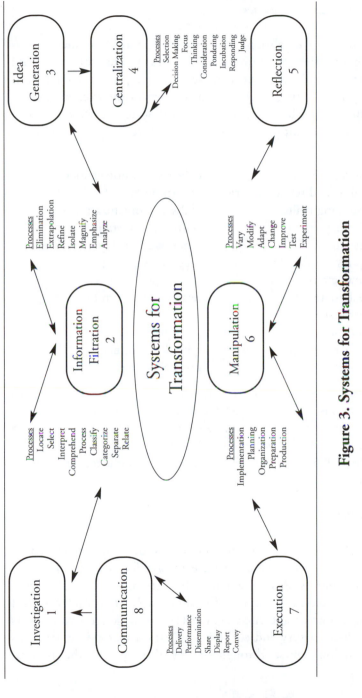

Figure 3. Systems for Transformation

Note. From *The Ultimate Guide for Student Product Development and Evaluation*, (p. 12), by F. A. Karnes and K. R. Stephens, 2000, Waco, TX: Prufrock Press. Copyright 2000 by Prufrock Press. Reprinted with permission.

Other Sharing Showcases

Products can also be attractively displayed in many areas throughout the community. This gives a sense of pride and importance to the student while serving as a great public relations tool by introducing to the rest of the world the excitement and learning that is being generated in the gifted classroom. Some places that student products may be displayed in your community are

bank lobbies	colleges and universities
public and school libraries	governmental offices
shopping malls	clubs and organizations
airports	train and bus stations
restaurants	school administrative offices
stores	magazines
newsletters	newspapers
real estate offices	retirement communities
hospitals	preschools
fairs or festivals	town halls
PTA meetings	school board meetings
post offices	business offices

Students may also choose to enter their products in various competitions. Information related to specific academic areas as well as fine and performing arts, leadership, and service learning can be found in the book *Competitions: Maximizing Your Abilities* (Karnes & Riley, 1996). The possibilities of potential audiences and display areas are abundant.

Evaluation

Evaluation of student products should be multidimensional so students can receive helpful and extensive feedback from a wide array of sources. Assessment may be determined by the teacher using preselected criteria, self-evaluation by the students, and feedback from an audience. Forster (1990) suggested that projects have self-regulatory and constant evaluation methods so students can stay on course throughout the duration of the project.

Students may wish to develop questionnaires to determine their audiences' perceptions of their products and presentations. Before beginning their projects, it may also be advisable that the students choose a support person with whom they can conference periodically to share progress and receive feedback. Gibbons (1991) suggested that this support person be an expert in the particular topic, if possible.

Establishing Criteria

Students should be involved in establishing the criteria for product evaluation. If they are familiar with the criteria prior to beginning work on the projects, students will be more apt to produce successful products. Establishing criteria for evaluating products that are complex in nature can be difficult. Byrnes and others (1982) have developed an easy-to-use scale for creative products such as drama, poetry, music, and dance. The scales contain glossaries of the important components of these unique products, making them easy for students and teachers to use effectively. Topic experts can also be asked to assist in developing criteria for certain products.

Renzulli, Reis, and Smith (1981) have developed the Student Product Assessment Form, which rates eight factors in product developing including purpose; problem focusing; level of resources; diversity of resources; appropriateness of resources; logic, sequence, and transition; action orientation; and audience.

Creating Rubrics

Once exemplary criteria for a particular product has been selected, a rubric can be constructed. A rubric is a framework for evaluating products on an established scale. The first step in constructing a rubric is to list all the components of the proposed product. For example, if the product is a poster, the basic components might include title, labels, graphics, and layout. Components will vary according to the expected complexity of the product and the abilities of the student. For example, older students may wish to add additional components beyond the basic ones.

After a list of components has been generated, exemplary characteristics of each component should be listed. For example

Title
- legible; neat
- prominent; visible
- representative of topic; appropriate
- correct spelling/grammar

Labels
- legible; neat
- appropriate placement
- correct spelling/grammar

Graphics
- clear; visible
- appropriate to theme
- securely attached

Layout
- balanced
- noncluttered
- interesting
- appropriate emphasis

Once the exemplary characteristics of each component have been listed, a scoring criteria or scale for each characteristic must be set. It is recommended that a four- or a six-point scale be used rather than an odd numbered scale. With odd numbered scales there is a tendency for the rater to select the middle value. In addition, if using a numbered scale, each value should be clearly defined. For example, a "1" may be designated as "Poor" or "Incomplete" while a "4" may designate "Superior" production (Karnes & Stephens, 2000).

Figure 4 is an example of a completed rubric that was created using the above procedure. Many ready-made rubrics can be found in books and on the Internet. Care should be taken in selecting and adapting such rubrics to meet your specific needs. A list of books and Internet sites that might be helpful in designing rubrics is included toward the end of this chapter.

Components	Characteristics	Ratings					
Title	• legible; neat	1	2	3	4	5	6
	• prominent; visible	1	2	3	4	5	6
	• representative of topic; appropriate	1	2	3	4	5	6
	• correct spelling/grammar	1	2	3	4	5	6
Labels	• legible; neat	1	2	3	4	5	6
	• appropriate placement	1	2	3	4	5	6
	• correct spelling/grammar	1	2	3	4	5	6
Graphics	• clear; visible	1	2	3	4	5	6
	• appropriate to theme	1	2	3	4	5	6
	• securely attached	1	2	3	4	5	6
Layout	• balanced	1	2	3	4	5	6
	• not cluttered	1	2	3	4	5	6
	• interesting	1	2	3	4	5	6
	• appropriate emphasis	1	2	3	4	5	6

1 = Incomplete; 2 = Needs Improvement; 3 = Fair;
4 = Emerging; 5 = Good; 6 = Superior

Figure 4. Completed Rubric

Note. From *The Ultimate Guide for Student Product Development and Evaluation*, (p. 17), by F. A. Karnes and K. R. Stephens, 2000, Waco, TX: Prufrock Press. Copyright 2000 by Prufrock Press. Reprinted with permission.

Evaluators

As mentioned earlier, evaluation of student products should be multidimensional. This can be achieved by having a variety of evaluators. They might include peers, audience members, teachers, the student, topic experts, or school administrators.

Celebration

What better motivator to work diligently and produce a high quality product than to have the chance to celebrate and reflect upon your accomplishments? Gibbons (1991) suggested that students have a pizza party and share their products with one another informally. In doing so, students see the wide variety of products they are capable of producing. Students can share the thought processes that went into designing the product and perhaps even have the opportunity to explore the topic further, as more questions are generated when great minds meet.

Product Fair

Celebration is an important component in product development. It allows students to build confidence and feel good about their achievements. A product fair can provide students with the opportunity to share products in a completely different type of stress-free setting. Renzulli and Reis (1991) suggested an end-of-year product fair, which includes coverage by local newspapers, television, and radio stations. Such coverage would expand the students' audience and provide excellent public relations for the gifted program. Through such an event they can also share the stages in the development, implementation, and evaluation of the product.

Reflection

As students pack up their products on the bus and depart for home, the time for reflection begins. Students should be encouraged to reflect on the entire process of creating their product from beginning to end. Is there anything else about the topic that needs further research? What could have been done differently? What really worked? These reflections will be a valuable contribution toward improvement as students begin a new journey into another product frontier. They will learn from both their successes and failures. In a sense, they will learn a great deal about themselves and others. Most of the time, people reflect on things often without even realizing it; but, by purposely doing so, a great deal can be learned that will be of value in the future.

Product Journals

One method students can use to reflect on their product producing experience is keeping a detailed journal. This will help students keep track of the steps of product development and will also serve as a way for them to remember and reflect on the entire process. Students will have gained an abundance of new knowledge through the research, planning, and creative problem-solving experiences.

How to Foster Product Development in the Classroom

There are many ways teachers can encourage and promote creative product development within their classrooms. By providing the necessary resources, creative ideas are more likely to be generated.

Posting a Product List

A simple way to encourage product development is by merely posting a list of products as seen in Figure 1 on the wall in the classroom. When students need an idea for a product, they can go to this list and select something that is appropriate to their topic and audience. By displaying the list, students are motivated to try their hand at a variety of different products, beyond the report and poster.

Product Portfolios and Inventories

Teachers can keep product portfolios and inventories on each student. This will allow teachers across grade levels to see what types of products a particular student has made during his or her school career. Visually, product portfolios provide an excellent way for students to see their growth and progress over the years. Figure 5 displays a technique that can be used to keep track of the various products a student develops.

Don't Throw It Away

Teachers throughout the school can send a notice home asking parents to donate a variety of items to the school or classroom that inspire creative product development. A designated corner in the classroom or closet within the school can house these materials to be utilized by the students when needed for product development. By having these necessary materials available, students will be encouraged to use their creative abilities. Requested materials might include

egg and milk cartons
aluminum foil
buttons
boxes (shoe, jewelry, etc.)
yogurt cups
ribbon
toilet paper tubes
wire coat hangers
nuts, bolts, screws
greeting cards
newspapers
clothespins
broken costume jewelry

cans (coffee, soup, etc.)
fabric scraps
plastic berry baskets
microwave meal trays
butter tubs
wrapping paper
paper towel tubes
packaging popcorn
colored paper scraps
old magazines
old keys
yarn/string
beads

Student _____

Date	Type of Product	Academic Subject	Grade Level/Teacher

Figure 5. Student Product Inventory

Product Resource Files

When students complete a product, they can take a photograph and write the directions and materials necessary for creating their product on a special form (see Figure 6). This form and photograph can be stored in a product resource file and used by other students to obtain ideas for new products. Students should be encouraged not merely to copy someone else's idea but to expand on it. How might they make that particular product better? How might they display information relating to the topic using a similar product?

Many of the products on the list may be unfamiliar to students, like a geodesic or triptych. Having a photograph and generic directions on how to create these unfamiliar products may assist students in better understanding what they are and how they are created.

"How To" Library

Having a library of books that describe how to create various products may further inspire students. Books designed for both students and professionals can be used to provide an abundance of information. A bibliography of several "How to" books is provided at the end of this chapter.

Internet Resources

There are many web sites that will assist students in developing products. Internet searches can be conducted to obtain information related to research and specific products. For example

holography	http://holo.com/holo/book/book1.html
family tree	http://www.genhomepage.com
web design	http://www.cnet.com/Content/Builder/Graphics/ Masters
animation	http://www.awn.com/

Such sites can provide an array of information with links to more resources that may not be found elsewhere. Students should perform Internet searches on the topics and product types as means of accumulating additional information for their endeavors.

Name: _____

Product: _____

Subject: _____

Materials: What You Need and Where to Get it!
                    What   Where
1.
2.
3.
4.
5.
6.

The Process: Procedures for Production
1.
2.
3.
4.
5.
6.
7.
8.
9.
10.

Comments:
        Pros:

        Cons:

        Advice:

        * Attach a photo of the product to this form *

Figure 6. Product Description

Computer Software

There is also an abundance of computer software that can assist students in the development of products. Software to make family trees, design multimedia presentations, learn origami, compose music, discover animation, and much more is available. Check your local computer supply store or preferred software catalog for the latest programs.

Summary

It is apparent that product development is an excellent way to encourage both creative and independent learning. Students can create original products to extend an idea or thought pertaining to a particular topic of interest. Students learn the value of flexibility when meeting time and material restraints during product construction. They engage in creative problem solving as they overcome obstacles during the process, and they learn that careful planning and organization can assist in making the product producing experience a positive one. Product development is an essential component in the gifted education program that assists in meeting the complex and advanced needs of gifted students as they become tomorrow's creative problem solvers and thinkers (Stephens, 1996).

Teacher Resources

Publications

Bauer, M. D. (1992). *What's your story?: A young person's guide to writing fiction.* New York: Houghton Mifflin.
Benjamin, S. (1996). *The public speaking handbook. Grades 8–12.* Glenview, IL: Goodyear Books.
Bentley, N., & Guthrie, D. (1996). *Putting on a play: The young playwright's guide to scripting, directing, and performing.* Brookfield, CT: Millbrook Press.

Chapman, G., & Robson, P. (1991). *Making books: A step-by-step guide to your own publishing.* Brookfield, CT: Millbrook Press.

Craig, D. (1993). *Making models.* Brookfield, CT: Millbrook Press.

Dearing, S. (1992). *Elegantly frugal costumes.* Colorado Springs, CO: Meriwether.

Draze, D., & Palouda, A. (1992). *Design studio.* San Luis Obispo, CA: Dandy Lion.

Everett, F., & Garbera, C. (1987). *Make your own jewelry.* London: Usbourne.

Gamble, K. (1994). *You can draw anything.* NSW, Australia: Allen & Unwin.

Gibbons, G. (1997). *Click: A book about cameras and taking pictures.* Boston, MA: Little, Brown & Company.

Gibson, R. (1993). *Masks.* London: Usbourne.

Gibson, R. (1995). *Paper mache.* London: Usbourne.

Gibson, R. (1995). *Stencil fun.* London: Usbourne.

Gibson, R. (1996). *Printing.* London: Usbourne.

Guthrie, D., Bentley, N., & Arnsteen, K. K. (1994). *The young author's do-it-yourself book.* Brookfield, CT: Millbrook Press.

Irvine, J. (1987). *How to make pop-ups.* New York: Beechtree Books.

Irvine, J. (1990). *Homemade holograms* . New York: TAB Books.

Karetnikova, I. (1990). *How scripts are made.* Carbondale, IL: Southern Illinois University Press.

Kronenwetter, M. (1995). *How to write a news article.* New York: Franklin Watts.

Lade, R. (1996). *The most excellent book of how to be a puppeteer.* Brookfield, CT: Millbrook Press.

Lightfoot, M. (1993). *Cartooning for kids.* Buffalo, NY: Firefly Books.

Needham, K. (1995). *Collecting things.* London: Usbourne.

Pearson, C. (1982). *Make your own games workshop.* Carthage, IL: Fearon Teacher Aids.

Pederson, T., & Moss, F. (1995). *Internet for kids: A beginner's guide to surfing the net.* Los Angeles, CA: Price Stern Sloan.

Phillips, K. (1995). *How to write a story.* New York: Franklin Watts.

Potter, T,. & Peach, S. (1987). *Graphic design.* London: Usbourne.

Provenzo, E. F., Provenzo, A. B., & Zorn, P. (1984). *Pursuing the past.* Menlo Park, CA: Addison Wesley.

Ryan, M. (1994). *How to give a speech.* New York: Franklin Watts.

Slafer, A., & Cahill, K. (1995). *Why design? Activities and projects from the national building museum.* Chicago: Chicago Review Press.

Wingate, P. (1996). *Projects for windows.* London: Usbourne.

Woods, H., Verboys, J., & Evans, G. (1990). *Lasers: Activities for the classroom.* Albany, NY: Delmar.

Addresses

The Center for Research on Evaluation, Standards,
and Student Testing
CRESST/UCLA
301 GSE&IS
Mailbox 951522
300 Charles E. Young Dr. N.
Los Angeles, CA 90095–1522
http://www.cresst96.cse.ucla.edu/index/htm

References

Atwood, B. (1974). *Building independent learning skills*. Palo Alto, CA: Learning Handbooks.

Baker, E. L., & Schacter J. (1996). Expert benchmarks for student academic performance: The case for gifted children. *Gifted Child Quarterly, 40*, 61–65.

Burnette, C., Norman, J. T., & Browning, K. (1997). *D-K12 designs for thinking*. Philadelphia: The University of the Arts.

Byrnes, P. A., & others. (1982, April). *Creative products scales-Detroit public schools*. Paper presented at the Annual International Convention of the Council for Exceptional Children, Houston, TX.

Davis, M., Hawley, P., McMullan, B., & Spilka, G. (1997). *Design as a catalyst for learning*. Alexandria, VA: Association for Supervision & Curriculum Development.

Feldhusen, J., & Kolloff, M. (1978). A three-stage model for gifted education. *Gifted Child Today, 1*, 53–58.

Forster, B. R. (1990). Let's build a sailboat: A differentiated gifted education project. *Teaching Exceptional Children, 22*(4), 40–42.

Gibbons, M. (1991). *How to become an expert: Discover, research, and build a project in your chosen field*. Tucson, AZ: Zephyr Press.

Karnes, F. A., & Riley, T. L. (1996). *Competitions: Maximizing your abilities*. Waco, TX: Prufrock Press.

Karnes, F. A., & Stephens, K. R. (2000). *The ultimate guide to student product development and evaluation*. Waco, TX: Prufrock Press.

Kettle, K. E., Renzulli, J. S., & Rizza, M. G. (1998). Products of mind: Exploring student preferences for product development using my way . . . an expression style inventory. *Gifted Child Quarterly, 42*, 49–60.

Maker, J. C., & Nielson, A. B. (1996). *Curriculum development and teaching strategies for gifted learners* (2nd ed.). Austin, TX: PRO-ED.

Renzulli, J. S. (1977). *The enrichment triad model: A guide for development defensible programs for the gifted and talented*. Mansfield Center, CT: Creative Learning Press.

Renzulli, J. S., & Reis, S. M. (1991). Building advocacy through program design, student productivity, and public relations. *Gifted Child Quarterly, 35*, 182–187.

Renzulli, J. S., Reis, S. M., & Smith, L. H. (1981). *The revolving door identification model*. Mansfield Center, CT: Creative Learning Press.

Stephens, K. R. (1996). Product development for gifted students: Formulation to reflection. *Gifted Child Today, 19*(6), 18–21.

Wiggins, G. (1996). Anchoring assessment with exemplars: Why students and teachers need models. *Gifted Child Quarterly, 40*, 66–69.

CHAPTER 7

Writing Units That Remove the Learning Ceiling

JULIA LINK ROBERTS
Western Kentucky University

RICHARD A. ROBERTS
Western Kentucky University

Rationale for Removing the Learning Ceiling

All children and youth can benefit from having the learning ceiling removed in order to become the best learners they can be. All children and youth must master basic skills and core content; yet, as they reach mastery, they need and deserve opportunities to continue learning at challenging levels. Learning experiences must be designed to make accommodations for each child to continuously progress, for a child cannot learn what he or she already knows. Yes, a teacher can teach what the child already knows, but a child cannot learn what he or she already knows. For all children to make continuous progress, learning experiences must be differentiated and the learning ceiling must be removed, allowing a student who is ready to learn at a more complex level and at a faster pace to continue learning each day.

All K–12 teachers have the responsibility to write and implement units that remove the learning ceiling, for the goal of teaching is to promote learning for all students, including those who are gifted and talented. Planning units that allow for continuous progress means expecting all students to perform academically at the highest level possible and providing opportunities for children who demonstrate readiness for advanced learning. All teachers must recognize that fairness is matching learning experiences to student need, rather than providing the same instruction for all.

Assessment is the key to knowing when it is appropriate and necessary to differentiate the curriculum. Prior to teaching a unit, teachers must assess what children know and are able to do. Otherwise, teachers may not know how much their students already know about the topic and assume that the assessment at the end of the unit revealed how much the students learned. Preassessment provides necessary information for teachers to plan challenging learning opportunities for all children who can demonstrate on the preassessment that they already know the core content and are ready to move on to more challenging learning experiences.

Support for differentiating instruction comes from the National Education Goals established at the 1989 Education Summit for Governors and the President in Charlottesville, VA, and later expanded from six to eight goals. Goal 3 in The National Education Goals specifies that, by 2000, American students will leave grades 4, 8, and 12 having demonstrated competency in challenging subject matter—including English, mathematics, science, foreign languages, civics and government, economics, arts, history, and geography; and every school in America will ensure that all students learn to use their minds well so they may be prepared for responsible citizenship, further learning, and productive employment in our nation's modern economy. What constitutes challenging subject matter will differ from student to student depending on what they already know and are able to do.

> These words are about excellence. Meeting them [the goals] will require that the performance of our highest achievers be boosted to levels that equal or exceed the performance of the best students anywhere. (U.S. Department of Education, 1991, p. 60)

To provide "challenging" subject matter requires differentiating so that the content and process match the different levels of readiness among children who are in the same age bracket. All children are not ready to achieve at the same high level and on the same time schedule any more than they are ready to wear the same size shoes when they reach a certain age. Teachers must address the needs of all children, including those who are gifted and talented in a specific academic content area or in all content areas (in the arts and humanities, as well as in social studies, mathematics, science, language arts, and foreign languages). Learning to use their minds well speaks to providing challenging levels of thinking and problem solving, as well as challenging content.

Prisoners of Time, the report released by the National Education Commission on Time and Learning in 1994, states that

> the strongest message this commission can send to the American people is that education must become a new national obsession as powerful as sports and entertainment, if we are to avoid a spiral of economic and social decline. (p. 10)

If the focus of schooling is on learning, flexibility must be built into planning and implementing instruction to accommodate children who require less time to learn and who need more challenging content if they are to reach their potential for high-level learning.

National Excellence: A Case for Developing America's Talent (U.S. Department of Education, 1993), the second national report on gifted and talented children and youth, emphasizes the importance of learning to work hard at challenging tasks. Winebrenner (1992) said that self-esteem is damaged by ongoing lack of challenge. When gifted students "rarely or never get to work on highly challenging tasks, they slowly lose confidence in their ability to take on difficult projects" (p. 8). Winebrenner (1999) stated "self-esteem actually is enhanced when success is attained at a task that has been perceived as difficult or challenging" (p. 13). Differentiating the curriculum for students who have already mastered much of the unit content prior to its implementation allows them to work hard at challenging academic tasks and enhance their self-esteem as capable learners.

Planning a Unit

If American students are to achieve the goals identified in Goals 2000, units of instruction must provide continuous progress for all students so that learning becomes a way of life, not an end-product. The teacher's focus for each unit must be on what students should know and be able to do, taking into account what students already know and are able to do prior to implementing the unit. Teachers must be knowledgeable of the content and be student-centered in order to plan and implement units that will be appropriately challenging for all students. What individual students know and are able to do in relation to the topic and content selected for the unit will guide the teacher in determining challenging learning experiences for individuals or clusters of students.

Before a school year begins, teachers should have an overview of the curriculum for the year, even though they often will design specific learning opportunities unit by unit. A unit does not imply a specific amount of time that will be needed, as some units may be planned for two weeks while others will need more time to optimize learning. Within a unit, the time to learn needed by individual students will differ; therefore, in planning the unit, the teacher must include options that allow all students to be challenged to work at high levels.

Model of the Relationship of Unit Components

The Model of the Relationship of Unit Components provides the broad overview for planning. The model (Figure 1) highlights the importance of the theme and generalizations that form the outer ring of the model, the unbroken ring encircling all other components. The universal theme and related generalizations provide the framework needed to develop a variety of topics within or across content areas. A theme and related generalizations encompass the topic and related content, the preassessment and postassessment, as well as all of the learning experiences. All of the components must relate to each other if the learning experiences are to be meaningful and appropriately challenging to the learners. If learning is to be maximized, unit planning will be focused on the

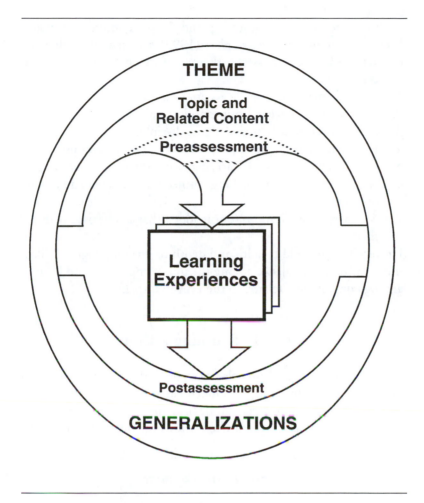

Figure 1. Model of the Relationship of Unit Components

components, and it will not be a loosely connected set of learning experiences.

A universal or broad-based theme maximizes the learning, for it can be used in various content areas to allow students to see how their learning in one context applies within other content areas or situations. They can see how learning inside school can apply to what they learn outside school and vice versa. Universal themes enhance the power of learning and help children and youth become life-long learners. Kaplan (1993) said that the following criteria can be used to assess a theme for its universal and broad-based nature:

1. Is the theme "universal" in its application?
2. Is the theme "timeless" in its application?
3. Is the theme equally usable across disciplines?
4. Is the theme appropriate for students across age groups?
5. Is the theme capable of "carrying" important information?
6. Is the theme useful in making connections between and among disciplines?
7. Are there generalizations (or big ideas) that can be used with the theme?

Universal themes add breadth and depth to learning. Figure 2 illustrates the need for balance among the unit components and balance among content areas related to the universal theme.

Steps in Planning a Unit

Either one of two starting places can be used to begin the planning process of a unit that can be differentiated. Selecting the universal theme or identifying the topic can be the appropriate starting place. If a universal theme is the point chosen for initiating the process, the

---

Steps in Unit Planning

1. Select a universal theme.
2. Develop generalizations related to the theme.
3. Identify the topic of study.
4. Identify core content and complex content related to the topic.
5. Design the postassessment or culminating activity.
6. Plan/identify preassessment strategies.
7. Design learning experiences incorporating content (core and complex content), process (basic and higher-level processes), and product (a variety of products).

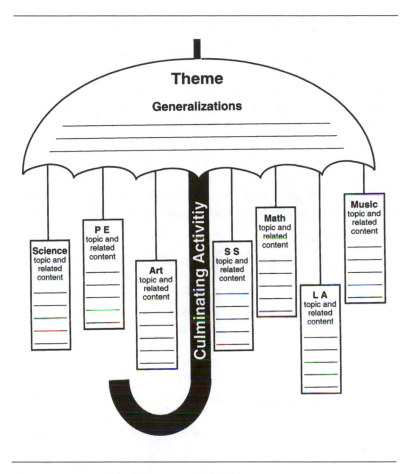

Theme

Generalizations

Science
topic and
related
content

P E
topic and
related
content

Art
topic and
related
content

Culminating Activitiy

S S
topic and
related
content

Math
topic and
related
content

L A
topic and
related
content

Music
topic and
related
content

**Figure 2. Picture of the Relationship
of Unit Components**

selection of the topic will come next. If the topic is chosen first, then it is important to next select a universal theme and develop the related generalizations. Both steps must be planned early in the unit-writing process to ensure that the unit maximizes the opportunities for learning. The topic and the universal theme work together to add power to units and remove the learning ceiling. Together, the topic and the universal theme provide criteria for the teacher to use when selecting and designing learning experiences for the unit.

The Universal Theme and Related Generalizations

A universal or broad-based theme is broader than a topic, and it must meet the following criteria. First, the theme must be applicable for the past, present, and future—not being place-bound. For example, the Roaring '20s and the age of dinosaurs are topics, not universal themes because they are limited by time and space. Second, the theme must be equally usable by teachers of all content areas, including mathematics, physical education, and the visual arts, without manufacturing content to fit into the "theme." Requiring all teachers to base instruction on a topic (often mistakenly called a theme) instead of a broad-based or

---

Examples of Universal Themes

Change
Patterns
Structures
Adaptation
Systems
Exploration
Power

---

universal theme, results in one or more teachers being forced to generate contrived learning experiences. For example, a physical education or math teacher has a difficult time developing meaningful learning activities on *bears* or *tropical rain forests*. A universal theme promotes interdisciplinary learning, and it establishes an optimum situation for differentiating learning opportunities. Finally, the universal theme is capable of carrying important information; generalizations can be developed that link major concepts to make statements about the universal theme.

Generalizations are statements related to the broad-based or universal themes. They are statements that will hold true across time and space. Generalizations allow interdisciplinary connections to be discovered by students or modeled by teachers as they can be applied to content across the disciplines and can be amplified as the student matures in his or her thinking.

Themes and generalizations empower learners when they are used by teachers across content areas over time. A universal theme can be used by a single teacher; however, the impact of the theme is greater when employed by a team of teachers, either by all the teachers at one grade level or by all the teachers in the school and rotated by the year. For example, *change* could be the

---

Example of a Universal Theme and Related Generalizations

CHANGE

1.   Change brings about change.
2.   Change can have positive and negative results.
3.   Change is universal.

There is no set number of generalizations. Teachers should develop generalizations that provide a broad view of the content for their students.

---

theme for the first school year, *patterns* for the next year, and *structures* for the third year. A schoolwide universal theme can be a powerful mechanism for enhancing interdisciplinary connection-making. A theme and related generalizations can be used for an entire year, but they also may be planned for shorter periods of time.

Some themes, while not universal, allow for the use of generalizations that are appropriate for a limited number of content areas. Examples of themes that are more applicable to one or a few rather than to all content areas are *revolutions, expression,* and *culture.* These themes differ from universal themes in that they are not equally applicable in all content areas, yet they are capable of carrying important information through their generalizations.

The Topic and Related Content

The topic describes the content of the unit in more specific terms. Examples of topics that are appropriate for various content areas at the elementary level include *basic machines, folk tales and legends, rhythm*

Sources of Content

1. Local curriculum guidelines
2. State curriculum frameworks or guidelines
3. National curriculum standards

---

and pitch, weather, and *multiplication.* Sample middle school topics include *ecosystems, state government, perspective,* and *probability.* High school topics are often the same topics that were learned during earlier school years; however, the topic is taught at a higher level and presupposes mastery at previous levels. For example, *social issues, chemical reactions, medical technology,* and *mathematical notation* are topics taught during high school. At all levels, topics are usually related to major concepts in specific disciplines. The power of topics to enhance student learning at all levels is increased when they are linked to universal themes, facilitating connections across disciplines.

Selecting the core and complex content follows the identification of the topic. The topic and the content of the unit come from three major sources: local curriculum guides, state curriculum frameworks or guidelines, and the national curriculum standards in mathematics, civics, history, geography, the arts, foreign languages, and science. Local and state curriculum documents are enhanced when used in conjunction with the Curriculum and Evaluation Standards for School Mathematics (National Council of Teachers of Mathematics, 1989), the National Standards for Civics and Government (Center for Civil Education, 1994), the National Standards for World History (National Council for History Standards, 1994c), the National Standards for American History (National Council for History Standards, 1994a; 1994b), the National Geography Standards (Geography Education Standards Project, 1994), the National

Standards for Arts Education (Consortium of National Arts Education, 1994), the National Science Education Standards (National Research Council, 1996), and the National Standards in Foreign Language Learning (National Standards in Foreign Language Education Project, 1996). Local, state, and national standards combine to provide the content to be considered when identifying topics and selecting the key content that will provide the focus of the unit.

As they have developed and issued curriculum standards, various professional organizations have responded to the call for high standards. These curriculum standards have spelled out the high-level content that should guide curriculum development.

The national standards in the various content areas are the benchmarks for which educators must plan. For all children, the national standards provide high standards that will require quality teaching if they are to be met. National standards provide the minimal standards for children who are gifted and talented. These standards should be in hand when planning curriculum, as they provide the bottom line for the level of content and process that must be mastered by students who can learn at complex levels and at rapid paces—students who are gifted and talented in specific academic areas, as well as those who are intellectually gifted. In line with the model presented in this chapter, preassessment for new units of instruction (related to the standards) will provide the needed information to indicate that differentiated learning experiences are needed in order for the student or clusters of students to continually progress.

Postassessment

Also encompassed by the universal theme and generalizations in Figure 1 is the postassessment, which may be a culminating activity or an exit exhibition. The postassessment should be planned after the topic and related content have been specified, and it should provide the opportunity for students to demonstrate the breadth of their learning during the unit in a context typical of real-life situations. It should be planned before designing learning experiences, for these experiences can be selected or developed to build skills and incorporate knowledge needed to successfully complete the culminating or exit activity. As a child learns to play a sport, he or she learns requisite skills one by one; however, the integration of knowledge and skills is necessary in order to play the sport well. The culminating activity requires a similar integration of what the student has learned and is able to do as a result of the learning experiences in the unit.

The postassessment or culminating activity is to the unit what a product is to the learning experience. In each case, the culminating activity and the product of the learning experience are the demon-

---

Example of a Culminating Activity

A student or group of students writes a play/short story that ties together what they have learned about the culture, politics, and history of ancient Rome.

---

stration of what the student knows and is able to do; however, the postassessment encompasses what the student knows and is able to do at the conclusion of the unit, rather than being the result of a single learning experience. The postassessment may be designed by the teacher or by the student(s). The activity may be a problem-solving task that requires integrating knowledge (content) and skill (process) into a demonstration of what a student or students working together in a cluster know and are able to do to solve the problem. A well-constructed essay exam can be an appropriate postassessment. A student or a cluster of students can design the culminating activity, a unique opportunity for students for whom the learning experiences have been differentiated in response to evidence that they already can meet the expectations of the core curriculum.

The Learning Experiences: Building Blocks of the Unit

Designing Learning Experiences

After the theme is chosen, the generalizations are identified, the topic and related content have been specified, and the culminating

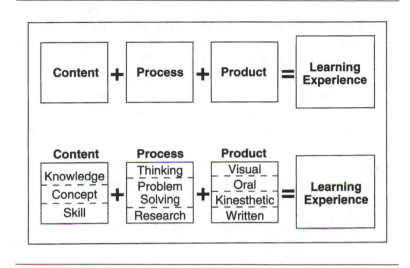

Figure 3. Elements of Learning Experiences

activity is planned, the next level of unit planning is the development of learning experiences. Learning experiences are the building blocks of units. Units contain numerous learning experiences, each of which is designed to teach important content, processes, and products. The Elements of Learning Experiences, as shown in Figure 3, illustrate how a learning experience is built by combining content, process, and product.

The content is what you want the students to know at the end of the unit. Related content includes the concepts and knowledge to be learned to reach unit learning goals. Content has been specified earlier in the unit planning process; each learning experience focuses on a concept or knowledge to be learned as the unit is implemented. If the concept to be taught is *the cell*, then the cell becomes the content of the learning experience. Teaching students how to produce a new or untried product can become the content for a learning experience. If the students have never produced a Venn diagram, the Venn diagram would be the content of the learning experience. If a new process skill is being introduced, that skill can become the content for that learning experience.

The process is the *what* the students are to be able to do. The process includes thinking, problem solving, and research skills. The national curriculum standards include process, as well as content within their standards. Although Bloom's (1984/1956) *Taxonomy of Educational Objectives* in the cognitive domain represents only one way of developing process skills, it is used within this model as the system for writing learning experiences at various levels. For example, on the level of knowledge/comprehension, the desired outcome of a learning experience could be to explain the functions of the various parts of the cell. At the analysis level, the student could learn to compare and contrast the structure of plant and animal cells.

Elements of a Learning Experience

Content:	Plant and Animal Cells
Process:	Analysis
Product:	Venn Diagram (visual/written)

Objective of the learning experience: The student will compare and contrast the structure of plant and animal cells producing a Venn diagram.

The product is the means used to demonstrate what one has learned. In other words, the product is how the teacher wants students to show what they know and are able to do as the result of being involved in the learning experience. Products may be visual, oral, kinesthetic, or written. Providing a balance in the types of products in learning experiences allows students the opportunity to show what they have learned in a preferred way or with a learning style that is a strength. Products that have been the traditional mainstays of the curriculum are papers (written), reports (oral or written), posters (visual), illustrations (visual), and laboratory experiments (kinesthetic). However, the possibilities for products are much broader than those most frequently used. In fact, a broad array of products can tap into student interests in learning.

Using different combinations of content, processes, and products allows teachers to create learning environments in which different needs of students can be addressed. A learning environment in which students have an element of choice and engage in learning experiences that are matched to their needs and interests is a positive one for teacher and students.

Differentiating Learning Experiences

In order to differentiate the content of learning experiences, the following three curriculum components must be in place:
1. The core content must be specified so that what all students should know and be able to do by the completion of the unit is public.
2. Strategies for ongoing assessment are planned in order to provide a solid rationale for compacting the curriculum and differentiating learning experiences.
3. Core and complex content, basic and higher-order processes, and a variety of products must be identified/developed in order to plan differentiated learning experiences to match the need and prior knowledge/experiences of students.

Because of their importance, each of these components will be discussed in more detail.

1. Identifying the core content in Step 4 of the unit planning sequence is necessary before proceeding with planning to differentiate learning experiences. It is not possible to plan to differentiate appropriately without specifying what all children in a particular grade and content area are expected to know and be able to do with the topic and related content by the conclusion of the unit of study. The core content must be specified so that what all students should know and be able to do by the completion of the unit is well understood. Planning the topic and related content at the core content level is a prerequisite for differentiating. Without this preplanning, there is no point of reference for compacting the curriculum. Likewise, it is difficult to know if the teacher and students reach the unit goals if they are not stated in advance.

Topics are usually large enough that teachers could go in numerous directions, and it is not possible to teach all content that could be tied to the topic. For example, a unit on the Civil War could be taught chronologically, or it could focus on battles, political events, or cultural history. Since it is possible to study the Civil War at the graduate level, during a two- or three-week unit, it is not possible for students to master all of the content on a meaningful level. Narrowing the topic and focusing the related content will provide the rationale for selecting/developing some learning experiences over others. Likewise, the universal theme and generalizations will facilitate making interdisciplinary connections and provide a criterion for designing learning experiences. For example, if the universal theme of change is used and generalizations include "change can be either good or bad" and "change brings about change," a learning activity that examines the Civil War in light of the generalizations could ask students to compare and contrast life on a plantation in a southern state before, during, and after the Civil War with a focus on change. Product choices could include a written diary or a series of illustrations. Thus, the learning experience is tied to the topic and core content, yet it also relates to the universal theme and generalizations. Learning is more powerful and long-lasting if it is consciously tied to a universal theme and related generalizations.

2. Strategies for ongoing assessment in Step 6 are planned in order to provide a solid rationale for compacting the curriculum and differentiating learning experiences. Without evidence from assessment, differentiating learning experiences for students will appear capricious, and the teacher will be subject to criticism. The purpose of differentiation is to match a learning experience to the need(s) of a student or a cluster of students for whom the learning experience is appropriately challenging. If everyone can complete the learning experiences planned for differentiation, then the learning experiences are not really appropriate for only some of the students, nor do they provide appropriately differentiated experiences. When assessment strategies demonstrate that the student already knows the content and is able to do what is expected at the conclusion of the unit, the rationale is provided for differentiating. Ongoing assessment can make it possible for all students to make continuous progress.

Preassessment is a critical element in unit planning. Different strategies for preassessment can provide variety and bring in information on students' prior knowledge and interests relative to the content.

Various assessment measures can be used to document what students know and what they need for differentiation, if the need exists.

Preassessment may take many forms. Four methods of preassessment are (1) using a pretest, the end-of-the-unit assessment given prior to teaching the unit; (2) asking the five most difficult questions to be learned in the unit before beginning the unit; (3) giving students the opportunity to design a mind map to visually share the information and the interrelationships they understand about the unit to be taught; and (4) providing the opportunity for students to individually tell/write what they already know about a topic and what they would like to know through a KW assessment or chart.

The pretest uses the end-of-the-unit assessment prior to beginning the unit and will reveal what students already know about the topic and provide the documentation of the need for differentiated learning experience. Another version of a pretest is to ask the five most difficult questions to be answered at the end of the unit (Winebrenner, 1992). A student who can answer the five most difficult questions that the unit is planned to teach prior to the teaching of the unit deserves to have alternate learning experiences. The teacher who is embarking on a unit on simple machines would have the opportunity to glean from students their responses to the five most difficult questions that the teacher plans to ask at the conclusion of the unit.

Preassessment measures may be constructing a mind map (Buzan, 1983) of the topic. A mind map provides the opportunity for the student to visually map out what he or she knows about the topic or focal subject matter of the unit, making connections between the major ideas or concepts. A mind map has some of the characteristics of webbing; however, the strategy depends upon using key words to detail what the student already knows about the topic. The mind map allows children who know a great deal about a topic to share the amount of information, as well as the experiences they have had, that relates to the topic or concept that will be studied. A mind map also allows the students to show the interrelationships they understand about the topic.

Another assessment measure that will show the need for differentiation is an individual KW Chart on which the student details what he or she knows (K) and wants to find out (W). Having the

- Pretest
- Five Most Difficult Questions
- Mind Map
- Individual KW Chart

student provide questions concerning what he or she wants to learn can provide a direction for differentiated learning opportunities. Students who are beginning a study of the Depression of the 1930s may be asked to make a KW Chart by listing what they already know about the Depression and what they would like to know about this period of history. With all four methods of preassessment above, the information allows students to bring in what they have learned about a topic in school and outside school. The value of the preassessment is the use the teacher makes of the information to allow individual students or clusters of students to learn more complex content and to have differentiated learning experiences based on what they already know and are able to do.

Planning for Differentiated Learning Experiences

- Identify/select the core content.
- Assess student knowledge of core content.
- Identify/plan core and complex content, basic and higher-level processes, and a variety of products.

3. Learning experiences are designed by combining content, process, and product. During planning, core and complex content, basic and higher-order processes, and a variety of products must be identified and developed in order to provide differentiated learning experiences. Learning experiences can be differentiated on one, two, or all three dimensions—content, process, and product. Complex content includes abstract concepts, issues and problems, and advanced

knowledge related to the core content, universal themes, and related generalizations. Complex/abstract content related to the core content allows students to continue learning about the same topic or universal theme with the rest of the class; however, it elevates the level of the content to match the student's or students' advanced knowledge of the content and readiness to process the information at higher levels.

Differentiated learning experiences must be appropriately matched to the student(s)' readiness to learn more complex content, use higher-level processes to demonstrate what they have learned, and develop a wide range of products. The same students may not always need differentiation in all subjects or in all topics within a content area. If preassessment documents that the core content is known at the 80% level or above, the content needs to be compacted to include differentiated learning experiences with a focus on complex content.

> Differentiated learning experiences use a variety of products that require the application of higher-level processes to complex content related to the topic and core content.

More and more states (for example, Kentucky) are specifying core content that requires thinking and problem solving for all children. Goals 2000, as mentioned previously, states that all children will learn to use their minds well. The national curriculum standards include content and process standards that all children and youth should reach before exiting grades 4, 8, and 12. Since thinking and problem solving are expectations for all children, more complex and challenging experiences must be available for children who have mastered them. The content for those gifted students who are ready for differentiated learning experiences must be complex, providing for continuous progress and the development of their academic capabilities. A variety of products can be used to demonstrate mastery of complex content.

To facilitate the planning process, the Planning Form for Learning Experiences was developed (Figure 4). The form can be used to plan differentiated learning experiences with core content and complex content. The planning form allows the planner to see the theme and related generalizations, as well as the topic and relat-

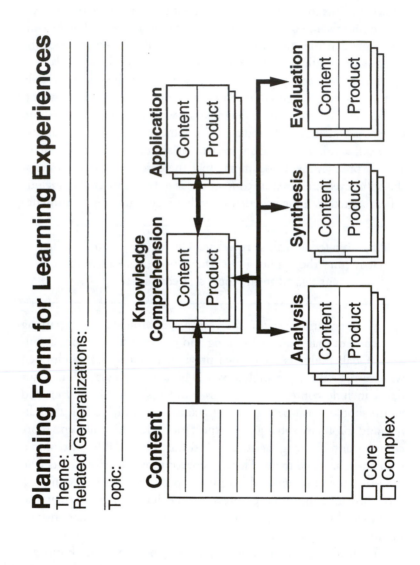

Figure 4. Planning Form for Learning Experiences

ed content, as he or she designs learning activities. The layering of the learning experiences boxes suggests that numerous learning experiences can be developed in relationship to the content. A check in the content area box allows for using the same planning form for differentiated learning experiences with core or complex content.

It should be noted that the process skills of knowledge, comprehension, application, analysis, synthesis, and evaluation are not arranged in the usual linear hierarchy. Instead, knowledge and comprehension form the foundation for all other process skills. A student cannot apply, analyze, synthesize, or evaluate using criteria without knowledge of the topic. Starting with knowledge and comprehension, learning experiences can be developed that require students to utilize the full range of process skills while addressing core and complex content.

Sample units provide examples of the finished product resulting from the steps described in this chapter. The completed planning forms for topical units on Ancient Egypt (middle school) in Figure 5, the Rain Forest (intermediate) in Figure 6, and Patterns (primary) in Figure 7 illustrate how the core learning experiences are planned in relationship to the universal themes and related generalizations. Examples of differentiated learning experiences with complex content show how the planning form can be used to remove the learning ceiling. The layered boxes on the form indicate that there can be several learning experiences at each level with the same content but with a variety of products. The examples can be expanded to provide more student choice and to take the learning into greater depth.

The sample units illustrate how differentiation can be planned for individual students or clusters of students based on information from the preassessment. They also show how learning experiences can be matched to needs, interests, and abilities. Not all children need to complete all learning experiences; rather, the match is the key to removing the learning ceiling. All children, including those who are gifted and talented, need challenging learning experiences in all content areas on an ongoing basis. They need to have the floor to learning raised and the ceiling removed.

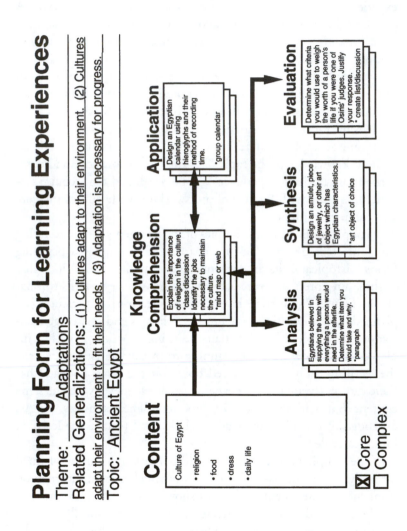

Figure 5. Example of Completed Planning Form
for Learning Experiences

Planning Form for Learning Experiences

Theme: Adaptations

Related Generalizations: (1) Cultures adapt to their environment. (2) Cultures adapt their environment to fit their needs. (3) Adaptation is necessary for progress.

Topic: Ancient Egypt

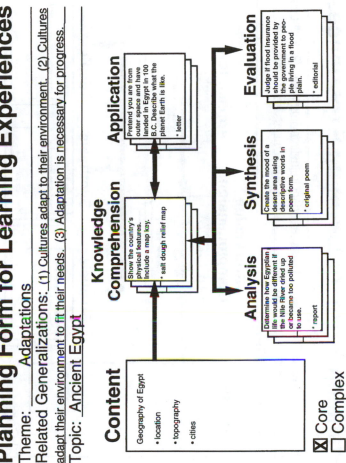

Content

Geography of Egypt
- location
- topography
- cities

☒ Core
☐ Complex

Knowledge Comprehension

Show the country's physical features. Include a map key.

• salt dough relief map

Application

Pretend you are from outer space and have landed in Egypt in 100 B.C. Describe what the planet Earth is like.

• letter

Analysis

Determine how Egyptian life would be different if the Nile River dried up or became too polluted to use.

• report

Synthesis

Create the mood of a desert area using descriptive words in poem form.

• original poem

Evaluation

Judge if flood insurance should be provided by the government to people living in a flood plain.

• editorial

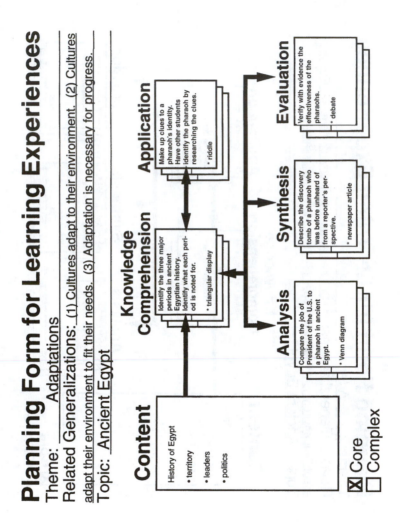

Planning Form for Learning Experiences

Theme: ___Adaptations___

Related Generalizations: ___(1) Cultures adapt to their environment. (2) Cultures adapt their environment to fit their needs. (3) Adaptation is necessary for progress.___

Topic: ___Ancient Egypt___

Content

History of Egypt

- territory
- leaders
- politics

☒ Core
☐ Complex

Knowledge Comprehension

Identify the three major periods in ancient Egyptian history. Identify what each period is noted for.

* triangular display

Application

Make up clues to a pharaoh's identity. Have other students identify the pharaoh by researching the clues.

* riddle

Analysis

Compare the job of President of the U.S. to a pharaoh in ancient Egypt.

* Venn diagram

Synthesis

Describe the discovery tomb of a pharaoh who was before unheard of from a reporter's perspective.

* newspaper article

Evaluation

Verify with evidence the effectiveness of the pharaohs.

* debate

Figure 5. Continued

Planning Form for Learning Experiences

Theme: Adaptations

Related Generalizations: (1) Cultures adapt to their environment. (2) Cultures adapt their environment to fit their needs. (3) Adaptation is necessary for progress.

Topic: Ancient Egypt

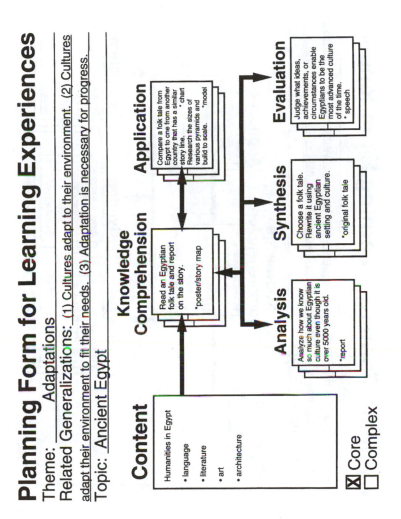

Content

Humanities in Egypt

- language
- literature
- art
- architecture

☒ Core
☐ Complex

Knowledge
Comprehension

Read an Egyptian folk tale and report on the story.

*poster/story map

Application

Compare a folk tale from Egypt to one from another country that has a similar story line.   *chart
Research the sizes of various pyramids and build to scale.   *model

Analysis

Analyze how we know so much about Egyptian culture even though it is over 5000 years old.

*report

Synthesis

Choose a folk tale. Rewrite it using ancient Egyptian setting and culture.

*original folk tale

Evaluation

Judge what ideas, achievements, or circumstances enable Egyptians to be the most advanced culture of the time.

*speech

Planning Form for Learning Experiences

Theme: __Adaptations__

Related Generalizations: __(1) Cultures adapt to their environment. (2) Cultures__
__adapt their environment to fit their needs. (3) Adaptation is necessary for progress.__

Topic: __Ancient Egypt__

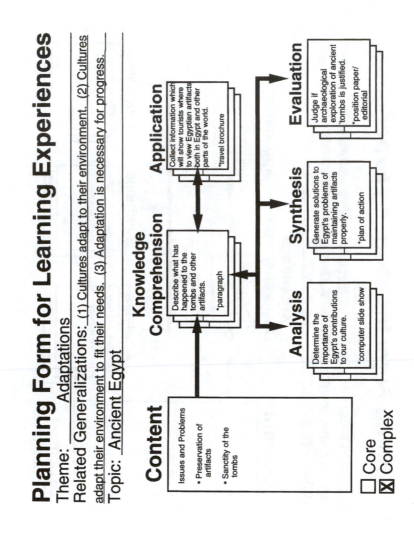

Figure 5. Continued

Planning Form for Learning Experiences

Theme: Adaptations

Related Generalizations: (1) Cultures adapt to their environment. (2) Cultures adapt their environment to fit their needs. (3) Adaptation is necessary for progress.

Topic: Ancient Egypt

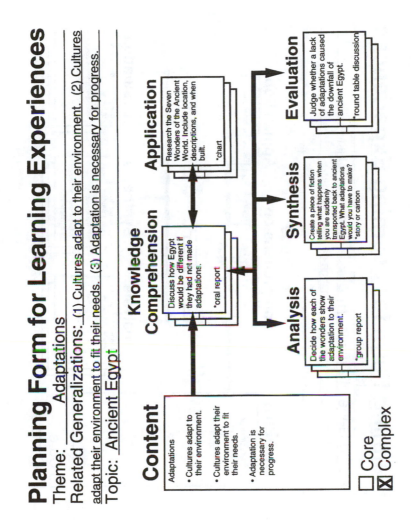

Content

Adaptations

- Cultures adapt to their environment.
- Cultures adapt their environment to fit their needs.
- Adaptation is necessary for progress.

Knowledge Comprehension

Discuss how Egypt would be different if they had not made adaptations.

*oral report

Application

Research the Seven Wonders of the Ancient World. Include location, descriptions, and when built.

*chart

Analysis

Decide how each of the wonders show adaptation to their environment.

*group report

Synthesis

Create a piece of fiction telling what happens when you are suddenly transported back to ancient Egypt. What adaptations would you have to make?

*story or cartoon

Evaluation

Judge whether a lack of adaptations caused the downfall of ancient Egypt.

*round table discussion

☐ Core
☒ Complex

Planning Form for Learning Experiences

Theme: Change

Related Generalizations: (1) Change can be good or bad.

(2) Change is continuous. (3) Change causes change.

Topic: Rain Forest

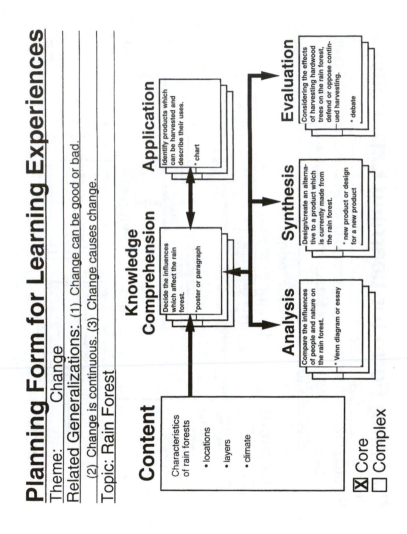

Content

Characteristics of rain forests

• locations
• layers
• climate

Knowledge Comprehension

Decide the influences which affect the rain forest.

• poster or paragraph

Application

Identify products which can be harvested and describe their uses.

• chart

Analysis

Compare the influences of people and nature on the rain forest.

• Venn diagram or essay

Synthesis

Design/create an alternative to a product which is currently made from the rain forest.

• new product or design for a new product

Evaluation

Considering the effects of harvesting hardwood trees on the rain forest, defend or oppose continued harvesting.

• debate

☒ Core
☐ Complex

**Figure 6. Example of Completed Planning Form
for Learning Experiences**

Planning Form for Learning Experiences

Theme: Change

Related Generalizations: (1) Change can be good or bad.
(2) Change is continuous. (3) Change causes change.

Topic: Rain Forest

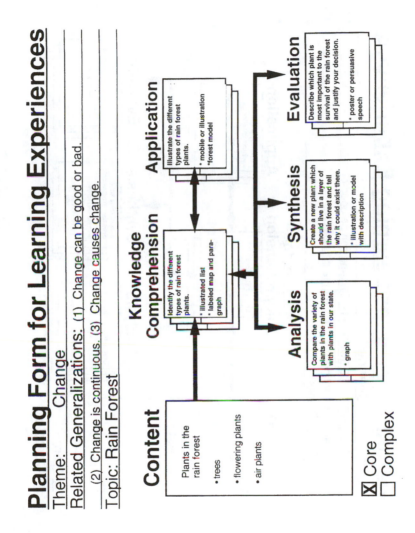

Content

Plants in the rain forest

• trees

• flowering plants

• air plants

Knowledge Comprehension

Identify the different types of rain forest plants.

* Illustrated list
* labeled map and paragraph

Application

Illustrate the different types of rain forest plants.

* mobile or illustration
*forest model

Analysis

Compare the variety of plants in the rain forest with plants in our state.

* graph

Synthesis

Create a new plant which should live in a layer of the rain forest and tell why it could exist there.

* illustration or model with description

Evaluation

Describe which plant is most important to the survival of the rain forest and justify your decision.

* poster or persuasive speech

☒ Core
☐ Complex

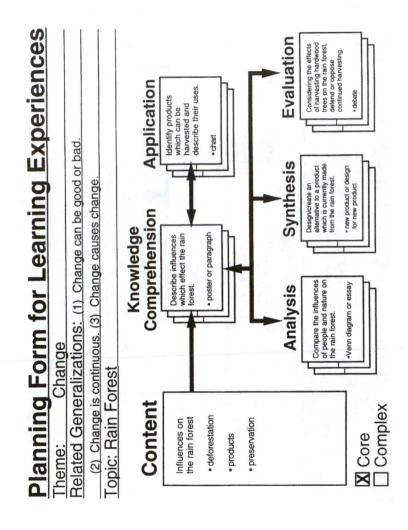

Planning Form for Learning Experiences

Theme: Change

Related Generalizations: (1) Change can be good or bad.
(2) Change is continuous. (3) Change causes change.

Topic: Rain Forest

Content

Influences on the rain forest

- deforestation
- products
- preservation

Knowledge Comprehension

Describe influences which effect the rain forest.

- poster or paragraph

Application

Identify products which can be harvested and describe their uses.

- chart

Analysis

Compare the influences of people and nature on the rain forest.

- Venn diagram or essay

Synthesis

Design/create an alternative to a product which is currently made from the rain forest.

- new product or design for new product

Evaluation

Considering the effects of harvesting hardwood trees on the rain forest, defend or oppose continued harvesting.

- debate

☒ Core
☐ Complex

Figure 6. Continued

Planning Form for Learning Experiences

Theme: Change

Related Generalizations: (1) Change can be good or bad.
(2) Change is continuous. (3) Change causes change.

Topic: Rain Forest

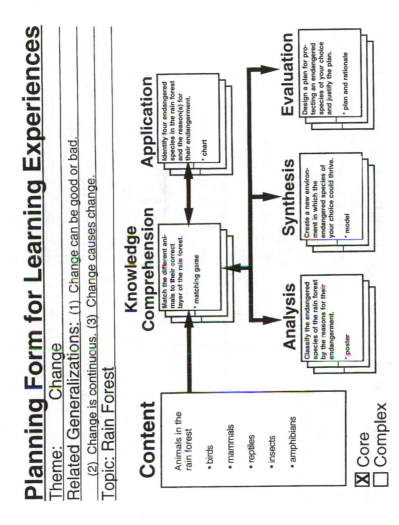

Content

Animals in the rain forest
- birds
- mammals
- reptiles
- insects
- amphibians

☒ Core
☐ Complex

Knowledge Comprehension

Match the different animals to their correct layer of the rain forest.
- matching game

Application

Identify four endangered species in the rain forest and the reason(s) for their endangerment.
- chart

Analysis

Classify the endangered species of the rain forest by the reasons for their endangerment.
- poster

Synthesis

Create a new environment in which the endangered species of your choice could thrive.
- model

Evaluation

Design a plan for protecting an endangered species of your choice and justify the plan.
- plan and rationale

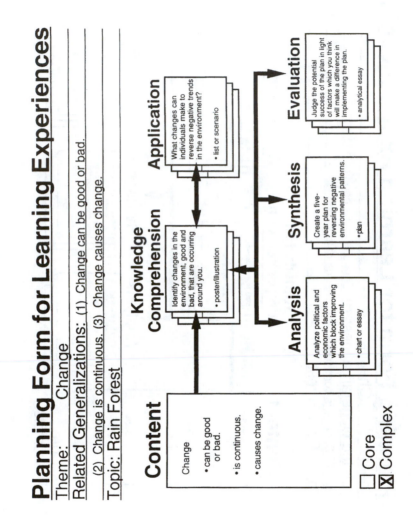

Planning Form for Learning Experiences

Theme: Change

Related Generalizations: (1) Change can be good or bad.

(2) Change is continuous. (3) Change causes change.

Topic: Rain Forest

Content

Change
- can be good or bad.
- is continuous.
- causes change.

Knowledge Comprehension

Identify changes in the environment, good and bad, that are occurring around you.
- poster/illustration

Application

What changes can individuals make to reverse negative trends in the environment?
- list or scenario

Analysis

Analyze political and economic factors which block improving the environment.
- chart or essay

Synthesis

Create a five-year plan for reversing negative environmental patterns.
- plan

Evaluation

Judge the potential success of the plan in light of factors which you think will make a difference in implementing the plan.
- analytical essay

☐ Core
☒ Complex

Figure 6. Continued

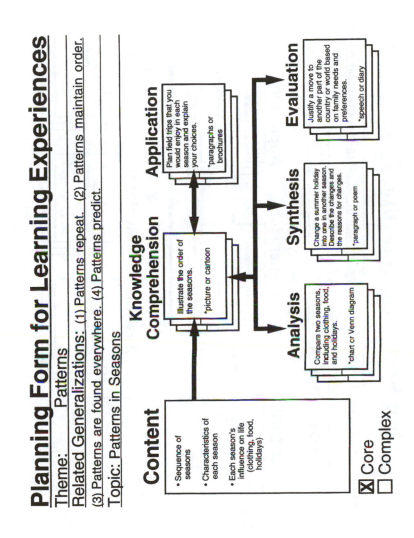

Figure 7. Example of Completed Planning Form
for Learning Experiences

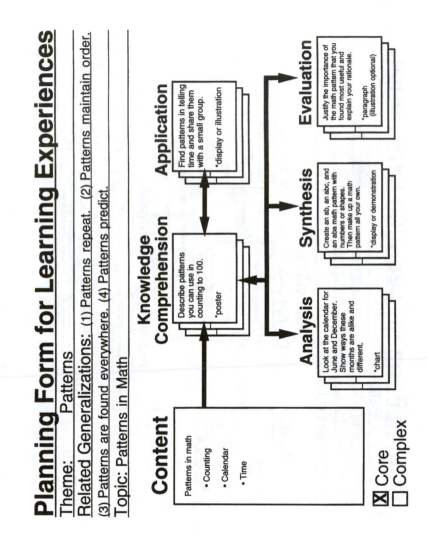

Planning Form for Learning Experiences

Theme: Patterns

Related Generalizations: (1) Patterns repeat. (2) Patterns maintain order.

(3) Patterns are found everywhere. (4) Patterns predict.

Topic: Patterns in Math

Content

Patterns in math
- Counting
- Calendar
- Time

☒ Core
☐ Complex

Knowledge Comprehension

Describe patterns you can use in counting to 100.

*poster

Application

Find patterns in telling time and share them with a small group.

*display or illustration

Analysis

Look at the calendar for June and December. Show ways these months are alike and different.

*chart

Synthesis

Create an ab, an abc, and an aba math pattern with numbers or shapes. Then make up a math pattern all your own.

*display or demonstration

Evaluation

Justify the importance of the math pattern that you found most useful and explain your rationale.

*paragraph (illustration optional)

Figure 7. Continued

Planning Form for Learning Experiences

Theme: Patterns

Related Generalizations: (1) Patterns repeat. (2) Patterns maintain order.

(3) Patterns are found everywhere. (4) Patterns predict.

Topic: Patterns in Families

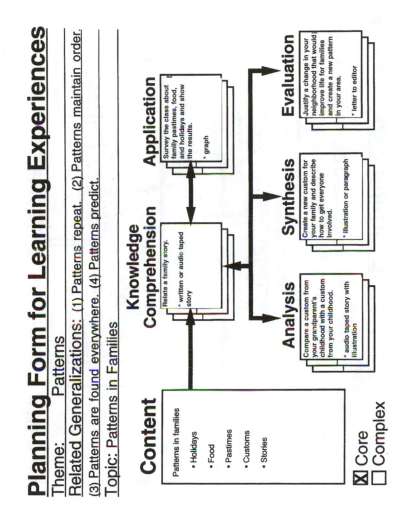

Content

Patterns in families

• Holidays
• Food
• Pastimes
• Customs
• Stories

☒ Core
☐ Complex

Knowledge Comprehension

Relate a family story.

• written or audio taped story

Application

Survey the class about family pastimes, food, and holidays and show the results.

• graph

Analysis

Compare a custom from your grandparent's childhood with a custom from your childhood.

• audio taped story with illustration

Synthesis

Create a new custom for your family and describe how to get everyone involved.

• illustration or paragraph

Evaluation

Justify a change in your neighborhood that would improve life for families and create a new pattern in your area.

• letter to editor

Planning Form for Learning Experiences

Theme: Patterns

Related Generalizations: (1) Patterns repeat. (2) Patterns maintain order. (3) Patterns are found everywhere. (4) Patterns predict.

Topic: Patterns

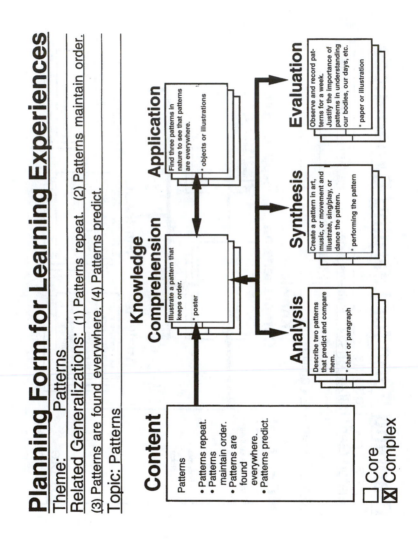

Content

Patterns

- Patterns repeat.
- Patterns maintain order.
- Patterns are found everywhere.
- Patterns predict.

Knowledge Comprehension

Illustrate a pattern that keeps order.

* poster

Application

Find three patterns in nature to see that patterns are everywhere.

* objects or illustrations

Analysis

Describe two patterns that predict and compare them.

* chart or paragraph

Synthesis

Create a pattern in art, music, or movement and illustrate, sing/play, or dance the pattern.

* performing the pattern

Evaluation

Observe and record patterns for a week. Justify the importance of patterns in understanding our bodies, our days, etc.

* paper or illustration

☐ Core
☒ Complex

Figure 7. Continued

Teacher Resources

Publications

Center for Gifted Studies. (1996). *Incorporating broad-based thematic units into the curriculum*. [Videotape]. Bowling Green, KY: Western Kentucky University.

Center for Gifted Studies. (1996). *Opening up the curriculum: Getting rid of the ceiling*. [Videotape]. Bowling Green, KY: Western Kentucky University.

Clarke, C. L., & Agne, R. M. (1997). *Interdisciplinary high school teaching: Strategies for integrated learning*. Needham Heights, MA: Allyn & Bacon.

Kaplan, S. N. (1993). *Developing thematic interdisciplinary curriculum for middle schools*. Bowling Green, KY: Western Kentucky University.

Paul, T., & Knickelbine, M. (1997, September). A new look at "higher-order" thinking and literature-based reading. *Advantage, 4*.

Samara, J., & Curry, J. (1994). *Developing units for primary students*. Bowling Green, KY: Kentucky Association for Gifted Education.

Shelton, K. (1996). *Rain forest*. [Unit]. Unpublished manuscript. Western Kentucky University.

Shuttlesworth, J. (1996). *Ancient Egypt*. [Unit]. Unpublished manuscript. Western Kentucky University.

VanTassel-Baska. J. (Ed.). (1998). *Excellence in educating gifted and talented learners*. Denver, CO: Love.

Web Sites

National Curriculum Standards—http://www.putwest.boces.org/Standards.html

References

Bloom, B. S. (Ed.). (1984). *Taxonomy of educational objectives: Cognitive domain.* Handbook I. New York: Longman. [Originally published in 1956]

Buzan, T. (1983). *Use both sides of your brain.* New York: E. P. Dutton.

Consortium of National Arts Education Associations. (1994). *National standards for arts education: What every young American should know and be able to do in the arts.* Reston, VA: Music Educators National Conference.

Center for Civic Education. (1994). *National standards for civics and government.* Calabasas, CA: Center for Civic Education.

Geography Education Standards Project. (1994). *National geography standards: Geography for life.* Washington, DC: National Geographic Society.

Kaplan, S. N. (1993). *Developing thematic interdisciplinary curriculum for middle schools.* Bowling Green, KY: Western Kentucky University.

National Council for History Standards. (1994a). *National standards for United States history: Expanding children's world in time and space, grades K–4.* Los Angeles: National Center for History in the Schools.

National Council for History Standards. (1994b). *National standards for United States history: Exploring the American experience, grades 5–12.* Los Angeles: National Center for History in the Schools.

National Council for History Standards. (1994c). *National standards for world history: Exploring paths to the present, grades 5–12.* Los Angeles: National Center for History in the Schools.

National Council of Teachers of Mathematics Commission on Standards for School Mathematics. (1989). *Curriculum and evaluation standards for school mathematics.* Reston, VA: National Council of Teachers of Mathematics.

National Education Commission on Time and Learning. (1994). *Prisoners of time.* Washington, DC: Author.

National Education Goals Panel (1997). National education goals report: *Executive summary: Mathematics and science achievement for the 21st Century.* Washington, DC: Government Printing Office.

National Research Council. (1996). *National science education standards.* Washington, DC: National Academy Press.

National Standards in Foreign Language Education Project. (1996). *Standards for foreign language learning: Preparing for the 21st century.* Yonkers, NY: National Standards in Foreign Language Education Project.

U.S. Department of Education. (1991). *America 2000: An education strategy.* Washington, DC: Author.

U.S. Department of Education. (1993). *National excellence: A case for developing America's talent.* Washington, DC: Office of Educational Research and Improvement.

Winebrenner, S. (1992). *Teaching gifted kids in the regular classroom.* Minneapolis, MN: Free Spirit Press.

Winebrenner, S. (1999). Shortchanging the gifted. *The School Administrator, 56*(9), *12–16.*

CHAPTER 8

Evaluating Learner and Program Outcomes in Gifted Education

CAROLYN M. CALLAHAN
University of Virginia

Educators committed to providing the highest quality programs for gifted students cannot neglect the process of evaluation. Collecting sound information about the short-term outcomes of on-going instruction and about the more long-term goals and objectives of services offered to our gifted students is critical for good decision making. Educators who plan and administer programs for gifted students need to systematically collect data about all aspects of their instructional programming to help determine those aspects of educational services that positively contribute to excellence in individual accomplishment of students and those practices that detract from maximum achievement.

The Importance of Assessing Learning Outcomes

The literature on assessment provides evidence that assessment data is useful in two critical ways in the instructional

253

process. First, theorists and researchers have shown that the most effective instruction will occur when learning activities are at a level where the learner is not quite capable of doing the task automatically or without effort, including the attainment of new knowledge and slightly more advanced skills and understanding. Yet, the learning activity must not be so difficult that the learner perceives the task is beyond reach. The difference between what a child can do on his or her own and what can be accomplished with a little assistance is called "the zone of proximal development" (Vygotsky, 1986/1934). Vygotsky believed instruction should be aimed slightly beyond what children currently know and can do. Hence, in order to fashion appropriate curriculum for any group of children, teachers must gather information about the current state of the learners' expertise.

For gifted students, this process is critical because they are likely to be out of the normative range of their age or grade peers. That is, teachers cannot rely on traditional assumptions about the developmental accomplishments or curricular achievements of fourth graders as a guide to the appropriate instructional level for gifted fourth graders. Similarly, teachers cannot make the mistake of assuming that all gifted students of the same age level are alike or that a particular gifted student is equally advanced across all disciplines or potential talent domains. In preparing instructional activities for gifted students, teachers of gifted students must recognize the great variability in achievement and aptitude across gifted students and within the individual gifted child.

Educators also cannot assume that an instructional activity or series of activities will be equally successful with all gifted students. Hence, making accurate judgments about student achievement in response to any curricular activity provides essential information about the success of instruction and about the current level of knowledge, skill, and understanding that is critical to inform the next stage of instruction. It provides essential information about the success of instructional interventions with individual students and across groups of gifted children in achieving the intended goals and objectives using the specified curriculum and instructional practices (and, perhaps, unintended outcomes as well). Thus, evaluation information provides critical data about what to teach next to an individual gifted child and to groups of gifted children.

Finally, students are entitled to feedback about their growth and achievements in response to the learning activities and in relation to expected outcomes and levels of performance. The establishment of procedures that provide students with information about what they have achieved, where their areas of strengths and weaknesses lie, and how their performance relates to standards of excellence serve to inform students of those standards and to reward efforts to achieve expertise.

The Importance of Evaluating Programs for Gifted Students

The evaluation of learning outcomes is a critical component of program evaluation. The major stakeholders in education programs (the identified gifted students, their parents, the funding agencies, the teachers, the administrators, and so forth) are all interested in the degree to which program expenditures (including student time, teacher effort, money, and so forth) result in student learning and achievement that would not be possible without the program.

Learner outcomes are important, but they represent only one aspect that we must look at in evaluating programs or services for the gifted. Program excellence can only be verified through the collection of data which demonstrates that the many goals and objectives of the program, including learner outcomes, have been achieved. Have the screening and identification procedures been fair, effective, and efficient in identifying all of the gifted and talented students? Do regular classroom teachers allow for development of full potential and demonstration of a wide range of talents? Are goals and objectives for gifted programs clearly specified at the district and classroom level? Are teachers well prepared to meet the needs of gifted students? Does the curriculum represent the most current theory and research about appropriate differentiation for the gifted? To what degree is the instructional program successful in helping gifted students achieve program goals and objectives?

Answers to these questions and others relating to the quality of all dimensions of gifted services are critical in ensuring that educators are making the best use of resources. The process of program evaluation can be used to answer these questions accurately and can make it possible to validate those components of a program that are working and to modify those that are not. That is, a carefully planned program evaluation will help administrators and teachers plan and modify services to gifted students that are more likely to deliver expected outcomes.

Unfortunately, in the process of developing or modifying programs for gifted students and in the development of curricular frameworks and instructional practice, the process of planning for evaluation is often an afterthought or is not given concentrated attention. If administrators fail to collect the kinds of evidence necessary to provide students with complete and accurate pictures of their accomplishments, if educators fail to examine the degree to which their instructional efforts have been successful, and if they hesitate in documenting the outcomes of programmatic efforts, then they will fail to provide the highest quality programs to gifted students. Neglecting to plan for accurate data gathering at the time program frameworks, curricula, and instructional strategies are developed may lead to missed opportunities to collect the most significant and meaningful information or may result in the failure to collect complete and necessary information.

Assessment of Learner Outcomes

Evaluation of learner outcomes serves many purposes. It provides students and their parents with information about the quantity and quality of student learning and performance; it serves as a basis for assessing the effectiveness of instruction; it is one variable to consider in future instructional planning; and it is a critical cornerstone of good program evaluation. In order for the assessment of program learner outcomes to be meaningfully interpreted, educators must carefully plan the evaluation process beginning with well articulated goals and objectives at the program, curricular, and daily lesson level. Of course, there are often unintended outcomes (positive and negative) which cannot be anticipated, but evaluation must begin with a clear sense of expectations for learning.

One of the most difficult tasks for teachers and other educators in the field of gifted education is the specification of the expected outcomes of instruction. However, to assess the degree to which an instructional activity or a curricular unit has been successful, educators must be able to specify the ways in which they expect the learner to be different as a result of the instructional experience. The levels of specificity of outcomes range from broad, general, and long-term statements of expectations as goals to specific activity-guiding objectives for the teachers to use on a daily basis. We must be able to specify what students will be expected to know, understand, and do as a result of the experiences provided by the instructional program.

Sources of Program Goal Statements Relating to Learner Outcomes

Many of the models proposed for developing programs or curriculum for gifted students have explicitly stated goals and many other implied goals. For example, a program basing its instruction on the Schoolwide Enrichment Model would be expected to have learner outcomes such as

- The student will demonstrate independent learning skills and self-directedness in planning and carrying out one or more investigative projects.
- The student will identify and develop the skills necessary to pursue his/her investigative problem (e.g., calculator, computer, scientific machines).
- The student will demonstrate advanced levels of competency in communication skills that reflect appropriate modes of expressing the results of their investigative and creative work. Such communication will take the form of various types of writing performances, constructions, and any or all additional forms of artistic expression. (Renzulli & Reis, 1985, p. 165)

Programs based on the Autonomous Learner Model would include objectives such as

- Students will comprehend the dynamics of the group process.
- Students will be able to apply the dynamics of group process to their environment (Betts, 1986, p. 39).

Specific curricular units developed using particular models should reflect the overall goals of the model or program but should also provide more specific assessment guidelines. For example, a unit based on Kaplan's model includes the following specific objective:

> Students will define, explain, and exemplify the statement that systems follow rules, procedures, and an order by studying the communications system of writing, the ecological system of the rain forest, the governmental system of how a bill becomes a law, and the mathematical system of measurement. (California Department of Education, 1994, p. 11–12)

Or, a program focusing on Renzulli's Enrichment Triad Model might elect to specify certain outcomes of Type II activities (process skill development) during a given time period. For example, the teachers might focus on objectives such as

- The students are able to generate clear, researchable, correctly-worded hypotheses.
- The students are able to discriminate between primary and secondary sources.
- The students are able to evaluate the relative reliability and validity of historical documents.

Programs not based on specific models must generate their own goals and objectives. One program might operate from a set of outcomes such as

- The students will exhibit improved critical thinking skills and problem-solving skills;
- The students will demonstrate greater independent learning;
- The students will produce products that represent excellence and creative productivity;
- The students will demonstrate greater self-esteem;
- The students will demonstrate positive attitudes toward school and excellence in learning; and

- The students will demonstrate in-depth understanding of the epistemology of at least one discipline (Callahan & Caldwell, 1993).

However, whether the program is directed by goals specified by model-developers or by goals and objectives that emanate from the administrators or teachers, outcomes specified for learners should come from both the cognitive and affective domains.

Content, Process, and Product Outcomes— The Cognitive Dimension

Content Assessment

Three dimensions are critical in the evaluation of student outcomes for gifted students. The first of these is the content dimension. While the dimensions of process, product, and content should be integrated in the instructional plan and can be most efficiently and effectively evaluated in a single product, they are separated here for ease of discussion only. There are also occasions when it is appropriate to assess the dimensions separately. These occasions would include attempts to assess the ways in which particular aspects of the instructional process have been effective in achieving goals in one of the domains. However, it is usually more efficient to measure them as they are integrated in our thinking and production processes.

Outcome evaluation will be more valid if the teacher is able to specify the aspects of content, process, and product to be evaluated. The examples that have been given thus far have suggested specific content. Within the example from the Kaplan model, the content to be assessed would come from the areas of mathematics, ecology, government, and communication. The teacher would identify the specific concepts, principles, and generalizations that would be taught and assessed.

Content objectives from the specific disciplines are available from recently developed compendia developed as part of the National Standards projects in mathematics (National Council of Teachers of Mathematics, 1993), science (National Research

Council, 1995; American Association for Science Literacy, 1993), social studies (National Council for History in the Schools, 1995), and the arts (Consortium of National Arts Education Associations, 1994). The highest levels of learning described by the documents reflect the discipline outcomes appropriate for gifted learners. Gifted programs based on both enrichment and acceleration models can easily find specific outcomes statements to serve as standards for assessing learner performance.[1] These references also indicate the ways in which content should be acted upon by learners to help them incorporate the content effectively into their cognitive structures, make meaning of the learning, apply content to meaningful situations, and extend their use of content to create new ideas and products. This leads to the second domain of assessment, process assessment.

Process Assessment

Within the process dimension-developers of curriculum for gifted learners should consider the domains of accomplishment relating to the application of skills of critical thinking, creative thinking, problem solving, and similar functions of thinking. Educators need to determine the accomplishments of students in the realm of making sense of and evaluating the new knowledge they encounter. They also need to evaluate the ways students use the new information to create new solutions to problems, new products, and ideas. Some of the outcomes specified in prior sections—such as the ability to generate clearly stated and researchable hypotheses, to discriminate between primary and secondary sources, and to evaluate the relative reliability and validity of secondary sources—represent objectives in the process domain. While the dimensions of process, product, and content have been addressed independently in some assessments to be discussed in this chapter, it is nearly impossible to separate process from content. Students think about something; students create products in some domain; and students critically examine evidence and ideas about some content.

One excellent source of process skill objectives relating to the development of critical thinking skills is the work of Robert

Ennis (1985, 1993). Ennis and his colleagues created a comprehensive list of skills in the critical thinking domain and developed tests that measure those skills. They also explored potential gender bias in the skill definitions and in the assessments (Wheary & Ennis, 1995). Burns and Reis (1991) wrote on the scope and sequence of process skills specific to instruction for gifted learners.

Product Assessment

Some designs for gifted programs explicitly call for product outcomes. For example, Renzulli's Enrichment Triad (1977) and Schoolwide Enrichment Models (Renzulli & Reis, 1985) explicitly call for Type III activities as hallmarks of appropriate curricular activities for the gifted. These activities are characterized as individual or small group "real life" investigations on a real problem with a real audience in mind. The definition of the expected product in the Schoolwide Enrichment Model provides an outline of the expectations for evaluation. Similarly, Kaplan's (1979, 1986) framework for curriculum development includes a component explicitly calling for products which serve as both tools of learning and verification of learning. Accordingly, educators have been urged to use authentic assessments to evaluate and provide feedback to gifted students (Reis, 1983).

The keys to making the use of product assessments meaningful in gifted programs are two-fold. First, creators of the assessment tools must find ways to set appropriate benchmarks for gifted learners. As Eva Baker and John Schacter (1996) suggest, the process of setting standards may require several stages including
- finding ways to set the high standards to be attained by looking for good descriptions of expert performance;
- describing that performance level in terms understood by both the teachers and their students; and
- translating the performance standards into scoring rubrics that are valid reflections of the standards.

Standards of excellence for gifted students have too often been set as "better than others the same age" rather than as the level of performance of those who are accomplished. As Wiggins (1993) indicated, it is critical to set high standards representing professional levels of performance, even though at a given grade level, the teacher may not have expectations that all students, or even any students will attain the standard. He spoke of the important distinction between expectations and standards: standards are set representing the highest level of performance and expectations represent how far a teacher might expect a given student to move toward the achievement of the standard at a particular point in time. Interestingly, children with talent in athletics and the arts learn at a very young age to look to models of adult accomplishment as their standard. They watch and seek to emulate Michael Jordan or Jean-Pierre Rampal.

Students not only need to know the standard, but to make performance assessment meaningful, students must come to know and understand both the standard and the steps necessary in the progression to the achievement of it. To look only at professional work without a sense of the progressive growth and development necessary to achieve the standard may simply frustrate both student and teacher. Well-developed rubrics will reflect stages of development toward the highest standards.

Affective Outcomes

The goals of services to gifted students are often from the affective realm, including the social behaviors and emotional adjustments of the students. These might include group process goals, such as those illustrated by the outcome expectations stated earlier from the Autonomous Learner Model. They might include expectations that students will learn social skills (ability to offer and accept constructive criticism, accept the role of follower in a group as appropriate, respect the ideas of others, and so forth) and that they will be able to adapt emotionally to their world. Within the realm of goals in this area are self-concept, self-esteem, and self-efficacy goals. Educators might also wish to assess the degree to which students' attitudes toward school and learning (in general or in specific academic areas) are influenced by the services offered. After all, of what value is helping students achieve high levels of performance in a given domain if the students simultaneously develop an aversion to ever studying this content again?

One group of outcomes that is not easily categorized as cognitive or affective is the set of behaviors including accepting responsibility for one's own learning, becoming an independent learner as in Treffinger's model for self-directed learning (1986), or becoming autonomous learners (Betts, 1986).

Individual Versus Group Outcomes

In many curricular frameworks designed for gifted learners and in many instructional strategies used in gifted classrooms, there are specific opportunities for the students to work in groups, either by direction of the teacher or by choice. The task itself may require group participation for successful completion. Illustrative units such as the Lunchroom Waste unit based on the Enrichment Triad Model, for example, might have been completed individually but are presented and evaluated as group investigations. Sharan and Sharan's Group Investigation Model (1992) and Elizabeth Cohen's model for cooperative learning (Cohen, Lotan, Whitcomb, Balderrama, Cossey, & Swanson, 1994), however, are specifically structured so that the students are required to do tasks that reflect individual student strengths, which must be combined for the greatest success in completion of the task. All cooperative learning models require some degree of group interaction and productivity. One of the critical issues for assessment is the clear specification of how the individual students will be evaluated in these settings. Slavin (1994) recommended there be clear individual accountability and assessment, as well as group assessments. The students should be clearly informed regarding the ways in which they will be evaluated.

Need for Specificity

One of the critical steps in the assessment process is to be sure the level of specificity and definition of expected outcomes will lead to using a valid assessment tool. For example, to say that one wishes to measure creativity is too broad and nebulous. Is the intent to measure the creative productivity of the student? What will be the specific characteristics of that productivity? To what degree are novelty, appropriateness of solution to the problem, technical quality of the product, and so forth, important in assessing the product? To what degree is it appropriate to include the process that the student goes through as important? What about attitudes and dispositions? Before selecting or constructing an instrument to assess student growth and achievement in any of the areas discussed thus far, it is critical to specify exact meanings for the terms used.

Instrumentation

The process of selecting or constructing the appropriate tools for assessing student progress toward achieving specified goals and objectives must be based on two critical judgments. First, the instrument or tool must be valid. It is important to ensure that there is evidence that the instrument and procedures selected measure the specified outcomes and objectives. Secondly, it is important that close attention is paid to ensuring that any tool selected or constructed is reliable (e.g., the score or rating given on one day should not be overly affected by how the student felt on that day, the scorer's mood on that day, error from confusion regarding directions, and so forth). The measure should yield consistent scores regardless of who administers or scores the test, performance, or product.

Types of Instruments

In the assessment process, a teacher or evaluator may choose to use either formal or informal instruments and procedures; standardized or nonstandardized instruments; self-report, peer evaluation, or teacher report; and paper and pencil, performance, or observational tools. These categories are not mutually exclusive.

For example, a formal assessment is one that is planned with specific guidelines for gathering information, while informal assessments are done in the course of everyday classroom activities. An observation may be formal or informal. Teachers always observe learners in the course of the day, but at times, they may observe for specific behaviors. Teachers may record their observations using a rating scale or check list to ensure that particular behaviors are (or are not) exhibited and to provide systematically collected data for reporting or planning purposes. Standardized instruments are those that are developed to be administered and scored according to very specific guidelines (e.g., the way directions are given, the timing of the test, and so forth). Most published achievement, personality, and aptitude tests are considered formal and standardized. A teacher's classroom test is usually formal, but not standardized. The reliability and validity, as well as the advantages and disadvantages of each approach, depend to some degree on the outcomes to be measured, the purpose for which data is being collected, the audience for the evaluation information collected, and the time available to construct and use the instrument or procedures.

Use of Tests to Assess Learner Outcomes

Up until the last several years, paper and pencil tests dominated classroom assessment, and nearly all large scale assessments of student progress at the district or state level depended on paper and pencil standardized assessments. The advantages of using multiple-choice or other objective formats in assessment are three-fold: (1) the range of topics or behaviors that can be assessed in a short period of time is very large, (2) the instruments can be administered to large groups and scored relatively inexpensively, and (3) they are reliable. The disadvantages of such assessments, particularly in measuring many of the goals and objectives of gifted programs, are the limited range of outcomes measured, the mismatch between the goals of gifted programs and the tests, and ceiling effects. A ceiling effect occurs when a test is unable to measure accurately the full extent of growth in gifted students. The ceiling effect may occur because gifted students score at the very top of an instrument on the pre-test, leaving very few or even no other items to answer correctly on the post-test. It may also occur because the instrument does not have a sufficiently broad range of content or processes assessed or enough difficult items to ensure it taps into the full extent of student growth on a posttest. In most cases, standardized achievement tests measure the traditional curriculum with most items focusing on knowledge or low-level understandings and processes. Gifted students often demonstrate mastery of grade-level expectations before instruction, so a standardized, on-grade-level test will not measure the impact of instruction. In some cases where acceleration is the service offered to gifted students, out-of-level testing may be used to demonstrate mastery of more advanced levels of learning within the traditional curriculum.

A limited number of tests of process skills claim to be discipline independent (although nearly all depend on reading and fluency with language). The most widely used are the Ross Test of Higher-Cognitive Processes (Ross & Ross, 1976), the Torrance Tests of Creative Thinking (Torrance, 1966), the New Jersey Test of Reasoning Skills (Shipman, 1983), the Watson-Glaser Critical Reasoning Appraisal (Watson & Glaser, 1980), the Cornell Critical Reasoning Test (Ennis, Gardiner, Guzzeta, Morrow, Paulus, & Ringel, 1964), and the Cornell Critical Thinking Test (Ennis & Millman, 1985). Other sources of instruments that measure process skills used within specific disciplines are available through professional organizations such as the National Council for the Social Studies, which published *Selected Items for the Testing of Study Skills and Critical Thinking* (Morse, McCune, Brown, & Cook, 1971).

Teachers may, of course, construct classroom tests to assess the success of gifted children in achieving instructional goals and objectives. These are not considered standardized tests.

In the domain of affective outcomes, there are many instruments that have been used to assess changes in students. Self-concept has been measured by such instruments as the Piers-Harris Children's Self-Concept Scale (Piers,1984), the Perceived Confidence Scale for Children (Harter, 1985), and the Self-Description Questionnaire (Marsh & O'Neil, 1984). One cautionary note in using these scales with expectations of documenting improved self-concept: gifted children generally exhibit higher self-concepts than average peers (Hoge & Renzulli, 1991); hence, expectations for growth may be unrealistic. However, educators should be sure that programming efforts do not have detrimental effects on students.

One affective area of concern that is often identified by parents, teachers, or counselors who work with gifted children is the stress and burnout a child might face in a program for gifted students. Instruments that have been used to monitor such effects are the Student Stress Inventory and the Maslach Burnout Inventory (Fimian, Fastenau, Tashner, & Cross, 1989). Social adjustments can be assessed through the use of sociograms.

Performance and Product Assessments

Many of the goals and objectives characterizing gifted programs cannot be assessed by traditional paper-and-pencil tests. Any goals that suggest creative productivity, the investigation of authentic problems, the use of alternative means of expression, or performance that emulates or represents the performance of professionals must be assessed using performance and product assessments. These products or performances may be stimulated or elicited by specific task descriptions that reflect extensions (in depth, complexity, abstractness, and so forth) or enrichment of traditional curricula. They allow for all students to engage in the activity with a set of clear standards representing appropriate expectations for gifted students and ways of dealing with advanced content, sophisticated processes, and authentic products. An example of a structured prompt for such an assessment is presented in Figure 1. Other products and performances may come from long-term assignments or projects such as those described earlier as part of the Schoolwide Enrichment Model. Performances in the arts have been traditionally evaluated by observation of both improvised and rehearsed presentations.

It is not sufficient to create the task and leave the definition of expectations and standards to chance or comparative evaluation. As noted in the earlier part of this chapter, it is critical that teachers explore what is considered the highest level of performance in the domain. Once appropriate standards of excellence or expert performance have been identified, educators must ensure that the rubrics (scoring guidelines) used to evaluate the student describe for the learner the clear progression of development from novice-level performance to expert performance.

Sample Mathematics Task and Rubric
How Deep is Deep? Grade 6

Purpose/Rationale
The purpose of this assessment is to engage students in thinking about, discussing, researching, and developing strategies for solving open-ended problems that contain relevant and extraneous variables or data. Students will also propose projected cost, equipment, personnel, and time necessary for an underwater exploration.

Objectives
Students will demonstrate their ability to
- distinguish relevant from irrelevant data in a problem;
- engage in research on an open-ended topic;
- find, interpret, and apply a strategy to solve a problem;
- work together cooperatively to find a solution to a problem; and
- engage in metacognition about their problem-solving process.

Related Ft. Worth Objectives
The learner will
- use concepts and skills associated with the understanding of numbers;
- develop and apply concepts of basic operations through use of calculators, computers, and manipulatives;
- solve problems designed to systematically develop students' problem-solving abilities through a variety of strategies and approaches; and
- use models and patterns to develop the algebraic concepts of relations and functions.

Context
Students may work together in pairs or individually in class to develop the strategy and solve the problem. Little teacher intervention is needed. Students should be given the rubric before beginning the problem.

Rater
This task is designed to be rated by the teacher with consideration for peer feedback in group presentations.

Use of Results
Results will be used primarily to make instructional decisions and provide feedback to students about their progress in problem solving.

Prerequisite Knowledge, Skills, and Dispositions
- Research Skills
- Experience working with mathematical strategies
- Experience working in groups to solve problems

Prompt
Prompt is designed for students who are functioning at grade level in mathematical and research skills. Planning sheets may be provided for struggling students who need more structure.

Rubric
See attached analytic rubric.

Source
Adapted from Houghton-Mifflin *Algebra 1* (Brown, 1992).

How Deep is Deep? Prompt 1

You are an oceanographer working on a project that requires you to investigate a sunken ship. For this particular project, you will need to know the depth of the ship lying on the ocean floor so that you can make preparations for exploring it. All you know is that a SONAR wave was sent down to the ship and returned in .076 seconds. You also know that the temperature of the water at the surface is 68° degrees Fahrenheit.

Work with a partner to do some preliminary research on SONAR using classroom resources, the Internet, the library, or any available resources that you feel might be helpful. Look for clues in the research that will help you develop a strategy to find out how far down the ship is. Indicate the depth of the ship and any other relevant information you found out from your research and hard work. Afterward, begin to brainstorm some ideas for exploring the ship. Make a proposal for you and your partner to present to the rest of your team (the class and your teacher). You and your partner will present your ideas to the team at our next meeting. Include the following in your proposal:

Figure 1. A Sample Performance Assessment Task

- the kind or equipment you will need;
- the projected cost of equipment;
- amount of oxygen needed and the cost of the oxygen;
- how many people will be needed;
- what time of year the exploration should begin; and
- how long you think the exploration will take.

In the mean time, you will need to describe how you came to your conclusions. Describe how and why you chose the strategy you did to figure out the depth of the ship. Show all of your work. In addition, describe and justify the proposal you will make to the team for exploring the ship. Include references to your research.

You will be evaluated on your selection of a strategy to solve the problem, the accuracy and authenticity of your response and proposal, your use of the research to propose the exploration parameters, and your cooperation with your partner. Make sure to read the attached rubric so you know exactly what you and your partner have to do to be successful.

Figure 1. Continued

Note.[2] From *Five-year study on Feasibility of High-end Learning in the Diverse Middle School 1995–2000,* by Rachel Cochran, 1991, Unpublished assessment tool, National Research Center on Gifted and Talented at the University of Virginia. Copyright 1991 by the NRC/GT. Reprinted with permission.

Schack (1994) effectively outlined such a rubric for adolescent research projects. The dimensions, along which she suggested evaluating research projects, included (1) formulating the research question, (2) generating hypotheses, (3) determining sample selections, (4) selecting and implementing data gathering techniques, (5) representing and analyzing data, (6) drawing conclusions, and (7) reporting findings. In Figure 2, the levels of performance that can be used to evaluate the degree to which students are learning the skills of reporting in a secondary level research project are illustrated. An example of one item on a rating scale to evaluate products produced by students completing a Type III activity enrolled in a Schoolwide Enrichment Program is provided in Figure 3.

Wiggins (1996) provided generic, initial dimensions or criteria for

Novice	**Apprentice**
Findings not presented or presentation is inaccurate or unclear; surface feature errors seriously interfere with comprehension	Findings communicated with some clarity; surface feature errors distract the reader

Proficient	**Distinguished**
Findings communicated clearly and accurately; appropriate format for audience; surface feature errors but are not distracting	Creative format or content; multiple ways of reporting (graphic, written, kinesthetic); few or no errors in surface features

Figure 2. Levels of Performance for Reporting Data as an Aspect of Secondary Research Projects

Note. From "Authentic Assessment Procedures for Secondary Students' Original Research, by G. D. Schack, (1994), *The Journal of Secondary Gifted Education, 6,* p. 39. Copyright 1994 by Prufrock Press. Reprinted with permission.

scoring the products of gifted students. He suggested teachers consider impact and evaluate the degree of the product's effectiveness (e.g., Does it solve the problem? persuade an audience? and so forth) and the level of the product's quality (e.g., Is it outstanding in its class?). He also suggested assessing the process of creating the product (e.g., Is it purposeful? efficient? adaptive? self-critical? Is it thoughtful? considerate? responsive? inquisitive? Did the student use the appropriate skills—those linked to the task and product and situation-specific for each product?).

Wiggins also suggested the form of the product be rated. He recommended looking to see if the product was well-designed (e.g., Does form follow function? Is the product authentic? elegant? clever? Is the product well-crafted? organized? priced? clear? mechanically sound? and so forth). Another dimension he listed as important was style. He recommended consideration of the voice (e.g., Is it authentic? Is the style of the product graceful?). And, of course, Wiggins would con-

In this rating scale, an example of performance is given that would represent the highest level of expectation.

Level of Resources

Is there evidence that the student used resources, materials, or equipment that are more advanced, technical, or complex than materials ordinarily used by students at this age/grade level?

For example, a sixth-grade student utilizes a nearby university library to locate information about the history of clowns from the 12th through the 16th century in major European countries.

5	4	3	2	1	NA

To a great extent   Somewhat   To a limited extent

**Figure 3. One Dimension of a Rating Scale
to Evaluate Type III Products**

Note. From *The Schoolwide Enrichment Model: A Comprehensive Plan for Educational Excellence* (p. 474–476), by J. S. Renzulli and S. M. Reis, 1985, Mansfield Center, CT: Creative Learning Press. Copyright 1985 by Creative Learning Press. Adapted with permission.

sider the content to be important. He included accuracy (correctness and validity), sophistication (depth, insightfulness, power, and expertise), and aptness or focus within this category.

Wiggins also provided examples of ways in which exemplary models have been collected for setting the highest level of performance we might require for gifted students. He suggested looking at the products of older students to identify models for younger students and examining the models of experts for the more advanced students. Others have suggested that students also identify accomplished works and derive the criteria from their own understanding of excellence. Other generic rubrics for performance-based assessments are outlined by Marzano, Pickering, and McTighe (1993).

Specific teacher learner outcomes should be reflected in the tasks developed by the teacher and the rubrics used to assess them. A rubric, designed to evaluate the task illustrated in Figure 1 and address the range of performance possible in a heterogeneous classroom including highly able learners, is presented in Figure 4. Sometimes, teachers wish to use a common rubric across many products over the course of a year's instruction to show student growth in particular areas. Several items from one teacher's rubric for scoring creative writing products illustrate this principle in Figure 5. The scoring rubrics in these examples are particularly exemplary in that they describe as the levels of expected performance at the top, middle, and bottom of the scale.

While all of these scales were designed for teacher assessment of student progress, students should be encouraged to use these scales to evaluate their own work and that of their peers. These skills in self-evaluation provide a base for students to develop intrinsic standards of performance. Using the scales to evaluate others can also be valuable in helping students with understanding the standards by seeing models of each level and discussing the meaning of the levels of performance.

Observations. The observation of musical and artistic performance and performances which may represent a student product should use carefully developed rubrics such as those described as performance assessment. However, teachers may do more informal assessments of student behaviors relevant to the goals of instruction. In particular, outcomes that are in the affective realm are often assessed using more informal observational strategies. Check lists or rating scales are often used to accomplish this assessment in a systematic fashion. An example of a teacher check list used to evaluate social outcomes, particularly in group work, is provided in Table 1. Table 2 provides an example of a rating scale that might be used by students to evaluate themselves on their social behavior in class.

Assessment of Program Outcomes

While learner outcomes are one critical set of goals for gifted programs, there are many other important aspects of a gifted program

Scoring Rubric: How Deep is Deep?

Preliminary Research
- Explorers engaged in preliminary research about the SONAR system to focus information so that they could solve the problem and generate a proposal for exploration.
- Explorers engaged in preliminary research about the SONAR system but were unable to find information to help solve the problem and generate a proposal for exploration or had trouble focusing the information so that they could uncover clues that would have helped them solve the problem and generate a proposal for exploration.
- Explorers did not engage in preliminary research about the SONAR system to help them solve the problem or generate a proposal for exploration.

Strategy and Proposal
- Explorers created or uncovered an appropriate strategy to find the depth of the ship as well as created a systematic plan to explore the ship which included all information specified in the task and additional, relevant information that the explorers uncovered along the way. Explorers left no stone unturned.
- Explorers created or uncovered a strategy to find the depth of the ship; however, the strategy needs work, is missing a variable, or incorporates an irrelevant variable (like the temperature of the water). Explorers created a proposal to explore the ship which included a great deal of relevant information but had large gaps that left the other team members with several questions and concerns.
- Explorers did not uncover or create a strategy to find the depth of the ship; or explorers used mostly irrelevant variables in their strategy; and explorers engaged mostly in guesswork to complete their proposal. Team members had trouble following the plan due to its sketchiness.

Calculations
- Explorers used their strategy to accurately approximate the depth of the ship, cost of materials, amount of oxygen necessary, time and personnel requirements, and so forth.
- Explorers applied their strategy appropriately, but minor errors in calculations prevented them from arriving at the most accurate depth, approximate cost of materials, amount of oxygen needed, time and personnel requirements, and so forth.

- Explorers applied their strategy inappropriately, or there were major or many calculation errors that prevented them from approximating the depth of the ship, cost of materials, time, personnel, and so forth.

Cooperation
- Explorers listened to each other's ideas. Both explorers contributed to the problem-solving process. Work was divided equally.
- Explorers listened to each other's ideas, but the work and contributions to the problem-solving process were divided unequally.
- Explorers did not work together to solve the problem. They required prompting to stay on task and listen to each other's ideas. Work was divided unequally.

Documentation and Defense
- Explorers discussed the way they solved the problems and addressed the requirements of the proposal in a way that would be reproducible by an outsider. Explorers included all research references, notes, and materials. There were no gaps in the logic of the process; each step "flowed" from the preceding one. The proposal is clearly a defensible one.
- Explorers discussed their problem-solving process but left some gaps in logic that would make it difficult for an outsider to understand the steps of the process and proposal development. However, the reader could gain a general sense of how the explorers solved the problem and generated the proposal. The proposal is still defensible. Explorers included all research references, notes, and materials.
- Explorers did not discuss their problem-solving process OR left many gaps in logic so that the reader could not follow the process or gain any sense of how the explorers solved the problem or created their proposal. The proposal is not defensible. The explorers failed to include all of their research materials and notes.

Figure 4. A Rubric for Scoring a Performance Task With a Full Range to be Used in a Heterogeneous Classroom

---

Note.[2] From *Five-year study on Feasibility of High-end Learning in the Diverse Middle School 1995–2000*, by Rachel Cochran, 1991, Unpublished assessment tool, National Research Center on Gifted and Talented at the University of Virginia. Copyright 1991 by the NRC/GT. Reprinted with permission.

The full rating scale is divided into two sections. The first is substance and includes clarity of ideas, fluency, description, and overall effectiveness. The second section is grammar and includes sentence structure, spelling, and neatness. The first two items illustrated in this figure are from the substance section; the third is from the grammar section.

Fluency

4 = The writing is very fluent and melodic. The writer uses language very effectively to create flow. Choice of words is often unusual and imaginative, but appropriate. The composition is not filled with clichés. The writer is not afraid to experiment with words or sentence structure and does so effectively.

3 = For the most part, the choice of words and sentence structure is successful. A few mistakes do not distract from the overall beauty and flow of the language of the piece.

2 = The writer uses clichés. The piece does not surprise the reader with its choice of words. The composition flows smoothly and is technically fluent, but it is not powerful because the language and wording is conventional. The writer uses no particularly descriptive or unusual words or seems to have used a thesaurus inappropriately.

1 = The writer uses words very poorly. There is no regard at all for whether the choice of words is suitable. The writing is disjointed and inappropriately short. Words are inappropriately simple or common.

Description

4 = The writer uses descriptive language well. Imagery is creative, imaginative, unusual, and clearly conveys a sense of that which is described. The reader can see or feel or taste that which is described. The setting for the theme is well developed. You are there. A clear mood is set. The characters and setting are vivid and three-dimensional.

3 = The writer provides a setting, describes character, and uses imagery, but the descriptions are sometimes flat. The choice of descriptive words sometimes brings a vivid image to mind, but sometimes common.

2 = The writer provides a setting, describes character, and attempts imagery, but the descriptions are flat. The choice of words does not

pull the reader into the setting or give the character life. The settings, characters, and scenes are not fully developed. You have an idea of where the writer wants you to be, but you are not there. The description lacks imagination.

1 = There is neither setting nor imagery. Characters are identified in the most mechanical terms. The writer makes no effort to set a scene or provide descriptive language.

Sentence Structure

4 = There are no major errors and only one or two minor errors in sentence structure (such as split infinitives). The sentence structure is correct regardless of the complexity of the sentence.

3 = There are very few major or minor errors in sentence structure; they occur in very complex sentences.

2 = There are a few serious errors in sentence structure and many minor errors, but the meaning remains clear. Errors occur in very complex and simpler sentences.

1 = The sentence structure is so full of errors that the meaning of the text is often obscured.

Figure 5. Selected Items From a Rating Scale to Score Creative Writing Compositions

---

Note. Adapted from *Creative Writing Compositions* by A. Moss, 1977, unpublished manuscript.

that also must be evaluated. These commonly fall into the categories of (1) identification and selection of students to be served, (2) the adequacy of a definition of giftedness and philosophy of gifted education, (3) teacher selection and training, (4) curriculum development and implementation of instructional strategies, (5) management of the program, and (6) communication. While each program will have different specific goals, examples of general evaluation concerns and questions that fall into each of these categories are given below.

- Identification and Placement of Students: Is the identification process effective and efficient in identifying students who reflect the stated definition of giftedness?
- Definition and Philosophy: Do the definition of giftedness and the philosophy of gifted education reflect current theory, research, and practice in the field? Are they defensible? Are they well articulated to administrators, teachers, parents, students, and community?
- Teacher Selection and Training: Does the staff development program provide teachers with the will and skills to develop and implement an instructional program appropriate for gifted students?
- Curriculum Development: Does the curriculum meet the could, would, and should test of Harry Passow? Is this a curriculum that only gifted students could, should, and would be successful in?
- Management: Are there adequate resources and facilities to implement this program?
- Communication: Does the plan for communication provide parents with sufficient information about the experiences of their children, expectations, and evaluation of student achievements?

Determining Areas of Concern and Evaluation Questions

The principle guides used in selecting priority areas for program evaluation are
- Does this reflect an important outcome of the program?
- Will the information collected about this area be of use to the key decision makers?
- Is this an area of critical concern to the stakeholders in the program (those most affected by program decisions)?
- Can studying this area help improve services to the students?

To decide which questions fit these criteria, it is very useful to establish an advisory committee made up of representatives of key decision makers and stakeholder groups.

In formulating the key evaluation questions, it is also critical to consider formative or in-process questions (e.g., Is the program being implemented as described and intended?), as well as outcome or summative questions (e.g., Did the students in this program produce cre-

Table 1. Check List for Evaluating
Social Behavior in Groups

The teacher can write students' names in the columns and then check behaviors as they occur.

Behavior to be Observed			
Is responsive to the needs of others.			
Willingly helps others solve problems.			
Listens to the ideas of others.			
Provides *constructive* criticism/suggestions.			
Respects others' contributions.			
Accepts suggestions and help.			
Works cooperatively with others.			
Accepts leadership role when appropriate.			
Accepts follower role when appropriate.			
Adheres to group decisions and plans.			
Encourages peers.			
Willingly shares ideas.			

Table 2. Student Self-Assessment Rating Scale

Getting Along With Others and Contributing to the Group

Directions:
Think about the ways in which you participate in our classroom. Then check the box which best describes how you think you respond to others.

	Always or nearly always	Usually	Sometimes	Never
I participate in class activities.				
I listen to my classmates' ideas.				
I volunteer to help others.				
I try to be a cooperative group member.				
I respect others' opinions.				
I stay with my assigned task in a group until I am finished.				
I wait until others finish speaking before I begin.				
I try not to dominate discussions and decisions in my group.				

ative, authentic products which addressed a real problem, use the tools of the discipline, and present the products to a real audience?) For an in-depth discussion regarding the selection of evaluation concerns and questions, see Callahan and Caldwell (1993).

Sources of Information

The next stage in program evaluation is to identify sources of information that will provide valid and reliable information. Several sources of data regarding student outcomes have been discussed in detail in the earlier section of this chapter, including tests, performance and product rating scales, and observations. Student performance on both formal and informal assessments can become part of the program evaluation process. It is also possible to use other data such as the results of Advanced Placement (AP) or International Baccalaureate exams; performance in competitions; awards and special recognition; surveys of students; parents and teachers; and interviews with students, teachers, and parents regarding student performance.

Parents are very good sources of information about communication of the program, the degree of challenge provided by the curriculum, and their children's reactions to program components. Teachers (both those who are specialists in gifted education and those who are regular classroom teachers) are also good sources of information about areas of concern regarding communication, as well as program management and the identification process.

Program documents could be reviewed by experts to determine whether the definition, philosophy, identification process, and curriculum meet the standard of best practice in the field. Of course, it is also critical to determine whether the documents reflect practice; so, in most cases, observation of classrooms will be necessary.

Data Collection

One of the primary issues in program evaluation is the question of who evaluates the program. Is it best to have an external evaluator, someone outside of the program or district? Or should the evaluation be done by school staff? The answer to this question depends on the purposes to be served, the demands of the audiences, and the expertise of staff.

In high stakes situations, if the program staff is presumed to be biased, then it is wise to consider bringing in an outside evaluator to construct and administer surveys and interviews, observe classes, analyze data, and make reports. If the staff does not have expertise in the field of evaluation, survey construction, interviewing, or data analysis, then outside expertise should be sought. Teachers of the students are in the best position to administer surveys to students; they are the most appropriate persons to administer tests because of student comfort with a familiar person. However, it may be necessary to have scoring done by persons considered less biased in those cases where subjectivity of scoring is an issue. One final consideration is staff time. If the tasks of evaluation will be done hurriedly with little attention to detail and accuracy, then the results will be useless at best and, at worst, damaging if bad decisions are made based on unreliable or invalid assessments or interpretations.

Quantitative and Qualitative Data. Quantifiable data is the data derived from test scores, scores on performance assessment scales, frequency counts of responses on surveys or questionnaires, or responses on observational scales. Qualitative data is derived from interviews, observations, analysis of program documents, or open-ended questions on surveys. When analyzing qualitative data, evaluators are looking for common themes and deeper insights into the perceptions, understandings, and explanations surrounding the program.

Surveys. The most common source of quantitative data in gifted program evaluations is survey data. A survey to one sample of constituents may be used to address many evaluation questions, or it may focus on one topic. For example, the items in the survey in Figure 6 were designed to assess the effectiveness of administrators of gifted programs. The questionnaire was given to central office and building level administrators, to principals, and to the staff of the program.

Rating Scales. Experts may use a rating scale to evaluate the quality of curriculum that has been developed for use with the gifted population. The survey in Figure 7 is an example of a survey designed for such use.

This survey should be accompanied by a letter explaining its purpose, whether or not the data will be confidential, anonymous, or neither, how the data will be used, and directions for completion and returning the survey.

Open-ended items or a space for comments might be added at the end to provide opportunities for the respondents to comment on areas not addressed in the survey. One example is provided.

Survey Directions:

Each of the statements below describes a characteristic desirable in a program administrator. Please place an X on the number that describes your perception of the degree to which (program administrator's name or title) displays this characteristic in your interactions with him (or her). Please consider the past two years; or if you have worked with the person less than two years, please consider the full time you have worked with him (or her).

Mark:

1   If you have not observed this characteristic.
2   If you have observed this characteristic only once or twice over the past two years.
3   If the program administrator usually exhibits this characteristic, but there are notable exceptions.
4   If you have observed this characteristic on nearly every occasion where it was applicable.
5   If you have not had an opportunity to judge this characteristic, or if the characteristic or activity is not applicable to your interactions with (program administrator's name or title).

Figure 6. A Management Survey

The program administrator has provided me with the type of information that is necessary to carry out my functions relating to this program.
1 2 3 4 5

The information I need to carry out my functions has been provided in a timely manner.
1 2 3 4 5

The information is presented in a clear and succinct manner.
1 2 3 4 5

I am provided with enough information to make good decisions in my role relating to this program.
1 2 3 4 5

I am allowed to participate in decisions when the decisions will affect my role or function in the program.
1 2 3 4 5

I (or a representative I am comfortable with) am/is allowed to provide input when decisions will affect my role or function in the program.
1 2 3 4 5

I feel the program administrator is honest with me.
1 2 3 4 5

The program administrator seeks to help me understand the reasons why certain decisions have been made.
1 2 3 4 5

When appropriate, the program administrator makes his (or her) attitudes and beliefs clear to me.
1 2 3 4 5

The program administrator tries to help me understand the reasons why certain decisions have been made.	1	2	3	4	5
When confronted with a difficult problem, the program administrator attempts to find a solution that will be at least partially acceptable to all without sacrificing the quality of decision and the likelihood the problem will be solved.	1	2	3	4	5
The program administrator gives reasonable consideration to my suggestions.	1	2	3	4	5
The program administrator attempts to put my suggestions into practice or provides me with an explanation as to why they cannot be implemented.	1	2	3	4	5
I feel that the program administrator makes the best use of my talents, ability to contribute to the program, and expertise.	1	2	3	4	5
The program administrator is just and considerate in the assignment of duties to subordinates.	1	2	3	4	5
The program administrator is available for consultation with me.	1	2	3	4	5

Figure 6. Continued

The program administrator is sensitive to staff morale.   1   2   3   4   5

The program administrator works to keep staff morale high.   1   2   3   4   5

The program administrator appears to operate from a well-organized plan.   1   2   3   4   5

The short and long range goals and direction of the program are clearly
communicated by the program administrator.   1   2   3   4   5

The program administrator sets realistic deadlines and attempts to see that
the deadlines are met.   1   2   3   4   5

The program administrator sees to it that the work of persons who play
different roles in the program are well-coordinated.   1   2   3   4   5

The program administrator is knowledgeable of pertinent details of his or her
subordinate's work.   1   2   3   4   5

The program administrator brings knowledge of the latest research and
development in the field of gifted education to staff.   1   2   3   4   5

The essential work of the program gets done on time.   1   2   3   4   5

The program administrator is adept at identifying and isolating problems.   1   2   3   4   5

The program administrator works to make gifted education an integral part of the school program.	1	2	3	4	5
The program administrator is flexible and adaptive to changes in events and circumstances.	1	2	3	4	5
The program administrator is open-minded and willing to change or modify original plans and objectives when the situation warrants adaptation.	1	2	3	4	5
When presented with a given problem, the program administrator explores a number of possible solutions before deciding which course of action to take.	1	2	3	4	5
The program administrator is open to new ideas.	1	2	3	4	5
The program administrator is able to develop and elaborate upon ideas and concepts.	1	2	3	4	5

How long have you worked with this person in his (or her) capacity as the administrator of the gifted program (or insert the name of the program)?

_____ Years and _____ Months

Figure 6. Continued

What is your role in the school division?

_____ Central Office Personnel
_____ Building Principal-Middle School
_____ Counselor
_____ Program Staff-Teaching

_____ Building Principal-Elementary
_____ Building Principal-High School
_____ School Psychologist
_____ Program Staff-Clerical

Comments:
In the space below, please feel free to provide further comments on the positive and negative aspects of the program administrator's performance. Specific examples or ideas for improvement of program functioning will be very useful.

Figure 6. Continued

Note. From Project Improve: Management Evaluation Form, by J. S. Renzulli and C. M. Callahan, 1972, In J. S. Renzulli, *A Guidebook for Evaluating Programs for the Gifted and Talented*, (pp. 181–184). Copyright 1972 by the Bureau of Educational Research at the University of Connecticut. Adapted with permission.[2]

Other Objective Assessment Strategies. One other useful strategy for assessing an affective outcome or social adjustment is the sociogram. If there is concern that the ways in which services are provided to gifted students create problems of isolation, a simple technique to test the hypothesis is to administer three simple questions: Who would you most like to sit near? Who would you most like to play with? Who would you most like to work with? Ask the students to list their three top choices (with all names written on the blackboard, so fear of misspelling does not influence choice). Then ask the same three questions in the negative form (e.g., Who would you least like to sit near?). The strategies for analyzing sociograms can be found in most introductory assessment textbooks (e.g., Gronlund, 1985).

Qualitative Data Collection. Interviews and observations form the basis for nearly all qualitative data collections. The process may be highly structured with specific interview questions or guides for observation, or they may be more open-ended, leaving the structure of the interview or observation open to the discretion of the person collecting the data. Structured interviews and observations are best used when there are very specific areas about which the evaluator is seeking data. When the purpose is to explore a more general sense of overall effectiveness and process, then a more open-ended approach is appropriate.

Data Analysis

The analysis of quantitative and qualitative data is the subject of whole courses in statistical and qualitative evaluation design courses. Questionnaire data is usually analyzed by presenting descriptive statistics—frequency counts of responses. And on rating scales, the mean and standard deviation of responses are presented if there is a sufficiently large number (more than 25 respondents) to make interpretation meaningful. These same strategies are used to report on ratings of curriculum, and so forth.

For reporting student outcome data, inferential statistics comparing learning of students receiving services with similar groups not receiving services may be used if there is a control or comparison group. However, most often results are compared to a standard or norm established by the program.

Curriculum Analysis Rating Scale

The items listed below were rated on a 4-point scale (1 = no attention to this principle, 2 = minimal attention to this principle—surface features only, 3 = some attention to the principle with good likelihood of substantial effectiveness, 4 = substantial and effective attention to the principle, NA = not applicable). In creating the actual instrument for use, include a column to the right of each item with opportunity for the raters to indicate their evaluations and comments.

In evaluating this curriculum document, please indicate the degree to which the framework addresses each principle.

The framework suggests an appropriate level of involvement of the gifted learner in decisions concerning choice of educational experience.	1	2	3	4	NA
Individual responsibility for learning is promoted.	1	2	3	4	NA
The teaching strategies selected and recommended replace the traditional superior/authority/dispenser of knowledge role of the teacher with the knowledgeable facilitator role.	1	2	3	4	NA
There is appropriate integration of content, process, and product goals.	1	2	3	4	NA
Instructional strategies are included that demand the application of hypothesizing, collecting and verifying data, predicting, and synthesizing that reflect a level of sophistication appropriate for gifted children of this age.	1	2	3	4	NA

	1	2	3	4	NA
The curriculum allows for differentiation for gifted learners who are at different levels of sophistication.	1	2	3	4	NA
Problem solving using the methodologies of professionals in this discipline is included.	1	2	3	4	NA
Recognition, analysis, and revisions of the process used to generate products receive as much focus as the evaluation of the product itself.	1	2	3	4	NA
Authentic problems are included when appropriate.	1	2	3	4	NA
Authentic or real products are encouraged as appropriate.	1	2	3	4	NA
Opportunities are provided for gifted and talented students to pursue areas of their own selection, individually or collectively.	1	2	3	4	NA
Content reflects a level of abstraction appropriate for gifted learners.	1	2	3	4	NA
Content reflects a level of depth and complexity appropriate for gifted learners.	1	2	3	4	NA

Figure 7. A Rating Scale for Use by Experts in Assessing Curricular Quality

	1	2	3	4	NA
The process dimension of instruction reflects a level of depth and complexity appropriate for gifted learners.	1	2	3	4	NA
Pacing of learning is appropriate for gifted learners.	1	2	3	4	NA
The curriculum allows for children of different ethnic, socioeconomic, or racial backgrounds to become engaged in learning.	1	2	3	4	NA
The content, process, and product dimensions of the curriculum reflect learning experiences that other students either could not, would not, or should not do.	1	2	3	4	NA
Students will have a better understanding of the epistemology of various disciplines.	1	2	3	4	NA
Learning experiences require students to engage in transformation of information, rather than mere memorization.	1	2	3	4	NA
Creative productivity is encouraged.	1	2	3	4	NA

Figure 7. Continued

Qualitative data has been the subject of many books, and those who are interested in pursuing this line of data collection and analysis should consult Guba and Lincoln (1981) or Yin (1990).

Decision Making

Whichever line of data collection and analysis is used for exploring program evaluation, the critical element is the use of the data. The evaluation data must reach appropriate decision makers for their use in evaluating the degree to which the program is functioning as intended. It must be presented in ways that decision makers can assess the degree to which results achieved match expectations or goals of the program. And it should be clear enough that they can use the information for directing the ways in which the program can be improved in order to achieve even greater success and move toward delivering a quality program, appropriate curriculum, and high quality learning experiences to gifted students.

All of these evaluation efforts, either at the classroom or program level, are to no avail unless the data is fed back into the decision-making process to allow for the teacher or administrator to do the most effective instructional and program planning. Further, the most effective planning will occur when the evaluation processes in the classroom and across program components are carried out regularly and systematically. Hence, planning for instruction and the planning for program modification must begin and end and begin again with effective evaluation.

The Instructional Circle

Too often the evaluation process is viewed as the end process of instruction or the inevitable evil that accompanies schooling. Effective educators adopt a different framework. The effectiveness of efforts to provide the highest quality services to gifted students will be greatest when
- the assessment and evaluation process become part of a cycle where information is used to provide feedback to teachers on

the effectiveness of instruction and for planning the next stage of instruction;

- assessments provide students useful information on how they are growing and changing;
- parents have meaningful information about the accomplishments of their children; and
- decision makers are able to use valid and reliable data to adjust program parameters to ensure the maximum effectiveness of services offered.

For these goals to be accomplished, each of the individuals responsible for the delivery of services—teachers and administrators—must assume responsibility for specifying the expected outcomes of instruction, for defining quality in programming, and then for selecting or designing and using assessment tools that will assess the important learning outcomes and the effectiveness related program components. To educate without systematically assessing the readiness for instruction is to do an injustice to students, and to fail to evaluate the results of instructional efforts is to do an injustice to students and the community.

References

American Association for Science Literacy. (1993). *Benchmarks for science thinking*. New York: American Association for the Advancement of Science.

Baker, E. L., & Schacter, J. (1996). Expert benchmarks for student academic performance: The case for gifted children. *Gifted Child Quarterly, 40*, 61–65.

Betts, G. T. (1986). The autonomous learner model for the gifted and talented. In J. S. Renzulli (Ed.), *Systems and models for developing programs for the gifted and talented* (pp. 27–56). Mansfield Center, CT: Creative Learning Press.

Brown, L. (1992). *Algebra 1*. Boston: Houghton-Mifflin.

Burns, D. E., & Reis, S. M. (1991). Developing a thinking skills component in the gifted education program. *Roeper Review, 14*, 72–79.

California Department of Education. (1994). *Differentiating the core curriculum for advanced and gifted students*. Sacramento, CA: Author.

Callahan, C. M., & Caldwell, M. S. (1986). Defensible evaluation of programs for the gifted and talented. In C. J. Maker (Ed.), *Critical issues in gifted education, Vol. 1: Defensible programs for the gifted* (pp. 277–296). Rockville, MD: Aspen.

Callahan, C. M., & Caldwell, M. S. (1993). *A practitioner's guide to evaluating programs for the gifted*. Washington, DC: National Association for Gifted Children.

Cochran, R. (1991). [untitled] Unpublished assessment tool designed while working on the five-year study on feasibility of high-end learning in diverse middle school 1995–2000. National Research Center on Gifted and Talented, University of Virginia.

Cohen, E. G., Lotan, R. A., Whitcomb, J. A., Balderrama, M. V., Cossey, R., & Swanson, P. E. (1994). Complex instruction: Higher-order thinking in heterogeneous classrooms. In S. Sharon (Ed.), *Handbook of cooperative learning methods* (pp. 82–96). Westport, CT: Greenwood Press.

Consortium of National Arts Education Associations. (1994). *National standards for art education: What every young American should know and be able to do in the arts*. Reston, VA: Music Educators National Conference.

Ennis, R. H. (1985). A logical base for measuring critical thinking skills. *Educational Leadership, 43*(2), 44–48.

Ennis, R. H. (1993). Critical thinking assessment. *Theory into Practice, 32*, 179–86.

Ennis, R. H., Gardiner, W. L., Guzzeta, J., Morrow, R., Paulus, D. L., & Ringel, L. (1964). *Cornell Conditional Reasoning Test.* Champagne, IL: Illinois Critical Thinking Project.

Ennis, R. H., & Millan, J. (1985). *The Cornell Critical Thinking Test.* Pacific Grove, CA: Midwest Publications.

Fimian, M. J., Fastenau, P. A., Tashner, J. H., & Cross, A. H. (1989). The measure of classroom stress and burnout among gifted and talented students. *Psychology in the Schools, 26,* 139–153.

Gronlund, N. E. (1985). *Measurement and evaluation in teaching.* New York: Macmillan.

Guba, E. G. & Lincoln, Y. S. (1981). *Effective evaluation.* San Francisco: Jossey-Bass.

Harter, S. (1985). The Perceived Competence Scale for Children. *Child Development, 53,* 87–97.

Hoge, R. D., & Renzulli, J. S. (1991). *Self-concept and the gifted child.* Storrs, CT: University of Connecticut, The National Research Center on the Gifted and Talented.

Kaplan, S. N. (1979). Language arts and social studies curricula in the elementary school. In A. H. Passow (Ed.), *The gifted and talented: Their education and development 78th Yearbook of the National Society for the Study of Education* (pp. 155–168). Chicago: University of Chicago Press.

Kaplan, S. N. (1986). The grid: A model to construct differentiated curriculum for the gifted. In J. S. Renzulli (Ed.), *Systems and models for developing programs for the gifted and talented* (pp. 180–193). Mansfield Center, CT: Creative Learning Press.

Marsh, H. W., & O'Neil, R. (1984). Self-Description Question-naire III: The construct validity of multi-dimensional self-concept ratings by late adolescents. *Journal of Educational Measurement, 21,* 153–174.

Marzano, R. J., Pickering, D., & McTighe, J. (1993). *Assessing student outcomes: Performance assessment using the dimensions of learning model.* Alexandria, VA: Association for Supervision and Curriculum Development.

Morse, H. T., McCune, G. H., Brown, L. P., & Cook, E. (1971). *Selected items for the testing of study skills and critical thinking.* Washington, DC: National Council for the Social Studies.

Moss, A. (1977). *Creative writing compositions.* Unpublished manuscript.

National Council for History in the Schools. (1995). *National standards for history.* Los Angeles: Author.

National Council of Teachers of Mathematics. (1993). *Curriculum and education standards for mathematics.* Reston, VA: Author.

National Research Council (1995). *National science education standards.* Washington, DC: Author.

Piers, E. (1984). *Piers-Harris Self-Concept Scale: Revised manual.* Los Angeles: Western Psychological Service.

Reis, S. M. (1983). Avoiding the testing trap. *Journal of the Education for the Gifted, 7,* 45–59.

Renzulli, J. S. (1977). *The enrichment triad model.* Mansfield, CT: Creative Learning Press.

Renzulli, J. S., & Callahan, C. M. (1972). Project improve: Management evaluation form. In J. S. Renzulli, *Project improve: Management evaluation form. A guidebook for evaluating programs for the gifted and talented,* (pp. 181–184). Bureau of Educational Research, University of Connecticut.

Renzulli, J. S., & Reis, S. M. (1985). *The schoolwide enrichment model: A comprehensive plan for educational excellence.* Mansfield Center, CT: Creative Learning Press.

Ross, J. D., & Ross, C. M. (1976). *Ross Test of Higher-Cognitive Processes.* Navato, CA: Academic Therapy.

Schack, G. D. (1994). Authentic assessment procedures for secondary students' original research. *The Journal of Secondary Gifted Education, 6,* 38–43.

Sharan, Y., & Sharan, S. (1992). *Expanding cooperative learning through group investigation.* New York: Teachers College.

Shipman, V. (1983). *New Jersey Test of Reasoning Skills.* Upper Montclair, NJ: Institute for the Advancement of Philosophy for Children.

Slavin, R. E. (1994). Student-teams-achievement divisions. In S. Sharon (Ed.), *Handbook of cooperative learning methods* (pp. 3–19). Westport, CT: Greenwood Press

Torrance, E. P. (1966). *Torrance Tests of Creative Thinking.* Bennsville, IL: Scholastic Testing Service.

Treffinger, D. J. (1986). Fostering effective, independent learning through individual programming. In J. S. Renzulli (Ed.), *Systems and models for developing programs for the gifted and talented* (pp. 429– 460). Mansfield Center, CT: Creative Learning Press.

Vygotsky, L. S. (1986). *Thought and language* (A. Kozuin, Trans.). Cambridge MA: MIT Press. (Original work published in 1934)

Watson, G. & Glaser, E. M. (1980). *Watson-Glaser Critical Thinking Appraisal.* San Antonio, TX: Psychological Corporation.

Wheary, J., & Ennis, R. H. (1995). Gender bias in critical thinking: Continuing the dialogue. *Educational Theory, 45,* 213–14.

Wiggins, G. P. (1993). *Assessing student performance: Exploring the purposes and limits of testing.* San Francisco: Jossey-Bass.

Wiggins, G. P. (1996). Anchoring assessment with exemplars: Why students and teachers need models. *Gifted Child Quarterly, 40,* 66–69.

Yin, R. K. (1990). *Case study research.* Newbury Park, CA: Sage.

Author Note

1. A useful source of information about standards at the state and national levels can be found at this web site: http://sccac.lacoe. edu/priorities/content.html.

2. The work reported herein was supported under the Education Research and Development Centers Program, PT/Award Number R206R5001, as administered by the Office of Educational Research and Improvement, U.S. Department of Education. The findings and opinions expressed do not reflect the positions or policies of the National Institute on the Education of At-Risk Students, the Office of Educational Research and Improvement, or the U.S. Department of Education. Permission to reproduce this material has been granted by The National Research Center on the Gifted and Talented, Joseph S. Renzulli, Director.

SECTION III

STRATEGIES FOR BEST PRACTICES

CHAPTER 9

Materials and Methods for Teaching Analytical and Critical Thinking Skills in Gifted Education

SANDRA PARKS

One common trait that differentiates gifted students from their age peers is their capacity to perceive information and use it productively to an unusual degree. Their analytical thinking skills are evaluated in the various cognitive ability instruments. To assess their cognitive abilities, students are given a variety of analysis tasks. They compare, contrast, or classify objects or ideas and recognize what part of a whole is missing, give definitions by stating categories and differentiating attributes, put objects or events in the correct order, and look for connections among facts. Because they analyze information intuitively and efficiently, they are able to learn quickly and effectively.

Students' critical thinking skills are seldom effectively measured in most assessment procedures. While they may be asked some "common sense" questions like, "What would you do if . . .," tests do not commonly assess their abilities to make well-founded judgments. Critical thinking tasks, such as evaluating the reliability of a source of information or deciding whether an inference is support-ed by evidence, are not commonly practiced in gifted student iden-tification.

Once students are placed in gifted programs, their teachers must organize and implement instruction appropriate to the high-er-order thinking capacities and needs of gifted students. While educators have shown considerable interest in critical thinking dur-ing the last decade, processes and principles of sound reasoning are seldom developed meaningfully in curriculum guides or textbooks. Thus, teachers of the gifted must select or design instruction that addresses inferential reasoning processes that are abstract, some-times requiring a technical understanding of logic.

While educators tend to differentiate between critical and cre-ative thinking, in everyday thinking tasks these mental processes are functionally inter-related. As shown in Figure 1, skillful decision making and effective problem solving require thoughtful analysis of an issue by considering creative alternatives and evaluating the rea-sonableness of alternatives or options (Swartz & Perkins, 1990). The methods, materials, and programs described in this chapter promote analytical and critical thinking, decision making, and problem solv-ing. Additional resources for creative thinking skills and processes are described in Cramond's chapter on Fostering Creative Thinking.

Analytical and Critical Thinking Instruction for Gifted Students

Instruction in thinking process addresses and extends the unusual cognitive abilities of gifted students. The analytical skills that have warranted differentiated instruction are refined and used effectively in academic tasks. They practice creative and critical thinking skills that may not have been assessed or that may be under-developed. They apply all these types of thinking processes in complex tasks. Students with creative or artistic talents employ crit-ical or analytical thinking in order to critique and explain more effectively their work. Students with leadership talent learn to be more organized and skillful in making judgments and to consider more original solutions.

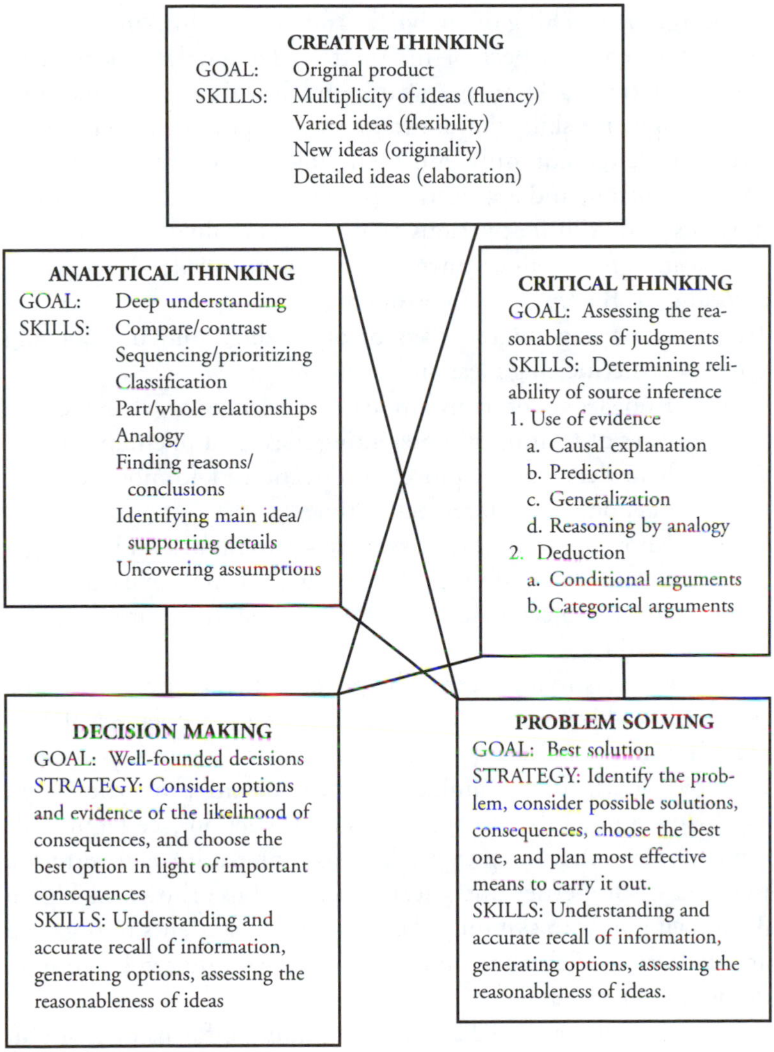

CREATIVE THINKING
GOAL: Original product
SKILLS: Multiplicity of ideas (fluency)
Varied ideas (flexibility)
New ideas (originality)
Detailed ideas (elaboration)

ANALYTICAL THINKING
GOAL: Deep understanding
SKILLS: Compare/contrast
Sequencing/prioritizing
Classification
Part/whole relationships
Analogy
Finding reasons/
conclusions
Identifying main idea/
supporting details
Uncovering assumptions

CRITICAL THINKING
GOAL: Assessing the reasonableness of judgments
SKILLS: Determining reliability of source inference
1. Use of evidence
   a. Causal explanation
   b. Prediction
   c. Generalization
   d. Reasoning by analogy
2. Deduction
   a. Conditional arguments
   b. Categorical arguments

DECISION MAKING
GOAL: Well-founded decisions
STRATEGY: Consider options and evidence of the likelihood of consequences, and choose the best option in light of important consequences
SKILLS: Understanding and accurate recall of information, generating options, assessing the reasonableness of ideas

PROBLEM SOLVING
GOAL: Best solution
STRATEGY: Identify the problem, consider possible solutions, consequences, choose the best one, and plan most effective means to carry it out.
SKILLS: Understanding and accurate recall of information, generating options, assessing the reasonableness of ideas.

Figure 1. Map of the Thinking Domain

Note. From *Teaching Thinking: Issues and Approaches.* (p. 133), by R. J. Swartz and D. N. Perkins, 1990, Pacific Grove, CA: Critical Thinking Press and Software (800) 458-4849. Copyright 1990 by Critical Thinking Press and Software. Adapted with permission.

Since gifted education curriculum is focused on higher-order thinking, the teaching of analytical and critical thinking processes is an essential aspect of instruction. For analysis, synthesis, and evaluation tasks to be meaningful learning, students must utilize cognitive skills that underlie these types of content objectives. Students not only must employ important knowledge, comprehension, and application processes in content lessons but must also be skillful at various analysis and evaluation processes.

Meaningful analysis involves many knowledge-level skills, according to Bloom's (1977) taxonomy:

1.20   Knowledge of the ways of organizing, studying, judging and criticizing ideas and phenomena;

1.21   Knowledge of conventions, knowledge of characteristic ways of treating and presenting ideas and phenomena;

1.22   Knowledge of the processes, directions, and movements of phenomena with respect to time;

1.23   Knowledge of the classes, sets, divisions, and arrangements which are regarded as fundamental or useful for a given subject field, purpose, argument, or problem. (p. 69–71)

Already classifying animals by phyla, students use at least one schema by which they understand important properties of animals. Teaching analysis skills shows students how to classify animals by criteria that examine other important properties (e.g., organizing animals by various means of protection [see Figure 2]). Students learn that the purpose for classifying animals determines the kind of properties one selects, such as those shown in Figure 3. Knowing how to skillfully classify prepares students to organize any collection of facts or objects by categories that will promote deeper understanding.

Just as well-developed analytical thinking informs meaningful analysis, well-developed critical thinking informs evaluation. Asking students to evaluate a work, an idea, or a principle without knowledge of the criteria, procedures, and principles for making such determinations results in an unsubstantiated opinion or statement of preference, rather than an informed, well-founded judgment. According to Bloom (1977), an evaluation task, the most complex form of higher-order thinking, involves

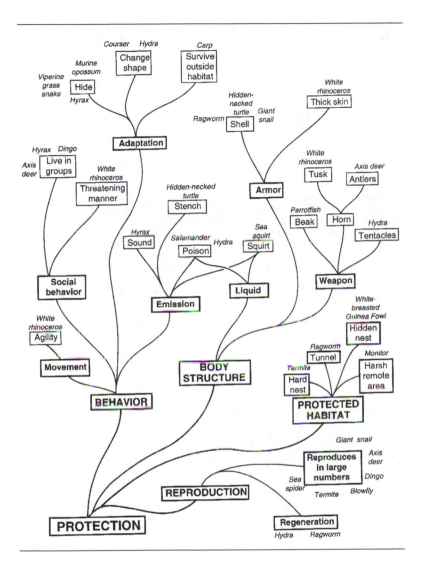

Figure 2. Classifying Animals by Types of Protection

Note. From *Infusing the Teaching of Critical and Creative Thinking into Content Instruction: A Lesson Design Handbook for the Elementary Grades* (p. 162), by R. Swartz and S. Parks, 1994, Pacific Grove, CA: Critical Thinking Books and Software (800) 458-4849. Copyright 1994 by Critical Thinking Books and Software. Reprinted with permission.

WAYS TO CLASSIFY	PURPOSE OF THE CLASSIFICATION	WHO WOULD USE IT AND WHY
Location	To indicate which animals inhabit a particular region. To indicate where in the world a particular animal can be found.	Traveler who wants to know what animals can be seen in an area. People who find animals for zoos.
Ecosystem	To indicate what kind of environment the animal needs to survive. To indicate what kinds of animals are likely to be found in a type of environment.	Environmentalists and government officials who try to preserve animals. Naturalists who want to find and observe animals in their natural environment. Zoo and aquarium workers who keep animals healthy.
Habitation (nest, den, hive, shell, etc.)	To indicate what kind of environment the animals need to survive. To indicate in what type of home the animal can be found.	Naturalists who want to find and observe animals in their natural environment. Zoo and aquarium workers who keep animals healthy. Architects who create homes and buildings based on natural principles of design. People who cultivate animals.
Outer covering	To indicate what kind of protection the animal needs to survive.	Environmentalists who try to preserve animals. Designers who create clothing based on natural design principles.
Body structure and functioning	To provide information about the bodies of animals. To indicate how animals function in their environment.	Biologists who explain diversity and evolution of animals. Doctors who treat ill animals. Zoo and aquarium personnel who keep animals healthy.
Benefit or harm to man	To indicate which animals can be used to benefit man. To indicate how various animals can benefit man. To indicate from which animals we need to protect ourselves.	Ranchers who cultivate animals for food. People who hunt animals for food (e.g., fishermen). Travellers who are going into the wilds. People who train animals.
Population/ species stability	To indicate size of population. To indicate which animals are endangered.	Environmentalists who try to preserve species of animals. People who hunt animals for food.

Figure 3. Purposes for Classifying Animals

Note. From *Infusing the Teaching of Critical and Creative Thinking Into Content Instruction: A Lesson Design Handbook for the Elementary Grades* (p. 161), by R. Swartz and S. Parks, 1994, Pacific Grove, CA: Critical Thinking Books and Software (800) 458-4849. Copyright 1994 by Critical Thinking Books and Software. Reprinted with permission.

making judgments about the value, for some purpose, of ideas, works, solutions, methods, materials, etc. It involves the use of criteria, as well as standards for appraising the extent to which particulars are accurate, effective, economical, or satisfying. . . . Evaluation represents not only an end process in dealing with cognitive behaviors, but also a link with the affective behaviors where values, liking, and enjoying are the central processes involved. (p. 185)

To make an informed evaluation, students should know some basic conventions for making judgments in various fields and must carry out certain types of analysis (Bloom, 1977):

1.24   Knowledge of the criteria by which facts, principles, opinions, and conduct are tested and judged;

1.25   Knowledge of the methods of inquiry, techniques, and procedures employed in a particular subject field, as well as those employed in investigating particular problems and phenomena (p. 71);

4.1   Analysis of elements: the ability to recognize unstated assumptions, to distinguish facts from hypotheses, and to distinguish a conclusion from the statements that support it; and

4.2   Analysis of organizational principles: the ability to infer an author's purpose, point of view, or traits of thought and feeling as exhibited in his work or to infer the author's concept of science as exemplified in his practice (p. 146).

In critical thinking instruction, students use knowledge and analysis principles to learn how to assess whether or not an evaluation report is reliable. The example in Figure 4 shows questions students generated about Percival Lowell's observations of Mars, in which he reported seeing lines on Mars that he described as canals. Students listed questions they wanted satisfied in order to decide whether the observation report was reliable. From their list of questions, they generated a strategy map of the factors that they would take into account when they evaluated the reliability of any observation report.

Using lines and color, students created a strategy map by "lining up" their questions with the types of questions represented on their list. Questions generally fell in four main categories: (1) ques-

QUESTIONS	TYPES OF QUESTIONS		
	OBSERVATION		**REPORT**
	OBSERVER	CORROBORATION	
What is his background?	—		
What is his scientific reputation?	—		
For whom was the report written?	———————————————		—
What kind of equipment did he use?	—————		
Did he use the same equipment for all sightings?	—————		
What was his state of mind? Was he clear-headed?	—		
Where was he when he made his observation?	—		
Did other accounts corroborate his report?	—	—	
In what form or publication did the report appear?	———————————————		—
Was the report a translation or his own words?	—		
What were the weather conditions?	—		
In what year did he make the observation?	—		
When did he write the report?	———————————————		—
Did he have normal sight?	—		
Was the equipment appropriately maintained?	—————		
Was he typically trustworthy?	—		
What did he expect to see?	—		
Did he know how to use the equipment?	—		
How often did he observe it?	—		
Is the lens scratched?	—		
How long did he observe it?	—		
Did he believe in life on Mars prior to the observation?	—		
Did he make accurate observations of other planets?	—		
Was he drinking before he made the observations?	—		
Was a model made to verify how formations should look?	—		
Was he paid for this account? If so, by whom?	—		

Figure 4. Questions About Reliability of Source Information

Note. From *Infusing the Teaching of Critical and Creative Thinking into Content Instruction: A Lesson Design Handbook for the Elementary Grades* (p. 159), by R. Swartz and S. Parks, 1994, Pacific Grove, CA: Critical Thinking Books and Software (800) 458-4849. Copyright 1994 by Critical Thinking Books and Software. Reprinted with permission.

tions about the observer (capacity, expertise, background, objectivity, and so forth), (2) the observation itself (the conditions, procedures, equipment, and so forth), (3) the nature of the report (type of publication, the reputation of the publication, audience, use of pictures or tables, and so forth), and (4) evidence that other observers corroborate the findings.

Once the types of questions were established and criteria for reliability were clarified, students then applied the strategy to evaluate the reliability of the Lowell's observation. The example in Figure 5 shows that students decided the technology available to Lowell and his predisposition to believe that there were canals on Mars biased his observation and outweighed his credentials and other scientific achievements.

While analytical and critical thinking is essential for meaningful content learning, these thinking processes promote students' decision making and problem solving. Developing students' analytical and critical thinking is not only one goal of the academic curriculum for the gifted; it is also integral to their personal growth and the development of leadership skills.

Approaches to Teaching Analytical and Critical Thinking

Deciding which approach to use is determined primarily by the gifted and talented service model employed in a specific gifted program whether it be in a homogeneous class, in cluster groupings, in a resource room, or in a mixed-ability classroom. The three approaches in the teaching of analytical and critical thinking, further summarized in Figure 6, include

- teaching thinking processes directly in a structured course of study or separate lessons;
- infusing analytical and critical thinking into content instruction; and
- using methods that promote thinking about content learning (Swartz & Parks, 1994).

These approaches have also proven effective in gifted education classes for different reasons, with different emphasis and with different results.

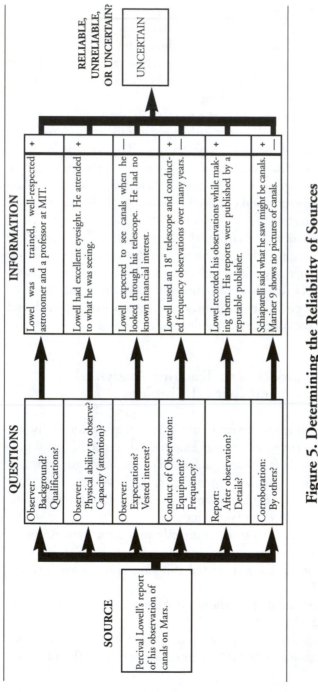

SOURCE

Percival Lowell's report of his observation of canals on Mars.

QUESTIONS

Observer:
Background?
Qualifications?

Observer:
Physical ability to observe?
Capacity (attention)?

Observer:
Expectations?
Vested interest?

Conduct of Observation:
Equipment?
Frequency?

Report:
After observation?
Details?

Corroboration:
By others?

INFORMATION

Lowel was a trained, well-respected astronomer and a professor at MIT. +

Lowell had excellent eyesight. He attended to what he was seeing. +

Lowell expected to see canals when he looked through his telescope. He had no known financial interest. —

Lowel used an 18" telescope and conducted frequency observations over many years. +

Lowel recorded his observations while making them. His reports were published by a reputable publisher. +

Schiaparelli said what he saw might be canals. Mariner 9 shows no pictures of canals. + —

RELIABLE, UNRELIABLE, OR UNCERTAIN?

UNCERTAIN

Figure 5. Determining the Reliability of Sources

Note. From *Infusing the Teaching of Critical and Creative Thinking into Content Instruction: A Lesson Design Handbook for the Elementary Grades* (p. 368), by R. Swartz and S. Parks, 1994, Pacific Grove, CA: Critical Thinking Books and Software (800) 458-4849. Copyright 1994 by Critical Thinking Books and Software. Reprinted with permission.

Teaching Analytical and Critical Thinking Directly in a Structured Course of Study or Separate Lessons

Two formats are commonly used for the direct teaching of thinking in gifted programs: (a) using separate courses with a clearly developed structure and objectives and (b) teaching a thinking process explicitly as a single, supplemental lesson. The systematic teaching of thinking processes is particularly effective for special populations whose development or language acquisition needs war-

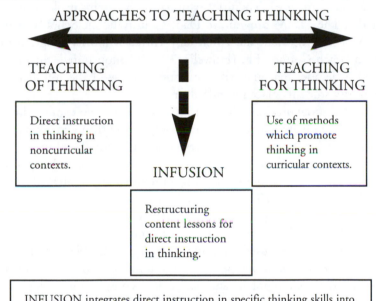

APPROACHES TO TEACHING THINKING

TEACHING
OF THINKING

Direct instruction
in thinking in
noncurricular
contexts.

INFUSION

Restructuring
content lessons for
direct instruction
in thinking.

TEACHING
FOR THINKING

Use of methods
which promote
thinking in
curricular contexts.

INFUSION integrates direct instruction in specific thinking skills into content area lessons. Lessons improve student thinking and enhance content learning.

Figure 6. Determining Reliability of Sources

Note. From *Infusing the Teaching of Critical and Creative Thinking into Content Instruction: A Lesson Design Handbook for the Elementary Grades* (p. 9), by R. Swartz and S. Parks, 1994, Pacific Grove, CA: Critical Thinking Books and Software (800) 458-4849. Copyright 1994 by Critical Thinking Books and Software. Reprinted with permission.

rant direct instruction. Bilingual, hearing-impaired, and learning-disabled gifted students benefit from sequentially developed cognitive instruction. Such programs offer practice in metacognition and employ the language of thinking.

Instruction in analysis skills is particularly significant to assure that special populations of gifted students (learning disabled, sensorially impaired, or minority students) have appropriate access to gifted or Advanced Placement programs (AP). Once access is gained, these students learn the academic skills for successful performance. The pool of potentially gifted minority students can be enlarged by the use of cognitive stimulation programs in elementary grades. The TEAM program in Dade County Public Schools (Rito & Moller, 1989) and the Potentially Gifted Minority program in Palm Beach County, FL, (Howells, 1992) demonstrated, for more than a decade, that analysis instruction increased the number of minority students placed in gifted programs.

Both programs identified minority students who exhibited the behaviors of being gifted but scored only in the fifth and sixth stanines in achievement testing. These students were placed in classes where they receive daily instruction in analysis skills. In both programs, after one year of instruction, approximately 25–30% of these students scored the 130 IQ required for placement in Florida's gifted programs. Follow-up studies show that these students perform successfully in gifted and advanced academic classes.

Both programs used *Building Thinking Skills* (Black & Parks, 1985), a cognitive development curriculum of figural and verbal lessons that develop key analysis skills—compare and contrast, sequencing, classification, and analogy. Lessons are sequenced by increasing complexity and provide cognitive stimulation and vocabulary acquisition for limited English proficiency or learning-disabled gifted students. *Building Thinking Skills* provides cognitive objectives, practice exercises, content transfer, and suggestions for metacognition. It is evaluated using normed cognitive skills tests and the mathematics comprehension, mathematics problem solving, and reading comprehension subtests of the *Stanford Achievement Test*.

In a similar secondary program in Jacksonville, FL, which also implemented analysis instruction, the number of minority students in AP classes tripled in a five-year period. Enrollment in AP classes for one predominately minority high school increased 3000%. After program implementation, one-third of the district's AP students were African American. SAT scores of black students in this school district topped the national average by 31 points—43 points above the state average (Potter & Dawson, 1988).

Critical thinking instruction as a separate course usually involves teaching logic, ethics, or aesthetics. *Critical Thinking I* (Harnadek, 1976) and *Critical Thinking II* (Harnadek, 1980) are two student books for specialized instruction in formal and informal logic. While the symbolic logic lessons may be taught in mathematics classes and the informal logic taught in English instruction, the actual implementation of the complete course requires at least 60 hours of instructional time. *Critical Thinking I* and *II* have been widely used by gifted education classes (grades 5–9) for more than 20 years. *Critical Thinking* (Ennis, 1996) is more appropriate for secondary gifted education instruction in English or humanities classes.

Philosophy for Children (Lipman, 1979) involves specialized instruction (primary grades through high school) in courses on logic, ethics, aesthetics, and scientific reasoning. It assists teachers in conducting class discussion of student novels. Training is necessary to teach the courses meaningfully. This program, featured on the National Diffusion Network, is evaluated using a critical thinking test developed for it by Education Testing Service.

Analytical and critical thinking courses have three common features. First, they contain objectives that are cross-disciplinary in content or application. Secondly, they involve a structured sequence of instruction to build competence in thinking skills. And, third, they rely heavily on class discussion of specialized student materials. Thinking objectives are clearly stated and measurable with cognitive abilities or critical thinking tests or performance assessment, such as debate or writing tasks.

Thinking courses are used primarily in resource rooms or enrichment centers because of their versatility across the curriculum and because a dedicated amount of time can be spent on them on a regular basis. A variety of direct instruction programs are listed in the summary of centers and networks in the appendix of this chapter.

Teaching Thinking Processes Explicitly as Single, Supplemental Lessons

Analytical and critical thinking may be taught in single lessons scheduled within the academic year as the content requires. Such instruction involves teaching a specific thinking strategy that supplements a content lesson. For example, teachers may teach a short lesson using a graphic organizer "scaffolding" to clarify various thinking or learning processes. Students may then utilize the strategy to make the content lesson more effective and meaningful. Students may modify the diagrams to fit individual styles, purposes, and interests. The goal of such instruction is self-initiated thinking and learning where the learner is proactive in conducting and managing his or her own mental tasks.

The graphic organizer shown in Figure 7 depicts the content of a lesson on information literacy. The strategy involves a variety of analytical and critical thinking skills and prompts the learner to reflect on (1) how to determine the type, quality, and availability of needed information, (2) how to retrieve and evaluate it, and (3) how to express or depict it for more effective understanding and decision making. The information explosion has made information literacy a timely curriculum initiative, particularly for independent study and research skills objectives for gifted curricula.

Students use a blank version of the diagram in Figure 7 to take notes, applying the strategy to a specific research inquiry of key questions: How does one define the type of information that is needed? How does one select a search strategy? How does one locate resources? How does one retrieve the needed data? How does one assess the accuracy and quality of information? How does one interpret, evaluate, and communicate that information? How does one draw well-founded judgments? and How does one produce creative products based on one's research?

A second example of teaching an analysis strategy involves using a modification of Hilda Taba's concept development model as a review tool (Eggen, Kauchek, & Harder, 1979). This process helps students assess how well they understand a concept. Each step of the process involves an analysis task: comparison and contrast, attribution, exemplification, and classification. If a student

HOW DO I FIND AND USE INFORMATION WELL?

WHAT INFORMATION DO I NEED?

WHAT KIND? Statistics, facts, observation reports, interpretations, depictions, creative works, explanations?

WHAT FORM? Text, tables, lists, maps, diagrams, outlines, pictures, interview, speeches, diaries?
WHAT MEDIUM? Print, film, videotape, videodisc, photograph, microfiche?

▼

HOW DO I FIND IT?

WHAT RESOURCES SHOW WHERE INFORMATION LIKE THIS IS LOCATED? *Books in Print, Reader's Guide*, Internet gopher, etc.

WHAT SEARCH PLAN WILL OFFER ADEQUATE INFORMATION EFFICIENTLY? Steps in search and retrieval?

▼

WHERE IS THE INFORMATION LOCATED?

TYPE OF SOURCE? Public libraries, specialized libraries, research or government agencies, computer file, Internet, CD rom?

SPECIFIC SOURCE? Title, author, publication, date, file name, volume, e-mail listing, publisher's address, telephone number?

▼

HOW DO I OBTAIN IT?

POLICIES? Authorization for access and use, limitations on volume and application, restrictions on photocopying, royalties, access fees?

HOW TRANSMITTED? Print material, computer disk, fax, e-mail? Time necessary? How converted? Technological compatibility?

▼

HOW RELIABLE IS THIS INFORMATION?

PRIMARY OR SECONDARY? RELIABILITY OF OBSERVATION REPORT? Observer? Procedures? Corroborated? Report documented?

REGARDED IN THIS FIELD? FITS KEY FACTORS IN THIS USE? Timeliness, comparable definitions, compatible procedures?

▼

HOW CAN I SHOW WHAT I LEARNED FROM THIS INFORMATION?

TYPE OF PRODUCT? Text display, performance, computer file?
AUDIENCE? Reader, listeners, size and background of audience?

CRITERIA FOR REPORTING? Documentation, standards for this type of product, citation, format, user-friendliness?

Figure 7. Graphic Organizer

Note. From *Learning on Purpose,* (p. 132), by B. Juarez, H. Black, & S. Parks, 1999, Pacific Grove, CA: Critical Thinking Books and Software (800) 458-4849. Copyright 1999 by Sandra Parks. Reprinted with permission.

DO I REALLY KNOW IT?

EXAMPLE: Money

WHAT KIND OF AN IDEA IS IT?
Objects that people exchange for goods and services.

CAN I NAME SOME EXAMPLES?
Pennies, nickels, dimes, quarters, dollar bills.

WHAT ARE SOME SIMILAR IDEAS?
Tokens used for bus or subway rides.

WHAT ARE SOME DIFFERENT IDEAS?
Checks, credit cards, barter.

WHAT ARE ITS IMPORTANT CHARACTERISTICS?
It represents a standard value that is backed up by the government. People recognize and must accept it for purchases within the country that issues it.

CAN I GIVE A FULL DEFINITION?
Money is an object exchanged for goods or services that is issued by the government and must be accepted for purchase within the country that issues it.

Figure 8. Concept Development

Note. From *Organizing Thinking II* (p. 335), by S. Parks and H. Black, 1990, Pacific Grove, CA: Critical Thinking Books and Software. Copyright 1990 by Critical Thinking Books and Software (800) 458-4849. Adapted with permission.

can answer six basic questions about a concept, he or she can be confident of his or her own conceptualization. The money example in Figure 8 shows how using the concept development model yields clear definitions. Lack of clarity about any of these questions shows the student the omissions or incomplete understandings that should be corrected.

While all students profit from using strategies such as this one, gifted students utilize these techniques in independent study and advanced academic programs. These strategies are useful in any gifted education service model and are particularly valuable when teaching gifted students in heterogeneous classrooms.

Infusing Teaching Analytical and Critical Thinking Into Content Instruction

The direct instruction examples described in the previous section involve either a structured course of study taught independently from content or cross-disciplinary lessons involving nonacademic exercises. The infusion approach involves the clarification and application of thinking processes within content lessons. It involves structured questions to form various kinds of judgments and graphic organizers to hold evidence and to guide students' thinking. The diagram in Figure 9 shows the key questions in the decision-making strategy and the steps in thoughtful decision making that can be taught in any discipline.

The decision-making graphic organizer in Figure 10 depicts students' research on Harry Truman's decision regarding the ending of World War II. Truman's options, the consequences of one option, information about the likelihood of various consequences, and consideration of the value of the consequences are summarized on the diagram. Students then evaluated each option to arrive at a judgment regarding the best alternative to end the war.

By "picturing" the decision-making process, the graphic organizer displays evidence for or against the likelihood of various consequences and records students' deliberations about the relative significance of them. By comparing graphics for several options, students "see" which options have significant positive and negative consequences.

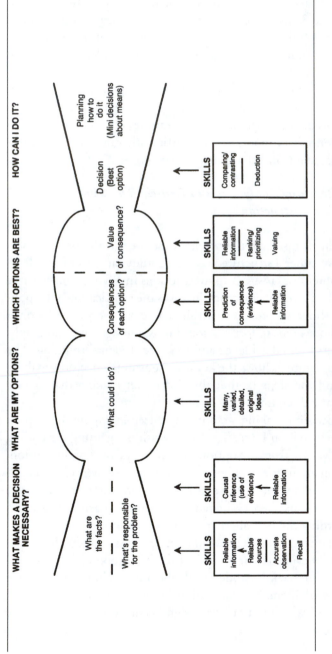

Figure 9. Thinking Skills Involved in the Decision-Making Process

Note. From *Issues and Approaches to Teaching Thinking* (p. 158), by R. Swartz and D. N. Perkins, 1990, Pacific Grove, CA: Critical Thinking Books and Software. Copyright 1990 by Critical Thinking Books and Software (800) 458-4849. Reprinted with permission.

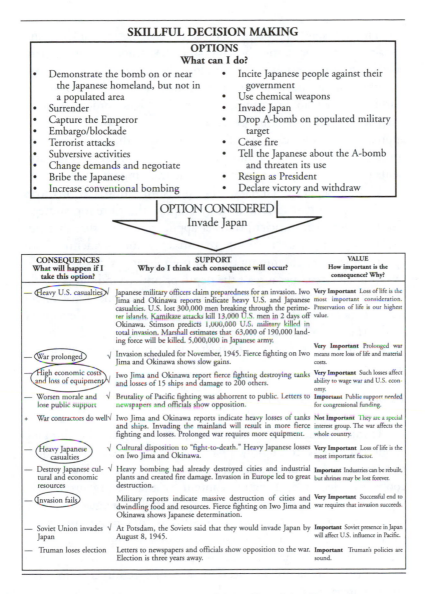

SKILLFUL DECISION MAKING

OPTIONS
What can I do?

- Demonstrate the bomb on or near the Japanese homeland, but not in a populated area
- Surrender
- Capture the Emperor
- Embargo/blockade
- Terrorist attacks
- Subversive activities
- Change demands and negotiate
- Bribe the Japanese
- Increase conventional bombing

- Incite Japanese people against their government
- Use chemical weapons
- Invade Japan
- Drop A-bomb on populated military target
- Cease fire
- Tell the Japanese about the A-bomb and threaten its use
- Resign as President
- Declare victory and withdraw

OPTION CONSIDERED
Invade Japan

CONSEQUENCES What will happen if I take this option?	SUPPORT Why do I think each consequence will occur?	VALUE How important is the consequence? Why?
— Heavy U.S. casualties √	Japanese military officers claim preparedness for an invasion. Iwo Jima and Okinawa reports indicate heavy U.S. and Japanese casualties. U.S. lost 300,000 men breaking through the perimeter islands. Kamikaze attacks kill 13,000 U.S. men in 2 days off Okinawa. Stimson predicts 1,000,000 U.S. military killed in total invasion. Marshall estimates that 63,000 of 190,000 landing force will be killed. 5,000,000 in Japanese army.	Very Important Loss of life is the most important consideration. Preservation of life is our highest value.
— War prolonged √	Invasion scheduled for November, 1945. Fierce fighting on Iwo Jima and Okinawa shows slow gains.	Very Important Prolonged war means more loss of life and material costs.
— High economic costs and loss of equipment √	Iwo Jima and Okinawa report fierce fighting destroying tanks and losses of 15 ships and damage to 200 others.	Very Important Such losses affect ability to wage war and U.S. economy.
— Worsen morale and lose public support √	Brutality of Pacific fighting was abhorrent to public. Letters to newspapers and officials show opposition.	Important Public support needed for congressional funding.
+ War contractors do well √	Iwo Jima and Okinawa reports indicate heavy losses of tanks and ships. Invading the mainland will result in more fierce fighting and losses. Prolonged war requires more equipment.	Not Important They are a special interest group. The war affects the whole country.
— Heavy Japanese casualties √	Cultural disposition to "fight-to-death." Heavy Japanese losses on Iwo Jima and Okinawa.	Very Important Loss of life is the most important factor.
— Destroy Japanese cultural and economic resources √	Heavy bombing had already destroyed cities and industrial plants and created fire damage. Invasion in Europe led to great destruction.	Important Industries can be rebuilt, but shrines may be lost forever.
— Invasion fails	Military reports indicate massive destruction of cities and dwindling food and resources. Fierce fighting on Iwo Jima and Okinawa shows Japanese determination.	Very Important Successful end to war requires that invasion succeeds.
— Soviet Union invades Japan √	At Potsdam, the Soviets said that they would invade Japan by August 8, 1945.	Important Soviet presence in Japan will affect U.S. influence in Pacific.
— Truman loses election	Letters to newspapers and officials show opposition to the war. Election is three years away.	Important Truman's policies are sound.

Figure 10. Decision-Making Graphic Organizer

Note. From *Infusing the Teaching of Critical and Creative Thinking into Social Studies Instruction: A Lesson Design Handbook for the Secondary Grades* (in process), by R. Swartz and S. Parks, in process. Copyright 1999 by Sandra Parks. Reprinted with permission.

The infusion approach emphasizes systematic thinking and metacognition about the thinking strategies students have experienced. Infusion lessons also employ the instructional methods described in the next section using cooperative or problem-based learning, using graphic organizers, and asking higher-order questions. Clarity about the thinking processes, as employed by the infusion approach, allows for clear transfer, in contrast to the more situation-specific character of such techniques so embedded in content that students may not recognize or remember the thinking involved.

Unlike separate courses, the infusion approach involves redesigning content lessons to fully employ the thinking strategy. Teachers also plan sufficient transfer applications to assure that students are competent in using the strategy independently. This approach is more commonly used in homogeneous classes or cluster-grouped classes because of the depth of understanding, research, and discussion of content involved in infusion lessons. Enrichment units, generally not offered in general curriculum in elementary grades (i.e., global studies, technology, anthropology, and so forth), provide thought-provoking contexts that are easily modified for infusion lessons.

Using Methods That Promote Thinking About Content

Using instructional methods to stimulate students' thinking about content is commonly practiced in gifted education. Staff development for teachers of the gifted frequently includes using cooperative learning, depicting content by graphic organizers, asking higher-order questions, employing Socratic dialogue or shared inquiry, using interactive computer software, designing instruction to honor multiple intelligences or various learning styles, implementing hands-on mathematics and process science, and engaging in inquiry or problem-based learning and integrating art into other content areas.

While these instructional methods may be used in any gifted education service model, they are especially useful in heterogeneous classes and cluster-grouped classes. Such methods promote deep understanding of content for all students, resulting in stimulating classroom activities. However, gifted students may utilize them at a more advanced level and with greater effectiveness. Gifted students demonstrate more complex applications of these techniques in class room activities, discussions, and assessment tasks.

For over two decades, teachers of the gifted learned to ask higher-order questions and conduct meaningful dialog through training in the Junior Great Books Program. Teachers facilitate discussions in which students examine great works of children's literature, using techniques of shared inquiry about the novels. While Junior Great Books is commonly employed in single-language, advanced academic programs, it has been effectively implemented in the Dade County, FL, gifted program that includes large numbers of gifted students whose primary language is not English.

Using Graphic Organizers

In previous examples, strategy maps have been supplemented by graphic organizers. Specialized diagrams depict how information is related, "picturing" issues so we can make informed interpretations or judgments. By using graphic organizers, teachers and students can access, organize, and display complex information involved in evaluating issues, solving problems, or making decisions. Graphic organizers may also be used to guide or stimulate thinking, to plan projects, and to assess students' learning.

Specially designed graphic organizers depict questions that thoughtful people ask and answer when they think critically: assessing the reliability of sources of information, evaluating reasons for conclusions, reasoning by analogy, evaluating causal explanation, making informed predictions, evaluating or forming generalizations, and using conditional or categorical reasoning. Notations on the graphic organizer summarize the information or evidence required in making such judgments and depict the steps in the evaluation process by symbols and design elements (arrows, circles, boxes, colors, and so forth).

Graphic organizers may be used for several purposes:
- to hold and organize information for research and evaluation;
- to show relationships;
- to stimulate or guide thinking; and
- to assess thinking and learning.

OPTIONS	RELEVANT CONSEQUENCES			
	EASE OF PRODUCTION	ENVIRONMENT	COST	AVAILABILITY
SOLAR Active Passive Photovoltaic	Easy, if location, latitude, and weather conditions are favorable. Little maintenance. Limited service for repairs. Photovoltaic not cost effective until improved technology makes it more efficient.	No undesirable air or water pollution. Unsightly equipment or circular fields of mirrors. Loss of trees. Environmental impact of manufacturing materials and equipment or disposing of batteries.	Start up is costly (could be reduced by mass manufacture). Low maintenance and repair. Operation costs are minimal. Research and development costly.	Limited by location, latitude, and weather. Seasonal in some areas. Distributing and storing resulting electricity is limited. Renewable.
NUCLEAR	Complex, requiring sophisticated instruments, specialized technicians, and unusual safety measures. Waste disposal is risky and requires long-term safeguards.	Radiation danger. Mining erosion and toxic tailings are produced to secure uranium. Storage of waste may result in radiation contamination. Production structures are huge.	Protective measures in operation and start-up costs are high. Licensing, certifying, and inspecting plants are expensive. Maintenance costs.	Uranium is scarce. Breeder reactors are controversial and limited.
PETRO-CHEMICAL	Complex, but commonly practiced.	Oil spills may result. Depletion of the oil supply. Hydrocarbons pollute the air, damage the ozone layer, and create acid rain. Processing pollutes air.	Exploration, research, distribution, and clean-up costs are high. Importing is costly; depends on international pricing. Valuable for uses other than energy.	Limited regional supplies. Nonrenewable.
COAL	Complex, but commonly practiced.	Strip and shaft mining scars the land. Use creates a grey film in the surfaces. Particulate emissions pollute the air. Acid rain pollutes air and water.	Research and development of soft coal use is costly. Labor, transportation, and conservation are costly.	Diminishing supply. Underutilize soft coal.

Figure 11. Completed Decision-Making Matrix

Note. From *Infusing the Teaching of Critical and Creative Thinking into Content Instruction: A Lesson Design Handbook for the Elementary Grades.* (p. 62), by R. Swartz and S. Parks, 1994, Pacific Grove, CA: Critical Thinking Books and Software (800) 458-4849. Copyright 1994 by Critical Thinking Books and Software. Reprinted with permission.

Graphics That Hold and Organize Information

Matrices are commonly used in textbooks, newspapers, and periodicals to organize complex information. The matrix in Figure 11 contains information involved in considering what energy sources our nation should develop and use. This matrix on alternative energy sources serves as a data retrieval chart—a graphic organizer to guide students' research and observations for conducting inductive reasoning. Students are not given this data but, instead, use the matrix to organize their research. The empty cells of the diagram in Figure 12 remind students of the kind of data needed in order to make an informed judgment.

In Figure 11, students listed their options (various types of energy sources) down the left side of the diagram. They labeled each column with a kind of consequence that should be considered in deciding energy use (availability, impact on the environment, cost to use and produce, and so forth). After each student group reported its findings about an energy source, their information was added to the matrix. A huge bulletin board can be used to organize and display the class' combined research on sources of energy.

Having organized this mass of information, students must interpret its meaning. Individually, in small groups, or as a whole class, students summarized information in each row and created a summary statement about a particular form of energy. For example, the student group responsible for gathering the data on solar energy prepared its summary statement to synthesize the important information that their research uncovered about solar energy.

Then, students summarized the information in each column to state a generalization that addresses the next important question: What kinds of consequences are more important than others? This summary statement addresses which factors in considering energy use warrant greater weight than others? By reflecting on the summary statements for the rows and the columns, students prepared a recommendation about which types of energy sources our nation should utilize.

OPTIONS	RELEVANT CONSEQUENCES			
	EASE OF PRODUCTION	ENVIRONMENT	COST	AVAILABILITY
SOLAR Active Passive Photovoltaic				
NUCLEAR				
PETRO-CHEMICAL				
COAL				

Figure 12. Blank Decision-Making Matrix

Note. From *Infusing the Teaching of Critical and Creative Thinking into Content Instruction: A Lesson Design Handbook for the Elementary Grades.* (p. 62), by R. Swartz and S. Parks, 1994, Pacific Grove, CA: Critical Thinking Books and Software (800) 458-4849. Copyright 1994 by Critical Thinking Books and Software. Reprinted with permission.

Graphics That Show Relationships

Most of the graphic organizers featured in textbooks or magazines are designed to show how information is related. Common graphics, such as matrices, flowcharts, Venn diagrams, branching diagrams, and concept maps, depict analysis: sequence, rank, classification, subdivision, analogy, part/whole relationships, or attribution.

Concept maps, also called "bubble maps" or "web diagrams," can be used to show a variety of relationships (attribution, classification, and part to whole relationships), can stimulate creative thinking, and are versatile for numerous instructional or personal uses. In the example in Figure 13, the concept map shows some key ideas students learn about in a unit on the Civil Rights Movement. This concept map may be the teacher's planning tool to design the course, a preinstruction assessment instrument, an advanced organizer for students (a framework to depict the concepts that students will learn in the course), or a review tool to summarize instruction when the unit is completed.

In this case, the concept map for the Civil Rights Movement is a mental model for any struggle for equality: the struggle against apartheid in South Africa, the labor movement, the women's movement, and so forth. Because gifted students tend to look for similar connections and applications, creating mental models that are as clearly "visible" as this one becomes a powerful tool for efficient learning and organized thought.

Graphics That Stimulate or Guide Thinking

Graphic organizers can be used to analyze or create a metaphor. Class discussions recorded on graphic organizers show how metaphors serve as idea bridges to convey other characteristics or images with playfulness and richness. Consider the cat metaphor in Carl Sandburg's poem "Fog." Using the diagram shown in Figure 14, students named a characteristic of a cat that was also true of fog, such as "silence." Students brainstormed words for silence, associated with either a cat or fog, and wrote these details or descriptors in the boxes on each side of the diagram. They then used the information on the graphic to critique

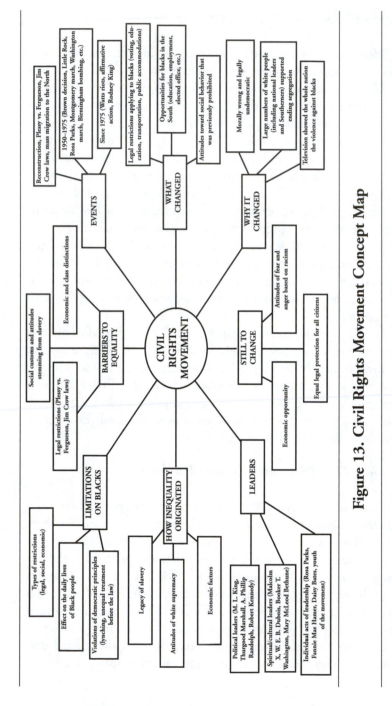

Figure 13. Civil Rights Movement Concept Map

Note. From *Design for Understanding.* (in press), by S. Parks, unpublished manuscript. Copyright 1999 Sandra Parks. Reprinted with permission.

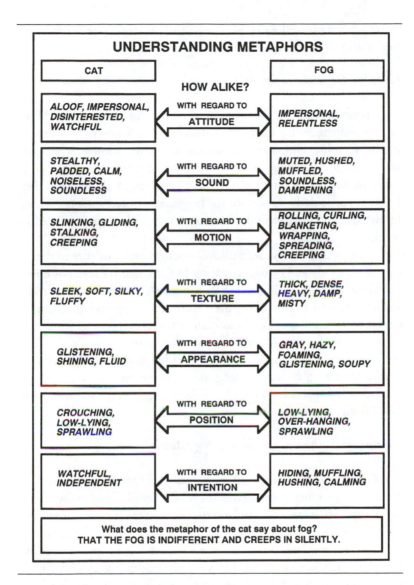

Figure 14. Graphic Organizer to Analyze Metaphors

Note. From *Organizing Thinking II* (p. 90), by S. Parks and H. Black, 1990, Pacific Grove, CA: Critical Thinking Books and Software (800) 458-4849. Copyright 1990 by Critical Thinking Books and Software. Reprinted with permission.

the effectiveness of the cat metaphor and created a poem that used fog as a metaphor for a cat.

Graphic Organizers for Assessment

Portfolio and performance assessment increasingly includes graphic organizers for teachers' evaluations and students' self-assessments. Graphics allow students to assess what they know, what they have learned, and what questions remain unanswered about concepts in an instructional unit. Using graphics to show what they know is particularly important for language-limited students whose knowledge and level of understanding may not be expressed well in writing.

Using graphic organizers allows teachers and students to depict learning quickly and easily, appealing to the cognitive styles of holistic, visual learners. While graphics are well-suited to show gains in learning factual information, the validity of inferences that can be drawn from using graphics in assessment warrants further investigation. Rubrics for the scoring of individual products and guidelines for interpreting graphics should be clarified and carefully reviewed before making quantitative judgments. However, as one indicator for broad interpretation of students' learning, concept maps provide helpful information.

Computer Software and Technology Tools

Computer technology offers access to an array of information resources, promotes interactivity between people, and allows users to manipulate images and information on a scale unprecedented in human thought. CD-ROMs hold enormous databases that make information available to us in word processing form that can be reorganized. Classroom teachers are only beginning to understand the richness of using data bases and videodiscs to access and hold information so that students can manipulate and draw interpretations from the information.

Interactive software allows the user to engage in inductive thinking in situations that cannot be modeled with concrete objects. For example, the software Gertrude's Puzzles™ (The

Learning Company, 1983) simulates using attribute blocks and Venn diagrams to show characteristics. However, students are not told the attributes of various sets and must inductively infer the characteristics of a set by observing whether their placement of the figures remains in the circle or falls out—an activity that one cannot carry out placing the actual blocks on a flat surface. Thus, concept attainment is superimposed to a classification task.

The HOTS program, featured on the National Diffusion Network, demonstrates the effectiveness of using computer software with higher-order questioning to increase the basic skills development of low performing students. Discussing the thinking involved in interacting with carefully selected interactive software involves both thinking skill development and metacognition. Designed for middle school and high school students, HOTS has been effectively used with elementary gifted students.

One of the key benefits of using computer software to stimulate ideas is demonstrated by Mindlink™ (Mauzy, 1991). This software is designed to guide the user, even if one has not been trained in creative thinking, through the synectics process. One principle of synectics is that the user has an enormous bank of background information that can be applied to a specific problem, if accessed analogically; the software is designed to access the user's stored, often unconscious, memory.

Mindlink™ prompts the user to generate new ideas in much the same way that "think tanks" work. The software is programmed to prompt metaphoric thinking as the user applies both the synectics process and his or her own background information to a particular problem. As an individual interacts with the software, he or she is guided to think and uncover new perspectives, different speculations, and more ideas than if he or she were working independently. Since the software takes the user down different lines of inquiry and provides different stimuli, at certain points in the process, the software also guides the user on a creative "bird walk." This is an imagery experience, seemingly unrelated to the problem, that diverts the user from the content of the specific problem and prompts analogical connections that one would perhaps not access if focused on the issue only.

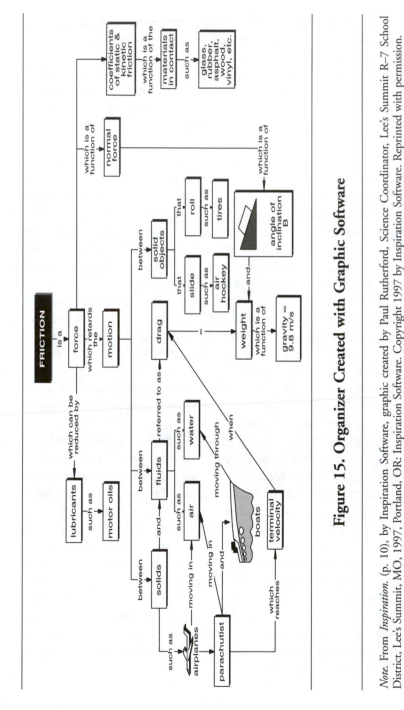

Figure 15. Organizer Created with Graphic Software

Note. From *Inspiration.* (p. 10), by Inspiration Software, graphic created by Paul Rutherford, Science Coordinator, Lee's Summit R–7 School District, Lee's Summit, MO, 1997, Portland, OR: Inspiration Software. Copyright 1997 by Inspiration Software. Reprinted with permission.

Since using graphic organizers allows us to depict ideas quickly and easily, computer software helps us "download" ideas onto diagrams. These diagrams become an aid to creative thinking, critical thinking, decision making, and planning. Some graphics software, such as Inspiration software in Figure 15, is programmed to reproduce standard design elements of graphic organizers (flowchart symbols, arrows, boxes, ovals, icons, clip art, and so forth) so that one can "doodle" with a computer. Templates to depict various analysis tasks are included in the software.

Because some spacing and size features are standardized, one can "draw out" his or her thought almost as quickly on the computer as he or she could sketch it on paper, thus producing a first-draft diagram of surprisingly good craftsmanship. Helping students use computer drawing to depict their thinking and learning improves students' motivation to show what they know and models the "thinking with a computer" skills that are becoming increasingly common in the workplace.

Video technology can provide the context for students to develop problem-solving skills contextualized in real-world problems. The Vanderbilt Learning Technology Center developed a series of videodiscs that presents complex, but authentic, problems in which students must generate and solve many subproblems in order to resolve the larger issue. One videodisc *The Adventures of Jasper Woodbury: Episode One* (Vanderbilt Learning Technology Center, 1996) presents a situation in which Jasper must decide what to do to get his boat home late in the afternoon, realizing that his boat has no lights. Based on a principle of embedded data design, the videodisc provides relevant and irrelevant data (time of sunset, a river map, weather conditions, and so forth) that middle school students use to define and solve Jasper's problem. The design features of this videodisc (embedded data, a videodisc format with random access capability, a context in which students must define problems, mathematics operations, and problem-solving skills) provide a rich source of data not commonly available in middle school mathematics classes and offer an authentic, cooperative problem-solving experience for students.

Assessing Analytical and Critical Thinking

Analytical and Critical Thinking Tests

Analytical thinking programs are commonly evaluated by cognitive abilities tests, such as those listed in the teacher resources. The Developing Cognitive Abilities Test (American College Testronics, 1990) provides data about the Bloom Taxonomy-related cognitive abilities in figural, symbolic, and verbal form. The Ross Test of Cognitive Processes (Ross & Ross, 1976) contains some analysis subtests and some inferential reasoning items. It is easily administered and is used commonly in gifted education programs.

Evaluating critical thinking by creating one's own objective tests requires considerable skill and background in test design and critical thinking. Guidelines for creating such assessment instruments, as well as an annotated bibliography of critical thinking tests, are available in Evaluating Critical Thinking (Ennis & Norris, 1980).

Assessing Students' Thinking in Writing

The effectiveness of analytical and critical thinking instruction is demonstrated dramatically in the quality of students' writing. Our writing is the hard copy of our thinking. If a student's thinking is fuzzy, disorganized, and incomplete, his or her writing will be similarly fuzzy, disorganized, and incomplete. Improvement in the quality of students' writing is the most dramatic and direct assessment of the efficacy of analytical and critical thinking instruction. Figure 16 shows the correlation of thinking processes to various kinds of writing prompts. While the questions in the thinking strategy may serve as standards for creating rubrics, students' thinking is often implicit, rather than explicit. Unless teachers review students' prewriting notes, one may not always know whether or not students have considered the key questions of various thinking strategies when preparing their papers.

Writing assessment increasingly involves using graphic organizers. Students frequently submit prewriting material so that the teacher can understand the process, as well as the product, of students' composition. While we must guard against artificial standardization of diagrams (such as proper or improper design of a student-generated graphic organizer), we can make assessment tasks more flexible by incorporating these tools into portfolio and performance assessment.

Assessing Thinking and Learning

One of the most complex issues in evaluating students' critical thinking and content learning involves planning appropriate assessment tasks, including performance assessments, and weighing students' work to assign a grade. For teachers in gifted classes in core

---

CORRELATING THINKING STRATEGIES TO TYPES OF WRITING

TYPES OF WRITING	USE THIS THINKING STRATEGY
NARRATIVE	
Create a story about this situation:	DECISION MAKING
EXPOSITORY	
Compare and contrast ___ and ___.	COMPARE AND CONTRAST
Describe the events that lead to ___.	SEQUENCING
What caused ___.	CAUSAL EXPLANATION
What would happen if ___.	PREDICTION
PERSUASIVE	
Why should ___ do ___?	REASONS/CONCLUSIONS
Why did ___ do ___?	CAUSAL EXPLANATION
Develop an argument for ___?	REASONS/CONCLUSIONS and UNCOVERING ASSUMPTIONS
What should be done to ___?	DECISION MAKING
CREATIVE	
Create a poem or story about ___.	CREATE A METAPHOR GENERATING POSSIBILITIES
DESCRIPTIVE	
Describe a ___.	PARTS OF A WHOLE or CLASSIFICATION
Describe how to ___.	SEQUENCING

Figure 16. Correlated Thinking Strategies to Types of Writing

---

Note. From *Design for Understanding*, by S. Parks, in process, Pacific Grove, CA: Critical Thinking Books and Software. Copyright 1999 by Sandra Parks. Reprinted with permission.

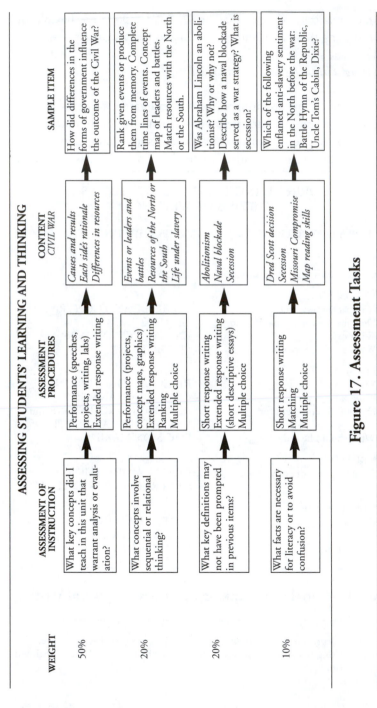

ASSESSING STUDENTS' LEARNING AND THINKING

WEIGHT	ASSESSMENT OF INSTRUCTION	ASSESSMENT PROCEDURES	CONTENT *CIVIL WAR*	SAMPLE ITEM
50%	What key concepts did I teach in this unit that warrant analysis or evaluation? →	Performance (speeches, projects, writing, labs) Extended response writing →	*Causes and results Each side's rationale Differences in resources* →	How did differences in the forms of government influence the outcome of the Civil War?
20%	What concepts involve sequential or relational thinking? →	Performance (projects, concept maps, graphics) Extended response writing Ranking Multiple choice →	*Events or leaders and battles Resources of the North or the South Life under slavery* →	Rank given events or produce them from memory. Complete time lines of events. Concept map of leaders and battles. Match resources with the North or the South.
20%	What key definitions may not have been prompted in previous items? →	Short response writing Extended response writing (short descriptive essays) Multiple choice →	*Abolitionism Naval blockade Secession* →	Was Abraham Lincoln an abolitionist? Why or why not? Describe how a naval blockade served as a war strategy? What is secession?
10%	What facts are necessary for literacy or to avoid confusion? →	Short response writing Matching Multiple choice →	*Dred Scott decision Secession Missouri Compromise Map reading skills* →	Which of the following enflamed anti-slavery sentiment in the North before the war: Battle Hymn of the Republic, Uncle Tom's Cabin, Dixie?

Figure 17. Assessment Tasks

Note. From *Design for Understanding* (in process), by S. Parks, unpublished manuscript. Copyright 1999 by Sandra Parks. Reprinted with permission.

content subjects, grading is always difficult, especially when class time and students' assignments have emphasized critical thinking. The diagram in Figure 17 shows examples of assessment tasks in a unit on the Civil War. Since higher-order thinking is best demonstrated in performances of skillful thinking and content understanding that requires considerable time and preparation for the students, such evaluation procedures should be weighted accordingly:

- evaluation tasks that involve critical or creative thinking require products that take considerable time and preparation and therefore receive the most credit,
- analysis tasks can be evaluated in forms that require less preparation and thought,
- knowledge, comprehension, and application tasks can be evaluated in test form, taking less time, requiring less thought, and receiving the least credit.

Staff Development on Improving Critical Thinking Skills

While staff development for teachers of the gifted commonly features analytical and critical thinking strategies, meaningful implementation of higher-order thinking instruction requires a long-term personal and professional development process. Robust teaching and learning involving critical thinking requires that teachers are themselves clear about the criteria and procedures of sound thinking. Since teacher education rarely offers sufficient background in analytical and critical thinking instruction, professional development becomes primarily an in-service function.

Critical thinking by its nature requires evaluating one's own strengths and weaknesses in higher-order thinking, as well as reflective practice regarding the quality of the analytical and critical thinking instruction that one offers students. Individual teachers must self-assess and self-select the kind of thinking processes that fit their disciplines and their own teaching styles. Then teachers must invest in their own intellectual growth, as well as expand their knowledge of teaching techniques.

The summaries of programs and centers in the Appendix of this chapter indicate sources of training and research to improve the quality of students' thinking and to enhance teachers' own personal and professional growth.

Teacher Resources

Publications

CTB-McGraw Hill. (1993). *Test of Cognitive Skills*. Monterey, CA: Author.

Harcourt Brace Educational Measurement. (1990). *Differential Aptitude Tests* (5th ed.). San Antonio, TX: Author.

Meeker, M., & Meeker, R. (1975). *Learning Abilities Test*. Vida, OR: Structure of Intellect Institute.

Thorndike, R., & Hagen, E. (1993). *Cognitive Abilities Test*. Itasca, IL: Riverside Publishing.

References

American College Testronics. (1990). *Developing Cognitive Abilities Test.* Iowa City, IA: Author.

Black, H., & Parks, S. (1985). *Building thinking skills.* Pacific Grove, CA: Critical Thinking Books & Software (formerly Midwest Publications).

Bloom, B. S. (Ed.). (1977). *Taxonomy of educational objective: Handbook 1 cognitive domain.* New York: Longman Publishers.

Eggen, P. D., Kauchek, D. P., & Harder, R. (1979). *Strategies for teachers: Information processing models in the classroom.* Englewood Cliff, NJ: Prentice-Hall

Ennis, R. (1996). *Critical thinking.* New York: Prentice-Hall.

Ennis, R., & Norris, S. (1980). *Evaluating critical thinking.* Pacific Grove, CA: Critical Thinking Books & Software (formerly Midwest Publications).

Harnadek, A. (1976). *Critical thinking I.* Pacific Grove, CA: Critical Thinking Books & Software (formerly Midwest Publications).

Harnadek, A. (1980). *Critical thinking II.* Pacific Grove, CA: Critical Thinking Books & Software (formerly Midwest Publications).

Howells, R. F. (1992, November). Thinking in the morning, thinking in the evening, thinking at suppertime. *Phi Delta Kappan,* 223–225.

Inspiration Software. (1994). *Inspiration.* Portland, OR: Inspiration Software.

The Learning Company. (1983). *Gertrude's puzzles.* Palo Alto, CA: Author.

Learning Technology Center. (1996). *The adventures of Jasper Woodbury: Episode one.* Nashville, TN: Vanderbilt University.

Lipman, M. (1979). *Philosophy for children.* Montclair, New Jersey: Institute for the Advancement of Philosophy for Children.

Mauzy, J. (1991). *Mindlink Internelis.* North Pomfret, VT: Mindlink, Inc.

Parks, S. (1999). *Design for understanding,* Unpublished manuscript.

Parks, S., & Black, H. (1990). *Organizing thinking II.* Pacific Grove, California: Critical Thinking Books & Software (formerly Midwest Publications).

Potter, P., & Dawson, J. W. (1988, October). National merit scholars by design, not by chance. *Educational Leadership,* pp. 54–56.

Rito, G. R., & Moller, B. W. (1989). Teaching enrichment activities to minorities: TEAM for success. *Journal of Negro Education,* 58(2), 212–219.

Ross, J. S., & Ross, K. T. (1976). *Ross Test of Cognitive Processes.* San Raphael, CA: Academic Therapy Publications.

Swartz, R., & Parks, S. (1994). *Infusing the teaching of critical and creative thinking into content instruction: A lesson design handbook for the elementary grades.* Pacific Grove, CA: Critical Thinking Press & Software.

Swartz, R., & Parks, S. (in process). *Infusing the teaching of critical and creative thinking into social studies instruction: A lesson design handbook for the secondary grades.* Unpublished manuscript.

Swartz, R., & Perkins, D. (1990). *Issues and approaches to teaching thinking.* Pacific Grove, CA: Critical Thinking Press & Software.

Woodcock, R. W., & Johnson, W. B. (1990). *Text of Cognitive Ability (Woodcock-Johnson).* Itasca, IL: Riverside Publishing.

Author Note

1. The summaries of programs, centers, and networks were prepared by the author and are updated on the web site of the Teaching Thinking Network of the Association for Supervision and Curriculum Development.

Appendix

Networks/Centers to Improve Cognitive Development

Network	*Purpose*	*Contact*
Accelerated Learning and Teaching	Information on school district implementation of accelerated learning	Association for Supervision and Curriculum Development Douglas McPhee 914 Robley Place Cardiff, CA 92007
COGNET	Share information on school district implementation and research on mediated learning	National Diffusion Network Katherine Greenburg College of Education University of Tennessee 131 Claxton Addition-Specia East Knoxville, TN 37996–3400 (615) 974-8145
Efficacy Institute	Implementation of instruction to improve the learning skills of minority students	Efficacy Institute Jeffrey Howard 128 Spring St. Lexington, MA 02173 (617) 862-4390
Gulfport Follow Through: UGA	Training on assessing and promoting cognitive development based on Piagetian principles	National Diffusion Network Gulfport Follow Through: UGA Model Gulfport Public Schools Barbara Thomas P.O. Box 220 Gulfport, MS 39501 (601) 865-4672
Institute for Learning and Development	Research and program development in learning disabilities and abilities	Institute for Learning and Development Lynn Metzer 3 Courthouse Lane Chelmsford, MA 01824 (508) 453-1992

Institute for Visual Thinking	Materials and staff development on visual education	Institute for Visual Thinking Box 332 Gaithersburg, MD 20887
Instrumental Enrichment	Staff development in the Instrumental Enrichment Program by Reuven Feurestein	International Renewal Institute, Inc. 200 East Wood St., Ste. 274 Palatine, IL 60067 (800) 348-4474 irisky@xnet.com
Intellectual Skills Development Center	Training and conferences on cognitive development	Intellectual Skills Development Center Lynne McCauley Moore Hall Western Michigan University Kalamazoo, MI 49008 (616) 387-4411
International Association for Cognitive Education	Share research on cognitive development	International Association for Cognitive Education Martin Miller Graduate School of Education and Psychology Touro College 350 5th Ave., 27 Ste. 1700 New York, NY 10119 (212) 643-0700
National Center for Developmental Education	Training and certification on developmental education	National Center for Developmental Education Elaini Bingham Appalachian State University Boone, NC 28608 (704) 262-3057 mockmt@appste.edu
Society for Accelerative Learning and Teaching	Research in the use of music to facilitate learning	Society for Accelerative Learning and Teaching Box 1216 Welch Station Ames, IA 50010
Society for Developmental Education	Development and conferences on developmental education and multiage classes	Society for Developmental Education 10 Sharon Rd. Peterborough, NH 03458 (800) 462-1478

Structure of Intellect Institute	Research, development and training on using J. P. Guilford's model of intelligence	Mary and Robert Meeker Structure of Intellect Institute P. O. Box D Vida, OR 97488 (503) 896-3936

Networks/Centers for Problem-Based, Experiential, or Cooperative Learning

Network	*Purpose*	*Contact*
Center for the Social Organization of Schools	Research, materials, and training on the implementation of cooperative learning	Center for the Social Organization of Schools Robert Slavin Johns Hopkins University 3505 North Charles St. Baltimore, MD 21218
Consortium for Problem-Based Learning	Staff development on designing, teaching, and assessing problem-based learning	Consortium for Problem-Based Learning Bill Stepien 1621 Nassau Rd. Charlotte, NC 28205
Cooperative Learning Center	Research on cooperative learning	University of Minnesota 202 Patte Hall 150 Pillsbury Dr. Minneapolis, MN 55455
Cooperative Learning Network	Information on school district implementation of cooperative learning	Association for Supervision and Curriculum Development Harlan Rimmerman 1405 N. E. 101 Terrace Kansas City, MO 64155 (816) 453-5050
Intercultural Research Development Association	Research and training on cooperative learning, specializing in bilingual education	Intercultural Research Development Association Juanita Garcia 5835 Callaghan Rd. San Antonio, TX 78228

Kagan Cooperative Learning	Research, materials, and staff development on the structured approach to cooperative learning	Kagan Cooperative Learning Spencer Kagan P.O. Box 72008 San Clemente, CA 92674–9208 (800) 933-2667 fax (714) 248-9662
Outward Bound	Research and staff development on an experiential program for team building	Outward Bound Harvard University Graduate School of Education Appian Way Cambridge, MA 02138
Problem-Based Learning	Staff development on designing, teaching, and assessing problem-based learning	Southern Illinois University School of Medicine Howard Barrows Department of Medical Education P.O. Box 19230 Springfield, IL 62794 (217) 782-0795
Problem-Based Learning Network	Information on implementing problem-based learning	Association for Supervision and Curriculum Development Linda Torp Center for Problem-Based Learning Illinois Mathematics and Science Academy 1500 W. Sullivan Rd. Aurora, IL 60506–1000 (708) 907-5956 fax (708) 907-5946 ltorp@msa.edu
Professional Development Associates	Staff development on conflict resolution and the implementation of cooperative learning	Professional Development Associates Laurie Stevarn 2015 Central Ave., N. E., #228 Minneapolis, MN 55418
Program for Complex Instruction	Research and training on a cooperative learning approach that involves classroom management aimed at improving higher order thinking	Program for Complex Instruction Center for Education Research Elizabeth Cohen Stanford University Stanford, CA 94305

Sarasota Thinks	Recognition and celebration of thinking in the community	The Education Foundation Ben Johnsen 950 Tamiami Trail S. Ste. 202 Sarasota, FL 34236 (813) 955-5405 fax (813) 952-0160
Serious Teens Acting Responsibly	Projects and thinking instruction in a community-based service program	STAR Veronica Primus-Thomas South Carolina State University 1890 Extension P.O. Box 7659 Orangeburg, SC 29117 (803) 536- 8855 fax (803) 536- 7102 vthomas@USCU.edu
Service and Experiential Learning Network	Information on implementing service learning or experiential learning programs	Association for Supervision and Curriculum Development Jan Schollenberger-Koenig Service Learning Coordinator Valparaiso, IN 46383 (219) 462-3986 jkoenig@mail.valpok12,in.us

Networks/Centers for Creating Thoughtful Schools

Network	*Purpose*	*Contact*
Autonomous Learner Program	Materials and staff development on implementing the Autonomous Learner Model	Autonomous Learner Model George Betts P.O. Box 2264 Greeley, CO 80632 (800) 345-2577 fax (970) 330-2391
Coalition of Essential Schools	Research and theory development on school reform to promote meaningful, humanistic learning	Coalition of Essential Schools Theodore Sizer Brown University Box 1969 Providence, RI 02912 (401) 863-3384

Council for Basic Education	Newsletter written by teachers to exchange classroom ideas	Council for Basic Education 1319 F. St. #900 Washington, DC 20004
Critical Skills Program	Reform in teaching, assessment, school culture, and student relationships	The Critical Skills Program Peter Epping Antioch New England Graduate School 40 Avon St. Keene, NH 03431–3516 (603) 357-3122
Developmental Studies Center	Provides collegial study packages and staff development to create learning communities and character building	Developmental Studies Center 200 Embardadero, Ste. 205 Oakland, CA 94606–5300 (800) 666-7270 fax (510) 464-3670 pub@devstu.org
High Success Network	Implementation of performance-based instruction	The High Success Network William Spady P.O. Box 1630 Eagle, CO 81631 (800) 642-1979 fax (303) 328-1698
Institute for Intelligent Behavior	Staff development on reflective practice and coaching to promote thoughtful teaching	Institute for Intelligent Behavior Bob Gramston 337 Guadalupe Dr. El Dorado Hills, CA 95630
Institute for Reality Therapy	Implementation of Reality Therapy to promote learning	Institute for Reality Therapy Barbara Hines Garner The Quality School 6913 Beeman St. Plano, TX 75023
Institute for Writing and Thinking	Sponsors a summer institute for writing and thinking	Institute for Writing and Thinking Judi Smith Bard College P.O. Box 50000 Annandale-on-Hudson, NY 12504–5000 (914) 758-7484

International Society for Exploring Teaching Alternatives	Annual conference for college and university faculty on innovative, individualized teaching techniques	International Society for Exploring Teaching Alternatives Ken Brown Office of Instructional Development Lakehead University Thunder Bay Ontario P7B 5E1 CANADA (807) 237-7631 or Susan Moncada Indiana State University Terre Haute, IN (812) 237-7631
Junior Great Books	Materials and staff development on conducting Shared Inquiry dialogue in classroom discussion	Great Books Foundation Debra Mantia 35 E. Wacker Dr., Ste. 2300 Chicago, IL 60601–2298 (800) 222-5870
Mississippi Writing and Thinking Institute	Professional development on writing and thinking	Mississippi Writing and Thinking Institute Tracia Bridges 104 Sis Circle Hattiesburg, MS 39402 (601) 325-7777
National Center for Accelerated Schools	Research, materials, and staff development on implementing the Accelerated Schools Model	National Center for Accelerated Schools Henry Levin CERAS 109 School of Education Stanford University Stanford, CA 94305–3084 (425) 725-1676
National Center for Restructuring Education, Schools, and Teaching	Research and professional development on reflective practice and school reform	Teacher's College Linda Darling-Hammond Columbia University 525 West 120th St. Box 110 New York, NY 10027

National Paideia Center	Implementation of the Paideia Program	National Paideia Center School of Education CB #2045 University of North Carolina Chapel Hill, NC 27599–8045 (919) 962-7379 fax (919) 962-7381
The Network, Inc.	Program and staff development on school reform	The Network, Inc. David Crandell 136 Fenno Dr. Rowley, MA 01969 (508) 470-1080
Network for Systems Thinking Chaos and Theory	Information on implementation of school reform based on systems thinking	Association for Supervision and Curriculum Development Barbara Vogl Change Management Systems 5300 Glen Haven Rd. Soquel, CA 95073 (408) 476-2905 fax (803) 476-0662 bvogl@aol.com
Network for Tech Prep	Information on implementing Tech Prep, including an emphasis on higher-order thinking	Association for Supervision and Curriculum Development Sandra Sarvis Lexington School District 4 P.O. Box 569 Swansea, SC 29160 (803) 568-1021 fax (803) 568-1020
Network for Wholistic Education	Information on implementation of school reform based on wholistic education	Association for Supervision and Curriculum Development John Palladino 81 Hill Dr. Oyster Bay, NY 11771 or Ontario Institute for Studies in Education Jack Miller Niagra Center 28 Prince St. St. Catherines, Ontario L2R 3X7 CANADA

Reading and Writing for Critical Thinking	Professional development for teachers in Eastern European, North, and South American nations on applying critical thinking skills	Orava Project Dr. Jeannie Steele or Dr. Kurt Meredith University of Northern Iowa Cedar Rapids, IA http://www.uni.edu/coe/rwet/ projdesc.html
Research for Better Teaching	Materials and staff development on school reform and study/ thinking skills	Research for Better Teaching John Saphier 56 Bellows Hill Rd. Carlisle, MA 01741 (508) 369-2294
School as a Home for the Mind	Materials and staff development on school reform, assessment, school culture, and student relationships	International Renewal Institute, Inc. 200 East Wood St. Ste. 274 Palatine, IL 60067 (800) 348-4474 irisky@xnet.com
Search Models Unlimited	Staff development on creating thoughtful schools and promoting thinking dispositions	Search Models Unlimited Arthur Costa P.O. Box 362 Davis, CA 95617–0362 (916) 956-7872 kwatsmu@aol.com
Smart Schools Network	Research on the implementation of the school reform principles described in "Smart Schools"	Project Zero David Perkins Longfellow Hall 13 Appian Way Cambridge, MA 02138 (617) 495-4342 fax (617) 495-9709 learn@pz.harvard.edu
Synthesis, Inc.	Staff development on higher-order thinking	Synthesis, Inc. Kathryn Merriam P.O. Box 4359 Pocatello, ID 83295
Thinking Possibilities	Faculty development on promoting thinking	Thinking Possibilities Harriet Chamberlin 1534 Scenic Ave. Berkeley, CA 94708

Thoughtful Schools Network	Information on school district experience creating a climate to promote thinking	Association for Supervision and Curriculum Development Silver and Strong Associates Aspen Corporation Park 1480 Rte. 9 North Woodbridge, NJ 07093 (800) 962-4432

Networks/Centers on Brain-Based Education, Learning Styles, and Multiple Intelligences

Network	*Purpose*	*Contact*
Affective Factors in Learning Network	Information on the effect of emotion in learning	Association for Supervision and Curriculum Development Harriet Arnold Bernerd School of Education University of the Pacific 3601 Pacific Ave. Stockton, CA 95211 (209) 946-2807 fax (209) 258-7984 harnold@vmsl.cc.uop.edu
Armstrong Creative Training	Professional development on multiple intelligences	Thomas Armstrong P.O. Box 548 Cloverdale, CA 95425 (707) 894-4646
Brain-based Education	Research on brain functions applied to education	Robert Sylwester University of Oregon College of Education Eugene, OR 97403
Caine Learning	Research, professional development, and system change based on brain research	Caine Learning Renate and Geoffrey Caine P.O. Box 1847 Idyllwild, CA 92549 (909) 659-0152 fax (909) 659-0242 gr@pe.net info@cainelearning.com

Foundation for Human Potential	Sponsors institutes on brain and environmental influences on intelligence	Foundation for Human Potential Andrea Gellin Shindler (847) 325-4769 AndreaFHP@aol.com
Gregoric Associates, Inc.	Materials and staff development on assessing learning styles and modifying instruction based on the Gregoric model	Gregoric Associates, Inc. Anthony Gregoric 15 Doubleday Rd. Columbia, CT 06237–0351 (203) 228-0093
Learner's Dimension	Materials and institutes on learning styles	Learner's Dimension Kathleen Butler P.O. Box 6 Columbia, CT 06237 (860) 228-3786 http://www.learnersdimension.com
Ned Herman Group	Professional development and materials on instruction based on brain research	Ned Herman Group Ned Herman 2075 Buffalo Creek Rd. Lake Lure, NC 28746
Network on Brain-based Education and Learning Styles	Share information on school district implementation of instruction based on brain research	Association for Supervision and Curriculum Development Center for the Advancement of Reform in Education Joan Caulfield Rockhurst College 1100 Rockhurst Rd. Kansas City, MO 64110 (816) 501-4651 or Institute for Instruction, Learning, and Teaching Wayne Jennings 2550 University Ave. Room 347–N St. Paul, MN 55114–1052 (612) 645-0200
New City School	Staff development and material on imple-mentation of multiple intelligences	New City School Sally Bergman 5209 Waterman St. St. Louis, MO 63108

Project Zero	Theory development and research on multiple intelligences	Project Zero Howard Gardner 321 Longfellow Hall 13 Appian Way Cambridge, MA 02138 (617) 495-4342 fax (617) 495-9709 learn@pz.harvard.edu http://www.pzweb.harvard.edu
Quantum Learning and Teaching	Materials, staff development, and summer camp for students based on brain-based education	Quantum Learning and Teaching 1725 Coast Highway Oceanside, CA 92054–5319 (619) 722-0072 fax (619) 722-3507 supercamp@aol.com
Teaching for Multiple Intelligences Network	Information on school district implementation based on multiple intelligences	Association for Supervision and Curriculum Development David Lazear New Dimensions of Learning 729 W. Waveland, Ste. G Chicago, IL 60613 (312) 525-6650
Turning Point	Materials and staff development on brain-based education	Turning Point P.O. Box 2551 Del Mar, CA 92014 (800) 325-4769 fax (619) 546-7560

Networks/Centers on Creative Thinking

Network	*Purpose*	*Contact*
American Creativity Association	Share information on creative thinking and thinking instruction	American Creativity Association P.O. Box 26068 St. Paul, MN 55126–0068 (612) 784-8375

Center for Creative Learning	Training, research, and materials on creative problem solving	Center for Creative Learning Donald Treffinger 4152 Independence Ct., Ste. C–7 Sarasota, FL 34234 (941) 351-8862 fax (941) 351-9061
Center for Studies in Creativity	Courses, graduate programs, research, and training on creative problem solving	Center for Studies in Creativity Scott Isaksen Buffalo State College 1300 Elmwood Ave. Buffalo, NY 14222 (716) 878-6223 fax (716) 878-4040
Creative Problem-Solving Institute	Develops instruction to improve abilities for creative learning, problem sensing, and solving	Creative Education Foundation Sidney Parnes 1050 Union Rd. Buffalo, NY 14224
Edward de Bono Programme for the Design and Development of Thinking	Offers training and conferences on creative thinking and problem-solving strategies by Edward de Bono	Programme for the Design and Development of Thinking Edward de Bono University of Malta Msida, Malta (365) 333903/6 fax 356-450
Future Problem-Solving Program	Sponsors a competition on future problem solving	FPSP Bonnie Jensen 318 W. Ann Ann Arbor, MI 48104 (313) 998-7377 fax (313) 998-7663
Institute for Creative Education	Materials and staff development on Paul Torrance's creative thinking model	Institute for Creative Education Monika Steinberg 700 Hollydell Court Sewell, NJ 08080 (609) 582-7000 fax (609) 582-4206

Inventive and Creative Education	Information on creativity applied to invention	National Inventive Thinking Association Leonard Molotsky P.O. Box 836202 Richardson, TX 75083
Mindlink	Computer software and staff development on the use of Synectics	Synectics Jeff Mauzy 17 Dunster St. Cambridge, MA 02138 (617) 868-6530
Odyssey of the Mind	Materials, training, and competitions on practical problem solving	OM Associates, Inc. C. Samuel Micklus P.O. Box 27 Glassboro, NJ 08028 (609) 881-1771 fax (609) 307-0645 http://www.creative-competitions.com
Talents Unlimited	Staff development on Calvin Taylor's creative thinking model	Talents Unlimited Deborah Hobbs Mobile County Public Schools 1107 Arlington St. Mobile, AL 30605 (205) 690-8060

Network/Centers on Critical Thinking

Network	*Purpose*	*Contact*
Center for Critical Thinking	Staff development on critical thinking	Center for Critical Thinking Baker University Baldwin City, KS 66006

Center for Critical Thinking and Moral Critique	Provides in-service programs in critical thinking and sponsors an annual critical thinking conference	The Center for Critical Thinking and Moral Critique Linda Elder Sonoma State University 1801 E. Cotati Blvd. Rohnert Park, CA 94928–3609 (707) 664-2940 fax (707) 664-4101 CCT@Sonoma.edu
Critical Thinking Center	Faculty development and conferences on critical thinking	University of East Anglia Alec Fisher School of Economics and Social Sciences Norwich NR47TJ ENGLAND
Critical Thinking Cooperative	Development of critical thinking materials and professional development on critical thinking	The Critical Thinking Cooperative LeRoi Daniels P.O. Box 62024 #143–4255 Arbutus RPO Vancouver, British Columbia V6J 1Z1 CANADA (604) 732-1907 fax (604) 732-1957 leroi.daniels@ubc.ca
Critical Thinking Exchange	Staff development on critical thinking	Critical Thinking Exchange Rock Valley College 3301 N. Mulford Rd. Rockford, IL 61111
Human Development Institute, Inc.	Staff development on critical thinking	Human Development Institute 140 La Grange, Ste. 18 La Grange, IL 60525
Institute for Critical Thinking	Produce a newsletter on critical thinking	Institute for Critical Thinking Mark Weinstein Montclair State University Upper Montclair, NJ 07043 (201) 893-5184

Institute for General Semantics	Training in Alfred Korzybski's general semantics approach to critical thinking and decision making	Institute for General Semantics 163 Engle St. Englewood, NJ 07631 (201) 568-0551 fax (201) 569-1793 Institute@General-Semantics.org http://www.General-Semantics.org
Institute for the Advancement of Philosophy for Children	International network connects teachers using the Philosophy for Children program	Institute for the Advancement of Philosophy for Children Montclair State College Upper Montclair, NJ 07043 (201) 893-4277
National Council for Excellence in Critical Thinking	Network of educators committed to quality in critical thinking instruction	The Center for Critical Thinking and Moral Critique Richard Paul Sonoma State University 1801 E. Cotati Blvd. Rohnert Park, CA 94928–3609 (707) 664-2940 fax (707) 664-4101 CCT@Sonoma.edu
New York Center For Critical Thinking and Language Learning	Share information for staff development on teaching and evaluating critical thinking and critical literacy	New York Center for Critical Thinking and Language Learning John Chafee The City University of New York Room E202A 31–10 Thomson Ave. Long Island City, NY 11101 (718) 482-5699 fax (718) 482-5599
Ohio Center for Critical Thinking	Staff development on critical thinking	Ohio Center for Critical Thinking Instruction 89 Grand Ave. Akron, OH 44303

Wisconsin Center for Excellence in Critical Thinking	Staff development and a summer institute on critical thinking	Wisconsin Center for Excellence in Critical Thinking Nancy Graese CESA #11 225 Ostermann Dr. Turtle Lake, WI 54889 (715) 986-2020 fax (715) 986-2040

Networks/Centers for Moral/Character Education and Conflict Resolution

Network	*Purpose*	*Contact*
American Institute for Character Education	Program development and training on character education	American Institute for Character Education 8918 Tesoro Dr. Ste. 220 San Antonio, TX 78217–6253 (512) 829-1727 (800) 284-0499
Character Education Group	Materials and training on character education	Character Development Group Dixon J. Smith P.O. Box 9211 Chapel Hill, NC 27515–9211 (919) 967-2110 fax (919) 967-2139
Conflict Resolution Network	Share information on school district implementation of conflict resolution instruction	Association for Supervision and Curriculum Development Mary Ellen Schaffer Elsie Johnson School 1380 Nautilus Lane Hanover Park, IL 60103 (708) 830-8770 or Steven Kline Elgin School District #46 335 E. Chicago St. Elgin, IL 60120 (708) 888-5357

Educators for Social Responsibility	Materials and share information on peace education	Educators for Social Responsibility 23 Garden St. Cambridge, MA 02138 (617) 492-1764
Facing History and Ourselves	Materials and training on moral education based on the study of the Holocaust	Facing History and Ourselves National Foundation Margot Stern Strom 25 Kennard Rd. Brookline, MA 02146 (617) 232-1595
Jefferson Center for Character Education	Materials development and training on direct instruction in character education	Jefferson Center for Character Education 2700 E. Foothill Blvd. Pasadena, CA 91107 (818) 792-8130 fax (818) 792-8364
Kenan Ethics Program	Research and conferences on moral education	Kenan Ethics Program Duke University P.O. Box 90432 Durham, NC 27708 (910) 228-1602 http://www.kenan.ethics.duke.edu.
National Center for Conflict Resolution Education	Staff development on the implementation of conflict resolution instruction	National Center for Conflict Resolution 110 Main St. Urbana, IL (217) 384-4118 fax (217) 384-8284
National Center for Dispute Resolution	Institutes on conflict resolution skills	National Center for Dispute Resolution 1726 M. St. N.W., Ste. 500 Washington, DC 20036–4502 (202) 466-4764 fax (202) 466-4769

Network for Character Education	Information on school district implementation of character education	Association for Supervision and Curriculum Development Center for the Advancement of Ethics and Character Kevin Ryan Boston University School of Education Room 356 605 Commonwealth Ave. Boston, MA 02215 (617) 353-3262
Peace Education Foundation	Program and staff development on conflict resolution and peer mediation	Peace Education Foundation Lloyd Van Bylevett 1900 Biscayne Blvd. Miami, FL 33132 (800) 749-8838
Personal Responsibility Education Process	Newsletters, conferences, and training on character education	Personal Responsibility Education Process Cooperative School Districts 13157 Olive Sour Rd. St. Louis, MO 63141 (314) 576-3535 (800) 478-5684 http://www.info.cds.org
Resolving Conflict Creatively	Program and staff development on the implementation of conflict resolution instruction	Resolving Conflict Creatively Linda Lantieri RCCP National Center 163 Third Ave., #103 New York, NY 10003
Social Decision Making and Problem Solving	Program and staff development on decision making in interpersonal relationships	University of Medicine and Dentistry of New Jersey-CMHC at Piscataway Thomas Schuyler 240 Shelton Rd. Piscataway, NJ 08854–3248 (201) 463-4939

Network/Centers to Improve a Variety
of Thinking Processes

Network	Purpose	Contact
Blanco Weiss Institute for the Development of Thinking	Faculty development on teaching a variety of thinking skills	Blanco Weiss Institute for the Development of Thinking 40 Hantke St. Jerusalem, ISRAEL 96782
British Psychological Society	Research and an international conference on developing thinking skills	University of London David Green 20 Bedford Way London, WC1HOAL UNITED KINGDOM
Center for Critical and Creative Thinking	Staff development on creative thinking and critical thinking	Center for Critical and Creative Thinking William Hayes P.O. Box 3234 Delta State University Cleveland, MS 38733 (662) 846-4247
Center for Guided Design	Staff development on decision making and problem solving in content instruction	Center for Guided Design Charles Wales Engineering Science Building West Virginia Morgantown, WV 26506–6101 (304) 293-4821, ext 213
Center for Thinking Skills	Research, staff development, and materials for teaching a variety of thinking skills	Center for Thinking Skills Robert Fisher West London Institute 300 Margarets Rd. Twickenham TW1 London TW1 1PT UNITED KINGDOM (801) 466-9365

Choices for the 21st Century	Materials and staff development on applying moral reasoning and decision-making skills to global issues	Choices for the 21st Century Thomas J. Watson Institute for International Studies Brown University Box 1948 Providence, RI 02912 (401) 863-3155
Critical Analysis and Thinking Skills	Staff development and materials for teaching critical thinking and decision making in grades 7–12	CATS Program Terry Applegate 4988 Kalani Dr. Salt Lake City, UT 84117–6421 (801) 466-9365
Critical and Creative Thinking Program	Staff development and a graduate program on critical thinking and creative thinking	Critical and Creative Thinking Program Delores Gallo University of Massachusetts 100 Morrissey Rd. Boston, MA 02125–3393
Developing Thinking Skills	Materials, research, and faculty development on teaching a variety of thinking skills	Instituto Technologico y de Estudios Superiores Margarita de Sanchez Topolobampo #463 Col. Las Brisad Monterrey Nuevo Leon 64790 MEXICO
Dimensions of Learning	Staff development and materials for designing instruction to promote thinking and learning	Mid-continent Regional Education Laboratory Robert Marzano 2550 South Parker Rd., Suite 500 Aurora, CO 80014
Dimensions of Learning Network	Share information on school district implementation of instruction based on Dimensions of Learning	Association for Supervision and Curriculum Development Diana Pearson Kenosha Unified School District Talent Development 3600 52nd St. Kenosha, WI 53144 (414) 653-7391 fax (414) 653-6005 dpearson2kusd.kusd.com

Faculty Development Project	Materials development and training on redesigning postsecondary instruction to promote thinking	Minnesota State College and University Center for Teaching and Learning Connie Stack and Joel Peterson North Hennepin Community College 7411 85th Ave. N. Brooklyn Park, MN 55445 (612) 424-0702 fax (612) 424-0965
Hamilton Association	Staff development and materials for teaching thinking skills through visual art	Hamilton Association Dorothy Hamilton Box 756 Columbia, MD 21045
Hartford Critical and Creative Thinking Center	Instruction on creative and critical thinking for schools, businesses, and communities	Hartford Critical and Creative Thinking Center Louise Loomis P.O. Box 12188 Hartford, CT 06132–0188 (860) 233-8650
International Center for the Teaching of Thinking	Implementation of Project Impact, provides regional training and workshops	International Center for the Teaching of Thinking S. Lee Winocur Field 5631 Marshall Dr. Huntington Beach, CA 92649 (714) 840-5772 fax (714) 840-2392
Kentucky Center for Critical Thinking	Staff development on a variety of instructional methods to improve thinking	Center for Critical Thinking Mac Luckey Morehead State University UPO 671 150 University Blvd. Morehead, KY 40351–1689 (606) 783-2813 fax (606) 783-2678
Korean Association for Thinking Development	Journal and staff development on teaching a variety of thinking skills	Korean Association for Thinking Development Department of Psychology Keumyung University Daego 704–701 KOREA

Maryland Center for Reasoning Studies	Staff development on a variety of approaches for teaching and assessing thinking and learning	Maryland Center for Reasoning Studies Toni Worsham Coppin State College 2500 W. North Ave. Baltimore, MD 21216 or Sarah Duff 6103 Gist Ave. Baltimore, MD 21215 or Phyliss Utterback 10818 Hunting Lane Columbia, MD 21044
National Center for Teaching Thinking	Staff development on infusing thinking instruction into content	National Center for Teaching Thinking Robert Swartz 815 Washington St., Ste. 8 Newtonville, MA 02160 (617) 965-4604 fax (617) 965–4674 AAVS48F@Prodigy.com
Research for Better Schools	Research and technical assistance in school reform and teaching thinking	Research for Better Schools Barbara Presseissen 444 N. 3rd St. Philadelphia, PA 19123 (215) 574- 9300
SAGE	Staff development and materials for teaching thinking in gifted education	Winch Park School Diane Modest 64 Prior Dr. Framingham, MA 07101 (508) 626-9190
South Carolina Center for Teaching	Staff development on a variety of instructional methods to improve thinking	South Carolina Center for Teaching Thinking Fran O'Tuel P.O. Box 1651 Irmo, SC 29063 (603) 777-2907

Teaching Thinking Network	Share information on a variety of approaches to teaching thinking	Association for Supervision and Curriculum Development Esther Fusco 24 Hopewell Dr. Stony Brook, NY 11790 (516) 751-4970
Thinking for a Change Society	Host for the 8th International Conference On Thinking	Thinking for a Change Society Arnold Ostfield 14323 101st. Ave. Edmonton, Alberta T5N OK7 CANADA (403) 426-2998 fax (403) 452-8859 arnie@arnold.ca

Networks/Centers to Assess Thinking

Network	*Purpose*	*Contact*
Assessing Thinking Skills and Dispositions	Materials, research, and staff development on assessing a variety of thinking skills and dispositions	CSU Philosophy Department Peter and Noreen Faccione 800 North St. CLG building Fullerton, CA 92634
Assessment Training Institute	Materials, research, and staff development on assessing thinking and learning	Assessment Training Institute Richard Stiggins 215 S.W. Washington, #201 Portland, OR 97204
Authentic Assessment Network	Information on school district implementation of authentic assessment practices	Association for Supervision and Curriculum Development Judith Dorsch Backes Carroll County Public Schools 55 North Court St. Westminister, MD 21157 (410) 751-3045 fax (410) 751-3003 or

Kathryn Alvestad
Calvert County Public Schools
1305 Darnes Beach Rd.
Pince Frederick, MD 20678
(410) 535-7254
fax (410) 535-7298

Center for Assessment and Research on Critical Thinking	Research and assessment of critical thinking processes and instruction	The Center for Critical Thinking and Moral Critique Richard Paul Sonoma State University 1801 E. Cotati Blvd. Rohnert Park, CA 94928–3609 (707) 664-2940 fax (707) 664-4101 CCT@Sonoma.edu
Center on Learning, Assessment, and School Structure	Research and staff development on assessing thinking and learning	Center on Learning, Assessment, and School Structure Grant Wiggins 648 The Great Rd. Princeton, NJ 08540
Classroom Connections, International	Training and staff development on collaborative assessment and student self-assessment	Classroom Connections, International Anne Davies RR4, Site 430 C–36 Courtnay, British Columbia V9-7J3 CANADA
Critical Thinking Interview Project	Development of a critical thinking interview procedure to assess students' critical thinking in academic contexts	Gail Hughes 141 Warwick S.E. Minneapolis, MN 55414 (612) 424-0964 ghughes@nh.cc.mn.us
Innovative Assessment	Training and computer equipment to document observation of thinking skills and behaviors	Innovative Assessment Charles Lavaroni 33 Aderney Rd. San Anselmo, CA 94960

| Maryland Assessment Consortium | Research and staff development on assessing a variety of thinking skills by performance assessment | Maryland Assessment Consortium Jay McTighe 10350 Whitewasher Way Columbia, MD 21044–3813 |
| Network for Designing District Evaluation Instruments for Math and Science Process Skills | Information on school district implementation assessment practices in mathematics and science | Association for Supervision and Curriculum Development Shelley Lipowich 6321 N. Canon del Pajaro Tucson, AZ 85750–1367 (520) 299-9583 fax (520) 577-3022 lipowich@aol.com or Bryan Wunar Loyola University of Chicago School of Education 6525 Sheridan Rd. #301 Sky Chicago, IL 60601 (312) 508-8383 fax (312) 508-8008 |

Networks/Centers to Improve Thinking Through Science and Technology

Network	*Purpose*	*Contact*
Coalition for Science Literacy	Professional development to improve thinking and problem solving in science education	Coalition for Science Literacy Gerre Meisels University of South Florida 100 5th Ave. S. St. Petersburg, FL 33701 (813) 553-3140 fax (813) 553-3145 gmeisels@acad.usf.edu

Council of Scientific Society Presidents	Research information on thinking and problem solving in science education	Council for Scientific Society Presidents Martin Apple 1550 M. St. N.W. Washington DC 20036 (202) 872-4452 fax (292) 872-4079
HOTS/Thinking With Computers	Staff development on using discussion of thinking processes involved in using interactive software	HOTS/Thinking With Computers Stanley Progrow HOTS Program 1643 N. Alvernon, Ste. 101 Tuscon, AZ 87512 (520) 795-2143 fax (520) 795-8837
Information Literacy Network	Information on school district implementation of instruction to improve information literacy, including computer technology	Association for Supervision and Curriculum Development Learning Resources and Technology Center John Cowley Joel Barlow High School 100 Black Rock Turnpike Redding, CT 06896 or Tally Negroni Stamford High School 55 Strawberry Hill Ave. Stamford, CT 06902 (203) 977-4902 fax (203) 977-4985
Interactive Learning Systems, Inc.	Professional development on using computer technology in assessment	Interactive Learning Systems, Inc. Barry Adams 71 Wimbledon Court Roxboro, NC 27573
Learning Technology Center	Product development and in-service training on using technology to create problem-solving contexts	Learning Technology Center John Bransford Vanderbilt University Box 45 Nashville, TN 37203

Media Laboratory	Research on artificial intelligence	Media Laboratory Massachusetts Institute of Technology 20 Ames St. Cambridge, MA 02139
National Center to Improve the Tools of Educators	Staff development on using CAI to promote higher-order thinking	National Center to Improve the Tools of Educators Douglass Carnine 805 Lincoln St. Eugene, OR 97401
Preparing for Tomorrow's World	Curriculum modules and staff development decision making, problem solving, and critical thinking applied to technology	Sopris West, Inc. 1140 Boston Ave. Longmont, CO 80501 (303) 651-2829
Technical Education Resource Center	Research and program development to use technology to improve thinking and problem solving	T.E.R.C. Jack Lockhead 2067 Massachusetts Ave. Cambridge, MA 02138

Networks/Centers for Improving Academic Skills

Network	Purpose	Contact
hm Learning and Study Skills	Materials and staff development on the hm Study Skills program	hm Study Skills Esther Davenport P.O. Box 95010 Newton, MA 02195 (617) 965-0048 fax (617) 965-0056 ctocbin1010@aol.com
Learning to Learn	Materials and staff development on a program to improve the learning effectiveness of high school students	Learning to Learn, Inc. Marcia Heiman 28 Penniman Rd. Allston, MA 02134 (617) 783-9292

National Learning Center	Information and staff development on improving learning	National Learning Center Lettie Battle 111 Lee Ave. Takoma Park, MD 20912
Practical Intelligences for Schools	Program development and research on teaching skills for successful school performance	Practical Intelligences for School Project Zero 321 Longfellow Hall 13 Appian Way Cambridge, MA 02138 (617) 495-4342 fax (617) 495-9709 learn@pz.harvard.edu http://www.pzweb.harvard.edu
Research for Better Teaching	Materials and staff development on a program to improve learning	Research for Better Teaching John Saphiere 56 Bellows Hill Rd. Carlisle, MA 01741
Study Skills Across the Curriculum	Material and staff development on middle school study skills program	Henry Sibley High School Patricia Olson 2897 Delaware Ave. West St. Paul, MN (612) 681-2376
Successful Learning Institute	Information on teaching a variety of thinking skills	Successful Learning Institute 36 Caldy Rd. West Kirby Rd. Mersey L48HG UNITED KINGDOM

C H A P T E R   1 0

Adapting Problem-Based Learning for Gifted Students

S H E L A G H   A .   G A L L A G H E R
University of North Carolina—Charlotte

Educational reform has spawned much experimentation with both curriculum and instruction. One approach that has gained popularity over the past decade is problem-based learning (PBL) (Barrows, 1985; Stepien & Gallagher, 1993). With explicit attention to authentic problem solving, hands-on learning, and self-directed learning, many teachers have embraced PBL as a way to improve curriculum and instruction for all their students. Others have claimed that PBL is perfect for gifted students. Can both these viewpoints be true? Of course, although it is true that PBL is appropriate for all students, it does not necessarily follow that PBL is exactly the same for all students. Certainly a fundamental similarity will always be evident because the *structural elements* of PBL are the same in any setting. The *substance* inside a PBL unit, however, can and should be adapted to meet the individual needs of the students who will be working with the problem. The purpose of this chapter is to present unique characteristics of gifted students as problem solvers and to show how PBL units can be adapted to extend their potential.

Matching Curriculum and Characteristics: Gifted Students and Problem Solving

Gifted students have cognitive and affective characteristics that distinguish them from the regular population of students. Interestingly enough, many of these traits are very similar to those that distinguish between expert and novice problem solvers. The characteristics that gifted students and expert problem solvers share in common provide a set of guidelines to use when thinking about adapting PBL for gifted students. Essentially, the goal of modifying PBL for the gifted is to narrow the gap between the special potential possessed by the child and the actual practice of expert adults. The similarities between expert problem solvers and gifted students are observed in four broad areas: knowledge base, conceptual reasoning, problem solving strategies, and dispositions.

Gifted Students Have the Capacity to Build an Expert's Knowledge Base

The cornerstone of an expert problem solver's expertise is a large knowledge base (Rabinowitz & Glaser, 1985). Experts acquire and retain large bodies of information by making connections among different facts. The large knowledge base serves to make experts both better informed and more creative: the more they know, the more opportunity they have to see unusual associations (Bruer, 1993). For example, an expert ecologist might remember the facts *fish, water,* and *aquatic plants* by connecting them all to a fishbowl. Using *fishbowl* as a central point of reference, experts can also use the idea to make associations with new information like gravel or fish food. In the future, when the expert needs this information, she need only recall the fishbowl, and all of the associated information will be retrieved as well.

The capacity to quickly learn and then retain information is also one of the most frequently cited characteristics of gifted children (Clark, 1996; Gallagher & Gallagher, 1994). However, to make effective use of their knowledge, gifted students need to learn how to use their information like an expert, making connections among pieces of information and creating new knowledge by making new associations.

Gifted Students Practice Conceptual Reasoning

Expert problem solvers and gifted students alike tend to look beyond the surface of the problem to find an underlying meaning. When searching for a helpful way to represent a problem, experts tend to look for its *deep structure*, using abstract concepts or principles to describe the heart of the dilemma. By contrast, novices tend to work with surface characteristics that may be more obvious but are less essential to developing an understanding of the heart of the problem. To go back to the previous example, the novice would try to solve a problem of dying fish in a fishbowl by looking at the fish food and the water in the tank—obvious targets but perhaps not the right ones. The expert, on the other hand, would look at the fishbowl as a water ecosystem. Recognizing that the elements in systems interact, the expert might look for interactions in the fishbowl and find that the gravel reflects sunlight, raising the water to a dangerously high temperature for the fish (Chase & Simon, 1973; DeGroot, 1965).

Gifted students give evidence of conceptual and abstract reasoning at an earlier age than their age-mates (Berliner, 1986; Bransford & Vye, 1989; Sternberg & Davidson, 1985). Similar to expert problem solvers, gifted students show the early promise of being able to develop skill in "deep structure" thinking.

Gifted Students Have Early Capacity for Problem Solving

Experts also tend to have *more* problem solving tools at their disposal than novices, and they know how to select among those skills according to their needs (Minstrell, 1989). While solving the problem of the fishbowl, the expert can switch easily from a content analysis of the water to a dissection of a dead fish to consultation with resources to fill in gaps in understanding. Without a similar repertoire of skills, the novice may simply conduct different variations of water analysis. Having looked at the data from many perspectives, the expert is also more likely to come up with a more creative or sophisticated problem definition. The expert's capacity for creative problem definition, or problem finding, provides the foundation for unique solutions (Getzels, 1979). Throughout the problem solving process, experts make greater use of metacognitive reflection, monitoring and controlling their thinking (Bransford & Vye, 1989) by reflecting on questions like Have I considered all the possibilities? What assumptions am I making about the effect of lamp light on the fishbowl water? and Is this strategy working? By contrast, novices might doggedly pursue the same unsuccessful strategy, unable to find their way out of a dead end.

Gifted students are more adept in problem finding than average ability students (Runco, 1986). Rogers (1986) found other similarities between the problem solving behaviors of experts and gifted students, including careful selection of strategies. While solving problems, gifted students also use metacognitive skills spontaneously, learning them more quickly and transferring them to new situations more readily than average ability students (Carr & Borkowski, 1986).

Gifted Students Have Expert-Like Dispositions

Eminent authors, scientists, and historians all emphasize the importance of exploration and the disposition to seek the unknown to their success (Judson, 1980; O'Connor, 1962; Tuchman, 1966). With the inclination to search for the unknown, experts are more likely to use forward problem solving, since they assume that the answer to their problem does not exist. Novices, on the other hand, would be more likely to pursue more predictable questions with verifiable solutions.

Taking an open-ended approach to problem solving requires believing that some problems have no predetermined "right" answer. Students who believe that all problems have a single, absolute right answer are not likely to look for many alternative answers in an ill-structured problem. Some have speculated that differences in these beliefs are "an educationally salient source of individual differences, especially when performance tasks are ambiguous and ill-defined" (Wilkinson & Maxwell, 1991). In other words, the belief that some questions have no single "right" answer is one factor that might determine a student's success in open-ended assignments.

A few studies investigating student dispositions give evidence that gifted students are more likely to believe that some questions have no predetermined answers (Goldberger, 1981; Murphy & Gilligan, 1980). In this attribute, gifted students are similar to adult experts.

Taken together, these research data give evidence that gifted students have a head start on their peers in developing expert problem solving capabilities, as demonstrated in Figure 1. At the same time, there is no doubt that gifted students have a long way to go in refining their raw potential into sophisticated skill. Having a head start is no guarantee of achieving the level of problem solving that a gifted student could well acquire. What must intervene is an education that moves gifted students from potential to skill and, hopefully, expertise along these dimensions.

While there is not, as of yet, a clear path from potential to expertise (Callahan, 1996), there are some hints as to how to begin developing an expert problem solver (Bransford & Vye, 1989; Bruer, 1993; Rabinowitz & Glaser, 1985). There is evidence that information is retained better when it is presented in a context that is meaningful to students (Brown, Collins, & Duguid, 1989). Students will learn to look for underlying concepts when they are

---

Qualities of an Expert Problem Solver	**Qualities of a Gifted Student**
• Broad knowledge base	• Acquires information quickly
• Looks for "deep structure" of problems	• Gives early evidence of conceptual thinking
• Has a large tool kit of skills; uses skills flexibly	• Carefully selects problem-solving strategies
• Monitors the problem-solving process	• Spontaneously uses metacognitive skills
• Uses dispositions supporting open-ended problem solving; uses forward thinking problem solving	• Early recognition that many questions have no single, absolute right answer

Figure 1. Shared Qualities of Expert Problem Solvers and Gifted Students

---

confronted with many representations of the same problem (Shoenfeld, 1989). Conceptual reasoning is enhanced when a teacher models the kind of thinking that reveals the conceptual level of activities (Bransford & Vye, 1989). Conversely, we know that expert-like understanding will not develop in environments where instruction is oversimplified, presented from a single perspective, context-independent, rigidly compartmentalized into structures, and passively transmitted (Spiro, Carlson, Feltovich, & Anderson, 1988). In other words, success in complex thinking happens only with repeated practice in complex learning environments.

A Promising Road to Expertise: Problem-Based Learning

Problem-based learning (PBL) provides the kind of complex learning environment that is well suited to developing expertise. The complex learning environment is created through the combined impact of the structural components of PBL: the ill-structured problem, the student as stakeholder, the self-directed learner, and the teacher as coach.

The Ill-Structured Problem

Perhaps the most noticeable difference between traditional instruction and PBL is that a PBL unit begins with the presentation of an ill-structured problem. The differences between traditional well-structured problems and ill-structured problems are embodied in the two examples in Figure 2.

These two problems have some surface similarities—they both deal with oranges, shortages, and customer dissatisfaction. Their differences are far more important than their similarities, for they are the characteristics that distinguish between a well-structured and an ill-structured problem. Characteristics of the ill-structured problems include

More information than is initially available is needed to understand the problem. In the example, Problem A can be solved quite easily once the appropriate formula is in place. In Problem B, much more is needed to understand the problem. Why is there an insufficient sup-

	ill-structured (handwritten)
Problem A	*Problem B*
You have two dozen oranges in your store. Mary comes in and buys six. Charles thinks about buying six but then changes his mind and gets a dozen. If Teresa buys four oranges and Ryan buys eight, is Brenda justified when she complains to you about not being able to find any oranges in the produce department?	You are the owner of the local food co-op. Your favorite customers have all come in complaining about the insufficient supply of oranges. What should you do?

Figure 2. PBL Problems

ply of oranges? What do the clients mean by *insufficient*? Did we run out? What are some ways of keeping oranges (and other fruit) in stock? The quality of the ill-structured problem is frequently referred to a *generative*. That is, the ill-structured problem actually generates questions.

No single formula exists for conducting an investigation to resolve the problem. In Problem A, there is a specific set of operations to conduct and solve the problem; and while some of the operations are reciprocal, there isn't much room for creative structure. In Problem B, however, there may be any number of different ways to deal with the client's complaints, depending, in part, on the exact nature of the problem.

As new information is obtained, the problem changes. In this case, Problem A has all the information needed to solve the problem supplied in the brief paragraph. In Problem B, the problem could shift considerably if students were to find either that there were restrictions on the import of citrus fruit or, on the other hand, that a new "orange diet" had caused a run on the fruit.

Students can never be 100% sure they have made the "right" decision. Problem A has a single, correct answer. In Problem B, the many possible options would have to be weighed to select the most reasonable one; and, even then, there would likely be negative, as well as positive consequences to the solution. Only rarely would an answer be absolutely right.

An important point to be made about PBL is that students are solving problems that are central to a field of study and designed around specific educational goals. Indeed, one of the reasons why PBL is considered defensible by many medical school programs is the care that is taken to create an apt reflection of learning and problem solving as they occur in the discipline (Boud & Feletti, 1991). Because an important goal of PBL is to integrate core content with authentic problem solving, the ill-structured problems used in the PBL classroom must meet additional criteria. To be considered educationally sound, PBL problems must

- be designed to ensure that students cover a predefined area of knowledge, preferably integrated from many disciplines;
- help students learn a set of important concepts, ideas, and techniques;
- successfully lead students to (parts of) a field of study; and
- hold intrinsic interest or importance, or represent a typical problem faced by the profession (Ross, 1991).

Thus, PBL is considered to be a more effective way to teach the core curriculum. In Problem B, students would run into much substantial content while trying to figure out why there are no oranges, including the growing cycle of oranges, import-export laws, the different varieties, or diseases that might infest oranges. All of these are associated with basic learning objectives at different grade levels. Taken together, the qualities of the ill-structured problem lead students to pursue questions and, in the process, extend their knowledge base in a meaningful context.

Student as Stakeholder

A second feature of PBL is the practice of placing students in a carefully selected stakeholder position. The stakeholder in a PBL unit is a person who has some level of authority, accountability, and responsibility for resolving some aspect of the problem. Students are assigned a specific role in each problem they encounter: a political advisor in a problem about district gerrymandering; a journalist in a problem about media in the court-room; a golf course groundskeeper in a problem about improving golf through grass selection. The goal of placing students in the shoes of a person actually involved in the problem is to make them an "apprentice" in that area. Like an artist's apprentice, students in a PBL problem experience the entire world of the problem solver and learn to adopt the appropriate dispositions, as well as content and skills. While in their apprenticeships, students learn many valuable lessons about problem solving from inside a discipline, including

- the way problem solving is approached in different disciplines;
- the role of bias and perspective in the problem-solving process;
- the subjective nature of all real-world problem solving;
- the need to understand many different ways to solve a problem (economic, scientific, political, ethical); and
- the intricate process of weighing the priorities of different points of view in a complex problem.

The Self-Directed Learner

The third change incorporated into the PBL classroom is that students are encouraged to take control of the learning process, thus becoming increasingly capable, self-reliant, and responsible learners. Teachers assist in this process by becoming a "tutor" who focuses on helping students develop a good tool kit of problem solving skills, assisting students as they learn to use it, and engaging students in a process of reflection about their own performance and the nature of problem solving.

The tutor also allows students to increasingly take on a set of responsibilities, including setting the learning agenda, facilitating the group process, and setting timelines or deadlines. Using metacognitive questioning and modeling good inquiry, the tutor reveals to students how professionals approach similar problems, helps students focus on a problem's central concepts, and probes to ensure that they understand all the data they gather. By reflecting on and evaluating their own thinking, students acquire better control over their thinking and feeling processes, ultimately resulting in better reasoning.

Adapting PBL for Gifted Students:
New Applications of Familiar Recommendations

PBL is not inherently appropriate for gifted students. Rather, it must be adapted and designed to match the unique needs of gifted learners. The appropriateness of PBL for gifted students is dependent upon the kinds of adaptations that are built into the problem design and instruction. For average-ability students, the first order of business in PBL might be to acquire the basics of metacognition and self-direction, the nature of concepts, and the skills of problem solving. Gifted students, on the other hand, need a different level of challenge in PBL, one that refines and extends existing skills that are already in place. The five adaptations recommended here may sound quite familiar, since the same recommendations are made for all sorts of curricula for gifted students (Maker, 1982; Kaplan, 1986; VanTassel-Baska, 1988). Recommended modifications of PBL for gifted students include

- ensuring advanced content;
- working with complex concepts;
- demonstrating interdisciplinary connections;
- practicing good reasoning, habits of mind, and self-directed action; and
- discussing conflicting ethical appeals.

Changes in any one of these five dimensions makes PBL problems more appropriate for gifted students; the benefits in learning accumulate and the number of adaptations increase. Perhaps the best way to demonstrate how a problem can be modified for instruction with gifted students is to work with a concrete example. For the purpose of discussion, consider the introduction to a problem involving an old oil platform, presented in Figure 3.

Students in this problem are in the stakeholder of the panel of scientists facing the problem of finding something to do with the defunct oil platform. After thinking about the problem, a group of gifted middle school students might develop a Learning Issues Board that looks something like the version presented in Figure 4.

The 40-story oil storage tank, named Brent Spar by its owner, the Shell Oil Company, is easy to spot, even in the cold choppy water of the North Sea. Its giant carcass, towering more than 90 feet above the surface and extending 370 feet below it, is temporarily anchored at 60° degrees north latitude, 50 kilometers west of the Shetland Islands. It has been there since June 1995. According to plans by Shell Oil, the storage tank should have been disposed of by now. But, Greenpeace became involved, and now the obsolete tank is riding the waves off Scotland.

The Brent Spar is now your problem! Shell Oil and Greenpeace have agreed to allow an impartial team of scientists decide what to do with the platform. This is where you and your team come in.

Shell Oil no longer wants to use the old storage tank, or any of the more than 100 of the old platforms, built in the 1970s. Last June, Shell Oil and the British government agreed to allow the oil company to scuttle the platform and let it settle to the bottom of the ocean. When Greenpeace heard of the plan, it organized a boycott against Shell Oil gasoline in Europe and landed protesters on the platform itself. A small group of protesters are still on the tank.

You and your team must decide what to do with the Brent Spar. As the boat approaches the platform, your team assembles to begin discussing the situation. What are your first thoughts about the situation? What do you think the group should know more about to solve the problem of the Brent Spar?

Figure 3. Brent Spar Problem

Note. From *Problem-Based Learning Across the Curriculum: An ACSD Professional Inquiry Kit* (Folder 4, Activity 1, p. 2), by W. J. Stepien & S. A. Gallagher, 1997a, Alexandria, VA: Association for Supervision and Curriculum Development. Copyright 1997 by ASCD. Reprinted with permission. All rights reserved.

Modification 1: Ensuring Advanced Content

One essential component of any PBL curriculum is to design the problem around an important and worthy body of knowledge. More specifically, the problems designed for gifted students should lead to advanced investigations that broaden and deepen their knowledge base. Teachers can ensure the presence of complex infor-

Hunches:

What seems to be going on here?
Shell Oil is trying to get out of a bind.
The oil barge will pollute the water if it stays where it is.
The barge should be towed ashore.

What We Know	What We Need to Know (Our Learning Issues)	Plan of Action
• Shell Oil owns the platform.	• Why is Greenpeace so upset?	• Build models of barges to sink.
• It is not in use anymore.	• Who is going to pay for all this?	• Look up information about the barge on the Internet.
• Greenpeace has protested on the barge.	• What are the effects of sinking the barge?	• Interview a physicist about sinking things.
• The barge is off the shore of Scotland.	• Why can't we just leave it out there?	• Look up Greenpeace in magazine articles.
• We are scientists.	• Could the barge be converted to another use?	
• We are supposed to come up with a plan to get rid of the barge.	• What are other ways of disposing of the barge?	
	• What kind of animal life is in the water?	

Figure 4. Sample Learning Issues Board for Brent Spar

mation by choosing problems that require the study of advanced information. For example, middle school students will be more challenged by the Brent Spar problem than by a problem about building a playground. Teachers can also arrange for students to "discover" resources with appropriately challenging information. In the case of the Brent Spar problem, this might take the form of prompting a guest speaker to raise issues of the regulation of ocean waters that might not otherwise emerge.

The content in a PBL problem can even be differentiated in a heterogeneous classroom. For example, in the Brent Spar problem, all students will encounter a foundation of understanding about the effects of oil on the ocean. During the course of small group research, the teacher/coach could help a small group of gifted students understand more challenging information about the physics involved in different approaches to sinking the platform.

Modification 2: Complexity of the Concept

Problem-based learning and concept-centered curriculum go hand in hand. In Brent Spar, the concept *change* is used to help students organize and think about the different components of the problem (Gallagher & Stepien, 1996). Discussion of the concept should not be reserved just for gifted students, since all students need to learn the fundamental nature of change. However, gifted students will be ready to appreciate the power of the concept at a more advanced level. Where regular students might benefit from a discussion centering around the fact that "change causes change," gifted students are ready for a more sophisticated application of the problem, such as "change is irreversible because of its interaction with time." Concepts can be drawn into the problem as a part of coaching, in Problem Log assessments, or during problem debriefing. At a more advanced level, teachers can use a concept to tie several problems together and let the concept develop as students transfer it from one problem to the next. Seeing the same concept in action in several problems should also help students develop the habit of looking for a conceptual structure to the problem (Gallagher, Sher, Stepien, & Workman, 1995; Stepien, Gallagher & Workman, 1993).

PBL in Action: Planet X

When pilot testing the PBL science units, commonly referred to as "the William and Mary units," "Planet X" was of special interest to us. Students were placed in the role of "mission specialists," charged with the job of creating a plant ecosystem that would help save the dying planet. It was the first time PBL had been tested with very young children, so we were eager to document as much as possible. A graduate assistant was in the classroom nearly every day to videotape the problem at work. Initially, we would have been satisfied with a very modest success; but, before long, we realized that we were onto something very, very special. The teachers working with the second graders were natural PBL coaches, and soon they were all on an adventure in plant ecosystems.

One day, the students were discussing how they might communicate with personnel on Planet X. The planet was just opposite the Earth on the other side of the sun, and it had exactly the same tilt and rotation. Being on the other side of the sun, the children were faced with the dilemma of how to send messages to their colleagues on the planet. They knew that sound travels in a straight line, which means that messages "beamed" to the planet would always bump into the sun. Their coach gently encouraged students to consider alternatives—drawing the Earth on a chalkboard and marking the path of a sound wave; and in a corner of the room, barely audible, you could hear someone murmur, ". . . mirror . . . ."

"What?" exclaimed the coach, seizing on the teachable moment. "What do you mean? Here, come up to the board and show us."

He handed the chalk to the second grader and stood back. The boy shuffled up to the chalkboard and drew a line above the picture of the Earth.

He said, "If we put a mirror up here . . . ."

"Yes! Yes!" the nearest girl shouted. "This will work because when we experimented with light, we bounced light!"

"Ah," the coach stepped in. "You mean that sound might reflect like light reflects? Could we use something like a satellite to get sound by the sun to Planet X? Would that work?"

"Yes!" shouted the class, overjoyed with their own cleverness.

That was just one moment in an amazing four months of PBL. That's right: four months. The unit lasted that long; not because the problem got out of control but because the teachers and students were both enjoying it and learning so much, they decided to keep it going for as long as they could. Even after four months, the students were disappointed when the adventure ended.

* "Planet X" has since been revised into the problem "Dust Bowl."

Modification 3: Interdisciplinary Connections and Interactions

Most real-world problems are interdisciplinary (Carter, 1988), which makes the goal of revealing connections and interactions among disciplines quite natural. However, the degree to which a problem is interdisciplinary can vary as a function of problem design and tutor guiding. A likely goal for teachers of the gifted would be to help gifted students explore intricate interconnections. As with the development of the concept, several layers of interdisciplinary interactions could be explored in Brent Spar. For example, while regular ability students think about the interactions of the energy use on the environment, gifted students might investigate other kinds of interactions, including the multi-faceted interactions of energy dependence, global governmental regulation, and territoriality.

Modification Four: Higher-Order Thinking Skills

A well-designed problem provides an environment where tutors can help students acquire sound inquiry skills (Schmidt & Moust, 1995). PBL provides an environment where students can be coached to improve their skills along many dimensions of good reasoning.

Critical Thinking Skills

Just as the problem can be designed to rely on more or less complex applications of a concept, so can students be encouraged to use more complex kinds of reasoning. Different phases of the problem draw on various kinds of reasoning skills. The first lesson of a problem, filling in the Learning Issues Board, requires analytical reasoning, discriminating between fact and inference, recognizing gaps in understanding, and prioritizing. Problem Definition, on the other hand, requires skills that include analysis and synthesis of information, determining bias, and summarizing understanding.

Beyond the basic problem solving and critical thinking skills, students will have an opportunity to learn discipline-specific skills related to the content matter of the problem. In Brent Spar, students have a natural opportunity to learn about scientific hypothesis posing, experimentation, and reporting. Students will also learn first-hand why it is important for scientists to be able to communicate with a variety of audiences, from other people in the science community to the lay public, as they try to explain to the press the rationale behind their decision.

Standards

Self-regulation is an integral part of self-directed learning, and becoming attentive to the standards of good reasoning is an integral part of becoming a self-regulating thinker. Paul (1992) provided a list of standards for good reasoning, including being clear, specific, relevant, logical, precise, accurate, consistent, and complete. With a list like Paul's as a point of reference, teachers could select a couple to emphasize with gifted students as they assess their own work. For example, teachers could raise the issue of standards with their students as they begin their experiments in Brent Spar. Particularly important to scientific research are standards of precision and accuracy. Assessments of the experiment could be designed to make the standards of clarity and precision a priority. As students become increasingly self-directed, they should be expected to adopt not only skills but standards as well.

Dispositions

Stakeholder positions, or the roles students take during the problem, can provide more than career exposure. Experts often emulate, or copy, the behaviors of a mentor before they create on their own (Storr, 1989). For this reason, mentorships are an often-mentioned recommendation for gifted students (Clark, 1996; Gallagher & Gallagher, 1994; Maker, 1982; Renzulli, 1977). While it may be impossible to provide all students with mentorship opportunities, teachers can help students understand different professions by judiciously selecting stakeholder positions. Immersion in the stakeholder point of view can be used to full benefit by requiring some reflection specifically about their role. As scientists sent to investigate the Brent Spar, students are encouraged to think like scientists and have first-hand experience with the difficulties of conducting science in a politically heated arena. Tutors maximize the apprenticeship by asking students to reflect about the scientist's dispositions: "As a member of the science team investigating Brent Spar, what are your priorities?" "Why is careful data recording so important?" and "What are you learning about the way scientists work?" Other questions could engage students in dialogue about the role of people who are involved in both science and community life. "What happens when business or government interferes in the course of science?" "If you are a scientist who works for the government or business, where is your first obligation: to the company or to the data?" Questions like these maximize the nature of the mini-apprenticeship created in the PBL classroom.

Metacognition

From the very beginning, students should be encouraged to reflect on their own problem-solving practices. Metacognition is important for all students. That is, all students need to learn how to self-assess their success in selecting priorities, implementing good problem-solving strategies, and using positive individual and cooperative work habits. As a part of the goal to promote self-directed learning, gifted students could be asked, either during discussion or in Problem Log activities, to reflect on their own attitudes toward problem solving and on key dispositions by asking them questions such as "How do your own personal biases affect your problem solving?" "Is it ever possible that the least supported idea is the right idea?" "What happens when we close off our options too early?" "Too late?" "What does it mean to have intellectual courage?" "Why would that be important while solving a problem?"

PBL in Action: Student Perspectives

One of the questions that perpetually pesters teachers is whether or not students "get it." In the case of PBL, we might ask whether or not students "get" the idea of complex problem solving. Recently, in Project P-BLISS (Problem-Based Learning in the Social Sciences), we became *very* interested in this question. We were working with disadvantaged gifted high school students, looking for curricula that would excite them and motivate them to engage in complex thought. To see if the students "got" the idea of complex problem solving, we used this question in their Problem Log: "What do you know about problem solving that you didn't know before?" Here are some representative responses:

- This unit taught me that if you want to be a good problem solver, you must be totally unbiased and look at both sides of the problem. I also learned that everything in a problem is not always as it seems, and many times you have to look into the facts deeper before you can come to a conclusion.

- This unit taught me that the solving process takes a while and is also a lot of work; but, once you get into the flow, it's fun. This process taught me how to compare and contrast and how to choose the right one. It also taught me how not to take sides in the matter because before you can understand what's going on, you have to get both sides of the story.

- I learned that, to solve a problem, it helps to break it down into a bunch of smaller problems that can be solved one at a time. And, doing this, you make it so you don't miss any parts of the problem that could play a good part in making it right. I also learned that, if you try to solve a problem without breaking it down, you can end up with a huge mess.

- You have to have lots of patience. Because everyone might not agree, everyone is not going to agree, and you have to stop and see it in two ways. Sometimes, when you think you've got somewhere, you have to go back 'cause you might have overlooked something.

- I did not realize the extent of how hard it is to make everyone agree on one topic, even though we all wanted essentially the same outcome.

Modification Five: Discussing Ethical Appeals

Complex, real-world problems often involve ethical dilemmas, and all students need to explore some dimensions of this side of any problem. Gifted students are unusually attuned to ethical issues and can benefit from discussions involving right, wrong, and best options. However, gifted students also appreciate complexity and realize that ethical discussions presenting one perspective as right are often too simplistic. Rather than point to one preferable perspective, an effective way to discuss ethics with gifted students is to look at the different ethical appeals evoked in the problem. Brody (1988) defined six ethical appeals: to rights, to consequences, to justice, to virtues, to benefit/cost, and to personhood. Each presents a different paradigm from which to view the problem. By looking at the problem through these different vantage points, students learn how problems become more complicated when different parties are using a different basis for their actions. In the problem of the Brent Spar, students/scientists would first see that the ethical appeal of their own perspective is an appeal to consequences: "What will happen if the oil platform isn't removed?" In order to develop a reasonable solution, they might also have to see that others involved with the problem use different ethical appeals. Environmentalists might be more interested in personhood—in this case the right of the individual to live in a clean, safe environment—and the owner of Shell Oil might be concerned about the benefit/cost of the spill.

Putting the Pieces Together

As mentioned above, changes in any one of the five recommended areas make the PBL environment more appropriate for gifted students. The degree of adaptation depends on the usual variables—teacher comfort and skill, student age and ability level, type of classroom adaptation, and everyone's familiarity with the PBL environment. Some teachers, working in heterogeneous groups, may only be able to adapt Problem Log activities for their gifted students, focusing on different kinds of self-reflection for different ability groups. Teachers in pull-out or self-contained settings may want to try more ambitious adaptations. A summary of all of the adaptations described above is presented in Figure 5.

Where and When to Use PBL

Complexity, especially the kind found in PBL curricula, can be fun; but it's not always easy. Because it is built to be multifaceted and complex, PBL requires a certain amount of time and continuity. Teachers of gifted students, on the other hand, work in a number of very different program configurations. Resource teachers can use PBL effectively, but it takes a little more organization and effort. The following list provides a brief set of guidelines to use when considering PBL for your classroom.

Continuous-Instruction-Classroom (Regular Classroom, Self-Contained Gifted Classroom, Daily Pull-Out Program). PBL can be used in any setting when students and teachers are together daily. While the regular classroom and self-contained classrooms offer different kinds of challenges to teachers, they are no different from the challenges presented by any curriculum. In the regular classroom, all students of varying abilities need to be stimulated. Making judicious use of the Learning Issues Board helps to differentiate, for the coach can help students find problems that they will find appropriately challenging. In the self-contained classroom or daily pull-out program, the challenge is in the design of the problem, since the whole problem should be made more advanced along the dimensions described above.

Resource Consultation. Another ideal configuration for PBL is resource consultation. Building on the collaborative relationship between the regular classroom teacher and the resource teacher, the two adults can build the program together and then share responsibility for differentiating instruction for within the problem. While in the classroom, the resource teacher could either work with the gifted students on a specific aspect of the problem or assist the regular classroom teacher with coaching strategies. The resource teacher could also help the regular classroom teacher develop assignments and activities to keep the high-ability students engaged with the problem between visits.

Area of Adaptation	Baseline Goals for Regular Ability Students	Additional Goals for Gifted Students
Content	• Roles governing ocean territories • Monetary conversions (pound to dollar) • Three alternative strategies to discard the Brent Spar • The impact of pipeline technologies • The impact of oil on the surrounding ocean ecosystem • Water flow rates	• Chemical composition of metals and oils • Radio nuclides • Differences between intensity and duration effects • Physics of fast and slow release options
Concept	• Most things change • Change causes change	• Adaptation and transformation are two different kinds of change and have different effects. • Change is irreversible because of its interaction with time.
Interdisciplinary	• Interaction of science (methods of sinking the barge; environmental impact) and social science (economics of each disposal option; business interest in benefit/cost)	• More complex interactions of social science (global regulation versus local regulation of water/local decision making impacts global arena) and economics (monetary versus human and/or animal costs) • Long-term effect of dependence on oil
Critical Thinking and Habits of Mind	• Experimentation, selection of problem solving strategies, and progress through the problem, including collaborative group work	• Additional reflection about the nature of problem solving, about the biases and assumptions of people with different points of view

Figure 5. Summary of Adaptations of PBL Problems for Gifted Students

Pull-Out Program, Occasional. The model has been adapted successfully for pull-out programs where students meet less frequently, but modifications must be made. The nature of the problem must be adapted along at least two dimensions. First, the story must be a little more episodic. Especially important is the use of "kickers" or "twists" to keep the story alive for students from week to week. Research tasks assigned for the periods in between meetings can help provide a link from one session to the next. Second, the problem must be somewhat less complex, since a huge, multifaceted problem would take the majority of the school year when students only meet once a week. Teachers who only see their students for an hour once a week may not be able to use PBL, but those with half-day blocks once a week will probably be successful if they think ahead about keeping the problem lively.

These guidelines are not meant to seem prescriptive, restrictive, exclusive, or exhaustive but rather to serve as a helpful blueprint as teachers experiment with PBL. Most of all, they are designed to answer the question: "Isn't this for *all* kids?" Yes, PBL is for all students, but adaptations help maximize its usefulness for different groups of students. It is true that all students should learn important concepts, but concepts differ in levels of abstraction and complexity. Gifted students are likely to need more complex applications of concepts to be appropriately challenged. All students need to understand relationships among disciplines, but they interact with each other in different ways. All students should be taught to self-assess their ability to analyze information, but gifted students will be ready earlier to think about their capacity to show intellectual honesty or integrity in their reasoning. With careful adaptation, teachers of the gifted can successfully use PBL to open the doorway to rich, challenging, and exciting learning experiences for gifted children.

Teacher Resources

Publications

Barrows, H. (1985). *How to design a problem-based curriculum for preclinical years.* New York: Springer.

Barrows, H. (1988). *The tutorial process.* Springfield, IL: Southern Illinois University School of Medicine.

Barrows, H. (1994). *Practice-based learning.* Springfield, IL: Southern Illinois University School of Medicine.

Benoit, B., McClure, T., & Kuinzle, R. (1997). Problem-based learning: Meeting real-world challenges. In J. H. Clarke & R. M. Agne (Eds.). *Interdisciplinary high school teaching: Strategies for integrated learning.* Boston: Allyn & Bacon.

Boyce, L. N., VanTassel-Baska, J., Burruss, J. E., Sher, B. T., & Johnson, D. T. (1997). A problem-based curriculum: Parallel learning opportunities for students and teachers. *Journal for the Education of the Gifted, 20,* 363–379.

College of William and Mary Center for Gifted Education. (1997a). *Acid, acid everywhere.* Dubuque, IA: Kendall/Hunt.

College of William and Mary Center for Gifted Education. (1997b). *Dust bowl.* Dubuque, IA: Kendall/Hunt.

College of William and Mary Center for Gifted Education. (1997c). *What a find.* Dubuque, IA: Kendall/Hunt.

College of William and Mary Center for Gifted Education. (1997d). *Electricity city.* Dubuque, IA: Kendall/Hunt.

College of William and Mary Center for Gifted Education. (1997e). *The Chesapeake Bay.* Dubuque, IA: Kendall/Hunt.

College of William and Mary Center for Gifted Education. (1997f). *No quick fix.* Dubuque, IA: Kendall/Hunt.

College of William and Mary Center for Gifted Education. (1997g). *Hot rods.* Dubuque, IA: Kendall/Hunt.

Cuozzo, C. C. (1996/7). What do lepidopterists do? *Educational Leadership, 53,* 34–37.

Delisle, R. (1997). *How to use problem-based learning in the classroom.* Reston, VA: Association for Supervision & Curriculum Development.

Dods, R. F. (1997). An action research study of the effectiveness of problem-based learning in promoting the acquisition and retention of knowledge. *Journal for the Education of the Gifted, 20,* 423–437.

Gallagher, S. A. (1997). Problem-based learning: What did it come from, what does it do, and where is it going? *Journal for the Education of the Gifted, 20,* 332–362.

Gallagher, S. A., Romanoff, B., Crossett, B., & Stepien, W. J. (1998a). *Gateways*. University of North Carolina at Charlotte.

Gallagher, S. A., Romanoff, B., Crossett, B., & Stepien, W. J. (1998b). *Kids at work*. University of North Carolina at Charlotte.

Gallagher, S. A., Romanoff, B., & Stepien, W. J. (1998). *A just prosecution: The adjudication of violent juveniles*. University of North Carolina at Charlotte.

Gallagher, S. A., Sher, B. T., Stepien, W. J., & Workman, D. (1995). Implementing problem-based learning in the science classroom. *School Science and Mathematics, 95*, 136–146.

Gallagher, S. A., Stepien, W. J., & Romanoff, B. (1998). *Impasse*. University of North Carolina at Charlotte.

Gallagher, S. A., Stepien, W. J., & Rosenthal, H. (1994). The effects of problem-based learning on problem solving. *Gifted Child Quarterly, 36*, 195–200.

Hmelo, C. E., & Ferrari, M. (1997). The problem-based learning tutorial: Cultivating higher-order thinking skills. *Journal for the Education of the Gifted, 20*, 401–422.

Johnson, T. (Producer), & Murphy, M. (Regional Director). (1998). *Problem-based learning: Using problems to learn*. [Film]. *(Available from Association for Supervision and Curriculum Development, 1703 N. Beauregard St., Alexandria, VA 22311–1714)*

Johnson, T. (Producer), & Murphy, M. (Regional Director). (1998). *Problem-based learning: Designing problems for learning*. [Film]. *(Available from Association for Supervision and Curriculum Development, 1703 N. Beauregard St., Alexandria, VA 22311–1714)*

Stepien, W. J. (Speaker). (1997). *Problem-based learning across the curriculum* (Cassette Recording). Reston, VA: Association for Supervision & Curriculum Development

Stepien, W. J., & Pyke, S. L. (1997). Designing problem-based learning units. *Journal for the Education of the Gifted, 20*, 380–400.

Stepien, W. J., & Gallagher, S. A. (1993). Problem-based learning: As authentic as it gets. *Educational Leadership, 50*(7), 25–29.

Stepien, W. J., & Gallagher, S. A. (1997). *Problem-based learning across the curriculum* (professional inquiry kit). Reston, VA: Association for Supervision & Curriculum Development.

Stepien, W. C., Gallagher, S. A., Romanoff, B., & Stepien, W. J. (1998). *To farm or not to farm.* University of North Carolina at Charlotte.

Stepien, W. J., Gallagher, S. A., & Workman, D. (1993). Problem-based learning for traditional and interdisciplinary classrooms. *Journal for the Education of the Gifted, 16,* 338–357.

Torp, L., & Sage, S. (1998). *Problems as possibilities: Problem-based learning in K–12 classrooms.* Reston, VA: Association for Supervision & Curriculum Development.

Web Sites

The Association for Supervision and Curriculum Development (ASCD)—http://www.ascd.org
A web-based listserv for educators interested in discussing PBL issues with their colleagues.

The Illinois Mathematics and Science Academy (IMSA)—http://www.imsa.edu
A web page that lists the major components of PBL and gives some specific examples of what they refer to as "mini-problems."

Howard Barrows—http://www.siumed/pblc/pblapp.html
Generally recognized as the modern father of PBL, Howard Barrows works at the Medical School at Southern Illinois University. Anyone who is interested in PBL should be familiar with Dr. Barrow's work and philosophy of PBL.

University of North Carolina at Charlotte—http://www.uncc.edu/sagallag/pbl/pbliss
The web site has a link to the PBL work of Shelagh Gallagher and William Stepien. The primary resource currently included on this web site relates to the new initiative Project P-BLISS: Problem-Based Learning in the Social Sciences.

A new project sponsored by the Jacob K. Javits Gifted and Talented Program is underway at the University of North Carolina at Charlotte to develop six PBL social studies units for use with gifted, disadvantaged students. Having been through two years of pilot testing and revision, the units are now available to teachers. The project also has produced self- and peer-assessment rubrics for tutoring skills, a web site to test the potential for downloading PBL materials, and a series of videotapes describing the project.

University of Delaware—http://www.udel.edu/pbl/
A web site for persons interested in the application of PBL in higher education (or for people looking for problems to use with advanced high school students). The University of Delaware presents an example of an undergraduate institution that is proactive in its support of the transformation from traditional to PBL structured classrooms. The web site offers an impressive list of classes offered using the PBL model.

College of William and Mary—The Center for Gifted Education—http://www.wm.edu/education/gifted/html
The only project to date that has resulted in nationally published PBL units. Information about these science units can be found at the Center for Gifted Education web page.

References

Barrows, H. (1985). *How to design a problem-based learning curriculum in the preclinical years.* New York: Springer-Verlag.

Berliner, D. (1986). Catastrophes and interactions: Comments on the mistaken metaphor. In C. J. Maker (Ed.), *Critical issues in gifted education: Defensible programs for the gifted* (pp. 31–38). Rockville, MD: Aspen.

Boud, D., & Feletti, G. (1991). *The challenge of problem-based learning.* New York: St. Martin's Press.

Bransford, J. D., & Vye, N. J. (1989). In L. B. Resnick & L. E. Klopfer, (Eds.) *Toward the thinking curriculum.* Reston, VA: Association for Supervision and Curriculum Development.

Brody, B. A. (1988). *Life and death decision making.* New York: Oxford University Press.

Brown, J. S., Collins, A., & Duguid, P. (1989). Situated cognition and the cultures of learning. *Educational Researcher, 18*(1), 32–45.

Bruer, J. T. (1993, Summer). The mind's journey from novice to expert. *American Education, 6*–46.

Callahan, C. M. (1996). A critical self-study of gifted education: Healthy practice, necessary evil, or sedition? *Journal for the Education of the Gifted, 19,* 148–163.

Carr, M., & Borkowski, J. (1986). Metamemory in gifted children. *Gifted Child Quarterly, 31,* 40–44.

Carter, M. (1988). Problem solving reconsidered: A pluralistic theory of problems. *College English, 50,* 551–565.

Chase, W. G., & Simon, H. A. (1973). Perception in chess. *Cognitive Psychology, 4,* 55–81.

Clark, B. (1996). *Growing up gifted* (3rd ed.). Columbus, OH: Merrill.

DeGroot, M. (1965). *Thought and choice in chess.* The Hague: Mounton.

Ennis, R. (1962). A concept of critical thinking. *Harvard Educational Review, 32*(1), 81–111.

Gallagher, J. J., & Gallagher, S. A. (1994). *Teaching the gifted child* (4th ed.). Boston: Allyn and Bacon.

Gallagher, S. A., Sher, B. T., Stepien, W. J., & Workman, D. (1995). Implementing problem-based learning in the science classroom. *School Science and Mathematics, 95,* 136–146.

Gallagher, S. A. & Stepien, W. J. (1996). Depth versus breadth in problem-based learning: Content acquisition in American studies. *Journal for the Education of the Gifted, 19,* 257–275.

Getzels, J. (1979). From art student to fine artist: Potential, problem finding and performance. In A. Passow (Ed.), *The gifted and the talented* (pp. 372–388). Chicago: University of Chicago Press.

Goldberger, N. R. (1981). Developmental assumptions underlying models of general education. Paper presented at Conference on General Education, William Paterson College of New Jersey, Wayne, 1979. Reprinted in *Liberal Education, 67,* 233–243.

Judson, H. F. (1980). *The search for solutions.* Baltimore, MD: Johns Hopkins University Press.

Kaplan, S. N. (1986). The grid: A model to construct differentiated curriculum for the gifted. In J. S. Renzulli (Ed.), *Systems and models for developing programs for the gifted and talented* (pp. 180–193). Mansfield Center, CT: Creative Learning Press.

Maker, C. J. (1982). *Curriculum development for the gifted.* Rockville, MD: Aspen Systems.

Minstrell, J. (1989). Teaching science for understanding. In L. B. Resnick and L. E. Klopfer, (Eds.), *Toward the thinking curriculum.* Reston, VA: Association for Supervision & Curriculum Development.

Murphy, J. M., & Gilligan, C. (1980). Moral development in late adolescence and adulthood: A critique and reconstruction of Kohlberg's theory. *Human Development, 23,* 77–104.

O'Connor, F. (1962). *Mystery and manners.* New York: The Noonday Press.

Paul, R. (1992). *Critical thinking: What every person needs to survive in a rapidly changing world.* Rohnert Park, CA: Foundation for Critical Thinking.

Rabinowitz, M., & Glaser, R. (1985). Cognitive structure and process in highly competent performance. In F. D. Horowitz & M. O'Brien (Eds.), *The gifted and talented: Developmental perspectives* (pp. 75–98). Washington, DC: American Psychological Association.

Renzulli, J. S. (1977). *The enrichment triad model: A guide to developing defensible programs for the gifted and talented.* Mansfield Center, CT: Creative Learning Press.

Rogers, K. (1986). Do the gifted think and learn differently: A review of recent research and its implications. *Journal for the Education of the Gifted, 10,* 17–40.

Ross, B. (1991). Toward a framework for problem-based curricula. In D. Boud & G. Feletti (Eds.), *The challenge of problem-based learning* (pp. 34–41). New York: St. Martin's Press.

Runco, M. A. (1986). Maximal performance on divergent thinking tests by gifted, talented, and nongifted children. *Psychology in the Schools, 23,* 308–315.

Schmidt, H. G., & Moust J. J. (1995). What makes a tutor effective? A structural-equations modeling approach to learning in problem-based curricula. *Academic Medicine, 70,* 708–714.

Shoenfeld, A. H. (1989). Teaching mathematical thinking and problem solving. In L. B. Resnick and L. E. Klopfer (Eds.), *Toward the thinking curriculum: Current cognitive research.* Reston, VA: Association for Supervision & Curriculum Development.

Spiro, R. J., Carlson, R. L., Feltovich, P. J., & Anderson, D. K. (1988). *Cognitive flexibility theory: Advanced knowledge acquisition in ill-structured domains.* Proceedings of the 10th annual conference of the Cognitive Society. Hillsdale, NJ: Lawrence Erlbaum.

Stepien, W. J., & Gallagher, S. A. (1993) Problem-based learning: As authentic as it gets. *Educational Leadership, 50,* 25–29.

Stepien, W. J., & Gallagher, S. A. (1997a). Self-study kit: Problem-based learning. (Folder 4, Activity 1). Alexandria, VA: Association for Supervision & Curriculum Development.

Stepien, W. J. & Gallagher, S. A. (1997b). *Problem-based learning across the curriculum: An ASCD professional inquiry kit.* Reston, VA: Association for Supervision and Curriculum Development.

Stepien, W. J., Gallagher, S. A., & Workman, D. (1993). Problem-based learning for traditional and interdisciplinary classrooms. *Journal for the Education of the Gifted, 16,* 338–357.

Sternberg, R. J., & Davidson, J. E. (1985). Cognitive development in the gifted and talented. In F. D. Horowitz & M. O'Brien (Eds.) *The gifted and talented: Developmental perspectives* (pp. 37–74). Washington, DC: American Psychological Association.

Storr, A. (1989). *Solitude: A return to the self.* New York: Ballentine Books.

Tuchman, R. (1966, March). Historian as artist. *New York Herald Book Week,* 14.

VanTassel-Baska, J. (1988). *Comprehensive curriculum for gifted learners.* Boston, MA: Allyn and Bacon.

Wilkinson, W. K., & Maxwell, S. (1991). The influence of college students' epistemological style of selected problem-solving processes. *Research in Higher Education, 32,* 333–350.

CHAPTER 11

Fostering Creative Thinking

BONNIE CRAMOND
University of Georgia

What is Creativity?

*I*t's almost like a riddle:

   What . . .
   . . . has been around as long as humans have?
   . . . exists in some form in all cultures?
   . . . can be exhibited by young and old, educated and uneducated,
      rich and poor?
   . . . is known to everyone?
   . . . Yet, can't easily be defined?

   Creativity!

Although all people think they can recognize it when they see it, there is not one commonly held definition. Our conceptions of creativity are filtered through our own overlays of culture, time, experience, values, belief systems, and so forth.

For example, the ancient Aztecs and Greeks viewed creativity as mystical, an inspiration "breathed in" from gods or muses (Rothenberg & Hausman, 1976). Many contemporary people and cultures feel the same way. Lionel Richie (Rader, 1993), a modern singer/songwriter and Grammy Award winner, described the composition process this way:

> It's like radio stations playing in my head. I'm in the shower singing along to this great song, and then I stop one moment and go, "Hey it's not on the radio." What's frightening about it is I'm not singing a song, I'm singing *along* with the song that's playing in my head. (p. 20)

He went on to say that he considered God his co-writer.

There are many other examples of this spiritual view, both ancient and modern. An excellent collection of original writings on various views of creativity (Rothenberg & Hausman, 1976) illustrates the diversity of conceptions of the nature of creativity. There is the psychoanalytic view of creativity as described by Freud and others that explains creative expression as a regression to a childlike way of thinking, or a way to safely express aggressive or sexual thoughts. Conversely, humanists such as Rogers or Maslow differentiated self-actualizing creativity as part of optimal mental health from special talent creativity that may accompany mental problems. The behaviorists led by Skinner have argued that creativity is simply a learned response to stimuli, and many cognitive psychologists, such as Weisberg, believe that creativity is a way of thinking that can be taught. Other views include the physiological view that creativity is related to brain organization or brain wave functions (Diamond, 1988; Ferguson, 1977; Restak, 1993). There is probably some truth to all of these views, yet each one is insufficient to explain the complexity that is creativity.

Some scholars prefer to think of creativity as a system that incorporates the person, process, product, and the environment (e.g. Sternberg, 1988; Feldman, Csikszentmihalyi, & Gardner, 1994). Such system views grant that within each of the four dimensions listed above there are many variables that determine the if, when, how, who, what, where, and why of creativity. For example, a person may be born with perfect pitch, a good auditory memory, and the creative capacity to write new music but not have the opportunity for music lessons, the manual dexterity to play an instrument, or the time, money, and encouragement to pursue a musical interest. Such a person would have some of the components necessary for the expression of musical creativity, but not others. So many variables must coincide in the right combinations for creativity to be manifested, that it is no wonder great creative accomplishments are rare.

On the other hand, such a person may create tunes for his children, pick out some songs on the harmonica at a party, and sing with a local group. He may think of imaginative ways to make his everyday job more interesting and his paycheck stretch. Everyday examples of creativity surround us.

Some people differentiate between big "C" creativity, that of the eminent, and little "c" creativity, such as in the examples given above. Others believe that creativity can be viewed hierarchically

---

Emergenative Creativity—entirely new principles or assumptions around which new schools, movements, and the like can flourish.

Innovative Creativity—improvement through modification involving conceptualizing skills.

Inventive Creativity—ingenuity is displayed with materials, methods, and techniques.

Productive Creativity—artistic and scientific products within restrictions.

Expressive Creativity—spontaneous drawings of children.

Figure 1. Taylor's Levels of Creativity

Note. From "The nature of the creative process," In P. Smith (Ed.), *Creativity,* (pp. 51–82), by I. A. Taylor, 1959, New York: Hasting House. Copyright 1959 by Hasting House.

(Taylor, 1959). In Taylor's model, outlined in Figure 1, the expressive art work of a child can be considered creative; however, it is not as high on the scale as a creative invention. The highest level, emergenative creativity, involves changing the structure of the field or starting a new field or movement. Freud's work in psychotherapy could be considered in such a category.

Sometimes, the only difference in the great and the everyday creatives is that someone has discovered and promoted them. Boorstin (1992) made the case in his tome, *The Creators*, that Shakespeare owes his success to the affection of his fellow actors as well as to his unquestionable talent.

> About three-fourths of the prolific output of playwrights in his lifetime has disappeared. But Shakespeare's fellow actors, as a token of friendship to him, did us the great service of preserving the texts of his plays when they arranged publication of the First Folio in 1623. (p. 317)

Luck plays a big part in creativity, too. However, luck and inspiration are not the only, or even the most important parts, of creativity. The hard work that is central to creativity was addressed when Pasteur said, "Chance favors the prepared mind."

What is creativity? There is some confusion in schools with the concept of creativity. Guilford (1967, 1977) included many creative abilities in his model of intelligence. However, many people assume that creativity is limited to artistic expression, which doesn't include the problem solving type of creativity that is invoked when making a scientific discovery, solving a social problem, or keeping restless children busy on a rainy day.

Another source of confusion arises from the use of the words *talented* or *gifted* along with *creative*. In some uses, talent refers to a point on the continuum of ability that is less than giftedness; for example, when one believes there are many talented musicians, but few truly gifted ones (Cox, Daniel, & Boston, 1985, p. 122). At other times, giftedness is used to refer to general intellectual ability and talent to specific ability; for example, a talented mathematician (Feldhusen, 1986; MacKinnon, 1978).

Still another view is Gagné's (1985), which conceptualized giftedness as ability and talent as performance. This is similar to

Bloom's (1985) definition of talent as a high level of *demonstrated* ability, rather than *aptitude* in a certain field of study or interest. It seems that in order for someone to demonstrate giftedness at the highest levels in any field, there is a need for the confluence of creativity, talent (or skill in a particular domain), and motivation.

Who is Creative?

There has been a great deal of interest over the years in describing the creative personality. Much of our information in this regard comes from retrospective research that has examined the lives of eminent creative people such as Mozart, Freud, Darwin, Einstein, and others. Another line of research has compared the personality characteristics of creative people in a specific field, such as architecture, with less creative people in the same field (MacKinnon, 1965, 1976). A third line of research has examined the personality characteristics of individuals who score high on a measure of creativity or produce something judged to be creative. From such research studies we have amassed a compendium of creative characteristics (see Figure 2).

Because so many of the behaviors that have been listed as indicative of creative individuals may also be used in identifying learning and behavior problems, teachers should be wary of attributing a negative cause to a child's "differentness." For example, an examination of the similarity in the behaviors attributed to both highly creative individuals and those diagnosed with Attention Deficit Hyperactivity Disorder (ADHD) indicates the possibility of an overlap in the conditions; (Cramond, 1994, 1995). Both individuals who are creative and those who have been diagnosed with ADHD may manifest similar characteristics, such as daydreaming, high energy, impulsiveness, risk-taking, preoccupation, difficult temperament, and poor social skills. In addition, there is evidence from both groups of mixed laterality and anomalies in cerebral dominance, more spontaneous ideation, higher levels of sensation seeking behavior, and higher energy or activity than in normal populations. (For more information, visit http://www.gifted.uconn.edu/cramond.html and http://www.bornto explore.org/addcre-1.html.)

Cognitive	Personality
• relatively high intelligence	• willingness to confront hostility and take intellectual risks
• originality	
• articulateness and verbal fluency	• perseverance
• good imagination	• curiosity
• metaphorical thinking	• openness to new experience
• flexibility	• driving absorption
• independence of judgment	• discipline and commitment to one's work
• ability to cope well with novelty	• high intrinsic motivation
• logical thinking skills	• tolerance for ambiguity
• internal visualization	• a broad range of interests
• ability to escape perceptual sets	• tendency to play with ideas
• ability to find order in chaos	• unconventionality in behavior
• questioning	• tendency to experience deep emotions
• alert to novelty and gaps in knowledge	• intuitiveness
• ability to use existing knowledge as a base for new ideas	• seeking interesting situations
	• opportunism
• aesthetic ability that allows recognition of good problems in the field	• conflict between self-criticism and self-confidence

Figure 2. Characteristics of Creative Individuals

Note. From "What do we know about creativity," In R. J. Sternberg (Ed.), *The Nature of Creativity: Contemporary Psychological Perspectives,* (pp 434–435), by T. Z. Tardiff & R. J. Sternberg, 1988, Buffalo, NY: Creative Education Foundation. Copyright 1988 by Creative Education Foundation, 1050 Union Rd., Buffalo, NY 14224. Reprinted with permission.

The best way to think of creativity may be analogous to our modern conceptions of intelligence. Psychologists generally agree that intelligence can be expressed in many ways, is affected by genetics and environment, may be nurtured or hindered by experiences, is at least partly defined by the culture, and is measured inexactly by any test. Substitute the word *creativity* for *intelligence* and you would have another true statement. Both creativity and intelligence are multidimensional constructs that all humans demonstrate to some degree. Although people readily admit they have no creativity, they rarely would claim to have no intelligence. It is our job as teachers to help students find and enhance their abilities in both areas.

How Can We Nurture Creativity in Ourselves and Others?

The single best way to nurture creativity in anyone may be to recognize and value it. In his 22-year follow-up of individuals first tested in elementary school, Torrance (1981) found that the "teachers who made a difference" were those who enabled their students to hold on to their creativity. These teachers were not always the most creative individuals themselves, but they recognized that spark in their students and encouraged it. As parents, teachers, colleagues, and friends (even to ourselves), we can refrain from joining the "murder committees" who try to kill every new idea with negativism and, instead, maintain an open mind for new possibilities. There are other more active ways to nurture creativity.

Environment

Psychological Safety

One way to enhance creativity is to maintain an environment conducive to it. Rogers (1954, 1976) pointed out that creativity is more likely to be expressed in a situation where there is *psychological safety*. Because coming up with an original idea requires taking a risk—that you'll be wrong, make a fool of yourself, be rejected—the less severe the consequences, the more likely the risk will be assumed. In other words, a classroom where ideas are valued as highly as answers and mistakes are viewed as learning opportunities is more encouraging of innovation than one where humiliation and punishment are frequently used.

Rewards

What about rewards? There is some debate about the role of rewards in the fostering of creativity. Amabile and her colleagues (1983) found that *any* evaluation of performance, even positive evaluation, can diminish creativity. Why would that be so? Think about the explanation of a psychologically safe environment. The expectation of a possible positive evaluation also carries with it the possibility of a negative one next time. In some cases, the more positive the first evaluation the harder it is to live up to it on subsequent tries. Thus, we have the writer who's blocked after one best seller or the artists who release one hit recording never to be heard again. Also, the reward can have a role in shaping the behavior. A person who is seeking a reward may opt to do that which is perceived to be most likely to be rewarded again rather than that which is truly creative. So, we have the artists who "sell out" to commercialism and the writers who continue to write books according to a hackneyed formula.

But, the relationship between reward and creativity is not so simple. There are individuals who are rewarded for their work and continue to produce creatively. In fact, some of them may not be so moved to be prolific without the financial incentive. Amabile and her colleagues conceded that the expectation of reward and other factors, such as self-esteem and the degree of intrinsic motivation, affect how the reward state is perceived. Other researchers have concluded that rewards do not dampen intrinsic motivation (Cameron & Pierce, 1994). For teachers, the key seems to be helping students find what they love and encouraging them to do it well. Students with strong *self-esteem* and strong *intrinsic motivation* are resistant to the possible deleterious effects of rewards (Amabile, 1983).

Balancing Stimulation and Reflection

Another environmental factor that can affect creativity is the amount and timing of stimulation. Although most parents and teachers know about the positive effects on brain development that are attributed to a stimulating environment, many are not aware that individuals also need quiet time to reflect and fantasize. Elkind (1989) warned against the stress that is cause to an over-scheduled child. In the 1960s,

Taba (1962) explained that a good lesson has proper pacing, alternating active lessons and quiet lessons. More directly related to this discussion, Torrance (1981; Torrance & Safter, 1990) advised that *stimulation* be alternated with times for *quiet reflection*. Without both, individuals lack the impetus for creative ideas or the time to develop them.

Wallas (1926, 1976) described the creative process as occurring in four parts: preparation, incubation, illumination, and verification. During preparation, materials and information are gathered. This phase may include the stimulation that could inspire a creative response. During incubation, the individual is not visibly working on the problem but may be fooling around with the materials. When illumination occurs, there is an idea, a solution to a problem, or a sentiment to express. Finally, during verification, the idea is carried out, the solution is applied, or the art is completed. Two of these, preparation and verification, are outwardly active periods. The other two are introspective. These may coincide roughly with the need for stimulation and peace, although the four stages do not occur so linearly as presented. They may occur out of order, be repeated, or vary in length and intensity.

Flow

A leading creativity theorist, Csikszentmihalyi (1990; Csikszentmihalyi & Csikszentmihalyi, 1988), studied the emotional and motivational aspects of creativity. After interviewing more than 300 people involved in creative activities, he concluded that they described their experiences during the creative process with the same phenomenological characteristics. Because several talked about being swept along, or other such terms, he called the experience *flow*. There are eight key conditions, all or many of which must pertain for flow to occur.

1. The challenges of the activity are well-matched to the individual's skills. If the activity is too easy, the individual is bored. If it is too difficult, anxiety is the result.
2. There are clear goals and clear feedback.
3. There is a merging of action and awareness; the individual often reports feeling like a conduit of the work.
4. Still, the individual feels a sense of control. There is motivation to continue but a feeling that one can stop at will.

5. The individual is concentrating only on the relevant stimuli and giving the task full attention.
6. There is an absence of self-awareness because of the focused attention on the task that sometimes, at its most challenging levels, becomes a transcendence of self.
7. Because of a change in consciousness, there is a distorted sense of time. One can work for hours without realizing how much time has gone by, or feel that an eon has passed in just a few seconds.
8. The process is an exhilarating experience that creates intrinsic motivation to engage in the same sort of activity again. However, the activity and the skills must continue to become more complex in order to fully engage the individual. Thus, flow may be seen as a dynamic force in evolution.

Most teachers can readily see that it is very difficult, if not impossible, to create such conditions in the regular school classroom. For example, the first condition, matching the task to the student's ability, is quite challenging with a heterogeneously grouped class. However, we can create flow experiences that children can continue to work on outside of school. These would include activities that come from the students' interests, have some degree of self-selection, are extended over some time, but have continual feedback.

Summary

In summary, an environment that is conducive to creativity is one that is psychologically safe, where the intrinsic rewards of accomplishment are emphasized over extrinsic rewards and controls, where students have opportunities to learn about their interests and pursue them with some autonomy, where there is a balance of stimulation and quiet time, and where challenges are matched to the abilities of the learners. Such an environment can be created for students at least some of the time, and they can learn to create such environments for themselves.

Space does not permit more detail about how to provide such an environment. Interested individuals could look at some curricular models that would assist in providing a good environment for creativity, such as the Schoolwide Enrichment Model (Renzulli & Reis, 1985), the Autonomous Learner Model (Betts, 1986), or the

Incubation Model (Torrance & Safter, 1990), which will be described later because of its emphasis on creativity development.

Strategies

Although providing the proper environment is very important for nurturing creativity, there are more active ways to promote creativity in the classroom. Through the use of specific creativity strategies, teachers can help students develop the thinking skills and attitudes important to the creative process. It is important to note that such skills and attitudes should be infused throughout the curriculum rather than taught separately. Just as with critical thinking activities, creative thinking activities should be ingrained in all subjects if students are to see their worth and apply them when suitable.

Warm-Up

Before any activity is undertaken, individuals should first participate in a *warm-up* activity. Just as it is important to warm-up your muscles before any vigorous exercise, so too is it important to warm-up our thinking, especially for creative thinking. You could use just about any creative activity as a warm-up. It's a good idea to use multimodal approaches—verbal, visual, musical, and physical activities can all be effective.

One example of a good warm-up activity is to have groups of four students sitting at a table with a fountain pen cartridge that has a small pin prick in one end, four sheets of art paper, and four pencils. Students should be instructed to number each edge of one side of the paper, 1–4. The students should then be instructed to squeeze a drop of ink in the center of the paper, fold the paper in half, and smooth it creating an ink blot. With the edge #1 facing them, give students 30 seconds to list all of the things the shape could be. At the end of 30 seconds, call time, and have each student pass his or her sheet to the next student on the right who will turn it to edge #2. Students again have 30 seconds to imagine what the ink blot could be from this angle. Repeat until all four edges have been titled. Then, have students show the pictures and share some of the titles.

A good, active, kinesthetic movement warm-up is one based upon complex contraptions. Explain that such a machine is like the one in the popular game *Mousetrap*, or show pictures of Rube Goldberg's inventions (1968). Students are asked to volunteer to get in front of the group and make a repeated machine-like movement. Then, other students can come up one-by-one and add a motion to the machine. When all volunteers are up and moving, remaining students are asked to brainstorm what the machine is and how the various movements work together. For example, students may decide that it is a baby-washing machine with a washer, dryer, powderer, and diaperer based upon the movements.

Humor is always a good warm-up. A simple use of humor is to share appropriate jokes or cartoons with the class. Another idea is to have students propose captions for cartoons chosen from children's magazines (Ziv, 1983).

The ideas for warm-ups are almost limitless. The main criteria for a good warm-up activity are that it is enjoyable, engages the students, gets them to think creatively, and promotes a relaxed atmosphere.

Ideation

There are several ideation strategies that can be used to warm-up or to restart creative thinking when things get bogged down. Perhaps the best known of these is *brainstorming*.

The principles of brainstorming are simple. First, there must be deferred judgment; and, second, quantity breeds quality. That is, while producing ideas, we must resist the urge to criticize our own ideas as well as those of others. The goal is to produce as many ideas as possible so that at least one good creative idea will be generated. Sometimes, even one person's silly idea will spark a creative idea in another. In accordance with these principles are the four rules listed in Figure 3.

Starters for brainstorming can be as simple as "Name all the things that you can think of that are green" or as thought-provoking as "Just suppose teachers did have eyes in the backs of their heads. What are some things that might happen?" Some other brainstorming starters are provided. "Name all the words you can

1. Criticism is ruled out. All evaluative comments, both positive and negative, must be withheld during the brainstorming process.
2. Free wheeling is welcomed. Individuals are encouraged to use free association to elicit as many different ideas as possible.
3. Quantity is wanted. All ideas are recorded.
4. Combination and improvement are sought. Individuals are encouraged to hitchhike or piggyback—embellish, adapt, or connect the ideas of others to create new ideas.

Figure 3. Rules of Brainstorming

think of that begin with a B." "What are some ways that we could make zoos better for animals?" "Name some things you can make with an old shoe box." There are many ways to start this process that are appropriate for the age and sophistication of the group.

One simple technique for encouraging ideation is called SCAMPER (Eberle, 1996). The letters of the word stand for the different methods for considering things in order to think of new ideas. For example, take the question, "What are some ways that we could make zoos better for animals?" We might use the SCAMPER method to brainstorm:

Substitute: put the people in enclosures and let the animals run free;

Combine: have the birds from the aviary in the same place with the monkeys;

Adapt: use climate control domes and vegetation to simulate their natural environment;

Magnify or minify: make zoos larger with more space; breed smaller versions of animals so that the space seems larger;

Put to other uses: give the animals activities to occupy them;

Eliminate: remove as many unnatural sensations as possible— sights, sounds, smells, foods, textures, and so forth; and

Reverse or rearrange: group animals and vegetation together as in the wild and let them hunt or forage for their own food.

Many of these ideas have been incorporated in some form or another in modern zoos. Other ideas may be unfeasible. The point at this juncture is just to generate thinking of as many, and as varied, ideas as possible. Ideally, many ideas could be listed under each category and sorted out in a subsequent step.

Metaphorical or Analogical Thinking

Other creative strategies use metaphorical or analogical thinking. One technique is to begin with a stem with the form: (Something) is like _____ because _____. Then, participants complete the phrase with an unlikely object and tell how they are alike. Here is a stem and some sample responses from *A Whack on the Side of the Head*:

> Life is like . . .
> . . . a jigsaw puzzle but you don't have the picture on the front of the box to know what it's supposed to look like. Sometimes you're not even sure you have all the pieces.
> . . . riding an elevator. It has a lot of ups and downs and someone is always pushing your buttons. Sometimes you get the shaft, but what really bothers you are the jerks. (von Oech, 1983, pp. 40–41)

A variation would be to have participants choose nouns at random by drawing word cards from a hat, picking words from a dictionary, and so forth. Then, they would have to find ways to force fit the two nouns to answer the question of how they are alike. For example, a student who chose *book* and *sponge* might say, "A book is like a sponge because they both can be absorbing."

Synectics

Gordon (1961) developed a method of systematically applying analogies in problem solving that he labeled *synectics*. Such thinking has been used in business for creating new products or improving existing products. One famous example is the Pringles™ potato chip. The problem was, "How can we package chips to minimize breakage and maximize the number of chips we can fit into a compact package?" The answer came from an analogy in nature. Leaves that are wet and pressed together dry together in a compressed shape. It wasn't too big a leap to figure how to apply this to chips. Science, too, has used analogies from nature to create products like the hypodermic needle (snake's fang) or the submarine (fish's swim bladder).

The idea of synectics is to solve problems using analogies and opposites to associate comparable responses. Then, force fit generated responses into a realistic solution for the problem. There are four types of analogies used: (1) *direct*, with the goal of making actual comparisons with similar situations in nature or elsewhere; (2) *personal*, with the goal of having the problem solver identify with some aspect of the problem in order to look at it in an unfamiliar way; (3) *symbolic*, with the goal of using an objective and impersonal image to represent some component of the problem, perhaps through putting two conflicting aspects of the problem together; and, (4) *fantasy*, which uses imaginary ideas to find ideal solutions (Gordon, 1961).

How could this be applied? Let's say the problem is how to reduce the noise in the school cafeteria, and we want a solution other than the age-old one of having students eat in silence. The analogies need not be used in any particular order.

- **Direct:** What materials muffle noise in nature?
  Brainstorm: cotton, water, earth.
  Force fit: Use some soundproof materials on the walls to absorb some of the noise.
- **Personal:** How would I like to be captured if I were a noise?
  Brainstorm: in a soft cloud, in an open field, with a close group of friends.
  Force fit: noise is diminished if it is absorbed, allowed to be in wide open spaces, or divided into smaller segments. We've already suggested an absorbent material for the walls, so change the configuration of the room so that there is more or less space.
- **Symbolic:** Take two conflicting aspects of the analogy and put them together into a short phrase or image.
  Force fit: We want to create a quiet noise. Perhaps we can teach children to speak quietly at lunch.
- **Fantasy:** Eat like at a picnic or a restaurant.
  Force fit: Eat out of doors on nice days or in smaller groups in smaller rooms.

Through this method, several possible solutions may be proposed to be used singularly or in conjunction. If our goal is to allow children to eat in the cafeteria and socialize with their friends without creating a great deal of noise, then we could put some absorbent, soundproofing material on the walls; reconfigure the room with dividers so that there are smaller, more intimate dining areas; incorporate lessons on speaking softly at the table; and eat out of doors on nice days.

Visualization

Another kind of exercise that can range from simple to complex is *visualization*. One way to promote visualization skills is through guided imagery. With this technique, students relax and close their eyes while the teacher verbally leads them through a succession of images. One language arts teacher in the Midwest took a group of middle school students on an imaginary trip to the beach. These students, who had never seen an ocean, were lead to imagine what the ocean looked like, smelled like, the salt of the water, the soft heat of the sand, the cawing of gulls overhead. The teacher used vivid sensory images to describe the scene. Then, she had the students write a story about a trip to the beach. She was amazed at the length of the stories and the students' use of descriptive words and phrases.

Another activity that uses visualization is the *encounter lesson*. Encounter lessons are activities to stimulate creativity and positive feelings of worth. They are active lessons, lasting from 15 to 20 minutes, that involve sensory imagination. The object is an encounter with ideas and others. The structure of an encounter lesson consists of five questions with lengthy pauses for the students to imagine their answers. Soft music can be played in the background. The type and order of the questions are (1) question of identity; (2) question of awareness; (3) question of isolation; (4) question of risk or danger; and (5) question of wisdom.

An example of an encounter lesson that could be used with a class studying about Native Americans is

Imagine you are a Native American ...
- What tribe do you belong to? (identity)
- What do you hear ... see ... feel ... smell ... taste? (awareness)

- You are away from the rest of the tribe. How do you feel? (isolation)
- You've been captured by an enemy. How do you feel? (danger)
- What have you learned from these experiences? What would you like to tell the world for posterity? (wisdom)

Then, students can take turns telling about their experiences. This would be a good introductory activity for the teacher to assess each student's background knowledge and preconceived ideas about a topic. It would also be a good cumulative activity whereby students use what they have learned to imagine the details of different Native American cultures.

Focusing on Attributes

Attributes are categories of characteristics. For example, attributes of people include hair color, eye color, height, weight, temperament, ethnicity, talents, and so forth. Attributes can include the physical, psychological, social, and other. According to Koberg and Bagnall (1991), "Attribute listing is easiest when you begin with general categories and work your way down to specifics." (p. 59)

By focusing on attributes, we can solve problems in several ways. Four techniques that use attributes are attribute listing, attribute analogy chains, morphological analysis, and morphological synthesis.

To use *attribute listing,* list all of the components or elements of the given problem in one column. List all the attributes or characteristics of each component in a second column. Generate ideas for improvement in a third and positive and negative features in a fourth. The problem should be stated in "how-to" fashion, as, for example, "How to improve the playground" (see Table 1).

Using this model, each positive and negative feature can then be translated into a new element of the problem to be run through the entire process again, making the creative activity self-perpetuating (Saletta, 1978, p. 1; see Table 2).

Another way to use attributes in problem solving is to look for a relationship between two very different things—even if this relationship has to be somewhat forced. Then, create *attribute analogy chains.* For example, if we wanted to improve the design of a television set, we could list its basic attributes as

Table 1. Attribute Listing Chart

Element	Attribute	Ideas for Improvement	Positive/Negative
1. Swings	Too high	Lower them	Small kids can swing; if too low, little kids can get hurt easier
2. Ground	Blacktop	Soften with mats, artificial turf	Safety; increases number of games playable and cost; effects of weather on mats

Table 2. Second Attribute Listing Chart

Element	Attribute	Ideas for Improvement	Positive/Negative
1. Children	Different ages	Separate in areas	Safer for small ones; less interaction
2. Cost	High	Fund-raiser	Effective; work

Name: television;

Form: geometric, angular, cube;

Function: entertain, educate, accompany.

To each of these attributes we might tag the following analogy ideas:

Name: videotube, idiot box, entertainment cube;

Form: prism, sphere, semicircle;

Function: live theater, school, conversation.

From these, we might produce the following alternative views:

- Change name to Entertainment Prism (EP).
- Try prism forms that allow for different screens at different angles—with ear phones, families can view different shows in the same room.
- Use at school to send different lessons to different groups within the same classroom—called Educational Prism (EP).

Morphological Analysis is another technique that uses attributes to develop new ideas. With this checkerboard technique, attributes from one dimension of the object are listed along the top and attributes of another dimension along the side. The new ideas are created when combinations are forced to fill in the squares of the grid. Example: Invent a new kind of bagel (see Figure 4).

Morphological Synthesis is a similar technique that requires you to list the attributes of the situation. Then, below each attribute, brainstorm as many alternatives as you can. When completed,

	Grain		
	Corn	**Barley**	**Kasha**
Fruit			
Kiwi	Kiwi corn	Kiwi barley	Kiwi kasha
Mango	Mango corn	Mango barley	Mango kasha

Figure 4. Morphological Analysis Grid

make many random runs across the lists of alternates, picking up a different one from each column and combining them into original forms.

Here is one way to do this to get an idea for writing a story.

List the main attributes that you want to use for the story starter: main character, supporting characters, conflict, setting.

Brainstorm as many ideas as you can under each attribute. In this case, I have listed six under each, but there are many more possibilities (see Figure 5).

Randomly pick one option from each of the columns. One way to do this is to use the last four digits of a phone number. For example, using the phone number 4246, I would choose the fourth option in column one, the second in column two, and so on. (If you're going to use this method, it helps to come up with at least 10 options in each column. Otherwise, with larger numbers you have to count down and then begin again at the top.)

Put your combination together. In this case, I would have a beauty queen involved in an international plot with circus acts at a TV station. Some television plots have been written this way. Author Terry Kay, who wrote *To Dance with the White Dog*, has used a method somewhat similar to this in writing scenes for television programs or chapters for books (T. Kay, personal communication, November 16, 1997).

Main Character	Characters	Supporting Conflict	Setting
dog	farm hands	property	mountain town
detective	circus acts	jealousy	Old West
murderer	talking animals	theft	New York
beauty queen	school children	international plot	Ancient Egypt
super hero	a family	war	farm
rock star	bikers	personal	TV station

Figure 5. Morphological Synthesis Grid

Lateral Thinking

Certainly, one of the most prolific authors in the area of creativity strategies has been Edward de Bono. He coined the term *lateral thinking* and defined it as pattern switching, a new way of looking at the world (1985a). He explained that lateral thinking is not the same as creativity; it is valueless, but it comprises both an attitude and a number of defined methods (1970, 1986).

Each of these methods is named with key letters that stand for the first letters in the words of the method. For example, EBS is a method that has participants *examine both sides* of an argument. A follow-up method called ADI has participants list the issues of the argument under the columns *agreement, disagreement, irrelevance.* This might be a good way to have students look at a concern in social studies or science and prepare to discuss it based on the issues.

Some of these methods are as complex as PISCO, which outlines the steps in a multi-step planning operation: *purpose, input, solutions, choice, operation.* (As you will see, this problem-solving method is similar in many ways to the Osborn/Parnes Creative Problem-Solving process and the Japanese Quality Circles to be discussed later.) One that I have found particularly useful for students when reading some new information is to have them list in columns ideas they think are positive, those they think are negative, and those that have no particular value but are worth noting. This method is called PMI for *plus, minus, interesting.* Although simple, it is an effective way to get students to interact with the reading and consider how they feel about what they are reading.

Another method that de Bono has used is from his book, *Six Thinking Hats* (1985b). (In 1991, he published *Six Action Shoes,* with a similar technique.) The six hats represent six different ways of thinking. White is worn by the neutral and objective thinker who is concerned with facts and figures. Red represents the emotional, intuitive view that acts on hunches and impressions, rather than on logical reasons. Black points out the negative aspects of a situation, the errors in logic, and possible consequences of a course of action. Yellow keeps up the optimistic, positive thinking and focuses on benefits and constructive ideas. Green represents creativity, deliberate innovation, and new approaches to problems.

Blue stands for control and organization of the thinking and of the other thinkers.

Students can be divided into groups and each given a hat made from construction paper in one of the six colors. When presented with a problem to solve or an issue to discuss, the students must stay in the role according to the hat they are wearing. This method helps make students aware of some of the ways in which people think about issues and helps them to focus on deliberate thinking.

One variation on this is to pair the students—white and red, black and yellow, green and blue—to discuss the issue. Another is to have them discuss for a certain amount of time, then switch hats. The Six Hats Method is particularly effective when students get to "try on" methods of thinking that are not natural to them.

The beginning of such a discussion might sound something like this:

White: "Our problem is to decide whether it is ethical for scientists to continue to conduct research with live animals."

Red: "Oh, the poor little monkeys!"

Black: "You can't just consider the animals. Without animal research many medical discoveries would not have been made. Many people are alive today because of such discoveries."

Red: "Thank goodness for that!"

Yellow: "Perhaps there is a way we can still get the benefits of animal research without too much pain and suffering."

Blue: "Let's stick to our problem at hand: Is research on live animals ethical?"

Green: "There wouldn't be such an ethical dilemma if we could think of a way to do the same quality of research without sacrificing animals. Let's think, how might we simulate animal reactions realistically so that we can conduct research without using live animals?"

Such a discussion might lead into a creative problem solving exercise to attempt to solve Green's stated question.

Creative Problem Solving

The Osborn/Parnes Creative Problem-Solving process (CPS) is composed of five steps: fact finding, problem finding, idea finding, solution finding, and acceptance finding (Parnes, 1981). This process incorporates both *divergent thinking*, or thinking of many possibilities, and *convergent thinking*, or thinking of the one right or best solution. During *fact finding*, information is gathered about the situation. *Problem finding* means identifying the central or most salient problem and any underlying subproblems. The *idea finding* refers to the process of generating many possible solutions (usually by brainstorming). The *solution finding* step involves applying criteria to choose the best solution. And *acceptance finding* involves "selling" the solution to the key individuals involved in decision making.

Although these steps are presented in a logical order, in real problem solving they do not always occur in this order. Sometimes, we are presented with a problem and have to go back and research the facts. Other times, we may be in a position to sell an idea to a constituency and find that the correct problem was not identified, and we have to go back to the problem finding step.

This was the case in the 1970s when the Detroit automakers lost money trying to sell luxury cars to a public that was seeking more energy-efficient and reliable vehicles. Therefore, strict adherence to an order or insistence in completing every step every time is artificial after students have learned the process.

There are some techniques, activities, and devices that have been found helpful in training others to use CPS. One standard device is the use of IWWMW . . . during problem finding. When students begin the problem statement with "In what ways might we . . . ." it is left open for creative attack.

Another standard device is the use of a criteria grid for evaluating solutions. The one in Figure 6 is shown with space to list five ideas along the left side, but many more are possible and desirable. It is also illustrated with spaces for six criteria across the top; but, again, this is an arbitrary number.

Here is an example. Suppose some high school students used CPS to solve the dilemma of what to do to celebrate their graduation. They worded the problem as, "In what ways might we celebrate our graduation?" During the fact finding step, they had discovered that most of them did not have much money to spend; they wanted to involve as many graduates as possible; they wanted to do some-

Ideas	Fun	Inexpensive	Interactive	Location	Weather	Total
1. picnic	3	5	4	5	1	18
2. party	5	4	5	2	3	19
3. dance	4	3	3	1	4	15
4. dinner	1	2	2	3	5	13
5. go out	2	1	1	4	2	10

←———— Criteria ————→

**Figure 6. Creative Problem-Solving Solution
Evaluation Grid**

thing fun and informal; and they had to plan it quickly. During idea finding, they brainstormed many possibilities (see Figure 6).

During solution finding, they chose the top five to consider further and listed them along the left side of the grid. They chose criteria based upon their fact finding and the realities of planning. Then, they applied each criterion to each idea and rank ordered the ideas with the highest number going to the best idea in that category. So, they decided the party would be the most fun, and the dinner the least. The dance was the hardest for which to find a location, and the picnic was most dependent on the weather. When all criteria had been used to rank all ideas, the numbers were totaled across the rows and entered in the last column.

The idea with the highest total is the best idea according to the listed criteria. In this case, the party was rated slightly higher than the picnic. The major considerations seem to be the possibility of inclement weather for the picnic and the possibility of finding a location to hold the party. At this point, the students could go back to fact finding and check the weather reports and availability of a party locale. Or, they could choose to go back to the problem finding step: "In what ways might we plan for the picnic so that weather would not ruin it?" Then, ideas might be generated about securing a shelter, picking the best date based on the forecast, and so forth.

Quality Circles

Like CPS, Quality Circles is a problem-solving process that is primarily used by groups. Developed by Japanese industrialists, it was brought to American industry in the 1960s (Bellanca, 1984; Dewar, 1980). Also like CPS, it requires shifting back and forth from divergent to convergent thinking. However, Quality Circles differs in its *emphasis* on convergent thought and analytical thinking and its formality. With CPS, members just call out ideas as they occur. With Quality Circles, members take turns around the circle, with each member saying one thing or opting to pass. There is a designated leader and a rotating role as recorder. The brainstorming ends when everyone passes. The basic steps for Quality Circles are these:

Problem Selection by Formal Brainstorming. This step is further broken down into problem listing, problem clarifying, discussion of the pros, discussion of the cons, participant voting, and data collection to ensure that the problem is the correct one to choose.

Cause-Effect Analysis. In this step, participants attempt to determine the causes of the problem situation and target the main cause. Once again, there is problem clarifying, discussion of the pros, discussion of the cons, participant voting, and data verification in an orderly, round robin fashion.

Solution Identification. In this step, participants use formal brainstorming and costs-benefits analysis, with the impediments to the solution as the costs and the expected positive outcome as the benefit. Then they vote.

The Recommendation. This is a formal presentation to decision makers that should include as much documentation of the project's history and the proposed plan as possible. This might include the goal, data gathered, action steps, timelines, responsibilities, obstacles, and a plan of evaluation.

Implementation. If the plan is approved, then each member of the circle takes on a specific responsibility to implement the plan. (If not, the circle goes back to address the problem again.)

Evaluation. Circle members conduct the evaluation and provide a final report.

Role-playing

Role-playing can be a wonderful outlet for creative expression as well as a very effective creative problem solving technique. Role-playing and creative dramatics have been recommended as part of the curriculum for gifted children, especially in the language arts (Cramond, 1993; Van Tassel-Baska, 1998). Most teachers are well aware that children enjoy such activities. In fact, a survey of a group of gifted middle school students indicated that role-playing and creative dramatics were among their favorite activities in school (Martin & Cramond, 1983).

However, fewer teachers seem to be aware of the need and methods for teaching problem solving through role-playing (Torrance, Murdock, & Fletcher, 1997). Based upon the techniques of sociodrama or psychodrama, role-playing in creative problem solving differs from each in the type of problem that is addressed and the depth of emotional involvement and disclosure of the participants. Although psychodrama can be a very powerful tool for individuals to address serious psychological problems, sociodrama can be the same for groups. Problem solving, through role-playing, can use many of the same techniques with less personal problems. For example, students could role-play to convince the principal to consider their bid for a change in cafeteria rules.

Using the terms of psychodrama (Blatner, 1973), the main roles are *protagonist(s)*, the main character in the problem situation; *director*, usually the teacher who guides the action and ensures that rules are followed and that the situation does not touch on matters too serious or sensitive for the classroom; and *auxiliaries*, others who take part in the enactment in supporting roles. There are three main parts to the enactment:

Warm-up may include group-building activities, as well as defining the problem; discussing the logistics, time, and rules; and choosing roles.

Action in which the protagonist(s) and auxiliaries enact the situation as if it were happening in the "here-and-now." The director monitors the action, adding other roles and players as may become necessary. The director also uses other techniques to move the problem along, such as the *mirror technique,* whereby other actors play the role of the protagonist to show him how he is behaving; *modeling* by other group members to show how they would act in the same situation; *role reversal* of the protagonist and his antagonists to enable individuals to see both sides of a conflict; and *repeat role-playing* with the protagonist trying a different solution each time.

Closure wherein the group discusses the action and evaluates the possible solutions that were generated. In some cases, this may begin another role-playing scenario during which members attempt to predict the outcome of the proposed solution.

There are many more techniques and variations on this basic creative problem-solving method through role-playing (Torrance, Murdock, & Fletcher, 1997). Teachers are cautioned to be alert during the action for any sensitive matters or strong emotional reactions from students that may warrant professional counseling. If these arise, the action should be stopped until the matter is addressed. The key to this method is to have students acting out and being emotionally involved in the problem at hand, not to cause stress.

Removing Blocks

Another effective way to encourage creativity is to remove blocks to individuals' creativity. These blocks are described, with exercises designed to help remove them, in Adams' (1986) book, *Conceptual Blockbusting: A Guide to Better Ideas. Perceptual Blocks* include:
- seeing what you expect to see—stereotyping;
- difficulty in isolating the problem;
- tendency to delimit the problem area too closely;
- inability to see the problem from various viewpoints;

- saturation; and
- failure to utilize all sensory inputs.

One exercise that illustrates how perceptual blocks can limit our thinking uses common materials. Give students a sheet with nine illustrations of a penny. Only one should have all of the elements correct and in the actual locations as on the penny. Most people, although we see pennies every day, are not able to easily complete this task of identifying the correct one. We handle pennies every day, but we no longer really see them. The same point could be made by asking students to draw a computer keyboard. How many could place all the letters and symbols correctly? When we don't pay attention to details, we can miss clues to solving a problem.

Emotional Blocks include
- fear to make a mistake, to fail, to risk;
- inability to tolerate ambiguity; overriding desires for security, order; "no appetite for chaos";
- preference for judging ideas, rather than generating them;
- inability to relax, incubate and "sleep on it";
- lack of challenge; problem fails to engage interest;
- excessive zeal; overmotivation to succeed quickly;
- lack of access to areas of imagination;
- lack of imaginative control; and
- inability to distinguish reality from fantasy.

How many students, especially bright students, have difficulty suspending disbelief long enough to consider that the improbable may be possible? Torrance reported that the great psychologist Thorndike presented prospective graduate students with an unlikely hypothetical situation and asked them to "just suppose" the outcome. Those who were unable to conjecture were considered too incurious for graduate study (Torrance, 1974). As an exercise, try a "just suppose" activity with students or friends. Or, discuss how often each of you has missed an opportunity because of fear of failure. These blocks prevent us from exercising our creativity.

Cultural Blocks include
- fantasy and reflection are a waste of time, lazy, even crazy;
- playfulness is for children only;
- problem solving is serious business, and humor is out of place;

- reason, logic, utility, practicality are good; feelings, intuition, qualitative judgments, pleasure are bad;
- tradition is preferable to change;
- any problem can be solved by scientific thinking and lots of money; and
- taboos.

An example of an activity that illustrates the power of taboos in hindering problem solving is given by Adams (1986). The problem may be shown as a visual or described accordingly:

> Imagine that you are one of a group of six people in a bare room along with the following objects: 100 feet of clothesline, a carpenter's hammer, a chisel, a box of Wheaties,™ a file, a wire coat hanger, a monkey wrench, and a light bulb. A steel pipe is stuck vertically in the concrete floor with a ping-pong ball lying at the bottom of the pipe. The inside diameter of the pipe is just slightly larger than the diameter of the ping-pong ball. Your task is to get the ball out of the pipe without damaging the ball, tube, or floor. How many ways can you think of to do this? (p. 54)

Depending on the nature of the group and the setting, participants can usually think of several possible solutions. However, the solution of urinating in the pipe to float the ball out is rarely suggested. When it is suggested, it is typically by a male, and it is often after there has been some whispering among the participants and laughing. Once that boundary has been breached, many other ideas come forth. This is not to say that these are the best ideas, but only that taboos can keep us from even considering some ideas and can limit our creativity.

Environmental Blocks include
- lack of cooperation and trust among colleagues;
- autocratic boss who values only his own ideas; does not reward others;
- distractions—phone, easy intrusions; and
- lack of support to bring ideas into action.

It is easy to demonstrate environmental blocks if you work in a school setting. Have students discuss the things that they find most distracting when they are trying to concentrate at home and at school. Then, have them sit silently for a prescribed amount of time in each location and record the number and types of distractions they observe. Finally, address how they may eliminate or mitigate against most distractions.

Another good activity to illustrate environmental blocks is to think of a new idea—maybe an invention or new way of doing things—that seems reasonably plausible. Then, seriously propose this idea to friends and, if you are brave, colleagues and others you meet from time to time. Note their reactions. Most often, people immediately form the murder committees discussed earlier and tell you all of the reasons your idea won't work. (This activity is especially potent in a faculty meeting.)

Intellectual and Expressive Blocks include
- solutions formed by solving the problem using an incorrect language;
- inflexible or inadequate use of intellectual problem-solving strategies;
- lack of, or incorrect, information; and
- inadequate language skill to express and record ideas (verbally, musically, visually, etc.).

Most of us have favorite languages (verbal, mathematical, visual, psychomotor) with which we attempt to solve most problems. For most people, verbal or mathematical skills are used most often to solve problems, probably because these are the kinds of problems we usually solve in school. Few of us are equally adept in all areas or are even facile at identifying problems that require a different language to solve.

Example: A favorite example is the Buddhist Monk problem as reported by Sternberg (1986). I've seen a couple of variations of this problem, but the essence is that a Buddhist monk walks up a mountain path to a temple at the top to pray. He leaves the bottom at six a.m., stops to eat lunch along the way, then continues until he reaches the top by six p.m. He prays and meditates through the night, then leaves at six a.m. the next morning to return to the bottom along the same path. Once again, he stops to rest and eat before arriving at the bottom near six p.m. The question: Is there a point along the path that the monk passes at the same time of day on both the days of his trip?

Solution: I have used the problem in my class and seen very bright adults struggle with the semantics or the numbers in trying to answer the question. The answer is yes, and the proof is visual. Instead of two days, imagine that there are two monks on one day. Of course they would meet somewhere along the narrow path as one ascended and the other descended. Another way to visualize this is to draw a graph (see Figure 7).

The key is not whether that graph exactly represents the path that the monk took but whether it is possible to draw any representative graph of his trip in which the lines do not intersect.

Example: Here is another example from Adams (1986). "Picture a large piece of paper, the thickness of this page. In your imagination, fold it once (now having two layers), fold it once more (now having four layers), and continue folding it over upon itself 50 times. How thick is the 50 times folded paper?" (pp. 71–72)

If you answered that it is impossible to fold a piece of paper, no matter how big or thin, 50 times, you are correct; but you need to practice suspending disbelief.

Solution: Your first fold would result in a stack two times the original thickness, your second would give you a stack 2 x 2 times the original thickness, and so on. So, the solution is 2^{50} times the

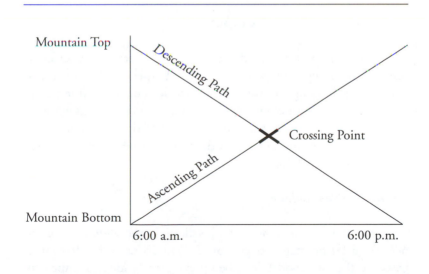

Figure 7. Graph of Buddhist Monk Problem

original thickness or about 1,100,000,000,000,000 times the original thickness. According to Adams, "if the paper is originally the thickness of typing paper, the answer is some 50,000,000 miles or over half the distance from the earth to the sun" (p. 72).

If you tried to use visualization on this problem, it probably did not work. Nor would verbal strategies be likely to result in a correct answer. Although it sounded like a problem that you should solve by doing or visualizing, the correct language for this problem was mathematics.

There are many problems that require expertise at verbal ability in books of riddles. A problem that requires spatial ability is to use six drinking straws to make four equilateral triangles with no overlap and no extraneous figures. Most people will struggle with this for some time before an enterprising individual realizes that the key is in "breaking the plane" and creating a three-dimensional pyramid with three straws as the base and three rising up as the pyramid.

The point of these exercises is to get people to realize that expert problem solvers spend time assessing the problem and devising a suitable strategy, rather than attacking every problem in the same way. Such flexibility in problem solving is an asset to creativity.

Competitions

Another important way that students can exercise their creative thinking is through competitions designed especially for encouraging creative thinking. For some people the idea of competition is an anathema to the idea of creativity; for many students competitions motivate, enhance their creativity, and provide them with opportunities that they would not have otherwise (Karnes & Riley, 1996; Torrance & Sisk, 1997).

Future Problem Solving

One of the best known competitions is the *Future Problem-Solving* (FPS) program. Begun by E. Paul Torrance in 1974, it is based on the CPS model described previously. Students compete at the local, state, and international levels in teams of four or as individuals. The students compete at the Junior level, grades 4–6; the

Intermediate level, grades 7–9; or the Senior level, grades 10–12. Students practice and train on "fuzzy" situations that are based on projected problems of the future. Some past "fuzzies" have dealt with prisons in space, famine, international terrorism, and the like. Students brainstorm the many possible problems inherent in the fuzzy, select and write one problem statement, then do research on the topic to gain as much information as possible.

They then apply the other steps of the CPS process to find possible solutions, apply criteria to choose the best solution, and devise a plan for selling their idea. Evaluation teams give students written feedback throughout the year on the three practice problems. The fourth problem is a qualifying problem, and teams that do well are invited to compete in the state bowl. Teams don't know ahead of time what the topic of the fuzzy will be at the bowl, just that it will be on one of the four areas they've researched that year.

Other newer components of the FPS Program include the Scenario Writing Competition, where students write stories set in the future about one of the four fuzzy topics, and the Community Problem-Solving Competition, where students identify a problem in their community and implement their solution.

Each state runs its own competitions a little differently and with different dates for the bowl; but the state bowl winners, as well as those from Australia, New Zealand, and Canada, are then invited to compete at the International FPS Bowl held in the United States in June. (There are other countries such as China and South Africa that participate in FPS but have not sent teams to compete.)

Odyssey of the Mind

This competition, begun in New Jersey in 1979 by Samuel Micklus, is similar to the FPS Competition in that there are problems that teams work on all year in order to prepare for the local, state, and world competitions. However, it differs from FPS in some key ways.

Although there are levels of competition, with Odyssey of the Mind (OM) there are four divisions from kindergarten through college. Perhaps most important, OM presents problems in a variety of domains. There are always five problems. One problem comes from each of the categories: structure, vehicle, and classical or literature.

Two additional problems are supplied from any of several areas: drama, invention, mathematics, speech, science, and writing. All include some performance aspect. This diversity may be the reason that it is the most popular of the national and international competitions; it appeals to children who express their creativity in many different ways. The content of the problems selected from the 1996–97 competition reflects this diversity: Pageant Wagon, Create and Animate, Morph Magic, Marvelous Mentor, and Camouflage Creation. Teams of no more than seven children work together on one of the problems throughout the year. Winners at the lower levels are qualified to present their winning product at the world level.

Other Competitions

Although FPS and OM are the only large-scale creative problem-solving competitions, there are many competitions for individuals who are creative in specific domains. Some of these include competitions for writing poetry, prose, plays, as well as, news articles, and editorial cartoons. There are competitions in business, mathematics, science, social studies, leadership, service, and technology, as well as in the performing and fine arts. It is probably safe to say that there are some types of competition involving any manner of creative expression. For detailed information about competitions in all of the above categories, refer to the Teacher Resources section at the end of this chapter and see *Competitions: Maximizing Your Abilities* (Karnes & Riley, 1996).

The Incubation Model

The Incubation Model is, as the name says, a model rather than a strategy for teaching creative thinking (Torrance & Safter, 1990). It was conceived as a way of addressing the whole of creativity, both rational and supra-rational.

> A supra-rational view of creativity suggests that individual consciousness transcends the boundaries of the deliberately rational creative process and experiences an altered state of consciousness, a holistic state of awareness, a state of instant communication among all the parts. (p. vii)

It is a challenge to become a great teacher and go beyond teaching students the rational creative thinking techniques and engage their curiosity, intuition, and emotions. Because incubation is often considered a vital part of the creative process, this model has the goal of fostering incubation in students by encouraging them to continue thinking about the lessons beyond the classroom. For example, many lesson plan formats have an initial activity, some developmental activities, and a culminating activity that is often some type of evaluation. With this type of lesson, the students' minds are opened up with the initial activity, then closed with the final, closing, or evaluation activity. The point of the Incubation Model is to open the students' minds and keep them open to learning about the topic when the formal lesson is ended. Accordingly, the steps of the Incubation Model and some short descriptions of instructional activities for each are

Stage 1: Heightening Anticipation
1. Confronting ambiguities and uncertainties;
2. Questioning to heighten expectation and anticipation;
3. Creating awareness of a problem to be solved, a possible future need, or a difficulty to be faced;
4. Building on the learners' existing knowledge;
5. Heightening concern about a problem or future need;
6. Stimulating curiosity and desire to know;
7. Making the strange familiar or the familiar strange;
8. Freeing from inhibiting mind sets;
9. Looking at the same information from different view points;
10. Questioning proactively to make the learner think of information in new ways;
11. Predicting from limited information;
12. Making the purposefulness of the lesson clear by showing the connection between the expected learning and present problems or future career;
13. Providing only enough structure to give clues and direction;
14. Taking the next step beyond what is known; and
15. Warming up physically or bodily to the information to be presented.

In using activities of the kind listed above, the teacher must keep in mind the purpose of such experiences. In essence, they are

- to create the desire to know;
- to heighten anticipation and expectation;
- to get attention;
- to arouse curiosity;
- to tickle the imagination; and
- to give purpose and motivation.

Stage 2: Encountering the Expected and Unexpected,
and Deepening Expectations
1. Heightening awareness of problems and difficulties;
2. Accepting limitations constructively as a challenge rather than cynically, improvising with what is available;
3. Encouraging creative personality characteristics or predispositions;
4. Practicing the creative problem-solving process in a disciplined systematic manner, with the problem and information at hand;
5. Deliberately and systematically elaborating upon the information presented;
6. Presenting information as incomplete and having learners ask questions to fill gaps;
7. Juxtaposing apparently irrelevant elements;
8. Exploring and examining mysteries and trying to solve them;
9. Preserving open-endedness;
10. Making outcomes not completely predictable;
11. Predicting from limited information;
12. Searching for honesty and realism;
13. Identifying and encouraging the acquisition of new skills for finding out information;
14. Heightening and deliberately using surprises; and
15. Encouraging visualization.

Stage 3: Going Beyond and "Keeping It Going"
1. Playing with ambiguities;
2. Deepening awareness of a problem, difficulty, or gap in information;
3. Acknowledging a pupil's unique potentiality;
4. Heightening concern about a problem;
5. Challenging a constructive response or solution;

6. Seeing a clear relationship between the new information and future careers;
7. Accepting limitations creatively and constructively;
8. Digging still more deeply and going beneath the obvious and accepted;
9. Making divergent thinking legitimate;
10. Elaborating the information given;
11. Encouraging elegant solution, the solution of collision conflicts, unsolved mysteries;
12. Requiring experimentation;
13. Making the familiar strange or the strange familiar;
14. Examining fantasies to find solutions of real problems;
15. Encouraging future projections;
16. Entertaining improbabilities;
17. Creating humor and seeing the humorous in the information presented;
18. Encouraging deferred judgment and the use of some disciplined procedures of problem solving;
19. Relating information to information in another discipline;
20. Looking at the same information in different ways;
21. Encouraging the manipulation of ideas and/or objects;
22. Encouraging multiple hypotheses; and
23. Confronting and examining paradoxes.

The Incubation Model was presented last under techniques for creative thinking because it could be used as an organizing framework within which the various activities described earlier could be incorporated. An example of how a teacher might use the steps of the Incubation Model might help illustrate the idea.

For example, in teaching a lesson on density in a science class, the teacher *heightens anticipation* by showing the students a tub of water and two cans of soda of the same brand—one regular and one diet. She asks the students to speculate about whether the cans will float or sink, questioning them about some of the principles they've learned about density.

After the students have discussed their predictions and reasons, the teacher drops the regular can of soda in the water and it sinks. By doing this the teacher guides the students to *encounter the expected* (for those who guessed correctly) *and unexpected* (for those who did not) *and deepen their expectations* by predicting whether the can of diet soda will sink or float. When the students have made their predictions, the teacher drops the diet soda into the tub and it floats.

Most lessons would conclude at this point with a wrap-up and summary of why the two cans reacted differently. However, the idea of the Incubation Model is to *keep it going* rather than wrap it up. So, before class ends, the students may be asked to think about another test that they could do to try to discover the principle behind the density difference. If students are intrigued enough, they will continue to think about the problem outside of class. Some may try to discover at home why some sodas sink and others float. Other students may propose another test to be done in class. At this point the teacher may incorporate other creativity and problem-solving strategies by having the students brainstorm the differences in the diet and regular sodas and create an attribute listing chart to compare sodas. With guidance, and a touch of drama, the teacher should be able to lead the students to discover that the sugar in the regular soda is what makes it denser than the diet soda. The students have learned about density, but they have also learned about problem solving, hypothesizing, testing ideas, and persisting with an idea beyond the boundaries of the classroom.

Summary

In order to nurture creativity in ourselves or others, we must first show that we value creativity by recognizing and respecting it in ourselves and others. Also, we can create a climate that is conducive to creativity: one that is psychologically safe and provides stimulation, as well as time for quiet reflection. Then, there are several techniques that we can use, first as warm-up, and as exercises to promote ideation, visualization, analogical thinking, lateral thinking, group and individual problem solving, and going beyond the rational for incubation. We can help identify and remove blocks to creativity, find competitions and other outlets for children's creativity, and provide opportunities and encouragement for expressive and problem-solving creativity whenever possible. If we do all of these things in the classroom, then perhaps we can be confident that we have become, like those reported in Torrance's longitudinal study (1981), the "teachers who made a difference."

Teacher Resources

A number of creative strategies have been described and some illustrative activities provided, but the preceding is not an all-inclusive list. There are many sources of activities designed to enhance creativity that are available to teachers. Some are from educational publishers; others are available from various sites on the Internet. A sample of these are listed in the resources section at the end of this chapter; however, these change, appear, and disappear so quickly that they should be reviewed frequently. There are also materials that are available to educators from companies that have provided grants.

Addresses

There are many publishers of materials appropriate for developing creativity in students. Some of these include

The Creative Education Foundation
1050 Union Rd., #4
Buffalo, NY 14224

Creative Learning Press, Inc.
P.O. Box 320
Mansfield Center, CT 06250

Free Spirit Publishing, Inc.
400 First Ave. North, Suite 616
Minneapolis, MN 55401-1730

The Future Problem-Solving Program
318 W. Ann St.
Ann Arbor, MI 48104-1337
http://www.fpsp.org/

Odyssey of the Mind Association, Inc.
P.O. Box 547
Glassboro, NJ 08028
http://mars. superlink.net/~lsemel/

Prufrock Press
P.O. Box 8813
Waco, TX 76714-8813
http://www.prufrock.com

Zephyr Press
3316 N. Chapel Ave.
P.O. Box 66006-C
Tucson, AZ 85728-6006

Web Sites

A recent search of the World Wide Web for sites on creativity listed 285 sites. On any given day there may be more or less. Many of these deal with creativity in business or some other specific domain. Others mention creativity in describing their products (such as "Use your creativity in customizing your home with our venetian blinds") or their creators ("Check out this creative personal web page"). Still others are more age specific, designed for adults or sophisticated older children. There is a site for creativity self-assessment that might be appropriate for adolescents and teens at http://www.volusia.com/creative/mag5.htm. The answers to the quiz are then given at http://www.volusia.com/creative/2mag6.htm. However, some of the ones that looked best are

American Creativity Association—http://www.BeCreative.org/

Creativity Based Information Resources database (CBIR)—http://www. Buffalostate.EDU/~cbir
A research site maintained by The Center for Studies in Creativity at Buffalo State College. Currently, the database contains over 10,300 annotated references of works focusing on creativity. You can actually search the database online.

Creativity Café—http://creativity.net/
A site featuring Storytellers of the New Millennium; live and cyber-space interactive programs like "KidCast For Peace" which are designed to "bring the community together and to create and enjoy evolutionary entertainment"; Earthday Broadcasts and KidCast Multicast; Creativity Camp which teaches Digital Storytelling tools, and a "living gallery" where all artists can show their art.

The Creativity Web—http://www.ozemail.com.au/~caveman/ Creative/ with links and resources on creativity and innovation

Cyberkids—http://www.cyberkids.com/ and *Cyberteens*—http:// www.cyberteens.com/
Connected sites that feature age appropriate games, contests, a magazine, and various outlets for creative expression. The launch-pad links visitors to sites for art, business, child safety, children's books online, computers, educational resources, entertainment, various academic subjects, museums, libraries, music, nature, sports, and more.

Enchanted Mind—http://enchantedmind.com/

Flow—http://www.flownetwork.com/

Gardner's *Project Zero* at Harvard—http://pzweb.harvard.edu/

The National Center for Creativity, Inc. (NCCI)—http://www.cre-ativesparks.org/

Wizard—http://www.thwww.com/mrwizard/wizardTOC.htm/
Many fun and safe links for kids as well as homework helpers in various content areas. With very cool animated graphics, kids are sure to enjoy this one.

Media

One of the best is the four-part film *The Creative Spirit* (Perlmutter, 1992) that appeared on PBS and was funded by IBM.

There is a book to accompany it (Goleman, Kaufman, & Ray, 1992), and a teacher's guide with activities and a computer disk. The teaching materials are available from The Creative Spirit, c/o TELED Inc., P.O. Box 933022, Los Angeles, CA 90099-2199.

References

Adams, J. L. (1986). *Conceptual blockbusting: A guide to better ideas.* Reading, MA: Addison Wesley.

Amabile, T. M. (1983). *The social psychology of creativity.* New York: Springer-Verlag.

Bellanca, J. (1984). Can quality circles work in classrooms of the gifted? *Roeper Review, 6,* 199–200.

Betts, G. T. (1986). The autonomous learner model for the gifted and talented. In J. S. Renzulli (Ed.), *Systems and models for developing programs for the gifted and talented,* pp. 27–56. Mansfield Center, CT: Creative Learning Press.

Blatner, H. A. (1973). *Acting-In: Practical applications of psychodramatic methods.* New York: Springer.

Bloom, B. S. (Ed.). (1985). *Developing talent in young people.* New York: Ballantine Books.

Boorstin, D.J. (1992). *The creators: A history of heroes of the imagination.* New York: Random House.

Cameron, J. & Pierce, W. D. (1994). Reinforcement, reward, and intrinsic motivation: A meta-analysis. *Review of Educational Research, 64,* 363–423.

Cox, J., Daniel, N., & Boston, B. (1985). *Educating able learners: Programs and promising practices.* Austin, TX: University of Texas Press.

Cramond, B. (1993). Speaking and listening: Key components of a language arts program for the gifted. *Roeper Review: A Journal on Gifted Education, 16* (1), 44–48.

Cramond, B. (1994). Attention-Deficit Hyperactivity Disorder and creativity—What is the connection? *The Journal of Creative Behavior, 28,* 193–210.

Cramond, B. (1995). The coincidence of ADHD and Creativity [Monograph]. *Research-Based Decision-Making Series.* Storrs, CT: The National Research Center for the Gifted and Talented.

Csikszentmihalyi, M. (1990). *Flow: The psychology of optimal experience.* New York: Harper.

Csikszentmihalyi, M., & Csikszentmihalyi, I. S. (Eds.) (1988). *Optimal experience: Psychological studies of flow in consciousness.* New York: Cambridge University Press.

de Bono, E. (1970/1986). *Lateral thinking.* New York: Harper & Row.

de Bono, E. (1985a). *de Bono's thinking course.* New York: Facts on File Publications.

de Bono, E. (1985b). *Six thinking hats.* Boston: Little, Brown, and Co.

de Bono, E. (1991). *Six action shoes.* New York: Harper Business.

Dewar, D. L. (1980). *The quality circle guide to participation management.* Englewood Cliffs, NJ: Prentice-Hall.

Diamond, M. C. (1988). *Enriching heredity: The impact of the environment on the anatomy of the brain.* New York: The Free Press.

Elkind, D. (1989). *The hurried child: Growing up too fast too soon.* Reading, MA: Addison-Wesley.

Eberle, B. (1996). *Scamper: Creative Games and Activities for Imagination and Development.* Buffalo, NY: D.O.K. Publishers.

Feldhusen, J. F. (1986). A conception of giftedness. In R. J. Sternberg & J. E. Davidson (Eds.), *Conceptions of giftedness.* (pp. 112–127). Cambridge: Cambridge University Press.

Feldman, D. H., Csikszentmihalyi, M., & Gardner, H. (1994). *Changing the world: A framework for the study of creativity.* Westport, CT: Praeger.

Ferguson, M. (1977). 'Mind mirror' EEG identifies states of awareness. *Brain/Mind Bulletin, 2*(30), 1–2.

Gagné, F. (1985). Giftedness and talent: Reexamining a reexamination of the definitions. *Gifted Child Quarterly, 29,* 103–112.

Goldberg, R. (1968). *Rube Goldberg vs. the machine age; a retrospective exhibition of his work with memoirs and annotations.* New York: Hastings House.

Goleman, D., Kaufman, P., & Ray, M. (1992). *The creative spirit.* New York: Dutton.

Gordon, W. J. (1961). *Synectics.* New York: Harper & Row.

Gordon, W. J. (1968). *The metaphorical way of knowing.* New York: Harper & Row.

Guilford, J. P. (1967). *The nature of human intelligence.* New York: McGraw-Hill.

Guilford, J. P. (1977). *Way beyond the IQ.* Buffalo, NY: Creative Education Foundation.

Karnes, F. A., & Riley, T. L. (1996). *Competitions: Maximizing your abilities.* Waco, TX: Prufrock Press.

Koberg, D., & Bagnall, J. (1991). *The universal traveler: A soft-systems guide to creativity, problem solving, & the process of reaching goals.* Menlo Park, CA: Crisp Publications.

MacKinnon, D. W. (1965/1976). Architects, personality types, and creativity. In A. Rothenberg and C.R. Hausman (Eds.), *The creativity question.* (pp. 175–189). Durham, NC: Duke University Press.

MacKinnon, D. W. (1978). *In search of human effectiveness.* Buffalo, NY: Creative Education Foundation.

Martin, C. E., & Cramond, B. (1983). Creative reading: Is it being taught to the gifted in elementary schools? *Journal for the Education of the Gifted, 6,* 70–79.

Parnes, S. J. (1981). *The magic of your mind.* Buffalo, NY: D.O.K. Publishers.

Perlmutter, A. H. (Producer), (1992). *The creative spirit.* [Film]. (Available from The Creative Spirit, c/o TELED Inc., P.O. Box 933022, Los Angeles, CA 90099-2199)

Rader, D. (1993, January 31). Why I walked away. *Parade,* 20–21.

Renzulli, J. S., & Reis, S. M. (1985). *The schoolwide enrichment model: A comprehensive plan for educational excellence.* Mansfield Center, CT: Creative Learning Press.

Restak, R. (1993). The creative brain. In J. Brockman (Ed.), *Creativity* (pp. 164–175). New York: Simon & Schuster.

Rogers, C. R. (1954/1976). Toward a theory of creativity. In A. Rosenthenberg & C. R. Hausmann (Eds.), *The creativity question* (pp. 296–305). Durham, NC: Duke University Press.

Rothenberg, A., & Hausman, C.R. (Eds.) (1976). *The creativity question.* Durham, NC: Duke University Press.

Saletta, P. (1978). *Creative thinking techniques.* (Contract No. 30076–0530). Washington, DC: Office of Gifted and Talented, U.S. Office of Education.

Sternberg, R. J. (1986). *Intelligence applied: Understanding and increasing your intellectual skills.* New York: Harcourt, Brace, Jovanovich.

Sternberg, R. J. (Ed.). (1988). *The nature of creativity: Contemporary psychological perspectives.* New York: Cambridge University Press.

Taba, H. (1962). *Curriculum development: Theory and practice.* NY: Harcourt, Brace.

Tardif, T. Z., & Sternberg, R. J. (1988). What do we know about creativity? In R. J. Sternberg, (Ed.). *The nature of creativity.* Buffalo, NY: Creative Education Foundation.

Taylor, I. A. (1959). The nature of the creative process. In P. Smith (Ed.), *Creativity* (pp. 521–82). New York: Hastings House.

Torrance, E. P. (1974). *Norms-technical manual: Torrance Tests of Creative Thinking.* Lexington, MA: Ginn.

Torrance, E. P. (1981). Predicting the creativity of elementary school children (1958–80) and the teacher who "made a difference." *Gifted Child Quarterly, 25,* 55–62.

Torrance, E. P., Murdock, M., & Fletcher, D. (1997). *Creative problem solving through role-playing.* Pretoria, South Africa: Benedic Books.

Torrance, E. P., & Safter, H. T. (1990). *The incubation model of teaching: Getting beyond the aha!* Buffalo, NY: Creative Education Foundation Press.

Torrance, E. P., & Sisk, D. A. (1997). *Gifted and talented children in the regular classroom.* Buffalo, NY: Creative Education Foundation Press.

VanTassel-Baska, J. (1998). *Excellence in educating gifted and talented learners* (3rd ed.). Denver: Love.

von Oech, R. (1983). *A whack on the side of the head.* New York: Warner Books.

Wallas, G. (1926/1976). Stages in the creative process. In A. Rothenberg and C. R. Hausman (Eds.), *The creativity question.* (pp. 69–73). Durham, NC: Duke University Press.

Ziv, A. (1983). The influence of humorous atmosphere on divergent thinking. *Contemporary Educational Psychology, 8,* 68–75.

CHAPTER 12

Developing Research Skills in Gifted Students

BARBARA MOORE
Mississippi University for Women

T om was an underachieving high school senior who had been identified as gifted in elementary school, but had not been achieving since sixth grade. When Tom was asked to describe the time he learned the most in school, he talked about his presentation on the Punic Wars in world history class. "I took a big sheet of poster board and made a model of the area of the Punic Wars and had the mountains and everything. I had the troops and I moved them all about and had them fight each other. . . . Everyone paid attention." Tom concluded that when the class ended, the only part of world history he remembered was the Punic Wars.

Keisha, a gifted eighth-grade student, vividly remembered fourth-grade science when the students created an ant farm and incubated chicken eggs. As the students observed the behavior of the ants and eggs, they speculated about the meaning of what they saw, created hypotheses based on their observations, tested these hypotheses by further observation, and read books from their school library.

Gifted students of all ages, whether they achieve in school or perform poorly in academic settings, share many characteristics that make them enjoy group or individual projects allowing them to be active investigators (Clark, 1988; Piirto, 1994). They are frequently interested in topics that are beyond the interests or capabilities of their age peers, and their task commitment allows them to investigate a subject of interest for extended periods of time. Their high degree of curiosity makes them want to probe, ask questions, and discover reasons why. Because of their ability to synthesize disparate information, they can work on complex projects and their insight allows them to find answers where others do not perceive questions. Yet, because of their ability to learn and retain information easily, they are often impatient with the pace of the curriculum and are bored in class.

The opportunity for gifted students to study topics in-depth is often limited to library searches. These "research" assignments usually consist of compiling information from encyclopedias and library books about a topic. This patchwork quilt variety of research projects often results in excruciatingly dull reports and does little to help gifted students experience the joy of discovery that true research can bring, except when creative students like Tom look beyond the school library for source material and find innovative ways to present their projects.

The science fair project, similar to Keisha's whole class investigations of ants and eggs, is another kind of research familiar to students and teachers, beginning in elementary school. In this kind of project, students' investigative endeavors are framed by the scientific method, beginning with a question that leads to a hypothesis, a research design, data collection, analysis, findings, and conclusions. Gifted students, who have a propensity to think in terms of "why" and "what if," can find this kind of project enjoyable as they test their theories about a variety of science-related topics such as the ability of goldfish to survive subfreezing temperatures, the relative effectiveness of various insulators, or the kinds of mold spores produced by different foods. One added benefit of this kind of assignment is that students' parents can become involved in the planning and implementation of the project. Any minor inconveniences that parents might have to endure, such as dead goldfish, moldy cheese, or other foreign objects in their refrigerators, are overshadowed by the opportunity to participate in their child's education in a meaningful way.

Original research can be used in other ways to enrich curriculum in gifted students' social studies, mathematics, and language arts classes. Just as these highly curious and motivated students can function as biological or physical scientists, they can also function as social scientists—creating surveys, observing, interviewing, and analyzing primary documents. Yet, few programs for gifted students include research projects based on the social sciences.

Gifted students have been described as those who will be our future inventors, creators, and leaders in their fields. Yet, many students do not understand how professionals in various fields related to social sciences conduct their work. What *does* a cultural anthropologist do all day? Who uses social studies in their careers? How are language arts skills used outside the fields of journalism and fiction writing? Students who begin to think and work like social scientists discover that history is not a collection of dates and events but is a complex interaction of human beings, their visions, values, strengths, and frailties.

A large part of the problem may be that many teachers, including teachers of the gifted, are unfamiliar with the research process as it relates to the social sciences. When teachers rely on textbooks that attempt to present a multitude of historical events that can be covered in a short period of time, students may lose the colorful details of the era, the individual human trees that make up the historical forest.

Today's teachers of the gifted are fortunate to have examples of television programs that use primary documents to tell a historical story. The Public Broadcasting System frequently airs programs that include the rich use of primary sources to capture an event in history. The most well-known examples of this kind of programming are Ken Burns' documentaries on the Civil War, the history of baseball, and his investigations into the lives of Thomas Jefferson and Lewis and Clark. In a trailer to his series on Lewis and Clark aired on PBS, Burns described a methodology different from the step-by-step linear process used by the scientist. He talked, instead, of a more intuitive, holistic approach in which gathering data, creating a script, and finding background music were accomplished simultaneously. LaRue (1995) described this process as being more like our everyday experience of history.

> For many of us, we are brought to our history in just this fashion—story, memory, anecdote. . . . These emotional connections become a kind of glue, which makes the most complex of past events stick in our minds and, particularly, in our hearts. (p. 1)

This experiential processing of historical data used by innovative professionals is seldom practiced in the classroom.

Thus, gifted students can pursue two paths to research. Like scientists, they can create experiments to test theories or, like social scientists, they can observe, interview, and analyze written documents to arrive at generalizations about their world.

Historical Perspective

The concept of student as researcher is over a century old. At the basis of Dewey's (1897) philosophy of education was the idea of students exploring their environment. Education, he stated, was not a succession of studies but was the development of new attitudes and interests in children toward the world around them (1901). He noted that in textbook-driven education, the content is preselected, there is usually one method of dealing with that content, and students have little opportunity to experiment or try new ideas. The ideal student in such a learning environment is passive and willing to submit to another's agenda. The child, Dewey (1901) argued, is a complex being who learns best when content is presented in a complex manner that mirrors real life. Dewey proposed a concept of education in which children carry out projects that are generated by their own curiosity. He believed that a school whose function is to give information, teach lessons, and form correct habits in children is not truly educational. The aim of education should be the growth of children, not the acquisition of skills they will need as adults. One attains power, he reasoned, by determining a personal issue or problem, selecting the means and materials needed to deal with that problem, and then using the processes of testing and experimentation to resolve the problem.

Piaget, in describing the behavior of children in terms of problem solving and internal motivation, reasoned, "A person won't ever solve a problem if the problem doesn't interest him" (Bringuier, 1980, p. 50). Piaget, too, was opposed to the concept of teaching as a transfer of knowledge from adult to child. "Everything one teaches a child prevents him from inventing and discovering" (p. 102). Although much attention has been paid to Piaget's stages of learning, Bruner (1977) noted that the focus of Piaget's observations was the way children learn—by actively exploring and interacting with their environments and by relying on trial and error to reach understandings.

Bruner (1977) believed that teaching should shift from the transfer of skills and understandings related to a field toward an understanding of the structure of the discipline being studied. Educators should "talk physics" to students rather than "talking about physics" (p. ix). He felt that it is more important for students to understand the underlying concepts, principles, attitudes, and problems of a field than to learn factual information related to that field. Like Dewey, Bruner noted that events in life are not isolated. Our physical and social world is made of a complexity of interwoven factors. Therefore, isolated facts are not easily remembered. To be retained, information must be placed in a meaningful structure or pattern. Bruner described the act of learning as a continuous process of problem solving in which the child acquires new information that often contradicts what the child already knows, manipulates the information to figure out why there is an apparent contradiction, and then checks to determine whether the manipulation of the information accomplished the task for which it was designed.

Ward (1961) was one of the first educational theorists to apply these principles to the field of gifted child education. Ward believed that gifted children differed from other children in the degree of their intrinsic motivation and in their ability to learn *about* content. One of his important contributions to the field of gifted education was to shift the focus from differentiating the content studied by gifted students to changing the process through which they learned. He viewed gifted students as needing to have academic experiences that teach them to become producers of knowledge because when these students become adults, they will be the ones to change and redefine the world. "Gifted students are those who will advance their culture, not just participate in it. Therefore, their education must be qualitatively different" (p. 80). He also stipulated that the education of gifted students needs to include opportunities to work alone, to use advanced resources and materials, to be allowed unstructured time, to be mentally and physically active, to try individualistic approaches to problems, and to exhibit creative behavior.

Renzulli's (1988) Multiple Menu Model incorporates many of the above ideas. He stated that students need to have *Knowledge Of,* a superficial familiarity of a subject; *Knowledge About,* a deeper understanding of the principles and theories related to a subject; and, *Knowledge How,* the understandings and tools needed to make a meaningful contribution to the field related to that subject. His Knowledge Menu includes the process of identifying problems within a subject area, gathering and analyzing data, drawing conclusions, and reporting findings.

From Dewey to Renzulli, educational theorists have emphasized the importance of helping students create real-world products. They believe in the importance of students' understanding and using a variety of methodologies that may be different for each content area. Practice applying knowledge in one setting to a specific problem can give students the tools they need to examine other problems in that field.

Program Models

Renzulli (1988) was also one of the first theorists in gifted education to create a program model that included the concept of gifted students as researchers. His Enrichment Triad Model developed in the 1970s is based on his Three Ring Conception of Giftedness, which describes gifted behaviors as resulting from the combination of above-average ability, task commitment, and creativity (Renzulli, 1988). Influenced by Bruner and Ward, Renzulli's Enrichment Triad Model focuses on helping gifted students develop behaviors exhibited by gifted adults who are successful in their fields. Because of this behavioral emphasis, Renzulli's model defines the gifted student in active terms, as a researcher, inventor, or creator.

Renzulli and Reis (1985) divided the research process into three phases or types of activities. Type I Enrichment activities consist of experiences that expose students to professionals in a variety of fields. Each Type I activity concludes with a debriefing in which students brainstorm current issues or problems that the gifted student with an interest in that field can pursue. For example, after listening to a Type I speaker describe the problem of water pollution, a group of students in Torrington, CT, decided to study water quality in their area. Type II Enrichment activities prepare students to function as professionals, teaching them the skills they will need to pursue their group or individual investigations. For example, the students studying water pollution needed to know ways of testing and analyzing water samples. During Type III Enrichment activities, students actually conduct their research and present their findings to a real audience. The students who studied water quality created a petition that they presented to their state legislature. In addition to teaching students the skills needed to research issues within a particular area, the inclusion of real products for real audiences helps students function as true researchers.

The Autonomous Learner Model (Betts, 1985) builds on Renzulli's concept of allowing gifted students to pursue areas of intense interests. Betts, too, believes that learning for gifted students should be self-directed, and the teacher of the gifted must help facilitate the pursuit of these interests. Like Renzulli, he described Explorations, Investigations, and In-Depth Study in which students develop knowledge, skills, and products within a particular field. His model differs from Renzulli's in that Betts placed a greater emphasis on the affective results of independent learning, such as increased self-direction and self-understanding that can result from the student being an active learner and researcher. Both models rely strongly on teaching gifted students the skills—such as problem solving, organization, decision making, writing, interviewing, and using computers—they will need to be successful creators of knowledge.

Most educational models for gifted students recognize the need to teach gifted students how to become researchers. For example, Tannenbaum (1986) included the use of mentors and apprenticeships in his model. The Purdue Model developed by Feldhusen and Kolloff (1986) includes teaching gifted students independent study skills so they can conduct independent investigations. In the latter model, students are encouraged to brainstorm problems their communities will face in the near future and, by using the creative problem-solving process, arrive at a solution to one of these problems.

The Research Process

Student research can occur in a variety of classroom environments. Some teachers prefer to have research projects conducted by an entire class. Deal and Sterling (1997) described using questions such as "Why do apples float and grapes sink?" to begin a unit on mass, volume, and density. Students were encouraged to use their senses to investigate the physical properties of a variety of objects but were also encouraged to read related reference materials and access experts by telephone or the Internet to increase their background knowledge about the subject.

In other instances, gifted students in mixed-ability classes or in pull-out classes can conduct their own independent or small group investigations. The following are suggestions for teachers who want to help their gifted students become researchers, either within the class for gifted students or in the mixed-ability classroom.

Steps in the Research Process

Student researchers, like their adult counterparts, can follow two paradigms, depending on the question they are researching. The quantitative paradigm uses the scientific method, consisting of creating and testing hypotheses. The qualitative paradigm, originating in social science research, uses observations, interviews, and document analysis to arrive at generalizations or hypotheses. With either paradigm, the student researchers will follow similar steps in the process of their independent or group investigations (Curry & Samara, 1991; Van Tassel-Baska, 1997):

Selecting a Topic Students explore topics related to a field through activities such as reading, brainstorming, discussing, and making webs.

Finding a Question or Problem to Research. Students generate a list of many possible questions and choose one that is interesting and has not already been answered.

Developing a Plan of Action. Students investigate how others in the field carry out research on similar problems; determine how they will collect and analyze data; and decide on a way to record their progress.

Gathering Information. Students determine sources of information; create a file of potential resources; determine guidelines for conducting interviews, observations, experiments, or surveys; locate existing information; and record their progress in meeting objectives.

Analyzing Information. Students analyze the data they have collected along with their notes; determine relevant findings; and organize all information.

Reporting Findings. Students determine an audience and decide on a product form.

Selecting a Topic

The first step in the research process is most important because it determines the direction in which the project will go and the quality of the research study. Sometimes it is helpful for students to talk to a teacher or other adult who shares an interest. For example, when Elvin was assigned a research project in his high school social studies class, he and his teacher discussed his interests during an after school meeting. Because the teacher knew that Elvin was interested in music, he suggested that Elvin talk to his music teacher. During their conversation, Elvin revealed that he had once attempted to make his own guitar and was curious about how stringed instruments were made. The music teacher provided Elvin with the addresses of instrument makers in the area and enlisted the support of Elvin's parents as drivers. Thus, Elvin's project was born.

Finding a Question or Problem to Research

Once students have decided their area of interest, they need to determine a question or problem to research within that area. Elvin's topic, Instrument Makers in Maine, became How are Stringed Instruments Made by Instrument Makers in Maine? The problem needs to be stated in such a way that student researchers can not answer it by merely reading what others have said about the problem. There are several ways in which students can change a topic into a problem:

- Students can use brainstorming techniques to list problems they perceive at school and in their community.
- They can interview the principal and other school personnel or invite them into the classroom to determine what they perceive to be problems. In one school, gifted students learned that the cafeteria workers were interested in knowing what foods served on a regular basis students really liked. The gifted students created a survey and administered it to all students in the school. When the cafeteria workers received the gifted students' analysis of the survey responses, they were surprised to learn that few of the students liked macaroni and cheese, so they discontinued serving it.
- Students can interview people in the community to determine problems that need innovative solutions. Olenchak (1996) used the Future Problem-Solving process to help teams, consisting of two adult members of the community and four students, identify a community problem and create an innovative solution to that problem. One such team found a historic building that was about to be demolished so the land could be used for commercial purposes. The winning team's solution was adopted by the town, and the building is now a historical museum.
- One form of Renzulli and Reis' (1985) Type I general exploratory experience involves inviting community members and experts in a variety of endeavors into the school to share their areas of expertise on topics related to the regular classroom curriculum. Type I speakers might include people knowledgeable about such diverse topics as robotics, acid rain, astronomy, or physical handicaps. As part of the debriefing process after the Type I activity, students determine problems that continue to exist in the field.
- College and university professors, especially those in the fields of social studies or science, are excellent sources of questions one might ask about the local community. These questions

might include the impact a new regional industry has on people and the environment, the reasons why certain groups migrated to a region, or the origins of local weather tales.

• Students can look for local landmarks that might merit their investigation, including old cemeteries, historical buildings, or historical events that took place in their area but have no marked site. Cooper (1985) suggested taking students on field trips through their local town and asking tantalizing questions such as the following: "How did the town get its name?" "How did your street get its name?" "Why did a particular industry decide to locate in your town?" "What famous people were born in your area?" "What was life in your town like a 100 years ago?" "Why was your town settled?" "Where is the oldest cemetery in town?" "Who was the first doctor in your community?" "How did your community change when the railroad came?" "Has your area ever experienced a natural disaster?"

Developing a Plan of Action

Although one goal of gifted education is to create students who are self-directed, independent learners, most students have few opportunities in the classroom to develop the skills that will allow them to reach that goal. Therefore, it is important for the teacher to help student researchers divide their project into manageable steps. Working with student researchers to create a structure and timeline for research projects allows students to work efficiently and effectively, minimizing off-task time. Winebrenner (1992) suggested creating a learning contract with each student. These contracts should include a section that stipulates the conditions under which the student agrees to work. These stipulations may include (1) recognizing that the teacher is not to be bothered when working with another group of students (one elementary school teacher solved this problem by wearing a colorful necklace when she was working with a small group and did not want to be disturbed); (2) using acceptable ways to obtain help when the teacher is busy; (3) knowing what to do if no help is immediately available; and (4) acknowledging students working on projects are not to bother other students or call attention to themselves. These rules are important in any classroom but are especially important in a mixed-ability class where gifted students have been compacted out of the regular assignments and are conducting individual or group research as a form of enrichment. A sample learning contract appears in Figure 1.

Tomlinson (1995) and Curry and Samara (1991) suggest several guidelines that can help the regular classroom teacher successfully implement a research program for gifted students:

- Each student needs to have a clear understanding of his or her project's objectives and the criteria that will be used to evaluate these objectives.
- Independent or group investigations need to be set up in small steps to ensure success. Help students plan projects carefully and allow for frequent check-in dates in which the teacher and students can discuss the progress of their projects.
- Skills need to be mastered before content acquisition (e.g., students need to be comfortable with interviewing skills before conducting an interview). Research skills can be introduced through whole group instruction.
- Parents need to understand about their child's projects, why they are being undertaken, when they are to be completed, how they can help, and how they should not help. This last point can not be over-emphasized. Parents who are informed can be a teacher's biggest fan club, but they need to know from the teacher of the gifted, and indeed from all teachers, the kinds of work the child will be doing and the rationale for this work.

Independent or group investigations that are carefully planned by the teacher, taking into account the above considerations, can be meaningful, challenging experiences for student researchers and will interfere minimally with the management of learning for other students in the class.

Gathering Information

Not all research studies will use the scientific method. Students and teachers must be aware of the kinds of research conducted by people in the field most closely related to the topic the student wishes to study. Some of these kinds of data collection methods are described below.

Chapter: _____

Name: _____

✓ Page/Concept	✓ Page/Concept	✓ Page/Concept
___ _____	___ _____	___ _____
___ _____	___ _____	___ _____
___ _____	___ _____	___ _____
___ _____	___ _____	___ _____
___ _____	___ _____	___ _____

Enrichment options: _____

special instructions

_____

_____

_____

Your idea:

_____

Working Conditions

_____

_____

_____

Teacher's Signature: _____

Student's Signature: _____

Figure 1. Learning Contract

Note. From *Teaching Gifted Kids in the Regular Classroom* (p. 24), by S. Winebrenner, 1992, Minneapolis, MN: Free Spirit. Copyright 1992 Free Spirit. Reprinted with permission.

Surveys. If students are going to construct surveys, there is a great deal they must understand first. Considerations include the following:

- Surveys need to be short for two reasons. First, a lengthy survey given to every student in a school can quickly become an overwhelming experience for student researchers. The process of recording responses to a long survey can take weeks of class time. When seniors at a high school in Maine were told that the school board was considering eliminating senior week before graduation, one senior decided to survey principals at the other high schools in the state to determine senior week practices in their schools. Although the survey ultimately provided the school with valuable information, the simple task of addressing more than a 100 envelopes demanded a great deal of the student's time. The second reason for keeping surveys short is that most people do not have the time to complete a lengthy survey. The response rate for a short survey can be far greater than for a longer one.
- Students need to decide who will be surveyed and under what conditions. Surveys can be administered to students in school during lunch time or to adults at a public place (shopping mall). In any case, arrangements and permission need to be completed in advance.
- Students need to determine whether they want to use open-ended questions ("My favorite novel is . . .") or Likert-scale questions in which, for example, people record their response to statements on a scale from *strongly agree* (SA) and *agree* (A) to *disagree* (D) and *strongly disagree* (SD) (e.g., "I enjoy the novels we read in class." SA, A, D, and SD).
- Students need to pilot their survey on a small sample of the population from whom they want information to determine whether the questions make sense, if the instructions are clear, whether people have difficulties with individual questions, and whether their survey will give them the information they need.
- Students need to decide how they will analyze the data once they receive it.
- Students need to decide in advance with whom they will share the results of the survey. Product forms can include a report to

the school board, the state legislature, the local historical society, or some other interested group; an article for the student newspaper; a bulletin board for the school; or a newsletter to parents.

Interviews. Interviews are another method of obtaining data for a research study. Students need a number of skills in order to conduct smooth interviews. First, they need to be at ease telephoning or writing to the person they will be interviewing. Indeed, interviews are a wonderful way to teach these skills. A student who is about to telephone the local veterinarian is usually highly motivated to practice telephoning in class.

Carey and Greenberg (1983) suggested the following check list for student interviewers: (1) decide on the source, then contact the person to establish a date, time, and place for the interview; (2) conduct background research before the interview in order to have some familiarity with the topic; (3) make a list of questions and practice asking them; (4) decide what equipment you will use and practice using it; and (5) prepare an introduction that will explain the purpose of the interview and how it will be used.

Student interviewers need to consider several aspects related to the use of tape recorders, including replacing batteries, testing the tape recorder at the beginning of the interview to determine whether it is working properly, determining the best placement for the tape recorder during the interview, and obtaining permission in advance to have the interview taped. Cooper (1985) gave several tips for recording interviews: (1) use a good quality tape and an external microphone, if you have one; (2) interview the person in a quiet place; (3) don't switch the recorder on and off; (4) help the person relax by talking about a childhood experience or asking about some object in the room; (5) give the person plenty of time to think (or even give them the interview questions in advance); and (6) listen carefully and probe for more information about an interesting story.

Students need to write their interview questions in advance and ask peers and teachers to critique their questions. Students should practice asking questions that are broad and general ("Tell me about your school.") rather than questions that require only short answers, ("Did you like school?") or that tend to suggest an answer. For example, "What did you like about school?" assumes that the respondent liked something about school. Students will also want to practice ways to begin and end interviews smoothly.

Once an interview is taped, students need to transcribe the interview or know someone who can. Parent volunteers or students in high school keyboarding classes will sometimes agree to do this laborious task. Students may also wish to photograph the interviewee and will need experience using a camera. A student with a camcorder may wish to use this equipment with the interviewee's permission. Although the skills needed to use this equipment seem basic, we cannot assume that all students are capable of using technology skillfully. Teachers need to build into the student researcher's curriculum opportunities to practice the many skills related to the interviewing process.

Primary Documents. If students are interested in examining primary documents, they need to know where these documents can be found. A trip to the local library can be extremely helpful for students researching local topics. If the librarian is notified in advance, he or she can pull books and documents for the students to peruse. A field trip to the county clerk's office is also helpful. Most students are not aware of the vast numbers of documents that can be found in county offices. Students may also be able to find primary documents by contacting local organizations such as the local historical society and national organizations such as National Geographic or by searching the Internet. Internet sites change regularly, but sites such as The Library of Congress or The Smithsonian are rich sources for primary documents and artifacts.

Students may also want to check with older residents in their communities about letters, diaries, photographs, and other documents that can help them in their searches. Teachers cannot assume that students know how to talk to a senior citizen, even if that person is the child's grandparent. Role-playing in class can make these contacts a lot less stressful for student and elder alike.

If students want to research one particular time period, a number of inexpensive books containing actual letters and diaries of individuals from that period can be found in college libraries or purchased through catalogues. For example, the Perspectives on History Series (published by Discovery Enterprises, Ltd., in Lowell, MA) publishes letters from Civil War soldiers in both armies and women who worked as nurses and spies.

Analyzing Information

Students do not have to be statisticians to analyze the data they collect. They do need to know how to organize information so that they can draw conclusions about their research. A variety of methods used by professionals can also be incorporated into student research projects.

Analyzing Surveys. With Likert-scale questions, students can look for frequencies or percentages for each response (e.g., 46% agreed and 54% disagreed) and report the frequencies in a bar graph or percentages on a pie chart. The students who surveyed their classmates about cafeteria foods reported the percent of students who selected each category response to their Likert-scale questions. Other students have used graphing software or books such as *Chi Square, Pi Charts, and Me* (Baum, Gable, & List, 1987) to organize their findings.

Responses to open-ended questions need to be analyzed using a more qualitative approach in which responses are labeled and separated into categories, with categories and category names continuously changing as new responses are analyzed. For example, one student researcher who asked about people who had influenced high school students' career choices began her analysis with categories of Politicians, Actors, and Athletes. Later she realized that all the responses in those three categories were related to people the students had seen on television, so she generated a new category called Television Personalities.

Analyzing Primary Documents. Research related to social science or literature frequently relies on a content analysis of primary documents such as letters, diaries, or newspapers from a particular period. The purpose of the content analysis may be as diverse as looking for a theme in a writer's body of work to analyzing letters and diaries in order to determine factual information or personal reactions to a historical event. Students can also analyze the content in many forms of current written and oral communication such as advertising, graffiti, song lyrics, television shows, or films. They can look at how written or visual communications have changed over time, such as the portrayal of women in advertisements found in *Life* or *Look* magazines over a 30-year period; changes in cartoons before, during, and after World War II; or changes in comic strips over the years.

Fraenkel and Wallen (1996) described three main types of content analysis: (1) frequency counts in which the researcher looks for a particular category of information, such as acts of violence in a movie, and counts the number of times that category appears; (2) nonfrequency analysis, in which the researcher looks for the presence of a category but does not count the instances, such as films in which people smoke; and (3) combinations of events in a communication, such as movies with violence and characters who smoke.

A fourth, more qualitative, approach to document analysis involves the researcher reading the document or viewing the communication without any predetermined categories in mind, looking to see what themes or concepts emerge. For example, a group of students reading first-hand accounts about slave ships determined that the writer's point of view greatly influenced the interpretation he placed on the events he described. A ship's doctor and a sailor described similar events in completely different ways.

Students need to understand that no matter what method they use, they can improve the reliability and validity of their findings by asking other student researchers to be peer reviewers, by dividing a document in half to determine whether a theme found in one half is also in the other half, by having two people analyze the same document separately, or by determining whether two aspects of the document (e.g., text and advertisements in a newspaper) reflect the same themes (Fraenkel & Wallen, 1996).

Individuals or groups of students can also research a particular time period by analyzing the paintings or photographs from that era. As with letters and diaries from another time period, students can create hypotheses about the period by analyzing the picture. They might want to discuss how the people are dressed, what the people seem to be doing, and what emotions the people seem to be feeling. They might want to speculate about the purpose of any objects in the picture. Students in Mississippi, examining Rigaud's painting of Louis XIV, concluded that Louis' primary concern was for people to see him as being wealthy and powerful. They then speculated about why he would want himself portrayed in this manner. These observations led to a deeper understanding of absolute monarchy when the students later studied Versailles and its kings.

Reporting Findings

Research products can take a variety of written and oral forms. Many lists of possible products can be found in literature on curriculum. One of the most handy lists is by Forte and Schurr (1996) who have created easy-to-use curriculum planners for each subject area that include lists of product forms divided according to Gardner's multiple intelligences.

A social studies teacher at the Mississippi School for Mathematics and Science had his students research the local cemetery. The project began with a class field trip to the cemetery. Before the trip, the teacher listed the names of all the people buried in the cemetery and gave the list to the local librarian. She checked through her archives to determine which individuals were on record in her archives. Each student selected a gravestone from the list and began a search of the library's archives and the county courthouse. After the students gathered biographical information, they synthesized and wrote it in the form of a monologue. After several weeks of practice, the students performed their monologues in character and appropriate period dress (often supplied by the local historical society). Judges reviewed these performances, and the winners made up the cast for that year's "Tales of the Crypt." People from around the country who visited the town during Pilgrimage each spring to tour the antebellum homes were also able to be audiences for "Tales" performances, which took place at night in the cemetery.

Foxfire, a journal begun by an English teacher from a school district in the Appalachian South, consists of the "recollections and reminiscences of living people about their past" (Sitton, Mehaffy, & Davis, 1983). Early *Foxfire* articles included topics such as "Moonshining as a Fine Art" and "Log Cabin Construction." Ultimately, the collection of articles was published by the editors of Doubleday, who were amazed when the book sold over 100,000 copies in the first month of publication (Sitton, Mehaffy, & Davis, 1983). Since then, many other *Foxfire*-type publications have chronicled history and folklore of communities around the country.

Sitton, Mehaffy, and Davis (1983) told about a three-year-old girl who was brought to the *Foxfire* offices by her parents to hear the tape of an interview with her grandfather who had died before she was born. The authors suggested that product forms can be written in the *Foxfire* format, dramatized, or simply kept as a tape archive in a local library.

Evaluating Student Researchers

When adults conduct research, their evaluations may be in the form of a publication in a distinguished journal or the response of peers after a presentation at a national conference. Often the most important evaluator is the researcher him or herself. A study that may be deemed unsuccessful by others may, nonetheless, have been meaningful to the researcher.

Evaluation of student research projects often has to be tied to grades, yet all the elements in evaluation of adult products also need to be present. Students must be allowed to fail. They need to understand that research is a kind of risk-taking behavior and may not result the way they had anticipated. It is important to determine in advance with students what the criteria will be to evaluate their projects and who the evaluators will be. An elementary school teacher in Maine not only establishes in advance with her students the criteria that will be used to evaluate the students' projects but also works with students to describe behavioral characteristics for each criterion. For example, if students decide they want to be evaluated on the quality of content and amount of creativity in their projects, they must determine what attributes constitute an A, B, C, D, or F (or acceptable, outstanding, not acceptable) for each criterion. In other words, how is A creativity different from B creativity? Although these discussions can become quite lengthy, they serve a variety of purposes. They teach students the skill of establishing criteria, force students to look at the standards of the field, and allow students to agree on specific concrete definitions of abstract concepts. Incidentally, this practice also helps the teacher develop the same skills.

Wiggins (1989) suggested that any authentic assessment of student products should include the following criteria:

- Skills of inquiry consist of the abilities to ask questions, analyze information, make decisions, and solve problems.
- Skills of expression consist of the abilities to communicate, orally and in writing, and interact with others.

If the research project is replacing curriculum that has been compacted in the regular classroom, Reis, Burns, and Renzulli (1992) suggested that these projects be evaluated because evaluation and feedback are important for the growth of any researcher, but they should not be graded. At the time the regular curriculum is compacted, students who compact out of certain skills or content should receive a grade of A for knowing that subject matter but do not need to receive an additional letter grade for the enrichment activities that replace the curriculum they already have mastered.

Research and Gifted Students With Learning Disabilities

Teaching gifted students to be active researchers can be especially helpful when working with atypical gifted students, particularly those who have been identified as having a learning disability. West (1991) speculated that students with learning disabilities may have neurological organizations that create difficulties with traditional educational tasks, such as memorization, short answer, or multiple choice assessments. He quoted Einstein's statement,

> As a pupil I was neither particularly good or bad. My principal weakness was a poor memory and especially a poor memory for words and texts. (p. 119)

The brains of learning-disabled gifted students may be more suited to tasks that involve finding and solving problems or creating original ideas. West noted that when a subject is approached in a more holistic manner, it more accurately reflects the world outside school. For example, he described mathematics as "a way of looking at and talking about the way plants grow, the way a bridge is stressed, the way music flows" (West, 1991, p. 207). West cited many famous people, such as Albert Einstein, Lewis Carroll, and Leonardo da Vinci, whose self-education, driven by their curiosity, led to their success in life.

Baum's (1988) description of her work with learning-disabled gifted students supports West's theoretical observations. The traditional curriculum for students with learning disabilities, regardless of the students' level of intelligence, usually focuses on remediation in the deficit area. As a result, these students frequently experience high levels of frustration in school which may lead to disruptive behavior in the classroom and negative feelings about school and about their own abilities (Baum & Owen, 1988). Baum (1988) observed, however, that in nonacademic settings, gifted students with learning disabilities are frequently productive and are able to learn rapidly. Using Renzulli's Triad Model, Baum helps LD gifted students investigate real problems. First they explore various areas of interest; next they are taught the skills they need to conduct their own investigation; and finally, they investigate a real problem, creating an authentic product for a real audience. Baum (1988) described one elementary school student with severe writing problems who audiotaped her research notes and created her own slide show called *A Day in the Life of Drusella Webster* which has been shown repeatedly at the Noah Webster House.

Baum and Owen (1988) noted two major benefits to students from this kind of research project. Students who completed projects expressed increased feelings of self-efficacy and demonstrated a great increase in time on task. The authors concluded that the students' feelings of self-efficacy increased because they had been successful in meaningful and challenging situations.

Baum, Renzulli, and Hébert (1995) reported successfully using research projects with underachieving gifted students. The researchers found that students not only made positive academic gains after the project but strengthened their relationships with teachers and peers.

Conclusions

Research projects can become a meaningful part of curricula for gifted students, whether students are homogeneously grouped or in a mixed-ability classroom. Research projects that investigate real problems allow gifted students to be excused from curricula that they already have mastered. These projects also give gifted students an understanding of how adults work in various fields of study. In addition, as the students work to complete research projects, they develop the many process skills, such as problem solving, observing, categorizing, and analyzing, that they will need in order to become independent learners.

Many articles in contemporary journals stress the need for problem-based learning, thematic instruction, and authentic assessment. On the other hand, some critics of these interdisciplinary strategies note that within each discipline lies a vast array of knowledge that can be explored and used. Prawat (1995), who is concerned with the superficiality of some project-based instruction, cited Dewey's statement made in 1931 that

> Many so-called projects are of such short time span and are entered upon for such casual reasons, that extension of acquaintance with facts and principals is at a minimum. In short they are too trivial to be educative. (p. 15)

Prawat concluded that, although students can benefit from studying interdisciplinary concepts such as power or conflict, they also need to be aware of the powerful ideas that are contained within each discipline. Student research projects can accomplish this task.

Teacher Resources

Publications

Burns, D. E. (1990). *Pathways to investigative skills.* Mansfield Center, CT: Creative Learning Press.

Shack, G. D. , & Starko, A. J . (1998). *Research comes alive: A guidebook for conducting original research with middle and high school students.* Mansfield Center, CT: Creative Learning Press.

Starko, A. J., & Shack, G. D. (1990) *Looking for data in all the right places.* Mansfield Center, CT: Creative Learning Press.

Addresses

Discovery Interprises
31 Laurelwood Dr.
Carlisle, MA 01741
(978) 287-5401

Foxfire
P.O. Box 541
Mountain City, GA 30562
http://www.foxfire.org

The Library of Congress
101 Independence Ave. S.E.
Washington, DC 20540
http://www.lcweb.lc.gov

National Geographic Society
1145 17th St. N.W.
Washington, DC 20036–4688
http://www.nationalgeographic.com

The Smithsonian Institute
Washington, DC 20560–0305
http://www.si.edu

References

References marked with asterisks are publications designed to help teachers incorporate student research in their classroom and are useful resources to have.

Baum, S. (1988). An enrichment program for gifted learning-disabled students. *Gifted Child Quarterly, 32,* 226–230.

Baum, S., Gable, R. K., & List, K. (1987). *Chi square, pie charts, and me.* Monroe, NY: Trillium Press.**

Baum, S., & Owen, S. V. (1988). High ability/learning- disabled students: How are they different? *Gifted Child Quarterly, 32,* 321–326.

Baum, S. M., Renzulli, J. S., & Hébert, T. P. (1995). Reversing underachievement: Creative productivity as a systematic intervention. *Gifted Child Quarterly, 39,* 224–235.

Betts, G. T., (1985). *Autonomous learner model.* Greeley, CO: Autonomous Learner Publications.

Bringuier, J. C. (1980). *Conversations with Jean Piaget.* Chicago, IL: University of Chicago Press.

Bruner, J. (1977). *The process of education.* Cambridge, MA: Harvard University Press.

Carey, H. H., & Greenberg, J. E. (1983). *How to use primary sources.* New York: Franklin Watts.**

Clark, B. (1988). *Growing up gifted.* New York: Macmillan.

Cooper, K. (1985). *Who put the cannon in the courthouse square?* New York: Walker & Company.**

Curry, J., & Samara, J. (1991). *Curriculum guide for the education of gifted high school students.* Austin, TX: Texas Association for the Gifted and Talented.

Deal, D., & Sterling, D. (1997). Kids ask the best questions. *Educational Leadership, 45*(6), 61–63.

Dewey, J. (1897). My pedagogic creed. *School Journal, 54,* 77–80 (cited in J. A. Boydston, (Ed.), 1972. *John Dewey: The Early Works 1882–1898,* Vol. 5, 1895–1898.). Carbondale, IL: Southern Illinois University Press.

Dewey, J. (1901). *Psychology and social practice.* Chicago, IL: University of Chicago Press.

Feldhusen, J., & Kolloff, P. B. (1986) The Purdue three–stage enrichment model for gifted education at the elementary level. In J. S. Renzulli (Ed.), *Systems and models for developing programs for the gifted and talented.* Mansfield Center, CT: Creative Learning Press.

Forte, I., & Schurr, S. (1996). *Curriculum and project planner for integrating learning styles, thinking skills, and authentic assessment.* Nashville, TN: Incentive Publications.**

Fraenkel, J. R., & Wallen, N. E. (1996). *How to design and evaluate research in education.* New York: McGraw–Hill.

LaRue, W. (1995, September 19). Ken Burns tries to "present the variety of existence." *The Syracuse Newspapers* [Online serial], Available http://web.syr.edu/~mssmit11/kenburns.burns. html.

Olenchak, R. (1996). *Rearing our village's children: Problem-solving partners.* Paper presented at the annual convention of the National Association for Gifted Children, Indianapolis, IN.

Piirto, J. (1994). *Talented children and adults.* New York: Macmillan.

Prawat, R. S. (1995). Misreading Dewey: Reform, projects, and the language game. *Educational Researcher, 24*(7), 13–22.

Reis, S. M., Burns, D. E., & Renzulli, J. S. (1992). *Curriculum compacting.* Mansfield Center, CT: Creative Learning Press.

Renzulli, J. S. (1988). The multiple menu model for developing differentiated curriculum for the gifted and talented. *Gifted Child Quarterly, 32,* 298–309.

Renzulli, J. S., & Reis, S. M. (1985). *The schoolwide enrichment model.* Mansfield Center, CT: Creative Learning Press.

Sitton, T., Mehaffy, G. L., & Davis, O. L. (1983). *Oral history: A guide for teachers (and others).* Austin, TX: University of Texas Press.**

Tannenbaum, A. J. (1986). The enrichment matrix model. In J.S. Renzulli (Ed.), *Systems and models for developing programs for the gifted and talented.* Mansfield Center, CT: Creative Learning Press.

Tomlinson, C. A. (1995). *How to differentiate instruction in mixed–ability classrooms.* Alexandria, VA: ASCD.

VanTassel-Baska, J. (1997). *Guide to teaching a problem-based science curriculum.* Dubuque, IQ: Kendall/Hunt.**

Ward, V. S. (1961). *Educating the gifted: An axiomatic approach.* Columbus, OH: Charles E. Merrill Books.

West, T. G. (1991). *In the mind's eye.* Buffalo, NY: Prometheus Books.

Wiggins, G. (1989). Teaching to the (authentic) test. *Educational Leadership, 46,* 41–46.

Winebrenner, S. (1992). *Teaching gifted kids in the regular classroom.* Minneapolis, MN: Free Spirit.**

CHAPTER 13

Affective Education and Character Development

Understanding Self and Serving Others Through Instructional Adaptations

JAMES R. DELISLE
Kent State University

Introduction

A story is told of a man who arrived in America from Europe in 1912, intact with dreams, hopes, ambitions, and naiveté. After several weeks in New York City, he wrote a letter home to those he had left behind. "I came to America because I heard the streets were paved with gold," he wrote. "When I got here I found out three things: first, the streets weren't paved with gold; second, they weren't paved at all; and third, I was expected to pave them."

What this man, and countless millions of others, learned throughout previous and future generations was that this is an interdependent world. People count on other people; dreams that come true are often as reliant on the faith or charity of others as they are on one's belief in the power of self. Undergirding this interdependence is an unspoken bond of emotional support; a bond that causes each individual to realize that, indeed, the old cliché is true: the human chain is only as strong as its weakest link.

Just as in 1912, roads still need to be paved and, if you look to your right and then your left, you will find those who work alongside you in their construction. If educators and parents are to benefit the children in their care most fully, an emphasis on this emotional aspect of learning and on the interdependence we all share is a prerequisite to self-appreciation, personal growth, and the development of empathy and character.

Affective Education: Its Roots and Its Purposes

There are many ideas and models for developing the emotional lives of children. Some of these have existed for decades; others are rather recent. And, although not every one of them focuses on gifted individuals as intended audiences, these approaches to affective education can benefit even the most able among us.

Maslow's hierarchy of human needs (1970) postulates that unless a child's most basic life needs are met—food, safety, belonging—the more extravagant needs of being in the service of others will seldom be reached. This is easy to understand: a child hungry for food or a home seldom feels the luxury of being concerned about world peace. Kohlberg (1964) and Gilligan (1982), though disagreeing about the specifics of moral development in boys and girls, do present "stage theories" that help explain how and when children transcend their egocentric selves and concern themselves with the physical and emotional plights of others. David Krathwohl and his colleagues (1965), in a much-ignored but very valuable undertaking, put forth an affective taxonomy that parallels the cognitive taxonomy designed by Benjamin Bloom. This six-level system helps explain how children's affective development grows in complexity as they mature into adulthood. Most recently, Gardner (1983) theorized that certain individuals possess interpersonal or intrapersonal intelligences. These can be noted in how people interact effectively in a helping role with others (interpersonal) or in their keen levels of self-understanding, which lead to an inner search for truth, beauty, or justice (intrapersonal). Taking these ideas several steps further and higher, Goleman (1995) wrote of emotional intelligence as being even more vital than a high IQ in the development of human potential.

When searching for thoughts about the unique affective development of gifted children, one will find that this quest has long been an accepted part of the education of gifted children. The work of Leta Hollingworth (1926; 1942) focused on the complex ways that even young gifted children interpret their world, often finding contradictions that cause them to question why one's actions are not always guided by one's own beliefs. "Political correctness" matters little to children intelligent enough to see through its thin veneer of rationality. This precocious understanding of logic, though, is not always accompanied with a sophistication of emotional judgment. Often, difficulties can arise when a very intelligent child's mind collides with the more typical aspects of his or her development. As expressed by Hollingworth,

> To have the intelligence of an adult and the emotions of a child . . . in a childish body is to encounter certain difficulties. . . . The years between four and nine are probably the most likely to be beset with the problems. (1942, p. 282)

Thus, when you meet a child who thinks like a 12-year-old, looks like a 9-year-old, has the emotions of a 6-year-old and argues like a middle-age, high-priced lawyer, certain life situations will cause stress or discontent for him. The focus of affective education for gifted children is to have them understand and accept that the differences within and between them are by-products of growing up gifted, and that the frustration and impatience that they often feel toward others' beliefs and actions is a natural (albeit uncomfortable) component of giftedness.

Annemarie Roeper, in an article relating how gifted children cope with their emotions (1995), mentions that if these uneven levels of development are left undiscussed, the child may grow to adopt unhealthy lifestyles, like perfectionism or extreme self-criticism. However, an emphasis on what Roeper calls "emotional education" can cause gifted children to "meet the experiences they encounter against a backdrop of emotional strength and balance" (p. 82).

The Meaning of Character

The idea of character is best noted by looking at its etymological roots, as the word itself, "character," originally meant a marking instrument that cuts indelible lines and leaves traces. Who can argue that such a description does not also relate to the people we acknowledge as leaving their own indelible personal impressions on their world? A related interpretation is expressed about the development of character, which is a natural and attractive link with affective education. Conceived by Lickona (1991), character development is seen as

> three interrelated parts: moral knowing, moral feeling, and moral behavior. Good character consists of knowing the good, desiring the good, and doing the good—habits of the mind, habits of the heart, and habits of action. (p. 51)

When these three aspects of character coalesce, they create a moral maturity, wherein by knowing and controlling ourselves, we can do right by others.

Hillman (1996) describes character in terms of both what it is and what it is not, stating that

> character is not what you do, it's the way you do it. . . . For character we look as much to the soldier's letter on the eve of battle and the families at home away from the action as to the plans laid out in a general's tent. (pp. 252; 254)

Hillman goes on to explain that although many people have talents, few have the character to realize those talents in ways that make them exceptional. Which, of course, begs the question as to how we can incorporate character development education into our schools.

Each of these statements about character shows the seamless weaving of thoughts and actions, an idea best expressed by Thomas Jefferson, who wrote that "whenever you do a thing, ask yourself how you would act were all the world looking at you, and act accordingly."

This development of character has long been seen as essential in the education of gifted children, who often share an awareness of the world around them that is uncannily mature. In my own experience as an educator, I have met seven-year-old Neil, whose saddest day of second grade was the morning he learned that Yitzak Rabin had been assassinated. He wanted to discuss during "classroom circle time" why someone would want to kill a man of peace. Then there was nine-year-old Jason, who began a newspaper in memory of his grandmother who died of pancreatic cancer. Half of the money he collects from his newspaper's distribution (it now has subscribers in more than 27 states and 8 nations) goes to the American Cancer Society, in hopes of finding a cure for the disease that took away his Nanny. Also, there is 13-year-old Emily, who read about the appalling conditions of some schools after apartheid ended in South Africa. So, she took it upon herself to collect books for the children who had few—at last count, she had collected and sent to Africa more than 56,000 books. Each of these children is "gifted in the heart," endowed with a special awareness and sensitivity that embodies the precepts of both affective and character education.

Where did these children learn these "skills?" Who were their teachers? And how can we, as the caring adults in charge of educating these young people, provide guidance and structure so that they can better understand and appreciate the world that is theirs? These are, perhaps, the most fundamental questions that thoughtful educators can ask.

What Affective and Character Education Are Not

Before the benefits of affective and character education can be discussed, several myths or misconceptions must be revealed. For even the goodness of spirit that underlies the actions of those who believe in their merits, there are critics who see such a focus as unnecessary or, even worse, coercive.

The first and most egregious misconception is that affective and character development are plots to inculcate our children with a specific set of liberal values and beliefs. Shades of the 1960s protest marchers and draft dodgers enter the minds of those who believe that educators interested in character and affective education harbor hopes of resurrecting the tie-dyed, drug-infested generation that lost faith in its country and its leaders. However, since the goals of legitimate practitioners of these ideas focus on skills such as integrity, perseverance, friendship, patience, and caring, it is hard to accept the "liberal values and beliefs" argument as valid. True educators of honest affective education and character development principles want children to learn the skills that underlie the reasons for their actions. In doing so, there is no room for indoctrination of one set of values that supersedes all others.

A second complaint is that the entire enterprise surrounding these endeavors is little more than fun, games, and touchy-feely exercises that seldom bear directly upon real life matters that gifted individuals confront in their lives. Instead, issues that can be raised with gifted children related to affective education might be "What do you think giftedness is, and do you fit your own definition?"; "Was there ever a time when being gifted proved to be uncomfortable or inconvenient?"; or "What expectations does society hold for people who are called *gifted and talented*?" Character development exercises might include investigating community resources that exist to help individuals or families in crisis, considering the qualities of people in your own life who helped develop your own character or defining what leadership is and how it is visible in different people and contexts. These concepts, as difficult as deciphering any mathematical theorem or determining the value of Shakespeare's *Hamlet* for 21st century readers, require thought and introspection, not bean bag chairs and classroom hijinks.

A third concern expressed, especially about character development, is that it is a sneaky way to make servants out of students. For example, the state of Maryland now requires all high school graduates to document 60 hours of community service that they have performed. Some parents have complained about this requirement— taken it to court, in fact—claiming that such a requirement is equivalent to involuntary servitude or forced volunteerism. Such hostile reactions, though rare, show that the principles underpinning the reasons for these requirements—self-actualization and interdependence—need to be expressed in ways that allow all parties to understand a school's intentions. The development of self-knowledge and leadership doesn't begin at some magic moment upon graduation from high school or college, and proponents of affective and character education understand this intimately.

Affective and Character Development: Working From the Inside-Out

Although some of the remaining portions of this chapter will include specific discussion of either affective or character education as if they were separate entities, it should be remembered that the two are linked together as naturally as a gourmet meal flows from course to course, a cacophony of blended flavors, yet each one distinct. As stated elsewhere,

> "To teach a child to read" may be our aim, but "to help a child appreciate the beauty of written words" is our mission. "Getting to know your community" is a laudable goal for our students, but "envisioning the possible ways you can serve your community" is a lifelong dream we seek for them. "Using higher-level thinking skills" will expand children's minds; "developing empathy and concern for others" will open their hearts. (Delisle & Delisle, 1996, p. 1)

This development of mind and spirit begins its journey inside the individual, as all boys and girls try to distinguish themselves as unique beings among the many. It is only when this self-awareness has begun to be personally absorbed that children can reach out to others in their families, schools, communities, and world. Once the groundwork has been laid so that the child feels safe enough—personally and psychologically—to respond to the needs of others, the emotional education has taken root. Children begin to see who they are and what they do does matter; the world would be a lesser place were they not included in it.

Figure 1 shows the emergence of the self from an interdependent model that relies on many factors. The diagonal (AEIOU) shows the components of this reliance, while the oval in the center shows how knowledge of self leads to awareness of one's place in the larger worlds of family, school, and community. The influences listed on the left column are some of the potential benefits and barriers to affective and character education, while the outcomes listed on the top right reveal some of the benefits of experiencing a life focused on the enhancement of self and others.

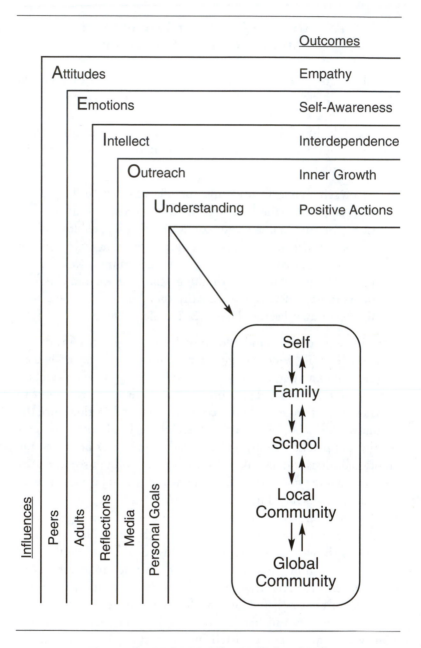

Figure 1. AEIOU: The Vowels of Life

Perhaps a specific example will clarify this idea. Mr. Joseph, a classroom teacher committed to the principles of affective and character education, begins each Monday with *New and Goods*, a 15-minute exercise where students (and the teacher) have a chance to mention anything new or good that has occurred in their lives since they last got together. Children may talk or they may simply say "pass." As reading class begins, and the children explore the Lois Lowry novel *The Giver*, each child is asked to reflect on whether utopia could ever exist and, if so, what it would look like. Also, keeping with the book's theme, students are asked how they would feel if they were selected as the only person in the nation to be given the ability to predict and plan the future. How would they use this power for the good of others? How might this authority be abused? What might this power cause them to learn about themselves?

During math, students listen to an architect talk about how she uses geometry and basic mathematical operations in the construction of her latest project: a Ronald McDonald House on the city's south side. Children are curious about how and why this "house" might be built differently from their own.

When social studies class begins, students are asked to review their latest *Person-To-Person* project ideas, a community-based program to give help to someone who needs it, or say "thank you" to someone who deserves it. On the bulletin board behind his desk, Mr. Joseph keeps a roster of what has been done so far this year:

PERSON-TO-PERSON PROJECTS

September—Wrote notes of encouragement in the shape of cigarettes to people beginning a stop-smoking program at City Hospital. Told them to crush out the notes after they were read.

October—Celebrated World Food Day by starting a campaign to not buy dessert at lunch for two days, giving the money you would have spent to charity. Four hundred twenty dollars was raised in the school district and sent to a local hunger relief center.

November—Prepared an "ecological calendar" for the new year ahead. Students were divided into groups, and each group focused on a specific environmental issue for each month. The calendars were copied and given to second-graders for their use, and each group taught a lesson on its topic.

December—Worked with preschoolers on decorating placemats. Brought these to the local nursing home and sang to residents and celebrated winter holidays.

As the day ends, Mr. Joseph bends down to eye level and shakes the hand of each of his students. As he says something positive to each of them, they do the same to him. This teacher, aware of the linkages between positive self-regard and an interest in helping to develop character, practices affective and character education on a daily basis. Hardly imaginary, teachers like Mr. Joseph exist in many schools but may be unaware of the importance of their cumulative actions.

Specific Activities to Enhance Affective and Character Education

Affective and character education are not prepackaged ideas one can pull off the classroom shelf and proclaim, "It's 2:15, children. Time to be affective!" Such cloying attempts to be authentic come off as exactly what they are: half-hearted and disingenuous. Rather, affective and character education begin with one's attitudes and beliefs about children and the educational process.

Two authors who propose a workable and theoretically-sound approach to the endeavor of meaningful educational experiences are William Purkey and John Novak (1996), whose book, *Inviting School Success*, is based on four principles:
1. people are able, valuable, and responsible and should be treated accordingly;
2. teaching should be a cooperative venture;
3. people possess untapped potential; and
4. this potential can be realized in an environment that respects individual differences and preferences.

How educators actualize the principles of Invitational Education is up to them, but Purkey and Novak (1996) suggest that all educators strive to become "intentional inviters" who focus on the positive and offer alternative behaviors when the student is practicing negative ones.

One way to establish this respectful, inviting climate is to post rules like this (Delisle and Delisle, 1996, p. 6):

CLASSROOM RULES

1. Walking in halls prevents accidents.
2. Be mature and serious during fire drills.
3. Enjoy chewing your gum at home.
4. When in groups, talk in six-inch voices.
5. Ask before you use.
6. People can be hurt by words and actions, so use both carefully.

Please remember: kindness is contagious!

Other ways to invite students intentionally would include
- marking the number of correct items on a test instead of the number of incorrect responses;
- writing positive comments on students' work instead of indiscriminately doling out stars or stickers;
- disciplining and praising in private (no names on the board for misbehavior!);
- inviting a group of students to have lunch with you to try to solve a classroom dilemma;
- telling students, "this subject is difficult, but we'll work at it together," rather than "this concept should be easy for kids as smart as you;"
- greeting students by name as they enter the classroom; and
- posting a suggestion box in the classroom so that students can safely ask for changes that are important to them.

There are literally thousands of ways that students can be invited to learn via the simple and direct routes of honesty and respect. *Inviting School Success* is recommended for those who wish to increase their abilities in this arena.

Once the classroom climate is conducive to students' learning—and this is more a process than an event—then the actual work on affective and character education can begin in earnest.

Affective Education Ideas for Gifted Students

No one can argue that the principles of invitational education apply only to gifted students. However, there are some areas of emotional concern to gifted students that arise due to their high intelligence. Addressing these issues directly builds a firm foundation for self-awareness and appreciation.

One of the first tasks of the teacher interested in helping gifted students better understand themselves is to ask them questions about their abilities. In a survey designed to determine the specific issues gifted students had about their intelligence, Galbraith and Delisle (1996) found that, among other things, gifted students wanted to know

- Is intelligence inherited, determined by environment, or do you pick it up on your own?
- If I don't use my intelligence, will I lose it?
- Are some ethnic groups more intelligent than others?
- Can a person be gifted and not do well in school?
- Why do people call me a "nerd" just because I'm gifted? (pp. 37–43)

These questions deserve answers; but, even more vitally, they need discussion. Doing so opens up both the minds and the hearts of students, as they come to realize they are not "minorities of one," the only smart kid asking questions that others might perceive to be dumb.

Other questions that can lead to intense and meaningful ruminations on the effects of giftedness on one's present and future lives are highlighted in Figure 2. If used in conjunction with real-life events that affect students, or in combination with young adult literature that addresses these topics (see the following section for suggested titles), these questions could be focused upon during an entire school year.

Two books that include numerous and diverse comments made by gifted students often serve to "prime the pump" in initiating these class discussions. Delisle's *Gifted Kids Speak Out* (1987) provides hundreds of one-liners from gifted elementary and middle school children about the high points and hassles of growing up gifted, while the American Association for Gifted Children's *On Being Gifted* (1978) provides extended essays from gifted teenagers

1. When were you identified as gifted? Do you recall if, and how, that label was explained to you? What do *you* think "gifted" means?
2. Is there a difference between being smart and being gifted? Explain.
3. Do you think your teachers understand giftedness? Why do, or don't you think so?
4. Was there ever a time when the gifted label was inconvenient or uncomfortable for you? Who or what made this so?
5. What misconceptions do people hold about gifted students? How can these misconceptions be changed?
6. Who has the highest expectations of you? Explain what these expectations are.
7. How would you respond to someone who said that gifted students don't need any special guidance or classes because they are already so smart?
8. What teacher attitudes and behaviors help you? Which ones hinder your learning?
9. What are your hopes, dreams, and goals for yourself, others, and your planet?
10. Is there anything you would like to ask me or ask each other?

Figure 2. Discussion Questions for Gifted Students to Increase Self-Awareness and Appreciation

on topics ranging from school to expectations to careers to self-understanding. Other helpful resources include Kerr's classic book, *Smart Girls, Gifted Women* (1985) and its sequel, *Smart Girls Two, (1995),* which explore the unique obstacles faced by gifted females; *Perfectionism: What's Bad About Being Too Good?* (Adderholdt-Elliott, 1998), which addresses one of the most pervasive and insidious problems related to giftedness; and Kincher's *Psychology for Kids* series (1988; 1995) which includes 80 psychological experiments that students can conduct on themselves, family, and friends to discover the reasons and purposes behind particular attitudes and behaviors.

Among the best aspects of self-discovery is learning that others share your same hopes, fears, biases, and questions. As unique as you may be, there are still some common bonds that unite us in this race we call "humanity." The teacher who takes the time and cares to address these life issues with gifted students is demonstrating the importance of such matters of the heart in the growth and development of individual children and adolescents.

Grooming for Character and Leadership: Activities That Matter

At the beginning of this chapter, a man came to see leadership as the willingness to pave roads that he presumed others had done before him. Yet this is only one form of expression; for, as noted by Roets (1996), we need other forms of leadership as well:

- *Entrepreneurs* who will create products and processes that will enable us to keep a roof over our heads, put bread on our tables, contribute to civilization, and leave a legacy for our children.
- *Philosophers* who will remind us how slowly human progress is made and how people who are fundamentally the same will differ profoundly in how that sameness is expressed.
- *Children* who must learn the current wisdom of the world and then selectively adopt and adapt that wisdom.
- *Public Service People* (police officers, teachers, doctors, etc.) who remember that they chose those professions to help people become independent, confident, competent, lifelong learners, and contributors to society.

The building of character takes each of us (the educators) and involves each of them (our students). We are not so rich a society that we can afford to dismiss or discount even the smallest inkling of leadership talent, however it is expressed. Here are some methods and materials that can serve as guideposts for helping leadership and character to blossom.

Lickona (1991) suggests that issues involving character can be taught through the required curriculum subjects, especially science and social studies. Since students (and their teachers) are inundated every day with issues that involve these content areas—for example, a petrochemical company's legal and ethical responsibilities after a major oil spill, or the issue of the purpose and promise of affirmative action programs—there is no way *not* to be aware of these moral and ethical issues without wearing blinders and earplugs. World and national history are other vehicles available for traveling the route to self-discovery. Nylen (1984) suggests that events such as the Boston Tea Party and the arrival of "the tired and poor" from Europe in the early 1900s be fodder for discussion on present-day issues involving rebellion and immigration. Also, discussion of how the lives of Harriet Tubman, Abraham Lincoln, Lewis and Clark, and Jackie Robinson could lead to a review of courage, honesty, respect, and justice as character traits that are universal in principle, even if not always in practice. Susan Kovalik's emphasis on *Integrated Thematic Instruction* (1994) is yet another useful model that can be used to introduce students to the elements of character. By focusing each week on a particular human characteristic—perseverance, patience, compassion, sense of humor, integrity—students begin to see the roles they can play in paving those roads that are still covered in dirt.

Based on their work in elementary and middle schools, Delisle and Delisle (1996) offered practical suggestions for "growing good kids." By emphasizing open-endedness and experiential student learning, they suggest 28 activities that encompass many facets of character education. One activity, "The Building Blocks of Character," has students build a three-dimensional set of "blocks" devoted to people in their lives who helped them to become the person they are today. Figure 3 is an example of a sixth grade boy's response to this lesson: a tribute to the brother who taught him so many things.

Another strategy that educators can use to introduce students to the elements of character in their lives is to share with them the wise words of others. Many large lessons can be learned from small collections of words collected by famous and not-so-famous individuals who had something to say, something to share. Figure 4 presents some of my favorite quotations, each one open to interpretation and much discussion.

In one Illinois junior high school, the language arts and art teachers combined classes to have students read famous quotes similar to these, write them using their newly-acquired skill of calligraphy, and hang them on posters throughout the school.

**Figure 3. Example of a Sixth-Grader's Response
to "The Building Blocks of Character"**

Note. From *Growing Good Kids*, (p. 113), by D. Delisle & J. Delisle, 1996, Minneapolis, MN: Free Spirit. Copyright 1996 Free Spirit. Reprinted with permission.

And Now, the Piece de Resistance!

The underlying purpose behind each of the preceding affective and character-based activities is something I call the "Iceberg Effect." If done right, with feeling and passion and heart, the activities themselves are only 10% of the goal; the other 90%, which is often hidden way below the obvious surface, is the resultant real-world action prompted by the students' awareness of the power they *do* possess to affect real-world change.

Some examples follow:

- When middle-school students in Ohio learned that a family of seven had lost all its possessions to a house fire, they rallied the community together to refurbish a newly-rented home, complete with furniture, appliances, toys, clothes—and hope.

"No person is your friend who demands your silence, or denies your right to grow." —Alice Walker

"There are no shortcuts to anyplace worth going." —Beverly Sills

"I don't know the key to success, but the key to failure is trying to please everybody." —Bill Cosby

"Birds sing after a storm, why shouldn't we?" —Rose Kennedy

"When I was growing up, I always wanted to be somebody, but I see now that I should have been more specific." —Lily Tomlin

"If you always do what interests you, at least one person will be pleased." —Katherine Hepburn

"It is fearful to know we're connected to everything in the universe, because then we're responsible." —Glenda Taylor

"If there is any kindness I can show, or any good thing I can do to any fellow being, let me do it now, as I shall not pass this way again." —William Penn

"If you judge people, you have no time to love them." —Mother Teresa

"A good listener is not only popular everywhere, but after a while, he knows something." —Wilson Mizner

Figure 4. The Logic of Life: Quotes To Live By

- When two classes of students in rural South Carolina learned that a community member needed a heart transplant, they sent him "the world's biggest greeting card," complete with well wishes and jokes to cheer him up. Even though the students could not afford a monetary gift, they chose to give of their hearts.
- A group of fifth-grade students in Utah was upset about toxic wastes in their community, so they lobbied the state legislature to pass a bill creating a "Superfund" to clean up these dangerous sites. House Bill 199 passed unanimously.

It all started out as a simple idea: have our sixth graders read lots of books; select their favorite characters, authors, and book endings; and hold a special "Academy Awards" event honoring both the nominees and the winners as selected by the students' secret votes.

The idea became a bit more complex when the science teacher added in a segment on the world's best chemists, physicists, astronomers, and biologists, which entailed reading biographies and searching Internet resources. Then, it got even more curious: The Academy of Motion Picture Arts and Sciences donated a limited-edition poster that we used as a raffle item. Parents donated baked goods, as well. The proceeds from the food sale and the raffle—about $165—were combined with the "entrance fees" collected on the evening of the awards ceremony. The entrance fee was a donated toy, book, canned good, or piece of clothing. At the end of the evening, over 500 pounds of items had been collected.

Then, it got funny. Our principal rented a tuxedo and served as our Master of Ceremonies. Kids dressed up as Gilly Hopkins, Copernicus, Louis the Swan (complete with white boa), Albert Einstein, and Curious George and the Man in the Yellow Hat. Winners were announced and acceptance speeches were given. Applause followed.

Then, it got poignant. At 9:00 the next morning, we all piled into a bus to deliver our donations to a local homeless shelter. There we met Steve, a recovering addict and drug dealer who talked about the pain of his earlier years and his hopes for the future. "I'm even learning to read, like you already do," he told us.

Then, it was complete. Upon returning to school, we discussed the Academy Awards and the homeless shelter. We wondered what life was like for famous authors, and we also wondered what life was like for Steve. To help with his reading lessons, the students decided to write him letters:

Dear Steve,
    I was one of the sixth-grade students who came to the shelter. . . . The speech you gave was what I would call a

great accomplishment. . . . I really was astonished by what you said about yourself. It was really amazing how you went from being a drug dealer and being in jail to becoming a well-rounded individual. . . . People can tell you not to do drugs, but it doesn't help until you see the effects of them. . . . Thank you for inviting us into your life just to make ours a better place. . . . You have the determination to escape from what you felt in your heart was wrong. . . . It takes a hero to save a group of people. But, before you can do that, you have to save your.

Good luck to you!

Your new friends

Watch out for those simple ideas. You never know where they are going to end up!

Figure 5. Affective Education, Character Development, and the Regular Curriculum: What a Bond!

Each of these stories is, of course, true. Each was made possible when teachers (or parents) got together with students and saw themselves, collectively, as part of a solution instead of part of a problem. And, most importantly, the tenor of each of these projects was based on the underlying belief that even a small change can have a major impact. As we are reminded by Stephen Wright, "It's a small world, but I wouldn't want to paint it!" A final example of a community service activity that was completed by two teaching colleagues and me (see Figure 5) gives evidence that the goals of character education can mesh well with more typical curricular areas, like reading, writing, and science.

There are dozens of resource books, agencies, and companies that are willing to help with financial and moral support of individual or class projects that involve the building of character and compassion in children. The Teacher Resources section at the end of the chapter lists just some of the many resources that provide all manner of helping hands to people who are willing to reach out and ask for support. If you were to purchase just one resource with your own funds, I would recommend *The Kid's Guide To Social Action* (Lewis, 1991), the definitive "how-to" resource guide that helps turn creative thinking into positive action.

Summary

This chapter began with a story; let it end with a parable:

Youth

Youth is not a time of life; it is a state of mind. It is not a matter of ripe cheeks, red lips, and supple knees; it is a temper of the will, a quality of the imagination, a vigor of the emotions. Nobody grows old by merely living a number of years. People grow old by deserting their ideals.
Years wrinkle the skin; but to give up enthusiasm wrinkles the soul.
Worry, doubt, self-distrust, fear, and despair—these are the long, long years that bow the heart and turn the greening spirit back to dust.
Whether 60 or 16, there is in every human being's heart the lure of wonder, the sweet amazement of the stars, the unfailing childlike appetite for what is next, and the joy of the game of living.
You are as young as your hope, as old as your despair.

—Anonymous

The people we grow to become tomorrow are all wrapped somewhere inside of the us we are today. By becoming aware of the characteristics that make us unique—our giftedness, our talents, our individual aspirations, and the size of our hearts—as well as those that make us all one—the need to belong, the desire to share, the willingness to grow—we will discover the collective spirits that have kept this world spinning since time began. With the guidance and support of a carefully planned school agenda that emphasizes character and personal growth, we can ensure that the next generation of adults will share an abundance of wealth that is measured in deeds, not dollars.

Teacher Resources

Web Sites

Character Counts—http://www.charactercounts.org
This site provides resources that provide children with the "six pillars or character": trustworthiness, responsibility, respect, fairness, caring, and citizenship.

Character Education Partnership—http://www.character.org
This is one of the most comprehensive sites on character education resources and programs, including the "Eleven Principles of Character Education."

Character Education: Teaching Kids to Care—http://www.aces.uiuc.edu/~uplink/SchoolsOnline/charactered.html
This site includes many activities that teachers can use to instill respect and responsibility in their students.

The Giraffe Project P.O. Box 759, Langley, WA 98260—http://www.giraffe.org
This K–12 program of character education and service learning teaches students that they have the ability and the responsibility to help make a better world. In addition to a highly engaging curriculum program, the Giraffe Project also distributes "Giraffe Awards" to risk-takers of all ages who are not afraid to "stick their necks out" in the service of others.

The Hardee's 'Rise and Shine' for Community Service Campaign (800) 872-7073—http://www.naesp.org/students/sslinks.htm
In this program, sponsored by Hardee's Restaurants, teachers are sent free copies of "An educator's guide to community service projects involving children," which details specific ways that such activities can be incorporated into classroom planning. Then, each year, Hardee's selects winners of their Rise and Shine competition, in which the sponsoring schools receive $5,000 to purchase school supplies or further extend student involvement in their communities.

The Peace Corps Partnership Program (800) 424-8580, Ext. 2227; 1990 K St., Washington, DC 20526—http://www.peacecorps.gov
For 30 years, this program has helped students understand other cultures and ways of life far different from their own. Peace Corps volunteers from across the world request funding for specific proposals (construction of a library, assistance to people trying to learn marketable trades, etc.). Individual schools in the U.S. "adopt" these projects and are kept in communication with both the Peace Corps volunteer and the local community as to the progress being made. Global connections become very real through this hands-on, beneficial program.

The Pizza Hut Kids' Hall of Fame Awards P.O. Box 92477, Libertyville, IL 60092—http://www.nationalgeographic.com/media/world/index.html
Co-sponsored with *National Geographic*, this program recognizes the accomplishments of children ages 14 and under who have made a positive difference in their world. Six students are inducted annually into the Hall of Fame in Washington, DC, and each receives a $10,000 college scholarship.

UNICEF (800) 367-5437—http://www.unicef.org/voy
Each year, UNICEF sponsors an essay contest for students in grades 4–8 on some aspect of global importance involving children (recent years' topics have included child labor and proper nutrition for young children). While providing information on the state of childhood across the planet, the program also involves students by asking them to become "youth ambassadors" for causes that interest them. Each year, two essay writers are selected to represent UNICEF at school assemblies around the nation.

Wiseskills: Character Education for grades K–8—http://www.wiseskills.com
This site provides many sample lessons, as well as a wealth of quotations for character education, conflict resolution, and career awareness

References

Adderholdt-Elliott, M. (1998). *Perfectionism: What's bad about being too good?* (2nd ed.). Minneapolis, MN: Free Spirit.

American Association for Gifted Children. (1978) *On being gifted.* New York: Walker.

Delisle, J. (1987). *Gifted kids speak out.* Minneapolis, MN: Free Spirit.

Delisle, D., & Delisle, J. (1996). *Growing good kids: Twenty-eight activities to enhance self-awareness, compassion, and leadership.* Minneapolis, MN: Free Spirit.

Galbraith, J., & Delisle, J. (1996). *The gifted kids survival guide: A teen handbook.* Minneapolis, MN: Free Spirit.

Gardner, H. (1983). *Frames of mind: The theory of multiple intelligences.* New York: Basic Books.

Gilligan, C. (1982). *In a different voice.* Cambridge, MA: Harvard University Press.

Goleman, D. (1995). *Emotional intelligence.* New York: Bantam Books.

Hillman, J. (1996). *The soul's code: In search of character and calling.* New York: Random House.

Hollingworth, L. (1926). *Gifted children: Their nature and nurture.* New York: Macmillan.

Hollingworth, L. (1942). *Children above 180 IQ, Stanford-Binet.* New York: World Book.

Kerr, B. A. (1985). *Smart girls, gifted women.* Scottsdale, AZ: Gifted Psychology Press (formerly Columbus, OH: Ohio Psychology Press).

Kerr, B. A. (1995). *Smart girls two.* Scottsdale, AZ: Gifted Psychology Press.

Kincher, J. (1988). *Psychology for kids.* Minneapolis, MN: Free Spirit.

Kincher, J. (1995). *Psychology for kids II.* Minneapolis, MN: Free Spirit.

Kohlberg, L. (1964). Development of moral character and moral ideology. In M. Hoffman & L. Hoffman (Eds.), *Review of child development* (pp. 383–431). New York: Russell Sage Foundation.

Kovalik, S. (1994). *ITI: The model: Integrated thematic instruction* (3rd ed.). Kent, WA: Books For Educators.

Krathwohl, D. R., Bloom, B. S., & Masia, B. B. (1965). *Taxonomy of educational objectives: The classification of educational goals, Handbook 2: Affective domain.* New York: David McKay.

Lewis, B. A. (1991). *The kid's guide to social action.* Minneapolis, MN: Free Spirit.

Lickona, T. (1991). *Educating for character: How schools can teach respect and responsibility.* New York: Bantam.

Maslow, A. (1970). *Motivation and personality* (2nd ed.). New York: Harper & Row.

Nylen, C. (1984, March). Integrating ethics into history. *Ethics in Education, 3,* 2–3.

Purkey, W. W., & Novak, J. (1996). *Inviting school success* (4th ed.). Belmont, CA: Wadsworth.

Roeper, A. (1995). How the gifted cope with their emotions. In *Annemarie Roeper: Selected writings and speeches* (pp. 74–84). Minneapolis, MN: Free Spirit.

Roets, L. (1996, February). Lois Roets on . . . leadership. In *The Newsletter.* Cedar Rapids: Iowa Association for the Gifted.

C H A P T E R   1 4

Teaching Gifted Students Through Independent Study

SUSAN K. JOHNSEN
Baylor University

A third-grade teacher announced to a small group of gifted students that they were going to begin their first independent study. She asked, "Does anyone know about independent study?"

A proud little girl immediately raised her hand and blurted, "It's when you write a research report!"

Most students might define an independent study in the same way as this third grader, but it is much more than reading books and writing papers. Independent studies may be used for solving community problems; uncovering new questions; creating a previously unknown history of a small neighborhood; and, most importantly, helping a student create a life-long love affair with learning.

Independent study is the most frequently recommended instructional strategy in programs for gifted students and is included in the majority of introductory texts as a means for differentiating and individualizing instruction (Clark, 1997; Colangelo &

Davis, 1991; Davis & Rimm, 1998; Feldhusen, VanTassel-Baska, & Seeley, 1989; Gallagher & Gallagher, 1994; Parker, 1989; Swassing, 1985; Treffinger, 1986). Independent study is also preferred by gifted students (Dunn & Griggs, 1985; Renzulli, 1977; Stewart, 1981). When compared to learning styles of more average students, gifted students like instructional strategies that emphasize independence such as independent study and discussion. However, while gifted students like these methods, they do not always have the necessary skills that are essential to self-directed learning; consequently, they need to learn them. Once they have acquired the critical independent strategies, gifted students are able to become life-long learners, capable of responsible involvement and leadership in a changing world (Betts, 1985).

Johnsen and Johnson (1986b) define independent study as "the process that you apply when you research a new topic by yourself or with others" (p. 1). Along with research, Kitano and Kirby (1986) added the important elements of planning and teacher involvement: "Students conduct self-directed research projects that are carefully planned with the teacher and are monitored frequently" (p. 114). Both Betts (1985) and Renzulli and Reis (1991) emphasize the importance of "real-world investigations" in their definitions. "In-depth studies are life-like for they provide an opportunity to go beyond the usual time and space restrictions of most school activities" (Betts, 1985, p. 55). Type III research projects are " . . . investigative activities and artistic productions in which the learner assumes the role of a first-hand inquirer—thinking, feeling, and acting like a practicing professional" (Renzulli & Reis, 1991, p. 131).

In summary, independent study is a planned research process that (a) is similar to one used by a practicing professional or authentic to the discipline; (b) is facilitated by the teacher; and (c) focuses on life-like problems that go beyond the regular class setting.

Independent Study Models

Models such as Renzulli's Enrichment Triad (1977a), Feldhusen and Kolloff's (1986) three-stage model, Treffinger's (1975) self-initiated learning model, and Betts and Kercher's (1999) Autonomous

Learner Model have inspired teachers to include independent study as an important component of their programs.

Renzulli's model (1977a) contains three qualitatively different phases that include Type I enrichment or general exploratory activities that introduce the student to a variety of topics and interest areas; Type II group training activities that develop creativity and research skills; and Type III investigations which encourage students to pursue real problems of personal interest to them (see Figure 1). Students move among and between the three types of activities as based upon their interest in a particular question, topic, or problem. When students arrive at Type III activities, the teacher helps them identify specific questions and methods to use in pursuing their

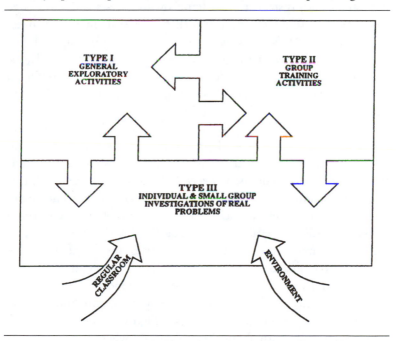

Figure 1. Renzulli's Enrichment Triad

Note. From *The Enrichment Triad Model: A Guide for Developing Defensible Programs for the Gifted and Talented* (p. 14), by J. S. Renzulli, 1977. Mansfield Center, CT: Creative Learning Press. Copyright 1977 by Creative Learning Press. Reprinted with permission.

independent studies. The teacher also provides feedback and helps the student find resources and audiences who might be interested in their products (Renzulli, 1979). Renzulli (1979) emphasizes the importance of finding "real" problems and using "authentic" methods during the Type III activities.

Feldhusen and Kolloff's (1986) three-stage inquiry model focuses on the development of basic divergent and convergent thinking abilities at Stage 1, more complex creative and problem-solving activities at Stage 2, and independent learning abilities at Stage 3 (see Figure 2). In the independent learning stage, gifted students are involved in research projects which focus on defining problems, gathering data, interpreting findings, and communicating results. At this stage, the students' own interests and knowledge base serve "to stimulate a deep intrinsic interest in an area of investigation" (p. 131). More recently, Feldhusen (1995) proposed The Purdue Pyramid (see Figure 3). Included in the wide array of learning experiences needed to develop talent and still occupying a prominent position is "independent study and original investigations" (p. 92).

Treffinger (1975) developed a four-step plan for teaching increasing degrees of independent, self-initiated learning (see Figure 4). At the *teacher-directed level*, the teacher prescribes all the activities for individual students; at *Level 1*, the teacher creates the learning activities and the student chooses the ones he or she wants to do; at *Level 2*, the student participates in decisions about the learning activities, goals, and evaluation; and at *Level 3*, the student creates the choices, makes the selection, and carries out the activity. The student also evaluates his or her own progress (see Figure 4).

Betts and Kercher (1999) divided their model into five major dimensions: orientation, individual development, enrichment activities, seminars, and in-depth study (see Figure 5). During orientation, the students learn about themselves and what the program has to offer. In individual development, the student focuses on developing skills, concepts, and attitudes that promote lifelong independent, autonomous learning. Enrichment activities assist students in deciding what they want to study independently. Seminars provide a forum for students in small groups to present their research to the rest of the group. Students learn how to promote understanding of

Stage I
Divergent & Convergent   **Examples of Resources**
    Thinking Abilities

Teacher-led short span activities   *Basic Thinking Skills* (Harnadek, 1976)
Emphasis on fluency, flexibility,   *New Directions in Creativity*
    originality, elaboration   (Renzulli & Callahan, 1973)
Application of skills in various   *Purdue Creative Thinking Program*
    content areas   (Feldhusen, 1983)
Balance between verbal and   *Sunflowering* (Stanish, 1977)
    nonverbal activities

Stage II
Development of Creative   **Examples of Resources**
    Problem-Solving Abilities

Teacher-led and student-initiated   *CPS For Kids* (Stanish & Eberle, 1996)
Techniques of inquiry, SCAMPER   *Problems! Problems! Problems!*
    morphological analysis,   (Gourley & Micklus, 1982)
    attribute listing, synectics   *Design Yourself!* (Hanks, Belliston, &
Application of a creative   Edwards, 1977)
    problem-solving model   *Hippogriff Feathers* (Stanish, 1981)

Stage III
Development of Independent   **Example of Resources**
    Learning Abilities

Student-led, teacher-guided   *Big Book of Independent Study* (Kaplan,
Individual or small group work on   Madsen, & Gould, 1976)
    selected topics   *Self-Starter Kit for Independent*
Application of research methods   *Study* (Doherty & Evans, 1980)
Preparation of culminating   *Up Periscope!* (Dallas Independent
    product for an audience   Schools, 1977)
                      Interest-A-Lyzer (Renzulli, 1977b)

Figure 2. Purdue Three-Stage Model

Note. From "The Purdue Three-Stage Enrichment Model for Gifted Education at the Elementary Level," by J. F. Feldhusen and P. B. Kolloff, 1986, in J. S. Renzulli (Ed.), *Systems and Models for Developing Programs for the Gifted and Talented* (p. 131), Mansfield Center, CT: Creative Learning Press. Copyright 1986 by Creative Learning Press. Reprinted with permission.

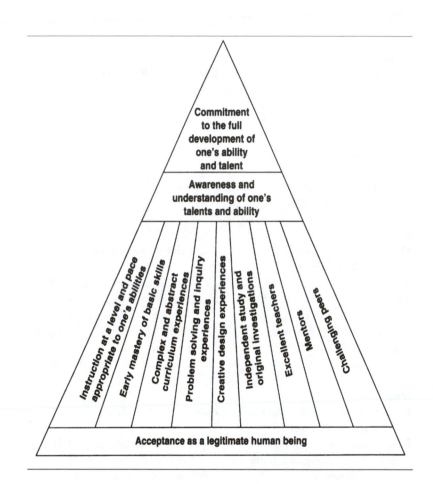

Figure 3. The Purdue Pyramid

Note. From "Talent Development: The New Direction in Gifted Education" by J. F. Feldhusen, 1995, *Roeper Review, 18*, p. 92. Copyright 1995 by Roeper Review, P.O. Box 329, Bloomfield Hills, MI 48303. Reprinted with permission.

their topics and facilitate the discussions. During the final in-depth study, students pursue areas of interest in long-term individual or small group studies similar to Renzulli's Type III projects.

While these and other models of independent study exist, empirical research is limited, with most of the studies focusing on

Decisions to be made	Teacher-Directed	Levels of Self-Direction		
		Self-Directed—Level 1	Self-Directed—Level 2	Self-Directed—Level 3
Goals and objectives	Teacher prescribes for total class or individuals.	Teacher provides choices or options for students.	Teacher involves learner in creating options.	Learner controls choices; teacher provides resources and materials.
Assessments of entry behaviors	Teacher tests, then makes specific prescription.	Teacher diagnoses, then provides several options.	Teacher and learner hold diagnostic conference; tests employed individually if needed.	Learner controls diagnosis; consults teacher for assistance when unclear about some need.
Instructional procedures	Teacher presents content, provides exercises and activities, arranges and supervises practice.	Teacher provides options for student to employ independently at his or her own pace.	Teacher provides resources and options, uses contracts that involve learner in scope, sequence, and pace decisions.	Learner defines project and activities, identifies resources needed, makes scope, sequence, and pace decisions.
Assessment of performance	Teacher implements evaluation procedures, chooses instruments, and gives grades.	Teacher relates evaluation to objectives and gives student opportunity to react or respond.	Peer partners used to provide feedback; teacher and learner conferences used for evaluation.	Learner does self-evaluation.

Figure 4. Treffinger's Model for Self-Directed Learning

Note. From "Teaching for Self-Directed Learning: A Priority for the Gifted and Talented," by D. J. Treffinger, 1975, *Gifted Child Quarterly, 19*, p. 47. Copyright 1975 by Prufrock Press. Reprinted with permission.

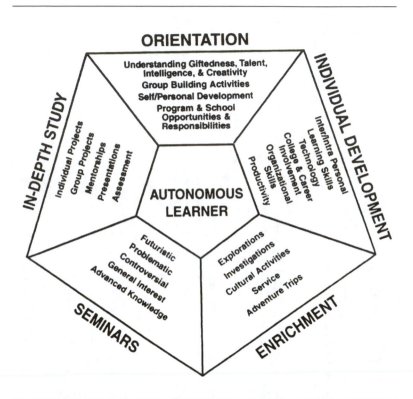

ORIENTATION

Understanding Giftedness, Talent, Intelligence, & Creativity
Group Building Activities
Self/Personal Development
Program & School Opportunities & Responsibilities

INDIVIDUAL DEVELOPMENT

Inter/Intra Personal
Learning Skills
Technology
College & Career Involvement
Organizational Skills
Productivity

IN-DEPTH STUDY

Individual Projects
Group Projects
Mentorships
Presentations
Assessment

AUTONOMOUS LEARNER

SEMINARS

Futuristic
Problematic
Controversial
General Interest
Advanced Knowledge

ENRICHMENT

Explorations
Investigations
Cultural Activities
Service
Adventure Trips

Figure 5. The Autonomous Learner Model

Note. From *The Autonomous Learner Model: Optimizing Ability* (p. 2), by G. T. Betts and J. J. Kercher, 1999, Greeley, CO: ALPS Publications. Copyright 1996, ALPS Publications. Reprinted with permission.

Renzulli's model. For example, students who completed Type III investigations reported that they were better prepared for research assignments, "were able to manage their time efficiently, and plan their work to meet their desired goal" (Hébert, 1993, p. 27). They have higher self-efficacy with regard to creative productivity and are more likely to pursue creative productivity outside of school (Starko, 1988). Delcourt (1993) found that students were more internally motivated toward projects they wanted to do and viewed other types of projects such as regular and gifted class assignments as "routine" or "regular" and not a part of creative activities. Olenchak and Renzulli (1989) found that students enrolled in Schoolwide Enrichment Model (SEM) schools had numerous creative products that exceeded the norm of typical student creative production. Gifted students who have participated in these programs feel that independent study has a positive influence on their motivation and career, their study habits and thinking processes, the degree of challenge, and the opportunity for self-expression in school (Renzulli & Gable, 1976; Zimmerman & Martinez-Pons, 1990).

Guidelines for Independent Study

While independent study is frequently used by teachers of gifted students, it is also one of the most abused strategies. Parents often find themselves struggling with their children's September-assigned research projects that are due in the spring. In these cases, teachers provide only grades with limited instruction and support. In effective independent studies, teachers are actively involved, facilitating each phase of the study as a student's interest emerges and develops. Teachers therefore need to remember the following guidelines when initiating independent studies with their students.

Don't Confuse Potential With Skill. While gifted students have a great potential for performing at a high level and producing complex products, they may not have the necessary skills for completing an independent study project. For example, they may not know how to identify good study questions or select a sample or use a systematic study method or gather information from a variety of sources. The teacher will need to teach many of these skills, particularly during the first independent study.

Identify Independent Study Skills. To facilitate the independent study, the teacher must be aware of the skills that are involved in every step of the process. For example, if the student is going to be conducting historical research, the teacher needs to know the specific steps in this method or be able to identify a historian.

Adapt as the Student Changes. While the teacher needs to have a thorough understanding of the steps in the process, the student's interest *must* guide the study. An interest cannot always be "turned on" according to schedule. Some flexibility must be built into the process so that students have choices of what, when, how, and how much they want to explore a topic.

Use Different Types of Research. "Don't take away my encyclopedia" is quickly being replaced with "Don't take away the Internet!" While both of these types of research are great resources to students, they also need to learn about first-hand or hands-on learning such as interviewing, experimenting, field studies, observing, surveying, discussing, and brainstorming with others. The type of research should match the question and method of study and be authentic to the discipline. For example, if the student is interested in roller coasters, then he might study them using the tools of a physicist.

Make it a Part of a "Regular" Program, Not an Addition. Sometimes independent study is something that students do when they finish the rest of their "regular" work. When this occurs, the student may never have enough time to pursue something of interest, may lose continuity, or worse yet, may view research as "extra" work. The teacher may wish to use curriculum compacting to "buy" class time for independent study (Renzulli & Reis, 1997).

Monitor Progress and Products. Establish a regular time to meet with students, facilitating various phases and stages, as they become more involved with their areas of study. This one-on-one time is important to identify needed research skills and to maintain each student's interest.

Develop an Appropriate Evaluation. The evaluation should match the characteristics of each step in the process and the student's experience with independent study. If the student is pursuing a topic independently for the first time, the teacher should consider this novice-level and evaluate accordingly. Evaluations should improve a student's study skills, encourage his or her interests, and increase a love for learning. If evaluations are too harsh initially, students will quickly lose motivation and follow teacher rules rigidly to receive the desired grade.

Believe in the Student's Ability and Be a Model. Nothing is more stimulating to students than others' interest in their independent studies. Teachers should make a point of noticing improvements and new ideas. Teachers who are engaged in their own research provide a model and can discuss their challenges in a collegial fashion with their students.

Remember that Independent Study Is Only One Way of Meeting the Needs of Gifted Students. Sometimes programs for gifted students are synonymous with independent studies. It is the only strategy that is used. Students quickly become bored with a repetition of projects leading to more and more products. Teachers will want to include many different strategies in their programs and limit independent studies to student-driven interests.

Steps in Independent Study

This section will describe nine steps that might be used in independent study. All of the steps may or may not be used in every independent study since the teacher and the student may already have defined some steps. For example, the teacher may present a problem and the students are responsible primarily for gathering information and sharing their results. Teachers who want students to find problems in their own interest areas may discover that all of these steps are helpful in teaching the process of independent study.

Introducing the Independent Study

In introducing the independent study, the teacher defines the process and gives each student a plan to manage his or her work (see Figure 1). At this stage, the teacher describes (a) various steps that will be used during the study; (b) the dates when different stages of the study are due; and, if known, (c) the audience who will be interested in the results of their study.

As mentioned earlier, the steps may vary depending upon the nature of the study. If the teacher has already identified the questions, the students may be focusing primarily on collecting information, developing and sharing a product, and evaluating the process.

At this initial step, the teacher must help students learn how to meet deadlines by establishing due dates. While researchers often dream of unlimited time to pursue topics of interest, reality generally dictates such a timeline.

Students also will be more involved in the independent study if the topic is of genuine interest to them and if they know it will be used or heard by an authentic audience. For example, when a second grade gifted class was introduced to the problem of limited recycling in their community, they immediately pinpointed the lack of curbside services as a contributing factor. With the help of their teacher, they identified the city council as an important audience because the members held the budgetary power to make changes in the current recycling program. Their entire study then focused not only on researching various aspects of recycling but also on how to sell their ideas to the council. Their enthusiasm and their professional video were rewarded with the desired change. Curbside recycling indeed improved the recycling program within their community.

Selecting a Topic

At this step, the students select something to study. It may be a problem they want to solve, an issue they want to debate, an opinion they want to prove, something they want to learn how to do, or simply something they want to know more about. Interesting ideas may be pursued immediately or collected over a period of time. For example, a bulletin board of expressed classroom opinions might be developed with the purpose of proving or disproving them later. Newspaper headlines can become issues or problems for community action studies. Ideas and new questions that grow from classroom units can be researched immediately or stockpiled for future investigations.

When students have difficulty selecting a single area for study, they may want to consider some of these questions: Which topic is most interesting to me? Which topic do I know the least about? Which topic do I know the most about? Which topic will be easy to find information? Which topic is the most unusual? Which topic will be the most useful to me? Which topic will be the most interesting to the audience?

This step frequently involves gathering more information about the topic. Students may investigate the Internet by contacting museums, agencies, universities, and state or national departments. They may send home letters to parents, put bulletins that request topic information in the teacher's lounge, interview experts in the field, call public radio and television stations, or, of course, browse through the school library. The teacher may also help by inviting experts to discuss their fields of study with the class, taking the class on field trips, or setting up learning centers that provide an overview of a specific topic. During this process, students may discover that they can't locate information about their topic, that the information is too technical or too difficult to understand, that the information is really not very interesting to them after all, or that another topic is more interesting. Throughout, the teacher lets the students know that seemingly good ideas don't work and that new ideas may appear accidentally or in unusual places. This step is important. If students are energized by their topics, the teacher may assume the role of facilitator rather than dictator.

For example, Alice happened to be in a fourth grade resource room with five other gifted children—all of whom were boys. The boys were very interested in discovering methods for designing new video games. Alice could care less about games; instead, she was really interested in penguins. While her choice created some difficulty for the teacher who had wanted a group-designed project, she eventually acquiesced to Alice's interest. The result was a beautifully designed zoo for Emperor Penguins.

Organizing the Study

Sometimes the teacher assists students in organizing or "mapping" their topics to help them find specific questions or problems. For example, if the teacher asks the students to brainstorm problems related to space explorations and the result includes only questions about UFOs and aliens, then this step is needed.

Organizational structures may include (a) descriptions, (b) comparisons, (c) causes and effects, or (d) problems and solutions. In *describing* space exploration, for example, the teacher might want to begin by creating categories for brainstorming. These categories may include space exploration's contributions, its future, its features, its history, its changes, its stages, or people's beliefs, feelings, or criticisms about it. Each of these broader categories form the hub of a wheel of student ideas and, eventually, questions.

Any of the descriptors generated about space exploration can be *compared* to other topics, models, theories, or rules. For example, the teacher might encourage the students to compare technological and human space exploration; historical and current beliefs about space exploration's contributions to science; or the features of early spacecraft with current or future ones. Again, questions begin to emerge from these comparisons or may lead to other organizational structures such as causes and effects or problems and solutions.

For example, if people have changed their feelings about space exploration, the student may want to consider the *causes and effects* of such a shift in attitudes. What might happen to space exploration's financial support? to scientific advances? to educational benefits? to scientists involved in cosmology? These effects may generate future *problems*. If financial support is withdrawn from space exploration, then the understanding of our solar system and the creation of a broader knowledge base may be limited.

All of these ways of examining a topic should lead to the most important step in the process: asking questions.

Asking Questions

After doing some preliminary research and organizing their topics, the students are ready to ask questions. Good questions lead to quality independent studies. Teachers need to teach students the characteristics of "good" study questions. But what are the criteria for such?

One criterion relates to its complexity. Can it be answered by a simple "yes" or "no" or by facts from a reference book? If so, the question may not be one that requires much research. Good study questions often produce several possible answers and may be pursued differently by various researchers. Two other criteria relate to practicality. Does the student have the time or resources to study the question? Finally, is the question useful or beneficial to the student or others? These criteria should help the student evaluate their questions.

Students may use their organizational categories to generate questions related to these stems: who, what, when, where, why, how, how much, how many, how long, and how far, along with what might happen if? For example, if a student were studying seals, they might ask descriptive questions such as, "What does a seal look like?" "Where does a seal live?" "When do seals breed?" or comparison questions, such as, "How are seals and penguins alike or different?" or cause and effect questions such as "How do treaties protect seals?" or problem questions such as, "Why is there a disagreement among countries over the hunting of seals?" The process of including categories with "W + H" stems should produce a great many questions. The teacher might wish to have the student select several questions for study or have the student examine the level of thinking required by each question.

In the latter case, some teachers choose to teach their students a framework for asking questions such as Bloom's Taxonomy. In this way, the student can determine the complexity of the question. One approach is to teach them the differences among "little thinking," "more thinking," and "most thinking" questions (Johnsen & Johnson, 1986a, p. 19). "Little thinking" (i.e., knowledge and comprehension) questions are those that the student can answer by simply copying or redoing something that someone else has done. "More thinking" (i. e, application and analysis) questions are those that can be answered if the student uses the information in new situations. "Most thinking" questions are those that can only be answered if the student creates and evaluates new information. Giving students these evaluation tools helps them create more complex questions that, in turn, influence the overall quality of the independent study. For example, in Alice's study of Emperor Penguins, she asked several "little thinking" questions such as, "What are the characteristics of Emperor Penguins?" "Where do they live?" "How do they breed?" and "What do they eat?" One "more thinking" question is, "How does the zoo in our city provide a habitat similar to the natural habitat of Emperor Penguins?" and one "most thinking" question is, "What might be an ideal zoo for an Emperor Penguin?"

Choosing a Study Method

Most of the time, students are aware of only a limited number of methods for gathering information to study a question in an area of interest: the library and, more recently, the Internet. In both cases, students often feel that their research is not quite complete without referring to the venerable encyclopedia. This one-type-of-method approach may not even address their study questions. How might Alice answer the question, "How does the zoo in our city provide a habitat similar to the natural habitat of Emperor Penguins" by gathering information in the library? Alice is going to need to visit the city zoo, talk to the zookeepers, and interview experts who know about Emperor Penguins. In Alice's and other students' studies, the questions should determine the study method.

There are many different kinds of study methods. Some of these methods include descriptive, historical, correlational, developmental, ethnographic, action, experimental, and quasi-experimental research (Issac & Michael, 1980). For example, if students want to know how different schools in their town were named, they would be interested in an historical study method. First, they might contact primary sources such as principals of different schools and people who were either at the school building when it was dedicated or know the person or place for whom/which the school was named. Second, they might locate secondary sources, such as newspaper stories that were written about the persons or places for which the schools were named. Third, they would interview their primary sources and take notes from their secondary sources. Fourth, they would review their interviews and notes, focus on facts, and delete biased or exaggerated information. Finally, they would verify information with their primary sources before sharing it with others.

Teachers will want to become acquainted with the research methods that address different kinds of questions so that their students will use authentic approaches that are frequently practiced by experts in each field. In addition, teachers will want to engage experts as mentors when students pursue topics in greater depth. What better way to study paleontology than to visit a "dig" with a practicing archaeologist? or to learn about theater with a director of drama? or to visit a courtroom with a practicing attorney? Authenticity is supported through the use of scientific methods, experts in various disciplines, a genuine student interest, and multiple approaches to gathering information, which is addressed in the next section.

Gathering Information

Both the study method and the information that is gathered flow naturally from the questions. If a student is interested in the relationship between the number of study hours at home and grades in school, then he or she will use a correlational method of research and gather information from students related to "study hours" and "grades." If students are interested in how an engineer spends his or her time during a workday, they will use a more ethnographic method of research, observing engineers during their workdays.

There are many ways of gathering information. Some of these include note taking, writing letters, surveying, interviewing, observing, reading, listening to focus groups, brainstorming with others, locating information on the Internet, going on field trips, or conducting controlled experiments in a laboratory. In each case, the teacher needs to clearly specify and teach the steps involved with the approach. For example, when interviewing, the student needs to know (a) how to select a person to interview; (b) how to make the initial contact and set up an appointment; (c) how to locate background information and prepare questions for the interview; (d) how to make a good impression during the interview; (e) how to ask questions and record information; (f) how to summarize interview notes; and (g) how to provide information to the interviewed person. With the advent of e-mail, interviews with experts are much more accessible for students. In using the web, the interested researcher may even take virtual tours of museums all over the world. Again, the teacher plays a valuable role by assisting the student in using search engines, locating reliable sources of information and/or experts, and critically evaluating the information.

Younger gifted children often gather information through hands-on activities, oral interviews, or surveys. For example, in learning about structures, children might build bridges with various materials, testing the strength of each design by placing toy cars or other objects on top. In deciding what businesses are needed in a classroom "city," they might conduct a "market analysis" through a survey of their classmates.

Remember that gathering information or paraphrasing written materials is a difficult task and should be taught to older students before they begin the process of independent study. In this way, interest in the topic and pacing of the project are not delayed by the frequently perceived "drudgery" of writing notes and outlining information. If students are already proficient in these tasks, then their studies can flow at a rate that maintains their enthusiasm.

In summary, information that is gathered should relate to the question, be authentic within the field of study, be clearly defined and taught to the students, and be appropriate for the age of the researcher.

Developing a Product

While most students believe that "independent study" is synonymous with "written report," information may be organized in a variety of ways. Products include books, diagrams, dioramas, videos, computer programs, games, graphs, posters, puppet shows, reports, tape recordings, timelines, debates, dramatizations, models, newspapers, poems, speeches, and many others.

If the product is an option, then students may select one or more that match their original questions. For example, Albert had several questions that related to his topic of interest, "bees." They included "What are the parts of a bee?" "What are the different kinds of bees?" and "Which wild flowers in my neighborhood do bees prefer?" Albert might have answered all of these questions with a written report or a Hyperstudio™ computer product, but he wanted to organize a display for parent open house. To answer the questions related to parts and kinds of bees, he drew a diagram of each one—comparing and contrasting coloration, size, and shape. He mounted these on a poster along with some photos in their natural habitats and labeled each part. For his study question that examined wild flower preferences among bees, he displayed his field notes, presenting the results in a series of graphs. He then prepared an audiotape in which he enthusiastically described the entire process of his independent study.

Similar to the step of gathering information, the product should be authentic within the field of study. For example, what product(s) might a naturalist develop to share his or her work? Did Albert share his bee study in a similar way? Indeed, a naturalist would keep a scientific journal, attach pictures or photos as examples, summarize results in a graph, and present information orally or in written form.

Again, the teacher will want to teach each step of product development. For example, in designing a timeline, the student might (a) determine which years will be included; (b) decide whether the time line will be horizontal or vertical; (c) decide whether to use pictures, drawings, special lettering, or other graphic designs; (d) decide the length of the line and each time period; (e) draw the line manually or use the computer; (f) divide the line into specific time periods; (g) write the dates and information beside the time line and attach any pictures or drawings; and (h) write a title.

Finally, the way that the information is organized should again match the age of the youngster. Hands-on, visual, and oral products are easier for younger children than written ones. For example, in presenting information gathered about an ancient culture, a class of young gifted students created a museum of artifacts with videos of "experts" describing each display. The teacher will find many resources to help in organizing information into products (see Teacher Resources at the end of this chapter).

Sharing Information

While information may be shared informally, students need to learn that there is life beyond the product. The teacher might discuss with the students some of these reasons for sharing information: students can learn from one another; students can improve their products; others can help evaluate the product; and students can gather support for the product.

There are two major ways of sharing information with an audience: through oral presentation or in a display. The best approach should be determined by the audience. Again, each step needs to be outlined and taught. For example, in designing an oral report, the student will need to (a) plan the report; (b) practice the report; (c) arrange materials in order; (d) stand in a visible spot; (e) introduce himself or herself; (f) look at the audience; (g) speak loudly enough to be heard; (h) hold the product or visuals where they can be seen; (i) state major points; (j) keep the talk short; (k) ask for questions; (l) have the audience complete the evaluation; and (m) thank the audience.

For an oral report, students should practice before their peers. During these practice sessions, each student should provide at least two positive comments to every one-improvement comment that relate to specific criteria. In this way, students' self-esteems and performances will improve.

Sometimes the process of independent study stops with the completion of a product. Products are graded, taken home, and eventually discarded. For products to *live*, students need to share their ideas, garner support, and develop new ideas that might intensify or create fresh interests in their topics. For example, Albert, who studied bees, might contact entomologists via e-mail or at a local university to discuss the results of his field study. He might improve his techniques through these communications or by actually working with an expert in planning his next study.

Evaluating the Study

The evaluation of independent studies is both formative and summative. With formative evaluation, students examine their performance in terms of the overall process. Criteria might include the following statements
- I had a well planned independent study.
- I used my time efficiently.
- I wrote a probing study question.
- I used varied resources.
- My research was extensive.
- I developed a fine product.
- My class presentation was effective.
- I have good feelings about the independent study. (Johnsen & Johnson, 1986b, p. 22)

Similar criteria may be developed for other evaluators, such as the teacher, peers, or both. The audience may also contribute their evaluation comments (see Figure 4). All of the evaluations can be collected and reviewed at a final teacher-student conference.

In addition to these types of formative evaluations, the student and teacher will want to use summative evaluation in judging the independent study products. Check lists or rubrics can be designed with specific criteria listed for each type of product. For example, evaluation characteristics for a pictograph might include
- Did the pictures relate to the collected data?
- Did the picture reflect the kind of information being expressed? For example, if the graph is about money, money signs ($) or pictures of coins might be used.

- Did each symbol represent the same amount?
- Did partial symbols represent fractions of the amount?
- Were the symbols the same size?
- Were the symbols aligned next to the labels?
- Did the graph have a title that represented the question?
- Was each line of pictographs labeled?
- Was there a key that indicated the amount that each pictograph represented?
- Was the overall graph neat and attractive?

Evaluations in independent studies should focus on what the student has learned and what he or she might do to improve the next research project. If evaluations are positive, the student will be encouraged to continue his or her study, looking for new questions or new areas. There are many evaluations that may be accessed in the literature such as Renzulli and Reis' (1997) Student Product Assessment Form. It examines the statement of the purpose; problem focus; level, diversity, and appropriateness of resources; logic, sequence, and transition; action orientation; and audience.

This chapter has provided a very brief overview of the critical steps involved in independent study and research. The reader is encouraged to use the following resources to learn more about this important instructional strategy with gifted students.

Teacher Resources

Publications

Betts, G. (1985). *The autonomous learner model for the gifted and talented.* Greeley, CO: ALPS Publications.
This 90-page book is a guide to the Autonomous Learner Model that describes each of the five-dimensions of the model and describes essential activities.

Burns, D. E. (1990). *Pathways to investigative skills: Instructional lessons for guiding students from problem finding to final product.* Mansfield Center, CT: Creative Learning Press.
This resource book contains 10 lessons designed to teach students

how to initiate a Type III investigation. Lessons focus on interest finding, problem finding, topic webbing, topic focusing, and creative problem solving.

Draze, D. (1986). *Blueprints: A guide for independent study projects.* San Luis Obispo, CA: Dandy Lion.
This book, for students in grades 4–8, provides directions for a written report, speech, model, debate, experiment, poster, book, survey, demonstration, learning center, multi-media project, problem solution, science project, game, special event, and display.

Garvin, K. (1991). *Research skills for beginners.* Greeley, CO: ALPS Publications.
This 36-page book is a practical, step-by-step approach for beginning researchers. It includes activities for various phases, from defining a topic to classifying information and from using resources to making the final presentation.

Heuer, J., Koprowicz, C., & Harris, R. (1980). *M.A.G.I.C. K.I.T.S.* Mansfield Center, CT: Creative Learning Press.
This activity book presents a collection of theme-based activities for Type I and Type II Enrichment experiences.

Johnsen, S. K., & Johnson, K. (1986). *Independent study program.* Waco, TX: Prufrock Press.
This program for students in grades 2–12 includes a teacher's guide with lesson plans for teaching research skills; student workbooks that correlate to the guide and are used for organizing the student's study; and reusable resource cards that cover all the steps of basic research.

Kramer, S. (1987). *How to think like a scientist.* New York: Crowell.
This book teaches students in grades 2–5 the steps in the scientific method: asking a question, collecting data/information, forming a hypothesis, testing the hypothesis, and reporting the results.

Leimbach, J. (1986). *Primarily research.* San Luis Obispo, CA: Dandy Lion.

This 64-page book includes eight units for primary-age children that present a different animal or pair of animals. Included with each unit are interesting facts and activities for structuring research.

Leimbach, J., & Riggs, P. (1992). *Primarily reference skills*. San Luis Obispo, CA: Dandy Lion.
This 64-page book helps students in grades 2–4 learn how to use the library. Reproducible worksheets teach the parts of a book, alphabetical order, dictionaries, encyclopedias, and finding books.

Polette, N. (1991). *Expanded first research projects for grades 1–4*. Dayton, OH: Pieces of Learning.
Using picture books, this 48-page book provides ideas for beginning research projects in the primary grades.

Polette, N. (1984). *The research book for gifted programs, K–8*. Dayton, OH: Pieces of Learning.
This 176-page book provides over 150 projects for primary, middle, and upper grades. Critical thinking skills are stressed.

Polette, N. (1991). *Research without copying for grades 3–6*. Dayton, OH: Pieces of Learning.
   This 48-page book describes practical approaches for reporting on topics in diverse ways. Different types of research are illustrated along with models.

Renzulli, J. S., & Reis, S. M. (1997). *The schoolwide enrichment model: A how-to guide for educational excellence*. Mansfield Center, CT: Creative Learning Press.
This resource book includes a collection of useful instruments, check lists, charts, taxonomies, assessment tools, forms, and planning guides to organize, implement, maintain, and evaluate different aspects of the SEM, K–12.

Wishau, J. (1985). *Investigator*. San Luis Obispo, CA: Dandy Lion.
This step-by-step guide for students in grades 4–7 includes activities in completing and presenting an in-depth research project. Specific information is provided for using the library, selecting a

research topic, writing a business letter, writing a biography, conducting an interview, taking a survey, and making a speech.

Woolley, S. (1992). *Writing winning reports.* San Luis Obispo, CA: Dandy Lion.
This set of guides for students in grades 4–7 includes instructions about how to write reports on specific topics such as animals, planets, countries, and explorers. Point breakdowns for grading are also included.

Web Sites

These web sites will provide teachers and students with information about independent study topics.

Art and Art History—http://humanites.ucsb.edu/shuttle/art.html
A major link to museums and galleries all over the world. It provides resources regarding artists and their work, art theory, art studios, auctions, cartography, design, clip-art, and teaching resources.

English Literature—http://humanites.ucsb.edu/shuttle/english.html
This collection of links helps you find literature resources by time period and genre. It includes references to drama and theater, fiction, poetry, creative writing, theory, cultural studies, and general humanities resources.

Human Languages—http://www.june29.com/HLP
This page is a catalog of language-related Internet resources. You may find online language lessons, translating dictionaries, native literature, translation services, software, language schools, or language information.

Kid's Web—http://www.npac.syr.edu/textbook/kidsweb
A subset of the Web that is simple to navigate and contains information at the K–12 level. Categories include the arts, sciences, social studies, miscellaneous, and other digital libraries.

Math Forum—http://forum.swarthmore.edu
This forum contains math resources by subject. Broad topics include numbers, chaos, cellular automata, combinatorics, fractals,

statistics, and topology. When exploring "numbers," you will find Archimedes' constant, Devlin's angle, Pi, favorite mathematical constants, and many other interesting topics that will link to other sites.

Science Gems—http://www-sci.lib.uci.edu
Great science discoveries are included among the 3,100 science links at this page. ExtraSolar planets, genome mapping, genetic testing, global ecosystem, and top quark may become interesting topics for students interested in science.

Social Studies & History—http://www.execpc.com/~dboals/boals.html
The major purpose of this site is to encourage the use of the Internet as a tool for learning and teaching and to help teachers locate and use resources. A wide selection of topics are included under the general headings of archaeology, genealogy, humanities, economics, history, government, research, and critical thinking.

Virtual Museum Library—http://www.comlab.ox.ac.uk/archive/other/museums/world.html
This site provides a comprehensive directory of online museums and museum-related resources. Museums are organized by country and by exhibitions. The USA link also lists the 57 "top museum" web sites.

Yahoo!—http://www.yahoo.com
You may search for specific topics using this page or use the listed resources to help you find information. Listed resources relate to arts and humanities, business and economy, computers and Internet, education, entertainment, government, health, news and media, recreation and sports, reference, regional, science, social science, and culture.

Yahooligans!—http://www.yahooligans.com
A search engine designed especially for elementary children. Sites include around the world, art and entertainment, computers and games, school bell, science and nature, and sports and recreation.

References

Betts, G. T. (1985). *The autonomous learner model for gifted and talented.* Greeley, CO: ALPS Publications.

Betts, G. T., & Kercher, J. K. (1999). *The autonomous learner model: Optimizing ability.* Greeley, CO: ALPS Publications.

Clark, B. (1997). *Growing up gifted: Developing the potential of children at home and at school* (5th ed.). Columbus, OH: Merrill.

Colangelo, N., & Davis, G. A. (1991). *Handbook of gifted education.* Needham Heights, MA: Allyn & Bacon.

Dallas Independent School District. (1977). *Up periscope! Research activities for the academically talented student.* Dallas, TX: Author.

Davis, G. A., & Rimm, S. B. (1998). *Education of the gifted and talented* (4th ed.). Needham Heights, MA: Allyn & Bacon.

Delcourt, M. A. B. (1993). Creative productivity among secondary school students: Combining energy, interest, and imagination. *Gifted Child Quarterly, 37,* 23–31.

Doherty, E. J., & Evans, L. C. (1980). *Self-starter kit for independent study.* Austin, TX: Special Education Associates.

Dunn, R., & Griggs, S. (1985). Teaching and counseling gifted students with their learning style preferences: Two case studies. *G/C/T, 14,* 40–43.

Feldhusen, J. F. (1983). The Purdue creative thinking program. In I. S. Sato (Ed.), *Creativity Research and Educational Planning.* Los Angeles, CA: Leadership Training Institute for the Gifted and Talented, 41–46.

Feldhusen, J. F. (1995). Talent development: The new direction in gifted education. *Roeper Review, 18,* 92.

Feldhusen, J. F., & Kolloff, P. B. (1986). The Purdue three-stage enrichment model for gifted education at the elementary level. In J. S. Renzulli (Ed.), *Systems and models for developing programs for the gifted and talented.* Mansfield Center, CT: Creative Learning Press.

Feldhusen, J. F., VanTassel-Baska, J., & Seeley, K. R. (1989). *Excellence in education of the gifted.* Denver: Love.

Gallagher, J. J., & Gallagher, S. A. (1994). *Teaching the gifted child* (4th ed.). Boston: Allyn & Bacon.

Gourley, T. J., & Micklus, C. S. (1982). *Problems! Problems! Problems!* Glassboro, NJ: Creative Competitions.

Hanks, K., Belliston, L., & Edwards, D. (1977). *Design yourself.* Los Altos, CA: William Kaufmann.

Harnadek, A. (1976). *Basic thinking skills: Critical thinking.* Pacific Grove, CA: Midwest Publications.

Hébert, T. P. (1993). Reflections at graduation: The long-term impact of elementary school experiences in creative productivity. *Roeper Review, 16*, 22–28.

Issac, S., & Michael, W. (1980). *Handbook in research and evaluation.* San Diego, CA: EdITS Publishing

Johnsen, S. K., & Johnson, K. (1986a). *Independent study program.* Waco, TX: Prufrock Press.

Johnsen, S. K., & Johnson, K. (1986b). *Independent study program student booklet.* Waco, TX: Prufrock Press.

Kaplan, S., Madsen, S., & Gould, B. (1976). *The big book of independent study.* Santa Monica, CA: Goodyear.

Kitano, M., & Kirby, D. F. (1986). *Gifted education: A comprehensive view.* Boston: Little Brown.

Olenchak, F. R., & Renzulli, J. S. (1989). The effectiveness of the school-wide enrichment model on selected aspects of elementary school change. *Gifted Child Quarterly, 33*, 36–46.

Parker, J. P. (1989). *Instructional strategies for teaching the gifted.* Boston: Allyn & Bacon.

Renzulli, J. S. (1977a). *The enrichment triad model: A guide for developing defensible programs for the gifted and talented.* Mansfield Center, CT: Creative Learning Press.

Renzulli, J. S. (1977b). *The Interest-A-Lyzer.* Mansfield Center, CT: Creative Learning Press.

Renzulli, J. S. (1979). The enrichment triad model: A guide for developing defensible programs for the gifted and talented. In J. C. Gowan, J. Khatena, & E. P. Torrance (Eds.), *Educating the ablest: A book of readings on the education of gifted children* (pp. 11–127). Itasca, IL: Peacock.

Renzulli, J. S., & Callahan, C. (1973). *New directions in creativity: Mark 3.* Mansfield Center, CT: Creative Learning Press.

Renzulli, J. S., & Gable, R. K. (1976). A factorial study of the attitudes of gifted students toward independent study. *The Gifted Child Quarterly, 20*, 91–99.

Renzulli, J. S., & Reis, S. M. (1991). The schoolwide enrichment model: A comprehensive plan for the development of creative productivity. In N. Colangelo & G. A. Davis (Eds.), *Handbook of gifted education* (pp. 111–141). Needham Heights, MA: Allyn & Bacon.

Renzulli, J. S., & Reis, S. M. (1997). *The schoolwide enrichment model: A how-to guide for educational excellence* (2nd ed.). Mansfield Center, CT: Creative Learning Press.

Stanish, B. (1977). *Sunflowering.* Carthage, IL: Good Apple.

Stanish, B. (1981). *Hippogriff feathers.* Carthage, IL: Good Apple.

Stanish, B., & Eberle, B. (1996). *CPS for kids.* Waco, TX: Prufrock Press.

Starko, A. J. (1988). Effects of the revolving door identification model on creative productivity and self-efficacy. *Gifted Child Quarterly, 32,* 291–297.

Stewart, E. D. (1981). Learning styles among gifted/talented students: Instructional techniques preferences. *Exceptional Children, 48,* 134–138.

Swassing, R. H. (1985). *Teaching gifted children and adolescents.* Columbus, OH: Merrill.

Treffinger, D. (1975). Teaching for self-directed learning: A priority for the gifted and talented, *Gifted Child Quarterly, 19,* 46–49.

Treffinger, D. (1986). Fostering effective, independent learning through individualized programming. In J. S. Renzulli (Ed.), *Systems and models for developing programs for the gifted and talented* (pp. 429–460). Mansfield Center, CT: Creative Learning Press.

Zimmerman, B. J., & Martinez-Pons, M. (1990). Student differences in self-regulated learning: Relating grade, sex, and giftedness to self-efficacy and strategy use. *Journal of Educational Psychology, 82* (1), 51–59.

CHAPTER 15

Extending Learning Through Mentorships

CHERYL PERILLOUX MILAM
Jefferson Parish Public School System,
Harvey, LA

Mentorships offer exciting opportunities to extend learning for students of any age. Some students may explore areas of interest in-depth with adults who share those same interests. Mentorships can offer expertise, experience, and resources that may be beyond the capabilities of the school setting. Some students might explore careers at an in-depth level to gain valuable knowledge, skills, and insight which will enable them to make informed decisions about their future careers, while still others may be paired with caring adult role models to aid in appropriate social/emotional development.

The value of mentorship programs for gifted students has been well documented (Beck, 1989; Beecher, 1995; Betts, 1986; Clasen & Clasen, 1997; Cox , Daniel, & Boston, 1985; Kaufmann, Harrel, Milam, Woolverton, & Miller, 1986; Reilly, 1992; Torrance, 1984), and is frequently incorporated into programs for gifted students throughout the country (Comer, 1989). Mentorship programs can provide rich learning experiences and resources beyond those that the school alone is able to provide.

Through collaborative efforts between the school and the community, mentors can assist their young protégés in building on their skills, knowledge, and interests to remove the barriers to advanced learning that schools unwittingly and ironically create. Tannenbaum (1983) asserted that school is actually a restrictive environment for gifted students who have a wide range of abilities and interests. If we are to successfully prepare gifted students to fulfill their roles as leaders in the global society of the 21st Century, then we must alter our image of education from that which occurs only within the four walls of the classroom directed by a teacher, to a vision of that which includes experiences in the community led by other significant adults, as well as the students themselves.

Defining Mentorship

A mentor is defined in the *New Webster's Encyclopedic Dictionary* (Thatcher, 1969) as a wise or faithful advisor or monitor. The word is derived from Homer's *Odyssey* (Eliot, 1937): Mentor, Ulysses' trusted friend and advisor, became the guardian and teacher of his son, Telemachus. Thus, the term *mentorship* has evolved to describe the relationship between those who have guarded, guided, and taught young people in a one-on-one learning experience. There are other terms in the literature that are often used interchangeably (Clark, 1988; Cox & Daniel, 1983) with mentorship, such as *internship* and *apprenticeship*. However, internship implies that classroom preparation has been completed and formal experiential training has begun, such as the case of a medical intern. Apprenticeship suggests that classroom preparation is limited in scope and the majority of preparation occurs in the field under the watchful eye of a master, such as a plumber's apprentice. Both terms suggest a systematic, formal training process at a specified point in time as preparation for a specific career and usually include a salary. However, a mentorship can occur at any time during a person's schooling or career. Mentorships may be formal in the sense that there is an on-going program to which students apply, may even receive high school credit, and are matched with an appropriate mentor. Mentorships may also be informal in that they are arranged, as needed, on an individual basis for students.

Benefits of Mentorships

From the observations of this writer and feedback from the various stakeholders, it can be concluded that there is much satisfaction to be derived by students and mentors in any mentorship experience. Students often gain new knowledge and skills, develop close relationships with caring adults, and gain self-confidence and a greater sense of well-being. Mentors frequently enjoy sharing their interests and expertise with bright young people, gain a healthy respect for the knowledge and abilities of their mentees, and develop long-term friendships with the students. In addition, the school benefits when mentors develop respect for the students and their schools, when students have access to sophisticated resources and technology, and when mentors turn into long-term partners in the educational process. These benefits, as well as others for students, mentors, and the schools, are listed below.

Benefits to the Student

Students can benefit significantly from the mentoring experience in a variety of ways including
- advanced skills, concepts, and information far beyond the classroom experience;
- assistance in career planning;
- a realistic idea of their unique talents and abilities;
- enhancement of self-esteem and self-confidence;
- developing creativity;
- knowledge of current education and training requirements for specific careers;
- establishment of a long-term friendship;
- networking with knowledgeable and influential people;
- a role model to emulate; and
- real-life experiences beyond the limits of the school.

Benefits to the Mentors

In addition to the benefits derived by the student, there are benefits for the mentor, which include
- an opportunity to work with a highly motivated, gifted student who possesses special talents, interests, and abilities similar to his or her own;
- assistance with special projects;
- good public relations for the mentor and his or her employer;
- personal satisfaction of participating in the selection, training, and instruction of gifted young people;
- stimulation of new ideas;
- establishment of a long-term friendship; and
- future source of highly able part-time or full-time employees.

Benefits to the School

Students and mentors are not the only beneficiaries of the mentorship experience. The school also benefits in the following ways
- establishment of community/school partnerships;
- good public relations and recruiting tool;
- extension of the school's limited resources through access to advanced materials, equipment, and settings; and
- assurance that classroom instruction is aligned with current employment trends and needs.

Types, Times, and Locations of Mentorships

Mentorships may be designed for a variety of purposes and in different settings at all age-levels. Mentorships may be organized formally or informally for the development of a student's interest area, a career investigation, or a student's affective development. Mentorships may occur outside the school in the community—a business, an industrial setting, a professional setting—within the school building, or even in the classroom.

Mentorships typically fall into three categories

1. *Development of an interest area* as a way of expanding or enriching the curriculum to enable students with special skills, knowledge, and interests to work with others having expertise in those areas;
2. *Career investigation* provides opportunities for career exploration; and
3. *Affective development* mentorships focus on issues of self-esteem, values, and emotional support and seek to provide role models for students.

Naturally, these categories are not mutually exclusive, and benefits may be derived during the mentorship from all of these areas; however, the student's primary need for the mentorship will determine the focus of the experience.

In addition to types of mentorships, they may occur for students at any age or grade-level—elementary, middle/junior, or senior high school. They may be of short duration (i.e., a few weeks for assistance with a specific project) or for an extended period of time (i.e., several months for career exploration or in-depth study of a specific topic). Mentorship opportunities may be arranged during school hours, after school, on weekends, and during the summer. They may take place at the school, in the community, or via the Internet. There is no one "right way" to establish mentorships. The important issue for anyone working with gifted children is to determine how best to serve a student's needs within the context of the local school culture and that of the school district.

Determining Need for a Mentor

Teachers must first determine if a student has a need for a mentor. A second-grader who wants to learn more about the weather, who understands water vapor and relative humidity, and who wants to create clouds; a middle schooler who wants to recreate an authentic holiday celebration at a nearby historic home; a senior who cannot decide if she wants to be a lawyer or a nuclear physicist—these are students who could benefit from having a mentor. Reilly (1992) suggested that a mentor is needed when a student has exhausted the resources of his or her school or school district or when his or her pace of learning greatly exceeds that of instruction in the classroom. This is especially critical for disadvantaged children and those in rural areas where the home environment cannot compensate for what may be inadequate resources available at school. Mentorships are also of critical importance for females, as documented by Kaufmann et al. (1986), in equalizing future earning power.

Because mentors are generally busy professionals who are willing to spend some of their valuable time working with young people, it is essential that teachers make certain that students have demonstrated their readiness to work with a mentor and that the mentor is not asked to provide information, resources, or experiences that are readily available at the school or local library. Students who have already learned a great deal about a particular interest area and still have unanswered questions about the topic may be good candidates for working with a mentor. However, these students should also exhibit the ability to work independently for extended periods of time. It is important that students who are working with a mentor in the community be mature and responsible individuals. Not only is the mentor giving his or her valuable time to a young person, but the mentor may be responsible for the student's behavior and well-being while at the work site. This is particularly true of middle or high school students who may be working with a mentor unchaperoned by a parent or teacher. Intentionally or not, the mentorship student will be an ambassador of the school and, as such, will create an indelible image of the school and the school district in the community. Even though elementary-age students should always be accompanied by a parent or teacher if the mentorship occurs outside of school, they, too, create a lasting impression on the mentor and represent their schools. Therefore, careful selection of elementary students is just as important as it is for middle and high school students.

Informal Mentoring Arrangements

Teachers may seek a mentor for a student when his or her needs cannot be met by available school resources and when he or she has demonstrated readiness for working with a mentor as observed by the teacher. Reilly (1992) devised a useful flow chart (see Figure 1) to help teachers in the process of identifying which children are ready for a mentor.

MENTOR PROGRAM IDENTIFYING AND USING RESOURCES		**START AT THE LOWEST LEVEL THAT WILL SERVE THE STUDENT**
	11	Arrange for a mentorship or internship, a long-term commitment from both the student and the expert. Best done during school time or during the summer so the experience is not tacked on the the end of a full day.
	10	Arrange for the student to meet with experts at their workplace. Meeting can be a short conversation and/or an observation, or shadowing, experience.
	9	Ask a specialist to visit the classroom to offer enrichment to all students while directly serving the one with a more in-depth need. Some programs arrange for specialists to visit schools regularly over a span of time.
	8	Ask a specialist within your school district to assist the student. With minimal inquiry, you will be amazed at the range of expertise within your district.
	7	Ask someone within the student's school to help the student one-on-one.
	6	Brainstorm possible activities and resources that will allow the student to advance his learning as independently as possible. Consider public libraries or specialized libraries located within museums, wildlife centers, or even businesses; community education classes; zoos, art, history, and science museums or galleries and/or their classes; local theaters and public park systems and/or their classes; private lessons such as dance, musical instruments or voice, theater, foreign language, or computer instruction. Local colleges and universities, businesses, human service agencies, clubs, or organizations may also offer resources for students from preschool through high school. Television and videotaped programs may offer information, culture, or a perspective on an issue. They are also helpful to those who prefer alternatives to reading.
	5	Add a list of what the student has already accomplished to your student profile. Include courses, clubs, books read, related activities, independent research, and work experiences.
	4	Ask parents how they have helped the student to date. Inquire about their availability and willingness to assist the student in pursuing new opportunities. Can they provide transportation? Field trips? Supplies and appropriate equipment? Space? If parents can't, who might be able to provide these resources?
	3	Find out what the student's needs are. What does he want to learn? How does she think would be the best way for her to learn? How much time and energy can he devote? Develop a student profile.
	2	Who perceives the need for additional enrichment? The student? The parent? The teacher?
	1	Decide who should be involved in the process of identifying the students' needs and planning for further learning and development.

START HERE!
Don't move up a level until you have exhausted the potential of the current level. Remember this chart has been designed to give you ideas. There are additional levels and opportunities not shown!

Figure 1. Mentorship Flow Chart

Note. From *Mentorship: The Essential Guide for Schools and Businesses* (p. 15), by J. M. Reilly, 1992, Scottsdale, AZ: Gifted Psychology Press (formerly Ohio Psychology Press). Copyright 1992 by Gifted Psychology Press. Reprinted with permission.

The steps in this chart will be particularly useful in determining if a student needs help in pursuing a particular interest area or addressing affective needs. For exploring career options, informal arrangements can also be effective, but by the time the student reaches high school, a more formal, structured program may be required.

On behalf of individual students, a teacher may arrange for a student to spend some time with a mentor either at school or at the mentor's work site for observing, interviewing professionals, participating in activities, assisting with a student project, or just talking about common areas of interest. These kinds of activities may be provided for individual students as the need arises. However, several students may exhibit the need for mentoring over an extended period of time, and a more formal approach can help the teacher in management tasks. Although the following procedures are designed to assist in establishing a formal mentorship program, teachers can use selected items and sample forms to assist with informal arrangements as well. Whether formal or informal, the first step is to determine what student needs are present.

Establishing a Mentorship Program

Developing a Proposal

Once the teacher has determined that there is a need for a formal mentorship program, a proposal must be developed and approval must be obtained through appropriate channels. This may include seeking approval for mentorship as a high school course for credit when possible. Each school district and state will have different procedures for securing approval for new programs and courses; however, the components of a proposal will generally include goals and objectives, a content outline, and an evaluation plan. Sample 1 in the Appendix includes each of these three major proposal components. For those seeking approval from a principal or school district for an individual student to work in a more informal setting with a mentor on an interest-based project or for an affective need, a similar proposal may be helpful.

Parent Communications

Parents should be made aware of the nature of both the mentorship program and their responsibilities. These should be specified in the initial correspondence to parents and students (see Sample 2 in the Appendix of this chapter for a sample parent letter) and include (1) permission for the student to participate in a mentorship; (2) ability to provide or arrange transportation; (3) proof of insurance; and (4) willingness to complete an evaluation at the end of the student's field experience with the mentor. Parents should also be encouraged to provide on-going feedback during the mentorship, particularly if they note any problems or difficulties.

Gifted middle/junior high students and their parents should be informed of the opportunities in high school for these students, including the mentorship program, so that they can plan ahead to ensure that students will meet the selection criteria when they are juniors or seniors. It is also highly desirable to have strong career exploration opportunities available prior to the senior year, which include shadowing (a short-term observation of a professional in the community, usually for a day or part of a day). Betts and Kercher's (1998) Autonomous Learner Model provides an excellent structure for career exploration and introduces autonomous learning to gifted students in an elective course. Students can interview and shadow adults in the community, thus enabling them to begin narrowing the focus of their career interests.

The teacher serving as the mentorship coordinator should distribute letters to gifted students and their parents while students are planning their schedules for the next school year. These letters (see Sample 2 in Appendix) will inform the students and parents of the components of the mentorship program and the criteria for selection. They should also be informed if there are any fees associated with the program that would allow the coordinator to purchase up-to-date career and college reference materials, career interest inventories and aptitude tests, software, videos, and consumables such as computer disks. If the school or school district can provide these materials for students, then a fee may not be necessary. The important issue is that students must have access to current resources and information.

Likewise, parents should be kept informed when a student is working with a mentor for the purpose of developing a student's interest area or for the purpose of affective development. It is essential to communicate regularly with parents, whether the mentorship setting is formal or informal.

Selecting Students for Mentorship

The next task is to select students who have demonstrated a need for such an arrangement. Generally, those students who "understand their topics, work hard at learning independently, and strongly desire the mentoring opportunity" (Reilly, 1992, p. 12) are good candidates for working with a mentor. It is strongly suggested that students experience a prementoring period of preparation before actually working with a mentor. One very effective model program is the Jefferson Parish Public School System's Mentorship Connection (Schwartz, 1989). This program consists of two semesters of mentorship for high school credit for seniors in which all gifted students may elect Mentorship I (preparation for field work), but only those who meet rigorous criteria are permitted to schedule Mentorship II (field work with a mentor). During Mentorship I, the first phase of the program, students concentrate on self-awareness and focus their interests through intensive career investigation. This is especially critical for gifted students who may be good at and are interested in everything. Mentorship I also provides an opportunity for the teacher of the gifted, working closely with school counselors, to help students combine two or more passion areas into a single career goal that encompasses a student's multiple interests and abilities. It also affords opportunities for students who seem to be avidly focused on a specific career to ascertain if that choice is founded on realistic expectations.

Selecting students who will actually work with a mentor in the community at the workplace is not a matter to be taken lightly. Criteria developed and publicized with program descriptions will be very helpful in identifying those students who need a mentorship experience and who will be successful. The following list of criteria is used by the Mentorship Connection (Schwartz, 1989) in Jefferson Parish Public Schools for admission to Mentorship II, the field experience with a mentor

- 3.0 grade point average;
- two years of honors/AP English/Social Studies or Science/Math;
- successful completion of an Autonomous Learner Model (Betts & Kercher, 1998) elective or Individual Projects (Type III) (Renzulli, 1977a) electives;
- three letters of recommendation (counselor, classroom teacher, and gifted teacher) (see Sample 3 in Appendix);
- letter to principal stating why the student should be selected for Mentorship II;
- interview by the mentorship coordinator;
- successful completion of Mentorship I;
- parent permission;
- ability to provide transportation; and
- proof of insurance.

These criteria assist in identifying not only those students who are ready for the field experience, but also students who will represent the school well in the community. Again, it must be emphasized that it is very important to select students (for either formal or informal programs) who will be dependable, responsible, and motivated. Certainly, other students can benefit from a strong mentor/mentee relationship; however, they may require a great deal of supervision and a more structured environment. If resources are available to provide the structure and monitoring they will need, then additional students might be considered.

For younger students, teachers might determine need through careful observation of students' task commitment and the quality of their school products. Those students who exhibit a desire to go beyond the scope of assignments, an interest in delving deeper into specific topics, and an unquenchable curiosity about a certain area are certainly good candidates for working with a mentor to further develop their passion areas.

Self-Awareness

When students begin the initial preparation for field work, they complete several interest, aptitude, and personality inventories such as COPSystem Career Measurement (Educational and Industrial Testing Service, 1992), the Interest-a-Lyzer (Renzulli, 1977b), JOB-

O (CPKE Career Materials, 1983), Major-Minor Finder (CPKE Career Materials, 1976), and Choices (ISM Careerware, 1998). The mentorship coordinator conducts individual and group meetings with students to discuss the results of these tests and inventories in the context of their grades, achievement test scores, ACT/SAT scores, high school courses, and community and extracurricular activities. Students use this information to narrow their focus to one or more career fields for intensive investigation. They begin with library research using such tools as *The Encyclopedia of Careers and Vocational Guidance* (J. G. Ferguson, 1997), *Occupational Outlook Handbook* (U.S. Department of Labor, 1998), and *The Dictionary of Occupational Titles* (U.S. Department of Labor, 1991). The computer program *Choices* (IMS Careerware, 1998), usually available to students through the school counselors, and the Internet are additional sources of good information. Guest speakers and interviews with several professionals yield more information about job descriptions, salary ranges, working conditions, education requirements, lifestyles, advantages and disadvantages of careers, and the job outlook.

Elementary and middle school students should also be prepared for a mentorship experience through activities that create self-awareness. These students should be made aware of their particular academic and intellectual aptitudes. This can be accomplished through the careful examination of a student's standardized test scores, classroom performances, and products and activities both within and outside of the school. It is helpful for students of any age to have accurate information about their abilities and to develop a healthy self-concept of their strengths and weaknesses. This will allow students to recognize that everyone has strengths and weaknesses, thereby combating the tendency many gifted children have toward perfectionism.

College and Scholarship Searches

Building on this intensive career investigation, students can explore postsecondary and scholarship opportunities that coincide with their career interests and abilities. The mentorship coordinator may assist students in using up-to-date resources such as *Peterson's Guide to Four-Year Colleges* (Peterson's Guides, 1999), *The College Blue Book* (MacMillan Library References, 1998), *The College Handbook*

(College Entrance Examination Board, 1998), *Career Choices: A Guide for Teens and Young Adults* (Bingham & Stryker, 1997), *The Scholarship Book* (Cassidy, 1999), and *America's Best Colleges* (Zuckerman, 1995). The coordinator or school guidance counselor also can help students explore college and scholarship opportunities via computer software or the Internet. Colleges and universities have produced informative videos and have established web sites to provide information to prospective students. Additionally, local and regional college fairs provide excellent opportunities for students to gather information to help in the decision-making process.

Students should write letters to colleges or postsecondary institutions, using a computer program, to request information, applications, and video previews. It is helpful for students to keep a log of their progress through the application process, either on paper or on a computer data base program, so they can keep track of where they are with respect to the various colleges to which they are applying. Students should be narrowing their searches to approximately five schools by the middle of the senior year. Additional attention should be given to writing application essays and preparing for college interviews. It is helpful if the mentorship coordinator leads the students in a discussion of application interviews and campus visits.

Individual Development

After this college and scholarship search, the mentorship teacher or coordinator may assist students in discovering their learning styles, improving communication skills, and developing good interpersonal skills. Together, the students and teacher set goals for individual development—include several of the following: writing resumes and cover letters to prospective mentors; learning word processing; acquiring interviewing techniques; brushing up on communication and research skills; mastering creative problem-solving strategies via creative and critical thinking processes; and using technology. These skills are taught through such strategies as role-playing, cooperative learning, a library scavenger hunt at a university library, and self-directed learning in individual or small group instructional settings.

Younger students also need to be aware of their personal strengths and weaknesses and should seek assistance in capitalizing on their strengths while improving their areas of weakness. The administration of any number of existing learning styles and interest inventories can aid the teacher in planning instructional activities to assist individual students in particular areas of need. For example, the teacher might have an elementary or middle school student practice his or her telephone skills or the social skill of making introductions through role-playing activities in the classroom. Good speaking and listening skills are essential for students of any age and should be an important part of a student's preparation to work with a mentor.

Teaching Social and Life Skills

Although social and life skills are not usually thought to be a necessary part of gifted education, preparation for a lunchtime appointment with a professional at an upscale restaurant can be intimidating for students who have not experienced anything but fast food restaurants. The mentorship coordinator should prepare students for such social and business encounters. Students need to practice everything from how to shake hands, to which utensils to use, to how to dress appropriately for the mentor's work site. This is just as necessary for high school students as it might be for elementary or middle school students.

Finding and Selecting Mentors

Finding good mentors is not an easy task. Sometimes, students already know someone, such as a relative or family friend. Other students find suitable mentors in their preliminary career explorations and intensive investigations through interviews. Sometimes, guest speakers volunteer to be mentors. The mentorship coordinator can locate additional prospects by using *The Community Talent Miner* (Jenkins-Friedman & Stewart, 1977) to survey the parents of the gifted students. Other opportunities may be available through friends and acquaintances of faculty members. Other gifted teachers in the district can sometimes provide leads. Excellent mentors can also be found through the yellow pages of the phone directory. Berger (1990) suggested that teachers use their own circle of friends and their contacts, parents of gifted students, local schools and universities, businesses and agencies, professional associations, local art groups, and organizations such as the American Association of Retired Persons.

It is important that there be a good rapport between the student and the mentor. Therefore, a great deal of care must be taken in selecting appropriate mentors. Davis and Rimm (1989) described the ideal mentor as one who possesses the following traits

- expertise in his or her specialized field,
- strong interest in teaching young people,
- enthusiasm and optimism,
- an "anticipation of tomorrow,"
- tact,
- flexibility,
- humor,
- tolerance,
- agility,
- creativity, and
- the ability to elicit higher levels of thinking and problem solving.

Similarly, Reis and Burns (1987) recommended that a mentor be knowledgeable, enthusiastic, able to communicate with students, and able to share his or her methodology and inquiry skills. All of these traits are those of any good teacher.

After initially contacting the prospective mentor through a cover letter explaining the program and its goals, the mentorship coordinator will, of course, want to interview prospective mentors with the student present so the teacher can judge whether or not the mentor is appropriate and if there seems to be good rapport between the student and mentor. During the interview, the teacher will discuss the program goals, expectations, responsibilities of each party, time requirements, scheduling, and evaluation. If the prospective mentor seems uncommunicative, uncomfortable, reluctant, or impatient, the search continues. If the student is uncomfortable with the prospective mentor, the search continues. However, most adults who are approached as prospective mentors are eager to serve as a mentor for a young person who shares his or her career interests. They welcome the opportunity to talk about their own experiences and share their expertise with students.

Preparing Mentors

A word of caution is necessary at this point. The students' safety and well-being are of primary importance. In addition to requiring evidence of insurance from the parent and assuring that the parent is responsible for transportation (although they may allow their high school-aged children to drive to the mentorship site), it is necessary to take reasonable precautions to ensure the student's safety at the workplace. This may even include a search for criminal records when feasible. Elementary-aged children should not be left without a parent or teacher at the mentorship site. Middle/junior high and high school students may be left alone at the workplace with a clear understanding among the mentor, the student, the parents, and the teacher of expected behavior, limitations of access to resources within the workplace, and areas that may be off-limits to the student. Additionally, mentors and students must be aware of inappropriate activities, however innocuous they may seem. For example, in his enthusiasm for the program and his mentee, a university history professor suggested that he and the female student could access a wealth of research material at his home. When the mentorship coordinator pointed out that that might suggest impropriety, the professor immediately apologized and explained that he had not considered that perspective. The student worked with this mentor at the university and had a wonderful experience as his mentee. Students should also be warned that any adult at the workplace whose actions or words make them uncomfortable should report this immediately to the parents and the mentorship coordinator, calling from the workplace if necessary. Students are also cautioned not to leave the workplace unless arrangements have been previously made and approved by the teacher and the parent. Although this writer has never experienced any inappropriate activities while coordinating a mentorship program, it is essential to take reasonable precautions to ensure the safety of the students.

Expectations and Responsibilities for Students, Parents, Mentors, and Teachers

If the mentorship experience is to be successful, the expectations and responsibilities for the students, parents, mentors, and the mentorship teacher must be clearly stated and understood.

As stated in *The Mentorship Connection* (Schwartz, 1989), student responsibilities include

- completing required assignments;
- attending regularly;
- making regular journal entries;
- displaying a cooperative attitude and willingness to learn;
- exhibiting honesty and courtesy;
- dressing appropriately;
- communicating any difficulties encountered at the mentorship site; and
- completing both formative and summative evaluations of the mentorship experience and a self-evaluation of performance.

Parent responsibilities include

- authorizing the student to participate;
- providing or arranging all transportation;
- providing evidence of medical or health insurance for the student;
- encouraging the student to fulfill his or her obligations;
- communicating any problems or difficulties to the mentorship teacher/coordinator; and
- completing an evaluation of the mentorship experience.

Mentor responsibilities include

- creating opportunities for mentor/student interaction;
- providing meaningful, hands-on experiences that contribute to the program's goals;
- assisting the student in developing a meaningful project of significance to both the student and the mentor;
- notifying the mentorship teacher/coordinator immediately if the student is injured or involved in an accident at the site;
- communicating any difficulties or problems with the student to the mentorship teacher/coordinator; and
- completing formative and summative evaluations of the student and, when appropriate, assigning a letter grade (when the mentorship is substituted for a regular academic course).

Mentorship teacher/coordinator responsibilities include

- training the student appropriately prior to mentorship placement;
- interviewing prospective mentors with students;
- facilitating the development of a meaningful project for the student at the mentor's workplace;

- monitoring student performance through regular site visits;
- assisting the student and the mentor in resolving any problems associated with the mentorship experience;
- planning an appropriate culminating activity for the purpose of sharing the student's experience with students, mentors, and parents;
- providing on-going feedback to the students, mentors, and parents; and
- completing an evaluation of the student and, when appropriate, assigning a final letter grade (Appendix, Sample 4).

It is helpful to conduct an orientation for mentors, students, and parents and to have a prepared packet of materials containing specific information regarding program goals and benefits, responsibilities, structuring of time, conversation starters, ideas for student participation, a checklist for preparing for the student's arrival, a time sheet, a project contract, and proof of insurance. It is best to conduct separate meetings for each of these groups so that participants may feel free to ask difficult questions and speak freely.

In a more informal arrangement, a packet of prepared materials may not be necessary; however, it is essential that the mentors, students, and parents have a clear understanding of the purpose of the arrangement, the expectations for all parties involved, the duration of the mentorship, and the logistics involved.

Planning the Field Experience

As noted previously, a mentor can meet with a student at a designated time and location at the school if it is not feasible for the student to work with his or her mentor at the workplace. However, the benefits to the student can increase greatly if the student is able to work with the professional at the work site. Prior to the start of the field experience, the mentorship coordinator should meet with the mentor and the student to review the goals of the mentoring experience, discuss the length and duration of the field experience, and decide upon the expectations, the activities, the possible projects, an attendance log, and an evaluation. It is important for both the student and the mentor to know what is expected and how the program will function.

For a mentorship as a high school course, the mentor will need to know if he or she is expected to play a role in grading the student's performance, projects, or both. He or she will also need to establish—with the student and under the approval of the teacher—a weekly schedule with the appropriate number of hours included. It is important at this point to note that the mentor must designate someone else at the site to supervise the student in the event that he or she is unexpectedly called away at a time when the student is scheduled to be there.

The mentorship coordinator should make subsequent visits to the work site to monitor the student's experience and determine if there are any problems that may have arisen. The teacher observes the student at the site and then meets with the student and the mentor to discuss the student's activities and to address any concerns or problems. It is important to follow up in this manner to avert potentially larger problems and to make certain that the student's activities and projects are appropriate.

One of the primary purposes for mentorship is to enlist professional assistance with a project for a student. This may be a project that evolves from a student's passion area or an extension of a classroom assignment. In the case of a mentorship as a high school course for career exploration, the project may be a requirement of the program and may be related to the ongoing work of the professional. In any case, projects will vary widely depending on the age and interests of the students and the mentors' areas of expertise. Generally, it is helpful for students to plan their projects and products around the framework of a Betts (1986) Autonomous Learner Model In-Depth Study or a Renzulli (1977a) Type III Management Plan. With the help of mentors, these kinds of management systems will allow students to set goals; plan activities; access materials, equipment, and resources; establish time lines; select criteria for evaluation; plan creative products; and share what they have learned and produced with an appropriate audience.

Mentorship students have produced some incredible projects. For instance, a high school student co-authored a journal article that was published in a national medical journal. Another student produced computer-generated graphics for a local television station's evening weather broadcast. One young female student assisted a veterinarian in surgery, and another created a year-long program of wellness activities for a senior citizens' group at a local mall. Another young man networked all the computers in the offices of an engineering firm. These are just a few examples of the kinds of projects or products that students might accomplish through an effective mentorship program. Likewise, elementary and middle school students gain valuable knowledge and skills and produce creative products far in advance of grade-level expectations and beyond the scope of what the classroom teacher is able to include in the regular curriculum. This level of success, however, is dependent on good planning and a clear understanding of expectations among all those involved.

Evaluation and Feedback

All of the responsible parties in the mentoring relationship—student, parents, mentor, and teacher—have a role in the evaluation of the experience, and it is essential to design an effective and appropriate evaluation plan at the outset of the mentorship experience. For example, in a formal secondary mentorship program specifically designed for career exploration, questionnaires both at the midpoint and at the end of the field experience will provide invaluable information and feedback for everyone. The questionnaires should be short, only a page or two, and reflect the program goals in terms of student performance and program success. All parties should complete a formal assessment, including student self-assessment, to determine if the student's personal goals and those of the program were met. A sample questionnaire is included in Sample 4 in the Appendix. In addition, there should be continual communication among all stakeholders to ensure that the mentorship is successful and rewarding for everyone.

Results of the evaluation should be shared with all parties, as well. Students need a realistic assessment of their performance; parents need to know if their child was successful and if the program was successful; mentors need to know if the student and the program were successful; and, of course, the teacher needs to determine if the student performed well and if the program was a success. This information will also allow the mentorship coordinator to make any changes necessary to improve the program to assist future students and mentors in achieving their goals. Whether the mentorship is a formal program or an informal arrangement for individual students as needed, evaluation is a key component to success.

Public Relations

The evaluation of the mentorship program will also provide information that can be used to publicize the program to the community and demonstrate its effectiveness to the school administration and school district personnel. Quotes from parents, mentors, and students can be effective tools in building support for mentorships and providing extended learning experiences for the students. Quotes from students such as the following can be useful in publicizing the mentorship program:

> I am getting great experience in the field of my choice by learning skills of research, etc. I get an idea of what I like and don't like about the certain area that I'm working in and that helps me make up my mind about future plans. I really enjoy working with Nick; he gives good advice and is an all-round nice guy and some of the mystery is dispelled about what goes on behind a publication. (Milam & Schwartz, 1991)

> My mentor is a person who I can look up to. She is what I want to be one day. Watching her and learning her tricks of the trade will one day aid me in my job. I absolutely agree that all learning cannot come from a book. There are things that I have learned at my mentorship that you would never learn in a classroom. I feel that my mentorship has been nothing but positive. It has helped me become more decisive and has given me valuable insight in the field of marketing. (Milam & Schwartz, 1992, p. 12)

Likewise, comments from mentors and parents such as those that follow can be helpful.

> Ames and I, as did our entire office, enjoyed working with Lisa during this brief mentorship period. Lisa is truly gifted and we all feel confident that she will make great strides in architecture or whatever profession she so chooses. We hope to keep in close contact with her during her college years and hope she, in turn, will feel comfortable to always stay in touch with us. (Milam & Schwartz, 1991)

The program is excellent and merits attention from school officials. Thank you for giving our child the opportunity to expand her knowledge in this learning/work experience. (Milam & Schwartz, 1992, p. 13)

These kinds of comments, as well as program descriptions, should be included in publicity efforts like brochures and videos, which can be made available to local business groups, realtors, parent groups, and others. In addition, a product fair might be held at the end of the year in which students describe their activities and display their products. This might be held in conjunction with a mentor reception at which students, parents, and mentors have the opportunity to meet one another. Representatives of the local media can also be invited. These suggestions are appropriate for both formal and informal mentorships and for mentorships that are career explorations, extensions of specific interest areas, or affective development.

Another essential element of good public relations is having students write personal thank-you letters to their mentors and the schools send generic thank-you letters. These letters not only genuinely express the students' and the school's gratitude to the mentors for sharing their expertise and taking time from their schedules to assist young people but also create a positive climate for asking the mentors to assist other young people in the future.

Telementoring

Telementoring is an exciting new source for mentoring and is now available for students who find it difficult or impossible to meet in person with their mentors, including students in remote or rural areas, students without the means to provide transportation to mentorship sites, and students who wish to explore careers that are very unusual. The Internet can provide an effective and inexpensive way for a student to communicate with a caring adult and to establish a long-distance mentorship experience.

The National Science Foundation has a web site (http://www.edc.org/CCT/Telementoring) for young women that provides much valuable information for teachers, parents, and students who are searching for a telementor in science, engineering, and computing. The index included at the web site provides information about mentors, parents and family, teachers, partners, resources, and project information. Another web site is the Hewlett-Packard Telementor (http://www.tele-mentor.org/hp). This program offers telementoring services to students in grades K–12 in math, science, professional communication skills, and career education and planning. There are October and December application deadlines, however, and a maximum capacity of 3,000 students.

The Electronic Emissary (http://www.tapr.org/emissary) offers a mentor database, links to other resources, suggestions for successful tele-mentoring, and a manual for facilitating telementoring projects. Tele-mentor Resources (http://www.iearn.org/circles/mentors. html) offers information about telementoring and links to telementoring projects.

In addition, teachers and students can find more sources for mentorships by merely inputting the word "mentor" or "telementor-ing" into a search engine. These searches yield results such as web sites offering links to articles and resources in telementoring (http://www.2learn.ca/Projects/together/KWORDS/telemenw. html) and an arts mentor program (http://www.smc. edu).

Other possibilities may occur by simply searching the Internet by topic, seeing whose name appears, and then corresponding by e-mail. The teacher could also put a want ad on the message board of a topic area or go through an association bulletin board that sub-scribes to a particular server.

In any case, it is the teacher's responsibility to screen the men-tor and supervise the student's activities on the Internet, just as he or she would in setting up a face-to-face mentorship. The safety and well-being of the student is of paramount importance. Nevertheless, telementoring can provide the student with a rich learning environ-ment and inspire the student to take charge of his or her own learn-ing as he or she gathers information in a new and interesting way while interacting with an adult who may live on the other side of the globe.

Conclusion

The mentorship experience may be designed for career investi-gation, the development of a specific interest area, or the development of affective growth. It may be formal or informal, in or outside the school. Whatever the circumstances, there are elements or components of the mentorship that are common to all these types and settings. These common elements include

- developing a mentorship proposal;
- communicating fully and frequently with parents;
- selecting students who need and are ready to work with mentors;
- defining the specific purpose of the mentorship;
- preparing students for the mentorship both academically and socially;
- identifying and selecting appropriate mentors;
- preparing the mentors for their interaction with the students;
- specifying the expectations and responsibilities for students, parents, mentors, and teachers;
- planning the mentorship experience—whether in the field or in the school—with close attention to student safety;
- developing a plan for on-going feedback and evaluation—both formative and summative evaluation; and
- designing the public relations component of the mentorship experience.

With careful attention to all of these components in planning any type of mentorship experience, students, mentors, and schools will be richly rewarded.

Teacher Resources

Publications

Barron's Educational Series. (1995). *Barron's profiles of American Colleges.* Hauppauge, NY: Author.

Covey, S. (1989). *The 7 habits of highly effective people.* New York: Simon & Schuster.

Featherstone, B. D., & Reilly, J. M. (1990). *College comes sooner than you think! The essential planning guide for high school students and their parents.* (2nd ed.). Scottsdale, AZ: Gifted Psychology Press.

Nash, D., & Treffinger, D. (1993). *The mentor kit: A step-by-step guide to creating an effective mentor program in your school.* Waco, TX: Prufrock Press.

Reilly, J. (1992). *Mentorship: The essential guide for schools and business.* Scottsdale, AZ: Gifted Psychology Press.

Addresses

Below are listed several mentorship programs throughout the country that might be helpful in establishing a mentorship program, either formal or informal.

Academic Mentoring Program
Fayette County Public Schools
701 East Main St.
Lexington, KY 40502

The Dakota County Mentor Program
Intermediate District 917
1300 145th St. East
Rosemount, MN 55068

Executive Assistant Program
Dallas Independent School District
3700 Ross Ave.
Box 159
Dallas, TX 75204

Internship Program
Academic and Performing Arts Complex
1120 Riverside Dr.
Jackson, MS 39202

The Mentorship Academy Program:
A School-Community Partnership for Developing Talent
Blue Valley Schools
15020 Metcalf, Box 23901
Overland Park, KS 66223-0901

The Mentorship Connection
Jefferson Parish Public School System
501 Manhattan Blvd.
Harvey, LA 70058

UCONN Mentor Connection:
An Inquiry-Based Summer Program for Talented Teens
362 Fairfield Rd., U-7
Storrs, CT 06269-2007

Web Sites

Arts Mentor Program—http://www.smc.edu/programs/artsmentor
Santa Monica College's Mentor Program in the arts provides gifted
students in the fine and applied arts with one-on-one support training by professionals in their specialized fields.

Chemistry Telementoring—http://www.washington.edu/
The Chemistry Telementoring site offers a discussion group for students in high school and college and their teachers, whose interests
(avocation, coursework, or career) lie in the area of chemistry.

Hewlett Packard E-Mail Mentor Program—http.//mentor.external.
hp.com/
The HP Telementor Program allows HP professionals worldwide to
help students through teacher supervised projects, in the critical
areas of math, science, professional communication skills, and
career/education planning. The HP Telementor Program is man-
aged by the International Telementor Center at Colorado State
University.

References

Beck, L. (1989). Mentorships: Benefits and effects on career development. *Gifted Child Quarterly, 33,* 22–28.

Beecher, M. (1995). *Developing the gifts and talents of all students in the regular classroom.* Mansfield Center, CT: Creative Learning Press.

Berger, S. L. (1990). Mentor relationships and gifted learners. (Report No. EDO-EC-90–5). Council for Exceptional Children, Reston, VA: Clearinghouse on Handicapped and Gifted Children. (ERIC Document Reproduction Service No. ED321491)

Betts, G. T. (1986). *Autonomous learner model.* Greeley, CO: ALPS Publications.

Betts, G. T., & Kercher, J. (1998). *Autonomous learner model* (2nd ed.). Greeley, CO: ALPS Publications.

Bingham, M., & Stryker, S. (1997). *Career choices: A guide for teens and young adults.* Santa Barbara, CA: Academic Innovations.

Briggs, I. M., McCaulley, M. H., Quenk, N. L., & Hammer, A. L. (1998). *MBTI manual (A guide to the development and use of the Myers-Briggs Type Indicator).* New Jersey: Consulting Psychologists Press.

Cassidy, D. J. (1999). *The scholarship book 2000: The complete guide to private-sector scholarships, fellowships, grants, and loans for the undergraduate.* Paramus, NJ: Prentice-Hall.

Clark, B. (1988). *Growing up gifted* (3rd ed.). New York: Merrill.

Clasen, D. R., & Clasen, R. E. (1997). Mentoring: A time-honored option for education of the gifted and talented. In N. Colangelo & G. A. Davis (Eds.), *Handbook of Gifted Education,* (pp. 218–229). Boston, MA: Allyn & Bacon.

College Entrance Examination Board. (1998). *The college handbook.* New York: College Board Publications.

Comer, R. (1989). A mentorship program for gifted students. *The School Counselor, 36,* 224–228.

Cox, J., & Daniel, N. (1983, September/October). The role of the mentor. *G/C/T, 29,* 54–61.

Cox, J., Daniel, N., & Boston, B. O. (1985). *Educating able learners: Programs and promising practices.* Austin, TX: University of Texas Press.

CPKR Career Materials. (1976). *Major-minor finder.* Belmont, CA: Author.

CPKR Career Materials. (1983). *JOB-O.* Meadow Vista, CA: Author.

Davis, G. A. & Rimm, S. B. (1989). *Education of the gifted and talented* (2nd ed.). Englewood Cliffs, NJ: Prentice-Hall.

Educational and Industrial Testing Service. (1992). *COPSystem Career Measurement.* San Diego, CA: Author.

Eliot, C. W. (Ed.). (1937). *The odyssey of Homer.* New York: P. F. Collier & Son Corporation.

Ferguson, J. G. (1997). *Encyclopedia of careers and vocational guidance* (vols. 1–4). Chicago: Author.

Gelles-Cole, S. (Ed.). (1985). *Letitia Baldrige's complete guide to executive manners.* New York: Rawson Associates.

Gourman, J. (1996). *The Gourman report: A rating of undergraduate programs in American and international universities* (9th ed.). Los Angeles: National Educational Standards.

IMS Careerware. (1998). *Choices 1998* [Computer software]. Clayton, NY: Author.

Jenkins-Friedman, R., & Stewart, D. (1977). *The community talent miner: A survey for locating community resources.* Mansfield Center, CT: Creative Learning Press.

Kaufmann, F. A., Harrel, G., Milam, C., Woolverton, N., & Miller, J. (1986). The nature, role, and influence of mentors in the lives of gifted adults. *Journal of Counseling and Development, 64,* 576–578.

MacMillan Library References. (1998). *The college blue book.* (25th ed.). New York: Simon & Schuster MacMillan.

Milam, C. P., & Schwartz, B. (1991). [Program evaluation: The mentorship connection]. Unpublished raw data.

Milam, C. P., & Schwartz, B. (1992). The mentorship connection. *G/C/T, 15*(3), 9–13.

Peterson's Guides. (1999). *Peterson's four-year colleges 2000.* Princeton, NJ: Author.

Reilly, J. M. (1992). *Mentorship: The essential guide for schools and business.* Dayton, OH: Ohio Psychology Press.

Reis, S. M., & Burns, D. E. (1987). A schoolwide enrichment team invites you to read about methods for promoting community and faculty involvement in a gifted education program. *Gifted Child Today, 49*(2), 27–32.

Renzulli, J. S. (1977a). *The Enrichment Triad Model: A guide for developing defensible programs for the gifted and talented.* Mansfield Center, CT: Creative Learning Press.

Renzulli, J. S. (1977b). *The Interest-a-lyzer.* Mansfield Center, CT: Creative Learning Press.

Schwartz, E. (1989). *The mentorship connection: Mentorship for gifted high school students: Rationale overview handbook.* Kenner, LA: Kinkos Copies. Elizabeth Adrian Schwartz, #12 D'Arbonne Ct., Kenner, LA, 70065.

Tannenbaum, A. (1983). *Gifted children.* New York: Macmillan.

Thatcher, V. S. (Ed.). (1969). *The new Webster encyclopedic dictionary of the English language.* Chicago: Consolidated Book.

Torrance, E. P. (1984). *Mentor relationships: How they aid creative achievement, endure, change, and die.* Buffalo, NY: Bearly Limited.

U.S. Department of Labor. (1991). *Dictionary of occupational titles* (4th ed., Vols. 1–2). Washington, DC: U.S. Government Printing Office.

U.S. Department of Labor. (1998). *Occupational outlook handbook.* (1998–1999 ed.). Chicago: VGM Career Horizons, NTC/ Contemporary Publishing Group.

Zuckerman, M. B. (Ed.). (1995). *America's best colleges, 1995 college guide.* Washington, DC: U.S. News & World Report.

Appendix

Sample 1
Mentorship Program Proposal

Objectives

The student will be able to
1. learn about professions through the use of first-hand experiences (interviews, lectures, shadowing, etc.);
2. develop a realistic view of professions through the use of a personal diary about a professional area;
3. develop and explore concepts necessary for a foundation in a professional area;
4. acquire specific cognitive knowledge, technical skills, and creative problem-solving strategies related to the professional area.
5. probe the concepts and ideologies of professions;
6. achieve growth in communication through interviews, surveys, and diaries;
7. integrate talents, skills, limitations, and expectations through the use of a personal inventory as applied to the specific area of study;
8. build communication skills through discussion, debate, role-playing, and drama;
9. utilize experts for first-hand experience of professionals at different stages in their professional lives;
10. present the diversity of the particular area of study via biographies, films, experts;
11. become oriented to the different critical issues within a profession;
12. build a model of the ideal person in his or her profession while having access to professional and leadership role models;
13. achieve an attitude of open exploration before decision making;
14. gain experience in the professional area by spending time with the professional in his or her work milieu;

15. speculate on future trends and issues in various areas;
16. explore areas of high interest and opportunities in professions;
17. gain a viable picture of the education and training necessary for professions; and
18. explore scholarships, grants, etc., available to persons pursuing specific professions.

Course Outline

I. Research in professional area.
II. Review of educational preparation required.
III. Interviews with professionals in field.
IV. Shadowing experience with professional.
V. Work experience with professional.
VI. Identify critical issues and trends in the professional area.
VII. Investigation of scholarships, grants, and other opportunities as related to the professional field.

Measurement of Course Objectives

At the end of the course, the mentorship teacher/coordinator will complete a course evaluation survey with input from mentors, students, and parents and assign a letter grade based on fulfillment of course objectives.

Qualifications of Instructor

Certifications for academically gifted and secondary education.

Note. From *The Mentorship Connection: Mentorship for Gifted High School Students—Rationale Overview Handbook,* (Section C, p ii), by E. Schwartz, 1989, Kenner, LA: Kinkos Copies. Copyright 1989 by Elizabeth Adrian Schwartz #12 D'Arbonne Ct., Kenner, LA 70065. Reprinted with permission.

Sample 2

[School Letterhead]

[Date]

TO: Prospective Mentorship Students and Their Parents

RE: The Mentorship Program for Gifted Students

The gifted program at [name of school] is offering a two-phase, two-semester Mentorship Program to gifted juniors and seniors. Each semester of this elective course is offered for honors credit. Upon successful completion of each semester the student will receive a letter grade and Carnegie Unit.

The first semester of the Mentorship Program is open to any gifted junior or senior. Students will participate in activities that will help them select a college, obtain scholarship information, and prepare for a mentor and a career. Activities in this preparatory phase include discovering interests and aptitudes, surveying of the job market, writing resumes, practicing interview techniques, exploring college/career/scholarship opportunities, discovering learning styles, and sharpening research skills.

The second semester of the Mentorship Program is open only to those gifted seniors who meet very specific criteria. In this phase, students spend a minimum of three hours per week with a mentor and three hours per week with their mentorship teacher for a period of 10 weeks. During the time spent with the mentor, the student will act as an observer, an interviewer, and a practitioner. The time spent with the resource teacher will be used to discuss mentorship experiences, complete assignments, complete college/scholarship applications, and make college and career decisions.

In order to obtain the necessary resource materials to maintain a quality program, a $25 fee is necessary for all students in the first semester of the Mentorship Program. These materials will include consumable, commercially published tests and inventories, videos, films, and up-to-date reference books.

The following criteria will be used to determine acceptance into the second semester of the Mentorship Program. The student must

1. Be currently identified as gifted and an active participant in the gifted program.
2. Have enough credits to be classified as a second-semester junior.
3. Have a 3.0 grade point average.
4. Have successfully completed two years of high school honors courses in science and math and/or English and social studies.
5. Have expressed a strong interest in participating in the program.
6. Have exhibited task commitment and maturity as evidenced in past performance in the gifted academic courses and electives.
7. Be able to schedule mentorship as an elective at the times offered.

8. Provide transportation to and from the mentorship site.
9. Write a letter to the principal expressing reasons for wanting to participate in the second semester of the Mentorship Program.
10. Submit three recommendation forms—one from a counselor, one from a core subject area teacher, and one from a gifted program teacher.
11. Be interviewed by a committee of gifted program teachers.

From the applicants for the second semester of the Mentorship Program, a screening committee of gifted program teachers will select those students whose applications and recommendations indicate a focused interest, motivation, ability to actively participate in a learning experience, and whose past record indicates task commitment and maturity.

If you have any questions or comments, please call the Gifted Department at [school name] between 8:00 a.m. and 2:00 p.m. [phone number].

Sincerely yours,

[mentorship teacher/coordinator's name]
Director, Mentorship Program

Detach and Return to the Gifted Department

If my child qualifies for Phase II of the Mentorship Program, I agree to the following and give my permission for my child to participate.

1. I will provide or arrange transportation to and from the mentorship site.
2. I will provide proof of medical/health insurance.
3. I will complete an evaluation of the Mentorship Program at the conclusion of Phase II.

_____   _____
        (student's name)   (parent's/guardian's signature)

                                             Date: _____

Note. From *The Mentorship Connection: Mentorship for Gifted High School Students—Rationale Overview Handbook,* (Section B, pp. 1–6), by E. Schwartz, 1989, Kenner, LA: Kinkos Copies. Copyright 1989 by Elizabeth Adrian Schwartz #12 D'Arbonne Ct., Kenner, LA 70065. Reprinted with permission.

Sample 3

TO: [name of teacher or counselor]

FROM: [name of mentorship teacher/coordinator]

RE: Prospective Mentorship II Students

Please complete the following appraisal of [student's name] who has applied for Mentorship II. Thank you for your assistance.

	Low	Average	High
Maturity			
Responsibility			
Task commitment			
Self-motivation			
Self-confidence			
Initiative			
Communication skills			
Interpersonal skills			

I DO _____/ I DO NOT _____ recommend the above student for Mentorship II.

Comments:

_____ GPA (counselor only)   _____
                                  (teacher's/counselor's signature)

Please return this form to [mentorship teacher's name] in room _____ or to his or her mailbox in the office as soon as possible. Thank you for your assistance.

Note. From *Unpublished Manuscript* for The Mentorship Connection, (p. 1), by C. P. Milam & A. V. Kent, 1990, Harvey, LA: Jefferson Parish Public Schools. Reprinted with permission from C. P. Milam.

Sample 4
Mentor Evaluation

Mentor's Name: _____

Student's Name: _____

Please circle the appropriate number and make additional comments:

SD= Strongly Disagree
D = Disagree
A = Agree
SA = Strongly Agree

		SD	D	A	SA
1.	The student was adequately prepared for his/her experience.	1	2	3	4
2.	Appropriate channels were used to contact prospective mentors.	1	2	3	4
3.	As a mentor, I was given an adequate explanation of the program.	1	2	3	4
4.	The mentor orientation packet was helpful.	1	2	3	4
5.	The method of student/mentor selection was appropriate.	1	2	3	4
6.	Time lines were realistic.	1	2	3	4
7.	The program demands were realistic.	1	2	3	4
8.	Upon entry into this mentorship, the student demonstrated adequate knowledge of the chosen career focus.	1	2	3	4
9.	The student displayed a positive attitude and enthusiasm toward the mentorship experience.	1	2	3	4
10.	The student displayed sound work habits such as appropriate appearance, dependability, promptness, and maturity.	1	2	3	4
11.	The student displayed knowledge of his/her interests, aptitudes, and ability.	1	2	3	4
12.	The student demonstrated knowledge of life style required by the career field, necessary personal characteristics, and responsibilities that accompany work in this field.	1	2	3	4
13.	My participation in this experience did not cause any significant inconvenience in the performance of my job.	1	2	3	4

Sample 4
Mentor Evaluation Continued

14. This student, in my opinion, is appropriately identified as gifted.   1   2   3   4

15. The student's project was well organized in terms of unity, development, and clarity.   1   2   3   4

16. The project demonstrated creativity in terms of either its fluency of ideas, originality, imaginative style, or theme.   1   2   3   4

17. The project demonstrated the use of a variety of resources.   1   2   3   4

18. The project demonstrated an advanced level of knowledge concerning the chosen subject matter.   1   2   3   4

19. The project demonstrated a possible practical application(s) for my organization.   1   2   3   4

20. I am interested in participating in the mentorship program again.   1   2   3   4

Please comment in the space below about any other observations you have made about the project itself and/or student productivity.

Using the following grading scale, please assign a letter grade to the student's overall performance and give reason for the grade.

$$
\begin{array}{lll}
95\text{--}100 & = & A \\
88\text{--}94 & = & B \\
78\text{--}87 & = & C \\
70\text{--}77 & = & D \\
69/\text{below} & = & F
\end{array}
$$

Grade _____

Reasons:

Thank you for participating.
Sincerely,
[mentorship teacher/coordinator]

Note. From *The Mentorship Connection: Mentorship for Gifted High School Students—Rationale Overview Handbook,* (Appendix, p. 15b.), by E. Schwartz, 1989, Kenner, LA: Kinkos Copies. Copyright 1989 by Elizabeth Adrian Schwartz #12 D'Arbonne Ct., Kenner, LA 70065. Reprinted with permission.

CHAPTER 16

Developing the Leadership Potential of Gifted Students

SUZANNE M. BEAN
Mississippi University for Women

FRANCES A. KARNES
The University of Southern Mississippi

A group of preschoolers negotiating the use of playground equipment . . . elementary-age students working on group projects . . . teenagers planning special events for the school . . .

These are examples of the experiences through which leadership potential is developed. Although the concept of *leadership* is often misunderstood and the process for developing good leaders is still debated, it is resolved that leadership skills can be developed, and more intentional endeavors must be made to cultivate bright, young leaders.

Of all the types of giftedness set forth in the various state and federal definitions, leadership is one of the most neglected areas. A recent (Javits, 1988) federal definition of gifted and talented students states

> The term "gifted and talented students" means children and youth who give evidence of high performance capabil-

ity in such areas as intellectual, creative, artistic, or leadership capacity, or in specific academic fields; and who require services or activities not ordinarily provided by the schools in order to develop such capabilities fully. (P.L.100–297, Sec. 4103. Definitions)

While most states accept this federal definition in their legislation and in their written program plans, the majority of special programs focus primarily on intellectual, academic, creative, and artistic capabilities. There are too few in-school programs designed for students with strong leadership potential that specifically focus on leadership development. Furthermore, every year millions of dollars are spent for leadership training in business and industry, the military, government, religion, and sports, but few dollars are spent for leadership education and development of children and youth in elementary and secondary schools.

The process of becoming a leader holds many valuable lessons in life. Interpersonal skills are necessary in every aspect of human endeavor—at home, school, work, and in the social arena. As one's leadership potential is nurtured, the ability to relate to others improves, and skills in communication, conflict resolution, decision making, and goal achievement are refined. While initiative and responsibility increase, self-concept and personal fulfillment flourish. Basic human needs of belonging, accomplishment, and reaching one's potential can be realized through the development of leadership. Leadership skills can make the difference between talents being fully utilized or unfulfilled.

The personal rewards for developing one's leadership potential are many, but the societal benefits of effective leaders may be even more significant. The call for more effective leaders must not be ignored. Perhaps at no other time in history has there been a greater challenge for positive human interaction and ethical leadership. These goals are critical to the progress of humankind.

Definitions

The word *leadership* means different things to different people. Most of the disagreement stems from the fact that leadership is a complex phenomenon involving the leader, the followers, and the situation. Some researchers have focused on the personality, physical traits, or behaviors of the leader; others have addressed the relationships between leaders and followers; still others have studied how aspects of the situation affect leaders' actions. According to Burns (1978), leadership is one of the most observed and least understood phenomena on Earth. It involves a range of experiences in the life of a person, which suggests the changing nature of this elusive concept.

Leadership has been defined in the following ways:

1. The directing and coordinating of the work of group members (Fiedler, 1967);

2. Leadership over human beings is exercised when persons with certain motives and purposes mobilize, in competition or in conflict with others, institutional, political, psychological, and other resources so as to arouse, engage, and satisfy the motives of followers (Burns, 1978);

3. The process of persuasion or example by which an individual (or leadership team) includes a group to pursue objectives held by the leader or shared by the leader and his or her followers (Gardner, 1990);

4. An interpersonal relation in which others comply because they want to, not because they have to (Hogan, Curphy, & Hogan, 1994); and

5. An activity or set of activities, observable to others, that occurs in a group, organization, or institution involving a leader and followers who willingly subscribe to common purposes and work together to achieve them (Clark & Clark, 1994).

Although the definitions differ in many ways, it is important to remember that there is no single *correct* definition. This variety points to the multitude of factors that affect leadership and the different perspectives from which to view it.

Unique parallels exist between the concepts of giftedness and leadership. Definitions in both areas are expanding, becoming more inclusive, and considering cultural and situational factors. Identification and assessment procedures for both giftedness and leadership have also developed to reflect the complexity and multidimensionality of the concepts.

Leadership Theories

One of the earliest leadership theories was the "Great Man" theory, which maintained that leaders were distinguishable from followers by fixed, inborn traits that were applicable across all situations (Galton, 1869). Research focused on identifying these abilities and traits believed to separate leaders from followers; but, for the most part, these efforts failed to find conclusive evidence that leaders and followers were truly different (Stogdill, 1974).

Since the Great Man theory, research efforts have fluctuated with respect to issues like the behavior of leaders, the modifications they make based on the followers and the situation, and the characteristics and effects of transactional and transformational leaders. "Situational Leadership" theory inspired further analysis of the relationship among leader behaviors, followers' satisfaction and performance, and the situation of the leadership experiences (Blake & Mouton, 1985; Hersey & Blanchard, 1982). Stogdill (1974) and Bass (1981) supported the notion that leadership effectiveness is highly dependent on the relationship between leader characteristics and the demands of specific situations. The past decade has seen an interest in "Transactional and Transformational" leadership theories (Bennis & Nanus, 1985; Hollander & Offerman, 1990; Yammarino & Bass, 1990). The basic difference in these two models is in the process by which the leader is thought to motivate followers. Transactional leaders motivate through contingency rewards and negative feedback, and transformational leaders inspire performance beyond ordinary expectations as they create a sense of mission and encourage new ways of thinking.

Current Research on Leadership and Youth

Although the majority of research in the area of leadership addresses adults, studies focusing on leadership and youth are increasing. Studies pertaining to leadership and gender in youth indicate some differences. Nemerowicz and Rosi (1995) found that both fourth- and fifth-grade boys and girls prefer to depict their own gender as the leader; however, boys did so 95% of the time as compared to 53% for girls. In a study of students in grades 6 through 11, Karnes and D'Ilio (1989, 1990) found that the girls in both groups perceived most leadership roles to be suitable for either gender, whereas the boys held more traditional stereotypical views. Karnes and D'Ilio (1989) also found significant differences favoring girls on emotional stability, dominance, and the secondary factor of independence using the High School Personality Questionnaire (HSPQ) with gifted students in grades 6 through 11.

Studies have shown that psychological type can be a good predictor of leadership style and behavior (Barr & Barr, 1989; Campbell & Velsor, 1985; Lawrence, 1982; McCaulley & Staff of the Center for Applications of Psychological Type, 1990; Myers & Myers, 1980). Alvino (1989) reviewed data collected using the Myers-Briggs Type Indicator (MBTI) with gifted students and young adults. He found that high school student leaders who were not necessarily identified as gifted fell predominantly into a group described as analytical managers of facts and details, practical organizers, imaginative harmonizers of people, and warmly enthusiastic planners of change. Leaders in student government activities fell predominantly into a group described as independent, enthusiastic, intuitive, aggressive, and innovative.

Several studies indicated that participation in extracurricular/community activities provides unique opportunities for students to belong and contribute to a group, as well as to experience success (Bass, 1981; Bennett, 1986; McNamara, Haensly, Lupkowski, & Edlind, 1985; Stogdill, 1974). Using the Leadership Strengths Indicator (Ellis, 1990) with disadvantaged youth ages 10 to 15, Riley and Karnes (1994a) found that the students' scores fell within the normal range. A significant difference favoring boys was found in the scale "High Level Participator in Group Activities." Slight nonsignificant differences were found between the scales "Enjoys Group Activities," "Journalistic," and "Courageous." The same measure was administered to intellectually gifted students in grades 4 through 6, and significant differences were found favoring girls on two scales, "Sympathetic" and "Conscientious," and the total score (Riley & Karnes, 1994b). Intellectually gifted students in grades 6 through 12 in suburban and rural settings also were administered the same instrument, and no significant differences were found (Abel & Karnes, 1993). These studies emphasized the importance of involvement in extracurricular activities and group work toward the development of leadership potential.

Leadership and Giftedness

Although gifted students are often deemed as being the future leaders at local, state, national, and international levels, little has been or is being undertaken to identify young leaders and help them develop their leadership potential. Foster and Silverman (1988) stated that schools must go beyond educating the gifted for followship and must become involved in understanding the fundamentals of leadership and incorporating it into the school curriculum. Lindsay (1988) said that leadership is the most controversial and neglected area in gifted education. Florey and Dorf (1986) stated that few gifted programs incorporate leadership into the curriculum for the gifted.

There are many connections between the characteristics used to describe an effective leader and a gifted individual. Effective leaders and gifted students are often highly verbal, socially sensitive, visionary, problem solvers, critical and creative thinkers, initiators, responsible, and self-sufficient (Black, 1984; Chauvin & Karnes, 1983; Plowman, 1981). Terman's (1925) classic study of the gifted revealed that gifted students were often the leaders in school. Hollingworth (1926) indicated that, among a group of children with average intelligence, the IQ of leaders was likely to fall between 115 and 130. Schakel (1984) found that, in comparison with nonintellectually gifted students, intellectually gifted students could be characterized as visionary leaders, whereas nongifted students seemed to be organizational leaders.

Using the HSPQ with students attending a self-contained high school for the intellectually gifted, Karnes, Chauvin, and Trant (1984) found that it failed to discriminate between individuals who held an "elected" leadership position and those who did not. Elected leaders, however, tended to be more tender-minded (sensitive, intuitive, tense, driven, group-dependent, and conscientious) than the nonelected group. In addition, females scored significantly higher than males on excitability, and males scored significantly higher on sensitivity (Karnes, Chauvin, & Trant, 1984). Although the need for more effective leaders is clear and gifted students typically possess the characteristics to become effective leaders, the development of leadership skills in gifted youth is often neglected.

Screening and Identification of Gifted Leaders

Identifying students for leadership training is a complex task. Conradie (1984) urged that leadership potential be identified early. The following leadership behaviors are often seen in preschool children: high verbal ability; sensitivity to the needs and concerns of others; popularity with their peers for companionship, ideas, and opinions; easy interaction with peers and adults; and easy adjustment to new situations (Hensel, 1991). Fukada, Fukada, and Hicks (1994) examined preschool children's leadership behavior during free play. Behaviors were recorded on a check list consisting of items such as initiating play, giving directions to others, monitoring the play, encouraging others, peacemaking, and so fourth. Results from this study indicated that leadership behavior is multidimensional, and the relationship between children's attributes and leadership behavior may depend on the dimension of leadership. Thus, more than one measure should be utilized to measure children's leadership.

Conradie (1984) also indicated the need for the identification of leadership potential to be continuous, because as children develop, social changes and leadership ability may emerge. A variety of methods may be utilized to identify leadership potential: parent/teacher/self-rating check lists, sociometric devices, self-esteem inventories, and commercially prepared screening and identification instruments.

The status of screening and identification instruments in leadership for elementary and secondary youth has been described as limited and in its infancy (Karnes & Meriweather-Bean, 1991). This is true several years later. Instruments with validity and reliability are limited in number. All vary on several aspects, including grades and/or ages, number of items specific to leadership, response modes, scoring procedures interpretation, and scores rendered. The current measures include

- The Leadership Characteristics (Part IV) of the Scale for Rating Behavioral Characteristics of Superior Students (SRBCSS) (Renzulli, Smith, White, Callahan, & Hartman, 1976);
- Rating Scale for Leadership (Roets, 1986a);
- The High School Personality Questionnaire (Cattell, Cattell, & Johns, 1984);
- Myers-Briggs Type Indicators (Myers & McCaulley, 1985);
- Murphy-Meisgeier Type Indicator for Children (Meisgeier & Murphy, 1987);
- Gifted Education Scale, (McCarney, 1987);
- Student Talent and Risk Profile (Institute for Behavioral Research in Creativity, 1990); and
- Khatena-Morse Multitalent Perception Inventory (Khatena & Morse, 1994).

Two additional standardized measures are commercially available: The Leadership Skills Inventory (Karnes & Chauvin, 2000a) and the Leadership Skills Indicator (Ellis, 1990). They have been designed for purposes other than screening and identification. The former was developed to be a diagnostic/prescriptive measure for instruction in leadership and the latter was designed to serve as a bases for discussion on the topics of leaders and leadership by counselors and teachers.

The Gifted Education Scale contains 48 items covering the five areas of giftedness in the 1987 federal definition: intellectual ability, creativity, specific academic aptitude, leadership, and performing and visual arts ability (McCarney, 1987). It was designed for students in grades kindergarten through 12. The teacher rates the students on a five-point scale; the leadership score is derived from 10 of the 48 items. It was nationally standardized on 2,276 students across the United States. It can easily be administered in approximately 20 minutes.

The Scales for Rating Behavioral Characteristics of Superior Students (SRBCSS) (Renzulli et al., 1976) was designed to assist teachers in their nominations of students for specialized programs for the gifted and talented. The original scales consisted of four rating areas or components: learning, motivation, creativity, and leadership. A criterion of the scales accepted early in the development process was that at least three separate studies in the literature had to specify the importance of a specific observable characteristic in order for it to be included in the instrument. In the first experimental edition, several districts offering programs for gifted and talented youth were involved. Validity and reliability studies were undertaken on all four scales. Part IV, Leadership Characteristics, was validated by comparing teachers' and peers' ratings through sociometric techniques (Hartman, 1969). The correlations were high for teachers and fourth-, fifth-, and sixth-grade students' ratings (Renzulli et al., 1976). By correlating the individual items with the total leadership ratings, the internal consistency of the leadership scale was verified by Renzulli et al.

Further studies included the investigation of the factor-analytical structure of the SRBCSS (Burke, Harworth, & Ware, 1982), which found that the Leadership Characteristics assessed many behavioral characteristics that typify leadership but concluded that they were descriptive of the type of leader who conforms and adapts to traditional expectations in a school setting.

A self-rating measure for students in grades 5 through 12 was constructed by Roets (1986a). A five-point scale is employed to rate 26 items. *Almost always, quite often, sometimes, not very often,* and *never* constitute the ratings. The instrument was administered to 1,057 youth living in the continental limits of the United States in both public and private schools. The validity was established by administering to 631 students in the standardization group two other measures of leadership with correlations of $r = .71$ and $.77$, respectively. The Spearman-Brown split-half formula established the reliability and correlation for the total sample at $r = .85$. Further investigation of reliability of the measure with the leadership scale of the SRBCSS indicated a correlation of $r = .55$.

Leadership—A Skill and Behavior Scale is a self-rating instrument developed by Sisk and Rosselli (1987). It contains the areas of positive self-concept, decision-making skills, problem-solving skills, group dynamics skills, communication skills, organizing, implementing skills, planning skills, and discerning opportunities. *Never, seldom, sometimes, often,* and *always* are the dimensions of the rating scale. Validity and reliability data are not provided.

A self-rating scale, the Khatena-Morse Multitalent Perception Inventory (KMMPT), contains the areas of artistry, musical, creative imagination, initiative, and leadership (Khatena-Morse,1994). The two forms of the instrument, A and B, contain four and six items in leadership, respectively. The standardization data, including extensive information on validity and reliability, are contained in the technical manual.

Seven check lists are contained in The Eby Gifted Behavior Index (Eby, 1989), six of which identify the behavioral processes of elementary and secondary school gifted youth in different talent areas. They are verbal, math/science/problem solving, musical, visual/ spatial, social/leadership, and mechanical/technical/inventiveness. An additional area was developed to provide criteria for the rating of original student products. Twenty items on the Social/Leadership Check List include active interaction with the environment, reflectiveness, perceptiveness, persistence, goal orientation, originality, productivity, self-evaluation, independence, and the effective communication of ideas. A five-point Likert-type rating format is provided for the teacher. The responses are "evidence of the behavior is shown rarely or never in social activities" to "evidence of the behavior is shown consistently in most social activities." The validity and reliability studies on the Social/Leadership Check list are reported in the manual.

The High School Personality Questionnaire (HSPQ) (Cattell, Cattell, & Johns, 1984) yields the Leadership Potential Score (LPS). Fourteen bipolar traits of personality are assessed: warmth, intelligence, emotional stability, excitability, dominance, enthusiasm, conformity, boldness, sensitivity, withdrawal, apprehension, self-sufficiency, self-discipline, and tension. The instrument designed for students ranging in age from 12 to 18 is a self-rating form, and it may be given individually or in groups. The 142-item instrument requires approximately 45 to 60 minutes to administer. Numerous studies attesting to validity and reliability of the instrument with a variety of youth samples are described in the manual (Cattell, Cattell, & Johns, 1984).

The LPS score is predicted from the HSPQ by an equation derived empirically by combining scores on the 14 primary scales using a specific formula (Johns, 1984). The LPS has been employed in several studies with intellectually gifted, creative, and leadership students. The mean scores of the subjects in each study were above those of the norming group (Karnes, Chauvin, & Trant, 1984; Karnes, Chauvin, & Trant, 1985; Karnes & D'Ilio, 1988a; 1988b).

The Student Talent and Risk (STAR) Profile (The Institute for Behavioral Research in Creativity, 1990) is based on Form U, Biographical Inventory, which was developed in 1976. Seven performance measures are provided: academic performance, creativity, artistic potential, leadership, emotional maturity, educational orientation, and at-risk. The student responds to 150 items based on the answer that is most like him or herself. Analysis on each student in the seven performance areas and on the group as a whole by percentile scores are provided through computer feedback. Validity, reliability, and research studies are provided in the technical manual.

Psychological type information, based on Carl Jung's theory of observable differences in mental functioning, is provided by the Myers-Briggs Type Indicator (MBTI) (Myers & McCaulley, 1985). Individuals create their "type" through the exercise of their individual preferences. Type theory provides a model for understanding the nature of differences among leaders (McCaulley et al., 1990). Each person has a predisposed preference for one of the bipolar attitudes (extroversion/introversion, judging/perceiving) and functions (sensing/intuition, thinking/feeling). The MBTI provides an interpretation of type as it relates to how an individual best perceives and processes information and how that individual prefers to interact socially and behaviorally with others. Psychological type is the combination of the two attitudes and functions preferred by the individual; therefore, all eight preferences are combined in all possible ways, with 16 types resulting. To administer the 166-item measure, approximately 45 to 60 minutes are needed. The instrument was designed and standardized to be a self-rating instrument for adolescents and adults. Reliability, validity, and other data are reported in the manual (Myers & McCaulley, 1985).

The Murphy-Meisgeier Type Indicator for Children (MMTIC) was developed based on Jung's theory of psychological type (Meisgeier & Murphy, 1987). The 70-item instrument designed for students in grades 2 through 8 was developed to measure the same four preference scales as the MBTI. A total of 4,136 students in grades 2 through 8 were included in the standardization process. Estimates of concurrent and content validity, reliability, and other data are reported in the manual.

These screening and identification instruments yield information about many leadership attributes and behaviors of developing young leaders. Because of the complex and multidimensional nature of leadership, it is recommended that more than one measure be used to assess students' leadership potential. The type of instructional program for leadership should be considered when selecting appropriate screening and identification instruments.

Instructional Programs and Materials for Leadership

The acquisition and application of the necessary leadership concepts and skills based on those identified as necessary to function as an adult leader in society is the basis for *The Leadership Development Program* (Karnes & Chauvin, 2000b). The diagnostic-prescriptive instrument, The Leadership Skills Inventory (LSI), has nine subscales: fundamentals of leadership, written communication, speech communication, character building, decision making, group dynamics, problem solving, personal development, and planning. Eight samples of students in grades 4 through junior college in seven states were included in the standardization. Criterion and content validity studies have been conducted (Karnes & D'Ilio, 1988a; Karnes & D'Ilio, 1988b, Karnes & Chauvin, 2000a). Reliability data are reported in the manual.

Upon beginning a leadership program, the students are administered the LSI, which is a self-rating and self-scoring instrument. After they complete the inventory, scores are plotted on the Leadership Skills Inventory Profile Sheet, which graphically depicts their strengths and weaknesses in leadership concepts and skills on the nine subscales. The concepts and skills that have been acquired and those in need of strengthening are immediately apparent. This information provides the teacher with the necessary data to assist the student in planning the appropriate instructional activities for every item on the LSI. One or more instructional strategies for each item are provided in *The Leadership Development Program* (Karnes

& Chauvin, 2000b). The teacher does not have to incorporate all the activities but only those which will provide the improvement necessary to become an effective leader based on the student's self-perceived strengths and weaknesses. Group discussions, simulations, and role-playing activities are the primary vehicle for learning, and they are student-centered rather than teacher-directed.

Crucial to the program is the application of the acquired leadership concepts and skills, which is facilitated through developing and implementing a "Plan for Leadership." After the completion of the instructional component, each student identifies an area in which he or she may initiate something new or change an already existing area of need in his or her school, community, or religious affiliation. The plan must have two major purposes: (a) to bring about desirable changes in the behavior of others and (b) to solve a major problem or work toward major improvements. Within the abilities of the students, it should be realistic, well-sequenced, and comprehensive. The student writes a plan with an overall goal with accompanying objectives, activities, resources, timelines, and methods for evaluation. Each plan developed is presented in class for peer review. An example of a completed plan and the types of plans prepared by male and female students for the school, community, and religious affiliation and the numbers of plans developed during each year of the program have been described (Karnes and Meriweather, 1989).

The instrument and the materials are the foundation of the Leadership Studies Program, a one-week summer residential experience, which has been validated (Karnes, Meriweather, & D'Ilio, 1987). The statistical analysis of the data collected in the programs indicates pre- and postassessment gains to be significant ($p = .01$) (Karnes, Meriweather, & D'Ilio, 1987).

After a careful analysis of all the program components, including the nine instructional areas necessary for being a leader and the plan for leadership, teachers, administrative decision makers, and community leaders can readily select the format of the program appropriate for their school and town. It may be an ongoing component of a resource enrichment program, conducted as a separate class at the junior or senior high school level; or the appropriate components may be included in English, speech, social studies, and other academic courses. Mentorship and internship provisions for leadership growth should also be made readily available to students after the completion of the instructional activities.

Another approach to examining leadership in youth is The Leadership Strengths Indicator (Ellis, 1990), a 40-item self-report questionnaire designed to obtain students' evaluations of their leadership traits and abilities. Eight cluster scores and an overall total leadership score are rendered on the 40-item self-report instrument. The eight clusters contain two to six items within the following areas: enjoys group activities, key individual in group activities, high level participator in group activities, journalistic, sympathetic, confident, courageous, conscientious, and self-confident. The response choices on the rating scale are *excellent, very good, better than most, okay,* and *not so good.* The indicator is intended to be a discussion starter for guidance and leadership development classes designed for students in grades 6 through 12. The psychometric properties, including validity and reliability, are reported in the manual.

Research has been conducted using the indicator with gifted. Disadvantaged gifted students ranging in age from 10 to 15 had scores within the normal range. A significant difference on Cluster Scale III, High Level Participator in Group Activities, was found favoring boys (Riley & Karnes, 1994a). Rural and suburban gifted high school youth were compared with no significant differences found (Abel & Karnes, 1993).

Parker (1989) proposed a leadership model designed to serve as the foundation for gifted programs. According to the theory on which her Leadership Training Model is based, leadership potential can be developed through the strengthening of four essential components: cognition, problem solving, interpersonal communication, and decision making. In one volume of the *Gifted Treasury Series* (Parker, in press), Parker includes an overview of leadership theory, suggested strategies for developing creative leadership in gifted students, and a variety of leadership units designed for use with gifted students of all ages.

For almost two decades, commercially prepared instructional materials for teaching leadership have been available. As early as 1980, Magoon and Jellen designed 25 strategies for developing leadership. Designed, according to the authors, to assist students in becoming future leaders by acquiring the skills of leading, the materials offer such instructional assistance as a check list for committee work, a group observation scale, and a listing of references.

The *Leadership Series,* which contains six instructional units in analyzing leadership, group skills, self-esteem, communication skills, values and goal setting, and social responsibility, was designed by House (1980). Based on Bloom's Taxonomy of Educational Objectives (1956), each unit contains 30 instructional activities. Objectives with emphasis on the high levels of thinking of analysis, synthesis, and evaluation are the basis of the program with reproducible worksheets.

A curriculum unit on leadership for upper elementary and junior high school gifted youth was developed by Gallagher (1982). Content specialists and teachers of the gifted worked to construct the instructional lessons, which had three specific objectives: to illustrate a particular leadership concept, to provide opportunities for the students to understand and internalize the concepts, and to develop the students' higher-level thinking skills. Three types of leaders were highlighted in the lesson plans: traditional, legal-rational, and charismatic. The activities in each lesson are grouped at three levels: awareness, instructional, and extension. Reproducibles for student use are included in the materials. An annotated bibliography on leadership and evaluation forms for students and parents are provided for the teacher.

Leadership: A Skills Training Program is an instructional program for students ages 8–18 (Roets, 1986b). The instructional activities are based on four themes: people of achievement, language of leadership, project planning, and debate and discussion. Suggested readings for young people, both fiction and nonfiction, and a listing of readings for adults are provided.

Several books directed to elementary and secondary school youth and teachers are available, and each contains many instructional activities for leadership training. The goals of the leadership materials presented in *Leadership Education: Developing Skills for Youth* (Richardson and Feldhusen, 1987), which had previously been developed by Feldhusen, Hynes, and Richardson (1977) with a grant in vocational-technical education, are to develop the social skills of leadership and an understanding on the part of the student as a potential leader. The 11 chapters include an introduction to leadership, outcomes of leadership education, personal characteristics of effective leaders, skills of a group leader, communication skills for leaders, leadership skills for group members, group goals development, group activity plans, committee organization, parliamentary procedure skills, and leadership and special abilities. Feldhusen and Kennedy (1986) reported evaluation results on the use of the materials in a summer leadership program with secondary gifted youth.

Sisk and Shallcross (1986) developed a guide to help clarify the meaning of leaders and leadership. The book is divided into 10 chapters: What is Leadership, Self-Understanding, Intuitive Powers, Visual Imagery, Communication, Motivation, Creative Problem-Solving Process, Futuristics, Women in Leadership Positions, and Learning Styles. Activities presented in each chapter may be used in a wide variety of instructional situations within schools. References for each topic are presented at the end of each chapter.

Sisk and Roselli (1987) coauthored *Leadership: A Special Kind of Giftedness* for the purpose of assisting in the understanding of the concepts of leadership and in applying current theories to personal lives and teaching. The book includes the definition of leadership, the theories, a model for planning and developing leadership training activities, a succinct summary of teaching/learning models, and a discussion on issues and trends in leadership. The four elements of the model developed by Sisk are characteristics of gifted leadership, selected teaching strategies, teaching/learning models, and key concepts. Twenty lessons are provided.

Lead On, designed by Hagemann and Newman (1999), helps educators and students address leadership problems more effectively. The book offers strategies for students and teachers to work together as they develop interpersonal and intrapersonal skills. Objectives, procedures, and extended activities provide cross-curricular connections, best practices, and real-life leadership applications for the 21st century.

The outstanding leadership stories of girls are highlighted in *Girls and Young Women Leading the Way* (Karnes & Bean, 1993). Twenty biographies of girls from elementary school through college are provided as role models for leadership. Each story contains personal information followed by a detailed overview of leadership accomplishment. There are questions to challenge the reader to leadership and a listing of appropriate agencies/organizations from which to gain more information. Motivation and inspiration are given by the quotations from nationally known female leaders. Suggestions for actions to record in a leadership notebook and an extensive reading list on female leaders from kindergarten to the young adult level are provided.

Leadership for Students: A Practical Guide (Karnes & Bean, 1995), a book for young leaders ages 8 through 18, contains guidance and advice about moving into leadership positions in the home, school, and community. The book contains chapters on leadership definitions, self-assessment of leadership, opportunities and training for leadership, influence and encouragement from others, great leaders, and advice to others. Figures 1, 2, 3, and Table 1 are examples of activities from the book that help extend students' views of leadership and assist them in planning for leadership. The book was designed to be interactive through the use of The Leadership Action Journal, which provides the opportunity for students to record their thoughts and actions pertaining to leaders and leadership. Stories of young leaders offer examples of peers and explain how they became leaders. Also featured is a listing of resources and addresses on leadership opportunities.

Incorporating Leadership into the Curriculum for Gifted Students

The goal of cultivating young leaders is of such critical importance to the individual and to society that it should be made an integral part of school and community programs for youth. Without more purposeful and intentional approaches to developing young leaders, only a few students are likely to emerge as adult leaders, and the world will continue the call for more effective leaders. Given the parallels between characteristics of effective leaders and gifted individuals, leadership education is a natural fit; and with the flexibility that often exists in the curriculum for gifted learners, programs and services for the gifted present environments that are most conducive to leadership development.

Toward this end, the concept of leadership must be a more direct part of the curriculum. It must also be broadened—from the narrow view of leadership as elected or appointed positions in politics, government, business, or industry to an expanded view of leadership permeating all dimensions of life, across all disciplines, ages, cultures, and levels of society. Leadership can and should be infused into the broad-based concepts, themes, and issues of the curriculum for gifted students. Leadership should be explored as it connects to *power, symbols, culture, patterns, relationships,* and *values.* The conceptual frameworks for

How is leadership connected to each of the parts of the web?

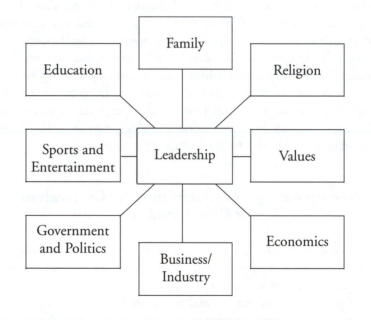

Figure 1. Leadership Web

Note. From *Leadership for Students: A Practical Guide for Ages 8–18,* (p. 125), by F. A. Karnes and S. M. Bean, 1995, Waco, TX: Prufrock Press. Used with permission. Copyright 1995 by Prufrock Press.

Table 1. Leadership Matrix

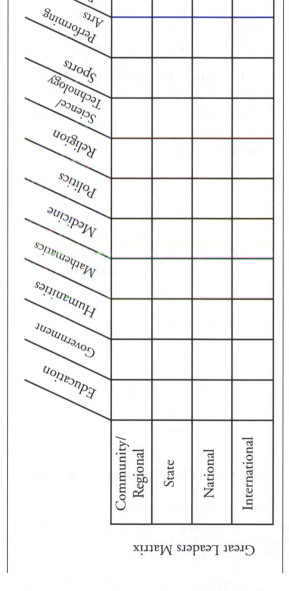

Great Leaders Matrix	Education	Government	Humanities	Mathematics	Medicine	Politics	Religion	Science/ Technology	Sports	Performing Arts	Business/ Industry
Community/ Regional											
State											
National											
International											

Note. From *Leadership for Students: A Practical Guide for Ages 8–18*, (p. 166), by F. A. Karnes and S. M. Bean, 1995, Waco, TX: Prufrock Press. Used with permission. Copyright 1995 by Prufrock Press.

thinking about leadership are valuable parts to one's leadership development.

There are many approaches that could prepare gifted learners for leadership roles. Instructional units on leadership should be taught in programs for the gifted. These units could include the study of the history of leadership, great leaders, ethical dimensions of leadership, theories and styles of leadership, leadership across cultures, leadership and futurism, and so on.

Changes in Leadership Over Time

Tribal Leadership _____

_____

_____

Leadership in Royalty _____

_____

_____

Democratic Leadership _____

_____

_____

Cooperative or Shared Leadership _____

_____

_____

Positive Aspects of Leadership in Today's Society _____

_____

_____

_____

Figure 2. The History of Leadership

Education about leadership is important, but it is not enough. Even those individuals with extensive knowledge about leadership may be poor leaders. Knowing what to do is not the same as knowing when, where, and how to do it. The *skills* of leadership are significant, too. Leadership through experience begins with the development of intrapersonal and interpersonal skills. Gifted students need guidance in self-understanding and access to one's own feelings and emotions, examining individual strengths and limitations, accepting those that cannot be changed, and setting goals to develop areas needed for personal growth and human relations.

My Goal _____

_____

_____

Objectives _____

_____

_____

Resources/Objectives _____

_____

_____

Other _____

_____

_____

Timeline _____

_____

_____

Figure 3. Leadership Development Plan

Note. From *Leadership for Students: A Practical Guide for Ages 8–18*, (p. 176), by F. A. Karnes and S. M. Bean, 1995, Waco, TX: Prufrock Press. Used with permission. Copyright 1995 by Prufrock Press.

Also critical to leadership skills is the ability to see events from the perspective of another, understand and relate positively to others, and perceive human needs and motivations. Gardner (1990) referred to these skills as the crowning capacity of the human condition, which supersedes and presides over other forms of intelligence. Teachers may use journaling, bibliotherapy, and other strategies for self-reflection and analysis. For interpersonal skills to flourish, teachers should intentionally plan group discussions and collaborative work. Problem-solving skills, conflict resolution, role-playing, and creative drama are all strategies that can be used to develop the seeds of early leadership development.

Schools could also offer structured courses on leadership for which credit is granted. Within these courses, students may assess their own leadership potential and develop plans of leadership to be implemented in schools, communities, and religious organizations. Students need the opportunity to examine areas of interest to which leadership experiences could be applied.

Mentorships and internships offer real-life experiences for adult leaders to collaborate with the schools for the purpose of developing young leaders. Pairing adult leaders with students interested in developing their leadership potential can be a positive practice for student and adult leaders, as well as the school and community.

Riley and Karnes (1996) recommended competitions as a vehicle for incorporating leadership in the curriculum and for recognizing and inspiring young leaders. Competitions such as the "I Dare You Leadership Award" and the "J. C. Penney Golden Rule Award" recognize those who have achieved in the area of leadership and reward promising young leaders with scholarships to attend an international leadership conference (Karnes & Riley, 1996). These and other such competitions not only can help inspire and recognize young leaders but can promote goal setting and a sense of autonomy and can provide the opportunity for students to meet other young leaders with similar interests and abilities.

Teachers must also be prepared to expose gifted learners to the array of choices for leadership opportunities outside the school. Youth leadership conferences, seminars, and weekend and summer programs are offered through colleges and universities, civic organizations, and business and industries across the nation. Such services and programs often serve as a spark to ignite the desire for becoming a leader and a boost in self-confidence, which is critical to effective leadership.

Educators must seek every opportunity to identify potential leaders at an early age and infuse leadership concepts and skills into the learning environment for gifted students. The ultimate goal is for each gifted student to understand the importance of leadership, realize his or her potential for leadership, gain the knowledge and skills necessary to be an effective leader, and be exposed to all avenues for leadership development within and outside the school environment.

Summary

Researchers are still struggling to generate appropriate definitions and theories of leadership. These conceptual frameworks for thinking about leadership bring meaning and relevance to one's leadership development. Although the majority of research on leadership centers around adults, studies focusing on leadership development of children and youth have emerged over the last decade. In particular, the similarities of characteristics and behaviors of effective leaders and gifted learners have been recognized. Leadership screening and identification instruments and instructional materials have been identified, and strategies for incorporating leadership into the curriculum for gifted learners have been discussed.

The primary goal is to heighten students' interest in the concept of leadership and help them to become more reflective and active in their individual pursuits of leadership potential. This goal requires support and commitment from all educators and other interested adults. Purposeful and creative approaches to leadership development must be pursued vigorously by those interested in the challenge.

References

Abel, T., & Karnes, F. A. (1993). Self-perceived strengths in leadership abilities between suburban and rural gifted students using the Leadership Strength Indicator. *Psychological Reports, 73,* 687–690.

Alvino, J. (1989). Psychological type: Implications for gifted. *Gifted Children Monthly, 10*(4), 1–2, 23.

Barr, L., & Barr, N. (1989). *The leadership equation.* Austin, TX: Eakin Press.

Bass, B. M. (1981*). Stogdill's handbook of leadership: A survey of theory and research.* New York: Free Press.

Bennett, W. J. (1986). *What works: Research about teaching and learning.* Washington, DC: U.S. Department of Education.

Bennis, W. G., & Nanus, B. (1985). *Leaders: The strategies for taking charge.* New York: Harper & Row.

Black, J. D. (1984). *Leadership: A new model particularly applicable to gifted youth* (Report No. EC171399). Indiana: Handicapped and Gifted Children Clearinghouse. (ERIC Document Reproduction Service No. ED 253 990)

Blake, R. R., & Mouton, J. S. (1985). *The managerial grid III.* Houston: Gulf.

Bloom, B. (Ed.). (1956). *Taxonomy of educational objectives. Handbook I: Cognitive domain.* New York: David McKay.

Burke, J. P., Harworth, C. E., & Ware, W. B. (1982). Scale for rating behavioral characteristics of superior students: An investigation of factor structure. *Journal of Special Education, 16,* 477–485.

Burns, J. M., (1978). *Leadership.* New York: Harper & Row.

Campbell, D., & Velsor, E. V. (1985). *The use of personality measures in the leadership development program.* Greensboro, NC: Center for Creative Leadership.

Cattell, R. B., Cattell, M. D., & Johns, E. F. (1984). *Manual and norms for the High School Personality Questionnaire.* Champaign, IL: Institute for Personality & Ability Testing.

Chauvin, J. C., & Karnes, F. A. (1983). A leadership profile of secondary gifted students. *Psychological Reports, 53,* 1259–1262.

Clark, K. E., & Clark, M. B. (1994). *Choosing to lead.* Charlotte, NC: Iron Gate Press.

Conradie, S. (1984). The identification of leadership potential. In J. Cawood, et al. (Eds.), *Climbing the ladder to leadership: A panel discussion* (Report No. ED20210). Paper presented at international conference on education for the gifted, Ingenium 2000, Stellenbosch,

South Africa. (ERIC Document Reproduction Service No. ED 292 228)

Eby, J. W. (1989). *Eby gifted behavior index (Administration manual)*. East Aurora, NY: D.O.K.

Ellis, J. L. (1990). *Leadership strengths indicator: A self-report leadership analysis instrument for adolescents*. Monroe, NY: Trillium Press.

Feldhusen, J. F., Hynes, K., & Richardson, W. B. (1977). Curriculum materials for vocational youth organizations. *Clearinghouse, 50,* 224–226.

Feldhusen, J., & Kennedy, D. (1986). Leadership training for gifted and talented youth. *Leadership Network Newsletter, 1*(2), 1–2.

Fiedler, F. E. (1967). *A theory of leadership effectiveness*. New York: McGraw-Hill.

Florey, J. E., & Dorf, J. H. (1986). *Leadership skills for gifted middle school students*. (ERIC Document Reproduction Service No. ED 273 404)

Foster, W. H., & Silverman, L. (1988). Leadership curriculum for the gifted. In J. VanTassel-Baska, J. Feldhusen, K. Seeley, G. Wheatley, L. Silverman, & W. Foster (Eds.), *Comprehensive curriculum for gifted learners* (pp. 356–360). Boston: Allyn & Bacon.

Fukada, S., Fukada, H., & Hicks, J. (1994). Structure of leadership among preschool children. *The Journal of Genetic Psychology, 155,* 389–395.

Gallagher, J. J. (1982). *A leadership unit*. New York: Trillium Press.

Galton, F. (1869). *Hereditary genius: An inquiry into its laws and consequences*. London: Macmillan. (Paperback edition by Meridan Books, New York, 1962)

Gardner, J. W. (1990). *On leadership*. New York: Free Press.

Hagemann, B., & Newman, C. (1999). *Lead on*. Marion, IL: Pieces of Learning.

Hartman, R. K. (1969). *Teachers' identification of student learners*. Unpublished paper, University of Connecticut, Storrs.

Hensel, N. H. (1991). Leadership giftedness: Social leadership skills in young children. *Roeper Review, 14,* 4–19.

Hersey, P., & Blanchard, K. H. (1982). Leadership style: Attitudes and behaviors. *Training and Development Journal, 36*(5), 50–52.

Hogan, R. J., Curphy, G. J., & Hogan, J. (1994). What do we know about personality: Leadership and effectiveness? *American Psychologist, 49,* 493–504.

Hollander, E. P., & Offerman, L. (1990). Power and leadership in organizations: Relationships in transition. In K. E. Clark & M. B. Clark (Eds.), *Measures of leadership*. West Orange, NJ: Leadership Library of America.

Hollingworth, L. S. (1926). *Gifted children: Their nature and nurture*. New York: Macmillan.

House, C. (1980). *The leadership series*. Coeur D'Alene, ID: Listos.

Institute for Behavioral Research in Creativity. (1990). *Student talent and risk profile*. Salt Lake City, UT: Institute for Behavioral Research in Creativity.

Javits, J. K. (1988). *Gifted and Talented Students Education Act* (Title IV, Part B of P.L. 100–297).

Johns, E. F. (1984). The relationship of personality and achievement to creativity and leadership behavior. In R. B. Cattell, M. D. Cattell, & E. Johns (Eds.), *Manual and norms for the High School Personality Questionnaire* (pp. 35-56). Champaign, IL: Institute for Personality and Ability Testing.

Karnes, F. A., & Bean, S. M. (1993). *Girls and young women leading the way*. Minneapolis: Free Sprit.

Karnes, F. A., & Bean, S. M. (1995). *Leadership for students: A practical guide*. Waco, TX: Prufrock Press.

Karnes, F. A., & Chauvin, J. C. (2000a). *Leadership skills inventory*. Scottsdale, AZ: Gifted Psychology Press.

Karnes, F. A., & Chauvin, J. C. (2000b). *The leadership development program*. Scottsdale, AZ: Gifted Psychology Press.

Karnes, F. A., Chauvin, J. C., & Trant, T. J. (1984). Leadership profiles as determined by the HSPQ of students identified as intellectually gifted. *Roeper Review, 7*, 46–48.

Karnes, F. A., Chauvin, J. C., & Trant, T. J. (1985). Validity of the leadership potential score of the High School Personality Questionnaire with talented students. *Perceptual and Motor Skills, 61*, 163–166.

Karnes, F. A., & D'Ilio, V. (1988a). Assessment of concurrent validity of the Leadership Skills Inventory with gifted students and their teachers. *Perceptual and Motor Skills, 66*, 59–62.

Karnes, F. A., & D'Ilio, V. (1988b). Assessment of criterion-related validity of the Leadership Skills Inventory. *Psychological Reports, 62*, 263–267.

Karnes, F. A., & D'Ilio, V. (1989). Leadership positions and sex-role stereotyping among gifted students. *Gifted Child Quarterly, 33*, 76–78.

Karnes, F. A., & D'Ilio, V. (1990). Sex-role stereotyping of leadership positions by student leaders. *Perceptual and Motor Skills, 70*, 335–338.

Karnes, F. A., & Meriweather, S. (1989). Developing and implementing a plan for leadership: An integral component for success as a leader. *Roeper Review, 11*, 214–217.

Karnes, F. A., & Meriweather-Bean, S. (1991). Leadership and gifted adolescents. In M. Bireley & J. Genshaft (Eds.), *Understanding the gifted adolescent: Educational, developmental, and multicultural issues* (pp. 122–138). New York: Teachers College Press.

Karnes, F. A., Meriweather, S., & D'Ilio, V. (1987). The effectiveness of the Leadership Studies Program. *Roeper Review, 9,* 238–241.

Karnes, F. A., & Riley, T. L. (1996). *Competitions: Maximizing your abilities.* Waco, TX: Prufrock Press.

Khatena, J., & Morse, D. T. (1994). *Khatena-Morse multi-talent perception inventory.* Binsonville, IL: Scholastic Testing Service.

Lawrence, G. (1982). *People types and tiger stripes: A practical guide to learning styles.* Gainesville, FL: Center for the Applications of Psychological Type.

Lindsay, B. (1988). A lamp for Diogenes: Leadership, giftedness, and moral education. *Roeper Review, 1,* 8–11.

Magoon, R. A., & Jellen, H. G. (1980). *Leadership development: Democracy in action.* Poquoson, VA: Human Development Press.

McCarney, S. B. (1987). *Gifted evaluation scale.* Columbus, MO: Hawthorne Educational Services.

McCaulley, M. H., & Staff of the Center for Applications of Psychological Type. (1990). The Myers-Briggs Type Indicator and leadership. In K. E. Clark & M. B. Clark (Eds.), *Measures of leadership* (pp. 381–418). New York: Center for Creative Leadership.

McNamara, J. F., Haensly, P. A., Lupkowski, A. E., & Edlind, E. P. (1985). *The role of extracurricular activities in high school education.* Paper presented at annual convention of National Association for Gifted Children, Denver, CO.

Meisgeier, C., & Murphy, E. (1987). *Murphy-Meisgeier type indicator for children.* Palo Alto, CA: Consulting Psychologists Press.

Myers, I. B., & McCaulley, M. (1985). *Manual: A guide to the development and use of the Myers-Briggs Type Indicator.* Palo Alto, CA: Consulting Psychologists Press.

Myers, I. B., & Myers, P. B. (1980). *Gifted differing.* Palo Alto, CA: Consulting Psychologists Press.

Nemerowicz, G., & Rosi, E. (1995). *Children's perceptions of leadership: A report of preliminary findings.* Aurora, NY: Women's Leadership Institute.

Parker, J. P. (1989). *Instructional strategies for teaching the gifted.* Boston: Allyn & Bacon.

Parker, J. P. (in press). Developing creative leadership. *The gifted treasury series.* Englewood, CO: Teacher Ideas Press.

Plowman, P. D. (1981). Training extraordinary leaders. *Roeper Review, 3,* 13–16.

Renzulli, J. S., Smith, F. H., White, A. J., Callahan, C. M., & Hartman, R. K. (1976). *Scales for rating the behavioral characteristics of superior students* (SRBCSS). Wethersfield, CT: Creative Learning Press.

Richardson, W. B., & Feldhusen, J. F. (1987). *Leadership education: Developing skills for youth.* New York: Trillium.

Riley, T. L., & Karnes, F. A. (1994a). Intellectually gifted elementary students' perceptions of leadership. *Perceptual and Motor Skills, 79,* 47–50.

Riley, T. L., & Karnes, F. A. (1994b). A leadership profile of disadvantaged youth based on Leadership Strengths Indicator. *Psychological Reports, 74,* 815–818.

Riley, T. L., & Karnes, F. A.(1996). *Competitions as an avenue for inspiring and recognizing young leaders.* Unpublished manuscript, The University of Southern Mississippi.

Roets, L. S. (1986a). *Leadership: A skills training program.* New Sharon, IA: Leadership.

Roets, L. (1986b). *Roets rating scale for leadership.* Des Moines, IA: Leadership.

Schakel, L. (1984). *Investigation of the leadership abilities of intellectually gifted students.* Unpublished dissertation, University of South Florida, Tampa.

Sisk, D. A., & Rosselli, H. C. (1987). *Leadership: A special kind of giftedness.* New York: Trillium.

Sisk, D. A., & Shallcross, D. J. (1986). *Leadership: Making things happen.* Buffalo, NY: Bearly Limited.

Stogdill, R. M. (1974). *Handbook of leadership.* New York: Free Press.

Terman, L. M. (1925). *Genetic study of genius: Vol. 1. Mental and physical traits of a thousand gifted children.* Stanford, CA: Stanford University Press.

Yammarino, F. J., & Bass, B. M. (1990). Long-term forecasting of transformational leadership and its effect among naval officers: Some preliminary findings. In K. E. Clark & M. B. Clark (Eds.), *Measures of leadership* (pp. 151–169). West Orange, NJ: Leadership Library of America.

CHAPTER 17

Cooperative Learning and Gifted Learners

MARY RUTH COLEMAN
University of North Carolina

ooperative learning (CL) is not an entirely new idea. The use of a variety of forms of group work for problem solving and learning dates back to early proponents of education, including John Dewey (Ellis & Whalen, 1990). However, cooperative learning has come to mean much more than just small groups of students working together on a shared task. Although cooperative learning can take many forms, the common denominators which usually distinguish CL from other small group work include
- positive interdependence among group participants;
- individual accountability for content, skills, and concept mastery;
- face-to-face interaction among group members;
- development of appropriate socialization skills; and
- group processing of learning and interactions (Johnson, Johnson & Holubec, 1990).

Other differences between small group work and cooperative learning may include the ways in which the groups are structured. Many proponents of CL recommend that groups be created with mixed-abilities to include high-, middle-, and low-ability students (Nelson, Gallagher & Coleman, 1993; Johnson & Johnson, 1991; Sharan, 1990). The grouping strategy, however, does not always have to include mixed-ability levels. Slavin (1990) pointed out that "cooperative learning has been used successfully within ability-grouped classes for very high achievers" (p. 7).

Three widely used models for cooperative learning were developed by David and Roger Johnson (1987), Robert Slavin (1988), and Spencer Kagan (1990). A brief overview of each shows how diverse cooperative learning approaches can be.

Johnson and Johnson's Model

The Johnsons' model strongly emphasizes social skills and group dynamics as key goals for cooperative learning (Johnson & Johnson, 1990). Students are assigned to groups that reflect the diversity of the overall classroom, and heterogeneity of the CL group is stressed. The ideal task is one that requires interdependence of the group, with every member making a meaningful contribution to the learning process. Students are assigned (or they may select) roles within the CL group to ensure smooth operating. These roles usually include functional jobs like materials gatherer or recorder but may also include social responsibilities like designated praiser or encourager (Ellis & Whalen, 1990). Groups are assessed regularly on both academic growth and social dynamics, and progress is recognized through group rewards (and sometimes group grades).

Slavin's Model

Robert Slavin's approaches to cooperative learning emphasize shared responsibility of learning with individual accountability for mastery and are highly content-driven. Competition across the CL groups, or teams, is frequently used to motivate and reward students. Team members work to support each other's learning while earning points for team progress and effort. Slavin has designed several specific methods, including Team Games Tournaments (TGT), Student Teams Achievement Division (STAD), Team Accelerated Instruction (TAI), and Cooperative Integrated Reading and Comprehension (CIRC). In addition to the strategy of blending competition with cooperation, Slavin has also focused on developing curriculum materials in math and reading to support his methods. In addition to helping teammates learn, students are also encouraged to move through the materials at a self-paced rate, allowing gifted students to accelerate when appropriate (Slavin, 1980; 1981).

Kagan's Model

Spencer Kagan's model relies on a variety of structures to organize interactions among students (Kagan, 1990). Examples of structures include *Think-pair-share*, where students reflect individually, discuss in pairs, and share with their CL group or the class; *Round Robin* where each group member shares in turn; *Numbered Heads Together*, where students consult (all heads in) to ensure that everyone in the group understands the answer; and *Jigsaw*, where individual members work across teams to become experts on a topic and then return to their home-team to share their knowledge. The use of structures gives teachers a number of ways to shift classroom "talk-patterns" so that more students can be actively involved in each lesson. Students' learning is assessed individually, but group rewards are used to build incentive.

Most teachers who use cooperative learning pull from each of these three models, as well as from others to create methods that work for them in their classrooms (Coleman, Gallagher, & Nelson, 1997).

Cooperative Learning with Gifted Students

The controversy over the use of cooperative learning with gifted students stems primarily from a heavy reliance on mixed-ability CL groups in a heterogeneous classroom (Allan, 1991; Gallagher & Coleman, 1994; Robinson, 1990; Sapon-Shevin & Schniedewind, 1993). When CL is used as the predominate method of instruction and groups are configured heterogeneously, gifted students may experience frustration (Mills & Durden, 1992; Robinson, 1991). Under these circumstances, gifted students in a national study expressed the following concerns

- worry when others in the group won't listen or work;
- anxiety that if they take over, others won't like them;
- frustration that they were being dragged down;
- annoyance at always being bugged for the answers; and
- angry when their grades were lowered as a result of the lack of effort on the part of others (Coleman & Gallagher, 1995).

Robinson (1990) captured the feeling these students expressed with a single word: exploitation.

In spite of the difficulties gifted students experienced, they also indicated that work in CL groups gave them a chance to feel helpful, be a leader, and get help when they needed it. Furthermore, they said that they were not always perfect, and sometimes they were the ones in trouble (Gallagher, Coleman, & Nelson, 1993; Matthews, 1992). The problems experienced by gifted students in these settings likely stem from a misuse of CL, rather than an appropriate use of a viable teaching/learning strategy (Coleman, 1994). In December, 1996, the National Association for Gifted Children issued a position paper which captures the main ideas of the controversy (see Figure 1).

When cooperative learning is used with groups of high ability students—in either advanced classes or in classes for gifted students—many of the difficulties disappear completely (Coleman et al., 1997). Gifted students working in CL groups with others of similar abilities seem to thrive on the interactive dynamic exchanges which this format promotes (VanTassel-Baska, 1998). The only drawback expressed by students regarding CL in these settings was that there never seemed to be enough talk time for everybody to share their ideas fully.

Strategies for CL with Gifted Students

The question is not "Should we use CL with gifted students?" but "How can we effectively use CL, in both its heterogeneous and

The National Association for Gifted Children (NAGC) periodically issues policy statements dealing with the issues, policies, and practices that have an impact on the education of gifted and talented students. Policy statements represent the official convictions of the organization.

All policy statements approved by the NAGC Board of Directors are consistent with the organization's belief that education in a democracy must respect the uniqueness of all individuals, the broad range of cultural diversity present in our society, and the similarities and differences in learning characteristics that can be found within any group of students. NAGC is fully committed to national goals that advocate both excellence and equity for all students, and we believe that the best way to achieve these is through differentiated educational opportunities, resources, and encouragement for all students.

Cooperative learning (CL) encompasses a variety of classroom practices which include the following attributes: group interdependence built around common goals, a focus on social skills or group dynamics, and individual accountability for material learned. Cooperative learning experiences can provide valuable opportunities to share ideas, practice critical thinking, and gain social skills.

When heterogeneous CL groups are the primary strategy in the classroom, gifted students' needs may not be met. Cooperative learning advocates often stress forming CL groups with students intentionally clustered by mixed-abilities. When gifted students are included in these CL groups, special care must be taken to differentiate the tasks appropriately. Cooperative learning is more likely to be effective for gifted learners when group tasks and goals:

- take into account differences in students' readiness levels, interests, and learning modes;
- focus on high-level tasks that require students to manipulate, apply, and extend meaningful ideas;
- ensure appropriate and balanced work responsibilities for all participants;
- ensure balanced opportunities for learners to work with peers of similar, as well as mixed readiness levels; and
- are balanced with opportunities for students to work independently and with the class as a whole.

Figure 1. NAGC Position on Cooperative Learning

When differentiation does not happen, gifted students may feel overburdened and responsible for the entire "workload."

Teachers who use CL with heterogeneous groups need additional support and preparation in how to structure the learning tasks to ensure that the instructional activities meet the cognitive and social needs of the most able students in the group. NAGC believes that cooperative learning should be viewed within a range of instructional strategies that may enhance some learning objectives for some gifted students some of the time but should not be used as a panacea to replace differentiated services addressing the educational needs of gifted students. When used in conjunction with an array of services to differentiate the education of gifted students, CL can be an appropriate strategy.

Figure 1. Continued

Note: From *Position Paper on Cooperative Learning* by National Association for Gifted Education (1996) Washington, DC: NAGC. Copyright 1996 NAGC. Reprinted with permission.

homogeneous forms, so that all students, including gifted learners, benefit?" A variety of strategies can be used to increase the likelihood that cooperative learning will meet the needs of gifted students. The following ideas should be considered:

- Offer some CL experiences in groups of high-ability students, such as honors and advanced classes, pull-out or gifted resource classes, and similar ability clusters within heterogeneous classrooms.

- Make sure that CL assignments reflect tasks that are differentiated for students' learning levels. For instance, if the group is finding locations on a globe using latitude and longitude, the locations should reflect a variety of difficulty levels to match student needs.

- Plan open-ended tasks so that all students can make meaningful contributions. Provide ample opportunities for students' contributions by creating a travel brochure for your state or designing a collage representing an African country.

- Use the *jigsaw* method to regroup students by task, interest, or level. If the task is creating a topographical map of a state, the students may regroup by ability for research and return to their main CL group with new information to help complete the assignment.

- Create CL groups as expert groups on a given topic, where students are allowed to self-select tasks to explore in greater depth. This can be an option for students who have mastered the basic curriculum before their classmates. In a U.S. history class, groups may form to study the roles of women during the Civil War or analyze early gospel music for themes/messages.
- Form CL groups across grade levels allowing advanced students to work with older students on projects of interest or to work in support roles with younger students in an area of strength. Students might join together to write computer programs or to create a nature path for the school.
- Use a variety of self-paced CL materials that encourage team members to move at their own learning rate while earning "progress points" for their team. Slavin (1991) designed several instructional materials that are appropriate for students in these settings.
- Use flexible CL groups where students can accomplish large tasks through the efforts of smaller strength and interest groups. For example, when putting on a class performance, students can choose from working on the sets; designing costumes; working on the programs, advertisements, and concessions; or writing, producing, and acting in the play.
- Form CL groups around problem-based learning activities (Gallagher, 1997; Hmelo & Ferrari, 1997) where students engage in working through an ill-structured problem. Problems focusing on high-interest concerns and curriculum content are integrated into the solution building process. For example, a science class could be asked to explain and make recommendations regarding a series of fish kills in a local water system.
- Provide a safety net for students who either do not want to work in a group (Li & Adamson, 1992) or who are experiencing great difficulty in group participation by planning alternatives for completing the assignments. Alternatives should be used when support offered still is not working and should not be seen as a punishment.

- Plan assessment strategies that recognize and reward group problem solving, innovation, and group dynamics and do not assign individual grades for students based on the groups efforts. CL groups could earn points/rewards for their team by working well and creating innovative solutions to given tasks; individual learning should be evaluated through other means.

The major theme of all of these strategies is building flexibility, choice, and challenge into the CL activities. This means that when we design CL lessons we should try to incorporate multiple levels of difficulty, use a variety of meaningful ways to contribute to the task, plan several opportunities for students to make decisions regarding the completion of the task/project, and use individual methods to assess/evaluate students' learning. This kind of CL takes a lot of planning and preparation. The next sections contain outlines of ideas and examples for CL activities.

Sample CL Activities for Different Grades and Settings

The following descriptions are meant to be used as examples on how CL activities might be structured to meet students' needs at multiple levels. Although the activities have been organized by subject area and grade level, they can be modified to fit different grades, depending on the needs of the students. The first description, "Room for Improvement," is presented in detail from the preparation through assessment phases. The remaining activities are briefly described.

Third Grade, Math, Measurement, and Area: Room for Improvement

The purpose of these activities is to reinforce measurement and the calculation of area. Students will work on both a CL home team (four to five students) and in jigsaw groups to gather information. The CL home team will be responsible for completing the main task and developing a proposal to redecorate the classroom. Each jigsaw group will work on a specific task to be folded into the home team proposal.

The difficulty levels of the individual tasks can be adjusted by assigning students to jigsaw groups. Students' choices are incorporated as they select the materials and design their proposal; individual students' strengths should be used in the preparation of the proposal itself. Time needed for completion of these activities will vary from one week to 10 days, depending on the amount of time designed each day.

Task Description. Each class in the school will be able to redecorate its room. We need to come up with a proposal to improve on our room. The principal will review our proposals and select one for the class. To develop the proposal, you will need a great deal of information. Here are some options you can use in your proposal: paint or wallpaper the walls; carpet part or all of the floor; put shelf-lining paper on the desks; get new window blinds; and add some bookshelves.

Each CL group is responsible for developing a proposal for the changes; the proposal serves as a bid for the job and must contain complete information on choices of colors, design ideas, and costs. The proposal must include enough information to complete the redecoration if it is the one selected. Each proposal must have a brief description of the proposed changes, a fact sheet with specific cost information (including the cost to paint the walls with the number of gallons of paint selected and the price per gallon); a design board that shows all the colors and combinations used; and a drawing of the room with the new changes.

Preparation. In the weeks before you begin, visit a hardware store and gather materials to build a resource bank for the project (this could be a field trip). You can use sample paint chips (make sure you list on each the cost-per-gallon and how much wall a gallon will cover—are two coats recommended?), wallpaper samples with cost/coverage information; swatches of carpet with price-per-square-foot (does it need a carpet backer?), samples of shelf-liner paper with cost and dimensions-per-roll, and window blind options with prices. If you want your students to look at bookshelves, you will also need information on boards, nails, and paint for these. Many hardware stores will donate yardsticks (and even hats with their logo) if you tell them it is for a school.

You will also need several measurement tools, such as tape measures, rulers, and yardsticks, as well as graph paper, pencils, and calculators. Materials for the proposals should also be handy (poster board, paper, colored pencils, or crayons).

CL Activities. Assign students to mixed-ability CL home teams (four to five per team). Present the "Room for Improvement" simulation and task and discuss the bidding process along with the principal's role in ultimately selecting the proposal (make sure your students know this is a simulation!). Assign students to jigsaw groups of appropriate difficulty level for data collection. Members of the jigsaw group will figure out how to calculate the area and cost of the items in their proposal—including floor area, type of carpet needed, and carpet prices. The five jigsaw groups (bookshelves, floor covering, desk tops with shelf paper, windows, and wall paper/paints) will carry this information back to their home CL team. You may want to design a worksheet for each group to record its data (see Figure 2).

Students in jigsaw groups should figure out how to measure and calculate the cost of the various options on which they are working (the more challenging tasks, such as calculating wall area and paint/paper cost, should be assigned to your top math students). During the process, students can explore a variety of problem-solving approaches to get the needed information. Once the jigsaw groups have their summary sheets, students return to their CL home team and share what they have learned.

The CL home team then selects the options it wants for its proposal. Once the options have been agreed on, the team assigns tasks for the proposal development (fact sheets, description, design board, and drawing).

Assessment of the CL Task. A sample rubric is included to present the CL home team's success in completing the assigned tasks (see Figure 3). The areas included in the sample assessment are
- group dynamics (ability of the students to work in harmony and ensure that all members make meaningful contributions);
- content of the proposal (comprehensiveness, accuracy, and integration of ideas);
- presentation (neatness, organization, and beauty); and
- innovation (ability to incorporate originality and uniqueness of style).

Name: _____ Surface area of walls: _____
Home team: _____ (square foot)

Paint:

	color	cost per gallon	square feet covered per gallon	2 coats? Yes No	total cost
1.					
2.					
3.					
4.					
5.					

Wall Paper:

	pattern	cost per roll	square feet covered per roll	total cost
1.				
2.				
3.				
4.				
5.				

**Figure 2. Room for Improvement:
Sample Worksheet for Data Collection**

These areas may change depending on what you want to emphasize. The teams can be given special recognition or rewards for their work based on the review of their success. The ultimate recognition would be the selection of their proposal by the principal as the winning bid.

Individual assessment of learning should be done using students' work samples, tests, and demonstrated mastery of content (in this case, measurement and calculation of area). Students may be given a smaller version of this task to complete independently, or they may be asked questions like "How many different ways can you figure out how much carpet will be needed to recarpet the principal's office?" Grades for math should reflect students' knowledge and mastery of the content and must be assigned through individual assessments.

Social Studies in the Sixth Grade

Many social studies classes in the middle grades are heterogeneously grouped with students of wide-ranging abilities. The ideas here are designed to allow the teacher to incorporate a variety of CL strategies to meet a range of student needs.

1. Create mixed-ability study teams to review material, compete in quiz bowls (make sure you offer challenge questions of increasing difficulty), and compete for accomplishment/improvement points. You can also award team points for homework completion as an extra incentive (Slavin, 1988).

2. Use pretests to assess mastery of basic information and allow students to challenge out of work they have mastered so they can pursue an area of interest. CL groups should be formed around topics related to the curriculum (e.g., study of the role of individuals in the early exploration of the West or changes in fashion across history). Products developed by the CL group can be shared with the class. Grades for these students should reflect individual mastery of the core content (pretest results) and success in completion of their part of the CL group work (often student contracts can help clarify expectations). If several students contribute to one product, ask that each student initial their contributions.

Title: Sample CL rubric for "Room for Improvement" Date _____
Topic: Math measurement and calculation of area Grade level _____

Level	Group Dynamics	Content of Proposal	Presentation	Proposal
5	Individuals worked in harmony and made meaningful contributions to group. Problems were handled in a positive manner.	Proposal incorporates all required elements and reflects accuracy and continuity of group thinking (integration of components).	Proposal presentation is neat, well-organized, colorful, and aesthetically pleasing.	Proposal ideas reflect original designs with unique style and/or combine existing components in an unusual fashion; has "flare."
4	The group worked well together completing the task and resolved problems in a positive manner.	Proposal is complete and accurate, and some attempt has been made to integrate parts.	Proposal is neat, well-organized, and colorful.	Ideas reflect some originality and unique combinations of components.
3	The group was able to complete task with minimum conflicts and was able to solve problems that arose with some support.	Proposal is complete and accurate but is somewhat disjointed (segments were not integrated).	Proposal is neat and well-organized.	Ideas reflect some originality.
2	The group was able to complete task with support to help them resolve conflicts.	Proposal is complete, but information is incorrect.	Proposal is well-organized but messy.	Ideas reflect little originality.
1	Group was unable to work together and problems overwhelmingly lead to conflicts.	Proposal is incomplete, and information is incorrect.	Proposal presentation is messy and poorly organized.	Ideas reflect little originality and represent a "copy."

Figure 3. Rubric Planner

3. Structure a large event—such as History Day, creation of an interactive History Museum, or a period play/reenactment; and form CL groups around students' interests and areas of strength to make contributions.

4. Complete an analysis of historical periods developing a cosmic calendar that shows the major event in politics, literature, the arts, science, inventions, fashion, and education. Your CL groups can select the topic to research and contribute their information to the overall calendar, or you can form home teams to create the calendars, and they can jigsaw out into the area study groups.

High School Physical Science Class

Most high school science classes are already leveled by ability or student self-selection. Within this setting, CL groups can provide motivation by capitalizing on students' interests. Whenever possible, students should be allowed to select the groups they will work in; if this is not possible, then the group members should be randomly assigned. Some ideas for CL activities include

1. CL groups may form to study areas of high interest that are not usually included in the curriculum, such as chaos theory, the Tao of Physics, the physics of baseball, the portrayal of physics in science fiction, or the history of physics. Students should self-select groups and contract to complete specific work assignments.

2. Science labs offer an ideal opportunity for CL groups to collaborate on problem solving. In addition to traditional labs, students can be given puzzlers and asked to design experiments to test, explain, or explore solutions. Puzzlers might include fairly straightforward physics applications like "What is the optimal wall covering for a music hall that accommodates for sounds during performances?" or more complex applications such as "Design an energy efficient dwelling that is as self-sustaining as possible." (This may be a space station or an underwater eco-sphere.)

3. High school science classes provide the perfect opportunity to infuse problem-based learning (PBL) activities. In a biology class, students may be asked to wrestle with "problems" as large as global warming or as close as a new shopping mall going up in the community. When CL groups are formed around PBL

activities, students work together as a team to research, debate, and present solutions to their problem.

4. Service learning opportunities are being provided for many high school students; in some districts, these are a requirement for graduation. Cooperative learning groups are an ideal vehicle for the development of service projects for the community or school. Service projects focus on needs and involve things like developing a playground for younger students, working with an after-school tutorial program, or monitoring the environment of a river for runoff and other pollution. These projects allow students to make meaningful contributions while exploring interests and career options.

Classes for Gifted Students

Special classes for gifted students offer a unique setting for CL. Students can be given the chance to pursue areas of high interest through CL groups, and the use of CL often reduces competitiveness through collaboration (Joyce, 1991). Although most students identified as gifted are socially competent (unlike the myth of the complete nerd), it may be necessary to review group dynamics and teach some skills to help build group cohesion (Joyce, 1991). These skills may be part of a leadership unit, or they may be built into a self-study approach as students get to know their learning and interaction styles (Ross & Smyth, 1995).

Role of the Teacher

The teacher's role in CL activities is different from her role in direct instruction. The primary work of the teacher actually happens before the CL activity takes place—the planning. Investment in planning time is essential to successful CL. The design of high quality CL lessons take time. When planning to use cooperative learning, the same kinds of decisions need to be made as with any other teaching strategy. As teachers, we continually reflect on questions like the following: Is the time going to be well spent? Does the topic lend itself to group work? Can I structure the task so all students can make meaningful contributions? What can I do for those who either will not, or cannot, work in groups? Is there a better way to engage my student?

During the CL lesson, teachers monitor the group work, help them trouble shoot, and, when necessary, intervene to help resolve group conflicts. Rules of thumb, such as "Ask three before me," help students understand that they should rely on their group first and the teacher second. Teachers' informal observations of students can often be done best when CL groups are meaningfully engaged. One strategy for this is to tell students that part of their grade for the project will be based on their participation in their group and that during the course of the project, you will be doing observations of each of them. Each day you can use sheets of mailing labels on a clip board to record observations and grades for specific students (peel off the sticker and place it in the student's portfolio or file). If you do not tell students when you are observing them specifically for their grade, you will find that they notice whenever you walk around with your clipboard.

Conclusions

When used appropriately, cooperative learning is a wonderful way to engage students in learning. Unfortunately, the mis-uses of CL, as either a teacher convenience or as a replacement for a variety of differentiated learning experiences, has caused problems for some gifted students. I hope this chapter will help to provide optimal learning experiences for all our students. Creating opportunities to engage students in exciting learning and allowing them to generate and share ideas is what schooling should be about. Cooperative learning is one option we have to reach and teach our students; we should use it wisely.

Teacher Resources

Publications

Churchill, R. (1992). *Amazing science experiments with everyday materials*. New York: Sterling.

More than 60 science experiments can be replicated at home so students, grades 2–8, can share their learning with family members.

Coffin, M. (1996). *Team science.* Tucson, AZ: Zephyr Press.
The outlines of science labs, appropriate for groups of students grades 4–8, foster cooperation while students learn about earth, life, or physical science topics.

Davidson, N., & Worsham, T. (Eds.). (1992). *Enhancing thinking through cooperative learning.* Williston, VT: Teachers College Press.
Practical ideas for implementation have been included to give the reader several ideas on how to build "cooperative thinking" into group activities.

Fogarty, R. (1997). *Problem-based learning.* Arlington Heights, IL: SkyLight.
While providing a variety of curricula frameworks, this book uses real-world problems to promote students' learning and thinking.

Addresses

Center for Gifted Education
The College of William and Mary
P.O. Box 8795
Williamsburg, VA 23187-8795
(757) 221-2362
fax (757) 221-2184
http://www.wm.ed/education/gifted.htm.
e-mail: cfge@facstaff.wm.edu
William and Mary Center for Gifted Education's Curriculum Units for Gifted Students provide an excellent platform for cooperative learning groups. Many of these units involve problem-based learning activities.

Prufrock Press
P.O. Box 8813
Waco, TX 76714–8813
(800) 998-2208
http://www.prufrock.com

SkyLight
2626 S. Clearbrook Dr.
Arlington Heights, IL 60005
(800) 290-6600

Teachers College Press
P.O. Box 20
Williston, VT 05495–0020
(800) 575-6566

Zephyr Press
P.O. Box 66006
Tucson, AZ 85728–6006
(800) 232-2187

References

Allan, S. (1991). Ability grouping research reviews: What do they say about grouping for the gifted? *Educational Leadership, 48*(6), 60–65.

Coleman, M. R. (1994). Using cooperative learning with gifted students. *Gifted Child Today, 17*(6), 36–37.

Coleman, M. R., & Gallagher, J. J. (1995). The successful blending of gifted education with middle schools and cooperative learning: Two studies. *Journal for the Education of the Gifted, 18*, 362–384.

Coleman, M. R., Gallagher, J., & Nelson, S. M. (1997). *Cooperative learning and gifted students: Report on five case studies.* Washington, DC: National Association for Gifted Children.

Ellis, S. S., & Whalen, S. F. (1990). *Cooperative learning: Getting started.* New York: Scholastic.

Gallagher, S. A. (1997). Problem-based learning: Where did it come from, what does it do, and where is it going? *Journal for the Education of the Gifted 20*, 332–362.

Gallagher, J. J., & Coleman, M. R. (1994). Cooperative learning and gifted students: Five case studies. *Cooperative Learning, 14*(4), 21–25.

Gallagher, J. J., Coleman, M. R., & Nelson, S. (1993). *Cooperative learning as perceived by educators of gifted students and proponents of cooperative education.* Chapel Hill, NC: University of North Carolina, Gifted Education Policy Studies Program.

Hmelo, C. E., & Ferrari, M. (1997). The problem-based learning tutorial: Cultivating higher-order thinking skills. *Journal for the Education of the Gifted 20*, 401–422.

Johnson, D., & Johnson, R. (1987). *Learning together and alone.* Englewood Cliffs, NJ: Prentice-Hall.

Johnson, D., & Johnson, R. (1990). Social skills for successful group work. *Educational Leadership, 47*(4), 29–32.

Johnson, D., & Johnson, R. (1991). What cooperative learning has to offer the gifted. *Cooperative Learning, 11*(3), 24–27.

Johnson, D., Johnson, R., & Holubnec, E. (1990). *Circles of Learning: Cooperation in the classroom* (3rd ed.). Edina, MN: Interaction Book.

Joyce, B. (1991). Common misconceptions about cooperative learning and gifted students. *Educational Leadership, 48*(6), 72–74.

Kagan, S. (1990). The structural approach to cooperative learning. *Educational Leadership, 47*(4), 12–15.

Li, A., & Adamson, G. (1992). Gifted secondary students' preferred learning style: Cooperative, competitive, or individualistic? *Journal for the Education of the Gifted, 16*, 46–54.

Matthews, M. (1992). Gifted students talk about cooperative learning. *Educational Leadership, 50*(2), 48–50.

Mills, C., & Durden, W. (1992). Cooperative learning and ability grouping: An issue of choice. *Gifted Child Quarterly, 36,* 11–16.

National Association for Gifted Children. (1996). Position paper on cooperative learning. Washington, DC: National Association for Gifted Children.

Nelson, S., Gallagher, J., & Coleman, M. R. (1993). Cooperative learning from two different perspectives. *Roeper Review, 16,* 117–121.

Robinson, A. (1990). Cooperation or exploitation? The argument against cooperative learning for talented students. *Journal for the Education of the Gifted, 14,* 9–27, 31–36.

Robinson, A. (1991). *Cooperative learning and the academically talented student.* Storrs, CT: The National Research Center on the Gifted and Talented.

Ross, J. A., & Smyth, E. (1995). Differentiating cooperative learning to meet the needs of gifted learners: A case for transformational leadership. *Journal for the Education of the Gifted, 19,* 63–82.

Sapon-Shevin, M., & Schniedewind, N. (1993). Why (even) gifted children need cooperative learning. *Educational Leadership, 50*(6), 62–63.

Sharan, S. (1990). Cooperative learning and helping behavior in the multi-ethnic classroom. In H. Foot, M. J. Morgan, & R. Shute (Eds.), *Children helping children* (pp. 151–176). New York: John Wiley.

Slavin, R. E. (1980). Cooperative learning. *Review of Educational Research, 50,* 315–342.

Slavin, R. E. (1981). Synthesis of research on cooperative learning. *Educational Leadership, 38*(8), 655–700.

Slavin, R. E. (1988). *Student team learning: An overview and practical guide.* Washington, DC: National Education Association.

Slavin, R. E. (1990). Ability grouping, cooperative learning, and the gifted. *Journal for the Education of the Gifted, 14,* 3–8, 28–30.

Slavin, R. E. (1991). What cooperative learning has to offer the gifted. *Cooperative Learning, 11*(3), 22–23.

VanTassel-Baska, J. (1998). *Excellence in educating gifted and talented learners.* (3rd ed.). Denver, CO: Love.

C H A P T E R   1 8

Teaching Through Simulations for the Gifted

DOROTHY A. SISK
Lamar University

S imulation games are experiential activities that, like Alice's Looking Glass, challenge assumptions, expand perspectives, and facilitate change. Just as Alice experienced the manipulation of time and space and gained personal insight, so do gifted students as they experience simulation and turn the present into the possible future.

Background and Definitions

Simulation as a teaching tool is not new by any means. For years, law students have participated in moot courts, and secondary students have conducted mock political conventions. Nevertheless, simulation techniques are experiencing significant growth in their development and use in teaching and education.

Simulation can be defined as constructing and operating on a model that replicates behavioral processes or a larger system of reality. In other words, a simulation is an operating imitation of a real process. A game can be defined as any contest (play) among adversaries (players) operating under constraints (rules) for an objective (winning, victory, or payoff). The term *game* is applied to simulations that work wholly or partly on the basis of players' decisions, because the environment and activities of participants have the characteristics of games; players have their goals, sets of activities to perform, constraints on what can be done, and pay-offs (good and bad) as consequences of the action. Although there are many wonderful simulation games available, the illustrations and examples given in this chapter have been used successfully in gifted programs (TAG GAME; BARNGA; Land of the Sphinx and Land of the Rainbow; BAFA' BAFA'; PARLE' and Uphill Controversy).

Why is Simulation Effective for Gifted Students?

Simulation has high motivational value because gifted students immediately see a useful reason to learn, to succeed, and to win the simulation game. "Playing to win" taps into their competitive nature. Simulation games also provide gifted students opportunities to do higher-level thinking such as critical and creative thinking, logical thinking, and decision making. Social values are taught through simulation and competition is experienced, but coopera-tion is necessary to experience a common goal: winning the game. Students also gain empathy for real-life decisions and a better understanding of the effects of various situations (Lee, 1994).

In simulations, gifted students act and interact as they become involved in the facts, the processes, and the key concepts to be learned in the game. Interactions becomes legitimate vehicles for learning—powerful and deep learning takes place while they are engaged in exciting and satisfying play (Sharon & Sharon, 1992).

Simulation games provide opportunities for gifted students to practice new behaviors and experiment with new attitudes and points of view in a nonthreatening, nonjudgmental environment. Maker and Neilson (1996) stressed the valuable social and leader-ship skills that are developed in these interactive group activities.

Simulation games are also particularly useful in building cross-cultural understandings because, in a very short time, students can stimulate cognitive and affective understandings of other cultures to broaden their perspectives. Duke and Seinder (1978) noted that simulations increase students' tolerance and their levels of acceptance of others' thoughts and ideas.

Major Benefits for Gifted Students Derived From Simulation Games

Critical Thinking. Simulation games motivate and reward critical thinking of gifted students as they analyze possible moves and probable consequences of those moves and rationally plan and think through countermoves. Simulation games also encourage and develop the intuitive thinking of gifted students as they make spontaneous decisions.

Understanding the Role of Chance. Simulation games demonstrate that life is not always affected by logical plans or intuitive solutions. We know from experience that rarely are we completely in control of our lives and, for that reason, most designers of simulations include chance variables.

Multi-Level Learning. Gifted students learn on three levels while participating: (1) learning facts and information embodied in the context and dynamics of the game;(2) learning processes simulated by the game; and (3) learning the relative costs, benefits, risks, and potential rewards of alternative strategies for making decisions. Through information, processes, and strategies, simulation provides students the experience of simultaneously operating on all three levels and demonstrates that decision making is not a simple process (Myers & Myers, 1995). Many gifted students operate on several levels simultaneously, and they particularly enjoy this engaging aspect of simulation.

Social Values. Simulation games teach social values, such as competition, cooperation, and empathy. Gifted students, with their worthy sense of values, appreciate opportunities to explore social values. In PARLE', students clearly see that players must cooperate in order to play and win. By cooperating on problems that affect the attainment of goals, gifted students come to understand and appreciate the social value of cooperation.

Personal Responsibility. As players make choices and receive rapid feedback, they see the consequences of decisions immediately. They learn that their actions affect others, as well as themselves. Gifted students experience the way decisions influence the future. Simulation games allow students to recognize their personal responsibility in dealing constructively and effectively with the environment and influencing plans for actions in the future.

Teacher/Student Dynamics. Simulation games involve a close working relationship between the teacher and the students. Since the teacher acts as facilitator and the rules of the game direct the participants, the teacher is viewed not as judge or jury but as an assistant to the process, allowing the student to focus attention on what is happening in the game. Learning is turned over to the participants, and gifted students, with their strong sense of independence, enjoy this aspect of simulation.

Knowledge and Skills. Simulation games build upon the knowledge and skills each student brings to the simulation, while at the same time, they increase the student's knowledge of specific terms, concepts, facts, structures, and relationships. In simulation, the teacher is able to help the students develop specific intellectual and social skills and change their attitudes. Simulation games encourage students to think and ask the kinds of questions that expand their understanding of social systems in a global situation. In a structured and safe situation, simulation games afford opportunities for gifted students to experiment, to try new ideas and behaviors, and to develop leadership skills.

With skillful debriefing, the teacher links game behavior to real-life problem solving. According to James Coleman, former director of the Johns Hopkins Center for Developing Simulation Games, the use of simulation reverses a common situation for the learner (Coleman, 1966). Instead of having learning as the primary goal, the student has learning of the material as a secondary motivation, a step necessary to reach the main goal, which is doing well in the simulation game. In simulation games, the students assimilate the material in order to efficiently carry out actions toward the game's goal.

Group Dynamics. Simulation establishes a sense of community among the students. The low-risk situation offers opportunities for self-awareness, and learning continues beyond the game as students experience insight within their own lives and those of others. The problem-solving situation in simulation actively involves the students and requires considerable interaction and communication. This quickly brings about a sense of trust in a group of students, and a high degree of motivation arises because the students enjoy playing games.

Simulation games are used at the highest levels of international policy study. Most people are naturally partisan; just as lawyers for two litigants are likely to do a better job of raising and investigating the issues involved in a dispute than if they sat as judges, so does role-playing in simulation make for a more intense and thorough investigation. In addition, most students trying to understand the reactions of others in complicated hypothetical situations are more effective if they actively identify with one of the participants. Teachers who successfully use simulation games are highly enthusiastic and report being more involved with their students in the learning process.

Description of the Method

To understand what a simulation game is, it is helpful to examine each part: activity, simulation, and game.

Teachers are familiar with group exercises that can be processed so that students learn by doing. For example, if you ask a small group of students to put together a puzzle and give each person a few of the pieces, they will set about doing it. When you stop them and ask what they learned from this activity, they might discuss teamwork, leadership, cooperation, power, or strategic planning. This activity is an exercise.

However, you could make this exercise into a simulation by asking the students what workplace roles would be appropriate for putting together the puzzle. They might suggest puzzle assemblers, frontline managers, executives, accountants, or legal counsel. Then, you could ask for volunteers to play each role and give them an appropriate identification badge. In this way, they could continue to put the puzzle together with new ways of relating to each other to get the job done. The activity now represents a simulation exercise.

To turn this simulation exercise into a simulation game, you would need to add game-like elements and rules. In this case, you might give some of the puzzle assemblers specific constraints such as blindfolds or a rule that they can only touch inside pieces—no edges. You could give chips to the accountant to be used as rewards or give chips to the managers who could pay the accountant when the assemblers make mistakes. You could give the executives the puzzle box with the picture of the completed puzzle or give the executives their own puzzle to complete. You could add payoffs by giving assemblers or managers chips each time a puzzle is completed. In this activity, you are now working with a simulation game that could provide a rich debriefing.

TAG GAME

Developed by Garry Shirts (1992) at Simulation Training Systems, this is a short, highly participative exercise that can be used to encourage a group of gifted students to focus on similarities and differences so they can be openly discussed in class sessions. Students wear tags of different shapes and colors, walk around silently, observe each other, and then, without any talking, the teacher asks them to group themselves. After a couple of rounds, the students hand in their tags and receive new, very unique tags. Again they are asked to observe but not to talk before they decide on how to group. Debriefing plus game time usually takes less than one hour. Gifted students usually list obvious similarities and differences among people, but eventually they begin to identify deeper, more abstract similarities and differences.

BARNGA

Created by Sivasailam Thiagarajan (1989), BARNGA's key concept is that cultural differences exist in subtle forms, but they are often swamped by obvious similarities. Students in groups of four learn and play a quick card game. The groups think they are all learning the same game, but each game is slightly different. After five minutes, players are asked to play silently and to settle any disputes by communication through gestures. After five more minutes, two players from each table are shifted to the next table, under the guise of a tournament. Because two sets of rules are now in operation, there are heated discussions expressed through gestures. After five minutes of play at this table, players shift once more to the next table. The game is terminated after five minutes.

Land of the Sphinx and Land of the Rainbow

This game was developed by Sisk (1983b) to assist a group of psychologists in understanding and experiencing learning styles and to explore the concept of cerebral differences. The game can take up to a half day with debriefing; however, it has been successfully played in two class periods with high school gifted students. The setting is the year 2050, and a minimum of four travelers are selected to visit two different lands, the Land of the Sphinx and the Land of the Rainbow. Each land is posed with the necessity of selecting three projects to shape their future: one in education, research, and environment. In small groups, the students identify their three projects and then receive the travelers. The scenario for the Land of the Sphinx describes them as being inhabited by people who trust logic, objectivity, and implicitly. Order is very important, as are schedules and routine. Conversely, the Land of the Rainbow is inhabited by people who are interested in a deeper, larger, all-embracing reality, and they follow hunches. Students in one land do not have the description or scenario of people in the other land.

In the simulation game, travelers experience different reactions to questions that they pose to members of the two lands. The travelers' instructions ask them to display enthusiasm and curiosity and to be bold, open, courageous, and to find out as much about the new country as possible. In the debriefing, students usually discuss whether or not they were comfortable in the land to which they were assigned, and then the travelers are asked to select the land where they would like to remain as a resident. This game can be played with as many as 100 students. Large numbers require the creation of several Lands of the Sphinx and Lands of the Rainbow and adding sufficient numbers of travelers to allow visits to all of the lands.

Discussion centers should be established as a forum to share which environment is conducive to aspiration, curiosity, and individual goal attainment. Students from different cultures often see similarities between the simulated countries and their own. Many will want to openly discuss whether their homeland is shaping a desirable future. This simulation activity has been used in leadership seminars with middle school and high school students and as an opening exercise with residential students in the Texas Governor's Honors program to help build a sense of community. Gifted students quickly point out the similarities of the travelers' characteristics to those of gifted students.

BAFA' BAFA'

In BAFA' BAFA' the students are divided into two cultures: Alpha and Beta. Separately, each group learns the rules specific to its own culture. Alpha is an in group/out group, touching culture, and Beta is a foreign language-speaking, task-oriented culture. Once students learn and practice the rules of their own culture, observers and visitors are exchanged. After each exchange, students return and try to describe their experiences in observing and interacting with the other culture. BAFA' BAFA' teaches that what seems irrational, contradictory, or unimportant to us in our culture may seem rational, consistent, and terribly important to a person from another culture. Shirts (1992; 1974) developed BAFA' BAFA' for the Navy to help military personnel coexist within different cultures.

PARLE'

This simulation game was developed by Sisk (1976) to provide students opportunities to become representatives of 10 imaginary countries (Shima, Myna, Ila, Usa, Pam, Bonay, Shivey, Lani, Ranu, and Bili). Each of the countries has a variety of factors to be considered: defense, resources, and demography. A major theme of PARLE' is negotiation and interdependence among countries. A number of crisis incidents are introduced, such as a revolution in

Ranu. The teacher/leader can vary the point of time to reflect the past or present or to project into the future. The only way countries can win in this simulation is by cooperating and pooling resources.

Elements of Simulation Games

Simulation games can be compared across a range of characteristics such as time, props, number of participants, and debriefing.

1. *Time.* Simulation games can take a short time; some, like TAG, PARLE' and BARNGA, can be done in under an hour. Or, they can take a long time, such as Land of the Sphinx and Land of the Rainbow and BAFA' BAFA', which can take up to a half a day.

2. *Props.* Some games use simple props or artifacts such as paper clips and construction paper for TAG GAME or more sophisticated ones like those used in BAFA' BAFA'. Others use only the instructions (Land of the Sphinx and Land of the Rainbow). In addition, simulation games can simulate whole cultures or only aspects of a culture, such as PARLE' and BAFA' BAFA'.

3. *Number of Participants.* PARLE' can be played with 40 to 80 people. It can also be played with as few as 14 people, although much of the richness of the involvement is lost. TAG GAME can be played with 9 people, but it is more effective with 16 to 20. It can also be played in a large area filled with tables, with 100 to 200 people. Most games have an optimum number for playing, but with some ingenuity on the part of the teacher, they can be shrunk or expanded to accommodate numbers. One simple way to expand a game is to run several simultaneous games.

4. *Debriefing Issues.* PARLE' is a nonthreatening simulation game that can serve as an excellent beginning for gifted students to learn how to discuss sensitive issues. Once the game ends, the teacher can debrief what happened in the simulation and encourage the students to draw analogies to real life. For example, one group of gifted high school students listed biased perceptions as a communication problem and noted a number of

misperceptions that were formed because they were viewing another culture from the viewpoint of their own culture. In debriefing simulation games that focus on multicultural issues, teachers will want to encourage gifted students to discuss specific real life situations the game simulates. For example, after playing Land of the Sphinx and Land of the Rainbow, the teacher can ask students to address what might be done when someone is placed in the predicament of not knowing the rules in a new culture—but thinking they do. "Processing" is the heart of simulation games, and debriefing usually focuses on what happened, what the consequences of the actions were, how misperceptions lead to mistakes, how certain strategies were effective, and so forth. May (1997) stressed the importance of the teacher observing and debriefing any stereotyping. These debriefings represent content issues such as cultural biases, values, and the needs for both adaptation and accommodation.

Using Simulations Effectively

When using simulation games with gifted students, it is important that the teacher/leader warm-up the students with a brief introduction of the game and explanation of the rules and patterns of play. It is important for the teacher to be clear and then move on, to accommodate the impatience and enthusiasm of gifted students who demand a fast pace. Clarity is essential, and it develops as the simulation game progresses. While the students are playing the game, the teacher's role is to be alert, observant, and as unobtrusive as possible. When asking the students to stop the game to debrief, a simple bridge from the game to debriefing can be: "Now, let's talk about what happened during the past half-hour or so . . ."

Flexibility and imagination are the keys to organizing gifted students to successfully experience simulation games. The high degree of student-to-student communication requires an atmosphere that allows physical and intellectual mobility. To facilitate this, the teacher will need to develop a sense of timing, knowing when it is appropriate to offer aid and support and when it is time to stop the simulation to process or debrief the action.

The processing, critiquing, or debriefing period is another essential element of simulation games; through analyzing their experience, students capitalize on the full learning potential. The importance of processing is reflected in the Chiodo and Flavin (1993) assertion that, until the opportunity to reflect is given to students, total learning has not taken place. In the postgame discussion, gifted students usually inductively arrive at a consensus of ideas, and the teacher's role is to direct the students' critical attention to the concepts and processes that the game simulated.

The debriefing format encourages students to share what they have experienced. Students will initially need to describe what happened. It helps for students to hear others' experiences in addition to sharing their own. As they talk about beliefs and feelings experienced during the simulation game, students can be encouraged to analyze why certain things happened or what was the basis from which certain observations were derived. The teacher can encourage the students to note the similarity of the game to the world's reality. With a little encouragement, debriefing sessions naturally move to summarizing and generalizing that which constitute the message or key concept simulated in the game.

Another effective technique for debriefing is to ask students to list or share specific ideas that have come forth during the discussion and to offer generalizations based on these ideas to draw conclusions. This approach is quite effective since generalizations and conclusions are more meaningful to gifted students when they come from themselves.

In addition, Clark (1985) cautioned teachers to be aware that gifted students' sensitivity and empathy may result in their becoming emotionally involved in the simulation game and losing their critical sense. Games also may trigger intense feelings, and occasionally arguments can lead to expressions of personal hostility. A skillful and sensitive teacher can help prevent these outbursts by closely observing the group during the simulation and making a special effort to resolve ill feelings as they become evident during the debriefing. When there are disagreements, the teacher can ask students which rules were ignored and why and encourage them to analyze their own behavior during the game. This aspect of the game addresses the interpersonal and intrapersonal behaviors of giftedness as described by Gardner (1983).

Teachers need to be sure simulation games are culturally appropriate, since participative learning is not traditional in all societies. Unfortunately, there is no rule of thumb for making the decision of whether or not to use a simulation game. Simulation games have been used successfully when there appeared to be little or no chance for success. The factors seem to be the teacher's comfort level with the method, the game's handling of the topic, the degree of trust developed, and an effective teacher to help frame the game in terms that are meaningful and relevant to the maturity level of the students. The best way to understand simulation games is to briefly examine several very different ones.

Designing a Simulation Game

Designing a simulation game is a complicated process, not to be undertaken lightly, and has a number of variables that need to be considered. First, decide what simulation game you want to teach: What are the key concepts on which to focus? Then, select the real-life situation the game will simulate. Next comes the structure of the game: What roles, goals, resources, interaction, sequence of events, and external factors need to be considered? Decide if there will be a board, tokens, score sheets, tables, graphs, chance cards, spinners or dice, and the like.

Then, write the rules. What is the order of play? What do players do? How does the game end? It is essential to test and revise games, adjusting them for realism, validity, comprehensiveness, and playability. Re-designing an existing game may be preferable to starting from scratch.

To demonstrate how teachers can devise their own games, a simple format developed by Avis Reid (1984) in her workbook *Turn to Page 84* can be helpful. First, start with a problem base for simulation. Decide on a concise statement of the problem such as *A communicable disease has broken out in a community.* Then, decide on the objectives of the game such as (1) *the students will experience group dynamics such as reaching a consensus;* (2) *the students will develop insight into their own personal value system and* that of others; and (3) *the students will explore various methods of decision making.*

After the objectives have been decided, scenarios or scenes should be written that could include past events, background information, the present time, setting, and conditions that will affect the game, such as *The community is multi-ethnic and comparatively isolated. It is midwinter and the decision concerning a communicable disease must be made in 24 hours.*

Characters and their goals are then identified: *Doctors, nurses, parents, teachers, principals, and students will be involved.* When writing the characters' brief descriptions—their physical characteristics and personalities—you may want to allow the students' creative role-playing to "flesh out" the characters. The final description may be as brief as the following: *The doctor is the only one who knows how the cure must be utilized. He is to be assisted by a panel of citizens including two nurses who are against the use of the serum.* Three roles can be either specifically spelled out, leaving no leeway, or leaving considerable leeway for the gifted students to create the characters with their own ideas and values.

Following the establishment of the characters and their goals, Reid (1984) suggested that an exact point in time be identified for the beginning of the game. She also suggested listing the resources to be used for the game, whether they be physical, social, economic, political, or personal. Resources give the game greater complexity and heighten the interest of the players.

Rules and their administration are the last to be included. Rules include those that govern the players, the game pattern, the scoring, and the implementation. In the case of the aforementioned communicable disease game, *Several people (15) have been exposed, and there is serum for only eight people. How can decisions be made to save eight people and sacrifice the lives of seven others? Each person is given a role on the advisory panel and a certain number of points. A consensus is required to make decisions, and there is a time constraint of one hour.*

The last areas to be considered in devising a game are debriefing and evaluation. During this time, lead the students to examine how decisions were made and how they felt about them. This is an opportunity for the teacher to reinforce positive social attitudes that have been observed and to arrange other experiences for information gathering to help the gifted students build greater understanding. Analogies can be made to both present and past situations from observations shared by the gifted students. Debriefing is extremely important and should be allotted to approximately one-fourth of

---

Name of the Game

**Statement
of the Problem**

Objectives

Scenario
Include past events, background information, the present time, setting, and the conditions that may affect the game.

Characters
Give a brief description of the physical characteristics, the personality, and the players' goals for the game.

Point in Time
The exact place and time when the game begins.

Resources
Props for the game—physical, social, economic, political, or personal.

Rules
To govern players, the game pattern and scoring, and implementation.

Evaluation and Feedback
Were objectives reached; can the game be improved?

Figure 1. Design Your Own

Note. From *Turn to Page 84,* by Reid, 1985 as cited in *Creative Teaching of the Gifted,* (pp. 114–117), by D. Sisk, 1985, New York: McGraw-Hill.

the playing time. If there is a 45-minute playing period, 15 minutes should be allowed for debriefing. The format for *Design Your Own* appears in Figure 1.

Uphill Controversy, designed by Pat Gilbert (1980), a teacher of the gifted, is an example of the Reid format entitled *Design Your Own* (see Figure 2). This is the first step in planning a game (Sisk, 1983a).

Name of Game   Uphill Controversy

Objectives
To gain insight into how a school system is organized, why changes are made, and who makes the decisions.

Scene
Uphill Elementary school was built in 1920. It has a fine reputation but dwindling numbers. Many families have lived in the neighborhood for 20 years.

Characters
Board of Education members, teachers, children, county financial advisors, and parents.

Point in Time
Press Release: Decision concerning possible closure of Uphill school to be made in three days. A PTA meeting is called to discuss the issue.

Resources
Maps showing high school attendance area, location of other elementary schools, and number of students in each. State and county guidelines for transportation.

Rules
- Each group will meet to prepare arguments for or against school closure. One member of the group may go to another group to try to form coalitions. Any number of group members may align themselves with another group, although the leader and the recorder must stay in the original group.
- Each group will present its proposal before the Board of Education. The Board will meet and vote on the decision. The Board will also vote for the group whose proposal is most convincing. The group receiving the most votes is declared the winner.

Evaluation and Feedback

Figure 2. Design Your Own: Uphill Controversy

Note. From Unpublished Manuscript, by P. Gilbert, 1980, COGS: University of West Virginia at Charleston as cited in *Creative Teaching of the Gifted*, (pp. 116–117), by D. Sisk, 1985, New York: McGraw-Hill.

Situations in Which Simulation Games Are Useful

Simulation games are effective in preparing gifted students for student exchange programs. At the Center for Creativity, Innovation, and Leadership (CCIL) at Lamar University in Beaumont, TX, simulation games have proved effective with the United States Agency for International Development foreign graduate students from mostly third world countries studying in the United States to prepare for re-entry to their homelands. For example, Land of the Sphinx and Land of the Rainbow, played with this group, encouraged open discussion of incidents of understanding, misunderstanding, and over-generalizing to either individuals or countries.

Many simulation games can be flexibly used with a wide age-span of gifted students to enrich their study of political science, geography, history, and current affairs. For example, PARLE' illustrates the influence of geography and natural resources on foreign policy. It also introduces students to the central problem facing foreign policy makers throughout history: the defense of one's country when it is surrounded by potentially hostile neighbors. In playing PARLE', gifted students learn the importance of personal diplomacy and how individual responsibility can transform sensitive international situations. Young gifted children can play PARLE' to develop an understanding of the importance of leadership and the interactive effect of resources and geography on a country. Prufrock Press publishes a series of multi-disciplinary simulation games such as *Endangered Species* (Beeler, 1994); *Medieval Destructions* (Beeler, 1992); *Western Exploration* (Beeler, 1992); *Earth Friendly* (Beeler, 1994); and *American Nostalgia* (Beeler, 1992). May (1997) compiled a number of simulation resources that are listed at the end of this chapter and categorized by subject area.

The intensity of involvement in simulation games helps gifted students learn quickly. Gifted programs that need to rapidly develop some key concepts in a limited time period will want to use this method. For example, Land of the Sphinx and Land of the Rainbow was used to help a school system hosting an international educational seminar understand the complexities of different cultures and different ways of behaving. The organizers used the insight they gained from the game to organize one of the most successful meetings ever attempted by their school system.

Simulation games are great levelers. Gifted students facing any new experience can play PARLE' and learn how to operate more efficiently in a group. During simulation activities, students become aware of each other's strengths and weaknesses and learn how to help one another reach goals. Parker (1989) stated that the most meaningful simulations are ones in which the students role-play by putting themselves in the place of others.

Benefits and Outcomes From Using Simulation Games

In a discussion concerning the use of simulation with Phil Phoenix, Professor Emeritus from Columbia University in New York, he stated that play is one of the fundamental factors in the creation of culture, and simulation games provide a means for making the topic at hand relevant to current reality. In a game where students take on future roles in the limited time and space framework of the simulation, choices are made to follow certain courses. For that moment, students turn the present into the future and sample the future. This manipulation of time and space can be one of the most meaningful and exciting aspects of simulation. Through simulation, students eliminate the interval between learning and applying; they tie the present, the future, skills, values, and knowledge together to make an ongoing situation relevant and useful. Simulations also provide opportunities for students to safely practice their behavior in the classroom (Axelson 1993).

Comparison With Other Teaching Methods

When simulation games are compared to other instructional methods such as written materials, textbooks, workbooks, lectures, and technological presentations on selected variables such as responsiveness and a variety of other input modes, one finds that simulation games require an active response from each student and respond to each student's actions. A survey of more than 350 students in a school for gifted indicated that the students overwhelmingly preferred collaborative experiences rather than individualistic experiences (Christensen, 1994). Simulation games incorporate a wide variety of input methods or ways for information to be presented such as speeches, prints, pictures, charts, maps, and diagrams. In addition, games often present

Advantages	Disadvantages
• Active involvement • Fun and challenging • Change of pace • Produces memorable, shared experience • Promotes deductive learning (i.e., child's play) • Makes drill and practice more palatable • Simplifies complicated issues or concepts • Encourages empathy • Allows risk taking and creativity in a safe environment • Promotes development of analytic skills • Makes theory and strategy tangible concepts	• Time-consuming • May have special space or equipment requirements • Expense of commercial games • Not considered legitimate training • Cultural issues among multicultural groups • Intense enthusiasm for active learning may cause resistance to more traditional learning • Oversimplifies complex issues or concepts • Momentum of game may mask objectives • Participants may have trouble or refuse to get out of game roles • All participants may not have the same experience

Figure 3. Advantages and Disadvantages of Simulation Games

Note. From "*Creating Participatory Learning Activities that Promote Effective Functioning of Multi-cultural Work Groups,*" by J. Blohm and J. Bradley, SIETAR 16th Congress, Kilkenny, Ireland, 1990. Copyright Judee Blohm. Reprinted with permission.

information by means of the physical position of tokens on a board, furniture in a room, or even the students themselves. Simulation games tend to take longer than more didactic methods, yet learning is quick and often more insightful since games are usually more active and more intense than many teaching methods. A list of advantages and disadvantages will be helpful in making a decision on when to use simulation as a teaching tool (see Figure 3).

Conclusion

Simulations have long been used in the military, business, medicine, administrative planning, and education. Their use as a teaching tool is substantial and simulations are particularly applicable to the study of issues by gifted students. Through simulation games, gifted students learn to make more intelligent decisions about life as they experience various processes such as interactive negotiation, communication, decision making, and creative problem solving. The intellectual jolt that simulation provides is often enough to start gifted students learning how to learn about a given topic of interest. This highly motivating nature of simulation makes it a complementary tool to well-integrated gifted programs.

Teacher Resources

Publications

Language Arts

Arner, B. (1995). *Library detective.* Carlsbad, CA: Interact.
A simulation of solving a mystery while learning how to find library information. A precious library manuscript has been stolen. Students join in cooperative learning teams and work to find the missing manuscript. Appropriate for grades 4–8.

Jaffe, C. (1991/1987). *Enchanted castle.* Carlsbad, CA: Interact.
A simulated journey through a fantasy world of fairy tales. Your students receive a Story Guide Map and Travel Tickets and plan a journey to an enchanted castle. Along the way, they stop to read fantasy fairy tales and complete intriguing activities. Appropriate for grades 2–4.

Jaffe, C., & Liberman, M. (1989). *Odyssey.* Carlsbad, CA: Interact.
A simulated journey through the world of classic Greek mythology where student teams meet heroes, heroines, gods, and goddesses. Students will read in teams at least eight classical myths. They will also work to climb Mt. Olympus (to work through each level, team members analyze the myths cooperatively, then complete a comprehension worksheet for group evaluation). Appropriate for grades 4–8.

Math

Middendorf, C. J., & White, F. (1991). *Math quest.* Carlsbad, CA: Interact.
An adventure simulation focusing on math problem-solving techniques, where cooperative learning groups explore four strange worlds in search of great treasure. Students apply several math problem-solving strategies while trekking through Dinosaurland, Fantasyland, Sportland, and Numberland. Appropriate for grades 3–8.

Bippert, J., & Steiger, J. (1989). *Shopping spree.* Carlsbad, CA: Interact.
A game show simulation teaching students calculator and estimation skills. As contestants on a game show, students reinforce their calculator skills, make purchasing decisions, and spend game show money in six different shops. Appropriate for grades 3–8.

Day, M. (1980). *Stock market.* Carlsbad, CA: Interact.
Stock Market. A math and economics simulation of buying and selling in the stock market. Students have an imaginary $100 bill to invest and try to make wise decisions by researching their purchases. Appropriate for grades 6–12.

Science

Bippert, J., & Vandling, L. (1995). *Project polaris*. Carlsbad, CA: Interact.
A simulation in which students build a space station while utilizing estimation and measurement. In cooperative learning space pods, students use estimation and hands-on measurements at each of 10 constellation stopping points in space. Their mission—build a space station where everyone convenes in a united effort to ensure galactic peace. Appropriate for grades 3–6

Flindt, M. (1990). *Zoo*. Carlsbad, CA: Interact.
A simulation of caring for animals in a modern zoo. In this simulation, the mayor and city council plan to close Zooland because it is outdated, the animals are poorly treated, and attendance is declining. Your students want to save Zooland and take action. Appropriate for grades 2–5.

Libetzky, J., & Hildebrand, J. (1993/1975). *Adapt*. Carlsbad, CA: Interact.
An interaction unit exploring the importance of physical environment to past, present, and future societies. Students become geographers examining the importance of physical environment to the lives of past and present human beings living in hunting and gathering societies. Appropriate for grades 6–9.

Wallace, D. (1991). *Clone*. Carlsbad, CA: Interact.
A simulation of a congressional hearing on genetic engineering. What makes us Human? If a human is cloned, does the clone also have human rights? Appropriate for grades 6–12.

Wesley, J. (1993/1971). *Ecopolis*. Carlsbad, CA: Interact.
A simulation of a community struggling to solve ecological problems. Students study a brief 150 year ecosystem history and then examine ecological issues in their imaginary city of Ecopolis, whose population has soared to 225,000. Appropriate for grades 6–9.

Social Studies

Broderbond/Learning Company. (1985). *Where in the world is Carmen San Diego?* San Rafael, CA: Broderbond/Learning.
Students in grades 5–12 learn geographic facts and skills while tracking Carmen across the globe.

Lacey, B. (1998/1995). *Calhoun vs. Garrison.* Carlsbad, CA: Interact. A confrontational talk show format. John C. Calhoun, Southern advocate, and William Lloyd Garrison, abolitionist, debate whether or not Americans should allow slavery to remain in their nation. Appropriate for grades 7–12.

Plantz, C., & Callis, J. M. (1995). *Pacific rim.* Carlsbad, CA: Interact. A simulation which helps students understand the growing importance of Pacific Rim countries, lands, people, and cultures. Students complete research projects and written reports. Students also simulate travel on a ship from Japan to New Zealand. Appropriate for grades 5–9.

Addresses

Association for Business Simulations and Experiential Learning (ABSEL)
Center for Business Simulations, LB 8127
Georgia Southern College
Statesboro, GA 30460–8127
http://www.towson.edu/~absel/
(912) 681-5457
Broderbund Software
17 Paul Dr.
San Rafael, CA 94903-2101

Electronic Arts
http://www.ea.com

Interact
1914 Palomar Oaks Way, #150
Carlsbad, CA 92008

Intercultural Press
P.O. 700
Yarmouth, ME 04096
International Simulation and Gaming Association (ISAGA) and the *Simulation and Gaming: An International Journal of Theory, Practice and Research* (Official Journal of ABSEL, ISAGA and NASAGA, edited by David Croohall)

Elyssabeth Leigh, President
Faculty of Education
University of Technology, Sydney
P.O. Box 123
Broadway NSW 2007
Australia
e-mail: Elyssabeth.Leigh@uts.edu.au
http://www.home.aone.net.au/ozsaga/what_is_isaga.htm

North American Simulation and Gaming Association (NASAGA)
P.O. Box 78636
Indianapolis, IN 46278

Prufrock Press
P.O. Box 8813
Waco, TX 76714–8813
(800) 998-2208
http://www.prufrock.com

Gary R. Shirts
BAFA' BAFA'
P.O. Box 910
Del Mar, CA 92014.
Simulation Training Systems
483 Avenida Primavera
Del Mar, CA 92014

S. Thiagarajan
BARNGA
4423 East Trailbridge Rd.
Bloomington, IN 47401

References

Axelson, J. (1993). *Counseling and development in a multicultural society.* Belmont, CA: Wadsworth.

Beeler, C. (1992). *Simulation Series: American Nostalgia.* Waco, TX: Prufrock Press.

Beeler, C. (1992). *Simulation Series: Medieval Destinations.* Waco, TX: Prufrock Press.

Beeler, C. (1992). *Simulation Series: Western Exploration.* Waco, TX: Prufrock Press.

Beeler, C. (1994). *Simulation Series: Earth Friendly.* Waco, TX: Prufrock Press.

Beeler, C. (1994). *Simulation Series: Endangered Species.* Waco, TX: Prufrock Press.

Blohm, J. (1997). *Use of games and simulations in team building.* (Unpublished manuscript) Conference paper at Intern-ational Water Environment Conference, Stockholm, Sweden.

Blohm, J., & Bradley, J. (1990). *Creating Participatory Learning Activities that Promote Effective Functioning of Multi-Cultural Work Groups.* Conference paper at SIETAR 16th Congress, Kilkenny, Ireland.

Chiodo, J. & Flavin, M. (1993). The link between computer simulations and social studies learning. *Debriefing Social Studies, 84*(3), 119–121.

Christensen, M. (1994). An investigation of gifted students' perceptions involving competitive and noncompetitive learning situations. In N. Colangelo, S. G. Assouline, & D. L. Ambroson (Eds.), *Talent Development, Vol. 2,* (pp. 505–507), Dayton, OH: Psychology Press.

Clark, B. (1985). *Growing up gifted.* Columbus, OH: Merrill.

Coleman, J. S. (1966). In defense of games. *American Behavioral Scientist, 10,* 3–4.

Dukes, R., & Seinder, C. (1978). *Learning with simulations and games.* Beverly Hills, CA: Sage Publications.

Gardner, H. (1983). *Frames of mind: The theory of multiple intelligences.* New York: Basic Books.

Gilbert, P. (1980). Unpublished manuscript. COGS: University of West Virginia at Charleston. In D. Sisk *Creative Teaching of the Gifted,* (p. 116–117), 1985. New York: McGraw-Hill.

Lee, T. (1994). *Effectiveness of the use of simulation in a social studies classroom* (ERIC Document Reproduction Service no. ED 381 448) Clearinghouse Identifier: SO024724

Maker, J., & Nielson, A. (1996). *Curriculum development and teaching strategies for gifted learners.* Austin, TX: PRO-ED.

May, D. (1997, March/April). Simulations: Active learning for gifted students. *Gifted Child Today, 20,* 28–35.

Myers, C., & Myers, L. (1995). *The professional educator.* New York: Wadsworth.

Parker, J. (1989). *Instructional strategies for teaching the gifted.* Boston, MA: Allyn & Bacon.

Reid, A. (1984). Turn to page 84. In D. Sisk, *Creative Teaching of the Gifted,* (p. 116–117), 1985, New York: McGraw-Hill.

Sharon, Y., & Sharon, S. (1992). *Expanding cooperative learning through group investigation.* New York: Teachers College Press.

Shirts, R. G. (1974). *BAFA' BAFA'* Del Mar, CA: Simulation Training Systems (formerly Simile II).

Shirts, R. G. (1992, October). Ten secrets of successful simulations. *Training 29,* 79.

Sisk, D. (1976). *PARLE': A simulation game:* Washington, DC: Department of Health, Education & Welfare.

Sisk, D. (1979). Simulation games and other innovative curriculum. *Gifted Child Quarterly, 23,* 227–236.

Sisk, D. (1983a). *Creative teaching of the gifted.* New York: McGraw Hill.

Sisk, D. (1983b). *Land of the Sphinx and Land of the Rainbow.* Beaumont, TX: Center for Creativity, Innovation, and Leadership, Lamar University.

Sisk, D. (1985). *Creative teaching of the gifted.* New York: McGraw-Hill.

Thijagarajan, S. (1989, June). *BARNGA: A simulation game on cultural clashes.* Yarmouth, ME: Intercultural Press.

SECTION IV

SUPPORTING AND ENHANCING GIFTED PROGRAMS

CHAPTER 19

Public Relations and Advocacy for the Gifted

JOAN D. LEWIS
University of Nebraska—Kearney

FRANCES A. KARNES
The University of Southern Mississippi

Y*ou are a fifth-grade teacher of the gifted who wants to acquaint the community with your students' accomplishments. Recently, they participated in a service learning project with the Keep America Beautiful campaign to clean the local river. Your reasons for sharing this information about your students might include (1) they made significant contributions beyond what might be expected for their ages; (2) they developed an extensive knowledge of the environment, local industrial processes, and public relations strategies; (3) you want to see children and youth receive positive recognition; and (4) you want to see gifted students and their instruction featured in the news so people will recognize that there are practical reasons for supporting their education.*

Another scenario might be that you are the enrichment specialist in your school, teaching elementary gifted students in resource classes and collaborating with teachers for their cluster groups in the regular classroom. Parents have come to you about extending the gifted program beyond the elementary school level. This has been a concern of yours for some time. You would like for your district to provide a comprehensive array of services for gifted learners at all grade levels. Your reasons might include (1) program options are limited in your district; (2) research supports qualitatively and quantitatively differentiated instruction for gifted learners; (3) gifted students are a heterogeneous group that cannot be served adequately with only one program option; and (4) atypically gifted students are more likely to receive services with expanded educational options.

Definition of Terms

The terms *advocacy, lobbying,* and *public relations* are at times used synonymously, yet their meanings differ. Consider the following dictionary definitions (*Merriam-Webster's*, 1993):

Advocacy: the act or process of advocating or supporting a cause or proposal.

Lobby: to conduct activities aimed at influencing public officials and especially members of a legislative body on legislation. (1) to promote (as a project) or secure the passage of legislation by influencing public officials. (2) to attempt to influence or sway (as a public official) toward a desired action.

Public relations: the business of inducing the public to have understanding for and goodwill toward a person, firm, or institution; also the degree of understanding and goodwill achieved.

West (1985) described public relations in education in a comprehensive manner that identifies some of the key concepts that will be employed throughout this chapter (as cited in Kowalski, 1996, p. 7):

Educational public relations: a systematically and continuously planned, executed, and evaluated program of interactive communication and human relations that employs paper, electronic, and people media to attain internal, as well as external support for an educational institution.

Rationale for Public Relations in Gifted Education

Professionals in gifted education have voiced their concerns regarding the lack of public relations and advocacy for over a decade. Gifted children and youth are often misunderstood and victims of myths and stereotyping (Karnes & Riley, 1991). Grika (1986) stated that these misconceptions could foster public resistance to funding for gifted education. Dettmer (1991) indicated that advocacy usually is conducted out of crisis rather than by design and that public relations have taken a lesser role to other issues in the field. Renzulli (1993) reminds us that researchers are guilty of "preaching" to the converted, and more emphasis should be put into writing for professionals in other areas of education. It is not only researchers but also practitioners in the classrooms that need to write and speak to other publics.

Advocates for gifted learners need to take the same approach as those who fought for the rights of students with disabilities. Supporters of the gifted need to educate school and community personnel about the characteristics and needs of high-ability learners. In addition, they need to provide teachers and their administrators with clear, concise reasons why it is not only appropriate but equitable to teach all students to the highest level of which they are capable. The issue is frequently viewed as a conflict between equity and excellence, yet these two philosophies need not be viewed as mutually exclusive. When all students receive an education that meets their cognitive and affective needs, both equity and excellence will be achieved.

Educators and the communities that support them must remember the diversity of today's classrooms. Students come from families with different socioeconomic, racial, ethnic, language, religious, geographic, moral, health, and experiential backgrounds, as well as with a range of physical and mental abilities. It is no small task for educators to meet the many and differing needs that are found in today's schools. It is critical that advocates for gifted students bear in mind this diversity. Gifted learners are not the only children with special needs; however, theirs are more likely to be ignored precisely because of this diversity and the prevailing belief that such bright children can "make it on their own" (Clark, 1992).

Historically educators have made little use of public relations. In the current era of school reform, greater value is being placed on these skills (Kowalski, 1996). The 1993 report from the U.S. Department of Education called *National Excellence: A Case for Developing America's Talent* states that

> to accomplish the goal of identifying and serving students with outstanding talent so that they reach their full potential, we must elicit the help of the entire community. Policymakers, educators, business leaders, civic organizations, and parents can all play important roles in improving education for America's most talented students. . . . Only a challenging educational environment that elevates standards for everyone can create the schools our students need to take their places in tomorrow's world. (Office of Educational Research and Improvement, 1993, p. 14)

Unfortunately, there has been resistance to gifted education (Clark, 1992), perhaps because giftedness is not well understood. It is all the more important for each of us to speak out for the needs of our students and educate ourselves with the necessary skills to employ various public relations strategies when appropriate so we can make the dream of high-quality education a reality.

Few articles about gifted learners and their education have been published in the popular press in recent years. An analysis of newspaper coverage of the gifted was conducted by Lewis and Karnes (1995) and Meadows and Karnes (1992). There were 180 news releases listed in NewsBank Electronic Index for 1986 through 1994. News coverage was steady for the first three years at about 20% of the total (18%, 21%, 22% of the total respectively) but dropped abruptly to 11% in 1989 and remained the same in 1990. The number of articles continued to decline to 3% in 1992, only five articles. A slight increase was seen during the two most recent years, from 4% to 6% in 1993 and 1994 respectively (Lewis & Karnes, 1995).

A similar investigation was conducted of magazines through the analysis of articles listed in *Readers' Guide to Periodical Literature* under various headings with the word "gifted," between January 1, 1982, and December 31, 1996 (Lewis & Karnes, 1996). The largest number of articles (73 or 43%) was published during the first five years, with 53 (31%) published during the next five years and only 44 (26%) during the last five years of the study. Thus, both investigations of print media articles—newspaper and magazine—indicated a sharp decline in information on the gifted during the 1990s. Lewis and Karnes (1995, 1996) urged parents, teachers, and other professionals in the field to write articles based on their knowledge and experiences to broaden the general public's understanding of gifted children.

Targeting Your Audience

The general population is comprised of many subgroups based on interests. When planning public relations, it is important to target the specific population or populations that will be most beneficial. The message and the way it is delivered may vary depending on the interests of these groups, even though the basic message remains the same.

Public relations may be viewed as planned and unplanned. Part of your planning will include identifying your target audiences and devising strategies that will best explain your goal and supporting purposes. Every person working on public relations activities must speak the same message to avoid confusing the audience. This is easier to accomplish when working toward a particular goal. It is, however, highly important the rest of the time too! Your unplanned interactions with people throughout your school and community also need to perpetuate a central message, otherwise your problems and complaints tend to be what is heard, not the positive aspects of gifted children and their education.

Audiences Internal to the Educational System

Audiences with a background or special interest in education will likely be more informed about general educational issues than individuals whose primary interests may be elsewhere. Even within this broad group, expertise will vary widely (see Figure 1). What they are likely to have in common is a strong interest in the education of young people.

- School boards
- Superintendents
- Assistant superintendents
- Principals

- Assistant principals
- Curriculum specialists
- Media specialists
- Guidance counselors
- School psychologists

- Special education directors
- Coordinators of gifted programs
- Teachers—elementary
- Teachers—secondary
  (specific content areas)
- Teachers—gifted/talented
- Support staff
- Students
- Parents/guardians
- Family members

Figure 1. Audiences Internal to the Educational System

When targeting parents or guardians and other family members, keep in mind their concern for providing what they believe is best for their children; however, the amount of time and energy they have to contribute may be limited. Remember that family members are both an audience and a potentially powerful force for advocacy. The students themselves are also an audience and can be excellent advocates. Who better to speak to the benefits of quality services than the students themselves? The categories of students and parents include all levels of ability and need, not only those with ties to gifted education. Public relations planners would be wise to take into consideration the needs and feelings of these diverse groups.

The manner in which you approach various groups may need to be different. To parents and guardians, the individual student is paramount. The difficulties of meeting the needs of a very heterogeneous population are often not recognized. Most educators, of necessity, tend to focus their primary attention on the majority. Keep in mind that your fellow educators have differing educational and experiential backgrounds, as well as exposure to gifted individuals. In addition, they already have enormous responsibilities that require their time and attention. It is not too surprising that research shows that they are inclined, if only by default, to let gifted children learn on their own (Archambault, Westberg, Brown, Hallmark, Zhang, &

- General public
- Neighbors
- Friends
- Relatives
- Civic and service organizations

- Arts
- Business and industry
- Media
- Political and government leaders
- Professionals
- Religious affiliation members

Figure 2. Audiences External to the Educational System

Emmons, 1993; Westberg, Archambault, Dobyns, & Slavin, 1993). Relative to the needs of the majority and the evident needs of students with disabilities, the needs of gifted learners do not seem very pressing. Sometimes, they may not be noticed at all.

Audiences External to the Educational System

The broadest of all audiences is the general public (see Figure 2). Within this group are people inside the educational system and individuals who are not overtly connected to the schools. Neighbors, friends, and relatives are people you see every day and often do not think of in terms of public relations. Similarly, you may not recognize your informal dealings with various organizations, religious affiliation members, and others within your community who can have a powerful impact on perceptions of gifted children and their education. The general public may also be thought of in terms of people in the arts, business and industry, the media, political organizations, the government, and the many professions. The way your message is packaged and delivered to the arts community may need to be a little different from the way it is presented to businesses or the media.

Public Relations Strategies

A wide variety of strategies are available for bringing your message to the attention of your targeted audience(s). These include nonprint, print, and other media as a means for information dissemination. An extensive shopping list of strategies is provided below with a brief description of each (see Tables 1, 2, and 3). Some of these methods are free while others range in price. When selecting the strategies, consider the overall cost, the effectiveness for reaching your targeted audience, and the ease of use. You want to be sure to get the most "bang for your bucks," and that does not always equate with free or inexpensive. It is worth the time to con-

Table 1. Nonprint Media

Nonprint Media	Example
Radio	Hard news, human interest stories, editorials, talk shows, interviews, public service announcements, and community calendar.
Teleconferencing	Staff development, classes, meetings, and interviews.
Telephone	Planned networks to spread news rapidly, and advertised hotlines.
Telephone answering machine	Organization and program updates, and class news made available on a publicized number at scheduled times.
Television	Hard news, human interest stories, editorials, talk shows, interviews, public service announcements, and community calendar. Use national experts, local professionals, gifted students, and others as appropriate.
Video	Professional, amateur, or student-made: Displays at meetings, malls, fairs, conferences; public interest segments on TV and ETV; news releases for TV; and staff development.

Table 2. Print Media

Print Media	Example
Advertising—donated, paid; display, classified	In newspapers, journals, magazines, radio, television, and Internet.
Advertising slugs	Specialized imprint designed to accompany stamp on postage meter for bulk mailings.
Articles—single, series	In newspapers, newsletters, journals, magazines, Internet, and other print media.
Bibliographies	Book listings on variety of topics.
Billboards	Unused space available rent-free for nonprofit groups.
Bookmarks	Print with organization logo, slogan, or key information.
Brochures	Provide information about gifted children in general, state and local organizations, program services, or specific topic.
Bus placards	Bus side panels, both inside and outside, donated on space-available basis.
Direct mail	Packets of selected information mailed to targeted groups.
Editorials—guest, invited	In newspapers, newsletters, journals, magazines; on radio, television, Internet.
Electronic signs	Banks, other businesses, schools have external message boards for short public service information.
E-mail	Individual and group mailings, news groups, bulletin boards, and mailing lists (listservs).
Fact sheet—single, series	Directed to specific audiences.

Table 2. Continued

Journals	Wide array of professional publications at state, national, and international levels. Send for publication guidelines.
Letters to the editor	Fact, opinion, and advice to give and solicit information, change attitudes, express gratitude, and build coalitions. Written by adults and students.
Magazines—local, state, national	Wide array of general and specific topic publications containing news releases, editorials, letters to the editor, articles (single or feature series), advertising (paid or donated), and calendars of up-coming events.
Newsletters	In-house publications for employees and members of organizations, businesses, and schools.
Newspapers	News releases, editorials, letters to the editor, articles (single or feature series), advertising (paid or donated; display or classified), public service announcements, and community calendars.
News releases	Immediate or continuing news coverage including feature stories, opinion pieces, brief summary of special events, and other items of interest.
Novelty items	Includes pens, pencils, other school items, buttons, refrigerator magnets, coffee cups, hats. Print with a logo or slogan.
Piggy-back mailing	Information included in another group's mail out.
Postcards	Quick reminders of meeting dates and calendar of special events, invitations, and special messages.
Posters—various sizes, colors, messages	Place on school bulletin boards; in business and store windows, libraries, and buses.
Rubber stamp	Imprinted with logo or slogan. Use with bright-colored ink on all outgoing material.

Stickers	Various sizes and colors with logo or slogan: Small stickers can make envelopes and other papers stand out; large stickers can attract attention on car bumpers.
T-shirts	Imprint with logo or program slogan for special events, trips, and gifts.
Wire service	Forward quality news articles for broader coverage and listing in news data bases.
World Wide Web home page	Numerous resources are linked providing broad access to a wide array of general and specific documents (single or series), news releases, advertising, and search tools for locating additional info.

Table 3. Other Media

Other Media	Example
Displays	Place in libraries, store windows, business and industry lobbies, and conferences.
Special events	Proclamations (governor announces state gifted month, mayor names local gifted week), ribbon cutting or wrapping, recognition of student or class contributions to the community, booths at conferences or malls, recognition ceremonies for supporters (with or without a meal, present certificates, gifts, or plaques), contests, sponsorships, conferences, panel discussions, seminars, and workshops.
Speeches at meetings, events, and conferences—local, state, national, and international	Business, civic, education, and social groups.
Student performances—local, state, national, international	Present at meetings, conferences, fairs, and mall events, etc.

sider carefully a suitable mix of strategies. For specific suggestions on writing techniques and media relations, see Alvino (1991), Karnes, Lewis, and Stephens (1999), Pentecost (1997), and Steinke and Steinke (1987). An example of an extensive and creative media campaign conducted by a state gifted organization in Wisconsin is described in Grika (1986). Many of her ideas could be used locally by scaling them down in size.

Basic Planning for Effective Public Relations

Public relations activities need to be approached with careful planning to maximize their effectiveness. Individual strategies in isolation do not work, as well as a coordinated plan for the year. If your time and resources are limited, start small with one or two activities. New strategies can be added each year. You can publicize class activities on your own, but it is easier and more efficient to share the load with others. Consider working with colleagues from your school or district, teachers from other districts, and parents of your students. Whether you are working as a member of a small group or for a large organization, it is important to develop a basic plan. It will save more time and energy than it consumes and enhance your effectiveness. Local parent support groups and state, national, and international gifted organizations need to appoint a standing committee charged with the development of a public relations plan for the organization.

Another important aspect of planning is to familiarize yourself with district policies that regulate publicity. Check with a school official about district guidelines. People in small schools need to follow the chain of administrative command, such as principal or superintendent. Large school systems usually have a person designated for public relations. Work closely with this individual to increase the effectiveness of your public relations efforts. Written parental permission is usually needed for using photographs of children and youth. Remember too that you are always under obligation to disseminate information in a clear and accurate manner so as not to misrepresent your position.

Be clear about what you want to achieve and why. Before selecting the public relations strategies you will use, it is critical that you are clear about what you want to achieve and why. Is your goal primarily to inform the community of your students' activities and accomplishments, or do you want to make something occur or to prevent some action? Write down what you want to do and why in clear, concise language. Note supporting reasons to explain why you are taking this action.

Agree on your goal and develop a goal statement. Everyone working on the public relations (publicity) activities needs to come to an agreement on a specific goal. A goal statement is then developed to help provide direction. Activities that do not effectively further this goal should be carefully reviewed, and decisions should be made on an individual basis.

Know your subject before working to convince others. Know your subject. This basic requirement is so obvious it can be overlooked. All participants in public relations activities should have an adequate knowledge of the needs of gifted children and be able to explain clearly how what you want to accomplish will further the goal of meeting these needs. Preparing a fact sheet for your own use will save time and reduce the chances of someone making a costly error. Confusion or misstatements can hinder the goal. An added bonus of this fact sheet is that it can double as one of your public relations strategies (see Table 2).

For accurate supporting information, contact the Council for Exceptional Children (CEC), the National Association for Gifted Children (NAGC), and the National Research Center on the Gifted and Talented (NRC/GT; see Teacher Resources). CEC has gathered together numerous digests and fact sheets on a variety of topics. One specific to the gifted and public relations has been developed by Karnes and Lewis (1997). The question and answer service at AskERIC, which is supported by CEC, will provide a quick response via e-mail from their web page, direct e-mail without using the Web, or the telephone. NAGC has developed a number of position papers that can prove a useful resource when you are gathering background information for your public relations. The 17 divisions specializing in critical areas of gifted education can provide supporting facts. Abstracts of recent research reports, as well as other useful material is available at NRC/GT.

Determine your target audience(s). Determining who comprises your primary audience(s) can save time, money, and energy. Your audience will be determined by what you want to accomplish. On-going public relations can increase collective understanding of the characteristics and educational needs of gifted learners by targeting the general public or specific individual groups.

Dealing with crisis management or implementing program change is somewhat different. Each requires separate strategies, but they can work in tandem. To meet a crisis or implement changes in policy requires that you identify those who wield the power and their advisors. Target people who can accomplish what you want rather than the general public. In the first scenario at the beginning of the chapter, you can easily accomplish your goal by targeting the general public. This is an example of on-going public relations. The second scenario is more complicated. Both general and specific audiences will need to be targeted. Your main audience to change district policy will be those individuals internal to the school, such as the superintendent, director of gifted programs or special education, curriculum developers, building principals, and teachers (gifted, regular, special education, and special content area) (see Figure 1). Target others who are likely to be affected. Disseminating *all* your information to everyone in the community may not be very efficient; however, including the general public when publicizing the unique characteristics and educational needs of gifted students will help raise general awareness in your community for future use. In addition, it can enhance economic development by building partnerships with key members of the business community. A strong educational system is an asset when attempting to attract new business and industry to locate in an area. Targeting the media is usually worthwhile regardless of the intended outcome. Members of the media can help you share your message with a wider audience.

Decide on your basic message. It is necessary to decide on the basic message you want to deliver so that your public relations plan, regardless of size, is focused and free of educational jargon that can be confusing. Next, all members of the public relations committee need to practice the message so that everyone speaks with the same voice. It is particularly important to be clear about what you want and why. Refer to the reasons and support statement you recorded earlier.

Establish a realistic timeline. A reasonable timeline needs to be developed based on the nature of your plan. Allowing either too little or too much time can lead to failure. Each individual activity should also have a specific time limit. These activities are placed on the calendar in a logical order, and the feasibility of completing them all in the time set aside is determined. The number of activities is then adjusted to make sure the overall time table can be kept. In the community scenario, the timeline would be short or the news is old. Fast-breaking stories need to be dealt with in a timely manner, such as the Keep American Beautiful community scenario. Expanding educational program options for gifted children may need several years, with shorter timelines for the various components necessary for achieving such a broad goal.

Determine evaluation criteria so you will know you have succeeded. Ask yourself what you will need to *see* to know your public relations strategies have been successful. These criteria will vary depending on your goals. Just writing letters to key people, publishing articles in the newspaper, or talking to school officials does not mean anything was accomplished. These are the activities, not the ends you are trying to achieve. In scenario one, a news article with a picture in the local paper and perhaps television coverage may be your criteria. In the second scenario, a preliminary criterion might be the formation of a committee to investigate possible educational options for gifted students. Later criteria might include implementation of a specified number of these options.

Get others involved. Organizations need to appoint a committee to coordinate their public relations activities. Individual teachers and parents who want to contribute to improving the public's view of gifted education should locate at least one or two others with whom they can work. They might even begin a special interest group or work within another organization. Public relations can be carried out by one person, but it is more effective to involve others. Once the nucleus of a committee has completed the basic planning, acquire as many volunteers to help as possible in order to broaden your support base and increase good will. Be certain these volunteers are also clear about the goal and the message.

The Message

You have decided on your basic message and selected one or more strategies to disseminate it. Figure 3 names some general topic ideas for articles for discussion on radio or television. Your message to the general public in scenario one will include topics 1, 2, and 4. For scenario two, topic 1 will be formatted in a considerably different manner when targeting the general public and school officials. You could also target the latter group with topic 4 and descriptions of exemplary classes and programs from around the country (a variation of topic 3).

Print media will be an important strategy, and there are several formats that can be effective (see Figure 4). Consider reaching out beyond your local newspaper as a publisher of your message, even for a local program or school issue. Newspapers with regional or state coverage can spread your message and possibly gather support from other communities that are working on similar problems. Newsletters for various community or even state organizations and businesses have broad audiences. You can increase your support base by involving others in reciprocal or collaborative projects. With so many people accessing the Internet, doing mass mailings using e-mail, a local or national listserv, or bulletin board or creating your own web page are additional ways to spread your message and elicit support.

Talent Identification

In the earlier sections of this chapter, we discussed a variety of public relations strategies. Now it is time to identify your Points of Personal Power (see Figure 5). What can you do as an individual to contribute to the development or implementation of a public relations plan? You have far more power than you realize and you know many others who will help once they know you need them. Our lives are comprised of many overlapping areas of influence. Your friends, colleagues, and acquaintances in each of these areas are not only your audience but also part of your support.

The purpose of your public relations is to convert members of your audience to supporters. Consider first those people with

1. General and specific information about gifted and talented children and their programs.
2. Descriptions spotlighting activities, projects, and individuals.
3. Details about special classes and programs from around country.
4. Focus on the ways society will benefit from providing these unique services.

Figure 3. Topics

- Format for publication
    News releases
    Editorials
    Letters to the editor
    Articles—single and feature series
    Paid or donated advertisements

- Publication sources for articles and news
    Local, state, and national newspapers
    Local, state, and national magazines
    Professional magazines
    Newsletters—organization, school district, business/industry
    National wire services
    E-mail
    Listservs (mailing lists)
    Electronic bulletin boards
    World Wide Web

Figure 4. Information Dissemination

whom you come in contact because of your career. These include not only co-workers but also support people, supervisors, business associates, and members of professional organizations to which you belong, to name just a few. For teachers, there will be

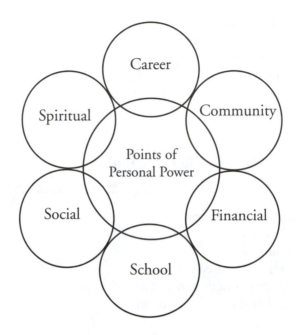

Figure 5. Points of Personal Power

considerable overlap of career and school. The school sphere includes people internal and external to the school (see Figures 1 and 2).

Who are your contacts when managing your money? Bankers, tellers, and loan officers are a few of the most common. Some people have financial advisors, stock brokers, or investment counselors. You may belong to a club or organization focusing on financial issues.

Socially there are many possibilities. Family and neighbors are important contacts. With whom do you spend time? This can be in person, on the phone, or even on-line. Include acquaintances, as well as your closest friends. You may know them from organizations, leisure activities, or work. Who do you know because of your religious affiliation? This can include spiritual and lay leaders and members of the congregation.

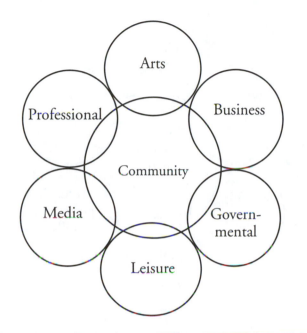

Figure 6. Community Subgroups

Community is an amorphous whole that can be subdivided into various groups such as those in Figure 6. The arts includes the fine arts of painting and sculpture, photography, dance, theater, the places that house the arts, and museums. There are many businesses in any town, such as supermarkets, drug stores, and specialty shops. Include large and small industries in this category, too. Government encompasses local, county, state, and national leaders and their supporters. Leisure can include sports, entertainment, exercise, crafts, reading, and much more. Newspapers, radio, and television comprise the media. And finally, the category of professionals includes doctors, nurses, dentists, lawyers, architects, and the people who work for them. Note whom you know in each of these areas that might be supportive or have skills that you can use. Remember to gather job and special interest information from the parents of your students. Each of these contacts can be included in a resource file for future use.

Figure 7. Talent Identifiers

The people you know in each of these dimensions are Points of Personal Power for you. Now it is time to begin identifying your own and others' talents (see Figure 7). To produce continuous public relations, gather committee members with talent in creative, development (obtaining money), interpersonal, organizational, speaking, and writing skills or with connections to people with expertise in these areas. The task can sound daunting until you consider the contacts you and your colleagues and parents can assemble together.

What are your unique talents? (See Figure 8.) Place your initials beside each of the skills that you consider a strength, adding examples as needed. Do the same for your collaborators. Now include names from your resource list to fill holes in critical areas. It is not necessary to have someone for each unique skill, particularly if your present plans are for a small publicity effort. More comprehensive public relations plans will utilize a larger number of talents.

Figure 8. Unique Skills

To appraise the community of your students' excellent work with the Keep America Beautiful committee (scenario one), you could write a news release for the local newspaper. That is a good beginning. Now consider additional options. You, a parent, another adult, or the students themselves could develop a videotape about their work, which could be used to raise awareness of community conservation efforts while increasing public understanding of gifted students' capabilities. Depending on the content, the tape could then be used as a community interest feature on television; at meetings of Keep America Beautiful, Rotary, Kiwanis, PTO/PTA, and other organizations; as a display in the mall; as an educational tool to share with other children in the school and district; and as staff development for district teachers. The children could create a before-and-after display at the library or in a store window. Your students could conduct a survey of their classmates and members of the community about environmental issues. They could share their results by writing letters to their legislators, letters to the editor, and a news article for the paper. Students could also share what they learned from their projects by making presentations to various organizations, at conferences, and on local radio and television talk shows. Legislators could be invited into the classroom or taken on a tour of the site while the students explain the conservation issues. The media are usually willing to cover the activities of dignitaries; and, by association, your students and your educational program would receive excellent news coverage. Meanwhile, your students learn useful interpersonal skills.

Involving Others

Everyday interactions with other teachers can influence their thinking about gifted education, whether you intended that or not. Remaining positive even with challenges facing you and your students is important. Collaborating with classroom teachers will help dispel notions of elitism and improve education for all students (Hertzog, 1998).

Visitors who have been invited to your classroom and people you meet while on field trips or other school outings are both an audience for public relations and potential new advocates for gifted education. The way you and your students present yourselves to the outside world influences the attitudes people form about gifted children in general. Preparing visitors and people you know you will meet on field trips for the kinds of questions gifted children ask will help them understand your students better and avoid embarrassment. People who are not used to little children who ask big questions can come away from such an encounter with negative feelings; when they know what to expect they are more likely to appreciate the children's advanced thinking.

Students can be empowered to advocate for themselves in many ways. Learning appropriate behavior for different social situations is a useful life skill that usually needs to be taught. Children need to learn about the unintended consequences of their actions or words. They can learn how to speak appropriately with school personnel, business leaders, and legislators. Class instruction can include how to write press releases, create videos, develop displays, conduct interviews, and design T-shirts.

Parents have a great deal of power. They can advocate for your students and your program in ways that you as a teacher cannot, such as talking with administrators about specific needs and concerns. Parents can be responsible for or help with publicity by writing news releases and newsletters. The latter can be disseminated to all parents, school personnel, community leaders, and legislators. Additional writing projects might include a letter to the editor congratulating the school district on its gifted and talented program and letters to legislators thanking them for their support. Parents can advertise coming events with posters and telephone trees and take photographs and videos for publicity. Use the talent identifier (see Figure 7) to find the unique skills (see Figure 8) of your students' parents and invite them to help build a strong, positive image for gifted learners.

Staff development targeted to gifted education is needed in every school. Few general educators have sufficient knowledge of the cognitive and social-emotional characteristics to prepare them to work effectively with gifted learners. New research on identification of underserved populations and improved instructional methods is being conducted. These are only two reasons for including the needs of gifted learners as one of the regular topics for staff development. When experts in the field are not available to give the training, video tapes can deliver needed information (Karnes & Lewis, 1996; Lewis & Karnes, 1997). Karnes and Lewis have provided an annotated listing by topic with publishers and contact information. This too is a form of public relations that should not be overlooked and utilized when appropriate.

Working within an organization can be a practical method for increasing public awareness and need for gifted education. Whether you help start a parent/teacher support group or you work with an established organization, you have the resources of many people to help disseminate the message. In either case, a public relations committee needs to be formed that will plan and coordinate all activities. You can be the catalyst that motivates the group to extend its informational reach beyond its current level. Ask to be on the agenda, and describe briefly the advantages of planning and working together. If your organization already has an active public relations program, you can suggest some of the strategies provided in this chapter. In addition, reaching out to other constituencies could provide useful collaboration (Riley & Karnes, 1993a).

Use of Organizers

The public relations work sheet is an easy way to begin motivating and organizing volunteers to become active participants in public relations (see Figure 9). It can be disseminated to groups such as those at staff development, educational and community meetings, conferences, and parent meetings to obtain a commitment to specific activities. Small and large organizations can also use the work sheet to survey their members for their strengths and interests when developing public relations. Items can be tailored to suit the specific needs of your classroom or group.

If one article or one activity can increase public awareness of gifted children and their unique needs, how much more effective is a year of coordinated strategies? The annual plan is a way to organize and coordinate your public relations, whether for your classroom; a school or district gifted program; a local, state, national, or international gifted organization; or other supporters of gifted education (see Figure 10). Even if your group can only fill in one or two activities, it is a beginning. Next year, or even next month, you may realize you can add another component. By keeping track of what you are doing, who is responsible, and how effective your technique is, you will discover you can use your planning time more efficiently. In addition, it will help you be more aware of whom you are reaching and whom you need to target.

Most schools have an open house in the early fall and holiday programs near the end of the year. These common activities pro-

I, _____, will work to see implemented or suggest the following public relations strategies to the local and/or state association for the gifted:

	Local	State	Activity
Bibliography			
Bookmark			
Brochure			
Display			
Fact sheet			
Magazine article			
News release			
Newsletter article			
Newspaper article			
Open house			
Postcard			
PTA/PTO program			
Speeches at meetings, events, conferences			
Survey of local/state groups to determine liaisons			
T-shirt			
Technology (conferencing, e-mail, Internet, staff development, WWW)			
Video			
Other			

Figure 9. Public Relations Worksheet

vide public relations opportunities. Decide how to make use of them and note them on your calendar. Plan to write about some of your students' special accomplishments and submit them to your local newspaper several times during the year. Organizations might include membership drives, fund raising plans, and conventions or special programs as their base activities. Writing news articles, a brochure, a fact sheet, and a web page and seeing that this information is disseminated appropriately might come next. These are only generic ideas with no plan behind them. To be effective, it is important to coordinate activities around a specific goal.

Involving Other Constituencies

One method for determining the degree of support for gifted education from the general public is to conduct a public opinion telephone survey. Karnes and Riley (1997) found the response from a representative, statistical sample of residents in a given state was very positive toward the gifted. Results were disseminated to key state representatives and senators to encourage increased state funding.

Teachers and other advocates in gifted education may wish to join together with specific educational groups and associations at local, state, and national levels to determine advocacy and public relations opportunities. One way to achieve this would be to assess the needs of their members through a mail survey. Two such studies have been conducted (Riley & Karnes, 1993a; Troxclair & Karnes, 1997). In each study, professional educational organizations were surveyed to determine such information as the total membership, publications, conferences, and the needs of each group pertaining to gifted education (see Figure 11).

Riley and Karnes (1993a) reported the results of a survey to 23 associations in Mississippi with 15 groups responding for 48% return rate. There were approximately 370,000 individuals within the 15 associations with memberships ranging from 125 to 66,000. All of the responding groups published a newsletter and three produced journals. All had state conferences with four providing one to three workshops and one offering four to six sessions

Month	Objectives	Strategies/Activities	Person Responsible	Date Due	Expected Outcome
August					
September					
October					
November					
December					
January					
February					
March					
April					
May					
June					
July					

Figure 10. Public Relations Annual Plan

Name of Organization: _____

I. *Association Information*

Person completing this survey:

Name: _____ Title: _____
Address: _____
_____
_____

Telephone No. _____
Approximate number of members in the association: _____

II. *Association Publications*

Journal Title: _____ No. Issues per year _____
Newsletter Title: _____ No. Issues per year _____

Approximate number of articles relating to gifted education
in your association's
journal during the past 3 years   _____
newsletter during the past 3 years   _____

Other publications addressing gifted education topics during the past 3
years (monographs, books, etc.). Give complete reference.
Number: _____
Reference: _____

III. *Association Conferences* (Please check appropriate responses.)

Approximate number of workshops or presentations devoted to gifted
education at association conferences during the last 3 years:
_____ 0
_____ 1–3
_____ 4–6
_____ 7–8
_____ 9 or more

Topics addressed at association conferences during the past 3 years:
_____ Characteristics of the gifted
_____ Identifying and screening the gifted
_____ Teaching strategies for the gifted
_____ Parenting the gifted
_____ Issues and trends in gifted education
_____ Curriculum development in gifted education
_____ Organization and administration of gifted education
_____ Legal issues in gifted education
_____ Funding gifted education
_____ The future of gifted education
_____ Gifted/Learning Disabled/ADHD
_____ Others _____

Would your group be interested in including gifted education workshops and presentations as you plan future conference programs?

_____ Yes (If yes, please circle topics listed on front of sheet in preceding section which would be of primary interest.) List additional topics here: _____

_____

_____ No

Conferences Scheduled:
2000   Location: _____
        Dates: _____
2001   Location: _____
        Dates: _____

IV. *Association Commitment*

Does your association have a position paper which is specific to or includes gifted children?

_____ Yes (If yes, please attach a copy of the statement.)
_____ No

Does your association have an active gifted education committee or special interest group?
_____ Yes (If so, provide group's name.) _____
_____ No

Please rate your association's interest in or commitment to gifted education on a scale of 1 (low) to 6 (high).

_____ 1 Lowest
_____ 2
_____ 3
_____ 4
_____ 5
_____ 6 Highest

Please mail this form and any attachments available to:

Figure 11. Gifted Education Survey

on the gifted over the prior three years. All groups responded positively to a question regarding interest in including sessions and presentations in gifted education at future conferences. The requested topics were characteristics of the gifted, learning-disabled gifted, personal and social problems of the gifted, and science fair projects for the gifted. None of the responding organizations had a position statement or an active committee on the gifted.

Similar information was rendered from the study conducted by Troxclair and Karnes (1997). Forty-one percent of the 40 organizations surveyed indicated that their total members were 156,823 with a range of 60 to 66,000 per group. Thirteen of those responding published a journal. Within the prior three years, four organizations published from one to three articles on the gifted. Twenty-six organizations published a newsletter with three groups having one or two articles pertaining to the gifted. Four groups held one to three sessions with topics pertinent to the gifted, and 18 organizations indicated they would welcome sessions on gifted/learning disabled/ADHD, teaching strategies for the gifted in specialized programs and in the regular classroom. One organization had a position paper and one had a committee on the gifted.

State organizations having these data available should develop both short- and long-range public relations plans. One strategy suggested by Riley and Karnes (1993b) was to establish an advocacy/public relations committee within the state gifted association. The committee would have multiple purposes such as to coordinate articles for newsletters and journals to other state professional associations, to establish a speakers bureau for conferences of other groups, and to assist those groups wanting to establish a committee or write a position paper for the gifted.

State associations have developed a variety of public relations tools for advocacy (Karnes, Lewis, & Pentecost, 1996; see Figure 12). The most widely used across all state associations was the newsletter. Next were brochures and proclamations by mayors and governors, followed by special events and student performances. Displays, T-shirts, posters, hotlines, buttons, videos, and bibliography listings were employed by some associations. Media contacts were most often through the newspapers using feature articles, editorials, and letters to the editor. Only one-third of the state associations employed radio and television for public relations. Less than 12% used paid advertisements. Half of the associations had a public relations committee, but only 14 indicated having planned media campaigns and 24 reported having an annual plan.

These studies were designed to be used as models for other states but can be easily adapted for groups at local and national levels to develop appropriate public relations and advocacy strategies. Both of the studies indicated the many opportunities for the development of collaboration and partnerships with other professionals. By networking with other organizations, greater results will transpire than are possible when working alone.

Summary

Public relations are a continuous need in gifted education. Selecting the appropriate target audience(s) for your public relations efforts is an important initial decision. In addition, you need to be sure that all participants understand the basic message and speak with one voice. To make this critical component easier to accomplish, it is recommended that the basic plan be clearly written. A wide variety of public relations strategies are available. The next step is to select the appropriate strategies for each target audience. Objective evaluation criteria are needed to determine if your public relations plan has been effective. Joining with other interested individuals and organizations gives you the potential to expand your ability to reach your chosen audiences. The goal of disseminating accurate information about gifted learners and their education is never-ending, yet worthwhile. How else will people outside the classroom learn about how your students contribute to their communities or why your students require a differentiated education to help them fulfill their considerable potential? Every person in gifted education needs to make a lifelong commitment to become public relations specialists for gifted children and youth.

Name of Organization: _____

I. *Association Information*

    Person completing this survey:

    Name: _____ Title: _____
    Address: _____
    _____
    Telephone No. _____

    Approximate number of members in the association: _____

Please respond yes or no to each of the following items if your organization has employed them for public relations.

II. *Association Printed Public Relations Materials*

Newsletter	yes _____	no _____
Affiliate Newsletter	yes _____	no _____
Journal/Magazine	yes _____	no _____

III. *Specialty Public Relations Strategies:*

Billboard	yes _____	no _____
Brochure		
About Organization	yes _____	no _____
Other topic	yes _____	no _____
Bibliographies	yes _____	no _____
Bookmarks	yes _____	no _____
Buttons	yes _____	no _____
Displays	yes _____	no _____
Posters	yes _____	no _____
Proclamation from mayor		
or governor	yes _____	no _____
Special events	yes _____	no _____
Examples _____		
Student performances	yes _____	no _____
T-shirts	yes _____	no _____
Telephone hotline	yes _____	no _____
Video		
About organization	yes _____	no _____
Gifted characteristics	yes _____	no _____

Teaching techniques	yes _____	no _____
Other	yes _____	no _____

IV. *Media Contacts for Public Relations*

Newspapers	yes _____	no _____
Editorials	yes _____	no _____
Feature articles	yes _____	no _____
Letters to the editor	yes _____	no _____
Paid ads	yes _____	no _____
Display	yes _____	no _____
Classified	yes _____	no _____
Television	yes _____	no _____
Radio	yes _____	no _____
Other	_____	

V. *Public Relations*

Do you have a public relations committee?	yes _____	no _____
Do you have a planned media campaign?	yes _____	no _____
Do you have an annual public relations plan?	yes _____	no _____
Do you network with other organizations?	yes _____	no _____
Do you contribute to other organization's newsletters?	yes _____	no _____
Do you provide speakers for other organizations?	yes _____	no _____
Do you have presidents of other organizations on your advisory board?	yes _____	no _____

VI. *Other Public Relations Ideas We Have Found Effective*

_____

_____

Thanks!   Thanks!   Thanks!

Figure 12. Public Relations Survey

Teacher Resources

Publications

Few materials are focused on developing public relations for special programs. Articles addressing the needs of public relations in gifted education are listed in the references. Books on public relations for schools are provided below.

Hanson, E. M. (1992). Educational marketing in the public schools: Policies, practices, and problems. *Educational Policy, 6*(1), 19–34.

Holcomb, J. H. (1992). *Educational marketing: A business approach to school-community relations.* Lanham, MD: University Press of America.

Kowalski, T. J. (1996). *Public relations in educational organizations.* Englewood Cliffs, NJ: Merrill.

Lober, I. M. (1993). *Promoting your school.* New Paltz, NY: Technomic.

Warner, C. (1994). *Promoting your school: Going beyond PR.* Thousand Oaks, CA: Corwin Press.

Yale, D. R. (1995). *Publicity and media relations check lists.* Lincolnwood, IL: NTC Business Books.

Addresses

AskERIC
ERIC Clearinghouse on Information and Technology
4-194 Center for Science and Technology
Syracuse University
Syracuse, NY 13244-4100
(800) 464-9107
http://www.ericir.syr.edu
askeric@askeric.org

Council for Exceptional Children (CEC)
1920 Association Dr.
Reston, VA 20191-1589
(888) 232-7733
fax (703) 264-9494
http://www.cec.sped.org
conteduc@cec.sped.org (professional development);
susans@cec.sped.org (CEC divisions and subdivisions)

National Association for Gifted Children (NAGC)
1707 L Street, N.W., Suite 550
Washington, DC 20036
(202) 785-4268
http://www.nagc.org

National Research Center on the Gifted and Talented
(NRC/GT)
University of Connecticut
362 Fairfield Rd., U-7
Storrs, CT 06269-2007
(860) 486-4676
fax (860) 486-2900
http://www.ucc.uconn.edu:80/~wwwgt/nrcgt.html

National School Public Relations Association (NSPRA)
15948 Denwood Rd.
Rockville, MD 20855
(301) 519-0496
fax (301) 519-0494
http://www.nspra.org

Web Sites

Numerous Internet sites are available that offer information about college and university classes on public relations, list agencies that provide public relations for businesses and organizations, or list other contacts in this field. These links are targeted primarily at the business community.

National School Public Relations Association (NSPRA)—http://www.nspra.org/
This site includes articles and online help for schools and several publications among its resources.

References

Alvino, J. (1991). Media relations: What every advocate should know about the tricks of the trade. *Gifted Child Quarterly, 35*, 204–209.

Archambault, F. X., Jr., Westberg, K. L., Brown, S. W., Hallmark, B. W., Zhang, W., & Emmons, C. L. (1993). Classroom practices used with gifted third- and fourth-grade students. *Journal for the Education of the Gifted, 16*, 103–119.

Clark, B. (1992). *Growing up gifted: Developing the potential of children at home and at school* (4th ed.). New York: Merrill.

Dettmer, P. (1991). Gifted program advocacy: Overhauling bandwagons to build support. *Gifted Child Quarterly, 35*, 165–171.

Grika, J. T. (1986). Gifted children—waste not, want not: The how-to's of a statewide g/c/t awareness campaign. *Gifted Child Today, 9*(1), 25–29.

Hertzog, N. B. (1998). The changing role of the gifted education specialist. *Teaching Exceptional Children, 30*(3), 39–43.

Karnes, F. A., & Lewis, J. D. (1996). Staff development through videotapes in gifted education. *Roeper Review, 19*, 106–110.

Karnes, F. A., & Lewis, J. D. (1997, May). *Public relations: A necessary tool for advocacy in gifted education.* (ERIC Digest E542).

Karnes, F. A., Lewis, J. D., & Pentecost, C. H. (1996, December). Use of public relations by state associations for the gifted. *NAGC Communique, 9*(2), 4.

Karnes, F. A., Lewis, J. D., & Stephens, K. R. (1999). Parents and teachers working together for advocacy through public relations. *Gifted Child Today, 22*(1), 14–18.

Karnes, F. A., & Riley, T. L. (1991). Public relations strategies for gifted education. *Gifted Child Today, 14*(6), 35–37.

Karnes, F. A., & Riley, T. L. (1997). Determining and analyzing public support for gifted education. *Roeper Review, 19*, 237–239.

Kowalski, T. J. (1996). *Public relations in educational organizations.* Englewood Cliffs, NJ: Merrill.

Lewis, J., & Karnes, F. A. (1995). Examining the media coverage of gifted education. *Gifted Child Today, 18*(6), 28–30, 40.

Lewis, J. D., & Karnes, F. A. (1996). *A portrayal of the gifted in magazines: An initial analysis.* (ERIC Document Reproduction Service No. ED 405 710)

Lewis, J. D., & Karnes, F. A. (1997). Videotapes in gifted education will enhance staff development. *Special Populations Division Newsletter, 6*(2), 8.

Meadows, S., & Karnes, F. A. (1992). Influencing public opinion of gifted education through the newspaper. *Gifted Child Today, 15*(1), 44–45.

Merriam-Webster's Collegiate Dictionary (10th ed.). (1993). Springfield, MA: Merriam-Webster.

Office of Educational Research and Improvement (1993). *National excellence: A case for developing America's talent.* Washington, DC: U.S. Government Printing Office.

Pentecost, C. H. (1997). Media relations in gifted education: A teacher's guide. *Gifted Child Today, 20*(5), 32–34, 36–37.

Renzulli, J. D. (1993). Research and you can make a difference. *Journal for the Education of the Gifted, 16*, 97–102.

Riley, T. L., & Karnes, F. A. (1993a). Joining together with other associations: Strategies for cooperation. *Roeper Review, 15*, 250–251.

Riley, T. L., & Karnes, F. A. (1993b). Shaping public policy in gifted education. *Gifted Child Today, 16*(2), 23–25.

Steinke, G. L., & Steinke, R. J. (1987). *Public relations for special education.* (ERIC Document Reproduction Service No. ED 345 431)

Troxclair, D., & Karnes, F. A. (1997). Public relations: Advocating for gifted students. *Gifted Child Today, 20*(3), 38–41, 50.

Westberg, K. L., Archambault, F. X., Jr., Dobyns, S. M., & Slavin, T. J. (1993). An observational study of classroom practices used with third- and fourth-grade students. *Journal for the Education of the Gifted, 16*, 120–146.

C H A P T E R   2 0

Getting What You Need

Locating and Obtaining Money and Other Resources

KRISTEN R. STEPHENS
University of North Carolina—Charlotte

FRANCES A. KARNES
The University of Southern Mississippi

A teacher of the gifted in a rural school district has worked diligently for several years to receive over $600,000 in grants. A staff development day for teachers of the gifted at a local university offered her an overview of researching funding sources and procedures for writing grant proposals. With a one-hour seminar as her introduction to the fund development processes, she successfully perfected her skills and now makes presentations on the topic to groups of teachers.

With the limited amount of money available in school districts for classroom materials and projects, finding external funding opportunities has become necessary for many teachers of the gifted. This chapter provides an overview of the types of funding agencies that exist and how to locate them, as well as how to develop an idea and write a grant proposal. Information on other sources of funding has also been given, as well as procedures for determining policies at the district level.

Status of Federal Funding For Gifted Education

At present, the only federal legislation which exclusively designates funds for gifted and talented education is the Jacob K. Javits Gifted and Talented Students Education Act. This act directs the Secretary of Education to make grants and contracts for programs and projects to meet the educational needs of gifted and talented students. Currently, funding is set at $6.5 million and is designated for a federal office, the National Research Center, and model projects.

Since gifted students are offered limited protection under both federal and state laws and are not covered under the Individuals with Disabilities Education Act (IDEA), many advocate that new legislation is essential to meet their unique educational needs. One of the more recent attempts is the Gifted and Talented Students Education Act (H.R. 637) which was introduced to the new congress on February 10, 1999. It proposes categorical grant money to state education agencies to support programs and services for the gifted and talented. Funding is based on the student population of the state, with each state receiving a minimum of $1 million. In addition, this act allows states to distribute money to public schools to provide for professional development, innovative programs and services, emerging technology, and technical assistance relating to the education of gifted and talented students. A total of $160,000,000 is authorized to be appropriated to carry out this act for the fiscal years of 1999 through 2003.

Another source of federal dollars that can be used for gifted programs is Title VI-The Innovative Education Program Strategies Program found in the reauthorized Elementary and Secondary Education Act of 1965. Local Education Agencies (LEA's) can apply for this funding directly through their state's department of education. Programs should focus on high standards for all students, professional experiences that better prepare teachers to teach to high standards, flexibility to stimulate local initiatives coupled with responsibility for results, and the promotion of partnerships among families, communities, and schools. Contact the Title VI representative from your state department of education for additional information.

Types of Funding

There are essentially two types of funding: public and private. Some projects will be appropriate for both types of funding while others may be best suited for one or the other. Private sources often will not support projects for which there are already substantial amounts of public funding available, such as in the area of children with disabilities. Furthermore, the purpose of public funds is set by legislation, whereas private funds focus on emerging needs and issues pertaining to special interest populations. It should be noted that funding within the school district and at the state department of education should also be explored. Some states have monies for instructional aids, technological equipment, and other materials.

Several other differences exist between public and private funding sources. For example, public funding sources generally have the most money to award and are more likely to pay all project costs. In contrast, private funders may be more restrictive in what expenses are covered; and most, with the exception of the major foundations, offer smaller amounts of money. The proposal format is another area in which the two funding types differ. Public sources use prescribed formats for proposals, which can be lengthy and complex, whereas proposals for private sources are often less formal.

Public funding can be located through federal, state, and local agencies. Some examples of federal agencies include the U.S. Department of Education, The National Institutes of Health, and The National Science Foundation. State and local agencies may be more geographic in scope, limiting their funds to specific regions in which they are involved.

Private funding sources include foundations, corporations, and professional and trade associations. Examples of foundations are The Carnegie Foundation, The Kellogg Foundation, and the Spencer Foundation. Corporations that provide grant monies include AT&T,™ Toyota,™ and Whirlpool.™ Some examples of associations providing grant monies are The American Association of University Women, The National Education Association, and The Council for Exceptional Children.

Once the project idea has been determined, the search for the funding source that best fits the need can begin. The funding agency's priorities must match project goals. The size of the awards offered, geographic focus, eligibility requirements, restrictions, and deadlines for submitting a proposal will all need to be considered. Thorough research into these key areas can assist the grant searching process.

Developing an Idea

Developing and refining a project idea should be the first step in the grant searching process. Taking the initial time to outline ideas and goals can assist in locating the most relevant funding source. Keep in mind that goals and priorities must match those of the selected funding agency.

The first step in cultivating an idea is to assess needs. What areas in the classroom, school, or community need to be initiated, need improvement, or need to be adequately addressed? A needs statement can give purpose to the project and will inform a potential funder of the importance of the proposed project. It is also necessary at this point to research any previous work that has been undertaken in the needs area to establish that the problem exists statewide and nationally. The further one can broaden the potential scope and impact of the idea, the more likely funding is assured. Also, the more innovative the idea, the better the chances of finding support for the project (see Figure 1).

After the area of need has been identified, compile a list of goals, objectives, and activities for the proposed project; this is the plan of action. It will help identify the population the project intends to address, the staffing areas that will be needed, and the time frame in which one will be operating. Ask colleagues for advice and assistance in the development of this phase of the plan. In some schools, teams of teachers work on schoolwide projects.

Determining a working budget will also be beneficial at this point. Since many funding sources have limited funds, establishing whether one needs $100,000 or $1,000 to execute a proposed project will have a substantial impact on identifying a funding source. In developing a budget, be sure to consider all expenses related to equipment and supplies, personnel, facilities, travel, communications, general operating expenses, and overhead, which includes light, heat, and

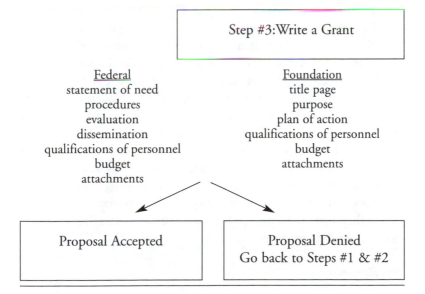

Step #1: Refine an Idea

- Assess your needs.
- Compile a list of goals, objectives, activities, and evaluation methods.
- Determine a working budget.

Step #2: Locate a Funding Source

- federal
- private
- corporate
- foundation
- state
- local

Step #3: Write a Grant

Federal	Foundation
statement of need	title page
procedures	purpose
evaluation	plan of action
dissemination	qualifications of personnel
qualifications of personnel	budget
budget	attachments
attachments	

Proposal Accepted

Proposal Denied
Go back to Steps #1 & #2

Figure 1. Steps in Securing Funds

so forth. Having a preestablished budget figure will assist in eliminating many funding agencies, making the information sifting easier.

Locating a Funding Source

Once the need has been identified, a plan of action has been created to address the need, and a general idea of the amount of money being requested has been determined, it is time to research potential funders. Several resources can assist during this endeavor: databases, libraries, and publications. Thorough research to locate a funding source whose priorities match project goals can be a challenging yet potentially rewarding experience.

Centers

The Foundation Center is a good place to begin research. The Center offers a collection of fund-finding publications and resources, including a database on CD-ROM that lists approximately 40,000 private and community foundations. The CD-ROM is available at the Center's Libraries in Washington, DC, New York, Atlanta, Cleveland, and San Francisco. To accommodate people who do not live near these locations, 100 Cooperating Collections exist across the United States. In each state, there is at least one library designated to have extensive holdings from the Foundation Center. Information on contacting the Foundation Center about its work and the Cooperating Collection is found at the end of this chapter.

If one lives near a college or university, many institutions of higher learning have Offices of Research and Sponsored Programs. These offices assist university faculty in developing proposals and finding grant sources. Although they may not provide direct assistance, they may be helpful in locating sources of funding information within the community.

Publications

The Catalog of Federal Domestic Assistance (CFDA) describes all the federal government's programs that give money. This source is published annually by the Office of Management and Budget (OMB), and it is also available at major libraries. The most current information relating to eligibility, application and award processes, addresses, and contacts are given.

The Chronicle of Philanthropy is a newspaper that includes articles on fund raising and philanthropy. Lists of recent grants and profiles of foundations and corporations are also given. The newspaper is published biweekly and is available through The Chronicle of Higher Education Inc. It can be found online and in most college and university libraries.

The Federal Register, which is published every weekday except on legal holidays, provides public regulations and legal notices issued by federal agencies. *The Federal Register* is published in paper and is available at most major libraries. An online database of *The Federal Register* is also available through the U.S. Government Printing Office (GOP).

The Congressional Record is a daily record of the activities within the U.S. Congress. Information is given on bills that are introduced and debated. Legislation is directly tied to funding availability for many programs; therefore, it is essential to stay abreast of the latest information from Washington. Copies of the Congressional Record can be found at most libraries.

The Education Funding News, published weekly by the Education Funding Research Council, provides information on what is happening in Washington and presents grants that are available in the field of education.

Information on how to contact or subscribe to the above publications is listed at the conclusion of this chapter. The above list is by no means comprehensive. Check local or college and university libraries for additional sources.

Analyzing Sources

Once information has been assessed on funding agencies, there are several things to identify:

What are the priorities of the agency, and do they match the proposed goals and objectives? For example, the agency may focus its efforts in urban areas, and the proposed project may be in a rural area.

What are past projects that this agency has funded? Request an annual report from the funding agency and look at what projects are currently being funded or have been funded in the past. Patterns may be present. For example, even though a foundation may say it funds projects nationally, 80% of the projects funded in the past may be located in the same state or geographic region.

What are the limitations and restrictions? Many agencies do not fund individuals, for-profit organizations, or political or religious associations. There may also be geographic restrictions. For example, many corporations and companies may restrict giving to areas in which there is a company presence. Also, there may be restrictions on how the money can be used. Equipment, salaries, and overhead may not be covered.

Is a letter of inquiry required? Many agencies—foundations in particular—want a brief letter explaining the organization, the goals and objectives of the project, and proposed budget prior to submitting a formal proposal. If the proposed idea matches the agency's priorities, a more detailed proposal will be requested.

Are there necessary application forms? Many agencies have standard application and cover forms that will need to be requested. Some agencies have these available for downloading from their web sites. Check to make sure that all the proposal guidelines are addressed, so the agency is provided with all the information requested.

What is the deadline? Most deadlines follow an annual pattern, meaning they are on the same date from year to year; however, since government programs depend on legislation for funding, many programs may be changed or cut. Furthermore, some government programs do not award grants annually. In retrospect, many foundations accept applications at any time with no established deadlines. Board members may meet periodically throughout the year to review proposals.

What is the average grant size? It is important to check and see what the average award is for each agency. For example, a specified project may need approximately $100,000 of support, but a particular agency may only make an award of up to $5,000. Find an agency that can financially support the proposed idea.

What is the length of support? Many federal grants will support projects for approximately three years. Continued support may be available if the project proves to have made an impact. Furthermore, many agencies want to know in the proposal how the program will be supported once funding is terminated. The potential sustainability of the program is paramount to funding agencies when making the decision to provide financial support to a project.

By addressing these above questions and thoroughly researching potential agencies, a lot of time and frustration can be saved. Nothing can be more disappointing than spending long hours developing a proposal and sending it to the wrong agency based on an overlooked detail. Research the funding agency inside and out. If there are legitimate questions, contact the agency or foundation before writing the proposal.

Major Components of a Grant Proposal

The major components and guidelines of a grant proposal differ slightly according to each funding agency. When making application to foundations and corporations, the following components are usually requested: title page, purpose, approach, qualifications, budget, and attachments. In addition to those components, state and federal agencies usually require information on the statement of need, procedures, evaluation, and dissemination.

Foundations and Corporations

The *title page* of a proposal to a foundation or corporation should have the title of the project; legal name of the submitting agency; address, name, and phone number of the contact person; a short summary; amount requested; signatures of approval; and other assurances, such as a nondiscrimination clause.

The *purpose* section should set forth the goals and objectives; description of those to be served, including geographic location and number; needs and significance of the project; and relevance to the donor's purposes.

The *approach* or the *plan of action* contains specific outcomes, staff responsibilities and training, and the evaluation design. Project dissemination activities are usually described as well. Donor recognition should be mentioned.

The *qualifications* of the key project staff should be given along with names of any consultants and all cooperating agencies. If special facilities, equipment, and so forth are needed and available, mention them to demonstrate capability to conduct the project.

A detailed *budget* is usually required, and all items essential to the project must be included. Asking for additional funds after the project has been approved is typically denied. Components of the budget may include, but are not limited to, personnel; travel; supplies and materials; data processing; printing/postage; facilities; equipment, if allowable; and indirect costs.

It is important to list indirect costs such as office space, lights, heat, equipment usage, and the like. Other items to be included would be monies from other agencies, often referred to as matching funds, if any; description of how the project will be supported after the requested funding period expires; and plans for additional fund raising, if appropriate. Consult the financial officer of your district or institution about matching funds and indirect costs.

The *attachments* requested from the potential donor may include the names of the members of the board of directors and their affiliations; copy of the IRS determination; organization's last annual report; information describing the organization; and letters of support.

Always be thorough in reviewing the requirements of the foundation or corporation because more or less information may be required. Only submit what has been requested, as these two groups are usually not interested in lengthy proposals.

State and Federal Agencies

The proposals forwarded to state and federal agencies usually require more detail and specificity. Components, again, differ somewhat from those required by foundations and corporations, and only those necessary components will be reviewed.

Following the title page, the abstract of approximately 200–500 words, the purpose, and the proposal to a state or federal agency should emphasize the *statement of need*. In this section, a thorough description should be given of the problem that is to be addressed and reasons why it is important. The emphasis should be on significance, timelines, and broad application of the solution. Recent local, state, and national statistics about the problem(s) should set forth the need in a clear and concise manner.

The *procedure* section varies somewhat as to a research or non-researched based project. In the latter, a general description should be offered, followed by details on the method, the participants, organization, and timelines. In the former, the data instruments should be described, as well as how the information is to be collected, analyzed, and reported.

The *evaluation* section of the grant proposal should include evidence that the purposes of the project have been accomplished. Information should include data collection, analysis, and evaluation; selection or the development of instruments to be utilized; and the reporting procedures.

Through the *dissemination* portion of the proposal, specifics should be given on how the findings or products of the project will be distributed (newspaper releases, presentations at conferences, journal articles, etc.). Reporting procedures to the funding agency, if and when required, should also be described.

Although the *qualifications* component has been briefly described in the above section on corporations and foundations, a few other points need to be considered when submitting to state and federal agencies. Resumés, along with a listing of publications, should be included for the key personnel and consultants. The amount of time each will give to the project with his or her responsibilities is usually required. A staff-loading chart, which depicts who will be responsible for selected activities, is often necessary.

A detailed budget with indirect costs and any matching funds is critical. Again, be sure to consult with the financial officer or grant writer in your district or institution.

Sources of Funding in Your Community

There are many other sources of funding available in addition to foundations, corporations, and state/federal agencies. Sources of private sector funding include denominational groups; neighborhood and fraternal charities; retail merchants; volunteer and business/professional associations; United Way; Chamber of Commerce; small and large businesses; local franchises of regional, state, and national companies; postsecondary institutions including community, four-year colleges, and universities; civic groups; and arts councils. Local philanthropists, celebrities, professional athletes, local decision makers, and agency directors may have discretionary funds. Some local private funding sources may have guidelines for requesting monies, so call or write to determine the procedure for requesting support. A one-page summary may be all that is necessary with the purpose, goals, activities, and budget required. Making an appointment with the person to discuss the request is sometimes the best procedure, while some associations or persons prefer to receive the information via the mail or e-mail.

At the local level, persons funding requests may either wish to be personally involved in the funded program or remain anonymous. Ask for preferences, so as not to cause any embarrassment.

For years, schools have developed fund-raising strategies for various projects. Gensheimer (1993) and Novelli (1994) shared many examples of how schools can solve the money mystery through local and state grants and fund-raising projects. Walsh (1990) suggested the following activities.

Balloon Blast-Off. Students, teachers, parents, and community members sponsor, for a specific fee, a balloon with their name, address, and phone number attached. The person with the balloon traveling the farthest receives a prize.

Auctions. These are great events. With items donated, the profits can be substantial.

Breakfast, Lunch, or Dinner With a Special Person. Everyone likes to have a meal with a celebrity such as a famous athlete, Easter Bunny, Santa Claus, TV personality, or local celebrity.

Palent (1985) advocated the following fund-raising activities: a marathon (running, walking, biking, etc.); a sale of goods (antique, baked goods, etc.); a sale of services (babysitting, car wash, house cleaning, yard work). Swan (1990) suggested contests (fishing, golf, tractor pulls, etc.); sale of items (candy, cards, light bulbs, etc.) and services (handyman, house sitting, window washing, lawn care, etc.).

Additional ideas include a Quarter Rally, where double stick tape is placed from one end of the mall to another, and shoppers are asked to put down a quarter in support of the cause; a wish list that can be published in a local newspaper or sent to area businesses, organizations, or past donors; advertisement by asking a local supermarket to print a message on its shopping bags for a month (this is not a direct fund-raising activity, but it does generate a lot of publicity); and Rock-a-Thons, where supporters get pledges to rock in rocking chairs for a day (ARCH, 1992).

Gensheimer (1993) directed ideas on fund raising to both teachers and parents. Ideas included a used goods sale, clothesline sales, knowledge-a-thon, and a school carnival. Two unique ideas were a birthday party and a penny war. The former can be held for local children at a school with a fee charged to cover all expenses. The latter idea is based on the fact that people don't like to carry extra pennies with them. Students decorate coffee cans and place them at various local locations for the public to dispose of extra pennies.

When planning for such fund-raising activities, be sure to keep the following steps in mind:
- Set a fund-raising goal for a specific purpose.
- Target potential donors or sponsors.
- Determine legal matters such as tort liability, taxes, insurance needs, and so forth.
- Choose a specific fund-raising event.
- Develop a realistic budget.
- Select a date(s).
- Organize volunteers.
- Publicize the event.
- Oversee all aspects of the activity.
- Thank all involved.
- Keep from one year to the next all ideas, public relations strategies, and volunteer lists (Stephens & Karnes, 1999).

Old Strategies/New Practices

Over the last decade, public elementary and secondary school districts and programs have successfully employed fund-raising strategies previously practiced primarily by postsecondary institutions: annual giving, endowments, commemorative planned giving, and unrestricted and restricted gifts. Local, state, and national associations are also engaging in fund development.

Annual giving is usually conducted toward a wide spectrum of groups. The most obvious are students, their families, and alumni. Others to be included within the school would be the board members, teachers, administrators, and staff. In the community, those targeted for annual giving should include vendors, service groups, professional organizations, small businesses, local corporations, foundations, and the general public. Giving may be requested through personal visits, telephone calls, and letters. Gifts may be monetary and nonmonetary. Monetary gifts include cash, checks, money orders, and charges to approved credit cards. Examples of nonmonetary gifts include bonds and securities, goods and services, real and personal property, royalties, copyrights and trademark rights, and insurance policies stating the school district or program as a beneficiary. Wereley (1992) suggests writing a clever "want ad" for a community partner. Publish the ad in the local newspaper or create a flyer and distribute to area businesses and organizations.

Commemorative gifts are becoming more popular within education. The gift is given "in memory of" or "in honor of" either a deceased or living person, and it may be restricted or unrestricted. A donor may wish to leave, either through a will or another instrument, an insurance policy for general or specific purposes. Large amounts of money may be given for endowments with the interest used as designated by the donor (Karnes, Stephens, & Samel, 1999).

Personal property could be art, equipment, cars, and so forth. Examples of real property include a residence, business, building, or undeveloped land. Real and personal properties must be assessed by a certified professional appraiser, and they are only helpful to districts if they can be used or sold. School districts engaged in fund development should have board-approved policies written within state and federal guidelines under the advisement of a tax attorney. They should also have developed policies on strategies to be used, such as methods of acknowledgment and recognition and confidentiality.

Summary

With the limited amount of money allotted to gifted education, it is imperative that teachers and administrators become knowledgeable in grant writing and in locating sources of funding.

Teacher Resources

Publications

There are many books that can assist in the funding process. A few of these are

Bauer, D. G. (1996). *Educator's Internet funding guide: Classroom connect's reference guide to technology funding.* Lancaster, PA: Wentworth Worldwide Media.

Brewer, E. W., Achilles, C. M., & Fuhriman, F. R. (1995). *Finding funding: Grantwriting and project management from start to finish.* Thousand Oaks, CA: Corwin Press.

Gensheimer, C. F. (1993). *Raising funds for your child's school.* New York: Walker & Company.

Graham, C. (1993). *Keep the money coming: A step-by-step strategic guide to annual fundraising.* Sarasota, FL: Pineapple Press.

Hall, M. (1988). *Getting funded: A complete guide to proposal writing.* (3rd ed.). Portland, OR: Continuing Education.

Ferguson, J. (1997). *Grants for schools: How to find and win funds for K–12 programs.* New York: Soho Press.

Orlich, D. C. (1996). *Designing successful grant proposals.* Alexandria, VA: Association for Supervision and Curriculum Development.

Ross, D. M. (1990). *Fund raising for youth: Hundreds of wonderful ways of raising funds for youth organizations.* Colorado Springs, CO: Meriweather.

Ruskin, K. B., & Achilles, C. M. (1995). *Grantwriting, fund raising, and partnerships: Strategies that work.* Thousand Oaks, CA: Corwin Press.

Addresses

AT&T Telecommunications
32 Sixth Ave.
New York, NY 10013
http://www.ATT.com/

American Association of University Women
1111 16th St. N.W.
Washington, DC 20036
http://www.aauw.org/

The Catalog of Federal Domestic Assistance
General Services Administration
300 7th St. S.W., Ste. 101
Washington, DC 20407
(202) 708-5126
http://www.gsa.gov/fdac/default.htm

The Carnegie Corporation of New York
437 Madison Ave.
New York, NY 10022
http:www.carnegie.org/

The Chronicle of Philanthropy
1255 23rd St. N.W.
Washington, DC 20037
http://www.philanthropy.com

Commerce Business Daily
Superintendent of Documents
Government Printing Office
Washington, DC 20402
(202) 512-1800
http://www.cbdnet.access.gpo.gov/

Congressional Record
Government Printing Office
Washington, DC 20402
(202) 512-1800

Council for Exceptional Children
1920 Association Dr.
Reston, VA 20191–1589
http://www.cec.sped.org/

Education Funding News
4301 North Fairfax Dr., Ste. 875
Arlington, VA 22203
(703) 528-1082

The Federal Register
The Superintendent of Documents
Washington, DC 20402
(202) 512-1800
http://www.access.gpo.gov/su_docs/aces/aces140.html.

Javits Gifted and Talented Students Education Program
Office of Educational Research and Improvement
555 New Jersey Ave., N.W.
Washington, DC 20208-5645

W. K. Kellogg Foundation
1 Michigan Ave. E.
Battle Creek, MI 49017–4058
http://www.WKKF.org

The National Education Association
1201 16th St. N.W.
Washington, DC 20036
http://www.nea.org/

The National Endowment for the Arts
Public Information Office
1100 Pennsylvania Ave. N.E.
Washington, DC 20506
(202) 682-5400
http://arts.endow.gov

The National Endowment for the Humanities
1100 Pennsylvania Ave. S.W.
Washington, DC 20506
(202) 786-0438
http://www.neh.gov

The National Institute of Health
49 Covent Dr., #Blee16
Bethesda, MD 20892–0001
http://www.nih.gov/

The National Science Foundation
4201 Wilson Blvd.
Arlington, VA 22230
(707) 306-1234
http://www.nsf.gov

Office of Educational Research and Improvement (OERI)
Education Information Branch
Capitol Plaza Building, Ste. 300
555 New Jersey Avenue S.W.
Washington, DC 20208
(202) 357-6556 or (800) 424-1616
http://www.ed.gov/offices/OERI

The Spencer Foundation
875 N. Michigan Ave., Ste. 3930
Chicago, IL 60611–1803
http://www.spencer.org/

Toyota Motor Sales USA, Inc.
P.O. Box 2991
Torrance, CA 90509
http://www.toyota.com/

Whirlpool Corporation
200 M-63 N.
Benton Harbor, MI 49022–0692
http://www.whirlpool.com/

Web Sites

Some useful web sites can also provide a substantial amount of information to get one underway in grantwriting.

The Foundation Center—http://www.fdncenter.org
Provides links to and information on nearly 100 private foundations, 54 corporate grant makers, and 18 grant-making charities.

Grant Sources for Educators—http://www.capecod.net/schrock-guide/business/grants.htm
Targeted at educators, this web site offers links regarding information on grants and fund-raising activities.

Grants Web—http://www.web.fie.com/cws/sra/resource.htm
A good place to begin, with easy accessibility to numerous links for federal and nonfederal grant sources.

Pitsco's Launch to Grants and Funding—http://www.pitsco.com/p/grants.html
A wide array of links to funding agencies and other resources helpful to educators as they pursue the grant writing endeavor.

U.S. Department of Education—http://gcs.edu.gov
Includes information on the Secretary's initiatives, agency publications, legislation, press releases, programs with application procedures, and agency personnel with contact information.

http://www.ipt.lpl.arizona.edu/IPT/Grant
The text of several successful education grants are found here. One has the option of reading the proposal on the Internet or downloading the text file itself.

http://www.ra.tec.edu//alliance/TEMPLATE/alliance_resources/pubs/TERCpubs/TERCGrantmanual/TOC.html
This manual was assembled to provide high school science teachers guidelines for submitting proposals for science education enhancement to foundations, government agencies, and local philanthropies. This is a comprehensive overview of how to successfully write educational grants.

Through careful research and innovation, an idea can be turned into a reality with the discovery and acquisition of a funding source. Although the process requires a lot of work, the rewards will be well worth the efforts. Good luck in the fund-finding adventure.

References

ARCH. (1992). *Creative fund-raising activities.* Chapel Hill, NC: ARCH National Resources Center for Crisis Nurseries and Respite Care Services.

Elementary and Secondary Education Act of 1965, 20 U.S.C. §36 (1988).

Gifted and Talented Students Education Act, H.R. 637, 106 Cong., 1st Sess. (1990).

Individuals with Disabilities Education Act, 20 U.S.C. §1401 et seq. (1990).

Gensheimer, C. F. (1993). *Raising funds for your child's school.* New York: Walker & Company.

Karnes, F. A., Stephens, K. R., & Samel, B. (1999). Fund development in gifted education: An untapped resource. *Gifted Child Today, 22*(5), 30–33, 52.

Novelli, J. (1994). You can get grants! *Instructor, 104*(1), 32–36.

Palent, S. A. (1985). *Fund raising for park, recreation, and conservation agencies.* Washington, DC: National Park Service.

Stephens, K. R., & Karnes, F. A. (1999). Creative ways to raise money for the gifted program. *Gifted Child Today, 22*(2), 48–51.

Swan, J. (1990). *Fund raising for the small public library.* New York: Neal-Schuman.

Title VI of the Elementary and Secondary Education Act of 1965, 20 U.S.C. §7311 et seq.

Walsh, E. (1990). Fund raising made easy. *Parks and Recreation, 25*(10), 60–63, 78.

Wereley, J. (1992). Developing and maintaining a school partnership. In C. S. Hyman (Ed.), *The school-community cookbook: Recipes for successful projects in the schools: A "how-to" manual for teachers, parents, and community* (pp. 88–93). Baltimore, MD: Jewish Community Federation of Baltimore; Children of Harvey and Lyn Meyerhoff Philanthropic Fund; Fund for Educational Excellence.

CHAPTER 21

Teaching on a Shoestring
Materials for Teaching Gifted Students

TRACY L. RILEY
Massey University, New Zealand

*P*icture this: gifted students working with community members to clean up a local beach. They have done their "homework." Charlotte describes the effects of pollution on sea creatures as she works with another volunteer. Terrance has developed a year-long action plan he will use to guide a group of younger children through a beach clean-up. Back in the resource room, the walls display maps showing water shortages throughout the region, and on the bookshelves are poems and stories about our most vital resource: water.

The teacher is beside himself. Not only can he see the growth and development in his students' eyes, but he can still see dollar signs in his budget. For just five dollars and a little effort, he has pulled off a great feat. He has been "teaching on a shoestring" using the Teacher's Water Education Resource Guide (1997), available from the nonprofit environmental group, Earth Day Resources.

Following this teacher's example, this chapter explores the vast potential of teaching materials suitable for gifted children, highlighting free and inexpensive items.

Materials for Teaching Gifted Children

Materials for teaching gifted children come in many shapes and sizes and with a variety of purposes. While text after text describes the importance of teachers of the gifted having a solid understanding of methods and materials for teaching the gifted, little has been established to answer the questions teachers might have regarding materials. For example, how and where are materials obtained? Perhaps more importantly, what constitutes suitable materials? This chapter addresses these two questions, beginning with a brief look at the general nature of materials for gifted students and criteria for their selection. Following is a lengthy discussion on the use of free and inexpensive materials, giving a rationale for their potential use with gifted students, as well as strategies for locating and using them effectively.

Materials for teaching gifted children may be teacher-developed or published locally, nationally, or internationally. Resources may be intended for teacher or student use. Some materials are specially designed for teaching the gifted child and are obtainable from publishing companies. Other materials may be intended for general audiences of learners but ideally work for gifted students due to their unique nature. The costs of the materials vary; yet, some materials may be free or inexpensive such as those created by governmental agencies, nonprofit organizations, or business and industry. With the variety of options available for supporting the learning goals and objectives for gifted children, it is important for teachers to have a good understanding of how to best select the materials that fill their desks and bookshelves.

Karnes and Collins (1985) gave a range of general, student, and teacher considerations related to the selection of materials for gifted students. See Table 1 for the selection of educational materials for gifted students. Of the criteria listed by Karnes and Collins, one stood out in this author's mind: Is the cost commensurate with the use and learning objectives? This is an important criterion; but, perhaps a more important reality check for some teachers might be to ask, Is the cost commensurate to the gifted program's budget? Teachers must be careful in their spending and should be highly selective in the purchase of materials. However, selectivity is not just a monetary necessity; it must occur if the needs of the gifted student are to be met. Thus, a set of criteria for selection should be utilized, alongside careful planning, goal setting, and organization. The purpose of any material selected for gifted students should be to provide a differentiated learning experience for this unique group of learners.

Partnering Differentiation for Gifted Learners With Free and Inexpensive Materials

Gifted children bring to the classroom a unique set of learning characteristics demanding recognition and attention. Maker and Nielson (1995) described four areas that need to be qualitatively differentiated for gifted learners: content, process, products, and the learning environment. In order to effectively influence change in each of these domains, the teaching and learning materials must be taken into consideration. This need for differentiation is based upon many characteristics of gifted learners—advanced knowledge and understanding, a grasp of global or conceptual issues, and a range of diverse, sometimes unusual, interests. Numerous free and inexpensive materials available to teachers also meet these three broad, yet defining, traits.

Just peruse *Instructor Magazine*'s web site of Best Bets, Freebies, Contests, and Other Good Deals (http://scholastic.com/instructor/freebies/contests.htm). Many of the featured items are of an advanced academic nature. The content is interdisciplinary and lends itself to an abstract nature. For example, literary classics such as *Romeo and Juliet*, *A Tale of Two Cities*, and *Sherlock Holmes* are brought into the spotlight for 6–12 year-olds in the PBS series *Wishbone*. Broad-based issues such as women's suffrage, environmental awareness, and communication are highlighted through videos, posters, discussion groups, and pictures. One cannot question diversity, as topics range from pizza farms to folk art to old-growth forests. Clearly, there is a suitable match between this sampling of freebies and the unique needs of gifted students.

Table 1. Criteria for the Selection of Educational Materials for Gifted Students

In order to facilitate the analysis of instructional materials under consideration for use in educational programs for gifted students, a check list entitled "Criteria for the Selection of Educational Materials for Gifted Students" has been designed. This check list has three basic components: General Considerations in Materials Selection, Student Considerations in Materials Selection, and Teacher Considerations in Materials Selection. General Considerations are applicable for the selection of all educational materials. Student Considerations pertain specifically to the educational needs of gifted students. This portion of the check list is designed to be the most helpful in determining whether a material promotes or allows for differentiated educational experiences for gifted students. Teacher Considerations are designed to promote the selection of those materials that will enhance the role of the instructor as a facilitator of the learning process. This check list is not viewed as all-inclusive. Additional items may be added to the check list to meet local considerations.

This check list is designed not as an evaluation instrument but rather as a screening device. The number of positive and negative responses should not determine final selection or rejection of a particular material, as no material will contain all facts incorporated into the check list. The selection of a specific educational material should be based on positive responses to those items that best express student, program, and teacher needs.

Modification of the check list for the selection of educational materials for gifted students to meet local or individual program needs is encouraged. This check list should not be perceived as all-inclusive. It is intended to serve as a guide to materials selection, and the questions included are suggested ones for consideration.

In some cases, items that reflect particular program goals may be added. In other cases, educators at the local level may wish to delete certain items and retain those they perceive to be the most important.

Numerical ratings have been intentionally omitted from this check list. We feel that including a rating scale would usurp professional judgment at the local level. Teachers and administrators of programs for gifted students may wish to devise their own rating system to use with this check list. When this is done at the local level, materials can then be rated and subsequently selected to fit individual programs and objectives.

Certain cautions are advised in the selection of commercial educational materials for gifted students. Materials marked "enrichment" should be carefully examined to determine the nature of the educational objective. Enrichment activities appropriate to the gifted should extend learning experiences and not reinforce concepts already mastered. Some enrichment materials which are attractively packaged lack depth and challenge.

Materials with specific indicators of age and/or grade level should be analyzed to determine if their content is appropriate to the development level, abilities, and interests of a gifted student. Using materials designed for particular grade levels at lower grade levels does not, in itself, constitute an appropriate educational program for gifted students. The overuse of games and puzzles in programming for gifted is discouraged, as well as the sole use of commercial instructional materials. Educational materials should not constitute the total instructional program for gifted students. The manner in which materials are utilized, adapted, and supplemented by teachers determines the direction, focus, and quality of differentiated programs for the gifted. These students should be allowed to assume responsibility for their own learning, including content, learning style, and rate.

General Considerations in Materials Selection	Yes	No
Does the material include general learning objectives?	——	——
Do the learning objectives of the material support the goals of the program?	——	——
Are the concepts presented in the materials valid?	——	——
Does the material have an attractive format and design?	——	——
Are the materials durable?	——	——
Are the materials conveniently packaged?	——	——
Are the materials portable?	——	——
Are the majority of the materials nonconsumable?	——	——
Is the cost of the material commensurate with the use and learning objectives?	——	——
Is the necessary equipment available for the utilization of the material?	——	——
Is the purchase of additional materials necessary?	——	——
Is the suggested grade or age level specified?	——	——
Is the material designed to be used individually?	——	——
Is the material appropriate for group instruction?	——	——
Is an instructional guide provided?	——	——
Are there sufficient numbers of students to utilize the material?	——	——
Are the learning materials presented in sequence?	——	——
Has the material been field tested?	——	——
Do the learning objectives justify the amount of time required for the activity?	——	——

Table 1. Continued

	Yes	No
Do the concepts presented in the materials conflict with community standards?	——	——
Are the materials presented in such a way so as to be nondiscriminatory in terms of culture, race, sex, or handicapping condition?	——	——

Student Consideration in Materials Selection for Gifted Students	Yes	No
Are the students' interests reflected in the materials?	——	——
Is the mode of presentation commensurate with the learning style of the student?	——	——
Can the concepts presented be employed by the student in other learning situations?	——	——
Is self-evaluation an integral part of the material?	——	——
Do the materials encourage the student to undertake further study and research in related areas?	——	——
Are appropriate references provided for use by the student?	——	——
Are the processes taught applicable to a variety of learning situations?	——	——
Is the content of the material consistent with the student's developmental level or prior experience or training in this area rather than grade-level oriented?	——	——
Do students develop products; and if so, are appropriate outlets for students' products suggested?	——	——
Does the material promote development in one or more dimensions of learning appropriate for the gifted?	——	——
A. Does the material foster and enhance the development of oral and written communication skills?	——	——
B. Does the material foster and enhance the development of higher-cognitive processes of analysis, synthesis, and evaluation?	——	——

C. Does the material foster and enhance the development in the affective domain, such as understanding ourselves and others? —— ——

D. Does the material foster and enhance the development of logical thinking, such as inductive and deductive reasoning and problem-solving skills? —— ——

E. Does the material foster and enhance the development of critical thinking, such as the judgement and decision-making processes? —— ——

F. Does the material foster and enhance the development of divergent production, such as open-ended responses and self-expression? —— ——

G. Does the material foster and enhance research skills such as library research skills and knowledge and application of the scientific method of research? —— ——

H. Does the material foster and enhance development in values clarification, such as defining, expressing, and assuming responsibility for personal values? —— ——

I. Does the material foster and enhance the development of group dynamics, group interaction processes, and communication and discussion techniques? —— ——

J. Does the material foster and enhance the development of creativity, such as fluency, flexibility, originality, and elaboration? —— ——

Teacher Considerations in Materials Selection for Gifted Students

	Yes	No
Are specific teaching suggestions provided?	——	——
Do materials allow for teacher initiative and adaptation?	——	——
Are guidelines given for making some of the necessary materials rather than purchasing them?	——	——

Table 1. Continued

If specialized training is required for teachers' utilization of materials, do instructions accompany the material?	——	——
Is the amount of required teacher preparation time consistent with the scope of the learning objectives?	——	——
Are appropriate references and resources suggested?	——	——
Is the teaching style suggested in the materials parallel with the instructional style of the teacher?	——	——
Are suggestions provided for the elevation of student progress?	——	——

Note. From *Handbook of Instructional Resources and References for Teaching the Gifted.* (pp. 15–20), by F. A. Karnes, 1984, Newton, MA: Allyn and Bacon. Copyright 1984 by Allyn and Bacon. Adapted with permission.

Furthermore, gifted educators have defined a set of content-related expectations for teaching gifted students. These include advanced content which is interdisciplinary in nature, has variety, is timely, and shows complexity and authenticity (Maker & Nielson, 1995; Renzulli, 1977; VanTassel Baska, 1997). The following defining characteristics of free and inexpensive materials are matched to the educational needs of gifted children.

Advanced Content. There is no age range or grade specification for many of the materials available at low-cost. Some items may be intended for adults, but the content can be readily digested by gifted students.

Interdisciplinary Nature. Many of the topics and themes featured in free and inexpensive materials range across the curriculum, weaving various subject matter into a tapestry, as opposed to separate threads.

Variety. The content includes a range of unique and intriguing themes.

Timeliness. Because many of these materials are produced by business and industry, the content is relevant and current. Hot topics are thoroughly covered with the latest information and ideas.

Complexity. The vocabulary, issues, and activities are not superficial but are of a complex nature suitable for the gifted child.

Authenticity. A range of free and inexpensive materials address real problems, relevant to today's world and the lives of gifted students.

Another example of content-differentiation is provided by the Anti-Defamation League in its resources for Holocaust education. The materials begin with suggestions for dividing information into appropriate themes. Each theme includes interactive writing exercises, suggested books, videos, posters, and options for helping students to define the relevance of the Holocaust by examining prejudice and bigotry today. Other sections of the catalog recommend books for children written by children, as well as videos and publications on Holocaust resistance and Holocaust rescue. Throughout the entire catalog is a timeline listing important historical dates, as well as maps and photos that serve as excellent documentary resources.

Consider process skills for a moment. Renzulli (1977) perhaps first defined process skills by way of Type II enrichment in the Enrichment Triad Model. These have been further explored by Karnes and Bean (1994) via the Process Skills Rating Scales. In the simplest of terms these are the "how" of teaching and learning. Suitable process skills for gifted students to explore within their education include "creative thinking and problem-solving skills, learning-how-to-learn skills such as classifying and analyzing data, advanced reference, and communication skills" (Renzulli & Reis, 1997, p. 137). These process skills may be planned and taught; however, there are other skills that may surface almost accidentally based upon a student's interests and strengths. For example, a child intrigued by cotton growth may be required to read advanced materials intended for agricultural specialists, conduct agricultural experiments, and take on broad complicated research methodologies related to the field.

Free and inexpensive materials for gifted students certainly address the skills highlighted in gifted programs but really begin to open doors for those individual skills necessitated by unique abilities and interests. Rather than focusing on steps or components of a particular process skill, whether it is research or problem solving, these materials often force students to apply the skills to their learning. This orientation of process skills is supported by Schiever and

Maker (1997), who stated that "fragmentation is not likely to promote transfer of the higher-thinking skills to other content areas or to daily problems or situations" (p. 113). Many of the authentic, timely, advanced materials available at little or no cost circumvent this fragmentation in the ways in which students and teachers alike utilize them in their classrooms. Examples of free and inexpensive materials that force students to utilize a differentiated set of process skills can be found on the Internet.

The application of process skills integrated in advanced content is another necessity in the education of gifted children. This is often carried out via small-group or independent study of a self-selected problem resulting in an authentic product (Renzulli & Reis, 1997). The products should be original and encourage both written and oral work (VanTassel Baska, 1997). Products are intended to demonstrate students' mastery of both content and processes and, as Howley, Howley, and Pendarvis (1986) stated, may be tangible or intangible. The shift in evidencing learning for gifted students should move from focus on check lists, worksheets, and tests to an array of possibilities reflecting advanced knowledge and methodology (Renzulli & Reis, 1997).

Because many of the free and inexpensive materials suitable for gifted students are designed by an audience outside of education, these materials naturally avoid the traditional view on mastery of skills and knowledge. This is an ideal match because, as Schiever and Maker (1997) asserted, learning in gifted classrooms must be different from that taking place in regular classrooms. If the materials being utilized reflect goals and objectives outside of the regular curriculum, the partnership of gifted kids with free and inexpensive, yet high-quality materials, allows for product development that also extends beyond the norm.

Examples of the assortment of opportunities may be found on the home page of the Federal Reserve Bank of San Francisco (http://www.frbsf.org/econedu/curriculum/index.html), which highlights teaching materials. Secondary students partaking in "The Muffin Market" establish their own muffin shop, and those with a successful economic venture clearly demonstrate their understandings of economics. Elementary students create their own storybook in which a character is making and spending money, or they write a play about how money may be used in the future.

Product development often requires instruction, and for those crafty students, the craftnetvillage (http://www.craftnetvillage. com/project_library/kids_crafts.html) provides instruction on how to design a range of crafts from topiaries to quilts to finger puppets. Students can learn cartooning basics with a live online lesson of how to draw a cat by cartoonist Duane Barnhart when visiting the Cartoon Connections home page (http://www.cartoonconnec- tions. com/). Or, students can create their own puzzles using the Puzzlemaker (http://www.puzzlemaker.com/). These free web sites are created as resources to teach children more about product development and as lessons that are necessary for quality products.

If the content, processes, and products are differentiated in a qual- itative manner, one can only assume that the learning environment will also look and feel different from the traditional classroom. Maker and Nielson (1995) described learning environments for gifted chil- dren that are child-centered as opposed to teacher-centered, in which teachers serve as facilitators rather than directors of learning. Using free and inexpensive materials allows—almost forces—teachers to change the learning environment. The sheer range of content, mixed with the variety of process skills utilized to develop unique products, is a free ticket for classroom teachers to create a learning environment focusing on special interests and abilities of students. Individuals are allowed freedom of choice, and self-direction is encouraged.

If a premise of gifted education is to provide depth and breadth by way of content, process, products, and learning environment, the consideration and inclusion of low-cost materials adds flair and vital- ity. It simply works! But, the theoretical underpinnings of teaching and learning for gifted children are just one set of reasons for educa- tors to explore this resource. They may well be the most important; however, one should not overlook the practicality, money-saving, and personal benefits of tapping into free and inexpensive materials.

Why Use Free and Inexpensive Materials for Teaching the Gifted?

Free and inexpensive materials are practical, user-friendly, low or no cost, and readily available. Teachers of the gifted are cited often in the literature as being flexible (Feldhusen, 1997). This flexibility often stems from necessity, as teachers are working in classrooms with students who are gifted but not homogenous. They possess diverse interests and abilities. Teaching effectively requires meeting the demand for variety, often in classrooms that have few resources. Teachers of the gifted all too often learn that, in order to have adequate materials to enhance their teaching and maximize student potential, they have to go to great extremes.

If teachers utilize free and inexpensive materials, then they should be able to avoid some of the added expense often associated with the lack of resources. Interestingly, Vest (1991) reported that purchasing items is the most common means of obtaining classroom resources, whereas donations are the least common. This is an unexpected reality considering the financial status of many schools, particularly gifted programs, coupled with the availability of free or inexpensive items. Rather than "beg, borrow, and steal," teachers of the gifted should begin to explore a variety of other practical and effective avenues at little or no cost. The fact that these materials are free (or almost free) is a reason in and of itself for their use.

A final free reward goes to the teacher (Cruickshank, 1990) who stated

> The public is particularly laudatory of teachers who, without benefit of special resources, overcome seemingly extraordinary obstacles to help their pupils succeed, thus demonstrating that other teachers could make a difference, too, if they tried harder or were more creative. (p. 16)

Finding solutions to challenges is rewarding, particularly if the greatest ones are student needs and limited resources. The positive outcomes are "great both in terms of resources found and . . . recognition" (Vest, 1991, p. 8).

In sum, it appears that by pairing gifted students with free and inexpensive materials, many rewards are gained: differentiating student needs are met with challenging and appropriate materials, practicalities are addressed, and teachers are fulfilled. Having established a rationale for the use of these materials, it is important to further examine how the resources can effectively be used to support the education of gifted students.

How Can Free and Inexpensive Resources Be Used With Gifted Students?

Low-cost teaching and learning resources cannot effectively meet the needs of gifted students without the skills of good teachers. While research indicates that teachers of the gifted need to possess the ability to develop materials for teaching the gifted (Hultgren & Seeley, 1982), teachers also need to be able to critically evaluate and appropriately select materials. The same principles related to the selection of all materials (as previously discussed in Table 1) apply here. There are also further considerations in using free and inexpensive materials:

- The materials should be used in tandem with other learning tools, including books and magazines, computer software, and resource people. As a stand-alone resource, many low-cost items may not be adequate for meeting learning goals and objectives.
- The reliability and authenticity of the information contained in free and inexpensive materials should be scrutinized.
- The suitability of the materials for matching student interests and abilities should be examined. For example, having a close look at the topic and reading level enhances their use.
- The actual cost involved may exceed a teacher's expectations. While some of the materials appear to be free, there are sometimes additional or hidden costs such as shipping and handling, supplementary materials needed for activities, or even the invisible costs of Internet access and usage.

From the selection of materials, the next step in their effective use reflects the competencies and skills of good teaching. When the materials are used in conjunction with Feldhusen's (1997) suggested competencies of teachers of the gifted, then success in their use can be better assured. These skills include fast-paced instruction, emphasis on creativity and thinking skills, appropriate grouping for instruction, including opportunities for independent learning, and curriculum differentiation. Common sense indicates that whether a material is low-cost or high-cost, in the hands of a well-trained and knowledgeable teacher, it is far more effective.

Included within these competencies is an underlying assumption that the teacher is reliant upon sound educational models and practices supported by current theory and research. These may encompass both enrichment and acceleration, the two most commonly referred-to vehicles for teaching gifted children. Ideally, the two should work in tandem (Townsend, 1996) and in support of one another. Acceleration, or vertical development through the curriculum, requires a vision of content at an academically advanced level. Enrichment—otherwise known as horizontal curriculum development—involves content that is beyond the boundaries of the regular curriculum. With careful selection, planning, and forethought, free and inexpensive materials can compliment the goals of both enrichment and acceleration.

Karnes and Collins (1985) further discussed these principles in stating,

> Educational materials should not constitute the total instructional program for gifted students. The manner in which materials are utilized, adapted, and supplemented by teachers determines the direction, focus, and quality of differentiated programs for the gifted. These students should be allowed to assume responsibility for their own learning, including content, learning style, and rate. (p. 20)

Perhaps the most important "how-to" skill for effectively using free and inexpensive materials with gifted children is good common teaching sense. Keeping in mind the necessity of careful selection and competent teaching based upon sound educational models and practices should ensure that materials for gifted children are maximized in meeting their needs. The reasons for using free and inexpensive materials are convincing only if they are used appropriately.

The Search Begins . . .

Having established why and how free and inexpensive materials can be used with gifted children, the next question is, "Where can teachers go to find educational resources at little or no cost?" Vest (1991) reported that there is a minimal amount of educational literature available to assist teachers in planning and pursuing this quest; however, there is a maximum amount of resources available for those ready and willing to search.

The quest for low or no-cost materials for teaching gifted children has many layers in which the community may be involved. A logical first place to look is locally. With today's technology and innovation, national and international possibilities are more easily accessible. Local, state, national, and international communities commonly share the four primary sources to be tapped. These are educational institutions, business and industry, families, and government agencies. Each source should be explored at every level. Lewis and Munn (1987) suggested asking six questions prior to the start of an investigation:

- What information do I want?
- Why do I want it?
- When do I need it?
- How do I collect it?
- Where can I find it? and
- From whom do I get it?

A good starting place for investigating free and inexpensive materials is print media. Vest (1991) gave a comprehensive listing of directories, recommending *Educator's Guide to Free Curriculum Materials and Free and Inexpensive Learning Materials*. These resources are often accessible though libraries and teacher resource centers at colleges and universities. *Free Stuff for Kids* (Free Stuff Editors, 1997) is a fun resource that is published annually. Another book worth checking out is *Free and Almost Free Things for Teachers* (Osborn, 1993). For information on similar publications, see the Teacher Resources section at the end of this chapter. The local library may have other similar publications; a chat with the reference librarian could be worthwhile.

The Internet also offers more, including a few recommended sites for obtaining free materials. When conducting a library or Internet search, some key words to consider are free, inexpensive, cost-effective, and economical. You can also visit the Barnes and Noble home page and do a subject search for the latest books (http://www.bn.com).

In addition to books and web sites, there are a couple of magazines that frequently offer information on free and inexpensive materials. For example, a recent issue of *Gifted Child Today* (1997) features free educational materials supporting the PBS series Nova, "Where in Time is Carmen San Diego?," and Science Odyssey. *Instructor Magazine* also offers teachers a variety of possibilities in "Best Bets," a regular feature of the magazine.

Renzulli and Reis (1985) recommended the creation of a source file. Starting a computer-based file or an index with information like that illustrated in Figure 1 would be beneficial. These files could be located in individual classrooms, but a schoolwide source would probably serve a wider audience of students and teachers. In addition to organized files, schools may also establish a centralized storage area for resources. A search based upon careful planning and organization can only lead to positive outcomes.

Tips for Teaching on a Shoestring

Planning and organizing the search for materials is certainly essential, but there are also some tricks of the trade that can be helpful. To begin, what constitutes suitable materials for gifted children? This topic has been explored previously in this chapter, and to highlight the key points, teachers should consider:

Concept/Theme: _____   Discipline Areas: _____

Age/Grade Level: _____

Author of Publication: _____   Date of Publication: _____

Title: _____   Address: _____

Cost: _____

Notes: _____

Figure 1. Sample Source File Card

- how the materials relate to learning goals and objectives;
- practicalities such as costs and durability;
- suggested uses and potential modifications; and
- content validity and appropriateness.

In regard to student considerations, student interests and strengths should be reflected, as well as opportunities for advanced content, process skill development, and original products. The same care should be given in the selection of free and inexpensive materials for gifted children as would be taken with any other materials. Vest (1991) suggested that teachers should initially request only one copy of the item of interest in order to check for suitability.

Once appropriateness has been established, there is a series of other mechanisms that can be put into place to aid in successful quests for free and inexpensive materials. Chayet (1994) advised teachers to read the local paper, particularly looking for garage sales. She also suggested contacting government agencies, getting placed on mailing lists, and utilizing teacher discounts. Additional practical tips include

- Start a letter-writing campaign.
- Spread the word to parents, teachers, friends, relatives, and, of course, students.
- Utilize the media: newspapers, magazines, posters, and even bulletin boards.
- Let your fingers do the walking. Use the yellow pages and call 800 numbers.
- Involve students in the search for free materials.
- Share your finds with colleagues.
- Always use the best manners (saying "please" and "thank you" goes a long way).
- Save everything. Recycle.
- Keep your eyes and ears open.

In addition to these tips, it is always wise to read and follow ordering directions carefully. Some agencies, for example, require a self-addressed, stamped envelope in order to distribute materials. Not reading carefully could lead to a delay or perhaps no response at all.

Effective positive communication is essential to the successful search for materials. Whether a request for materials is communicated via a phone call, letter, advertisement, or e-mail message, it should be clear, concise, and specific. Consider including the following details

- age/grade level of students;
- topic, theme, or subject of interest;
- specific material (if known);
- number of copies; and
- return address.

Always end the communication with a positive note of thanks— even if it is an unsuccessful request. A sample letter is shown in Figure 2. Remember that students can also be involved in communication of this nature. In this author's experience, a thank-you note written by two 12-year-old students resulted in a second donation of books for the enrichment classroom.

The ABC's and 1–2–3's of Free and Inexpensive Materials

Exactly what resources are available on a free or low-cost basis? The variety ranges from people-power to consumable classroom

---

Dear Colleague,

My fifth-grade gifted class is studying a unit on space exploration. I am seeking materials on this topic. If you have any complimentary materials available, please forward them to the address below:

Your School
Anytown, USA

Thank you for your generous contribution in enriching the lives of my young students.

Sincerely,
Teacher of the Gifted

Figure 2. Communication that Works

---

materials. Figure 3 displays the array of items for use by gifted students and their teachers. Upon beginning and pursuing a quest for resources and materials, teachers will surely add to this list. The content areas covered by these resources are also expansive, with science, language arts, social studies, health and nutrition, art, technology, mathematics, foreign languages, and careers adequately represented. An integrated approach to learning can easily be supported by many of the free and inexpensive materials available to teachers.

A   activity books, annotated bibliographies, art supplies
B   book covers, booklets, bookmarks, bumper stickers
C   coloring pages, charts, curriculum guides, cassette tapes, crosswords
D   decals, discussion topics
E   experiments, experts
F   fact sheets, fun packs, flags, films, food
G   games, garage sale specials, guest speakers
H   hands-on fun
I   inexpensive items, Internet sites
J   journals
K   keypals
L   literature, leaders
M   maps, magnets, manipulatives, magazines, mentors
N   newsletters, newspapers
O   on-line assistance
P   prints, puzzles, posters, pamphlets, photos, pictures
Q   quizzes
R   riddles, reinforcers, recipes, reproducibles
S   software, seeds, science supplies, stamps
T   tattoos, toys, teaching guides
U   used goods
V   videos, valuable information, volunteers
W   workbooks, writing utensils
X   "xtra, xciting" stuff
Y   yardsticks
Z   zany and zappy things

**Figure 3. An Alphabetic Array of Free
and Inexpensive Materials**

Having discussed the many dimensions of teaching gifted students on a shoestring, in closing it is essential to remember the importance of organization and follow-through. A word of thanks, accurate record keeping, and sharing of resources can only lead to positive outcomes. Tapping into the many levels of community ensures great results for teachers and students alike. Weaving into the search are the fundamental principles of curriculum differentiation which are based upon sound educational theory and, when practiced, further enhance the educational outcomes for gifted students. Using materials to teach the gifted—whether they are high- or low-cost—requires forethought, planning, and careful evaluation.

Yet, remember, "enriching your classroom and curriculum need not be expensive" (Osborn, 1993, p. 7). Supplementary materials and resources are available at little or no cost—just for the asking. On a shoestring, teachers can bring the world right into their own classrooms, opening doors for gifted students and making learning more exciting than ever.

Teacher Resources

Publications

Brown, D. (1993). *Finding free and low-cost resources for teaching.* Brookfield, VT: Ashgate Publishers.
The 1995–1996 "gold mine" find for educators.

Freebies Magazine. (1997). *The official freebies for teachers.* (5th ed.) Kansas City, MO: Lowell House.
An annual publication jam-packed with great deals for teachers.

Harrington, B., & Christensen, B. (1995). *Unbelievably good deals that you absolutely can't get unless you're a teacher.* Chicago: NTC Contemporary.
An amazing variety of low-cost teaching aids.

Addresses

Anti-Defamation League Material Resource Center
744 Northfield Ave.
West Orange, NJ 07052
(800) 343–5540
fax: (201) 652–1973
ask for the *Holocaust Mini-Catalog: Rescue and Resistance,
Tools for Teachers.*

Web Sites

American Society for Microbiology—http://www.asmusa.org/edurc/
edu29.htm
Go to this site to hook gifted students up with mentors who
are members of the society. The process skills related to interpersonal relationships are particularly highlighted using this
method, as well as skills related to research, leadership, and
communication.

Create Your Own Newspaper—http://crayon.net
Students can join over 200,000 others who have used this site for
creating their own online newspaper. As the site says "news minus
paper = news!" Process skills highlighted include research and writing skills and, of course, computer how-to-skills.

Fabulous Freebies: Free Materials for Teachers!—http://www.educa-
tion -world.com/a_curr/curr110.shtml
This site, by Education World, tells visitors about some worthwhile
shoestring teaching materials. Topics include diet and nutrition, pet
care, money, recycling, and gardening, as well as some free software
sites for educators.

Free Stuff for Kids and Teachers—http://www105.pair.com/ free 4kid/
This web page contains suggested materials for both teachers and their
students available on the web, through a phone call, or mail. The range
of items includes, but is not limited to, curricular materials and software, lesson plans, crafts, and coloring pages.

Free Things for Educators—http://www.geocities.com/Heartland/ Oaks/9122/
Designed by a teacher, this is one of the most comprehensive listings of free and inexpensive materials on the Internet. With links to all suggested materials, the page is also divided into different age groups, or users can search by subject. The page is updated regularly.

MORE Fabulous Freebies: Free Materials for Teachers!—http://www. education-world.com/a_curr/curr109.shtml
Visitors at this site get a glance of the highlights of fabulous freebies and details on how to obtain them. Teaching materials span across the grades, including geography resources from the U.S. Geological Survey; science experiments for elementary/middle graders from the Edison Foundation; and a free magazine aimed at helping teens develop skills and character (and helping teachers and counselors learn to help teens to do the same).

The National Budget Simulator—http://garnet.berkeley.edu:3333/ budget/budget.html
Students visiting this site incorporate both cognitive and affective process skills as they attempt to balance the U.S. government's budget. They may take the easy route, which is a quick version addressing only the basics, or they may endeavor to understand a more comprehensive picture, absorbing all the "nitty gritties."

PBS's Arthur's Teacher's Corner—http://www.pbs.org/wgbh/arthur/ teachers/activities/index.html
Activities designed for classrooms cover a range of skills, including cooking, creative thinking, problem solving, dramatic play, creative music, and social/emotional development.

U.S. Department of Labor Educational Resources *"Jobs for Kids Who Like . . ."*—http://stats.bls.gov/k12/html/edu_over.html
Students can explore career choices, focusing on the utilization of their skills of interviewing and writing to obtain information. Planning and forecasting skills are also enhanced through the effective use of this resource.

References

Best bets. *Instructor Magazine,* (1994, July/August). 45–50.

Chayet, B. (1994, July/August). 20 penny-pinching ways to double your classroom library. *Instructor Magazine,* 51–53.

Cruickshank, D. R. (1990). *Research that informs teachers and teacher educators.* Bloomington, IN: Phi Delta Kappan.

Feldhusen, J. F. (1997). Educating teachers for work with talented youth. In N. Colangelo & G. A. Davis (Eds.), *Handbook of gifted education* (pp. 547–552). Needham Heights, MA: Allyn & Bacon.

Free educational materials accompany PBS series. (1997). *Gifted Child Today, 20*(6), 8.

Free Stuff Editors. (1997). *Free stuff for kids.* New York: Simon & Schuster.

Howley, A., Howley, C. B., & Pendarvis, E. D. (1986). *Teaching gifted children.* Boston, MA: Little, Brown.

Hultgren, H. W., & Seeley, K. R. (1982). *Training teachers of the gifted: A research monograph on teacher competencies.* Denver: University of Denver, School of Education.

Karnes, F. A., & Bean, S. B. (1994). *Process skills rating scales.* Austin, TX: PRO-ED.

Karnes, F. A., & Collins, E. C. (1985). *Handbook of instructional resources and references for teaching the gifted.* Boston, MA: Allyn & Bacon.

Lewis, I., & Munn, P. (1987). *So you want to do research! A guide for teachers on how to formulate research questions.* UK: Scottish Council for Research in Education.

Maker, J., & Nielson, A. B. (1995). *Teaching models in the education of the gifted* (2nd ed.). Austin, TX: PRO-ED.

Osborn, S. (1993). *Free and almost free things for teachers.* New York: Pergiee.

Renzulli, J. S. (1977). *The enrichment triad model: A guide for developing defensible programs for the gifted and talented.* Mansfield Center, CT: Creative Learning Press.

Renzulli, J. S., & Reis, S. M. (1985). *The schoolwide enrichment model: A comprehensive plan for educational excellence.* Mansfield Center, CT: Creative Learning Press.

Renzulli, J. S., & Reis, S. M. (1997). The schoolwide enrichment model: New directions for developing high end learning. In N. Colangelo & G. A. Davis (Eds.), *Handbook of gifted education* (pp. 136–154). Needham Heights, MA: Allyn & Bacon.

Schiever, S. W., & Maker, C. J. (1997). Enrichment and acceleration: An overview and new directions. In N. Colangelo & G. A. Davis (Eds.),

Handbook of gifted education (pp. 113–125). Needham Heights, MA: Allyn and Bacon.

Teacher's water education resource guide. (1997). San Francisco, CA: Earth Day Resources.

Townsend, M. (1996). Enrichment and acceleration: Lateral and vertical perspectives in provisions for gifted and talented. In D. McAlpine & R. Moltzen (Eds.), *Gifted and talented: New Zealand perspectives* (pp. 361–376). Palmerston North: Education Research Development Center.

VanTassel Baska, J. (1997). What matters in curriculum for gifted learners: Reflections on theory, research, and practice. In N. Colangelo & G. A. Davis (Eds.), *Handbook of gifted education* (pp. 126–135). Needham Heights, MA: Allyn & Bacon.

Vest, B. J. (1991). Free classroom resources: Conducting a successful search. (ERIC Documents Reproduction Service No. ED 348 985).

EDITORS

Frances A. Karnes, Ph.D., is a professor of special education and director of the Frances A. Karnes Center for Gifted Studies at The University of Southern Mississippi. Dr. Karnes, who is also director of the Leadership Studies Program at USM, has become widely known for her research, publications, innovative program developments, and service activities in gifted education and leadership training. The primary focus of her research has been the education of gifted children, legal issues, gifted girls, and the development of the leadership potential of all youth. She is author or coauthor of more than 185 papers published in scholarly journals, numerous monographs and book chapters, and is coauthor of 15 books in gifted education and related areas.

Suzanne M. Bean, Ph.D., is a professor of education at Mississippi University for Women (MUW). She has served for the past 20 years in the field of gifted studies as a teacher of gifted students, director of the Mississippi Governor's School, and founder and director of various other programs for gifted students and their teachers and parents. She is currently serving as coordinator of gifted youth programs and graduate programs in gifted studies and instructional management at MUW. Dr. Bean has coauthored five books for young adults and has had numerous publications in professional journals. She serves on the editorial review board for *Gifted Child Quarterly* and *The Journal for Secondary Gifted Education*. She has been President of the Mississippi Association for Talented and Gifted and is currently serving as a delegate to the executive board of the National Conference on Governor's Schools. For the past two decades, she has made numerous presentations at the state, regional, and national levels. Dr. Bean was selected by MUW students as Faculty Member of the Year for 1998.

CONTRIBUTORS

Elissa F. Brown is director of the Chesapeake Bay Governor's School and a doctoral candidate at the College of William and Mary. Her interests include strengthening the linkages among policy, practice, and professional development in gifted education. She has for a number of years served as a teacher of gifted students and as an administrator of gifted programs. She has also presented at numerous state and national conferences and is president-elect of the Virginia Association of the Gifted. In 1998, she received the School of Education, College of William and Mary outstanding doctoral student award and in 1999 was a recipient of the outstanding doctoral student award from the National Association of Gifted Children.

Carolyn M. Callahan, Ph.D., professor in the Curry School of Education, University of Virginia, is also associate director of the National Research Center on the Gifted and Talented. She teaches courses in the areas of education of the gifted and is executive director of the Summer Enrichment Program. Dr. Callahan has authored more than 130 articles and 25 book chapters and monographs in gifted education focusing on creativity, the identification of gifted students, program evaluation, and the issues faced by gifted girls. Dr. Callahan has received recognition as Outstanding Faculty Member in the Commonwealth of Virginia and was awarded the Distinguished Scholar Award from the National Association for Gifted Children. She is a past-president of The Association for the Gifted and the National Association for Gifted Children. She also sits on the editorial boards of *Gifted Child Quarterly, Journal for the Education of the Gifted,* and *Roeper Review.*

Mary Ruth Coleman, Ph.D., is the director of project U-STARS, Using Science, Talents, and Abilities to Recognize Students, a Javits Gifted and Talented Student Education Program. She is a fellow at the Frank Porter Graham Child Development Center, University of North Carolina at Chapel Hill, and clinical associate professor in the School of Education. She served as the associate editor of the *Journal* *for the Education of the Gifted* for more than nine years and has put together two special issues of *JEG*—the first on gifted girls and women and the second on underserved gifted. She also guest edited *The Journal of Secondary Gifted Education* focus issue on gifted students with learning disabilities. Dr. Coleman serves as president of The Association for Gifted (TAG) and has served two terms on the board of the National Association for Gifted Children (NAGC). The NAGC recognized her with their 1992 Early Leader Award.

Bonnie Cramond, Ph.D., is an associate professor of gifted and creative education in the department of educational psychology at the University of Georgia and a research fellow with the Torrance Center for Creative Studies. She has had experience teaching and parenting gifted children, has published papers and chapters on giftedness and creativity, and has presented at local, national, and international conferences. Currently, she teaches graduate-level courses in giftedness and creativity. Her research interests are in creativity assessment and the nurturance of creative abilities in children, especially those who are seen as misfits in the regular classroom.

James R. Delisle, Ph.D., is professor of education at Kent State University in Ohio where he directs the undergraduate and graduate programs in gifted child education. The author of nine books and more than 150 articles, Dr. Delisle is best known for his *Gifted Kids' Survival Guide* (with Judy Galbraith) and *Growing Good Kids: 28 Activities to Enhance Self-Awareness, Compassion, and Leadership* (with Deb Delisle). His newest book, *Once Upon a Mind: The Stories and Scholars of Gifted Child Education,* was published in 2000 by Harcourt Brace College Publishers. For almost a decade, Dr. Delisle has taught one day each week in a local public school. These experiences in middle school classrooms serve as the basis for much of his writing (including the chapter included in this book) and a majority of his professional credibility.

Shelagh A. Gallagher, Ph.D., is an assistant professor of education at the University of North Carolina at Charlotte where she runs a master's degree program in the education of the gifted. She currently directs Project P-BLISS, a Javits grant to develop and disseminate social studies PBL units. Dr. Gallagher was also project manager of the Javits Science Grant at the College of William and Mary, overseeing the development of seven PBL science units. She first learned about PBL while at the Illinois Math and Science Academy, where she was a part of the Science, Society, and Future project. Other areas of interest include gifted girls and the academic needs of gifted adolescents. Dr. Gallagher is coauthor of *Teaching the Gifted Child*.

Barbara G. Hunt, Ed.D., is an assistant professor in gifted studies at the Mississippi University for Women. Previously, she worked in Texas in gifted education for 12 years as a teacher of sixth-grade gifted students. She continues doing workshops and conference presentations, especially in the area of meeting the social/emotional needs of the gifted. She currently teaches a graduate class on counseling the gifted child. She has studied gifted programs in England and the Netherlands. Dr. Hunt serves as an officer in the Mississippi Association for Gifted Children. Her article, "The Effect on Mathematics Achievement and Attitude of Homogenous and Heterogeneous Grouping of Gifted Sixth-Grade Students" was published in *The Journal of Secondary Gifted Education* in 1997.

Susan K. Johnsen, Ph.D., is an associate professor in the department of educational psychology and the associate dean in the School of Education at Baylor University. Currently, she directs and teaches courses in the area of education of the gifted at the undergraduate and graduate levels. She is editor of *Gifted Child Today* and serves on the editorial boards of *Gifted Child Quarterly* and *The Journal for Secondary Gifted Education*. She is the coauthor of the *Independent Study Program* and four tests that are used in identifying gifted students: *Test of Mathematical Abilities for Gifted Students* (TOMAGS), *Test of Nonverbal Intelligence* (TONI-3), *Screening Assessment for Gifted Students* (SAGES), and *Screening Assessment for Gifted Students–Primary Version* (SAGES-P). She has published numerous articles and is a frequent presenter at state, national, and international conferences. She is past-president of the Texas Association for Gifted and Talented and recently received an Award of Excellence for Outstanding Leadership from The Association for Gifted (TAG).

Sandra N. Kaplan, Ed.D., is a clinical professor in learning and instruction at the University of Southern California. She has authored articles and books in gifted education, specifically in the areas of differentiated curriculum and instruction, learning centers, and early childhood. She has been president of the California Association for the Gifted and the National Association for the Gifted. Currently, her interests are in the development of depth and complexity as a way of differentiating content and providing higher levels of knowing for gifted students.

Joan D. Lewis, Ph.D., is assistant professor of special education at the University of Nebraska at Kearney where she directs the graduate program in gifted education for the University of Nebraska system. She has published widely and speaks frequently at local, state, national, and international conferences in the areas of gifted girls, public relations and advocacy, self-actualization and self-concept, and Internet resources and techniques in gifted education and university-level instruction. Her work with the local and state associations in gifted education has spanned 18 years.

Cheryl Perilloux Milam, Ph.D., is currently the instructional programs consultant for the Jefferson Parish Public School System in south Louisiana where she supervises the gifted and talented programs among her other responsibilities. She was an award-winning classroom teacher for 24 years, 16 of which were spent instructing gifted students in grades 6–12. Dr. Milam has been an adjunct instructor of both graduate and undergraduate education courses. She is an educational consultant, as well as a presenter at national, state, and local conferences. She is the author of several journal articles and the coauthor of a chapter on gifted education in a special education text. Dr. Milam has served as the president of a local parents' organization for gifted education and has created a professional organization for gifted educators in southeast Louisiana. She is the recipient of the John C. Gowan Graduate Student Award from NAGC, the 1997 Excellence in Education award from the Louisiana Association for Gifted and Talented Students, and the award for Outstanding Contributions to Gifted and Talented Education from the Southeast Louisiana Professional Chapter of the Association for Gifted and Talented Students.

Barbara Moore, Ph.D., is an assistant professor of gifted studies and director of graduate studies at Mississippi University for Women. She received her Ph.D. from the University of Virginia, where she focused on curriculum and academic underachievement among gifted high school students. Dr. Moore is the chair of the Rural Focus Group for NAGC and is working through foundations and grants to help teachers in rural Mississippi schools enhance their curriculum. She recently began the Summer Odyssey Program, a summer residential program for gifted middle school students, at Mississippi University for Women.

Sandra Parks has served as a curriculum and staff development consultant on teaching thinking for schools and school districts since 1978. Since 1983, she has presented professional development institutes for the Association for Supervision and Curriculum Development at national and regional conferences. She conducted research on teaching critical thinking at the Indiana State University Laboratory School and was founding president of the Indiana Association for the Gifted. She taught gifted education courses at the University of North Florida and the University of Miami. She currently serves as the facilitator of the Teaching Thinking network of the Association for Supervision and Curriculum Development.

Sally M. Reis, Ph.D., is a professor of educational psychology at the University of Connecticut where she also serves as principal investigator of The National Research Center on the Gifted and Talented. She was a teacher for 15 years, 11 of which were spent working with gifted students on the elementary, junior high, and high school levels. She has authored more than 100 articles, 8 books, 30 book chapters, and numerous monographs and technical reports. She is coauthor of *The Schoolwide Enrichment Model, The Secondary Triad Model, Dilemmas in Talent Development in the Middle Years,* and *Work Left Undone: Choices and Compromises of Talented Females.* Sally serves on the editorial board of *Gifted Child Quarterly* and is the president of the National Association for Gifted Children.

Tracy L. Riley, Ph.D., teaches undergraduate and graduate courses in gifted education as a lecturer at Massey University in New Zealand. As an enrichment room teacher, Dr. Riley became interested in free and inexpensive materials out of necessity and has since presented numerous workshops on the topic. Dr. Riley has many publications in gifted education, both nationally and internationally. She is presently serving on the editorial board of *Gifted Child Today* and is coeditor of *APEX: The New Zealand Journal of Gifted Education.*

Julia Link Roberts, Ed.D., is director of The Center for Gifted Studies and professor of teacher education at Western Kentucky University. In 1998, she was named Distinguished Professor. Dr. Roberts is a member of the boards of the Kentucky Association of Gifted Education and the National Association for Gifted Children. She has developed and directed extensive programming for children, parents, and educators.

Richard A. Roberts, Ed.D., is professor of education in the School of Integrated Studies in Teacher Education at Western Kentucky University. Dr. Roberts has been a developer of the Kentucky Teacher Internship Program, and he has directed the program for the university. He has been actively involved in providing support for programs offered by The Center for Gifted Studies.

Robert W. Seney, Ed.D., is an associate professor in gifted studies at Mississippi University for Women and the director of the Mississippi Governor's School. He is active in the World Council for Gifted Children, the National Association for the Gifted and Talented, the Mississippi Association for Gifted Children, and the Texas Association for Gifted Children. He is a regular presenter at their annual conferences and has served in leadership positions in each of these organizations. Currently, he serves on the editorial advisory board of NAGC's *Parenting for High Potential,* and he is a contributing editor of *Roeper Review.* Before university service, he served as coordinator of gifted programs for a large Houston, TX., school district and as a teacher of the gifted. He has served more than 20 years in gifted education.

Dorothy A. Sisk, Ed.D., specializes in the field of gifted education, focusing on creative behavior and leadership development. She is currently a professor in education at Lamar University where she holds the C.W. and Dorthy Ann Conn Chair for Gifted Education and directs the Center for Creativity, Innovation, and Leadership. She also coordinates teacher training in gifted education. Dr. Sisk has authored and coauthored numerous chapters, articles, and papers, as well as books. She has served as the director of the U.S. Office of the Gifted and Talented; president, vice president, and executive administrator of the World Council for Gifted and Talented Children; and president of The Association for the Gifted (TAG). She was the first president of The American Creativity Association (ACA) and currently serves on the board of directors. She also served as editor of the *Gifted International* journal and is an associate editor of the *Journal for Creative Behavior* and *Gifted International.*

Melissa A. Small is a doctoral candidate in educational psychology at the University of Connecticut, with areas of concentration in gifted and talented education and evaluation and measurement. She is also a staff member at the Neag Center for Gifted Education and Talent Development. Her areas of research interest include mathematically talented students and gifted females' career development. She frequently works with school districts to provide in-service training in the Schoolwide Enrichment Model, curriculum compacting, and differentiation. She is a former Future Problem Solving Program coach and has evaluated for Michigan, Maine, and Connecticut FPSP competitions. Prior to her work in gifted education, she taught secondary mathematics.

Kristen R. Stephens, Ph.D., is a clinical assistant professor in the department of counseling, special education, and child development at the University of North Carolina at Charlotte. She has authored and coauthored several journal articles and has presented at local, state, national, and international conferences on numerous topics relating to gifted education.

Joyce VanTassel-Baska, Ed.D., is the Jody and Layton Smith Professor of Education at the College of William and Mary, where she initiated and serves as the director of the Center for Gifted Education. Formerly, she established and directed the Center for Talent Development at Northwestern University. Dr. VanTassel-Baska has also served as state director of gifted programs in Illinois and as a regional director, a local coordinator of gifted programs, and a teacher of gifted high school students. Her major research interests include the talent development process and effective curricular interventions with the gifted. She is the author of several books and has authored more than 200 publications on gifted education. She is the editor of *Gifted and Talented International,* a world-wide refereed journal in gifted education. Dr. VanTassel-Baska received the Outstanding Faculty Award from the State Council of Higher Education in Virginia in 1993 and the Distinguished Scholar Award in 1997 from the National Association of Gifted Children.